Principles
of Digital Audio

Principles
of Digital Audio

3rd Edition

Ken C. Pohlmann

McGraw-Hill, Inc.

New York San Francisco Washington, D.C. Auckland Bogotá
Caracas Lisbon London Madrid Mexico City Milan
Montreal New Delhi San Juan Singapore
Sydney Tokyo Toronto

McGraw-Hill

A Division of The **McGraw·Hill** *Companies*

pbk   6 7 8 9 FGRFGR 9 0 0 9 8

hc   1 2 3 4 5 6 7 8 9 FGRFGR 9 0 0 9 8 7 6 5

Library of Congress Cataloging-in-Publication Data
Pohlmann, Ken C.
    Principles of digital audio / by Ken C. Pohlmann. — 3rd ed.
      p.   cm.
    Includes bibliographical references and index.
    ISBN 0-07-050468-7   ISBN 0-07-050469-5 (pbk.)
    1. Sound—Recording and reproducing—Digital techniques.
  I. Title.
    TK7881.4.P63 1995
    621.389'3—dc20   95-17259
                                        CIP

Acquisitions Editor: Steve Chapman
Editorial team: Joanne Slike, Executive Editor
              Andrew Yoder, Supervising Editor
              B.J. Peterson, Book Editor
Production team: Katherine G. Brown, Director
              Janice Ridenour, Computer Artist
              Jeffrey Miles Hall, Computer Artist
              Wanda S. Ditch, Desktop Operator
              Nancy K. Mickley, Proofreading
              Joann Woy, Indexer
Design team: Jaclyn J. Boone, Designer   EL1
            Katherine Lukaszewicz, Associate Designer   0504695

Contents

Preface to the Third Edition

In 1984, a fast-talking publisher persuaded me to write a book describing the fundamentals of digital audio. I assumed the book would appeal only to a few analog misanthropes. *Principles of Digital Audio* was published in 1985. My assumption was incorrect.

The book's publication coincided with a tremendous surge in the research and development of digital audio technology. Instead of a technical paper or two, entire conferences were devoted to the subject; the rapidity of evolution surprised even the most optimistic engineer and gratified even the most driven marketing director. Digital audio had entered our lives.

A few years later, the idea of a second edition was broached. Having completely forgotten about the minor inconvenience of writing the original, I was again easily duped. The challenge of fitting this expanding subject between two covers proved to be formidable. Nevertheless, the book was published in 1989. I figured that the technology had matured, and that the second edition was definitive. This assumption was also severely incorrect.

Digital audio exploded. There was not a part of the entertainment, telecommunications, signal processing, or computer sciences that was not revolutionized, and entirely new industries have appeared. Perceptual coding, multimedia publishing, digital broadcasting, and video gaming have joined the wonders of modern life. Digital audio has thoroughly changed our lives. In the same way that a rising tide lifts all ships (this is also my investment strategy), the second edition sold well and helped to introduce many readers to this new science.

In 1994, the need for a third edition was clearly apparent. Acting against all rational thought, I set to work. Readers of earlier editions will observe radical changes. Several new chapters have been added, and all of the existing chapters have been heavily reworked, with obsolete material stricken and much new material added. Even many descriptions of bedrock basics have been revised because researchers have discovered new facets to them and, because of classroom teaching, my faculty of explanation has improved. In short, the third edition is a whole new ball game.

The third edition is also the last edition. I have given up trying to keep pace with fast-changing technologies. My next title is *Principles of Steam Locomotion*; I suspect that one edition will suffice. I certainly promise that I will never write a fourth edition describing digital audio. Unless, of course, the technology continues to astound us with its ingenuity and there are people anxious to learn about it.

A final note: a particularly astute Chinese curse condemns an individual to live in exciting times. On behalf of all the enormously creative and hard-working engineers who breathe life into the science of digital audio, I hope you find this book, a chronicle of their endeavors, to be exciting.

Ken C. Pohlmann
Coral Gables, Florida

Introduction

Readers familiar with earlier editions of *Principles of Digital Audio* may be surprised at the extent of the revisions in this third edition. Clearly, the essential nature of theoretical topics such as sampling and quantizing have not changed, but our understanding of them has. Similarly, the relative importance of topics continually undergoes change; advances in technology diminish the magnitude of some issues, while simultaneously magnifying others. In the same way that history continually rewrites itself, our understanding of scientific principles evolves. Moreover, and even more significantly, in the interim following the last edition, numerous entirely new digital audio applications have been developed. In short, this third edition is both needed, and is long overdue.

Examination of this new edition will show that over one-half of the text has been extensively revised. A number of topics have been eliminated to conserve the page count (and cost), a number of discussions have been significantly expanded, and a variety of new topics, both theoretical and practical in nature, have been introduced. Specifically, readers will find a considerable amount of entirely new material on channel codes, jitter, optics, optical storage, compact disc formats, digital audio interfaces, networks, psychoacoustics, perceptual coding, the MiniDisc, digital audio broadcasting, multimedia applications, digital filters, digital signal processing, low-bit conversion, noise shaping, and other subjects.

An introductory approach is retained, but the greater depth given to some material has somewhat increased the reading sophistication required; of course, readers may pick and choose according to their level and need. Also, the wider scope of topics should serve to better satisfy a broader range of students and professional practitioners. The latter will certainly notice an increased emphasis on applications-oriented material.

One thing has not changed. This book is neither a compendium of every possible fact nor an advanced treatise. It is an introductory text that attempts to provide the most lucid explanations possible, and to strike that all-important balance between mere information, and understanding. In other words, this is a learning tool, brought to you by someone who enjoys spending time on both sides of the lectern. With this in mind, the chapter contents can be summarized:

Chapter 1 introduces the most elemental concepts of sound pressure functions, as well as binary arithmetic and Boolean algebra. This nomenclature lays the foundation for everything to follow.

Chapter 2 presents the fundamentals of digital audio theory. Principles such as discrete time sampling, amplitude quantization, aliasing, and dither are alien to the analog world, but essential to the digital realm. This chapter carefully introduces each of these topics in an understandable way.

Chapter 3 describes the recording side of a audio digitization system, using a PCM architecture as its model. The hardware design of this encoder includes the anti-aliasing lowpass filter, sample-and-hold circuit, and A/D converter. In addition, this chapter includes a discussion of channel coding, the ultimate objective of an encoding system.

Chapter 4 explains the output processing required to transform binary data into an analog waveform. The hardware blocks of the decoder, D/A converter, output sample-and-hold circuit, and anti-imaging filter are described. Because all practical digital audio players now use digital filters, these devices are described. In addition to the PCM architecture, many specialized coding systems have been devised. In addition, this chapter includes a section on time-base correction, describing the need to control jitter tolerances throughout a digitization chain.

Chapter 5 surveys the field of error correction, a highly mathematical endeavor that is critical to the successful storage of high-density digital audio data. Basic error detection techniques such as parity are described, along with simple detection codes. Error correction schemes such as block and convolutional codes, interleaving, and Reed-Solomon codes are discussed in theoretical terms, as are practical implementations such as the Cross-Interleave Reed-Solomon Code. In addition, error concealment is described.

Chapter 6 examines magnetic tape, a venerable and still vital form of digital storage. A discussion of magnetic recording theory precedes descriptions of the most prominently used magnetic storage systems, including stationary and rotary head systems, with attention to the constraints underlying any particular format.

Chapter 7 presents the Digital Audio Tape (DAT) format, a rotary-head system used to record two audio channels, along with extensive subcode. DAT design is examined, including azimuth recording, track format, modulation, and error correction. Professional DAT applications of timecode recording and editing are also presented.

Chapter 8 discusses optical storage and transmission. The chapter begins with a review of optical phenomena such as diffraction, resolution, and polarization. Both nonerasable and erasable optical disk systems are discussed. Each system may be implemented with a variety of technologies. The chapter also considers fiber optics. The advantages of fiber optics, the operation of such a system, and limitations of fiber-optic interconnection are discussed.

Chapter 9 is devoted to the audio compact disc, and its many variations. The physical characteristics of discs and the nature of the data encoded on discs are presented. The theory of operation of the player is described; the laser pickup, EFM, CIRC, subcode, manufacturing, and other topics are discussed. Alternative CD formats are described including CD-ROM, CD-I, CD-WO (CD-R), Photo CD, Video CD, and DVD.

Chapter 10 describes the numerous professional and consumer digital interfaces that are used to interconnect digital audio devices. These include the SDIF-2, AES3 (AES/EBU), and AES10 (MADI), and S/PDIF protocols. In addition, SCMS and AES11, as well as sample rate conversion, are described. The chapter further discusses communications topics such as ISDN and file transfer, as well as computer networks, including the Internet.

Chapter 11 explores the increasingly important topic of perceptual coding, also known as low bit-rate coding. Data compression techniques such as Huffman coding are described. Psychoacoustics forms the basis for perceptual coding, whether the architecture employs subband or transform coding. The ISO/MPEG standard is described in detail, along with AC-3 and other coders. Key to the development of perceptual coders is the means used to evaluate their transparency. Finally, the MPEG-1 video standard is considered.

Chapter 12 presents the MiniDisc format, as used in both consumer and professional applications. The disc physical design, optical pickup, magneto-optical recording, ATRAC perceptual coder, disc mastering and manufacturing, and other topics are all explained.

Chapter 13 describes the rapidly evolving topic of digital audio broadcasting. Satellite transmission, a particularly powerful distribution method, is explained, including direct broadcast satellite applications. Technical considerations such as multipath performance and bandwidth are important to any digital broadcasting system. Both the Eureka 147 and IBOC systems are explained.

Chapter 14 examines the widespread use of digital audio workstations, following the introduction of digital mixing consoles. Workstations have changed post-production methods in many professional audio and multimedia applications; however, the multiplicity of file formats can complicate this environment. Specific examples of workstation operation are presented.

Chapter 15 tackles the topic of digital signal processing. Subjects such as linearity, time-invariance, impulse response, convolution, and transforms are explained in a largely nonmathematical fashion. Digital filter theory is discussed, with a look at both FIR and IIR filters. Parameters for filter design are presented, as are DSP hardware chips and DSP programming and their respective roles in a digital system. The chapter concludes with a look at applications such as delay, reverberation, and noise removal.

Chapter 16 describes low-bit converters, sometimes known as sigma-delta converters. With the help of noise shaping, low-bit D/A converters can provide an extremely low in-band noise floor and distortion. Similarly, low-bit A/D converters use a high sampling rate and decimation to achieve excellent performance. Several practical chip examples are considered. When converting a long wordlength file to a shorter length, it is important to preserve information with the use of psychoacoustically optimized noise shaping techniques.

Much of the material in this book stems from the work of the many pioneers and leaders in the field of digital audio technology. We owe a tremendous debt to them for their efforts in developing and fulfilling the potential of this young science. Clearly, their vision has profoundly changed both our industry and society.

1
CHAPTER

Sound and Numbers

Digital audio is a highly sophisticated technology. It pushes the envelope of many diverse engineering and manufacturing disciplines. Although the underlying concepts have been well understood since the 1920s, commercialization of digital audio did not begin until the 1970s because theory had to wait 50 years for technology to catch up. The complexity of digital audio is all the more reason to begin the discussion with the basics. Although this book deals with digital topics, at least one analog topic must be included—sound. Once we understand the nature of sound, we can begin to explore ways to encode the information contained in an audio event and process and store it digitally.

Physics of Sound

It would be a mistake for a study of digital audio technology to forget the acoustic phenomena for which the technology has been designed. Music is an acoustic event. Whether it originates from instruments radiating in air or from the direct creation of electrical signals, all music ultimately finds its way into the air, where it becomes a matter of sound and hearing. It is therefore appropriate to briefly review the nature of sound.

Acoustics is the study of sound and is concerned with the generation, transmission, and reception of sound waves. The circumstances for those three phenomena are created when energy causes a disturbance in a medium. For example, when a kettle drum is struck, its drum head disturbs the surrounding air (the medium). The outcome of that disturbance is the sound of a kettle drum. The mechanism is simple: the drum head is activated and it vibrates back and forth. When the drum head pushes forward, air molecules in front of it are compressed. When it pulls back, that area is rarefied. The disturbance consists of regions of pressure above and below the equilibrium atmospheric pressure. Nodes define areas of minimum displacement, and antinodes are areas of maximum (positive or negative) displacement. The displacement is quite small; in normal conversation, particle displacement is about one millionth of an inch. A crowd's acoustic outpouring might cause displacement of one thousandth of an inch.

Sound Waves

Sound is propagated by air molecules through successive displacements that correspond to the original disturbance. In other words, air molecules colliding one against the next propagate the energy disturbance away from the source. Sound transmission thus consists of local disturbances propagating from one region to the next. The local displacement of air molecules occurs in the direction in which the disturbance is traveling; thus sound undergoes a longitudinal form of transmission. A receptor (like a microphone diaphragm) placed in the sound field will similarly move according to the pressure acting on it, completing the chain of events. Incidentally, the denser the medium, the easier is the task of propagation. For example, sound travels more easily in water than in air.

We can access an acoustical system with transducers, devices able to change energy from one form to another. These serve as sound generators and receivers. For example, a kettle drum changes the mechanical energy contributed by the mallet to acoustic energy. A microphone responds to the acoustic energy by producing electrical energy. A loudspeaker reverses that process to again create acoustical energy from electrical.

The pressure changes of sound vibrations can be produced either periodically or aperiodically. A violin playing concert A moves the air back and forth periodically at a fixed rate. (In practice, things like vibrato make it a quasi-periodic vibration.) However, a cymbal crash has no fixed period; it is aperiodic. One sequence of a periodic vibration, from pressure rarefaction to compression and back again, determines one cycle. The number of vibration cycles that pass a given point each second is the frequency of the sound wave, measured in Hz (hertz). A violin playing concert A, for example, generates a waveform that repeats about 440 times per second; its frequency is 440 Hz. Alternatively, the reciprocal of frequency, the time it takes for one cycle to occur, is called the period. Frequencies in nature can range from very low, such as changes in barometric pressure around 10^{-5} Hz, to very high, such as cosmic rays at 10^{22} Hz. Sound is loosely described to be that narrow, low-frequency band from 20 Hz to 20 kHz—roughly the range of human hearing. Digital audio devices are designed to respond to frequencies only in that range.

Wavelength is the distance sound travels through one complete cycle of pressure change and is the physical measurement of the length of one cycle. Because the velocity of sound is relatively constant—about 1130 ft/s (feet per second)—we can calculate the wavelength of a sound wave by dividing the velocity of sound by its frequency. Quick calculations demonstrate the enormity of the differences in the wavelength of sounds. For example, a 20-kHz wavelength is about 0.7 inch long, and a 20-Hz wavelength is about 56 feet long. No transducers (including our ears) are able to linearly receive or produce that range of wavelengths. Their frequency response is not flat, and the frequency range is limited. The range between the lowest and highest frequencies a system can accommodate defines a system's bandwidth. If two waveforms are coincident in time with their positive and negative variations together, they are in phase. When the variations exactly oppose one another, the waveforms are out of phase. Any relative time difference between waveforms is called a phase shift. If two waveforms are relatively phase shifted and combined, a new waveform results from constructive and destructive interference.

Sound Pressure Level

Amplitude describes the sound pressure displacement above and below the equilibrium atmospheric level. In absolute terms, sound pressure is very small; if atmospheric pressure is 15 psi (pounds per square inch), a loud sound might cause a deviation from 14.999 to 15.001 psi. However, the range from the softest to the loudest sound, which determines the dynamic range, is quite large. In fact, human ears (and hence audio systems) have a dynamic range spanning a factor of millions. Because of the large range, a logarithmic ratio is used to measure sound pressure levels. The decibel (dB) uses base 10 logarithmic units to achieve this. A base 10 logarithm is the power to which 10 must be raised to equal the value. For example, an unwieldy number such as 100,000,000 yields a tidy logarithm of 8 because $10^8 = 100,000,000$. Specifically, the decibel is defined to be 10 times the logarithm of a power ratio:

$$\text{Level} = 10\log\left(\frac{P_1}{P_2}\right)\text{dB}$$

where P_1 and P_2 are values of acoustic or electrical power.

If the denominator of the ratio is set to a reference value, standard measurements can be made. In acoustic measurements, intensity levels (IL) can be measured in decibels by setting the reference intensity to the threshold of hearing, which is 10^{-12} W/m^2 (watts per square meter). Thus the intensity level of a rock band producing a sound of 10 W/m^2 can be calculated:

$$\text{Intensity level} = 10\log\left(\frac{P_1}{P_2}\right)\text{dB}$$

$$= 10\log\left(\frac{10^1}{10^{-12}}\right)$$

$$= 130 \text{ dB SPL (sound pressure level)}$$

When ratios of currents, voltages, or sound pressures are used (quantities whose square is proportional to power), the above decibel formula must be multiplied by 2.

The zero reference level for acoustic sound pressure level measurement is a pressure of 0.0002 dyne/cm^2. This level corresponds to the threshold of hearing, the lowest SPL humans can perceive, which is equal to 0 dB SPL. The threshold of feeling, the loudest level before discomfort begins, is 120 dB SPL. Sound pressure levels can be rated on a scale in terms of SPL. A quiet home might have an SPL of 35 dB, a busy street might be 70 dB SPL, and the sound of a jet engine in close proximity might exceed 150 dB SPL. An orchestra's pianissimo might be 30 dB SPL, but a fortissimo might be 110 dB SPL. Thus its dynamic range is 80 dB.

The logarithmic nature of these decibels should be considered. They are not commonly recognizable, because they are not linear measurements. Two motorcycle engines, each producing an intensity level (IL) of 80 dB, would not yield a combined IL of 160 dB. Rather, the logarithmic result would be a 3-dB increase, yielding a combined IL total of 83 dB. In linear units, those two motorcycles each producing sound intensities of 0.0001 W/m^2 would combine to produce 0.0002 W/m^2.

Harmonic Structure

The simplest form of periodic motion is the sinewave; it is manifested by the simplest oscillators, such as pendulums and tuning forks. The sinewave is unique because it exists only as a fundamental frequency. All other periodic waveforms are complex and comprise a fundamental frequency and a series of other frequencies at multiples of the fundamental. Aperiodic complex waveforms, such as the sound of motorcycle engines, do not exhibit this relationship. Many musical instruments are examples of the special case in which the harmonics are related to the fundamental through simple multiples. For example, a complex pitched waveform with a 150-Hz fundamental will have overtones at 300 Hz, 450 Hz, 600 Hz, 750 Hz, etc.

Overtones extend through the upper reaches of human hearing. The relative amplitudes and phase relationships of those overtones account for the timbre of the waveform. For example, a cello and trumpet can both play a note with the same fundamental pitch; however, their timbres are quite different because of their differing harmonic series. When a cellist plays the note D4 as a natural harmonic, the open D string is bowed, which normally produces a note of pitch D3, and the string is touched at its midpoint. The pitch is raised by an octave because the player has damped out all the odd-numbered harmonics, including the fundamental. The pitch changes; because the harmonic structure changes, the timbre changes as well. Harmonic structure explains why the ear has limited ability to distinguish timbre of high-frequency sounds. The first overtone of a 10-kHz tone is at 20 kHz; most people have trouble perceiving that overtone, let alone others even higher in frequency. Still, to record a complex waveform properly, both its fundamental and harmonic structure must be preserved, at least up to the limit of hearing.

The harmonic nature of periodic waveforms is summarized by the Fourier theorem. The Fourier theorem states that all complex periodic waveforms are composed of a harmonic series of sinewaves; complex waveforms can be synthesized by summing sinewaves. Furthermore, a complex waveform can be decomposed into its sinewave content to analyze the nature of the complex waveform. A mathematical transform can be applied to a waveform represented in time to convert it to a representation in frequency. For example, a square wave would be transformed into its fundamental sinewave and higher-order odd harmonics. An inverse transform reverses the process.

Other Phenomena

Sound will undergo diffraction, in which it bends through openings or around obstacles. Diffraction is relative to wavelength; longer wavelengths diffract more apparently than shorter ones. Thus, high frequencies are considered to be more directional in nature. Try this experiment: hold a magazine in front of a loudspeaker—high frequencies will be blocked by the barrier, and longer wavelengths will go around it.

Sound also can refract, in which it bends because its velocity changes. For example, sound can refract because of temperature changes, bending away from warmer temperatures, and toward cooler ones. Specifically, velocity of sound in air increases by about 1.1 ft/s with each increase of 1°F. Another effect of temperature on the velocity of sound is well known to every wind player. Because of the change in the speed of sound, the instrument must be warmed up before it plays in tune (the difference is about half a semitone).

The speed of sound in air is relatively slow, 740 mph. The time it takes for a sound to travel from a source to a receptor can be calculated by dividing the distance by the speed of sound. For example, it would take a sound about one-sixth of a second to travel 200 feet. Sound is absorbed as it travels. The mere passage of sound through air acts to attenuate the sound energy. High frequencies are more prominently attenuated in air; a lightning strike close by is heard as a sharp clap of sound, and one far away is heard as a low rumble because of high-frequency attenuation. Humidity affects air attenuation; specifically, wet air absorbs sound better than dry air. Interestingly, moist air is less dense than dry air (water molecules weigh less than the nitrogen and oxygen they replace) causing the speed of sound to increase.

Given the evident complexity of acoustical signals, it would be naive to believe that analog or digital audio technologies are sufficiently advanced to capture fully and convey the complete listening experience. To complicate matters, the precise limits of human perception are not known. One thing is certain: at best, even with the most sophisticated technology, what we hear being reproduced through an audio system is an approximation of the actual sound.

Digital Basics

Acoustics and analog audio technology are mainly concerned with continuous mathematical functions, but digital audio is a study of discrete values. Specifically, a waveform amplitude is represented as a series of numbers. That is an important first principle, because numbers allow us to manage audio information very efficiently. Using digital techniques, the capability to process information is greatly enhanced. The design nature of audio recording, signal processing, and reproducing hardware has followed the advance of digital technology; the introduction of software programming into the practical audio environment has been simply revolutionary. Thus, digital audio is primarily a numerical technology. To understand it properly, begin with an understanding of number systems.

The basic problem confronting any digital audio system is the representation of audio information in digital form. Although many possibilities present themselves, the logical choice is the binary number system. This base 2 representation is ideally suited for storing and processing numerical information. Fundamental arithmetic operations are facilitated, as are logic operations.

Number Systems

It all begins with numbers. With audio, we are dealing with information and numbers, as opposed to analog representation. Numbers offer a fabulous way to code, process, and decode information. In digital audio, numbers entirely represent audio information. We usually think of numbers as symbols. The symbology is advantageous because the numerical symbols are highly versatile; their meaning can vary according to the way we use them.

For example, consider my classic 1962 BMW R50/2 motorcycle, 500 cubic centimeters, registered as 129907 and shown in Fig. 1-1. Several numbers describe this machine; not so obvious is the important context of each. R50/2 represents the motorcycle's model number, 1962 is the year of manufacture, and 500 represents the quantity of cubic centimeters of engine displacement. The license number 129907 represents specifically coded information that allows my speeding tickets to be properly credited to my account. These various numbers are useful only by virtue of their arbitrarily assigned contexts. If that context is confused, then information encoded by the numbers goes awry. I could end up with a motorcycle with license number 1962, manufactured in the year 500, with an engine displacement of 129907 cubic centimeters.

1-1
The author's classic 1962 BMW R50/2 motorcycle.

Similarly, the numerical operations performed on numbers are matters of interpretation. The tally of my moving violations determines when my license will be suspended, but the sum of my license plate numerals is less problematic. Numbers, if properly defined, provide a good method for storing and processing data. The negative implication is that numbers and their meanings have to be used carefully.

For most people, the most familiar numbers are those of the base 10 system, apparently devised in the ninth century by Hindu astronomers who conceived of the 0 numeral to represent nothing and appended it to the nine other numerals already in use. Earlier societies were stuck with the unitary system, which used one symbol in a series of marks to answer the essential question: how many? That is an unwieldy system for large numbers; thus, higher-base systems were devised. Babylonian mathematicians invented a number system that used 60 symbols. It was a little cumbersome, but even today, 3700 years later, the essence of their system is still used to divide an hour into 60 minutes, a minute into 60 seconds, and a circle into 360 degrees.

Selection of a number system is a question of preference, because any integer can be expressed using any base. Choosing a number system simply questions how many different symbols we think are most convenient. The base 10 system uses 10 numerals; the radix of the system is 10. In addition, the system uses positional notation; the position of the numerals shows the quantities of ones, tens, hundreds, thousands, etc. In other words, the number in each successive position is multiplied by the next higher power of the base. A base 10 system is convenient for 10-fingered organisms, such as humans, but other number bases might be more appropriate for other applications. In any system, we must know the radix; the numeral 10 in base 10 represents the total number of fingers you have, but 10 in base 8 is the number of

Table 1-1. Four common number systems.

Hexadecimal (Base 16)	Decimal (Base 10)	Octal (Base 8)	Binary (Base 2)
0	0	0	0000
1	1	1	0001
2	2	2	0010
3	3	3	0011
4	4	4	0100
5	5	5	0101
6	6	6	0110
7	7	7	0111
8	8	10	1000
9	9	11	1001
A	10	12	1010
B	11	13	1011
C	12	14	1100
D	13	15	1101
E	14	16	1110
F	15	17	1111

fingers minus the thumbs. Similarly, would you rather have 10,000 dollars in base 6, or 100 in base 60? Table 1-1 shows four of the most popular number systems.

The Binary Number System

Gottfried Wilhelm von Leibnitz, philosopher and mathematician, devised the binary number system on March 15, 1679. That day marks the origin of today's digital systems. Although base 10 is handy for humans, a base 2, or binary, system is more efficient for digital computers and digital audio equipment. Only two numerals are required to satisfy the machine's principal electrical concern of voltage being on or off. Furthermore, these two conditions can be easily represented as 0 and 1; these binary digits are called bits (*bi*nary dig*its*). From a machine standpoint, a binary system is ruthlessly efficient, and it is fast. Imagine how quickly we can turn a switch on and off; that speed represents the rate at which we can process information. Imagine a square wave; the wave could represent a machine operating the switch for us. Consider the advantages in storage. Instead of saving infinitely different analog values, we only have to remember two values. Only through the efficiency of binary data can digital circuits process the tremendous amount of information contained in an audio signal.

Whatever information is being processed—in this case, whatever kind of audio signal has been converted to binary form—no matter how unrelated it might appear to be to numbers, a digital processor codes the information in the form of numbers, using the base 2 system. To better understand how audio data is handled inside a digital audio system, a brief look at the arithmetic of base 2 will be useful. In fact, we will consistently see that the challenge of coding audio information in binary form is a central issue in the design and operation of digital audio systems.

In essence, all number systems perform the same function; thus, we can familiarize ourselves with the binary system by comparing it to the decimal system. A given number can be expressed in either system and converted from one base to another. Several methods can be used. One easy decimal-to-binary conversion algorithm for whole numbers divides the decimal number by 2 and collects the remainders to form the binary number, as shown in Fig. 1-2A. Similarly, binary-to-decimal conversion can be accomplished by expressing the binary number in power of 2 notation, then expanding and collecting terms to form the decimal number, as shown in Fig. 1-2B.

$26.125_{10} = ?_2$

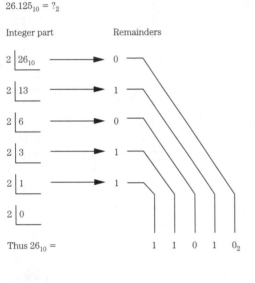

Integer part   Remainders

Thus 26_{10} =   1   1   0   1 0_2

Fractional part

2(0.125) = 0 + 0.250
2(0.250) = 0 + 0.500
2(0.500) = 1 + 0.000
Thus $0.125_{10} = 0.001_2$
Thus $26.125_{10} = 11010.001_2$

A

$11010.001_2 = ?_{10}$

Integer part

$$11010 = 1 \times 2^4 + 1 \times 2^3 + 0 \times 2^2 + 1 \times 2^1 + 0 \times 2^0$$
$$= 1 \times 16 + 1 \times 8 + 0 \times 4 + 1 \times 2 + 0 \times 1$$
$$= 16 + 8 + 2$$
$$= 26_{10}$$

Thus $11010_2 = 26_{10}$

Fractional part

$$0.001 = 0 \times 2^{-1} + 0 \times 2^{-2} + 1 \times 2^{-3}$$
$$= 0 \times 0.5 + 0 \times 0.25 + 1 \times 0.125$$
$$= 0.125_{10}$$

Thus $0.001_2 = 0.125_{10}$
Thus $11010.001_2 = 26.125_{10}$

B

1-2 Conversion of base 10 and base 2 numbers. A. Conversion of a decimal number to binary. B. Conversion of a binary number to decimal.

The conversion points up the fact that the base 2 system also uses positional notation. In base 2, each successive position represents a doubling of value. The rightmost column represents 1s, the next column is 2s, then 4s, 8s, 16s, etc. It is important to designate the base being used; for example, in base 2 the symbol 10 could represent a person's total number of hands.

Just as a decimal point is used to delineate a whole number from a fractional number, a binary point does the same for binary numbers. The fractional part of a decimal number can be converted to a binary number by multiplying the decimal number by 2. Conversion often leads to an infinitely sustaining binary number, so the number of terms must be limited.

As in the base 10 system, the standard arithmetic operations of addition, subtraction, multiplication, and division are applicable to the base 2 system, as shown in Fig. 1-3. As in any base, base 2 addition can be performed using the addition rules needed to form an addition table. The procedure is the same as in the decimal system; however, the addition table is simpler. There are only four possible combinations, compared to the more than 100 possible combinations resulting from the rules of decimal addition. The generation of the carry, as in the decimal system, is necessary when the result is larger than the largest digit in the system. The algorithms for subtraction, multiplication, and division in the binary system are identical to the corresponding algorithms in the decimal system.

$$
\begin{array}{cccc}
 & 0 & 0 & 1 & 1 \\
\text{Addition:} & +0 & +1 & +0 & +1 \\
\hline
 & 0 & 1 & 1 & 10 \quad \text{(with carry)}
\end{array}
$$

$$
\begin{array}{cccc}
 & 1 & 1 & 0 & 10 \quad \text{(with borrow)} \\
\text{Subtraction:} & -1 & -0 & -0 & -1 \\
\hline
 & 0 & 1 & 0 & 01
\end{array}
$$

$$
\begin{array}{cccc}
 & 0 & 0 & 1 & 1 \\
\text{Multiplication:} & \times 0 & \times 1 & \times 0 & \times 1 \\
\hline
 & 0 & 0 & 0 & 1
\end{array}
$$

$$
\begin{array}{cc}
 & 0 & 1 \\
\text{Division:} & \div 1 & \div 1 \\
\hline
 & 0 & 1
\end{array}
$$

1-3 Basic arithmetic operations of a base 2 number system.

Thus, a number is what we make it, and the various systems—differing only by base—operate in essentially the same way. A computer's use of the binary system is a question of expediency; it presents no real barrier to an understanding of digital techniques. It is simply the most logical approach. Ask yourself, would you rather deal with 10, 60, an infinite analog number, or 2 voltage levels?

Binary Codes

Although the abstractions of binary mathematics form the basis of digital audio systems, the implementation of these primitives requires higher level processing. Specifically, the next step up the evolutionary ladder is the coding of binary information. For example, individual binary bits or numbers can be ordered into words with specific connotations attached. In this way, both symbolic and numeric information is more easily processed by digital systems.

Just as the digits in a motorcycle license number carry a specially assigned meaning, groups of binary numbers can be encoded with special information. For example, a decimal number can be converted directly to its equivalent binary value; the binary number is encoded as the binary representation of the decimal number. Obviously, there is a restriction on the number of possible values that can be encoded. Specifically, an n-bit binary number can encode 2^n numbers. Three bits, for example, could encode eight states: 000, 001, 010, 011, 100, 101, 110, and 111. These could correspond to the decimal numbers 0, 1, 2, 3, 4, 5, 6, and 7.

Negative numbers present a problem because the sign must be encoded (with bits) as well. For example, a 1 in the left-most position could designate a negative number, a 0 could designate a positive number, and the remaining bits represent the absolute value of the number. This kind of coding is called a signed-magnitude representation. The 3-bit words 000, 001, 010, 011, 100, 101, 110, and 111 might correspond to +0, +1, +2, +3, –0, –1, –2, –3. One problem is the presence of both +0 and –0. Other methods can be used to better represent negative numbers.

Because we live in a decimal world, it is often useful to create binary words coded to decimal equivalents, preserving the same kind of decimal characteristics. Unfortunately, there is no binary grouping that directly represents the 10 decimal digits. Three bits handle the first seven decimal numbers, and four bits handle 16. For greater efficiency, a more sophisticated coding method is desirable. This method is easily accomplished with groups of four bits each, with each group representing a decimal digit:

First decimal group	Second decimal group	nth decimal group
$a_3 a_2 a_1 a_0$	$b_3 b_2 b_1 b_0 ...$	$n_3 n_2 n_1 n_0$

Given this approach, there are many ways that the 10 decimal digits can be encoded as four-bit binary words. Specifically, there are approximately 2.9×10^{10} possibilities. Given these choices, it makes sense to find a method that provides as many benefits as possible. For example, a good code should facilitate arithmetic operations and error correction, and minimize storage space and logic circuitry. Similarly, whenever digital audio designers select a coding method, they examine the same criteria.

Weighted Binary Codes

In some applications, weighted codes are more efficient than many other representations. In a weighted code, each binary bit is assigned a decimal value, called a weight. Each number represented by the weighted binary code is calculated from the sum of the weighted digits. For example, weights w_3, w_2, w_1, w_0 and bits a_3, a_2, a_1, a_0 would represent the decimal number $N = w_3 \times a_3 + w_2 \times a_2 + w_1 \times a_1 + w_0 \times a_0$.

The BCD (binary coded decimal) code is commonly used in digital applications. BCD is a positional weighted code in which each decimal digit is binary coded into four-bit words. It is sometimes called the 8-4-2-1 code, named after the values of its weights. The BCD representation is shown in Table 1-2, along with several other binary codes. The 8-4-2-1 and 6-3-1-1 codes are weighted; the others are not. Any decimal number can be represented with the BCD code. For example, the number 5995 would be 0101 1001 1001 0101. Note that the resulting binary number is quite different from that obtained by direct decimal-to-binary conversion. The BCD code solves the binary problem of representing large decimal numbers; systems interfacing with decimal numbers often use BCD code for this reason. Thus, they incorpo-

Table 1-2. Examples of several binary codes.
The 8-4-2-1 and 6-3-1-1 codes are weighted; the others are unweighted.

Decimal Digit	8-4-2-1 Code	6-3-1-1 Code	Excess-3 Code	2-out-of-5 Code	Gray Code
0	0000	0000	0011	00011	0000
1	0001	0001	0100	00101	0001
2	0010	0011	0101	00110	0011
3	0011	0100	0110	01001	0010
4	0100	0101	0111	01010	0110
5	0101	0111	1000	01100	1110
6	0110	1000	1001	10001	1010
7	0111	1001	1010	10010	1011
8	1000	1011	1011	10100	1001
9	1001	1100	1100	11000	1000

rate binary-to-BCD, and BCD-to-binary conversion programs. The 6-3-1-1 code is another example of a weighted code. For example, using the weights assigned to the 6-3-1-1 code, the code word 1001 represents the decimal number $N = 6 \times 1 + 3 \times 0 + 1 \times 0 + 1 \times 1 = 7$.

Unweighted Binary Codes

In some applications, unweighted codes are preferred. Several examples of unweighted codes are excess-3, 2-out-of-5, and Gray code. The excess-3 code is derived from the 8-4-2-1 code by adding 3 (0011) to each code word. In other words, the decimal digit d is represented by the four-bit binary number $d + 3$. In this way, every code word has at least one 1. The 2-out-of-5 code is defined so that exactly two out of the five bits are 1 for every valid word. This definition provides a simple way to check for errors; an error could result in more or less than two 1s.

Other unweighted codes can be defined, for example, so that no code word has less than one 1 or more than two 1s. This minimizes transitions in logic states when changing words, a potential cause of errors or distortion in output circuitry. In a Gray code, sometimes called a reflected code system, only one digit can change value when counting from one state to the next. A disadvantage of an unweighted code is that generally the corresponding decimal value cannot be easily computed from the binary values.

Two's Complement

Although it is comforting to define binary operations in terms familiar to humans, clearly such an enterprise would not be expedient. It makes more sense to specify numbers and operations in ways most easily handled by machines. For example, when binary numbers are stored in complemented form, an adding operation can be used to perform both addition and subtraction. Furthermore, when binary numbers are stored and processed through registers, a modular number system is often preferable.

Simple binary arithmetic operations can present problems when the result is stored. For example, given a three-bit system, suppose the numbers 110 and 100 are added. The answer is 1010. The left-most bit is a carry digit from the addition process. However, in a three-bit system, the carry digit would be lost, and the remaining answer would be 010. This is problematic unless the system can identify that an overflow has occurred. With modular arithmetic, such a result is easily reconciled.

Overflow is inherent in any system with a finite number of digits. Overflow requires an adjustment in our thinking. When an infinite number of digits is available, the task of adding, for example, 6 and 4 could be visualized by joining two straight line segments of lengths 6 and 4 together to obtain a line segment of 10. However with a finite number of digits, it is better to visualize a circular system, or better yet, to consider Fig. 1-4, which shows a representation of a three-bit binary system.

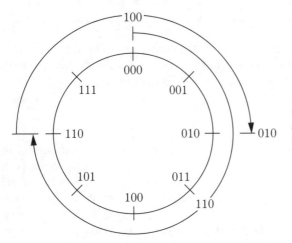

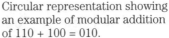

1-4
Circular representation showing an example of modular addition of 110 + 100 = 010.

When we add 6_{10} (110_2) and 4_{10} (100_2), the appropriate circular segments are joined, leading to a result of 2_{10} (010_2). The resulting number 2 is the remainder obtained by subtracting 8, that is, (2^3), from the sum of 10. Two numbers A and B are equivalent in modulo N if A divided by N yields a remainder that equals the remainder obtained when B is divided by N. For example, if $A = 12$ and $B = 20$, then $A = B$ (mod 8) because 12/8 = 1 + remainder 4 and 20/8 = 2 + remainder 4. The remainders are equal, thus the numbers are equivalent in modulo 8. Modulo 2 arithmetic is used in many binary applications; in general, when performing numerical operations with n-bit words, modulo 2^n arithmetic is used.

Modular Arithmetic

As noted, negative numbers can be expressed in binary form with a sign bit. Although convenient for humans, it is illogical for machines. Independent circuits would be required for addition and subtraction. Instead, using a special property of modulo number systems, an addition operation can be used to perform subtraction as well. Although a carry operation is still required, a borrow is not. Specifically, rather than store a negative number as a sign and magnitude, it can be coded in a base complemented form. Two kinds of complements exist for any number system. A radix-minus-one complement is formed by subtracting each digit of the number from the radix-minus-one of the number system. This is known as the nine's complement in the decimal system and the one's complement in the binary system. A true complement is formed by subtracting each digit of the number from the radix-minus-one, then adding 1 to the least significant digit. The true complement is called the ten's complement in the decimal system, and the two's complement in the binary number system. With base complement, a number added to an existing number will result in the full next power of the base. For example, the ten's complement of 35 is 65 because $35 + 65 = 10^2 = 100$, and the two's complement of 1011 is 0101 because $1011 + 0101 = 2^4 = 10000$. From this, note that a complement is the symbol complement plus 1, and the symbol complement is found by subtracting the original number from the highest symbol in the system.

Forming the one's and two's complement in the binary system is easily accomplished and expedites matters tremendously. Because the radix is 2, each bit of the binary number is subtracted from 1. Thus, a one's complement is formed by replacing 1s by 0s, and 0s by 1s, that is, complementing the digits. The two's complement is formed by simply adding 1 to that number and observing any carry operations. For example, given a number 0100, its one's complement is 1011, and its two's complement is 1100. It is the two's complement, formed from the one's complement, that is most widely used. For example, Table 1-3 shows a representation of numbers from +7 to –7 with two's complement representation of negative numbers. A positive two's complement number added to its negative value will always equal zero.

Recalling the discussion of modulo number systems, we observe how subtraction can be replaced by addition. If $A + B = 0$ in a modulo system N, then B is the negative of A. There are in fact many Bs such that $B = kN - A$ where $k = 0, 1, 2, \ldots$ When $k = 1$, when A is less than N, then $B = N - A$ behaves as a positive number less than

Table 1-3. A table of values showing a two's complement representation of positive and negative numbers.

Decimal Number	Binary Number
7	0111
6	0110
5	0101
4	0100
3	0011
2	0010
1	0001
0	0000
−1	1111
−2	1110
−3	1101
−4	1100
−5	1011
−6	1010
−7	1001

N. We can use $B = N - A$ in place of $-A$ in any calculation in modulo N. For example, $C = D - A$ is equivalent to $C = D + (N - A)$. In other words, if we can obtain $N - A$ without performing subtraction, then subtraction can be performed using addition. After some thought on the matter, we observe that, conveniently, $N - A$ is the two's complement of A.

Complement subtraction can be performed with addition. With binary, first consider standard subtraction:

$$\begin{array}{r} 10001 \\ -\,01011 \\ \hline 00110 \end{array}$$

However, the same operation can be performed by adding the two's complement of the subtrahend:

$$\begin{array}{r} 10001 \\ +\,10101 \\ \hline 1\ 00110 \text{ (the carry is discarded)} \end{array}$$

When a larger number is subtracted from a smaller one, there is no carry. For example, $2 - 8$ becomes $2 + (10 - 8)$ or $2 + 2 = 4$. Notice that the answer 4 is the ten's complement of the negative result that is $-(10 - 4) = -6$. Similarly, when a larger number is subtracted from a smaller one in binary:

$$\begin{array}{r} 101 \\ -\,11011 \\ \hline -\,10110 \end{array}$$

In two's complement:

$$\begin{array}{r} 101 \\ +\,00101 \\ \hline 01010 \end{array}$$

The answer is negative, but in two's complement form. Taking the two's complement and assigning a negative sign results in the number -10110. When performing two's complement subtraction, the final carry provides the sign of the result. A final carry of 1 indicates a positive answer, and a carry of 0 indicates a negative answer, in its two's complement, positive form.

If base complementing seems tedious, it is redeemed by its advantages when handling positive and negative (bipolar) numbers, which might, for example, represent an audio waveform. The MSB (most significant bit) is the sign bit. When it is 0, the number is positive, and when it is 1, the number is negative. In true binary form, the number 5 can be represented by 00000101 and -5 by 10000101. By representing negative numbers in two's complement form, -5 becomes 11111011, and the sign is handled automatically. All additions and subtractions will result in positive numbers in true binary form and all negative numbers in two's complement form, with the MSB automatically in the proper sign form. Humans appreciate two's complement because the left digit always denotes the sign. Digital processors appreciate it because subtraction can be easily performed through addition.

Boolean Algebra

The binary number system presents tremendous opportunities for the design of electronic hardware and software, including, of course, digital audio applications. Boolean algebra is the method used to combine and manipulate binary signals. It is named in honor of its inventor, George Boole, who published his proposal for the system in 1854 in a very curious work entitled: *An Investigation of the Laws of Thought, on Which Are Founded the Mathematical Theories of Logic and Probabilities.* Incidentally, historians tell you that Boole's formal education ended in the third grade.

Boolean Operators

Boolean logic is essential to digital applications because it provides the basis for decision making, condition testing, and performing logical operations. Using Boolean algebra, all logical decisions are performed with the binary digits 0 and 1, a set of operators, and a number of laws and theorems. The on/off nature of the system is ideally suited for realization in digital systems. The set of fundamental logic operators provides the tools necessary to manipulate bits and hence design the logic that comprises useful digital systems. Everything from vending machines to super computers can be designed with this powerful mathematics.

The Boolean operators are shown in Fig. 1-5. The operators OR, AND, and EXCLUSIVE OR (XOR) combine two binary digits to produce a single digit result. The Boolean operator NOT complements a binary digit. NAND and NOR are derived from the other operators. The operators can be used singly or in combinational logic to perform any possible logical operation.

The complement, or NOT operation, complements any set of digits. The complement of 0 is 1, and the complement of 1 is 0. A bar is placed over the digit to represent a complement.

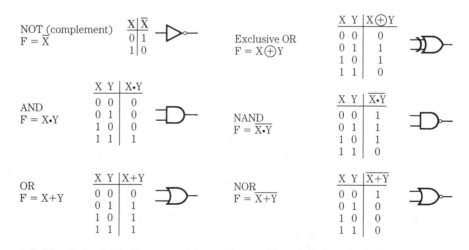

1-5 The six basic Boolean operators can be used to manipulate logical conditions.

The AND operation is defined by the statement: If X AND Y are both 1, then the result is 1; otherwise the result is 0. Either a dot symbol or no symbol is used to denote AND.

The OR operation is defined by the statement: If X OR Y, or both, are 1 then the result is 1; otherwise the result is 0. A plus sign is usually used to denote OR.

EXCLUSIVE OR differentiates whether binary states are the same or different. Its output is 1 when X differs from Y, and is 0 when X is the same as Y. The XOR function thus represents binary (mod 2) addition. A circled plus sign is used to denote XOR.

Combining AND and NOT produces NAND, and combining OR and NOT produces NOR; their results are the NOT of AND and OR, respectively.

Boolean Expressions

The Boolean operators can be combined into meaningful expressions, giving statement to the condition at hand. Moreover, such statements often lead to greater insight of the condition, or its simplification. For example, a digital system needs only the OR and NOT function because any other function can be derived from those functions. This relationship can be shown using De Morgan's theorem, which states:

$$\overline{A \cdot B} = \overline{A} + \overline{B}$$

$$\overline{A + B} = \overline{A} \cdot \overline{B}$$

Using De Morgan's theorem, observe that the expression:

$$A \cdot B = \overline{\overline{A} + \overline{B}}$$

generates AND from OR and NOT, and the expression:

$$A \oplus B = \overline{(\overline{\overline{A}} + B)} + \overline{(A + \overline{B})}$$

generates XOR from OR and NOT.

This example shows that Boolean operators can be combined into expressions. In this case, De Morgan's theorem is used to form the complement of expressions. This ability to form logical expressions allows us to use Boolean operators, along with one or more variables or constants, to solve applications problems. Parentheses are used to define the order in which operations are performed; operations are initiated within parentheses. When parentheses are omitted, complementation is performed first, followed by AND and then OR.

Logical expressions correspond directly to networks of logic gates, realizable in hardware or software. For example, Fig. 1-6A shows a logical expression and its equivalent network of logic gates. An expression can be evaluated by substituting a value of 0 or 1 for each variable, and carrying out the indicated operations. Each appearance of a variable or its complementation is called a literal. A truth table, or table of combinations, can be used to illustrate all the possible combinations contained in an expression. In other words, the output can be expressed in terms of the input variables. For example, the truth table in Fig. 1-6B shows the results of the logic circuit in Fig. 1-6A.

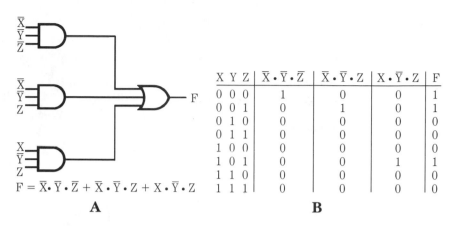

X Y Z	$\overline{X} \cdot \overline{Y} \cdot \overline{Z}$	$\overline{X} \cdot \overline{Y} \cdot Z$	$X \cdot \overline{Y} \cdot Z$	F
0 0 0	1	0	0	1
0 0 1	0	1	0	1
0 1 0	0	0	0	0
0 1 1	0	0	0	0
1 0 0	0	0	0	0
1 0 1	0	0	1	1
1 1 0	0	0	0	0
1 1 1	0	0	0	0

$F = \overline{X} \cdot \overline{Y} \cdot \overline{Z} + \overline{X} \cdot \overline{Y} \cdot Z + X \cdot \overline{Y} \cdot Z$

A   **B**

1-6 Boolean expressions can be realized through hardware or software, as circuits or logical statements. A. The logic realization of a Boolean expression. B. A truth table verifying solution to a Boolean expression.

Boolean Theorems

Given a set of operators and ways to combine them into expressions, the next step is to develop a system of Boolean algebraic relations. That set forms the basis of digital processing in the same way that regular algebra governs the manipulation of the familiar base 10 operations. In fact, the base 2 and base 10 algebraic systems are very similar, to the point of confusion. Relations such as complementation, commutation, association, and distribution, as shown in Fig. 1-7, form the mathematical logic needed to create logical systems. Remember that these laws hold true for Boolean algebra, but they are often uniquely defined.

Double complementation results in the original value. In other words, if 1 is complemented it becomes 0, and when complemented again, it becomes 1 again. Commutative laws state that the order in which terms are combined (with addition and multiplication operators) does not affect the result. Associative laws state that when several terms are added or multiplied, the order of their selection for the operation is immaterial. Distributive laws demonstrate that the product of one term multiplied by a sum term equals the sum of the products of the first term multiplied by each product term.

Most of these laws can be proved using proof by perfect induction. For example, consider the idempotence law, stating that $X + X = X$. We know that X can have only the value of 0 or 1. If X has the value 0, then $0 + 0 = 0$, and if X has the value 1, then $1 + 1 = 1$. Therefore $X + X = X$. By similar means, the rest of the Boolean laws can be proved. Although somewhat underwhelming in their simplicity, the power they wield is considerable.

Using Boolean theorems and other reduction theorems such as De Morgan's theorem, complex logical expressions can often be untangled to provide simple results. For example, consider these expressions:

$$F = X \cdot Y + X \cdot \overline{Y} + \overline{Y}(X + \overline{X})$$
$$F = X \cdot Y + X \cdot \overline{Y} + \overline{X} \cdot \overline{Y}$$

1. Special properties of 0 and 1

   $0 + X = X$ $\qquad$ $0 \cdot X = 0$
   $1 + X = 1$ $\qquad$ $1 \cdot X = X$

2. Idempotence laws

   $X + X = X$ $\qquad$ $X \cdot X = X$

3. Involution

   $\overline{\overline{X}} = X$

4. Complementation laws

   $X + \overline{X} = 1$ $\qquad$ $X \cdot \overline{X} = 0$

5. Commutative laws

   $X + Y = Y + X$ $\qquad$ $X \cdot Y = Y \cdot X$

6. Associative laws

   $X + (Y + Z) = (X + Y) + Z = X + Y + Z$
   $X \cdot (Y \cdot Z) = (X \cdot Y) \cdot Z = X \cdot Y \cdot Z$

7. Distributive laws

   $X \cdot (Y + Z) = (X \cdot Y) + (X \cdot Z)$
   $X + (Y \cdot Z) = (X + Y) \cdot (X + Z)$

8. Absorption laws

   $X + (X \cdot Y) = X$ $\qquad$ $X \cdot (X + Y) = X$
   $X + (\overline{X} \cdot Y) = X + Y$ $\qquad$ $X \cdot (\overline{X} + Y) = X \cdot Y$

1-7 Some of the principal laws of Boolean algebra.

$$F = X{\cdot}Y + X{\cdot}\overline{Y} + \overline{Y}$$
$$F = \overline{Y} + Y{\cdot}X$$
$$F = X + \overline{X}{\cdot}\overline{Y}$$
$$F = X + \overline{Y}$$

All these functions call for different Boolean manipulations, but their outputs are identical. Whether the end result of an expression is a hardware circuit or software program, simplification is understandably critical. For example, idempotence, distribution, and complementation can be applied to the expression in Fig. 1-6, resulting in a much simpler expression, as shown in Fig. 1-8. In this case, the original circuit required three AND gates, one OR gate, and three NOT circuits. The simplified circuit requires one AND, one OR, and two NOTs. The important point is that both circuits perform the same function, with identical outputs for any possible inputs.

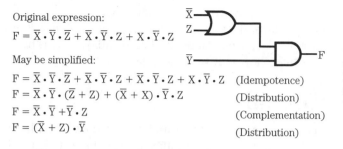

Original expression:

$$F = \overline{X} \cdot \overline{Y} \cdot \overline{Z} + \overline{X} \cdot \overline{Y} \cdot Z + X \cdot \overline{Y} \cdot Z$$

May be simplified:

$$F = \overline{X} \cdot \overline{Y} \cdot \overline{Z} + \overline{X} \cdot \overline{Y} \cdot Z + \overline{X} \cdot \overline{Y} \cdot Z + X \cdot \overline{Y} \cdot Z \quad \text{(Idempotence)}$$
$$F = \overline{X} \cdot \overline{Y} \cdot (\overline{Z} + Z) + (\overline{X} + X) \cdot \overline{Y} \cdot Z \quad \text{(Distribution)}$$
$$F = \overline{X} \cdot \overline{Y} + \overline{Y} \cdot Z \quad \text{(Complementation)}$$
$$F = (\overline{X} + Z) \cdot \overline{Y} \quad \text{(Distribution)}$$

1-8
Complex logical expressions can be simplified with Boolean laws to permit simpler hardware or software realization.

The process of reduction requires an understanding of the Boolean laws, as well as a few clever techniques. For example, canonical forms using minterms and maxterms are powerful reduction methods. The canonical sum of products can be used to realize circuits using only NAND gates, and the canonical product of sums can be used for NOR gate circuits.

Using these tools, useful digital hardware and software can be conceived to manage information or perform processing. For example, consider the design of an adder to sum two binary words. The simplest case is that of one-bit words. The desired truth table is shown in Fig. 1-9A. It shows the two input words X and Y, and output sum S and carry C. From this truth table, logical expressions can be written to realize the desired summation, as shown in Fig. 1-9B. The resulting network is called a half-adder. One possible realization is shown in Fig. 1-9C.

More generally, Boolean algebra can be applied to many types of problems. Even word problems posed in English can be converted to Boolean form and solved. For example, consider the syllogism with these three premises:

1. Babies are illogical
2. Nobody is despised who can manage a crocodile
3. Illogical persons are despised

By applying the principles of symbolic logic, the irrefutable, absolutely logical conclusion is:

4. A person able to manage a crocodile is no baby.

Whether the problem involves babies, crocodiles, motorcycle engines, or violin tones, binary logic can be applied with great finesse when the problem can be reduced to a binary state. From that elemental simplicity, tremendous complexity can be addressed. In this respect all digital systems are alike. They differ, however, ac-

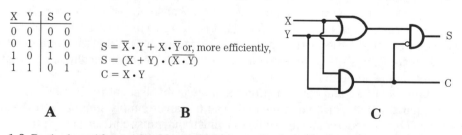

X	Y	S	C
0	0	0	0
0	1	1	0
1	0	1	0
1	1	0	1

$S = \overline{X} \cdot Y + X \cdot \overline{Y}$ or, more efficiently,
$S = (X + Y) \cdot (\overline{X \cdot Y})$
$C = X \cdot Y$

A   **B**   **C**

1-9 Beginning with a truth table, a half-adder can be logically expressed, and realized. A. The truth table for a half-adder function. B. The logical expressions for a half-adder function. C. A half-adder circuit.

cording to the kinds of information they process and what data manipulations they are called upon to accomplish. A digital audio system is thus a unique digital system specially configured to process audio data. Nonintuitively, digital audio systems have more in common with syllogisms than they do with analog audio systems.

Analog Versus Digital

Digital audio entails entirely new concepts and techniques, distinct from those employed in analog technology. From the very onset, we must think of information and its storage and processing in a new light. In that respect, a few comparisons between analog and digital technology might be helpful in showing the vast differences between them, as well as some of the advantages and disadvantages of each technology.

An analog signal can be compared to a digital signal; consider a bucket of water compared to a bucket of ball bearings. Both water and ball bearings fill their respective containers. The volume of each bucket can be characterized by the amount of its contents, but the procedures for each bucket would be different. With water, we could weigh the bucket and water, pour out the water, weigh the bucket alone, subtract to find the weight of the water, then calculate the volume represented. Or we could dip a measuring cup into the bucket and withdraw measured amounts. In either case, we run the risk of spilling some water or leaving some at the bottom of the bucket; our measurement would be imprecise.

With a bucket of ball bearings, we simply count each ball and calibrate the volume of the bucket in terms of the number of ball bearings it holds. The measurement is relatively precise, if perhaps a little tedious (we might want to use a computer to do the counting). The ball bearings represent the discrete values in a digital system, and demonstrate that with digital techniques we are able to quantify the values and gain more accurate information about the measurement. In general, precision is fundamental to any digital system. For example, a bucket that has been measured to hold 1.6 quarts of water is less useful than a bucket that is known to hold 8263 ball bearings. In addition, the counted ball bearings provide repeatability. We might fill another bucket with water, but that bucket might be a different size and we could easily end up with 1.5 quarts. On the other hand, we could reliably count out 8263 ball bearings anywhere, anytime.

The utility of a digital system compared to an analog system is paradoxical. Conceptually, the digital system is much simpler, because counting numbers is easier than measuring a continuous flow. That is, it is easier to process a representation of a signal rather than process the signal itself. However, in practice, the equipment required to accomplish that simple task must be more technologically sophisticated than any analog equipment.

Audio recording and reproduction technology involves more than buckets. But the comparison between analog and digital audio can be simply summarized. An analog signal chain, from recording studio to living room, must convey a continuous representation of amplitude change in time. This need is problematic because every circuit and storage medium throughout the chain is itself an analog device, contributing its own analog distortion and noise. This unavoidably degrades the analog signal as it passes through. In short, when an analog signal is processed through an analog chain with inherent analog artifacts, deterioration occurs.

With digital audio, the original analog event is converted into a stream of binary data, which is processed, stored, and distributed as a numerical representation. The reverse process, from data to analog event, occurs only at playback, thus eliminating many occasions for intervening degradation. The major concern lies in converting the analog signal into a digital representation, and back again to analog. Nevertheless, because the audio information is carried through a numerical signal chain, it avoids much spurious analog distortion and noise. In addition, digital circuits are less expensive to design and manufacture, they can be flexibly modified, they offer increased noise immunity, age immunity, temperature immunity, and greatly increased reliability. The power of logic is inherent in every binary number system from the simplest light switch, to the most sophisticated computer.

In theory, digital audio systems are quite elegant, suggesting that they easily surpass more encumbered analog systems. In practice, although digital systems are free of many analog deficiencies, they can exhibit some substantial anomalies of their own. The remaining chapters only scratch the surface of the volume of knowledge needed to understand the complexities of a digital audio system. Moreover, as with any evolving science, every new insight only leads to many more questions.

2
CHAPTER

Fundamentals of Digital Audio

The use of digital techniques for the recording, reproduction, storage, processing, and transmission of digital audio signals entails concepts foreign to analog audio methods. In fact, the inner workings of digital audio systems bear little resemblance to analog systems. Because audio itself is analog in nature, digital systems employ sampling and quantization, the twin pillars of audio digitization, to transform the audio information. Any sampling system is bound by the sampling theorem, which defines the relationship between message and sampling frequencies. In addition, the theorem dictates that the message be bandlimited. Special precautions must be taken to prevent a condition of erroneous sampling known as aliasing. Quantization error occurs when the amplitude of an analog waveform is represented by a binary word; effects of the error can be minimized by dithering the audio waveform prior to quantization.

Discrete Time Sampling

With analog recording, a tape is continuously modulated or a groove is continuously cut. With digital recording, numbers must be used. The first question is how to create those numbers. In other words, how do we record a data point from a changing waveform? Digitization uses time sampling and amplitude quantization to encode the infinitely variable analog waveform as discrete amplitude values in time. These techniques are considered in this chapter. First, consider the idea of discrete time sampling, the essence of digital audio.

Time seems to flow continuously. The hands of an analog clock sweep across the clock face covering all time as it passes by. A digital readout clock also tells time, but with a discretely valued display. In other words, it displays sampled time. Similarly, music varies continuously in time and can be recorded and reproduced either continuously or discretely. Discrete time sampling is the essential mechanism that defines a digital audio system, permits its analog-to-digital conversion, and differentiates it from an analog system.

However, a nagging question immediately presents itself. If a digital system samples discretely, what happens between samples? Haven't we lost the information occurring between sample times? The answer, intuitively surprising, is no. Given correct conditions, no information is lost due to sampling between the input and output of a digitization system. The samples contain the same information as the conditioned unsampled signal. To illustrate this, try a conceptual experiment.

Suppose we attach a movie camera to the handlebars of a BMW motorcycle, go for a ride, then return home and process the film. Auditioning this piece of avantgarde cinema, we discover that the discrete frames of film successfully reproduce our ride; it looks great. But when we traverse bumpy pavement, the picture is blurred. We determine that the quick movements were too fast for each frame to capture the change. We draw the following conclusions: if we increased the frame rate, using more frames per second, we could capture quicker changes. If we complained to City Hall and the bad pavement was smoothed, there would be no blur even at slower frame rates. The movie would fully reproduce the motorcycle ride. We settle on a compromise—we make the roads reasonably smooth, and then we use a frame rate adjusted for a clean picture.

Although the analogy is somewhat clumsy, the discrete frames of a movie create a moving picture, and similarly the samples of a digital audio recording create a signal. As noted, sampling is a lossless process if the input signal is properly conditioned. Thus, in a digital audio system, we must smooth out the bumps in the incoming signal. Specifically, the signal is lowpass filtered; that is, the frequencies too high to be properly sampled are removed. We observe that a signal with a finite frequency response can be sampled without loss of information; the samples contain all the information contained in the original signal. The original signal can be completely recovered from the samples. Generally, we observe that there exists a method for reconstructing a signal from its amplitude values taken at certain spaced points in time.

The Sampling Theorem

The idea of sampling occurs in many disciplines, and the origin of sampling theorems comes from many sources. Most audio engineers recognize American engineer Harry Nyquist as the author of the sampling theorem that founded the discipline of modern digital audio. The recognition occurred because Nyquist expressed the theorem in terms that are familiar to communications engineers. However, the story of sampling theorems predates Nyquist.

When he was not busy designing military fortifications for Napoleon, French mathematician Augustin-Louis Cauchy contemplated sampling. In 1841, he showed that functions could be nonuniformly sampled and averaged over a long period. At the turn of the century, it was thought (incorrectly) that a function could be successfully sampled at a frequency equal to the highest frequency. In 1915, Scottish mathematician E.T. Whittaker, working with interpolation series, devised perhaps the first mathematical proof of a general sampling theorem, showing that a bandlimited function can be completely reconstructed from samples. In 1920, Japanese mathematician K. Ogura similarly proved that if a function is sampled at a frequency at least twice the highest function frequency, the samples contain all the information in the function, and can reconstruct the function. Also in 1920, American engineer John Carson devised an unpublished proof that related the same result to communications applications.

It was Nyquist who first clarified the application of sampling to communications, and published his work. In 1925, in an article titled "Certain Factors Affecting Telegraph Speed," he proved that the number of telegraph pulses that can be transmitted over a telegraph line per unit time are proportional to the bandwidth of the line. In 1928, in an article titled "Certain Topics in Telegraph Transmission Theory," he proved that for complete signal reconstruction, the required frequency bandwidth is proportional to the signalling speed, and that the minimum bandwidth is equal to half the number of code elements per second. Subsequently, Russian engineer V.A. Kotelnikov published a proof of the sampling theorem in 1933, and in 1949 American mathematician Claude Shannon unified many aspects of sampling and founded the larger science of information theory. Today, engineers usually attribute the sampling theorem to Shannon or Nyquist. The half-sampling frequency is usually known as the Nyquist frequency. Nyquist, who was born in Sweden in 1889, and died in Texas in 1976, worked for Bell Laboratories and authored 138 U.S. patents.

Whoever gets the credit, the sampling theorem states that a continuous bandlimited signal can be replaced by a discrete sequence of samples without loss of any information and describes how the original continuous signal can be reconstructed from the samples; furthermore, the theorem specifies that the sampling frequency must be at least twice the highest signal frequency. This principle is widely applied throughout engineering and mathematics, in diverse areas such as optics, holography, meteorology, and oceanography, to name a few.

The sampling theorem can be applied to audio signals. The input audio signal is lowpass filtered, so that it is bandlimited with a frequency response entirely below the Nyquist frequency. Ideally, the filter is designed so that the only signals removed are those high frequencies that lie above the high frequency limit of human hearing. The signal can now be sampled to define instantaneous amplitude values. The sampled bandlimited signal contains the same information as the unsampled bandlimited signal. At the system output, the signal is reconstructed, and there is no loss of information (due to sampling) between the output signal and the input filtered signal. From a sampling standpoint, the output signal is not an approximation; it is exact. The bandlimited signal is thus re-created, as shown in Fig. 2-1.

Consider a continuously changing analog function that has been sampled to create a series of pulses. The amplitude of each pulse, when determined through quantization, ultimately yields a number that represents the signal amplitude at that instant. To quantify the situation, we define the sampling frequency as the number of samples per second. Its reciprocal, sampling rate, defines the time between each sample. For example, a sampling frequency of 40,000 samples per second corresponds to a rate of 1/40,000 second. A quickly changing waveform—that is, one with high frequencies—would require a higher sampling frequency. Thus, the digitization system's sampling frequency determines the high frequency limit of the system. The

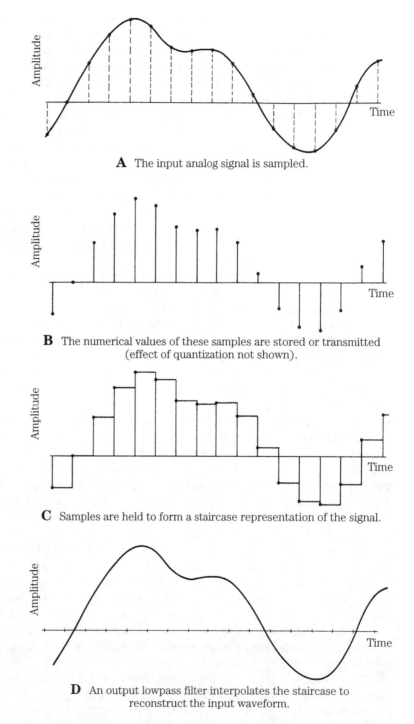

A The input analog signal is sampled.

B The numerical values of these samples are stored or transmitted (effect of quantization not shown).

C Samples are held to form a staircase representation of the signal.

D An output lowpass filter interpolates the staircase to reconstruct the input waveform.

2-1 With discrete time sampling, a bandlimited signal can be sampled and reconstructed without loss because of sampling.

choice of sampling frequency is thus one of the most important design criteria of a digitization system, because it determines the audio bandwidth of the system.

The sampling theorem precisely dictates how often a waveform must be sampled to provide a given bandwidth. Specifically, a sampling frequency of S samples/second is needed to completely represent a waveform with a bandwidth of $S/2$ Hz. In other words, the sampling frequency must be at least twice the highest audio frequency to achieve lossless sampling. For example, an audio signal with a frequency response of 0 to 20 kHz would theoretically require a sampling frequency of 40 kHz for proper sampling. It is crucial to observe the sampling theorem's criteria for limiting the input signal to no more than half the sampling frequency (the Nyquist frequency). An audio frequency above this would cause aliasing distortion, as described in this chapter. A lowpass filter must precede the sampling circuit to remove frequencies above the half-sampling frequency limit. A lowpass filter is also placed at the output of a digital audio system to remove high frequencies created internal to the system. This filter reconstructs the original waveform. Reconstruction is discussed in more detail in chapter 4.

Another question presents itself with respect to the sampling theorem. We observe that low audio frequencies are easily sampled; because of their long wavelengths, many samples are available to represent each period. But as the audio frequency increases, the periods are shorter and there are fewer samples per period. Finally, in the theoretical limiting case of critical sampling, at an audio frequency of half the sampling frequency, there are only two samples per period. However, even two samples can represent a waveform. For example, consider the case of a 40-kHz sampling frequency and an input 20-kHz audio sinewave. The sampler produces two samples, which will yield a 20-kHz square wave. In itself, this waveform is quite unlike the original sinewave. However, the 20-kHz square wave is comprised of odd harmonics—sinewaves at 20, 60, 100, 140, and 180 kHz, etc. A lowpass filter at the output of the digital audio system removes all frequencies higher than the half-sampling frequency. With all higher harmonics removed, the output of the system is a reconstructed 20-kHz sinewave, the same as the sampled waveform. We know that the sampled waveform was a sinewave because the input lowpass filter will not pass higher waveform frequencies to the sampler. As far as our ears are concerned, a sinewave is perfectly suitable because the harmonics of any complex 20-kHz waveform are above the audible frequency range. The first partial, for example, would be located at 40 kHz. Similarly, a digitization system can reproduce all information from 0 to $S/2$ Hz, including reproduction at $S/2$ Hz; even in the limiting case, the sampling theory is valid. Conversely, all information above $S/2$ is removed from the signal. We can state that higher sampling frequencies permit recording and reproduction of higher audio frequencies. But given the design criteria of an audio frequency bandwidth, higher frequencies will not improve the fidelity of those signals already within the bandlimited frequency range.

For critical sampling, there is no guarantee that the sample times will coincide with the maxima and minima of the waveform. Sample times could coincide with lower-amplitude parts of the waveform, or even coincide with the zero-axis crossings of the waveform. In practice, this does not pose a problem. Critical sampling is not attempted; a sampling margin is always present. As we have seen, to satisfy the sam-

pling theorem, a lowpass filter must precede the sampler. Lowpass filters cannot attenuate the signal precisely at the Nyquist frequency; a guard band is employed. The filter's cutoff frequency characteristic starts at a lower frequency, allowing several thousand hertz for the filter to attenuate the signal sufficiently. This ensures that no frequency above the Nyquist frequency enters the sampler. The waveform is not critically sampled; there are always more than two samples per period. Furthermore, the phase relationship between samples and waveforms is never exact because acoustic waveforms cannot synchronize with a sampler. In any case, the output signal is not reconstructed sample by sample; rather, it is formed from the response of many samples, in the same way that the ear does not hear each part of a waveform, but instead hears the average of sound over time.

Note that the need to bandlimit the audio signal is not as detrimental as it might first appear. The upper frequency limit of the audio signal can be extended as far as needed, so long as the appropriate sampling frequency is employed. The trade-off, of course, is the demand placed on the speed of digital circuitry and the capacity of the storage or transmission medium. Higher sampling frequencies require that circuitry operate faster and that larger amounts of data be conveyed. Both are ultimately questions of economics. Manufacturers have selected a sampling frequency of 44.1 kHz for the compact disc, for example, because of desirable size, playing time, and cost of the medium.

The entire sampling (and desampling) process is illustrated in Fig. 2-2. The signals involved in sampling are shown at various points in the processing chain. Moreover, the left half of the figure shows the signals in the time domain and the right half portrays the same signals in the frequency domain. In other words, we can observe a signal amplitude over time, as well as its frequency response. We observe in Fig. 2-2A and B that the input audio signal must be bandlimited to the half-sampling frequency $S/2$, using a lowpass anti-aliasing filter. This filter removes all components above the Nyquist frequency of $S/2$. The sampling signal in Fig. 2-2C and D recurs at the sampling frequency S, and its spectrum consists of pulses at multiples of the sampling frequency, S, $2S$, $3S$, etc. When the audio signal is sampled, as shown in Fig. 2-2E and F, the signal amplitude at sample times is preserved; however, this sampled signal contains images of the original spectrum centered at multiples of the sampling frequency. To reproduce the sampled signal, as in Fig. 2-2G and H, the samples are passed through a lowpass anti-imaging filter to remove all images above the $S/2$ frequency. This filter interpolates between the samples of the waveform, re-creating the input, bandlimited audio signal. As described in chapter 4, the output filter supplies an impulse response that uniquely changes the sample pulses into a continuous waveform.

The sampling theorem is unequivocal: a bandlimited signal can be sampled; stored, transmitted or processed as discrete values; desampled; and reconstructed. No information is lost through sampling. Sampling theorems such as the Nyquist theorem prove this conclusively. Of course, after it has time sampled the signal, a digital system also must determine the numerical values it will use to represent the waveform amplitude at each sample time. This question of quantization is explained subsequently in this chapter. For a more detailed discussion of discrete time sampling, and a concise mathematical demonstration of the sampling theorem, refer to the appendix.

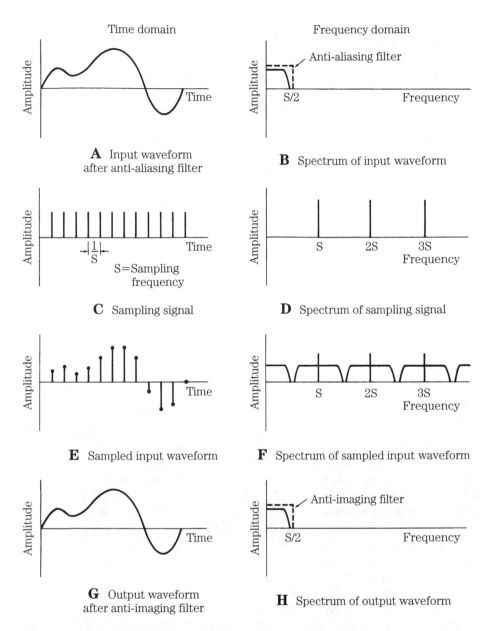

A Input waveform
after anti-aliasing filter

B Spectrum of input waveform

C Sampling signal

D Spectrum of sampling signal

E Sampled input waveform

F Spectrum of sampled input waveform

G Output waveform
after anti-imaging filter

H Spectrum of output waveform

2-2 Time domain (left column) and frequency domain (right column) signals illustrate the effect of bandlimited waveform sampling, and reconstruction.

Aliasing

One particular challenge to a digital audio system designer is that of aliasing, a kind of sampling confusion that can occur in the recording side of the signal chain. Just as a criminal can take many names and thus confuse identity, aliasing can cre-

ate false signal components. These erroneous signals can appear within the audio bandwidth and are impossible to distinguish from legitimate signals. Obviously, it is the designer's obligation to prevent such distortion from ever occurring. In practice, aliasing is not a limitation. It merely underscores the importance of observing the criteria of sampling theory.

We have observed that sampling is a lossless process under certain conditions. Most important, the input signal must be bandlimited; that is, a lowpass filter must precede the sampler. If this is not done, the signal is undersampled, which can create aliasing. Consider another conceptual experiment: focus a motion picture camera on me while I get on my BMW and drive away. In the film, as I accelerate, the spokes of the wheels rotate forward, appear to slow and stop, then begin to rotate backward, rotate faster, then slow and stop, and appear to rotate forward again. This action is an example of aliasing. The motion picture camera, with a frame rate of 24 frames per second, cannot capture the rapid movement of the wheels.

Aliasing is a consequence of violating the sampling theorem. The highest audio frequency in a sampling system must be equal to or less than half the sampling frequency. If the audio frequency is greater than half the sampling frequency, aliasing will occur. As the audio frequency increases, the number of sample points per period decreases. When the Nyquist frequency is reached, there are two samples per period, the minimum needed to record the bipolar nature of the waveform. If we sample even higher audio frequencies, the sampler will continue to produce samples at its fixed rate, but the samples create false information in the form of alias frequencies. As the audio frequency increases, a descending alias frequency is created. Specifically, if S is the sampling frequency, F is a frequency higher than the half-sampling frequency, and N is an integer, then a new frequency F_f is created at $F_f = \pm NS \pm F$. In other words, alias frequencies appear back in the audio band (and the images of the audio band), folded over from the sampling frequency. In fact, aliasing is sometimes called foldover. Although disturbing, this is not totally surprising. Sampling is a kind of modulation; in fact, sampling is akin to the operation of a heterodyne demodulator in an AM (amplitude modulation) radio. A local oscillator multiplies the input signal to move its frequency down to the standard IF (intermediate frequency). Although the effect is desirable in radios, aliasing in digital audio systems is not desired.

Consider a digitization system sampling at 44 kHz. Further, suppose that a signal with a frequency of 36 kHz has entered the sampler, as shown in Fig. 2-3. The primary alias component results from $S - F = F_f$ or $44 - 36 = 8$ kHz. The sampler produces the improper samples, faithfully recording a series of amplitude values at sample times. Given those samples, no device, digital or otherwise, could determine which was the intended frequency: 36 kHz or 8 kHz. Furthermore, recall that a lowpass filter at the output of a digitization system smoothes the staircase function to reconstruct the original signal. The output filter cutoff is the half-sampling frequency. Thus, frequencies above that frequency are removed. In this case, following the output filter, the 36-kHz signal would be removed, but the 8-kHz alias signal would remain, containing samples as innocuous as a legitimate 8-kHz signal. That unwanted signal adds distortion to the audio signal.

There are other manifestations of aliasing. Although only the $S - F$ component appears as an interfering frequency in the audio bandwidth, an alias component will

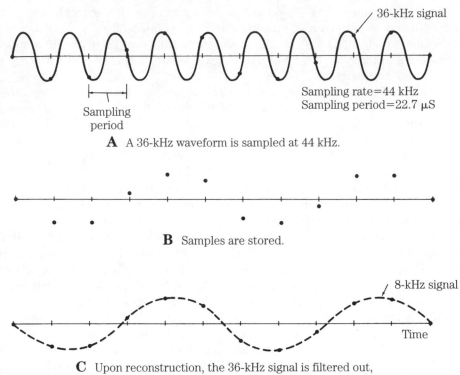

A A 36-kHz waveform is sampled at 44 kHz.

B Samples are stored.

C Upon reconstruction, the 36-kHz signal is filtered out, leaving an aliased 8-kHz signal.

2-3 An input signal greater than the half-sampling frequency will generate an alias signal, at a lower frequency.

appear in the audio bandwidth, no matter how high in frequency F becomes. Consider a sampling frequency of 44 kHz; an input frequency from 0 to 22 kHz would sound fine, but as the frequency ranges from 22 kHz to 44 kHz, it returns as a frequency descending from 22 kHz to 0. If the input frequency is raised from 44 kHz to 66 kHz, it appears again from 0 to 22 kHz, etc. Figure 2-4 shows how different aliased frequencies appear in the audio band from 0 to 22 kHz, as the input frequency increases.

Alias components occur not only around the sampling frequency, but also in the multiple images produced by sampling (see Fig. 2-2F). When the sampling theorem is obeyed, the audio band and image bands are separate, as shown in Fig. 2-5A and B. However, when the audio band extends past the Nyquist frequency, the image bands overlap, resulting in aliasing as shown in Fig. 2-5C and D. All of these components would be produced in an aliasing scenario: $\pm S \pm F$, $\pm 2S \pm F$, $\pm 3S \pm F$, etc. For example, given a 44-kHz sampler and a 27-kHz input signal, some of the resulting alias frequencies would be: 17, 61, 71, 105, 115, 149, 159 kHz, as shown in Fig. 2-5D.

More complex tones exaggerate the problem. With a sinewave, foldover is limited to the one and only partial of a sinewave. With complex tones, alias frequencies are generated separately for each harmonic. For example, the second harmonic of a complex waveform with an 11 kHz fundamental is 22 kHz, which would be critically

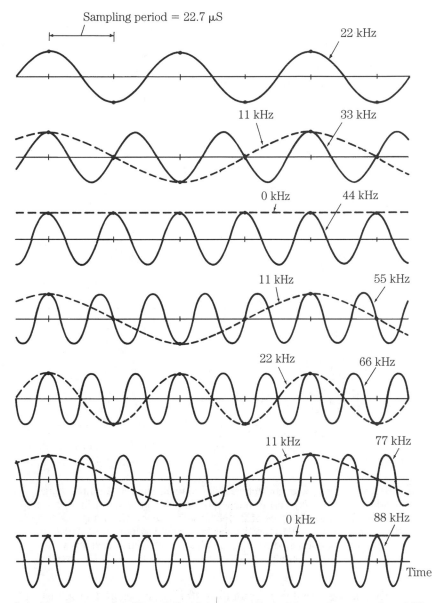

2-4 Alias frequencies (dotted lines) in the audio band vary between 0 and 22 kHz as the input frequency (solid lines) increases.

sampled by a 44-kHz sampler. However, the third harmonic at 33 kHz is aliased back at 11 kHz to add to the fundamental. The sixth harmonic at 66 kHz aliases at 22 kHz to add to the second harmonic. More typically, the fundamental and its harmonics would not be submultiples of the sampling frequency. For example, a complex periodic frequency of 5 kHz produces a fifth harmonic at 25 kHz, which aliases at 19 kHz; the sixth harmonic at 30 kHz aliases at 14 kHz; the seventh harmonic at 35 kHz

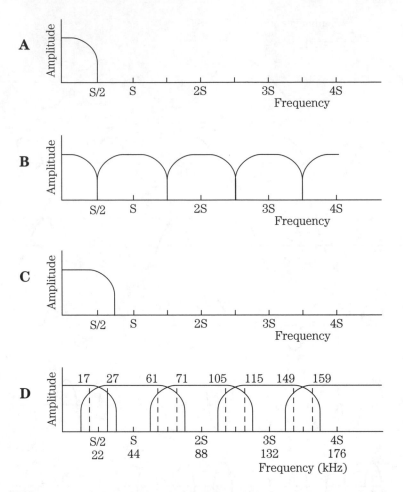

2-5 A spectral view of correct sampling, and aliasing. A. An input signal bandlimited to the Nyquist frequency. B. Upon reconstruction, images are contained within multiples of the Nyquist frequency. C. An input signal that is not bandlimited to the Nyquist frequency. D. Upon reconstruction, images are not contained within multiples of the Nyquist frequency; this spectral overlap is aliasing; a 27-kHz signal will alias in a 44-kHz sampler.

aliases at 9 kHz; and the eighth harmonic at 40 kHz aliases at 4 kHz, just below the fundamental.

Alias Prevention

In practice, the problem of aliasing can be overcome. In fact, in a well-designed digital recording system, aliasing does not occur. The solution is straightforward: the input signal is bandlimited with a sharp lowpass filter (anti-aliasing filter) designed to provide significant attenuation at the Nyquist frequency, to ensure that the sampled signal never exceeds the Nyquist frequency. An ideal filter would have a "brick-wall" characteristic with instantaneous and infinite attenuation in the stopband. However, in practice, the filter cannot achieve this. Rather, it is designed with a transition band in which attenuation is achieved over a steeply sloping characteristic. In addition, the filter provides attenuation to the limits of the amplitude resolution of the system. This ensures that the system meets the demands of the sampling theorem; thus, aliasing cannot occur.

It is critical to observe sampling theory, and lowpass filter the input signal in a digitization system. If aliasing is allowed to occur, there is no technique that can remove the aliased frequencies from the original audio bandwidth. Extremely low level aliasing can occur after the anti-aliasing filter, because of quantization error. A noise signal called dither is used to alleviate this distortion.

Quantization

A measurement of a varying event is meaningful only if both the time and the value of the measurement are stored. Sampling represents the time of the measurement, and quantization represents the value of the measurement, or in the case of audio, the amplitude of the waveform at sample time. Sampling and quantization are thus the fundamental components of digitization, and together can characterize an acoustic event. Both sampling and quantization become variables that determine, respectively, the bandwidth and resolution of the characterization. An analog waveform can be represented by a series of pulses; the amplitude of each pulse yields a number that represents the analog value at that instant. With quantization, as with any analog measurement, accuracy is limited by the system's resolution. Because of finite word length, a digital audio system's resolution is limited, and a measuring error is introduced. This error is often similar to the noise in an analog audio system; however, perceptually, it is more intrusive because its character varies with signal amplitude.

With uniform quantization, an analog signal amplitude is mapped into a number of quanta of equal height. The infinite number of amplitude points on the analog waveform must be quantized by the finite number of quanta levels; this introduces an error. A high-quality representation requires a large number of levels; for example, a high-quality music signal might require 65,536 amplitude levels or more. However, a few PCM levels can still carry information content; for example, two amplitude levels can (barely) convey intelligible speech.

Consider two voltmeters, one analog and one digital, each measuring the voltage corresponding to an input signal. Given a good meter face and a sharp eye, we might read the analog needle at 1.27 V (volts). A digital meter with only two digits might read 1.3 V. A three-digit meter might read 1.27 V, and a four-digit meter might read 1.274 V. Both the analog and digital measurements contain error. The error in the analog meter is caused by the ballistics of the mechanism and the difficulty in reading the meter. Even under ideal conditions, the resolution of any analog measurement is limited by the measuring device's own noise.

With the digital meter, the nature of the error is different. Accuracy is limited by the resolution of the meter—that is, by the number of digits displayed. The more digits, the greater the accuracy, but the last digit will round off relative to the actual value; for example, 1.27 would be rounded off to 1.3. In the best case, the last digit would be completely accurate; for example, a voltage of exactly 1.3000 would be shown as 1.3. In the worst case, the rounded off digit will be one-half interval away; for example, 1.250 would be rounded off to 1.2 or 1.3. If a binary system is used for the measurement, we say that the error resolution of the system is one-half the LSB (least significant bit). For both analog and digital systems, the problem of measuring an analog phenomenon such as amplitude leads to error. As far as voltmeters are concerned, a digital readout is an inherently more robust measurement. We gain more information about an analog event when it is characterized in terms of digital data. Today, an analog voltmeter is about as useful as a slide rule.

Quantization is thus the technique of measuring an analog event to form a numerical value. A digital system uses a binary number system. The number of possible values is determined by the length of the binary data word—that is, the number of bits available to form the representation. Just as the number of digits in a digital voltmeter determines resolution, the number of bits in a digital audio recorder also determines resolution. In practice, resolution is primarily influenced by the quality of the A/D (analog-to-digital) converter.

Sampling of a bandlimited signal is theoretically a lossless process, but choosing the amplitude value at sample time certainly is not. Any choice of scales or codes shows that digitization can never completely encode a continuous analog function. An analog waveform has an infinite number of amplitude values, but a quantizer has a finite number of intervals. All the analog values between two intervals can only be represented by the single number assigned to that interval. Thus, the quantized value is only an approximation of the actual.

Signal-to-Error Ratio

With a binary number system, the word length determines the number of quantizing intervals available; this can be computed by raising the word length to the power of 2. In other words, an n-bit word would yield 2^n quantization levels. The number of levels determined by the first $n = 1$ to 24 bits are listed in Table 2-1. For example, an 8-bit word provides $2^8 = 256$ intervals and a 16-bit word provides $2^{16} = 65{,}536$ intervals. Note that each time a bit is added to the word length, the number of levels doubles. The more bits, the better the approximation; but as noted, there is always an error associated with quantization because the finite number of amplitude levels coded in the binary word can never completely accommodate an infinite number of analog amplitudes.

It is difficult to appreciate the accuracy achieved by a 16-bit measurement. An analogy might help: if sheets of typing paper were stacked to a height of 22 feet, a single sheet of paper would represent one quantization level in a 16-bit system. Longer word lengths are even more impressive. In a 20-bit system, the stack would reach 352 feet. In a 24-bit system, the stack would tower 5632 feet in height—over a mile high. The quantizer could measure that mile to an accuracy equal to the thickness of a piece of paper. If a single page was removed, the least significant bit would change from 1 to 0. Looked at in another way, if the distance between New York and Los Angeles were measured with 24-bit accuracy, the measurement would be accu-

$$2^1 = 2$$
$$2^2 = 4$$
$$2^3 = 8$$
$$2^4 = 16$$
$$2^5 = 32$$
$$2^6 = 64$$
$$2^7 = 128$$
$$2^8 = 256$$
$$2^9 = 512$$
$$2^{10} = 1024$$
$$2^{11} = 2048$$
$$2^{12} = 4096$$
$$2^{13} = 8192$$
$$2^{14} = 16384$$
$$2^{15} = 32768$$
$$2^{16} = 65536$$
$$2^{17} = 131072$$
$$2^{18} = 262144$$
$$2^{19} = 524288$$
$$2^{20} = 1048576$$
$$2^{21} = 2097152$$
$$2^{22} = 4194304$$
$$2^{23} = 8388608$$
$$2^{24} = 16777216$$

Table 2-1. Number (N) of quantization intervals in a binary word is $N = 2n$ where n is the number of bits in the word.

rate to within 9 inches. A high-quality digital audio system thus requires components with similar tolerances—not a trivial feat.

At some point, the quantizing error approaches inaudibility. Most manufacturers have agreed that 16 to 20 bits provide an adequate representation; however, that doesn't rule out longer data words or the use of other signal processing to optimize quantization and thus reduce quantization error level.

Word length determines the resolution of a digitization system and hence provides an important specification for evaluating system performance. Sometimes the quantized interval will be exactly at the analog value; usually it will not be quite exact. At worst, the analog level will be one-half interval away—that is, there is an error of half the least significant bit of the quantization word. For example, consider Fig. 2-6. Suppose the binary word 101000 corresponds to the analog interval of 1.4 V, 101001 corresponds to 1.5 V, and the analog value at sample time is unfortunately 1.45 V. Because 101000½ is not available, you must round up to 101001 or down to 101000. Either way, there will be an error with a magnitude of one-half of an interval.

Quantization error is the difference between the actual analog value at sample time and the selected quantization interval value. At sample time, the amplitude value is rounded to the nearest quantization interval, as shown in Fig. 2-7. At best (sample points 11 and 12 in the figure), the waveform coincides with quantization intervals. At worst (sample point 1 in the figure), the waveform is exactly between two intervals. Quantization error is thus limited to a range between $+Q/2$ and $-Q/2$, where Q is one quantization interval. Note that this selection process, of one level or another, is the basic mechanism of quantization, and occurs for all samples in a digi-

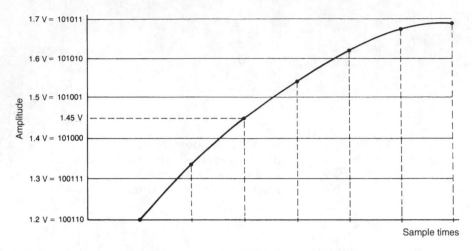

2-6 Quantization error is limited to one-half LSB.

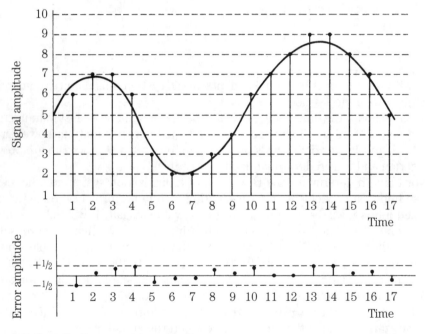

2-7 Quantization error at sample times.

tal system. This error results in distortion that is present for any amplitude audio signal. When the signal is large, the distortion is relatively small and masked. However, when the signal is small, the distortion is relatively large and might be audible.

In characterizing digital hardware performance, we can determine the ratio of the maximum expressible signal amplitude to the maximum quantization error; this determines the S/E (signal-to-error) ratio of the system. The signal-to-error ratio of a digital system is closely akin, but not identical to the S/N (signal-to-noise) ratio of an analog system. The S/E relationship can be derived using a ratio of signal-to-error voltage levels.

Consider a quantization system in which n is the number of bits, and N is the number of quantization steps. As noted:

$$N = 2^n$$

where one bit is a sign bit.

Half of these 2^n values will be used to code each part of the bipolar waveform. If Q is the quantizing interval, the peak values of the maximum signal levels are $\pm Q2^{n-1}$. Assuming a sinusoidal input signal, the maximum rms (root mean square) signal S_{rms} is:

$$S_{rms} = \frac{Q2^{n-1}}{(2)^{1/2}}$$

The energy in the quantization error also can be determined. When the input signal has high amplitude and wide spectrum, the quantization error is statistically independent and uniformly distributed between the $+Q/2$ and $-Q/2$ limits, and 0 elsewhere, where Q is one quantization interval. This dictates a uniform probability density function with amplitude of $1/Q$; the error is random from sample to sample; the error spectrum is flat. Ignoring error outside the signal band, the rms quantization error E_{rms} can be found by summing (integrating) the product of the error and its probability:

$$E_{rms} = \left[\int_{-\infty}^{+\infty} e^2 p(e)\,de \right]^{1/2} = \left[\frac{1}{Q} \int_{-\frac{Q}{2}}^{+\frac{Q}{2}} e^2\,de \right]^{1/2} = \left[\frac{Q^2}{12} \right]^{1/2} = \frac{Q}{(12)^{1/2}}$$

The power ratio determining the signal to quantization error is:

$$\frac{S}{E} = \left[\frac{S_{rms}}{E_{rms}} \right]^2 = \frac{\left[\dfrac{Q2^{n-1}}{(2)^{1/2}} \right]^2}{\left[\dfrac{Q}{(12)^{1/2}} \right]^2} = \frac{3}{2}(2^{2n})$$

Expressing this ratio in decibels:

$$\frac{S}{E} \text{ (dB)} = 10\log\left[\frac{3}{2}(2^{2n}) \right] = 20\log\left[\left(\frac{3}{2}\right)^{1/2}(2^n) \right]$$

$$= 6.02n + 1.76$$

Using this approximation for signal-to-error ratio, we observe that ideal 16-bit quantization yields an *S/E* ratio of about 98 dB, but 15-bit quantization is inferior at 92 dB. In other words, each additional bit reduces the quantization noise by 6 dB, or a factor of two. Longer word lengths increase the data signal bandwidth required to convey the signal. However, the signal-to-quantization noise power ratio increases exponentially with data signal bandwidth. This is an efficient relationship that approaches the theoretical maximum, and it is a hallmark of coded systems such as PCM (pulse-code modulation) described in chapter 3. The figure of 1.76 is based on the statistics (peak-to-rms ratio) of a sinusoidal waveform; it will differ if the signal peak-to-rms ratio differs from that of a sinusoid.

It also is important to note that this result assumes that the quantization error is uniformly distributed, and quantization is accurate enough to prevent signal correlation in the error waveform. This is generally true for high amplitude complex audio signals, where the complex distortion components are uncorrelated, spread across the audible range, and perceived as white noise. However, this is not the case for low amplitude signals, where distortion products can appear.

Quantization Distortion

Analysis of the quantization error of low-amplitude signals reveals that the spectrum is a function of the input signal; the error is not noise-like (as with high-amplitude signals), it is correlated. At the system output, when the quantized sample values reconstruct the analog waveform, the in-band components of the error are contained in the output signal. Because quantization error is a function of the original signal, it cannot be described as noise; rather, it must be classified as distortion.

As noted, when quantization error is random from sample to sample, the rms quantization error $E_{rms} = Q/(12)^{1/2}$. This equation demonstrates that the magnitude of the error is independent of the amplitude of the input signal, but depends on the size of the quantization interval; the greater the number of intervals, the lower the distortion. However, the relevant number of intervals is not only the number of intervals in the quantizer, but also the number of intervals used to quantize a particular signal. A maximum peak-to-peak signal (as used in the preceding analysis) presents the best case scenario because all the quantization intervals are exercised. However, as signal level decreases, fewer and fewer levels are exercised. For example, given a 16-bit quantizer, a half-amplitude signal would be mapped into half of the intervals. Instead of 65,536 levels, it would see 32,768 intervals. In other words, it would be quantized with 15-bit resolution. The problem increases as the signal level decreases. A very low-level signal, for example, would receive only one-bit quantization or might not be quantized at all. In other words, as the signal level decreases, the percentage of distortion increases. Although the distortion might be virtually unmeasurable at 0 dB, it increases significantly at low amplitude (for example, –90 dB) levels. As described in a following section, dither must be used to alleviate the problem.

The error floor of a digital audio system differs from the noise floor of an analog system, because in a digital system the error is a function of the signal. The nature of quantization error varies with the amplitude and nature of the audio signal. For broadband, high amplitude input signals (such as are typically found in music), the quantization error is perceived similarly to white noise. A high level complex signal shows a pattern from sample to sample; however, its quantization error signal shows no pattern from sample to sample. The quantization error is thus independent of signal (and thus assumes the characteristics of noise) when the signal is high level and complex. The only difference between this error noise and analog noise is that the range of values is more limited for a constant rms value. In other words, all values are equally likely to fall between positive and negative peaks. On the other hand, analog noise is Gaussian distributed, so its peaks are higher than its rms value.

However, the perceptual qualities of the error are less benign for low-amplitude signals and high-level signals of very narrow bandwidth. This fact is similar to the fact that white noise is perceptually benign, because successive values of the signal are random, whereas predictable noise signals are more perceptible. For broadband high-level signals, the statistical correlation between successive samples is very low; however, it increases for broadband low-level signals and narrow bandwidth, high-level signals. As the statistical correlation between samples increases, error initially perceived as benign white noise becomes a more complex kind of distortion.

Quantization distortion can take many guises. For example, the quantized signal might contain components above the Nyquist frequency; thus, aliasing might occur. The components appear after the sampler, but are effectively sampled. As Barry Blesser notes, the effects of sampling the output of a limiter or limiting the output of a sampler are indistinguishable. If the signal is high level or complex, the alias components will add into the other complex, noiselike errors. If the input signal is low level and simple, the aliased components might be quite audible. Consider a system with sampling frequency of 50 kHz, bandlimited to 25 kHz. When a 7-kHz sinewave of amplitude of one quantizing step is applied, it is quantized as a sampled 7-kHz square wave. Harmonics of the square wave appear at 21, 35, and 49 kHz. The latter two alias back to 15 and 1 kHz, respectively. Other harmonics and aliases appear as well.

The aliasing caused by quantization can create an effect called granulation noise, so called because of its gritty sound quality. With high-level signals, the noise is masked by the signal itself. However, with low-level signals, the noise is audible. This blend of gritty, modulating noise and distortion has no analog counterpart and is audibly unpleasant. Furthermore, if the alias components are near a multiple of the sampling frequency, beat tones can be created, producing an odd sound called "bird singing" or "birdies." A decaying tone presents a waveform descending through quantization levels; the error is perceptually changed from white noise to discrete distortion components. The problem is aggravated because even complex musical tones become more sinusoidal as they decay. Moreover, the decaying tone will tend to amplitude modulate the distortion components. Dither addresses these quantization problems.

Other Quantization Methods

Quantization is more than just word length; it also is a question of hardware design and architecture. There are many techniques available to accomplish quantization, and different strategies determine how the analog signal is assigned to the intervals. For example, a quantizer can use either a linear or nonlinear distribution of quantization intervals along the amplitude scale. An alternative is a delta modulation system, in which a one-bit quantizer is used to encode amplitude, using the single bit as a sign bit. In other cases, oversampling and noise shaping can be used to shift quantization error out of the audio band. Those algorithm decisions influence the efficiency of the quantizing bits, as well as the relative audibility of the error. For example, as noted, a linear quantizer produces a relatively high error with low-level signals that span only a few intervals. A nonlinear system using a floating point converter can increase low-level signals to utilize the greatest possible interval span. Although this improves the overall signal-to-error ratio, the noise modulation by-product might be undesirable. Historically, after examining the trade-offs of different quantization systems, manufacturers have determined that a fixed, linear quantization scheme is most suitable for music recording. However, newer perceptual coding systems challenge this assumption. Alternative digitization systems are examined in chapter 4. Perceptual coding is examined in chapter 11.

Dither

With large amplitude complex signals, there is little correlation between the signal and quantization error; thus the error is random and perceptually similar to analog white noise. With low-level signals, the character of the error changes as it becomes correlated to the signal, and potentially audible distortion results. A digitization system must suppress any audible qualities of its quantization error. Obviously, the number of bits in the quantizing word can be increased, resulting in a decrease in error amplitude of 6 dB per additional bit. This is uneconomical, and many bits are needed to satisfactorily reduce the audibility of quantization error.

Dither is a far more efficient technique. With dither, a small amount of noise is added to the audio signal prior to sampling to linearize the quantization process. Essentially, with dither the audio signal is made to shift with respect to quantization levels. The averaging process smooths the effect of incremental quantization levels and decorrelates the error from the signal. This randomizes the effects of the quantization error to the point of total elimination. However, although it greatly reduces distortion, dither adds some noise to the output signal.

Dither does not mask quantization error; rather, it allows the digital system to encode amplitudes smaller than the least significant bit, in much the same way that an analog system can retain signals below its noise floor. A properly dithered digital system far exceeds the signal to noise performance of an analog system. On the other hand, an undithered digital system can be inferior to an analog system, particularly under low-level signal conditions. A high-quality digital audio system demands dithering prior to quantization at the A/D converter. In a very conceptual sense, dither is similar to high frequency bias in an analog magnetic tape recorder. In addition, digital computations should be dithered prior to requantization at a D/A converter.

Consider the case of an input audio signal with amplitude on the order of one quantization interval. It would either move within the interval, resulting in a dc (direct current) signal, or move back and forth across the interval threshold, resulting in an output square wave, as shown in Fig. 2-8A and B. The square wave demonstrates that quantization ultimately acts as a hard limiter; in other words, severe distortion takes place. The effect is quite different when a dither noise signal is added to the audio signal. The result shown in Fig. 2-8C and D is a pulse signal that preserves the low-level information of the audio signal. The quantized signal switches up and down as the dithered input varies, tracking the average value of the input signal. This information is encoded in the varying width of the quantized signal pulses. This kind of information storage is known as pulse-width modulation, and it accurately preserves the input signal waveform. The average value of the quantized signal moves continuously between two levels, alleviating the effects of quantization error. Similarly, analog noise would be coded as a binary noise signal; values of 0 and 1 would appear in the LSB in each sampling period, with the signal retaining its white spectrum. The perceptual result is the original signal with added noise—a more desirable result than a quantized square wave.

Mathematically, with dither, quantization error is no longer a deterministic function of the input signal, but rather becomes a zero-mean random variable. In other words, rather than quantizing only the input signal, the dither noise and signal are

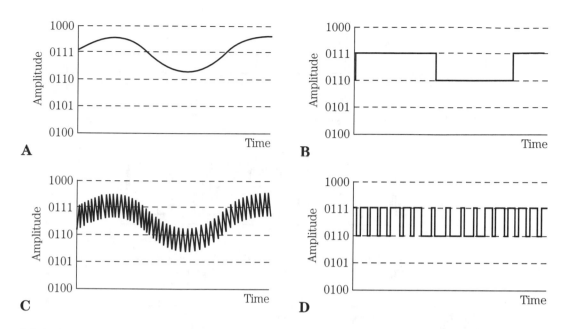

2-8 Dither is used to alleviate the effects of quantization error. A. An undithered input signal with amplitude on the order of one LSB. B. Quantization results in a coarse coding over two levels. C. A dithered input signal. D. Quantization yields a PWM waveform that codes information below the LSB.

quantized together, and this randomizes the error. This linearizes the quantization process. This technique is known as nonsubtractive dither because the dither signal is permanently added to the audio signal; the total error is not statistically independent of the audio signal, and errors are not independent sample to sample. However, nonsubtractive dither does manipulate the statistical properties of the quantizer, statistically rendering conditional moments of the total error independent of the input, effectively decorrelating the quantization error of the samples from the signal, and from each other. The power spectrum of the total error signal can be made white. Subtractive dithering, in which the dither signal is removed after requantization, theoretically provides total error statistical independence, but is more difficult to implement.

John Vanderkooy and Stanley Lipshitz have demonstrated the benefit of dither with a 1-kHz sinewave with a peak-to-peak amplitude of one LSB, as shown in Fig. 2-9. Without dither, a square wave is output from the digital-to-analog converter. When Gaussian dither with an rms amplitude of ⅓ LSB is added to the original signal, a pulse-width-modulated waveform results. The encoded sinewave is revealed when the signal is averaged over many periods. A sinewave emerges from the PWM output signal. The averaging illustrates how the ear responds in its perception of acoustic signals; that is, the ear is a lowpass filter that averages any signal. In this case, a noisy sinewave is heard, rather than a square wave.

The ear is quite good at resolving narrow-band signals below the noise floor, because of the averaging properties of the basilar membrane. The ear behaves as a one-

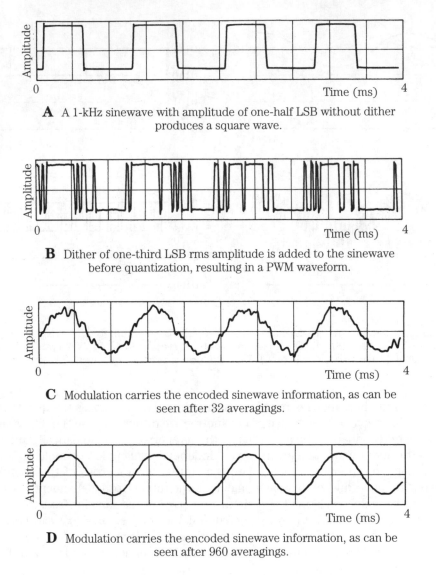

A A 1-kHz sinewave with amplitude of one-half LSB without dither produces a square wave.

B Dither of one-third LSB rms amplitude is added to the sinewave before quantization, resulting in a PWM waveform.

C Modulation carries the encoded sinewave information, as can be seen after 32 averagings.

D Modulation carries the encoded sinewave information, as can be seen after 960 averagings.

2-9 Dither permits encoding of information below the least significant bit.
Vanderkooy and Lipshitz

third octave filter with a narrow bandwidth; the quantization error, which is given a white noise character by dither, is averaged by the ear, and the original narrow-band sinewave is heard without distortion. In other words, dither changes the digital nature of the quantization error into a white noise, and the ear can then resolve signals with levels well below one quantization level.

This conclusion is an important one. With dither, the resolution of a digitization system is far below the least significant bit; theoretically, there is no limit to low-level resolution. By encoding the audio signal with dither to modulate the quantized signal, that information can be recovered, even though it is smaller than the smallest quantizer interval. Furthermore, dither can eliminate distortion caused by quantization, by reducing those artifacts to white noise. Proof of this is shown in Fig. 2-10, illustrating a computer simulation performed by John Vanderkooy, Robert Wannamaker, and Stanley Lipshitz. The figure shows a 1-kHz sinewave of 4.0 LSB peak-to-peak amplitude. The first column shows the signal without dither. The second column shows the same signal with triangular pdf (probability density function) dither (explained in the following paragraphs) of 2.0 LSB peak-to-peak amplitude. In both cases, the first row shows the input signal. The second row shows the output signal. The third row shows the total quantization error signal. The fourth row shows the power spectrum of the output signal (this is estimated from sixty 50% overlapping Hanning windowed 512-point records at 44.1 kHz). The undithered output signal (D) suffers from harmonic distortion, visible at multiples of the input frequency, as well as inharmonic distortion from aliasing. The error signal (G) of the dithered signal shows artifacts of the input signal; thus, it is not statistically independent. However, surprisingly, this error signal sounds like white noise (although it clearly does not look like white noise) and the output signal sounds like a sinewave with noise. This is supported by the power spectrum (H) showing that the signal is quite free of signal-dependent artifacts, with a white noise floor. However, we can see that dither increases the noise floor of the output signal.

Types of Dither

There are several types of dither signals, generally differentiated by their pdf (probability density function). Given a random signal with a continuum of possible values, the integral of the probability density function describes the probability of the values over an interval. The probability that the signal falls between the interval is the area under the function. For example, the probability might be constant over an interval, or it might vary. For audio applications, interest has focused on three dither signals: Gaussian pdf, rectangular (or uniform) pdf, and triangular pdf, as shown in Fig. 2-11. For example, we might speak of a statistically independent, white dither signal with a triangular pdf having a level or width of 2 LSB. Generally, dither signals have a white spectrum; however, the spectrum can be shaped by correlating successive dither samples without modifying the pdf; for example, a highpass triangular pdf dither signal could be created. All three dither types are effective at linearizing the transfer characteristics of quantization, but differ in their results. Although rectangular and triangular pdf dither signals add less overall noise to the signal, Gaussian dither is easier to implement in the analog domain.

Rectangular and triangular pdf dither of constant and precise amplitude are costly to generate in the analog domain; for example, the signal from a pseudo-random number generator could be applied to a D/A (digital-to-analog) converter to create a rectangular pdf signal. Therefore, designers often employ Gaussian noise as dither prior to A/D conversion. Gaussian dither is easy to generate with common

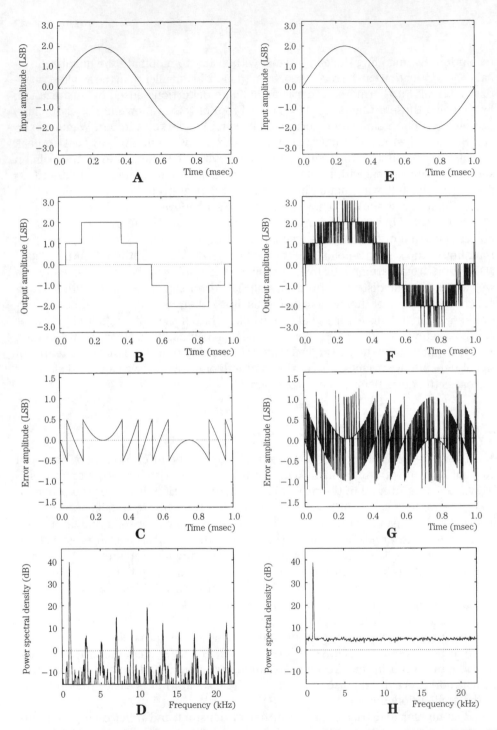

2-10 Computer-simulated quantization of a low-level 1-kHz sinewave without, and with dither. A. Input signal. B. Output signal (no dither). C. Total error signal (no dither). D. Power spectrum of output signal (no dither). E. Input signal. F. Output signal (triangular pdf dither). G. Total error signal (triangular pdf dither). H. Power spectrum of output signal (triangular pdf dither). Lipshitz, Wannamaker, and Vanderkooy

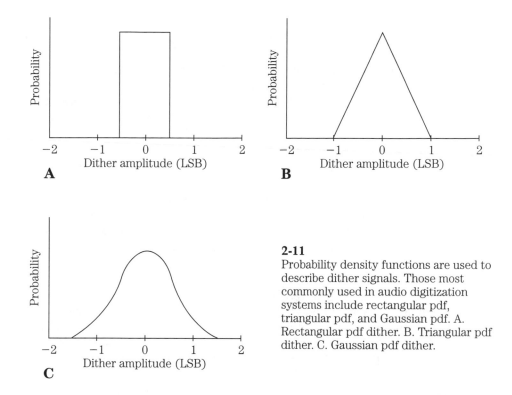

2-11
Probability density functions are used to describe dither signals. Those most commonly used in audio digitization systems include rectangular pdf, triangular pdf, and Gaussian pdf. A. Rectangular pdf dither. B. Triangular pdf dither. C. Gaussian pdf dither.

analog techniques; for example, a diode can be used as a noise source. The dither noise must vary between positive and negative values in each sampling period; its bandwidth must be at least half the sampling frequency. Gaussian dither with an rms value of ½ LSB will essentially linearize quantization errors; however, some noise modulation is added to the audio signal. The undithered quantization noise power is $Q^2/12$ (or $Q/(12)^{1/2}$ rms).

Gaussian dither contributes noise power of $Q^2/4$ so that the combined noise power is $Q^2/3$ (or $Q/(3)^{1/2}$ rms), where Q is one LSB. This increase in noise floor is significant.

Rectangular pdf dither is a uniformly distributed random voltage over an interval. Rectangular pdf dither lying between ±½ LSB (that is, a noise signal having a uniform probability density function with a peak-to-peak width that equals 1 LSB) will completely linearize the quantization staircase and eliminate distortion products caused by quantization. However, rectangular pdf does not eliminate noise floor modulation. With rectangular pdf dither, the noise level is more apt to be dependent on the signal, as well as width of the pdf. This noise modulation might be objectionable with very low frequencies or dynamically varied signals. Rectangular pdf dither of ±$Q/2$ adds a noise power of $Q^2/12$ to the quantization noise of $Q^2/12$; this yields a combined noise power of $Q^2/6$ (or $Q/(6)^{1/2}$ rms).

It is believed that the optimal nonsubtractive dither signal is a triangular pdf dither of 2 LSB peak-to-peak width, formed by summing (that is, by convolving the density functions) of two independent rectangular pdf dither signals each 1 LSB peak-to-peak width. Triangular pdf dither eliminates both distortion and noise floor modulation; however, the noise floor is higher than in rectangular pdf dither. Triangular pdf dither adds a noise power of $Q^2/6$ to the quantization noise power of $Q^2/12$; this yields a combined noise power of $Q^2/4$ (or $Q/2$ rms).

Thus, using these optimal dither amplitudes, relative to a nondithered signal, rectangular pdf dither increases noise by 3 dB, triangular pdf increases noise by 4.77 dB, and Gaussian pdf dither increases noise by 6 dB. In general, rectangular pdf might be preferred for testing purposes because of its expanded signal-to-error ratio, but triangular pdf seems preferable for listening purposes, in spite of its slightly higher noise floor. Clearly, Gaussian dither has a noise penalty. Because rectangular and triangular pdf dither are easily generated in the digital domain, they are preferable to Gaussian dither in requantization applications prior to D/A conversion. When measuring the low-level distortion of digital audio products, it is important to use dithered test signals; otherwise, the measurements might reflect distortion that is an artifact of the test signal and not of the hardware under test.

The amplitude of any dither signal is an important concern. Figure 2-12 shows how a quantization step is linearized by adding different amplitudes (width of pdf) of Gaussian pdf and rectangular pdf dither. In both cases, quantization artifacts are decreased as relatively higher amplitudes of dither are added. As noted, a Gaussian pdf signal with an amplitude of ½ LSB rms provides a linear characteristic. With rectangular pdf dither, a level of 1 LSB peak-to-peak provides linearity. In either case, too much dither overly decreases the signal-to-noise ratio of the digital system.

The increase in noise yielded by dither is usually negligible given the large signal-to-error ratio inherent in a digital system, and its audibility can be minimized, for example, with a highpass dither signal. This can be easily accomplished with digitally generated dither. For example, the spectrum of a triangular pdf dither can be processed so that its amplitude rises at high audio frequencies. Because the ear has a relative insensitivity to high frequencies, this dither signal will be less audible than broadband dither, yet noise modulation and signal distortion are removed. Such techniques can be used to audibly reduce quantization error, for example, when converting a 20-bit signal to a 16-bit signal. More generally, signal processing can be used to psychoacoustically shape the quantization noise floor to reduce its audibility. Noise-shaping applications are covered in chapter 16.

Designers have observed that the amplitude of a dither signal can be decreased if a sinewave with a frequency just below the Nyquist frequency, with an amplitude of 1 or ½ quantization interval, is added to the audio signal. The added signal must be above audibility yet below the Nyquist frequency to prevent aliasing. It alters the spectrum of quantization error to minimize its audibility and overall, does not add as much noise to the signal as broadband dither. For example, discrete triangular pdf dither might yield a 2-dB penalty, as opposed to 4.77 dB. However, a discrete dither frequency might lead to intermodulation products with audio signals. Wideband dither signals alleviate this artifact.

An additive dither signal necessarily decreases the S/N ratio of the digitization system. Barry Blesser proposed a subtractive dither signal that would preserve the

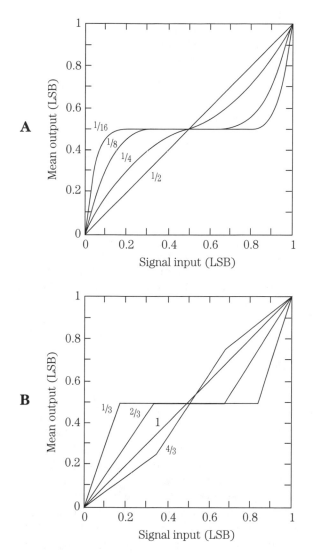

2-12
Input/output transfer
characteristic showing effects of
dither of varying amplitudes A.
Gaussian pdf dither of ½ LSB rms
linearizes signal. B. Rectangular
pdf dither of 1 LSB linearizes
signal. Vanderkooy and Lipshitz

S/N ratio, as shown in Fig. 2-13. Rectangular noise is a random-valued signal, which might be simulated by generating a quickly changing pseudo-random sequence of digital data. This can be accomplished with a series of shift registers and a feedback network comprised of EXCLUSIVE OR gates. This sequence is input to a D/A converter to produce analog noise, and the signal added to the audio signal to achieve the benefit of dither. Then, following A/D conversion, the dither can be digitally subtracted from the audio signal, preserving the dynamic range of the original signal. A further benefit is that inaccuracies in the A/D converter are similarly randomized. Other additive-subtractive methods call for two synchronized pseudo-random signal generators, one adding rectangular pdf dither at the A/D

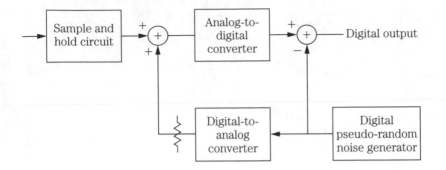

2-13 An example of a subtractive digital dither circuit using a pseudo-random number generator.

converter, and the other subtracting it at the D/A converter. Alternatively, in an autodither system, the audio signal itself could be randomized to create an added dither at the A/D converter, then re-created at the D/A converter and subtracted from the audio signal to restore dynamic range.

Digital dither must be used to decrease round-off error when signal manipulation takes place in the digital domain. For example, the truncation associated with multiplication can cause objectionable error, as described in chapter 15.

For the sake of completeness, Jim MacArthur has pointed out that one of the earliest uses of dither came in World War II; bombers used mechanical computers to perform navigation and bomb trajectory calculations. Curiously, these computers (boxes filled with hundreds of gears and cogs) performed more accurately when flying on board the aircraft, and less well on ground. Engineers realized that the vibration from the aircraft reduced the error from sticky moving parts—instead of moving in short jerks, they moved more continuously. Small vibrating motors were built into the computers, and their vibration was called dither from the Middle English verb "didderen," meaning "to tremble." Today, when you tap a mechanical meter to increase its accuracy, you are applying dither, and modern dictionaries define dither as "a highly nervous, confused, or agitated state." In minute quantities, dither successfully makes a digitization system a little more analog in the good sense of the word.

Conclusion

Sampling and quantizing are the two fundamental criteria for a digitization system. The sampling frequency determines signal bandlimiting and thus frequency response. Although complex, sampling is based on well-understood principles; the cornerstone of discrete time sampling yields completely predictable results. Aliasing occurs when the sampling theorem is not observed. Quantization determines the dynamic range of the system, measured by the signal-to-error ratio. Although bandlimited sampling is a lossless process, quantization is one of approximation. Quantization artifacts can severely affect the performance of a system. However, dither can eliminate quantization distortion, and maintain the fidelity of the audio digitization system. In general, a sampling frequency of 44.1 kHz or 48 kHz and a dithered word length of 16 to 20 bits yields fidelity comparable to or better than the best analog systems, with advantages such as longevity and fidelity of duplication.

Postscript: Fast Sampling Frequencies

Before ending our discussion of discrete time sampling, consider a hypothesis concerning the nature of time. Time seems to be continuous. However, some physicists have suggested that, like energy and matter, time might come in discrete packets. Just as this book consists of a finite number of atoms and could be converted into a finite amount of energy, the time it takes you to read the book might consist of a finite number of time particles. Specifically, the indivisible period of time might be 1×10^{-42} second (that's a 1 preceded by a decimal point and 41 zeros). The theory is that no time interval can be shorter than this because the energy required to make the division would be so great that a black hole would be created and the event would be swallowed up inside it. If any of you out there are experimenting in your basements with very fast sampling frequencies, please be careful.

Digital Audio Recording

The hardware design of a digital audio recorder embodies fundamental principles such as sampling and quantizing. The analog signal is sampled, converted to digital numerical form, and processed prior to digital storage, transmission, or further processing. Subsystems such as dither circuits, anti-aliasing filter, sample-and-hold, analog-to-digital converter, and channel code modulator constitute the hardware encoding chain. Although other architectures have been devised, the linear pulse-code modulation (PCM) system is the most illustrative of the nature of audio digitization and indeed is the most widely used system. This chapter and the next focus on the PCM hardware architecture. Such a system accomplishes the essential pre- and post-processing for either a digital recorder or real-time digital processor.

Pulse-Code Modulation

In theory, an almost endless number of techniques could be used to encode audio signals digitally. They are fundamentally identical in their operation of representing analog signals as digital data, but in practice they differ widely in relative efficiency in required bandwidth, and signal-to-noise ratio. Modulation is nothing more than a means of encoding information for the purpose of transmission or storage. Techniques such as amplitude modulation (AM) and frequency modulation (FM) have long been used to modulate carrier frequencies with analog audio information for radio broadcast. Because these are continuous kinds of modulation, they are referred to as wave-parameter modulation. AM and FM are illustrated in Fig. 3-1.

When conveying sampled information, various types of pulse modulation present themselves. For example, a pulse width, or position in time might represent the signal amplitude at sample time; pulse-width modulation (PWM) is an example of the former, and pulse-position modulation (PPM) is an example of the latter. In both cases, the original signal amplitude is coded and conveyed through constant amplitude pulses. A signal amplitude also can be conveyed directly by the modulation pulses; pulse-amplitude modulation (PAM) is an example of this approach. The am-

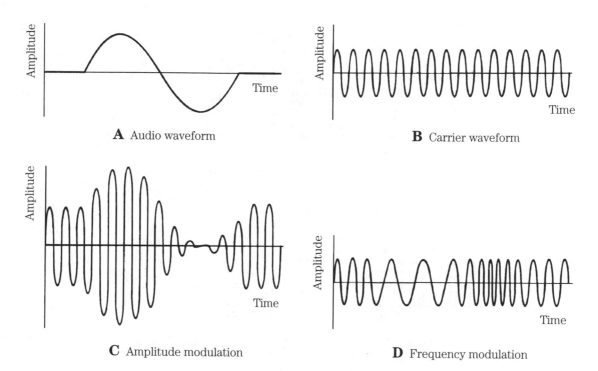

A Audio waveform

B Carrier waveform

C Amplitude modulation

D Frequency modulation

3-1 Amplitude modulation (AM) and frequency modulation (FM) are examples of wave-parameter modulation.

plitude of the pulses equals the amplitude of the signal at sample time. PWM, PPM, and PAM are shown in Fig. 3-2A through D. In other cases, sample amplitudes are conveyed through numerical methods. For example, in pulse-number modulation (PNM), the modulator generates a string of pulses; the pulse count represents the amplitude of the signal at sample time; this is shown in Fig. 3-2E and F. However, for high resolution, a large number of pulses is required. Although PWM, PPM, PAM, and PNM are often used in the context of conversion, they are not suitable for transmission or recording because of error or bandwidth limitations.

The most commonly used modulation method is pulse-code modulation (PCM). PCM was devised in 1937 by Alec Reeves while he was working as an engineer in the International Telephone and Telegraph Company laboratories in France; (Reeves also invented PWM). In PCM, the input signal must undergo sampling, quantization, and coding. By representing the measured analog amplitude of samples with a pulse code, binary numbers can be used to represent amplitude. At the receiver, the pulse code is used to reconstruct an analog waveform. The binary words that represent sample amplitudes are directly coded into PCM waveforms as shown in Fig. 3-2G.

With methods such as PWM, PPM, and PAM, only one pulse is needed to represent the amplitude value, but in PCM several pulses per sample are required. As a result, PCM might require a channel with higher bandwidth. However, PCM forms a very robust signal in that only the presence or absence of a pulse is necessary to read the signal. In addition, a PCM signal can be regenerated without loss. Therefore the

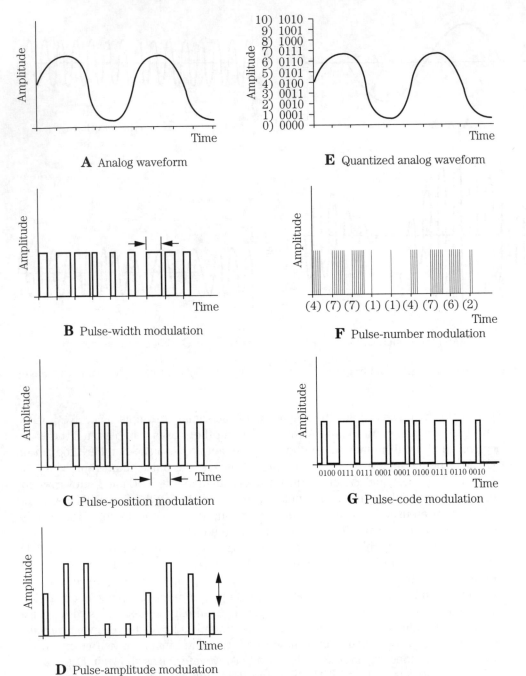

A Analog waveform

E Quantized analog waveform

B Pulse-width modulation

F Pulse-number modulation

C Pulse-position modulation

G Pulse-code modulation

D Pulse-amplitude modulation

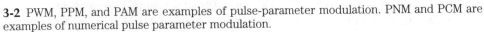

3-2 PWM, PPM, and PAM are examples of pulse-parameter modulation. PNM and PCM are examples of numerical pulse parameter modulation.

quality of a PCM transmission depends on the quality of the sampling and quantizing processes, not the quality of the channel itself. In addition, depending on the sampling frequency and capacity of the channel, several PCM signals can be simultaneously conveyed with time-division multiplexing. This ability greatly expedites use of PCM; for example, stereo is easily conveyed. Although other techniques presently exist and newer ones will be devised, they will measure their success against that of the pulse-code modulation digitization system. In most cases, highly specialized channel codes are used to modulate the signal prior to storage. These channel modulation codes arc also described in this chapter.

The architecture of a PCM system closely follows a readily conceptualized means of designing a digitization system. The analog waveform is filtered and time sampled and its amplitude is quantized by an analog-to-digital (A/D) converter. Binary numbers are represented as a series of modulated code pulses representing waveform amplitudes at sample times. If two channels are sampled, the data can be multiplexed to form one data stream. Data can be manipulated to provide synchronization and error correction, and auxiliary data can be added as well. Upon playback, the data is demodulated, decoded and error-corrected to recover the original amplitudes at sample times, and the analog waveform is reconstructed by a digital-to-analog (D/A) converter and lowpass filter.

The encoding section for a conventional stereo PCM recorder consists of input amplifiers, a dither generator, input lowpass filters, sample-and-hold circuits, analog-to-digital converters, a multiplexer, digital processing and modulation circuits, and a storage medium such as digital tape or disk. An encoding section block diagram is shown in Fig. 3-3. This hardware design is a practical realization of the sampling theorem. An audio digitization system is really nothing more than a transducer, which processes the audio signal for digital storage or transmission, then processes it again for reproduction. Although that sounds simple, the hardware must be carefully engineered; the quality of the reproduced audio depends entirely on the system's design. Each subsystem must be carefully considered.

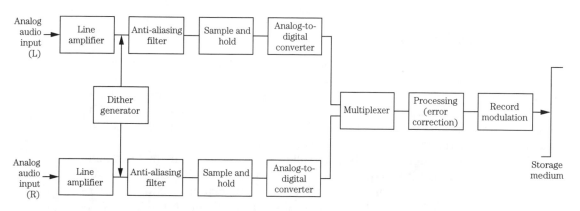

3-3 A linear PCM record section showing principal elements.

Aside from requirements of analog audio fidelity, such as low distortion and high signal-to-noise ratio, the input analog amplifiers have no special design features from a digital standpoint.

Dither Generator

Dither is a noise signal added to the input audio signal to remove the artifacts of quantization error, as described in chapter 2. Dither causes the audio signal to vary between adjacent quantization levels. This action decorrelates the quantization error from the signal, removes the effects of the error, and encodes signal amplitudes below the amplitude of a quantization increment. However, although it reduces distortion, dither adds noise to the audio signal. Perceptually, dither is beneficial because noise is more readily tolerated by the ear than distortion.

Analog dither, applied prior to an A/D converter, causes the A/D converter to make additional level transitions that preserve low-level signals through duty cycle, or pulse-width modulation. This linearizes the quantization process. Harmonic distortion products, for example, are converted to wideband noise. Several types of dither signals, such as Gaussian, rectangular, and triangular probability density function can be selected by the designer; in some systems, the user is free to choose a dither signal. The amplitude of the applied dither also is critical. In some cases, the input signal might have a high level of residual noise. For example, an analog tape might have a noise floor sufficient to dither the quantizer. However, the digital system must provide a dynamic range that sufficiently captures all the analog information, including the signal within the analog noise floor, and must not introduce quantization distortion into it. The word length of the quantizer must be sufficient for the audio program, and its LSB must be appropriately dithered. Whenever the word length is reduced, for example, when a 20-bit master recording is transferred to the 16-bit CD format, dithered must be applied, as well as noise shaping. Dither is discussed more fully in chapter 2; psychoacoustically optimized noise shaping is described in chapter 16.

Input Lowpass Filter

In a conventional encoder (nonoversampling), the analog signal is lowpass filtered by a very sharp cutoff filter; this bandlimits the signal and its entire harmonic content to frequencies below the half-sampling Nyquist frequency. For example, on a professional recorder with a sampling frequency of 48 kHz, the filter cutoff will be set around 22 kHz to allow for maximum attenuation at the half-sampling point. The input filter is sometimes called the anti-aliasing filter.

The input lowpass filter must attenuate all frequencies above the half-sampling frequency, yet not affect the lower frequencies. Thus, an ideal filter is a high-order filter with a flat passband, an immediate or brick-wall filter characteristic, and an infinitely attenuated stopband, as shown in Fig. 3-4A. In addition to these frequency-response criteria, an ideal filter must not affect the phase of the signal. Although in practice an ideal filter can be approximated, its realization presents a number of en-

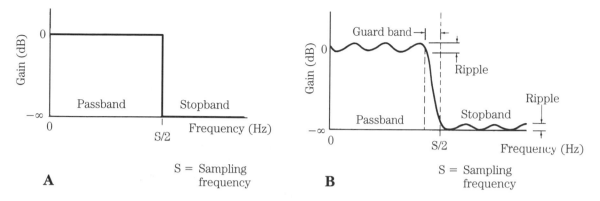

3-4 Lowpass filter characteristics. A. An ideal lowpass filter has flat passband response and instantaneous cut-off. B. In practice, filters exhibit ripple in the stopband and passband, and sloping cutoff.

gineering challenges. A brick-wall cutoff demands compromise on other specifications such as flat passband and low phase distortion. To alleviate the problems created by a brick-wall response, filters can use a more gradual cutoff, because this reduces phase nonlinearities. However, a low-order filter with a gradual response will roll-off audio frequencies, hence its passband must be extended to a very high frequency. To avoid aliasing, the sampling frequency must be extended to ensure that the filter provides sufficient attenuation at the Nyquist frequency. A higher sampling frequency, perhaps three times higher than required for a brick-wall filter, might be needed and data bandwidth requirements would be raised. To limit the sampling frequency and make full use of the passband below the half-sampling point, a brick-wall filter is mandated. It is ironic that this filter presents difficulties, because it is of analog design. After the A/D converter, the same filtering can be accomplished digitally with fewer complications. As discussed in this chapter, and in detail in chapter 16, oversampling A/D converters accomplish that.

In nonoversampling encoders with a sampling frequency of 48 kHz, the input filters are designed for flat response from dc to 22 kHz. This arrangement provides a guard band of 2 kHz to ensure that attenuation is sufficient. The passband must have flat frequency response; in practice some frequency irregularity, called ripple, exists, but can be designed to be ±0.1 dB or less. The stopband attenuation is designed to equal or exceed the system's dynamic range, as determined by the word length. For example, a 16-bit system requires stopband attenuation of over 95 dB. A stopband attenuation of −80 dB yields 0.01% alias distortion under worst case conditions. A practical lowpass filter characteristic is shown in Fig. 3-4B.

Other important filter criteria are overshoot, ringing, and phase linearity. Sharp cutoff filters exhibit resonance near the cutoff frequency and this ringing can cause coloration in frequency response. The sharper the cutoff, the greater the propensity to ringing. Certain filter types have inherently reduced ringing. Phase response also is a factor. Analog tape machines, microphones, and loudspeakers have always introduced phase distortion; lowpass filters exhibit frequency-dependent delay, called group delay, near the cutoff frequency, causing phase distortion. This can be corrected with an analog circuit preceding or following the filter, which introduces compensating delay to achieve overall linearity; pure delay, which is inaudible, results. In the cases of ringing and group delay, there is debate on the threshold of audibility of such effects; it is unclear how perceptive the ear is to such high-frequency phenomena.

Filter Design

Analog filters are often classified according to the mathematical polynomials that describe their characteristics. There are many filter types; Bessel, Butterworth, and Chebyshev are often used. For each of these, a basic design stage can be repeated or cascaded to increase the filter's order and to sharpen the cutoff. Thus, higher-order filters more closely approximate the ideal filter's brick-wall frequency response. For example, a passive Chebyshev lowpass filter is shown in Fig. 3-5; its cutoff slope becomes steeper when the filter's order is increased through cascading. However, phase shift also increases as the filter order is increased. The simplest lowpass filter is a cascade of RC (resistor-capacitor) sections; each added section increases the roll-off slope by 6 dB/octave. Although the filter would not suffer from overshoot and ringing, the passband would exhibit frequency response anomalies, and could not be used as an anti-aliasing filter.

Resonant peaks can be positioned just below the cutoff frequency to smooth the passband response of a filter but not affect the roll-off slope; a Butterworth design

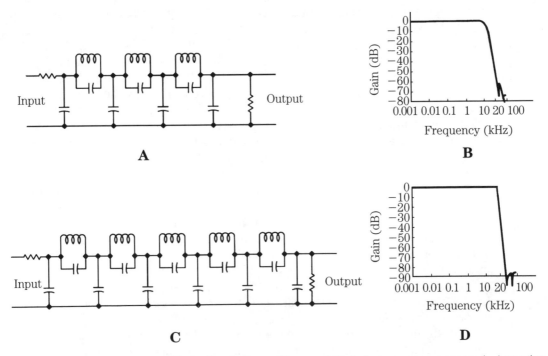

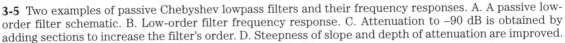

3-5 Two examples of passive Chebyshev lowpass filters and their frequency responses. A. A passive low-order filter schematic. B. Low-order filter frequency response. C. Attenuation to –90 dB is obtained by adding sections to increase the filter's order. D. Steepness of slope and depth of attenuation are improved.

accomplishes this. However, a high-order filter is required to obtain a sharp cutoff and deep stopband. For example, a design with a transition band 40% of an octave wide and a stopband of –80 dB would require a 33rd-order Butterworth.

A filter with a narrow transition band can be designed, at the expense of pass-band frequency response. This can be achieved by placing the resonant peaks somewhat higher than in a Butterworth design. This is the aim of a Chebyshev filter. A 9th-order Chebyshev filter can achieve a 0.1-dB passband ripple to 20 kHz, and stopband attenuation of 70 dB at 25 kHz.

One characteristic of most filter types is that attenuation continues past the necessary depth with frequencies beyond the half-sampling frequency. If the attenuation curve is flattened, the transition band can be reduced. Anti-resonant notches in the stopband are often used to perform this function. In addition, reactive elements can be shared in the design, providing resonant peaks and anti-resonant notches. This reduces circuit complexity. The result is called an elliptical, or Cauer filter. An elliptical filter has the steepest cutoff for a given order of realization. For example, a 7th-order elliptical filter can provide a 0.25-dB passband ripple, 40% octave transition band, and a –80-dB stopband. In commercial applications, a 13-pole design might be required.

In general, for a given filter order, Chebyshev and elliptical lowpass filters give a closer approximation to the ideal than Bessel or Butterworth filters, but Chebyshev filters can yield ripple in the passband and elliptical filters can produce severe phase nonlinearities. Bessel filters can approximate a pure delay and provide excellent phase response; however, a higher-order filter is needed to provide a very high rate of attenuation. Butterworth filters are usually flat in the passband, but can exhibit slow transient response. Generally, no filter is ideal, and there is a trade-off between high rate of attenuation and acceptable time-domain response. In practice, because of the degradation introduced by analog brick-wall filters, analog designs have been superseded by digital techniques employing in low-bit conversion, as described in chapter 16. However, whatever method is used, an input filter is required to prevent aliasing of any frequencies higher than the Nyquist frequency.

Sample-and-Hold Circuit

As its name implies, the sample-and-hold (S/H) circuit performs two simple yet critical operations. It time samples the analog waveform at a periodic rate, putting the sampling theorem into practice. It also holds the analog value of the sample while the analog-to-digital converter outputs the corresponding digital word. This is important because otherwise the analog value could change after the designated sample time, causing the A/D converter to output incorrect digital words. The input and output responses of a sample-and-hold circuit are shown in Fig. 3-6. The circuit is relatively simple to design; however, it must accomplish both of its tasks accurately. Samples must be captured at precisely the correct time and the held value must stay within tolerance.

As we have seen, time and amplitude information can completely characterize any acoustic waveform. The sample-and-hold circuit is responsible for capturing

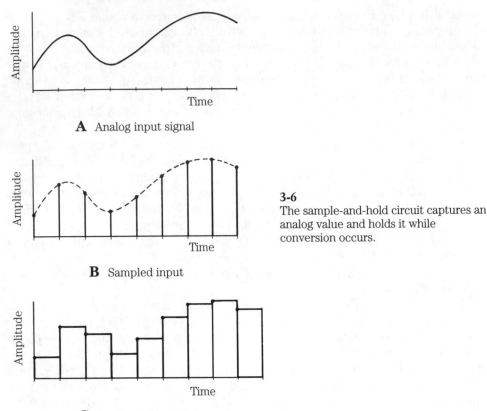

A Analog input signal

B Sampled input

3-6
The sample-and-hold circuit captures an analog value and holds it while conversion occurs.

C Analog held output

both informational aspects from the lowpass filtered analog waveform. Samples are taken at a periodic rate and reproduced at the same periodic rate. The sample-and-hold circuit accomplishes this time sampling. A clock, an oscillator circuit that outputs timing pulses, is set to the desired sampling frequency, and this command signal controls the S/H circuit.

Conceptually, an S/H circuit is a capacitor and a switch. The circuit tracks the analog signal until the sample command causes the digital switch to isolate the capacitor from the signal; the capacitor holds this analog voltage during A/D conversion. An ideal sample-and-hold circuit is shown in Fig. 3-7. The S/H circuit must have a fast acquisition time that approaches zero; otherwise, the value output from the A/D converter will be based on an averaged input over the acquisition time, instead of the correct sample value at an instant in time. In addition, varying sample times result in acquisition timing error; to prevent this, the sample command must be accurately clocked and the S/H circuit must be carefully designed.

Variations in absolute timing, called phase jitter, shown in Fig. 3-8, add noise to the sampled signal, and must be limited in the clock switching the S/H circuit. Jitter is particularly significant in the case of a high-amplitude, high-frequency input signal; jitter must not interfere with correct sampling of the LSB. The timing accuracy

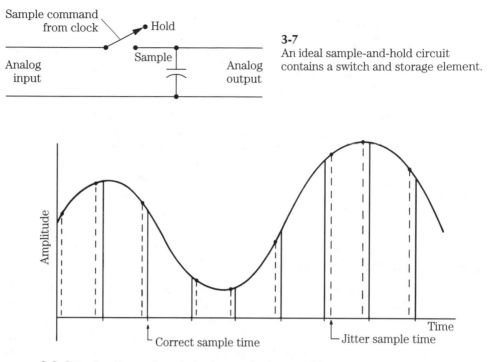

3-7
An ideal sample-and-hold circuit contains a switch and storage element.

3-8 Jitter is a time-axis variation in sample times, yielding noise and distortion in the output analog signal.

required for A/D conversion is considerable. By one analysis, jitter at the S/H circuit must be less than 200 ps to allow 16-bit accuracy from a full amplitude, 20-kHz sinewave, and less than 100 ps for 18-bit accuracy. Only then would the jitter components fall below the quantization noise floor. Clearly, S/H timing must be controlled by a clock designed with a highly accurate crystal quartz oscillator. Jitter is discussed in detail in chapter 4.

Acquisition time is the time between the initiation of the sample command and the taking of the sample. This time lag results in a sampled value different from the one that occurred at the correct sample time. A fixed delay can be corrected; however, the delay is a function of the amplitude of the analog signal. The best solution is prevention; therefore, it is important to design for minimum acquisition time. The S/H circuit's other primary function is to hold the captured analog voltage while conversion takes place. Note that this voltage must remain constant, because any variation greater than a quantization increment will result in an error at the A/D output. In practice, the held voltage is prone to droop because of current leakage. Droop is the decrease in hold voltage as the capacitor leaks between sample times. Care in circuit design and selection of components can limit droop to less than one-half a quantization increment over a 20 μs period. For example, a 16-bit, ±10-V range A/D converter must hold a constant value to within 1 mV during conversion. Acquisition time error and droop are illustrated in Fig. 3-9.

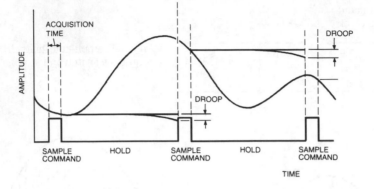

3-9 Two error conditions in the sample-and-hold circuit: acquisition time and droop.

Sample-and-Hold Circuit Design

The demands of fast acquisition time and low droop are in conflict in the design of an S/H circuit. For fast acquisition time, a small capacitor value is better, permitting faster charging time. For droop, however, a large-valued capacitor is preferred, because it is better able to retain the sample voltage at a constant level for a longer time. Circuit designers have found that capacitor values of approximately 1 nF can satisfy both requirements. In addition, high-quality capacitors made of polypropylene or Teflon dielectrics are often specified. These materials can respond quickly, hold charge, and minimize dielectric absorption and hysteresis—phenomena that cause voltage variations.

In practice, an S/H circuit must contain more than a switch and a capacitor. Active circuits such as operational amplifiers must buffer the circuit to condition the input and output signals, speed switching time, and help prevent leakage. Only a few specialized operational amplifiers meet the required specifications of large bandwidth and fast settling time. Junction field-effect transistor (JFET) operational amplifiers usually perform best. Thus, a complete S/H circuit might have a JFET input operational amplifier to prevent source loading and speed switching time, isolate the capacitor, and supply capacitor charging current. The S/H switch itself is probably a JFET device, selected to operate cleanly and accurately with minimal jitter, and the capacitor is high quality with low hysteresis. A JFET operational amplifier is usually placed at the output to help preserve the capacitor's charge. An example of a practical sample-and-hold circuit is shown in Fig. 3-10. Switch A is closed to sample. After conversion, switch B is closed to discharge capacitor C and prepare for another sample. The sample-and-hold circuit thus time samples and momentarily stores analog values for conversion. Its output signal is an intermediate signal, a discrete PAM staircase representing the original analog signal, but is not a digital word.

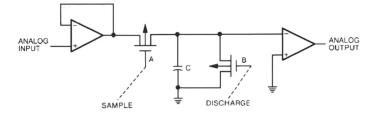

3-10 Example of a practical sample-and-hold circuit with JFET switches and buffered input and output.

Analog-to-Digital Converter

The analog-to-digital converter lies at the heart of the encoding side of a PCM audio digitization system, and it is the single most critical component in the entire electronic system. Any errors introduced by the A/D converter will accompany the audio signal throughout the remaining signal chain and ultimately, back into its analog state. Essentially, this circuit must examine the sampled input signal, determine the quantization level nearest to the sample's value, and output the binary code that is assigned to that level—accomplishing those tasks in a sampling period of 20 μs or less. The precision required is considerable: 15 parts per million for 16-bit resolution, four parts per million for 18-bit resolution, and one part per million for 20-bit resolution. There are two conventional multibit analog-to-digital design approaches: the input analog voltage can be compared to a variable reference voltage within a feedback loop to determine the output digital word, or the input voltage can be allowed to decrease and the time it takes to reach zero can be timed with a counter that generates an output digital word. Successive approximation methods are examples of the former; integration methods are examples of the latter. Oversampling A/D converters are considered in this chapter and in detail in chapter 16.

The A/D converter must perform a complete conversion at each sample time, for example, 48,000 conversions per second per channel in a professional audio digitization system. Furthermore, the digital word it provides must be an accurate representation of the input binary voltage. In a 16-bit linear PCM system, each of the 65,536 intervals must be evenly spaced throughout the amplitude range, so that even the least significant bit in the resulting word is meaningful. Thus, speed and accuracy are key requirements for an A/D converter. Of course, any A/D converter will have an error of ±½ LSB, an inherent limitation of the quantization process itself; furthermore, dither must be applied.

The conversion time is the time required for an A/D converter to output a digital word. For an A/D converter used in an audio digitization system, conversion time must be within the span of one sampling period. Achieving accurate conversion from sample to sample is sometimes difficult because of settling time or propagation time errors. The result of accomplishing one conversion might influence the next. If a converter's input moves from voltage A to B and then later from C to B, the resulting digital output for B might be different because of the device's inability to properly settle in preparation for the next measurement. Obviously, dynamic errors grow more severe with demand for higher conversion speed. In practice, speeds required for low noise and distortion can be achieved. Indeed, some A/D converters simultaneously process two waveforms, alternating between left and right channels; however, cost is always relatively high for any A/D with fast conversion time.

Accuracy is another important consideration. Several specifications have been devised to evaluate the performance of A/D converters. Integral linearity measures the straightness of A/D converter output. It describes the transition voltage points, the analog input voltages at which the digital output changes from one code to the next, and specifies how close they are to a straight line drawn through them. In other words, integral linearity determines the deviation of an actual bit transition from the ideal transition value, at any level over the range of the converter. Integral linearity is illustrated in Fig. 3-11A. Integral linearity is tested, and the reference line is drawn across the converter's full output range. Integral linearity is the most important A/D specification and is not adjustable. An *n*-bit converter is not a true *n*-bit converter unless it guarantees at least ±½ LSB integral linearity. The converter in Fig. 3-11A has a ±¼ LSB integral linearity.

Differential linearity error is the difference between the actual step height and the ideal value of 1 LSB. It can be measured as the distance between transition voltages, that is, the widths of individual input voltage steps. Differential linearity is shown in Fig. 3-11B. Ideally, all of the steps of an A/D transfer function should be 1 LSB wide. A maximum differential linearity error of ±½ LSB means that the input voltage might have to increase or decrease as little as ½ LSB or as much as 1½ LSB before an output transition occurs. If this specification is exceeded, to perhaps ±1 LSB, some steps could be 2 LSBs wide and others could be 0 LSB wide; in other words, some output codes would not exist. Quality A/D converters are assured of having no missing codes over a specified temperature range. The converter in Fig. 3-11B has an error of ±¾ LSB; some levels are ¼ LSB wide, others are 1¾ LSB wide. Conversion speed can affect both integral linearity and differential linearity errors. Quality A/D converters are guaranteed to be monotonic; that is, the output code either increases or remains the same for increasing analog input signals. If differential error is greater than 1 LSB, the converter will be non-monotonic.

Absolute accuracy error, shown in Fig. 3-11C, is the difference between the supposed level at which a digital transition occurs and where it actually occurs. A good A/D converter should have an error of less than ±½ LSB. Offset voltage, gain error, or noise error can affect this specification. For the converter in Fig. 3-11C, each interval is ⅛ LSB in error. In practice, otherwise good A/D devices can sometimes drift with temperature variations and thus introduce inaccuracies.

Code width, sometimes called quantum, is the range of analog input values for which a given output code will occur. The ideal code width is 1 LSB. A/D converters can exhibit an offset error as well as gain error. An A/D connected for unipolar operation has an analog input range from 0 V to positive full scale. The first output code transition should occur at an analog input value of ½ LSB above 0 V. Unipolar offset error is the deviation of the actual transition value from the ideal value. When connected in a bipolar

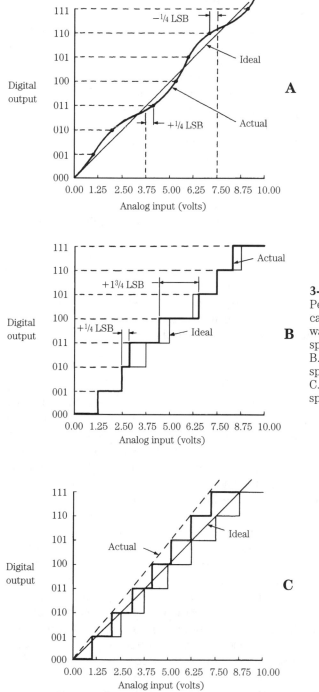

3-11
Performance of an A/D converter can be specified in a variety of ways. A. Integral linearity specification of an A/D converter. B. Differential linearity specification of an A/D converter. C. Absolute accuracy specification of an A/D converter.

configuration, bipolar offset is set at the first transition value above the negative full-scale value. Bipolar offset error is the deviation of the actual transition value from the ideal transition value at ½ LSB above the negative full-scale value. Gain error is the deviation of the actual analog value at the last transition point from the ideal value, where the last output code transition occurs for an analog input value 1½ LSB below the nominal positive full-scale value. Gain and offset errors are often trimmed at the factory, and might be further zeroed with the use of external potentiometers. Multiturn potentiometers are recommended for minimum drift over temperature and time.

The maximum analog input signal should be scaled as close as possible to the maximum input conversion range, to utilize the converter's maximum signal resolution. Generally, a converter uses a low input impedance that should be driven by a very low impedance source such as the output of a wideband, fast-settling operational amplifier. Transitions in an A/D converter's input current might be caused by changes in the output current of the internal D/A converter as it tests bits. The output voltage of the driving source must remain constant while supplying these fast current changes.

Changes in the dc power supply can affect an A/D converter's accuracy. Power supply deviations can cause changes in the positive full-scale value, resulting in a proportional change in all code transition values, that is, a gain error. Normally, regulated power supplies with 1% or less ripple are recommended. Power supplies should be bypassed with a capacitor—for example, 1 to 10 µF tantalum—located close to the converter, to obtain noise free operation. Noise and spikes from a switching power supply must be carefully filtered.

Successive Approximation A/D Converter

There are many types of A/D converter designs appropriate for various applications. For audio digitization, the necessity for both speed and accuracy limits the choices to a few types. The successive approximation register (SAR) A/D converter perhaps best exemplifies the task of performing accurate analog-to-digital conversion. An SAR converter is shown in Fig. 3-12. This converter uses a digital-to-analog converter in a feedback loop, a comparator, and a control section. In essence, the converter compares the analog input with its interim digital word converted into analog, until the two agree within the given resolution. In operation, the device follows an algorithm that, bit by bit, sets the output digital word to match the analog input.

For example, consider an analog input of 6.92 V and an 8-bit SAR A/D converter. The operational steps of SAR conversion are shown in Fig. 3-13. The most significant bit in the SAR is set to 1, with the other bits still at 0; thus the word 10000000 is applied to the internal D/A converter. This word places the D/A output at its half value of 5 V. Because the input analog voltage is greater than the D/A converter's output, the comparator remains high. The first bit is stored at logical 1. The next most significant bit is set to 1 and the word 11000000 is applied to the D/A converter, with an interim output of 7.5 V. This voltage is too high, so the second bit is reset to 0 and stored. The third bit is set to 1, and the word 10100000 is applied to the D/A converter; this produces 6.25 V, so the third bit remains high. This process continues until the least significant bit is stored and the digital word 10110001, representing a converted 6.91 V, is output from the A/D converter.

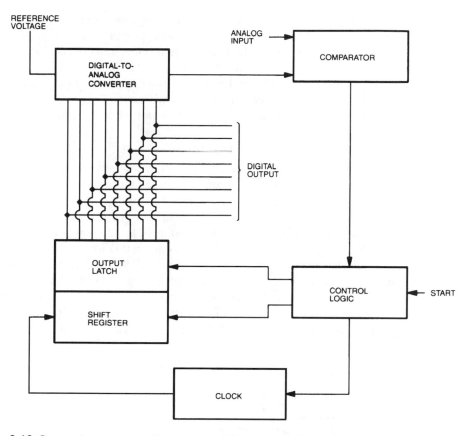

3-12 Successive approximation register A/D converter showing internal D/A converter and comparator.

SUCCESSIVE APPROXIMATIONS:

10000000 =	5.00000 v	OK
11000000 =	7.50000	RESET
10100000 =	6.25000	OK
10110000 =	6.87500	OK
10111000 =	7.18750	RESET
10110100 =	7.03125	RESET
10110010 =	6.95312	RESET
10110001 =	6.91406	OK

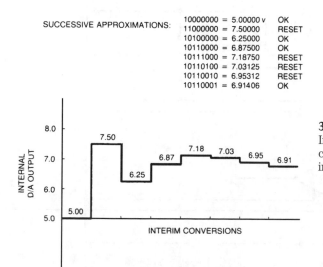

3-13 Intermediate steps in an SAR conversion showing results of interim D/A conversions.

This successive approximation method requires n D/A conversions for every one A/D conversion, where n is the number of bits in the output word. In spite of this recursion, SAR converters offer relatively high conversion speed and are cost effective. However, the converter must be precisely designed. For example, a 16-bit A/D converter ranging over ±10 V with ½ LSB error requires conversion accuracy of 3 mV. A 10-V step change in the D/A converter must settle to within 0.001% during a period of 1 μs. This period corresponds to an analog time constant of about 100 ns.

Dual-slope Integrating A/D Converter

Dual-slope conversion is another method for performing analog-to-digital conversion. In a single-slope converter, a reference value is allowed to integrate as a ramp function, and the time required for the ramp voltage to equal the input sample voltage is measured by a high-speed counter. The count is output as the digital word representing the analog value. For 16-bit conversion in 10 μs, the clock must run at a frequency of 6 GHz, which is too fast for conventional digital circuits.

In a dual-slope design, the integrating method is modified by using two counters; both are timed to yield eight bits each. The clock must run at 50 MHz, which is an attainable frequency. In a dual-slope converter, as shown in Fig. 3-14, two current sources can be switched to the integrator. The coarse ramp and the fine ramp are both timed by digital counters, which output the data word. The first unity current is

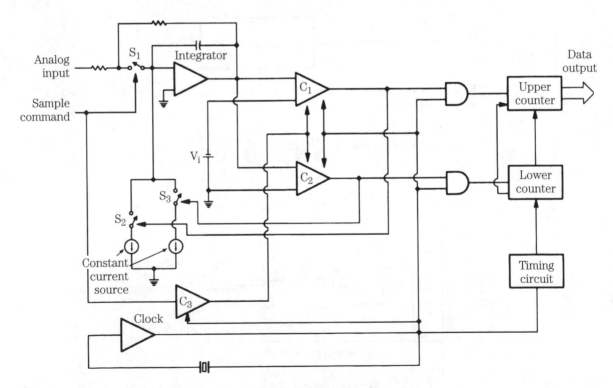

3-14 A dual-slope integrating A/D converter showing integrator and counters.

switched to form the coarse ramp, and this is timed with the first counter. One counting period equals 256 periods of the second counter. Then $\frac{1}{256}$ of the first current is switched to form the fine ramp, which is similarly timed by the second counter. The most and least significant eight bits are joined to form a 16-bit digital output word. Linearity of a dual-slope A/D converter largely depends on the dielectric loss of the capacitor. This method has been successfully integrated onto a single chip.

Oversampling A/D Converter

As noted, analog lowpass filters suffer from problems such as noise, distortion, group delay, and passband ripple, and it is difficult for multibit A/D converters to achieve resolution beyond 18 bits. In many applications, analog input (anti-aliasing) filters and multibit A/D converters have been replaced by oversampling A/D converters with digital filters. Note that implementation of a digital anti-aliasing filter is problematic because the analog signal must be sampled and digitized prior to any digital filtering. This conundrum has been resolved by clever engineering; in particular, a digital decimation filter is employed and combined with the task of A/D conversion. Operation of digital filters is discussed in detail in the next chapter, but the principles behind an oversampling A/D converter are presented here.

In oversampling A/D conversion, the input signal is first passed through a simple analog anti-aliasing filter, which provides sufficient attenuation, but only at a high frequency. The filtered signal is sampled at a high frequency to extend the Nyquist frequency, and quantized. After quantization, a digital lowpass filter uses decimation both to reduce the sampling frequency and prevent aliasing at the new, lower sampling frequency. Quantized data words are output at a conventional frequency (for example, 48 kHz). The decimation lowpass filter removes frequency components beyond the Nyquist frequency of the output sampling frequency to prevent aliasing when the output of the digital filter is resampled (undersampled) at the system's sampling frequency. Consider the oversampling A/D converter and D/A converter (both using two-times oversampling) shown in Fig. 3-15. An analog anti-aliasing filter restricts the bandwidth to $1.5f_s$, where f_s is the sampling frequency. The relatively wide transition band, from 0.5 to $1.5f_s$, is acceptable, and promotes good phase response. For example, a 7th-order Butterworth filter could be used. The signal is sampled and held at $2f_s$, and converted. The digital filter limits the signal to $0.5f_s$. With decimation, the sampling frequency of the signal is undersampled and hence reduced from $2f_s$ to f_s. This action is accomplished with a linear-phase FIR digital filter, with uniform group delay characteristics. Upon playback, an oversampling filter doubles the sampling frequency, samples are converted to yield an analog waveform, and high-frequency images are removed with a low-order lowpass filter.

Many oversampling A/D converters use a very high initial sampling frequency, and take advantage of that high rate by using low-bit conversion of the audio signal. Because the sampling frequency is high, word lengths of one or a few bits can provide high resolution. A sigma-delta modulator can be used to perform noise shaping, to lower audio band quantization noise. A decimation filter is used to convert the low-bit coding to 16-bit (or higher) coding, and a lower sampling frequency. Consider an example in which one-bit coding takes place at an oversampling rate R of 72;

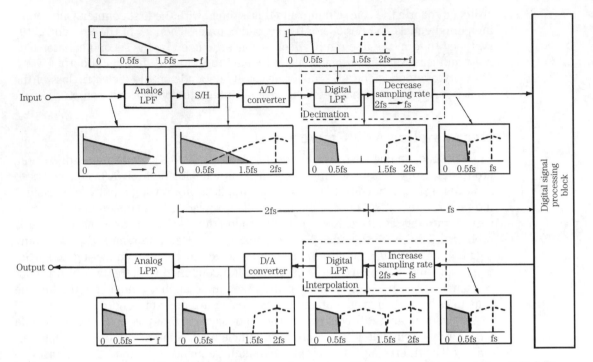

3-15 A two-times oversampling A/D and D/A conversion system. Decimation and interpolation digital filters increase and decrease the sampling frequency while removing alias and image signal components. Pioneer Electronics Corporation

that is, 72×44.1 kHz $= 3.1752$ MHz, as shown in Fig. 3-16. The decimation filter provides a stopband from 20 kHz to the half-sampling frequency of 1.5876 MHz. One-bit A/D conversion greatly simplifies the digital filter design. An output sample is not required for every input bit; because the decimation factor is 72, an output sample is required for every 72 bits input to the decimation filter. A transversal filter can be used, with filter coefficients suited for the decimation factor. Following decimation, the result can be rounded to 16 bits, and output at a 44.1-kHz sampling frequency.

In addition to eliminating brick-wall analog filters, oversampling A/D converters offer other advantages over conventional A/D converters. Oversampling A/D converters can achieve increased resolution compared to SAR methods. For example, they extend the spectrum of the quantization error between analog input and digital output far outside the audio band. Thus the in-band noise can be made quite small. The same internal digital filter that prevents aliasing also removes the out-of-band noise components. Increasingly, low-bit A/D converters are employed. This type of low-bit sigma-delta conversion is discussed in detail in chapter 16.

Successive approximation register A/D converters use a D/A converter in a loop to test a digital word, convert it and compare the analog result to the original input, then correct the approximation until a digital word has been determined and output. Integrating A/D converters use a timing circuit; a capacitor stores a voltage, and a timer counts as the voltage is integrated as a ramp. The number of counts in that

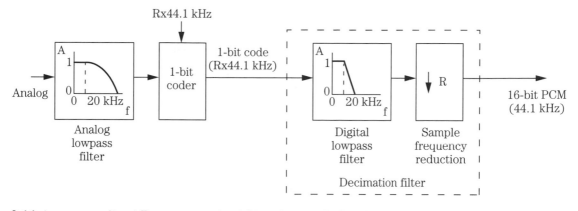

3-16 An oversampling A/D converter using 1-bit coding at a high sampling rate, and a decimation filter. _{Philips}

timing forms the output digital word. Oversampling converters operate at a high sampling frequency to obviate the brick-wall filter, then decimate the signal to a low sampling frequency, digitally removing any components that would alias; low-bit conversion provides high resolution. Whichever method is used, the goal of digitizing the analog signal is accomplished, as data in two's complement or other form is output from the device.

For digitization systems in which real-time processing such as delay and reverberation is the aim, the signal is ready for processing through software or dedicated hardware. In the case of a digital recording system, further processing is required to prepare the data for the storage medium.

Record Processing

After the analog signal is converted to binary numbers, several operations must occur prior to storage or transmission. Although specific processing techniques vary according to the type of output channel, PCM systems generally multiplex the data, add redundancy for error correction, perform interleaving, and provide channel coding. Although there is an uninteresting element of bookkeeping in this processing, any drudgery is critical to prepare the data for the output channel and ensure that playback will be accomplished satisfactorily.

Some digital audio programs are stored or transmitted with emphasis, a simple means of reducing noise in the signal. Pre-emphasis equalization boosts high frequencies prior to storage or transmission. At the output, a corresponding de-emphasis equalization attenuates high frequencies. The net result is a reduction in noise floor. A common emphasis characteristic uses time constants of 50 μs and 15 μs, corresponding to frequency points at 3183 and 10,610 Hz, with a 6-dB per octave slope between these points, as shown in Fig. 3-17. Use of pre-emphasis must be identified in the program material, so that de-emphasis equalization can be applied at the output.

In analog recording, an error occurring during storage or transmission results in degraded playback. In digital recording, error detection and correction minimize the ef-

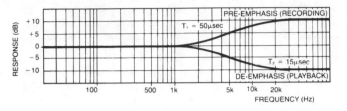

3-17 Pre-emphasis boosts high frequencies during recording, and de-emphasis reduces them during playback to reduce perceived noise.

fect of such defects. Without error correction, the quality of digital audio recording would be greatly diminished. Several steps are taken to combat the effects of errors. During encoding, coded parity data is added; this is redundant data created from the original data to help detect and correct errors. To prevent a single defect from destroying both the original data and the data required to correct it, interleaving is employed; this scatters data through the bit stream so the effect of an error is scattered when data is de-interleaved during playback. A complete discussion of parity, check codes, redundancy, interleaving, and the entire error correction system is presented in chapter 5.

Multiplexing is used to form a serial bit stream. Most digital audio recording and transmission is a serial process; that is, the data is processed as a single stream of information. However, the output of the A/D converter can be parallel data; for example, 16-bit words of two's complement data are output simultaneously. Before it is output, this parallel data must be converted to serial data. A data multiplexer accomplishes this transformation; the multiple input circuit accepts parallel data words and outputs the data one bit at a time, serially, to form a continuous bit stream.

Raw data must be properly formatted to facilitate its recording or transmission and later recovery. Several kinds of processing are applied to the coded data. The time-multiplexed data code is usually grouped into frames; to prevent ambiguity, each frame is given a synchronization code to delineate frames as they occur in the stream. A synchronization code is a fixed pattern of bits that is distinct from any other coded data bit pattern in much the same way that a comma is distinct from the characters in a sentence. In many cases, data files are preceded by a data header with information defining the file contents.

Addressing or timing data can be added to frames to identify data locations in the recording. This code is usually sequentially ordered and is distributed through the recording to distinguish between different sections. As noted, error correction data also is placed in the frame. Identification codes might carry information pertinent to the playback processing. For example, specification of sampling frequency, use of pre-emphasis, table of contents, timing and track information, and even copyright information can be entered into the data stream.

Channel Codes

Although analog-to-digital conversion is critical to the quality of a digital audio signal, the signal must undergo additional processing for successful storage, processing, or transmission. Channel coding is perhaps the most important example of a less visible, yet critical element in any digital audio system. Channel codes have been aptly described by Thomas Stockham as the handwriting of digital audio.

Channel code modulation must occur prior to storage or transmission. Digital audio is commonly considered to involve 1s and 0s, but the binary code is usually not conveyed directly. Rather, a modulated channel code represents audio samples and other conveyed information. It is thus a modulation waveform that is interpreted upon playback to recover the original binary data and thus the audio waveform. Modulation facilitates data reading by further delineating the recorded logical states. Moreover, through modulation, a higher coding efficiency is achieved; although more bits might be conveyed, a greater data throughput can be achieved overall.

A channel code describes the way information is modulated into a channel signal, stored or transmitted, and modulated back again. In particular, information bits are transformed into channel bits. The transfer functions of digital media create a number of specific difficulties that can be overcome through modulation techniques. A channel code should be self-clocking to permit synchronization at the receiver, minimize low-frequency content that could interfere with servo systems, permit high data rate transmission or high-density recording, exhibit a bounded energy spectrum, have immunity to channel noise, and reveal invalid signal conditions. Unfortunately, these requirements are largely mutually conflicting, thus only a few channel codes are suitable for digital audio applications.

Note that the decoding clock in the receiver must be synchronized in frequency and phase with the clock (usually implicit in the channel bit patterns) in the transmitted signal. In most cases, the frames in a binary bit stream are marked with a synchronization word. Without some kind of synchronization, it might be impossible to directly distinguish between the individual channel bits. Even then, a series of 1s or 0s form a static signal upon playback. If no other timing or decoding information is available, the time information implicitly encoded in the channel bit periods is lost. Therefore, such data must often be recorded in such a way that pulse timing is delineated. Codes that provide a high transition rate, that are suitable for regenerating timing information at the receiver, are called self-clocking codes.

Thus, one goal of channel modulation is to combine a serial data stream with a clock pulse to produce a single encoded waveform that is self-clocking. Generally, code efficiency must be sacrificed to achieve self-clocking because clocking increases the number of transitions, which increases the overall channel bit rate. The high-frequency signal produced by robust clocking content will decrease a medium's storage capacity, and can be degraded over long cable runs. A minimum distance between transitions (T_{min}) determines the highest frequency in the code, and is often the highest frequency the medium can support. The ratio of T_{min} to the length of a single bit period of input information data is called the density ratio. From a bandwidth standpoint, a long T_{min} is desirable in a code. T_{max} determines the maximum distance between transitions sufficient to support clocking. From a clocking standpoint, a shorter T_{max} is desirable.

Time-axis variations such as jitter are characterized by phase variations in a signal, observable as a frequency modulation of a stable waveform. The constraints of channel coding and data regeneration fundamentally limit the maximum number of incremental periods between transitions, that is, the number of transitions that can be detected between T_{min} and T_{max}. An important consideration in modulation code design is tolerance in locating a transition in the code. This is called the window margin, phase margin, or jitter margin and notated as T_w. It describes the minimum difference between code wavelengths; the larger the clock window, the better the jitter immunity. The efficiency of a code can be measured by its density ratio (DR) that is the ratio of the number of information bits to the number of channel transitions. The product of *DR* and T_w is known as the figure of merit (FoM); by combining density ratio and jitter margin, an overall estimate of performance is obtained; the higher the numerical value of *FoM*, the better.

Storing binary code directly on a medium is inefficient. Much greater densities with high code fidelity can be achieved through methods in which modulation code fidelity is low. The efficiency of a coding method is the number of data bits transmitted, divided by the number of transitions needed to convey them. Efficiencies vary from about 50% to nearly 150%. In light of these requirements, pulse-code modulation, for example, is not suitable for recording; thus, other channel modulation techniques must be devised. Although binary recording is concerned with storing the 0s and 1s of the data stream, the signal actually recorded might be quite different. Typically, it is the transitions from one level to another, rather than the amplitude levels themselves, which represent the channel data. In that respect, the important events in a digitally encoded signal are the instants in time at which state of the signal changes.

An efficient coding format must restrict dc content in the coded waveform, which could disrupt timing synchronization. The dc content is the fraction of time the signal is high during a string of 1s or 0s minus the fraction of time it is low. It results in a nonzero average amplitude value. For example, an NRZ signal (in which binary values are coded as high- or low-signal amplitudes) with all 0s or 1s would give a dc content of 100%. The dc content can be monitored through the digital sum value (DSV); the DSV of a code can be thought of as the difference in accumulated charge if the code was passed through an ac coupling capacitor. In other words, it shows the dc bias that accumulates in a coded sequence. Figure 3-18 shows two different codes and their DSV; over the measured interval, the first code does not show dc content, the second does. The dc content might cause problems in transformer coupled magnetic recording heads; magnetic heads sense domains inductively and hence are inefficient in reading low-frequency signals. The dc content can present clock synchronization problems, and lead to errors in the servo systems used for radial tracking and focusing in an optical system. These systems generally operate in the low-frequency region. Low-frequency components in the readout signal cause interference in the servo systems, making them unstable. A dc-free code improves both the bandwidth and signal-to-noise ratio of the servo system. In the compact disc system, the frequency range from 20 kHz to 1.5 MHz is used for information transmission; the servo systems operate on signals in the 0-Hz to 20-kHz range.

A single sampling pulse is easy to analyze because of its periodic nature in the time domain; Fourier analysis clearly shows its spectrum. However, a data stream differs in that the data pulses occur aperiodically, and in fact can be considered to be random. The power spectrum density, or power spectrum, shows the response of the

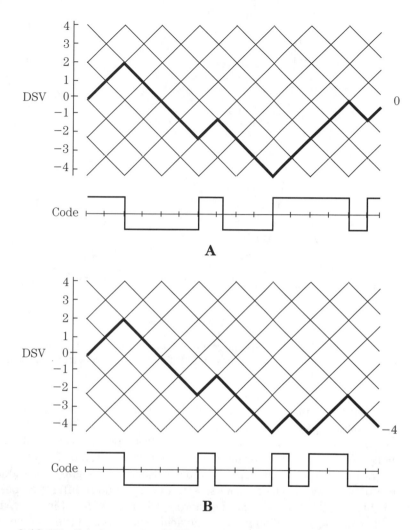

3-18 The digital sum value (DSV) monitors the dc content in a bit stream. A. A coded waveform that is free of dc content over the measured interval. B. A coded waveform that contains dc content.

data stream. For example, Fig. 3-19 shows the spectral response of three types of channel coding, nonreturn to zero (NRZ), modified frequency modulation (MFM), and biphase, with random data sequences. A transmission waveform ideally should have minimal energy at low frequencies to avoid clocking and servo errors, and minimal energy at high frequencies to reduce bandwidth requirements. Observe that the NRZ code has severe dc content. Biphase codes (there are many types, one being binary FM) yield a spectrum that has an energy distribution that is broadband. The MFM code exhibits a very narrow spectrum. The MFM and biphase codes are similar because they have no strong frequency components at low frequencies (lower than $0.2f$ where $f = 1/T$). If the value of f is 500 kHz, for example, and the servo signals do

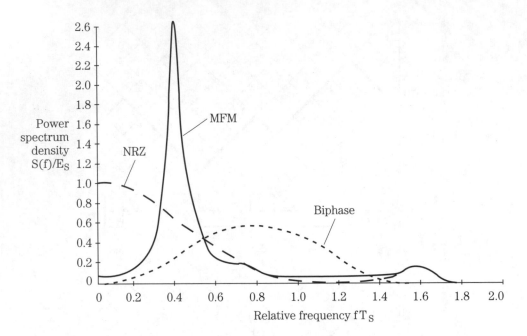

3-19 The power spectral density shows the response of a stream of random data sequences. NRZ code has severe dc content; MFM code exhibits a very narrow spectrum; biphase codes yield a broadband energy distribution.

not extend beyond 15 kHz, these codes would be suitable. The NRZ code has strong dc content and could pose problems for a servo system.

To minimize decoding errors, formats can be developed in which data is conveyed with data patterns that are as individually unique as possible. For example, in the 8-to-14 (EFM) code devised for the compact disc format, eight-bit symbols are translated into 14-bit symbols, carefully selected for maximum difference between symbols. In this way, invalid data can be more easily recognized. Similarly, a data symbol could be created based on previous adjacent symbols and the receiver could recognize the symbol and its past history as a unique state. A state pattern diagram is used in which all transitions are defined, based on all possible adjacent symbols.

As noted, in many codes, the information is contained in the timing of transitions, not in the direction (low to high, or high to low) of the transitions. This is advantageous because the code is thus insensitive to polarity; the content will not be affected if the signal is inverted. The EFM code used in the compact disc enjoys this property.

Simple Codes

The channel code defines the logical 1 and 0 of the input information. We might assume a direct relationship between a high amplitude and logical 1, and a low amplitude and logical 0. However, many other relationships are possible; for example, in one version of frequency-shift keying (FSK), a 1 corresponds to a sine burst of 100 kHz and a 0 corresponds to a sine burst of 150 kHz. The method of using only two values gives the inherent advantage of digital storage; relatively large variations in the medium do not affect data recovery. Because digitally stored data is robust, high packing densities can be achieved. Various modulation codes have been devised to encode binary data according to the medium's properties. Of many, only a few are applicable to digital audio storage, on either magnetic or optical media; a number of common channel codes are shown in Fig. 3-20.

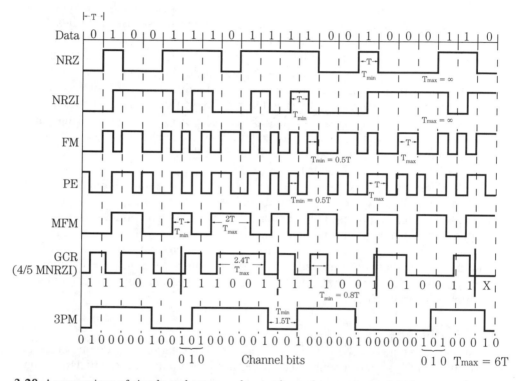

3-20 A comparison of simple and group-code waveforms for a common data input.

Perhaps the most basic code sends a pulse for each 1 and does not send a pulse for a 0; this is called return to zero (RZ) code because the signal level always returns to zero at the end of each bit period.

The nonreturn to zero (NRZ) code also is a basic form of modulation: 1s and 0s are represented directly as high and low levels. The direction of the transition at the beginning or end of a bit period indicates a 1 or 0. The minimum interval is T, but the maximum interval is infinite (when data does not change) thus NRZ suffers from one of the problems that encourages use of modulation: strings of 1s or 0s do not produce transitions in the signal, thus a clock cannot be extracted from the signal. In addition, this creates dc content. The data density (number of bits per transition) for NRZ is 1.

The nonreturn to zero inverted (NRZI) code is similar to the NRZ code, except that only 1s are denoted with amplitude transitions (low to high, or high to low); no transitions occur for 0s. For example, any flux change in a magnetic medium indicates a 1, with transitions occurring in the middle of a bit period. With this method, the signal is immune to polarity reversal. The minimum interval is T, and the maximum is infinite; a clock cannot be extracted. A stream of 1s generates a transition at every clock interval thus the signal's frequency is half that of the clock. A stream of 0s generates no transitions. Data density is 1.

In binary frequency modulation (FM), also known as biphase mark code, there are two transitions for a 1 and one transition for a 0; this is essentially the minimum frequency implementation of FSK. Biphase space code reverses the 1/0 rules. The minimum interval is $0.5T$ and the maximum is T. There is no dc content. In the worst case, there are two transitions per bit, yielding a density ratio of 0.5, or an efficiency of 50%. This code is used in the AES3 standard, described in chapter 10.

In phase encoding (PE), also known as phase modulation (PM), biphase level modulation or Manchester code, a 1 is coded with a negative-going transition, and a 0 is coded with a positive-going transition. Consecutive 1s or 0s follow the same rule, thus requiring an extra transition. These codes follow phase-shift keying techniques. The minimum interval is $0.5T$ and the maximum is T. This code does not have dc content, and is self-clocking. Density ratio is 0.5.

In modified frequency modulation (MFM) code, sometimes known as delay modulation or Miller code, a 1 is coded with either a positive- or negative-going transition in the center of a bit period, for each 1. There is no transition for 0s; rather, a transition is performed at the end of a bit period only if a string of 0s occurs. Each information bit is coded as two channel bits. There is a maximum of three 0s and a minimum of one 0 between successive 1s. In other words, $d = 1$ and $k = 3$. The minimum interval is T and the maximum is $2T$. The code is self-clocking, and might have dc content. Density ratio is 1.

Group Codes

Simple codes such as NRZ and NRZI code one information bit into one channel bit. Group codes use more sophisticated methods for great coding efficiency and overall performance. Group codes use code tables to convert groups of input words (each with m bits) into patterns of output words (each with n bits); the output patterns are specially selected for their desirable coding characteristics, and uniqueness that helps detect errors. The code rate for a group code is m/n. The value of the code rate equals the value of the jitter margin. In some group codes, the correspondence between the input information word and output code word is not fixed; it might vary adaptively with the information sequence itself. These multiple modes of operation can improve code efficiency.

Group codes also can be considered as run-length limited (RLL) codes. In particular, this coding approach recognizes that spacings between transitions do not have to be integer multiples of the clock period. In fact, transition spacings can be any multiple of the period, as shown in Fig. 3-21. This breaks the distinction between data and clock transitions and instead specifies a minimum number d and maximum number k of 0s between two successive 1s. These T_{min} and T_{max} values define the code's run length and specifically determine the code's spectral limits; clearly, data

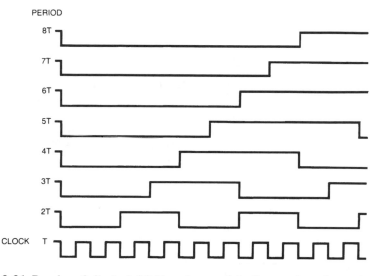

3-21 Run-length limited (RLL) codes regulate the number of transitions representing the channel code. In this way, transition spacings can be any multiple of the channel period, increasing data density.

density, dc content, and clocking are all influenced by these values. The value of the density ratio equals the value of T_{min}, such that $DR = T_{min} = (d + 1)(m)/n$. Similarly, jitter margin $T_w = m/n$ and $FoM = (d + 1)(m^2)/n^2$.

As always, density must be balanced against other factors, such as clocking. Generally, d is selected to be as large as possible for high density, and k is selected to be as large as possible while maintaining stable clocking. Note that high k/d ratios can yield code sequences with high dc content; this is a shortcoming of RLL codes. The minimum and maximum lengths determine the minimum and maximum rates in the code waveform; by choosing specific lengths, the spectral response can be shaped.

RLL codes use a set of rules to convert the information bit stream into a stream of channel bits by defining some relationship between them. A channel bit does not correspond to one information bit; the channel bits can be thought of as short timing windows, fractions of the clock period. Data density can be increased by increasing the number of possible transitions within a bit period. Channel bits are often converted into an output signal using NRZI modulation code; a transition defines a 1 in the channel bit stream. The channel bit rate is usually greater than the information bit rate, but if the run lengths between 1s can be distinguished, the overall information density can be increased. Generally, RLL codes are viable only in channels with low noise; for example, the required S/N ratio increases as minimum length d increases. Fortunately, optical disks are suitable for RLL coding. Technically, NRZ and NRZI are RLL codes because $d = 0$ and $k = \infty$; MFM could be considered as a (1,3) RLL code.

In the group coded recording (GCR) code, data is parsed into 4 bits, coded into 5-bit words using a look-up table as shown in Table 3-1, and modulated as NRZI signals. This implementation is sometimes known as 4/S MNRZI (modified) code. There is a transition every three bits, because of the 4/S conversion, the minimum interval

Data bit	Channel bit
0000	11001
0001	11011
0010	10010
0011	10011
0100	11101
0101	10101
0110	10110
0111	10111
1000	11010
1001	01001
1010	01010
1011	01011
1100	11110
1101	01101
1110	01110
1111	01111

Table 3-1. Conversion for the GCR (or 4/5 MNRZI) code. Groups of four information bits are coded as 5-bit patterns, and written in NRZI form.

is $0.8T$, and the maximum interval is $2.4T$. Adjacent 1s are permitted ($d = 0$) and maximum number of 0s is 2 ($k = 1$). The code is self-clocking with great immunity to jitter, but exhibits dc content. The density ratio is 0.8.

The three-position modulation (3PM) code is a (2,7) run-length limited adaptive code. Three input bits are converted into a 6-bit output word in which T_{min} is $1.5T$ and T_{max} is $6T$, as shown in Table 3-2. There must be at least two channel 0s between 1s. When 3PM words are merged, a 101 pattern might occur; this violates the T_{min} rule. To prevent this, 101 is replaced by 010; the last channel bit in the coding table is reserved for this merging operation. The 3PM code is so called because of the three positions ($d + 1$) in the minimum distance. The code is self-clocking. For comparison, the duration between transitions for 3PM is $0.5T$ and for MFM is T. Thus, the packing density of 3PM is 50% higher than MFM. However, its maximum transition is 100% longer, and its jitter margin 50% worse. 3PM exhibits dc content. Data density is 1.5.

As noted, RLL codes are efficient because the distance between transitions is changed in incremental steps. The effective minimum wavelength of the medium becomes the incremental run lengths. Part of this advantage is lost because it is neces-

Data bit			Channel bit					
			P1	P2	P3	P4	P5	P6
0	0	0	0	0	0	0	1	0
0	0	1	0	0	0	1	0	0
0	1	0	0	1	0	0	0	0
0	1	1	0	1	0	0	1	0
1	0	0	0	0	1	0	0	0
1	0	1	1	0	0	0	0	0
1	1	0	1	0	0	0	1	0
1	1	1	1	0	0	1	0	0
⊢—T—⊣			⊢——T——⊣					

Table 3-2. Conversion for 3PM (2,7) code. Three input bits are coded into a 6-bit output word in which the minimum interval is maintained at $1.5T$ through pattern inversion.

sary to avoid all data patterns that would put transitions closer together than the physical limit. Thus all data must be represented by defined patterns. The EFM code is an excellent example of this kind of RLL pattern coding. The incremental length for EFM is one-third that of the minimum resolvable wavelength. Data density is not tripled, however, because 8 data bits must be expressed in a pattern requiring 14 incremental periods. To recover this data, a clock is run at the incremental period of $1T$.

Eight-to-fourteen modulation (EFM) code is used to store data on a compact disc; it is an efficient and highly structured (2,10) RLL code. Blocks of 8 data bits are translated into blocks of 14 bits using a look-up table that assigns an arbitrary and unique word. The 1s in the output code are separated by at least two 0s ($d = 2$), but no more than ten 0s ($k = 10$). That is, T_{min} is 3 channel bits and T_{max} is 11 channel bits. A logical 1 causes a transition in the medium; this is physically represented as a pit edge on the CD surface. High recording density is achieved with EFM code. Three merging bits are used to concatenate 14-bit EFM words, so 17 incremental periods are required to store 8 data bits. This decreases overall information density, but preserves other advantages in the code. T_{min} is $1.41T$ and T_{max} is $5.18T$. The theoretical recording efficiency is thus calculated by multiplying the three-fold density improvement by a factor of 8/17, giving 24/17, or a density ratio of 1.41. That is, 1.41 data bits can be recorded per shortest pit length. For practical reasons such as S/N ratio and timing jitter on clock regeneration, the ratio is closer to 1.25. In either case, there are more data bits recorded than are transitions on the medium. The merging bits completely eliminate dc content, but reduce efficiency by 6%. The conversion table was selected by a computer algorithm to optimize code performance. From a performance standpoint, EFM is very tolerant of imperfections, provides very high density, and promotes stable clock recovery.

Zero modulation (ZM) coding is an RLL code with $d = 1$ and $k = 3$; it uses a convolutional scheme, rather than group coding. One information bit is mapped into two data bits, coded with rules that depend on the preceding and succeeding data patterns, and written in NRZI code. As with many RLL codes that followed it, ZM uses data patterns that are optimal for its application (magnetic recording) that were selected by computer search. Generally, the bit stream is considered as any number of 0s, two 0s separated by an odd number of 1s or no 1s, or two 0s separated by an even number of 1s. The first two types are coded as Miller code, and in the last the 0s are coded as Miller code, but the 1s are coded as if they were zeros, but without alternate transitions. The density ratio is approximately 1. There is no dc content in ZM.

The HDM-1 code used in professional digital recorders constructed with the DASH format is discussed in chapter 6. The 8/10 code used in the DAT format is discussed in chapter 7. Specifications for a number of simple and group codes are listed in Table 3-3.

Code Applications

In spite of different requirements, there is similarity of design between codes used in magnetic or optical recording. Practical differences between magnetic and optical recording codes are usually limited to differences designed to optimize the code for the specific application. Some codes such as 3PM were developed for mag-

Table 3-3. Specifications for a number of simple and group codes.

Parameter		NRZ NRZI	PE FM	MFM	ZM	GCR	3PM	EFM	HDM-1	8/10
Window margin	(T_w)	T	0.5T	0.5T	~0.5T	0.8T	0.5T	0.471T	0.5T	0.8T
Minimum transition	(T_{min})	T	0.5T	T	~T	0.8T	1.5T	1.41T	1.5T	0.8T
Maximum transition	(T_{max})	∞	T	2T	~2T	2.4T	6T	5.18T	4.5T	3.2T
DC content	DC	yes	no	yes	no	yes	yes	no	yes	no
Clock rate	CLK	no	2/T	2/T	2/T	1.25/T	2/T	17/8T	2/T	10/8T
Density ratio	DR	1	0.5	1	~1	0.8	1.5	1.41	1.5	0.8
Figure of Merit	$T_w T_{min}$ (T^2)	1	0.25	0.5	0.5	0.64	0.75	0.664	0.75	0.64
Maximum/Minimum ratio	T_{max}/T_{min}	∞	2	2	2	3	4	3	3	4

netic recording, but later applied to optical recording. Still, most practical applications use different codes for either magnetic or optical recording.

Optical recording requires a code with high density. Jitter performance is less a concern in optical recording, where media are largely jitter-free. Similarly, run lengths can be longer in optical media because clock regeneration is more easily accomplished. The clock content in the data signal provides synchronization of the data, and motor control. Because this clock must be regenerated from the readout signal (for example, by detecting pit edges) the signal must have a sufficient number of transitions to support regeneration, and the maximum distance between transitions ideally must be as small as possible. In an optical disk, dirt and scratches on the disk surface change the envelope of the readout signal, creating low-frequency noise. This decreases the average level of the readout signal. If the signal falls below the detection level, it can cause an error in readout. This low-frequency noise can be attenuated with a highpass filter, but only if the information data itself contains no low-frequency components. A code without dc content thus improves immunity to surface contamination by allowing insertion of a filter. RLL codes offer good performance in these areas and are suitable for optical disk recording.

The maximum run length of codes used for magnetic recording is greatly limited because magnetic systems will not respond to dc. They use a short run length to provide clocking for jitter-prone magnetic media, but this makes them inefficient. Because magnetic tape is a flexible medium, it is more prone to jitter than an optical disk. In the presence of jitter, the number of incremental periods that can pass before a further transition arrives is limited by the need to avoid any ambiguity in the number of incremental periods between transitions. Therefore, magnetic tape channel encoding has a lower limit on the maximum pattern length. Jitter is discussed in more detail in chapter 4. Ultimately, a detailed analysis is needed to determine the suitability of a code for a given application.

In many receivers and players, a phase-locked loop circuit is used to reclock the channel code, for example, from a storage medium. The channel code acts as the input reference, the loop compares the phase difference between the reference and its own output, and drives an internal voltage-controlled oscillator to the reference frequency, decoupling jitter from the signal. The comparison occurs at every channel transition, and interim oscillator periods count the channel 0s, thus recovering the code. A synchronization code is often inserted in the channel code to lock the phase-locked loop (PLL). In an RLL code, a pattern violating the run-length can be used for synchronization; for example, in the CD, two $11T$ patterns precede an EFM frame; the player can lock to the channel data, and not misinterpret the synchronization patterns as data.

Following encoding, the data is ready for storage or transmission. For example, in a digital tape recorder, the data is applied to a recording circuit that generates the current necessary for saturation recording. The flux reversals recorded on the tape thus represent the bit transitions of the modulated data. The recorded waveforms might appear highly distorted; this does not affect the integrity of the data, and permits higher recording densities. In optical systems such as the compact disc, the modulation code might result in pits. Each pit edge represents a binary 1 channel bit, and spaces between represent binary 0s. In any event, storage to media, transmission, or other real-time digital audio processing marks the end of the digital recording chain.

4
CHAPTER

Digital Audio Reproduction

Digital audio recording and reproduction processors serve as input and output transducers to the digital domain. They convert the analog audio waveform into a signal suitable for digital storage or transmission, then reconvert the signal to analog form. In a linear pulse-code modulation (PCM) system, the functions of the reproduction circuits are largely reversed from those in the record side. Reproduction functions include time-base correction, demodulation, demultiplexing, error correction, digital-to-analog conversion, output sample-and-hold circuit, and output lowpass filtering. Oversampling digital filters, preceding D/A conversion, are universally used.

Reproduction Processing

Reproduction processing comprises a signal chain that accepts a degraded coded signal and ultimately converts it to a high-fidelity analog waveform, as shown in Fig. 4-1. The reproduction circuits must minimize the effects of data storage or transmission. For example, every storage medium suffers from limitations such as mechanical variations and potential for damage to data. With analog storage, problems generally must be corrected within the medium itself; for example, to minimize wow and flutter, a turntable's speed must be precise. With digital systems, because of high data density, the potential for degradation is much greater. However, digital processing also offers the opportunity to correct many faults. For example, the reproduction circuits buffer the data to minimize the effects of timing variations in the data, and perform error correction.

To achieve high data density, the fidelity of the stored or transmitted channel code waveform is allowed to deteriorate. Thus, the signal does not have the clean characteristics of the original data. For example, a recorded digital signal as read from a tape head is not sharply delineated, but instead is rounded with pulses corresponding to the original data. A waveform shaper circuit identifies the transitions

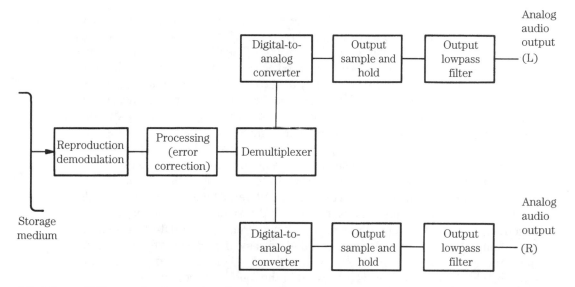

4-1 A linear PCM reproduction section. In practice, digital oversampling filters are used.

and reconstructs a valid data signal. In this way, data can be recovered without penalty for the waveform's deterioration.

Synchronization pulses and other clocking information in the bit stream are identified and used with time-base correction circuits to synchronize the playback signal, delineate individual frames, and thus determine the binary content of each pulse. In most cases, the signal contains timing errors such as jitter as it is received for playback. A data buffer is used to overcome this problem. A buffer can be thought of as a pail of water: water is poured into the pail carelessly, but a spigot at the bottom of the pail supplies a constant stream. Specifically, a buffer is a memory into which the data is fed irregularly, as it is received. However, data is clocked from the buffer at an accurately controlled rate, ensuring precise data timing. Samples can be reassembled at the same rate at which they were taken. Time-base correction is discussed in more detail later in this chapter.

The modulated audio data, whether it is HDM-1, EFM, MFM, or another code, is typically demodulated to NRZ code, that is, a simple code in which amplitude level represents the binary information, as discussed in chapter 3. The audio data thus regains a readable binary form and is ready for further reproduction processing. In addition, demultiplexing is performed to restore parallel structure to the audio data. The demultiplexer circuit accepts a serial bit input, counting as the bits are clocked in. When a full word has been received, it outputs all of the bits of the word simultaneously, to form parallel data.

The audio data and coded error-correction data are identified and separated from other peripheral data. Using the error-correction data, the data signal is checked for errors that have occurred following encoding. Because of the data density used in digital recording and transmission, errors occur with certainty; only their frequency and severity vary. The error correction circuits must de-interleave the data. Prior to recording, the data is scattered in the bit stream to ensure that a defect does not affect consecutive data. With de-interleaving, the data is properly re-assembled in time, and errors caused by intervening defects are scattered through the bit stream, where they are more easily corrected. The data is checked for errors using redundancy techniques. When calculated parity does not agree with parity read from the bit stream, an error has likely occurred in the audio data. Error correction algorithms are used to calculate the correct values. If within tolerance, errors can be detected and corrected with absolute fidelity to the original data, making digital recording and transmission a highly reliable technique. If the error is too extensive for correction, error concealment techniques are used. Most simply, the last data value is held until valid data resumes. Alternatively, linear interpolation calculates new data to form a bridge over the error. A more complete discussion of error correction techniques can be found in chapter 5. The serial bit stream consists of the original audio data, or at least data as original as the error correction circuitry has achieved. On leaving the reproduction processing circuitry, the data has regained timing stability, been demultiplexed, been de-interleaved, and incurred errors have been corrected. The data is ready for digital-to-analog conversion; digital filtering, which precedes D/A conversion, is discussed in the following section.

Digital-to-Analog Converter

The digital-to-analog (D/A) converter is one of the most critical elements in the reproduction system. Just as the analog-to-digital (A/D) converter largely determines the overall quality of the encoded signal, the digital-to-analog converter determines how accurately the digitized signal will be restored to the analog domain. Conventional multibit D/A converters can exhibit nonlinearity similar to that of A/D converters; low-bit converters, operating on a time basis rather than an amplitude basis, overcome this deficiency but must use noise shaping to reduce the in-band noise floor. Fortunately, high-quality D/A converters are available at relatively low cost.

Multibit D/A converters process parallel data words, usually operating at an oversampling rate; they are prone to many of the same errors as A/D converters, as described in chapter 3. In practice, resolution is chiefly determined by absolute linearity error and differential linearity error. Absolute linearity error is a deviation from the ideal quantization staircase and can be measured at full signal level; it is smaller than ±½ LSB. Differential linearity error is a relative deviation from the ideal staircase by any individual step. The error is uncorrelated with high signal levels but correlated with low signal levels; as a result it is most apparent at low signal levels as distortion.

Differential nonlinearity appears as wide and narrow codes, and can cause entire sections of the transfer function to be missing; this is shown in Fig. 4-2. Differential nonlinearity is minor with high-amplitude signals but the errors can dominate low-level signals. For example, any signal 80 dB below full scale will pass through only six or seven codes in a 16-bit quantizer; if half of those codes are missing, the result will be 14-bit performance. Depending on bias, the differential linearity error in a 16-bit D/A converter for a –90 dB sinewave signal can result in generated levels ranging

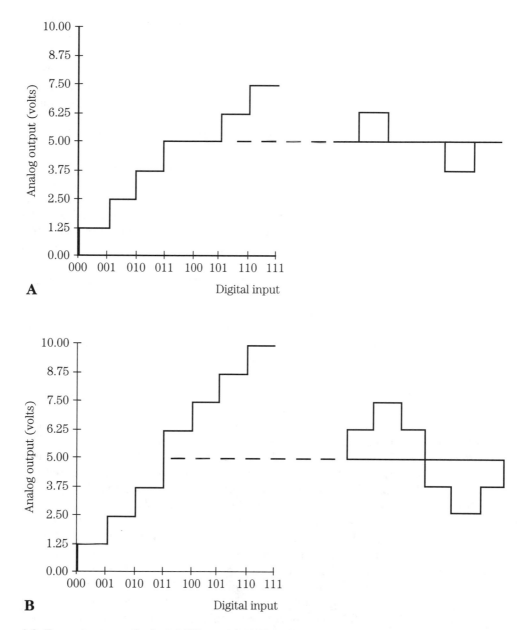

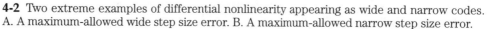

4-2 Two extreme examples of differential nonlinearity appearing as wide and narrow codes. A. A maximum-allowed wide step size error. B. A maximum-allowed narrow step size error.

from –85.9 dB to –98.2 dB. Because the bits and their associated errors switch in and out throughout the transfer function, their effect is signal dependent. Thus, harmonic and intermodulation distortion and noise vary with signal conditions. Because this kind of error is correlated with the audio signal, it tends to be perceptible. Nonmonotonicity is an extreme case of nonlinearity; an increase in a particular digital code does not result in an increase in the output analog voltage; most converters are guaranteed against this.

A linearity test measures the converter's ability to record or reproduce various signals at the proper amplitude. Specifically, linearity refers to the converter's ability to output an analog signal that directly conforms to a digital word. For example, when a bit changes from 1 to 0 in a D/A converter, the analog output must decrease exactly by a proportional amount. Any nonlinearity results in distortion in the audio signal; the amount that the analog voltage changes depends on which bit has changed. Every PCM digital word contains a series of binary digits, arranged in powers of two. The most significant bit (MSB) accounts for a change in fully half of the analog signal's amplitude, and the least significant bit (LSB) accounts for the least change, for example, in an 18-bit word, an amplitude change of less than four parts per million. Physical realities conspire against this accuracy. Conventional multibit converters exhibit differential nonlinearity because of bit weighting errors; thermal or physical stress, aging, and temperature variations are also factors.

To help equipment manufacturers use D/A converters to their best advantage, many D/A chips provide a means to calibrate the converter. Consider a 16-bit D/A converter offering calibration of the MSB. Because the MSB is so much larger than the other bits, an MSB error of only 0.01% (one part in 10,000) would completely negate the contributions of the two least significant bits (which account for one part in 21,845 of the total signal amplitude). An error of 0.1% in the MSB would swamp the combined values of the five smallest bits. Some converters offer calibration of the four most significant bits. It is interesting to note that fully 93% of the total analog output is represented through these four most significant bits. These MSBs largely steer the converter's output amplitude; when they are properly calibrated, the entire output signal of a well-designed D/A converter will be more accurate. This accuracy is most significant at low levels, usually below –60 dB. As noted, any nonlinearity in D/A conversion will be apparent as a deviation from a nominal amplitude. Moreover, such nonlinearity can be heard; for example, by using a test disc containing a dithered fade to silence tone, poor D/A linearity is audible.

Using tests for D/A linearity, the low-level performance of D/A converters can be evaluated. For example, Fig. 4-3 shows a D/A converter's low-level linearity. Reproduced signals lower than –100 dB in amplitude show nonlinearity. For example, a –100-dB signal is reproduced at an amplitude of –99 dB, and a –110-dB signal is reproduced at approximately –105 dB. Depending on signal conditions, this kind of error in low-level dynamics might audibly alter low-amplitude information.

In practice, linear 16-bit conversion is insufficient for 16-bit data. Converters must have a greater dynamic range than the audio signal itself. No matter how many bits are converted, the accuracy of the conversion, and hence the fidelity of the audio signal, hinges on the linearity of the converter. Linearity errors in converters generally result in a stochastic deviation; it varies randomly from sample to sample. However, relative error increases as level decreases. The linearity of a multibit D/A converter, and not the number of bits it uses, measures its accuracy.

A D/A converter must have fast settling time; the criteria for settling time are shown in Fig. 4-4. Settling time for a D/A converter is the elapsed time between a

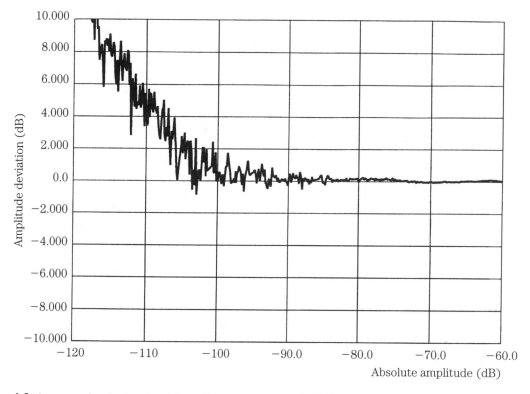

4-3 An example of a low-level linearity measurement of a D/A converter showing increasing non-linearity with decreasing amplitude.

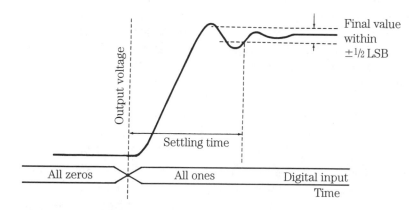

4-4 The settling time for a D/A converter is measured over the duration of a complete word change.

new input code and the time when the analog output falls within a specified tolerance (perhaps ±½ LSB). The settling time can vary with the magnitude of change in the input word.

Most D/A converters operate with a two's complement input. For example, an 8-bit D/A converter would have a most positive value of 01111111 and a most negative value of 10000000. In this format the MSB is complemented to serve as a sign bit. To accomplish this, the MSB can be inverted before the word is input to the D/A converter, or the D/A converter might have a separate, complementing input for the MSB.

Digitally generated test tones are often used to measure D/A converters; it is important to choose frequencies that are not correlated to the sampling frequency. Otherwise, a small sequence of codes might be reproduced over and over, without fully exercising the converter. Depending on the converter's linearity at those particular codes, the output distortion might measure better, or worse, than normal performance. For example, when replaying a 1 second, 1 kHz, 0-dB sinewave sampled at 44.1 kHz, only 441 different codes would be used over the 44,100 points. A 0-dB sinewave at 997 Hz would use 20,542 codes, giving a much better representation of converter performance. Standard test tones have been selected to avoid this anomaly. For example, some standard test frequencies are: 17, 31, 61, 127, 251, 499, 997, 1999, 4001, 7993, 10,007, 12,503, 16,001, 17,989, and 19,997 Hz.

Weighted-Resistor Digital-to-Analog Converter

Various types of digital-to-analog converters are used for audio digitization. Operation of multibit converters are quite different from low-bit converters. The former are most easily understood; we begin with an illustration of the operation of a simple multibit D/A converter. A digital-to-analog converter accepts an input digital word and converts it to an output analog voltage or current. The simplest kind of D/A converter, known as a weighted resistor D/A converter, contains a series of resistors and switches, as shown in Fig. 4-5.

A weighted-resistor converter contains a switch for each input bit; the corresponding resistor represents the binary value associated with that bit. A reference voltage generates current through the resistors. A digital 1 closes a switch and contributes a current, and a digital 0 opens a switch and prevents current flow. An operational amplifier sums the currents and converts them to an output voltage. A low-value binary word with many 0s presents many open switches, and a small voltage results. A high-value word with many 1s closes many switches and a high voltage results. Consider this example of an 8-bit converter:

$$V_{\text{out}} = -V_{\text{ref}}\left(\frac{b1}{2} + \frac{b2}{4} + \frac{b3}{8} + \frac{b4}{16} + \frac{b5}{32} + \frac{b6}{64} + \frac{b7}{128} + \frac{b8}{256}\right)$$

where $b1$ through $b8$ represent the input binary bits. For example, suppose the reference voltage is 1, the input word is 11010011, and $V_{\text{ref}} = 10$ V:

$$V_{\text{out}} = -10\left(\frac{1}{2} + \frac{1}{4} + \frac{0}{8} + \frac{1}{16} + \frac{0}{32} + \frac{0}{64} + \frac{1}{128} + \frac{1}{256}\right)$$

$$= -10\left(\frac{1}{2} + \frac{1}{4} + \frac{1}{16} + \frac{1}{128} + \frac{1}{256}\right)$$

$$= -8.24 \text{ V}$$

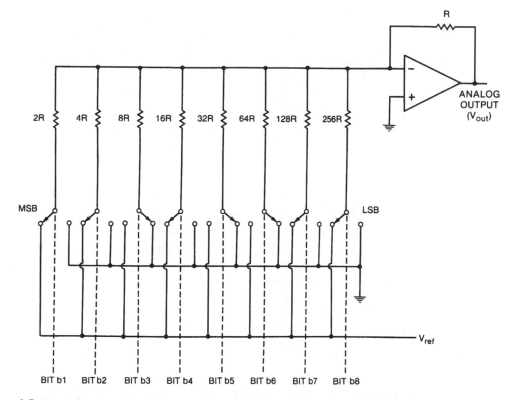

4-5 A weighted resistor D/A converter uses resistors related by powers of two, which limits resolution.

Although this design looks good on paper, it is rarely used in practice because of the complexity in manufacturing resistors with sufficient accuracy. It is extremely difficult to manufacture precise resistor values so that each next resistor value is exactly a power of two greater than the previous one. For example, in a 16-bit D/A converter, the largest-to-smallest resistor ratio is $2^{16} = 65,536$. If the smallest resistor value is 1 kΩ, the largest is over 65 MΩ. Similarly, the smallest current might be 30 nA and the largest 2 mA. In short, this design demands manufacturing conditions that cannot be efficiently met.

R-2R Ladder Digital-to-Analog Converter

A more suitable design approach for a D/A converter is the *R-2R* resistor ladder, as shown in Fig. 4-6. This circuit contains resistors and switches; however, there are two resistors per bit. Each switch contributes its appropriately weighted component to the output. The current splits at each node of the ladder, resulting in currents through the switch resistors that are weighted by binary powers of two. If a current *I* flows from the reference voltage, *I*/2 flows through the first switch, *I*/4 through the

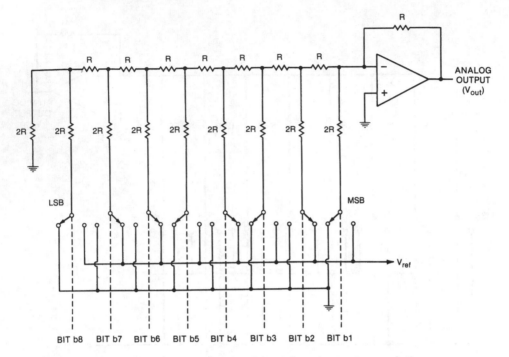

4-6 An R-2R D/A converter uses only two resistor values, improving resolution.

second switch, *I*/8 through the third switch, etc. Digital input bits are used to control ladder switches to produce an analog output:

$$V_{\text{out}} = -V_{\text{ref}}\left(\frac{b1}{2} + \frac{b2}{4} + \frac{b3}{8} + \frac{b4}{16} + \frac{b5}{32} + \frac{b6}{64} + \frac{b7}{128} + \frac{b8}{256}\right)$$

With an input word of 01010110 and $V_{\text{ref}} = 10$ V,

$$V_{\text{out}} = -10\left(\frac{1}{4} + \frac{1}{16} + \frac{1}{64} + \frac{1}{128}\right) = -3.36 \text{ V}$$

The R-2R network is preferred because it can be efficiently manufactured; only two values of resistors are needed. As noted, in many converters, one or several MSBs can be calibrated to improve linearity. In some designs, stability with respect to temperature is achieved with a compensation feedback loop. A high precision signal is generated and compared to the signal generated by the D/A converter. The difference between the two is applied to a memory, which in turn outputs a correction word to the input of the D/A converter. Errors caused by variations in the components are thus self-corrected and distortion is minimized.

Integrating Digital-to-Analog Converter

An alternative approach to the design of the digital-to-analog converter is the dual-slope integrating converter. Its operation is similar to that of the integrating A/D converter. The inherent accuracy of conventional ladder D/A converters depends on the precision of the resistor values. Even a small error in the value of the most significant bit or second most significant bit resistors can greatly affect the accuracy of the output voltage. Integration techniques do not require a ladder, and if internal reference currents are carefully regulated, high accuracy is obtained. A dual-slope integrating D/A converter can accept a 16-bit input word, dividing the word into the most significant and least significant 8 bits. An output integrating amplifier accepts the two current sources for timed intervals and outputs an analog voltage proportional to the timing ramps.

Zero-Cross Distortion

A quality D/A converter must be highly accurate. A 16-bit D/A converter with an output range of ±10 V has a difference between quantization levels of 20/65,536 = 0.000305 V. For example, the output from the input word 1000 0000 0000 0000 should be 0.3 mV larger than that from the input word 0111 1111 1111 1111. In other words, the sum of the lower 15 bits must be accurate to that precision, compared to the value of the highest bit. The lower 15 bits should have a relative error of one-half quantization level, as should the MSB. However, differential linearity error is greatest for the MSB, which produces the largest output voltage. Moreover, the MSB changes each time the output waveform passes through zero. Difficulty in achieving accuracy at the center of a multibit D/A converter's range leads to zero-cross distortion.

Zero-cross distortion occurs at the zero-cross point between the positive and negative polarity portions of an analog waveform. When a resistor ladder D/A converter is switched around its MSB, that is, from 1000 0000 0000 0000 to 0111 1111 1111 1111 to reflect a polarity change, an internal network of resistors must be switched. Current fluctuations and variations in bit switching speeds conspire to create considerable differential nonlinearity and glitches, as shown in Fig. 4-7. Collectively, these defects are known as zero-cross distortion. Because musical waveforms continually change between positive and negative polarity, twice each cycle, the zero axis is crossed repeatedly as the MSB is turned on and off. The error is particularly troublesome when reproducing low-level signals, because the fixed-amplitude glitch is proportionally large with respect to the signal. Further, the audibility of zero-cross distortion can be aggravated by dithering because of the increase in the number of transitions around the MSB.

Ideally, when there is no error difference between the smallest and largest resistors in the ladder, there is no error. However, the MSB generally has an error large compared to the LSB; the error can be larger than the value of the LSB itself. This is because the MSB in a 16-bit converter must be represented by a current value with an accuracy greater than 1/65,536 of the LSB. (This demonstrates why adjustment of the MSB is paramount in achieving converter linearity.) Similarly, error can occur when the 2nd, 3rd, and 4th bits are switched; however, the error proportionally decreases as signal level increases. By the same token, error is relatively greatest for low-level audio signals. When longer word-length converters are used, it is proportionally difficult to match resistor values.

Zero-cross distortion can be alleviated by careful calibration of the converter's most significant bits. Zero-cross distortion can also be reduced by providing a D/A

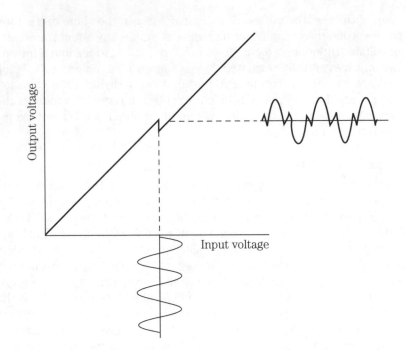

4-7 Crossover distortion occurs at the zero cross point when the input of a D/A converter changes polarity, resulting in a glitch in the output waveform.

converter for each waveform polarity. In this way, total switching of digits never occurs. The digital signal must be split between two D/A converters; an upstream processor chip performs this switching digitally, glitch-free. Zero-cross distortion is not present in low-bit converters, as described in chapter 16.

High-Bit D/A Conversion

Some manufacturers have introduced 18- or 20-bit (or higher) converters into 16-bit PCM reproduction systems to provide greater playback fidelity for 16-bit recordings. The rationale for this lies in flaws inherent in D/A converters. Except in theory, 16-bit converters cannot fully decode a 16-bit signal without a degree of error. When, for example, 18 bits are derived from 16-bit data and converted with 18-bit resolution, errors can be reduced and reproduction specifications improved. In order to realize the full potential of audio fidelity, the signal digitization and processing steps must have a greater dynamic range than the final recording.

The choice of 16-bit words for the CD, DAT, and other formats was determined primarily by the availability of 16-bit D/A converters and the fact that longer word lengths diminish playing time. However, 18-bit converters, for example, can provide better conversion of the stored 16 bits. When done correctly, 18-bit conversion improves amplitude resolution by ensuring a fully linear conversion of the 16-bit signal. An 18-bit D/A converter has 262,144 levels, exactly four times as many output levels as a 16-bit converter. Any nonlinearity is correspondingly smaller, and increasing the quantization word length at the conversion stage results in an increase in S/N ratio. Simultaneously, any quantization artifacts are diminished. In other words, an 18-bit converter gives better 16-bit conversion. In fact, the two extra bits of a linear 18-bit converter do not have to be connected to yield improved 16-bit performance.

The intent of high-bit D/A converters can be compared to that of oversampling: while the sampling frequency is increased, the method does not create new information; it makes better use of the existing information. Oversampling provides the opportunity for high-bit conversion of 16-bit data. When a 44.1-kHz, 16-bit signal is oversampled, both the sampling frequency and number of bits are increased—the former because of oversampling, and the latter because of filter coefficient multiplication. The digital filter must be appropriately designed so the output word contains useful information in the bits below the 16-bit level.

It is not meaningful to gauge the performance of a multibit D/A or A/D converter by its word length. More accurately, the signal-to-noise ratio measures the ratio between the maximum signal and the noise in the absence of signal. Because systems mute the output when there is a null signal, low-level error, such as zero-crossing distortion, is removed. A dynamic range measurement is more useful when measured as the ratio of the maximum signal to the broadband noise (0 Hz to 20 kHz), using a –60-dB signal. This provides a measure of low-level distortion. Using the dynamic range measurement, a converter's ENOB (effective number of bits) can be calculated:

$$ENOB = \frac{(\text{dynamic range} - 1.72)}{6.02}$$

For example, a 16-bit converter with a dynamic range of 90 dB provides 14.7 bits of resolution; 1.3 bits are mired in distortion and noise.

In many designs, low-bit D/A converters are used. They minimize many problems inherent in multibit converters, such as low-level nonlinearity and zero-cross distortion. Low-bit systems use very high oversampling rates, noise shaping, and low-bit conversion. A true 1-bit system outputs a binary waveform, at a very high rate, to represent the audio waveform. Other low-bit systems output a multivalue step signal that forms a PWM representation of the audio signal. Because of inherently high noise levels, low-bit systems must use noise shaping algorithms. Low-bit conversion is discussed in detail in chapter 16.

Output Sample-and-Hold Circuit

Many digital audio systems contain two S/H (sample-and-hold) circuits: one at the input to sample the analog value and maintain it while the A/D converter performs its task, and another S/H circuit on the output to sample and hold the signal output from the D/A converter, primarily to remove irregular signals called switching glitches. Because it can also compensate for a frequency response anomaly called aperture error, the output S/H circuit is sometimes called the aperture circuit.

Many D/A converters can generate erroneous signals, or glitches, which are superimposed on the analog output voltage. Digital data input to a multibit D/A converter requires time to stabilize to the correct binary levels. In particular, input bits might not switch states simultaneously. For example, during an input switch from

01111111 to 10000000, the MSB might switch to 1 before the other bits; this yields a momentary value of 11111111, creating an output voltage spike of one-half full scale. Even D/A converters with very fast settling times can exhibit momentary glitches. If these glitches are allowed to proceed to the digitization system's output, they are manifested as distortion.

An output S/H circuit can be used to deglitch the D/A converter's output signal. The output S/H circuit acquires a voltage from the D/A converter only when that circuit has reached a stable output condition. That correct voltage is held by the S/H circuit during the intervals when the D/A converter switches between samples. This ensures a glitch-free output PAM signal. The operation of an output S/H circuit is shown in Fig. 4-8.

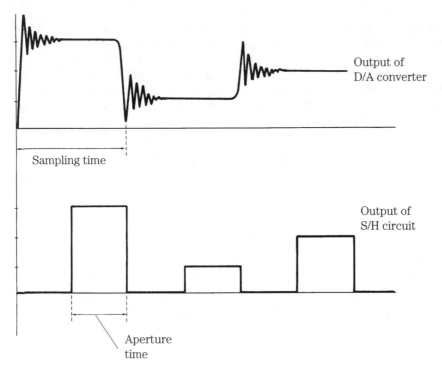

4-8 An output S/H circuit can be used to remove glitches in the signal output from the D/A converter.

From a general hardware standpoint, the output S/H circuit is designed similarly to the input S/H circuit. In some specifications, such as droop, the output S/H circuit might be less precise. Any droop results in only a dc shift at the digitization system's output, and this can be easily removed. In other respects, the output S/H circuit must be carefully designed and implemented in a digital audio system. Because of its differing utility, the output S/H circuit often requires special attention to specifications such as hold time and transition speed from sample to sample.

The S/H circuit is occasionally used to correct for aperture error, an attenuation of high frequencies. Different approaches can also be used. Aperture error stems from the width of the output samples. In this case, the narrower the pulse width, the less the aperture error. Given ideal (instantaneous) A/D sampling, the output of an ideal D/A converter would be an impulse train corresponding to the original sample points; there would be no high-frequency attenuation. However, an ideal D/A converter is an impossibility. The PAM staircase waveform comprises pulses each with a width of one sample period. (Mathematically, the function is a convolution of the original samples by a square pulse with width of one sample period.) The spectrum of a series of pulses of finite width naturally attenuates at high frequencies. This differs from the original flat response of infinitesimal pulse widths; thus a frequency response error called aperture error results, in which high audio frequencies are attenuated. Specifically, the frequency response follows a lowpass $|\sin(x)/x|$ function. When the output pulse width is equal to the sample period, the frequency response is zero at multiples of the sampling frequency, as shown in Fig. 4-9A. The attenuation of the in-band high-frequency response and that of high-frequency images can be observed.

At the half-sampling frequency, the value is 0.64, or about a 4-dB attenuation. This can be corrected with S/H circuits by approximating the impulse train output from an ideal D/A converter; the duration of the hold time is decreased in the S/H circuit. Sampling theory shows us that the bandwidth of the response is determined by the pulse width. The shorter the duration of the pulse, the greater the bandwidth. Specifically, if the output pulse width is narrowed with a shorter hold time, the attenuation at the half-sampling frequency can be decreased, as shown in Fig. 4-9B, where pulse width is halved. If hold time is set to one-quarter of a sample period, the amplitude at the Nyquist frequency is 0.97 or about a 0.2-dB attenuation. This is considered optimal because a shorter hold time degrades the signal-to-noise ratio of the system.

Another solution for aperture error is frequency compensation of the data prior to D/A conversion; this can be built into the digital lowpass filter that precedes the S/H circuit. This high-frequency boost, offset by aperture error, produces a net flat response, and the S/N ratio is not degraded. A boost could also be designed into the succeeding analog lowpass filter. Alternatively, a pre-emphasis high-frequency boost could be applied at the system input; the naturally occurring de-emphasis at the output S/H circuit would result in a flat response.

An output sample-and-hold circuit is primarily used to eliminate switching errors caused by the D/A converter during transition; however, the S/H circuit must avoid introducing transition errors of its own. An S/H circuit outputs a steady value while in the hold mode. When switching to the sample (or acquisition) mode, a slow transition introduces incorrect intermediate values into the staircase voltage. This problem is extraneous in the input S/H circuit because the A/D converter accomplishes its digitization during the hold mode and ignores the transition mode. However, the output S/H circuit is always connected to the system output and any transition error appears at the output. In other words, not only are the levels themselves part of the output signal, but the way in which the S/H circuit moves from sample to sample is included as well.

Distortion is greatest for high frequencies because they have a large difference between values. A 20-Hz signal does not change appreciably in one sampling

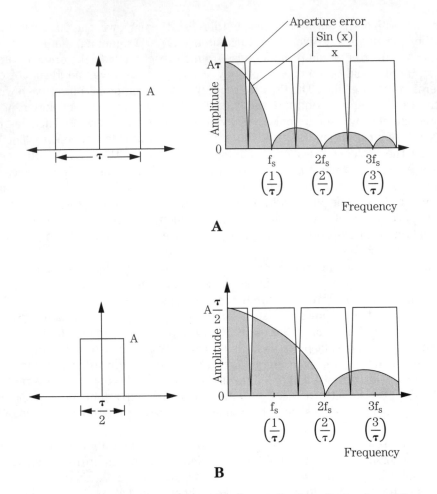

4-9 Aperture error can be minimized by decreasing the output pulse width. A. A pulse width equal to the sample period yields an in-band high-frequency attenuation. B. In-band high-frequency response improves when pulse width is one-half the sample period.

interval; however, a high-level 20-kHz signal will traverse almost the full amplitude range. Although the distortion products themselves can be removed by the output filter, they can internally beat with the sampling frequency to generate in-band distortion as well. To overcome this problem, the output S/H circuit must switch as quickly as possible from hold to sample mode. (A square-wave response would be ideal.)

In theory, this eliminates the possibility of distortion caused by transition, but in practice it is impossible to achieve the necessary high slew rate, which Barry Blesser has calculated to be as high as 5 V/ns (volts per nanosecond). Thus, an additional modification to the basic S/H circuit can be applied. An exponential change in amplitude from one quantization interval to the next does not create nonlinearity in the signal. Following output filtering, this exponential acquisition results in a linear response. It can be shown that an exponential transition from sample to sample causes only a slight high-frequency de-emphasis at the output, but no distortion or nonlinearity. An S/H circuit that integrates the difference between its present and next value results in such an exponential transition. The attenuation of high frequencies in an integrate and hold circuit is less than that produced by the sample-and-hold process itself, and also can be equalized.

The output S/H circuit thus removes switching glitches from the D/A converter's output voltage. Hold time can be set to less than a sample period to minimize aperture error. Many D/A converters are stringently designed to operate without an S/H circuit; aperture error is corrected in the digital filter. In some cases, the S/H function is included in the converter chip. Whichever method is used, the PAM staircase analog signal is ready for output filtering, and final reconstruction.

Output Lowpass Filter

The first and last circuits in an audio digitization system are lowpass filters, known as anti-aliasing and anti-imaging filters, respectively. Although their analog designs can be almost identical, their functions are very different. In lieu of classic analog anti-imaging filters, digital filter designs using oversampling techniques have replaced brick-wall analog filters.

Given the criteria of the Nyquist sampling theorem, the function of the input lowpass filter is clear: it must remove all frequency content above the half-sampling frequency, to prevent aliasing. Similarly, a lowpass filter at the output of the digitization system must remove all frequency content above the half-sampling frequency. This filter converts the output pulse amplitude modulation (PAM) staircase to a smoothly continuous waveform, thus reconstructing the original filtered input signal. The PAM staircase is an analog waveform, but contains artifacts of the sampling process. The shifts in level represent high-frequency components not present in the original signal. An output lowpass filter converts the staircase into a smoothly continuous waveform by removing the high-frequency components, leaving the original waveform (see Fig. 2-2). The staircase signal is smoothed; the output filter is sometimes called a smoothing filter.

The design criteria for an analog output lowpass filter are similar to those of the input filter. The passband should be flat and the stopband highly attenuated. The cutoff slope should be steep. Audibility of phase shifts caused by brick-wall filters must be considered. As with brick-wall anti-aliasing filters, group delay occurs and might cause audible artifacts. Phase correction circuits can be used; when placed at the output (or input) of a digitization system, they make group delays constant so the overall phase shift is linear with respect to frequency, and thus inaudible. One consideration unique to output lowpass filters is transient response. Unlike the input filter, it must process the amplitude changes in the staircase waveform. Just as a slow S/H circuit can introduce distortion, the output filter can create unwanted by-products unless its transient response is adequate. One consideration not commonly addressed is the possible presence of extreme high-frequency components of several megahertz, which might be contained in the output signal. Because of its high-speed operation, digital processing equipment can create this noise, and the filtering characteristics of most audio lowpass filters do not extend to those frequencies.

Viewing the output filtering process from a more mathematical standpoint, we can observe how sampling creates the need for filtering. Sampling multiplies the time domain audio signal with the time domain sampling (pulse) signal. In terms of the spectrum of these two sampled signals, this convolution produces a new sampled spectrum identical to the original unsampled spectrum. However, additional spectra are infinitely repeated across the frequency domain at multiples of the sample frequency. For example, an original 1-kHz sinewave sampled at 44 kHz also creates components at 43, 45, 87, and 89 kHz, etc. Although the sample-and-hold process substantially reduces the amplitude of the extraneous frequency bands, significant components still remain after the S/H circuit, particularly in the region near the audio band (see Fig. 4-9). To convert the sampled information back into correct analog information, the image spectra must be removed, leaving only the original baseband spectrum. This is accomplished by lowpass filtering.

Some might question the need to filter out frequencies above the Nyquist frequency because they lie above the presumed limit of human audibility. The original waveform is reproduced without filtering, but the accompanying spectra could cause modulation in other downstream equipment through which the signal passes. This in turn could negatively affect the audio signal. Other digital systems might be immune because their input filters remove the high frequencies, but oscillators in analog recorders or transmitters could conceivably create different frequencies in the audible band. Clearly, in systems with lower sampling frequencies (eg. 8 kHz) any images above the Nyquist frequency would be audible, and thus must be removed.

Impulse Response

Logically, when an impulse is input to a device such as a lowpass filter, the output is the filter's impulse response. As shown in chapter 15, the impulse response can completely characterize a system: A filter can be described by its time-domain impulse response or its frequency response; these are related by the Fourier transform. Furthermore, observe that multiplying an input spectrum by a desired filter transfer function in the frequency domain is equivalent to convolving the input time-domain function with the desired filter's impulse response in the time domain. Meanwhile, observe the action of lowpass filtering, and the impulse response, as shown in Fig. 4-10. In this example, the input signal comprises two sinewaves of different frequencies A; their spectra consist of two lines at the sinewave frequencies B. Suppose that we wish to lowpass filter the signal to remove the higher frequency. This is accomplished by multiplying the input spectra with an ideal lowpass filter characteristic D, producing the single spectral line F. The time-domain impulse response of this ideal lowpass filter follows a $\sin(x)/x$ function C; if the input time-domain signal is convolved with the $\sin(x)/x$ function, the result is the filtered output time-domain

Time domain

Frequency domain

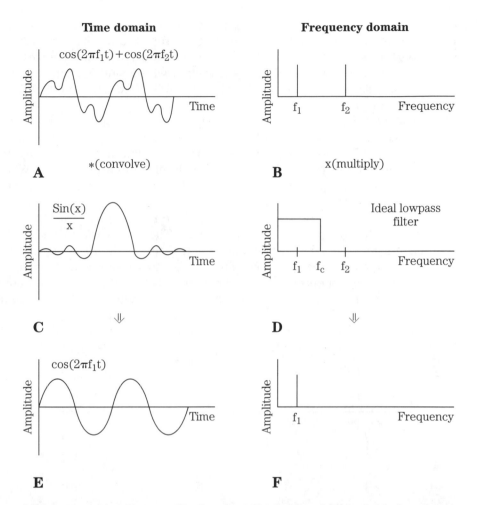

4-10 An example of lowpass filtering shown in the time domain (left column) and the frequency domain (right column). A. The input signal comprises two sinewaves. B. Spectrum of the input signal. C. Impulse response of the desired lowpass filter is a $\sin(x)/x$ function. D. Desired lowpass filter transfer function. E. Output filtered signal is the convolution of the input with the impulse response. F. Spectrum of the output filtered signal is the multiplication of the input by the transfer function.

signal E. In other words, a time-domain, sampled signal can be filtered by applying the time-domain impulse response that describes the filter's characteristic. In digital systems, both the signal and the impulse response are represented by discrete values; the impulse response of an ideal reconstruction filter is zero at all sample times, except at one central point.

The output filter reconstructs the audio waveform. Although the idea of smoothing the output samples to remove high frequencies is essentially correct, a more analytical analysis shows exactly how waveform reconstruction is accomplished by lowpass filtering. An ideal brick-wall lowpass filter is needed to exactly reconstruct the output waveform from samples; the sampling theorem dictates this. As noted, an ideal brick-wall lowpass filter has a $\sin(x)/x$ impulse response. When samples of a bandlimited input signal are processed (convolved) with a $\sin(x)/x$ function, the bandlimited input signal represented by the samples will be exactly reproduced; the sampling theorem guarantees this.

Specifically, as shown in Fig. 4-11A, when a single rectangular audio sample passes through an ideal lowpass filter, after a filter delay it emerges with a $\sin(x)/x$ response. If the lowpass filter has a cutoff frequency at the half-sampling point ($f_s/2$) then the $\sin(x)/x$ curve passes through zero at multiples of $1/f_s$. When a series of audio samples pass through the filter, the resulting waveform is the delayed summation of all the individual $\sin(x)/x$ contributions of the individual samples, as shown in Fig. 4-11B. Each sample's impulse response is zero at the $1/f_s$ position of any other sample's maximum response. The output waveform has the value of each sample at sample time, and summed response of the impulse responses of all samples between sample points. This superposition, or summation, of individual impulse responses forms all the intermediate parts of the continuous reconstructed waveform. In other words, when the high-frequency staircase com-

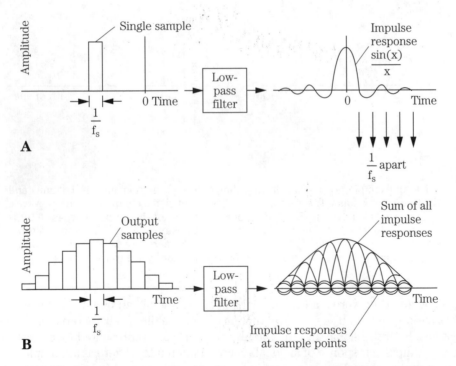

4-11 The impulse response of an ideal lowpass filter reconstructs the output analog waveform. A. The impulse response of an ideal lowpass filter is a $\sin(x)/x$ function; it is truncated in this drawing. B. When a series of impulses (samples) are lowpass filtered, the individual impulse responses sum to form the output waveform.

ponents are removed, the remaining fundamental passes exactly through the same points as the original filtered waveform.

Output filtering, with an ideal lowpass filter, yields an output audio waveform that is identical to the input lowpass filtered audio waveform. In other words, it is the filter's impulse response to the audio samples that reconstructs the original audio waveform.

Digital Filter

Because of the phase shift and distortion they introduce, analog brick-wall output filters have been abandoned by manufacturers, in favor of digital filters. A digital filter is a circuit (or algorithm) which accepts audio samples and outputs audio samples; the values of the throughput audio samples are altered to produce filtering. In this case, the digital filter simulates the process of ideal lowpass filtering and thus provides waveform reconstruction. Rather than suppress high-frequency images after the signal has been converted to analog form, digital filters perform the same function in the digital domain, prior to D/A conversion. Following D/A conversion, a gentle, low-order analog filter removes remaining images, at very high frequencies. In most cases, finite impulse response (FIR) digital filters using oversampling techniques are used. With oversampling, additional sample values are computed by interpolating between original samples. Because additional samples are generated (perhaps two, four, or eight times as many), the sampling frequency of the output signal is greater than the input signal. A transversal filter architecture is typically used; it comprises a series of delays and multipliers, and an adder.

The task of an oversampling filter is two-fold: to re-sample, and to filter through interpolation. The signal input to the filter is sampled at f_s, and has images centered around multiples of f_s, as shown in Fig. 4-12A and B. Re-sampling begins by increasing the sampling frequency. That is accomplished by injecting 0-valued samples between original samples at some interpolation ratio. For example, for four-times oversampling, three 0 samples are inserted for every original sample. The oversampling sampling frequency equals the interpolation ratio times the input sampling frequency, but the spectrum of the oversampled signal is the same as the original signal spectrum as shown in Fig. 4-12C and D. In this case, for example, with an input sampling frequency of 44.1 kHz, the oversampling frequency is 176.4 kHz. This data enters the lowpass digital filter with a cutoff frequency of $f_s/2$, operating at an effective frequency of 176.4 kHz. Although the original data was sampled at 44.1 kHz, with oversampling it is conceptually indistinguishable from data originally sampled at 176.4 kHz. The output from the filter is an interpolated digital signal, with images centered around multiples of the higher oversampling frequency f_a, as shown in Fig. 4-12E and F. To obtain the interpolated values in Fig. 4-12E, the zero-packed signal must be passed through a digital lowpass filter with the impulse response and transfer function shown in Fig. 4-12G and H. The fixed sample values in Fig. 4-12G, occurring at the oversampling frequency, are the coefficients of the digital transversal lowpass filter.

To recapitulate, interpolation is used to create the intermediate sample points. In a four-times oversampling filter, the filter outputs four samples for every original

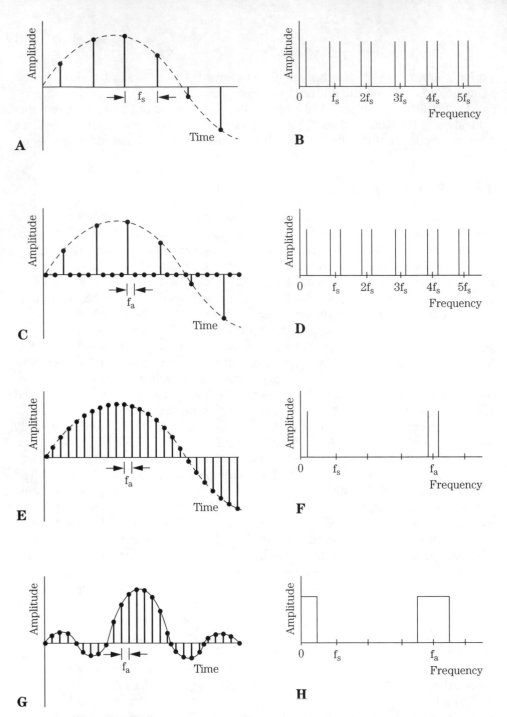

4-12 An oversampling filter resamples, and interpolates the signal, using the impulse response; this is shown in the time domain (left column) and frequency domain (right column). A. The input signal is sampled at f_s. B. The signal spectrum has images centered around multiples of f_s. C. With re-sampling, 0-valued samples are placed between original samples at some interpolation ratio. D. The spectrum of the oversampled signal is the same as the original signal spectrum. E. The digital filter performs interpolation to form new sample values. F. The output filtered signal has images centered around multiples of the oversampling frequency, f_a. G. The values of a sampled impulse response correspond to the coefficients of the digital filter used to form the interpolated sample values. H. The transfer function of the filter shows passbands in the audio band, and oversampling band.

sample. However, to be useful, these samples must be computed according to a certain algorithm. Specifically, each intermediate sample is multiplied by the appropriate $\sin(x)/x$ coefficient corresponding to its contribution to the overall impulse response of the lowpass filter in the time domain (see Fig. 4-11B). The $\sin(x)/x$ function in the time domain has zeros exactly aligned with sample times, except at the sample currently being interpolated. Thus every interpolated sample is a linear combination of all other input samples, weighted by the $\sin(x)/x$ function. The multiplication products are summed together to produce the output filtered sample. The conceptual operation of a digital filter thus corresponds exactly to the summed impulse response operation of an ideal analog brick-wall filter. Spectral images appear at multiples of the oversampled sampling frequency. Because the distance between the baseband and sidebands is larger, a gentle analog filter can remove the images without causing phase shift or other artifacts.

The oversampling ratio can be defined as:

$$R = \frac{f_a}{f_s}$$

where

f_a is the oversampling frequency,
f_s is the input sampling frequency.

Oversampling initially requires insertion of $(R-1)$ zero samples per input sample. The samples created by oversampling must be placed symmetrically between the input samples. A lowpass filter is used to band limit the input data to $f_s/2$, with spectral images at integer multiples of $(R \times f_s)$. Moreover lowpass filtering creates the intermediate sample values through interpolation. Rather than perform multiplications on zero samples, redundancy can be observed to design a more efficient filter.

Figure 4-13 shows a four-times oversampling digital filter, generating three intermediate samples between each input sample. The filter consists of a shift register of 24 delay elements, each delaying a 16-bit sample for one input sampling period. Thus each sample remains in each delay element for a sample period before it shifts to the next delay element. During this time each 16-bit sample is tapped off the delay line and multiplied four times by a 12-bit coefficient stored in ROM, a different coefficient for each multiplication, with different coefficients for each tap. In total, the four sets of coefficients are applied to the samples in turn, thus producing four output values. The 24 multiplication products are summed four times during each period, and are output from the filter. The filter characteristic ($\sin(x)/x$ in this case) determines the values of the interpolated samples. Each 16-bit data word is passed to the next delay (traversing the entire delay line), where the process is repeated. Because many samples are simultaneously present in the delay line, the computed impulse responses of these many samples are summed. The product of each multiplication is a 28-bit word ($16 + 12 = 28$). When these products are summed, a weighted average of a large number of samples is obtained. Four times as many samples are present after oversampling, with interpolation values calculated by the filter. The sampling frequency is increased four times, to 176.4 kHz. The result is the multiplication of the sampling frequency, and a cutoff filter characteristic. Through proper selection of filter coefficients, length of delay line, and time interval between taps, the desired lowpass $\sin(x)/x$ response is obtained—yield-

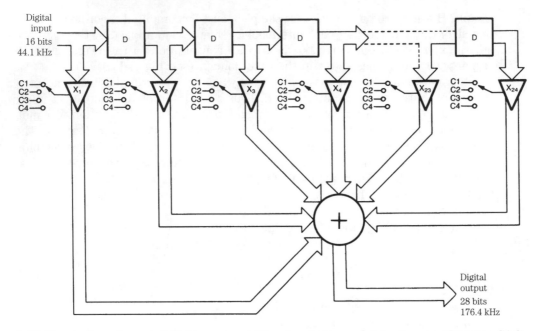

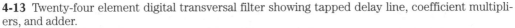

4-13 Twenty-four element digital transversal filter showing tapped delay line, coefficient multipliers, and adder.

ing correct waveform reconstruction. Because of the movement of the data across the shift register, this design is often called a transversal filter.

Figure 4-14 graphically shows how an oversampling digital filter simulates the effect of an analog filter in waveform reconstruction; specifically, it shows how interpolated samples are computed in a four-times oversampling filter. The input samples I_3, I_2, I_1, and I_0 are treated as $\sin(x)/x$ impulses placed relative to the center of the filter. Their maximum $\sin(x)/x$ impulse response amplitudes are equal to the original sample amplitudes, and the width of the impulse responses are determined by the response of the filter, in this case a filter with a cutoff frequency at the Nyquist frequency of the input samples. The summation of their unique contributions forms the interpolated samples (in practice, as noted, many more than four samples would be present in the filter). Each of the three interpolated samples is formed by adding together the four products, as shown in the figure. Original input samples pass through the filter unchanged by using one set of filter coefficients that contains three zero coefficients and one unity coefficient. In this way, the output sample that coincides with the input sample is unchanged. By multiplying each group of samples (four in this case) with this coefficient set, and three others, interpolated samples are output at a four-times rate.

The overall effect of four-times oversampling filtering is shown in Fig. 4-15. A brick-wall filter must sharply bandlimit the output spectra; with oversampling filtering, the images between 20 kHz and 156.4 kHz (centered at 44.1, 88.2, and 132.3 kHz) are suppressed, leaving the oversampling images. The output S/H circuit can be used to further suppress the oversampling spectra. In practice, a num-

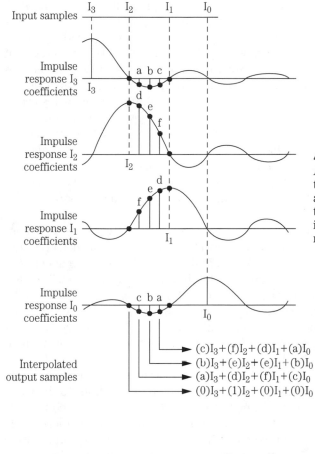

Input samples

I_3 I_2 I_1 I_0

Impulse
response I_3
coefficients

a b c

I_3

Impulse
response I_2
coefficients

d

e

f

I_2

4-14
A four-times oversampling filter
treats input samples as points on
a $\sin(x)/x$ curve; this reconstructs
the output waveform, as in an
ideal lowpass filter. In practice,
many more samples are needed.

Impulse
response I_1
coefficients

e d

f

I_1

Impulse
response I_0
coefficients

c b a

I_0

Interpolated
output samples

$\longrightarrow$ (c)I_3+(f)I_2+(d)I_1+(a)I_0
$\longrightarrow$ (b)I_3+(e)I_2+(e)I_1+(b)I_0
$\longrightarrow$ (a)I_3+(d)I_2+(f)I_1+(c)I_0
$\longrightarrow$ (0)I_3+(1)I_2+(0)I_1+(0)I_0

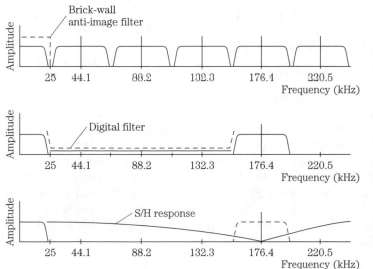

Brick-wall
anti-image filter

Amplitude

25   44.1   88.2   132.3   176.4   220.5
                                  Frequency (kHz)

Amplitude

Digital filter

25   44.1   88.2   132.3   176.4   220.5
                                  Frequency (kHz)

Amplitude

S/H response

25   44.1   88.2   132.3   176.4   220.5
                                  Frequency (kHz)

4-15
Image spectra in
non-oversampled, and
oversampled
reconstruction. A. A
brick-wall filter must
sharply bandlimit the
output spectra. B. With
four-times oversampling,
images appear only at the
oversampling frequency.
C. The output S/H circuit
can be used to further
suppress the
oversampling spectra.

ber of considerations determine the design of oversampling filters. The $\sin(x)/x$ waveform extends to infinity in both the positive and negative directions, so theoretically all of the values of that infinite waveform would be required to reconstruct the analog signal. Although an analog filter can theoretically access an infinite number of samples for each reconstruction value, a finite impulse response filter, as its name implies, cannot. Thus the oversampling filter is designed to accommodate the number of samples required to maintain an error less than the system's overall resolution. In the example above, only four coefficients were used with 300 28-bit coefficients preferred; in practice, perhaps 100 coefficients would suffice. However, because the $\sin(x)/x$ response is symmetrical, only half the coefficients need to be stored in memory; the table can be read bi-directionally. As noted, the multipliers in a digital filter increase the output word length; the output word cannot simply be truncated; this would increase distortion. The word should be redithered.

These examples have used a four-times oversampling filter. However, two-times, four-times, or eight-times digital filters can be used, in which a 44.1-kHz sampling frequency is oversampled to 88.1 kHz, 176.4 kHz, or 352.8 kHz respectively. For example, in an eight-times oversampling filter, seven new audio samples are computed for each input sample, raising the output sampling frequency to 352.8 kHz. Sampling modulation artifacts are shifted to a band at 352.8 kHz where they are easily removed with a simple analog lowpass filter. At any rate, most oversampling digital filters are similar in operation. However, the characteristic of the analog lowpass filter must vary. The lower the oversampling frequency, the closer to the audio band the image spectrum will be, hence the steeper the analog filter response required. When using multibit D/A converters, a practical limit to the oversampling frequency is reached (around eight times) because most D/A converters cannot operate at faster speeds. On the other hand, D/A converters can more easily convert an oversampling waveform because the successive changes in amplitude are smaller in an oversampled signal. More precisely, the slew rate, the rate of variation in the output waveform, is lower. This, along with less ringing and less overshoot, reduces intermodulation distortion. Some designers feel that in oversampling designs of eight times or more, the remaining image spectrum is at such a high frequency that no analog filtering is needed, or can be accomplished with a simple one-pole filter.

For performance, digital filters represent a great improvement over analog filters because a digital filter can be designed with considerable and stable precision, but an analog filter design is inherently limited. Because digital filtering is a purely numerical process, the characteristics of digital filtering, as opposed to analog filtering, cannot change with temperature, age, and so on. A digital filter might provide an in-band ripple of ±0.00001 dB, with stopband attenuation of 120 dB. A digital filter can have almost perfectly linear phase response. High-frequency attenuation due to aperture error can be compensated for in the transversal filter by choosing coefficients to create a slightly rising characteristic prior to cutoff. Digital filter theory is discussed in chapter 15.

Noise Shaping

Another important benefit of oversampling is a decrease in audio band quantization noise. For example, when the data leaves the filter at a four-times frequency, the quantization noise power is spread over a band that is four times larger, reducing its power density in the audio band by one-fourth, as shown in Fig. 4-16. This gives a 6-dB reduction in noise. Higher oversampling ratios yield corresponding lower noise (for example, eight-times yields an additional 6 dB).

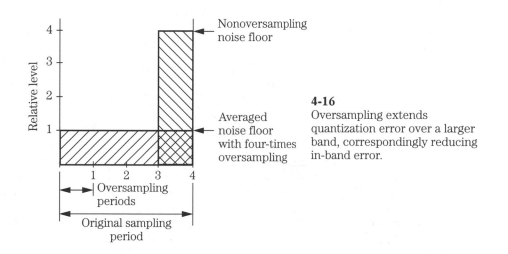

4-16
Oversampling extends quantization error over a larger band, correspondingly reducing in-band error.

Spectral shaping, called noise shaping, can reduce in-band noise even further. This is accomplished by requantizing the signal prior to D/A conversion. When quantization errors are independent, the spectrum is white; by selecting the nature of the dependence of the errors, the spectrum can be shaped. This is performed by an algorithm that produces desired statistically dependent errors. In a simple noise shaper, for example, 28-bit data words from the filter are rounded off and dithered to create the most significant 16-bit words. The 12 least significant bits are delayed by one sampling period and subtracted from the next data word, as shown in Fig. 4-17A. The result is a shaped noise floor, decreased by 7 dB in the audio band. At frequencies approaching 88.2 kHz, this feedback comes back in phase with the input, and noise increases, as shown in Fig. 4-17B. However, this out of band noise is attenuated by the S/H circuit and output analog filter. Noise shaping is discussed in detail in chapter 16.

Output Processing

Following digital filtering, the data is converted back to analog form with a D/A converter. In the case of four-times oversampling, the aperture effect of an output sample-and-hold circuit creates a null at 176.4 kHz, further suppressing that oversampling image. As noted, designing a slight high-frequency boost in the digital filter

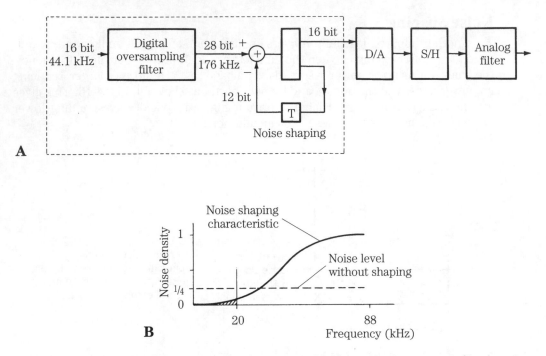

4-17 Noise shaping following oversampling decreases in-band quantization error. A. Simple noise-shaping loop. B. Noise-shaping suppresses noise in the audio band; boosted noise outside the audio band is filtered out.

can compensate for the slight attenuation of high audio frequencies. The remaining band around 176.4 kHz can be completely suppressed by an analog filter. This low-order anti-imaging filter follows the converter. Because the oversampling image is high in frequency, a filter with a gentle, 12 dB/octave response and a –3 dB point between 30 and 40 kHz is suitable; for example, a Bessel filter can be used. It is a non-critical design, and its low order guarantees good phase linearity; phase distortion can be reduced to ±0.1° across the audio band. Oversampling can decrease in-band noise by 6 dB, and noise shaping can further decrease in-band noise by 7 dB or more. Thus, with an oversampling filter and noise shaping, a 16-bit D/A converter can deliver good performance.

Alternate Coding Methods

Linear PCM is considered to be the classic digitization scheme, capable of high-quality audio performance. Other digitization methods offer both advantages and disadvantages compared to PCM. Although a linear PCM system presents a fixed scale of equal quantization intervals into which the analog waveform is mapped, specialized systems offer modified or wholly new mapping techniques. One advantage of specialized techniques is often data reduction, in which fewer bits are needed to encode the audio signal. They are thus more efficient. On the other hand, a penalty in reduced audio performance might be incurred.

In a fixed linear PCM system the quantization intervals are fixed over the signal's amplitude range, and they are linearly spaced as well. The quantizer word length determines the number of quantization intervals available to encode the analog amplitude. The intervals are all of equal amplitude and are assigned code words in monotonic order. However, both of these parameters can be varied to yield new digitization architectures.

Longer word lengths reduce quantization error; however, this requires a corresponding increase in data bandwidth. In addition, although uniform PCM quantization is optimal for a uniformly distributed signal, the probability distribution of most audio signals is not uniform. In alternative PCM systems, quantization error is minimized by using nonuniform quantization step sizes. Such systems attempt to tailor step sizes to suit the statistical properties of the signal. For example, speech signals are best served by an exponential-type quantization distribution; this assumes that small amplitude signals are more prevalent than large signals. Many quantization levels at low amplitudes, and fewer at high amplitudes should result in decreased error. Companding, with dynamic compression prior to uniform quantization, and expansion following quantization, can be used to achieve this result. Floating point and companding systems use range-changing to vary the signal's amplitude to the converter, and thus expand the system's dynamic range. A greatly modified form of PCM is a differential system called delta modulation. It uses only one bit for quantizing; however, a very high sampling frequency is required. Other forms of delta modulation include adaptive delta modulation, and companded and predictive delta modulation. Each offers unique strengths and weaknesses. Perceptual coding, based on psychoacoustics, is discussed in chapter 11.

Floating-Point Systems

Floating-point systems use a PCM architecture modified to accept a scaling value. It is an adaptive approach, with nonuniform quantization. In true floating-point systems, the scaling factor is instantaneously applied from sample to sample. In other cases, as in block floating-point systems, the scale factor is applied to a relatively large block of data.

Instead of forming a linear data word, a floating-point system uses a nonuniform quantizer to create a word divided into two parts: the exponent (scalar) and mantissa (data value). The mantissa represents the waveform's value, and its scaled amplitude is determined by the exponent. In other words, the exponent acts as a scalar that varies the gain of the signal in the PCM A/D converter. By adjusting the gain of the signal the A/D converter is used more efficiently. Low-level signals are boosted and high-level signals are attenuated; specifically, a signal's level is set to the highest possible level that does not exceed the converter's range. This effectively varies the quantization step size according to the signal amplitude. Following D/A conversion, the gain is again adjusted to correspond to its original value.

For example, consider a floating-point system with a 10-bit mantissa (A/D converter), and 3-bit exponent (gain select), as shown in Fig. 4-18. The 3-bit exponent provides 8 different ranges for a 10-bit mantissa. This is the equivalent multiplicative range of 1 to 128. The maximum signals are −65,536 to 65,408. In this way, 13 bits

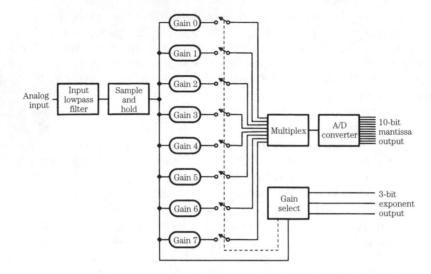

4-18 A floating-point converter uses multiple gain stages to manipulate the signal's amplitude to optimize fixed A/D conversion.

cover the equivalent of a 17-bit dynamic range, but only a 10-bit A/D converter is required. However, large range and small resolution are not simultaneously available in a floating-point system because of its nonuniform quantization. For example, although 65,408 can be represented, the next smallest number is 65,280. In a linear PCM system, the next smallest number is, of course, 65,407. In general, as signal level increases, the number of possible quantization intervals decreases; thus quantization error increases and S/N ratio decreases. In particular, the signal-to-noise ratio is signal dependent, and less than the dynamic range.

A floating-point system uses a short-word A/D converter to achieve a moderate dynamic range, or a longer-word converter for a larger dynamic range. For example, a floating-point system using a 16-bit A/D converter and a 3-bit exponent adjusted over a 42-dB range in 6-dB steps would yield a 138-dB dynamic range (96 dB + 42 dB). This type of system would be useful for encoding particularly extreme signal conditions. In addition, this floating-point system only requires a split 19-bit word, but the equivalent fixed linear PCM system would require a linear 23-bit word. In addition, when the gain stages are placed at 6-dB intervals, the coded words can be easily converted to a uniform code for processing or storage without computation. The mantissa undergoes a shifting operation according to the value of the exponent.

Although a floating-point system's dynamic range is large, its nature differs from that of a fixed linear system; its dynamic range is inherently less than its S/N ratio. This can be seen by considering that dynamic range measures the ratio between the maximum signal and the noise when no signal is present. With the S/N ratio, on the other hand, noise is measured when there is a signal present. In a fixed linear system, the dynamic range is approximately equal to the S/N ratio when a signal is present. However, in a floating-point system, the S/N ratio is approximately determined by the resolution of the fixed A/D converter (approximately $6n$), which is independent of the larger dynamic range. Changes in the signal dictate changes in the gain structure, which affects the relative amplitude of quantization error.

The S/N ratio thus continually changes with exponent switching. For example, consider a system with a 10-bit mantissa and 3-bit exponent with 6-dB gain intervals. The maximum S/N ratio is 60 dB. As the input signal level falls, so does the S/N ratio, falling to a minimum of 54 dB until the exponent is switched, and the S/N again rises to 60 dB, as shown in Fig. 4-19. For longer-word converters, a complex signal will mask the quantization error. However, in the case of simple tones, the error might be audible. For example, modulation noise from low-frequency signals and quantization noise from nearly inaudible signals might result. Another problem can occur with gain shifting: inaccuracies in calibration might present discontinuities as the different amplifiers are switched.

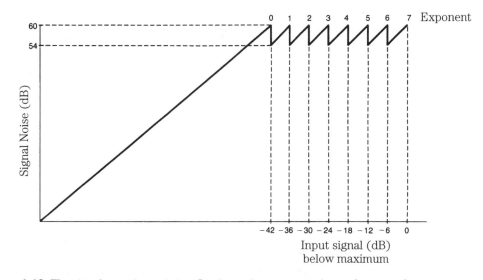

4-19 The signal-to-noise ratio in a floating-point system varies as the prescale gain varies.

The way in which the gain structure is changed affects the audibility of the error. Instantaneous switching from sample to sample tends to accentuate the problem. Instead, gain switching should be performed with algorithms that follow trends in signal amplitude, based on the type of program to be encoded. For example, syllabic algorithms are adapted to the rate at which syllables vary in speech. Gain decreases are instantaneous, but gain increases are delayed. This approximates a block floating-point system, as described below. In any event, the gain must be switched to prevent any overload of the A/D converter.

Block Floating-Point Digitization

The block floating point architecture is derived from the floating-point architecture. Its principal advantage is data reduction, for example, making it useful for transmission via satellite or other means where transmission time determines cost.

In addition, a block floating-point architecture facilitates syllabic or other companding algorithms.

In a block floating-point system, a fixed linear PCM A/D converter precedes the scalar. A short duration of the analog waveform, perhaps 1 millisecond, is converted to digital data. A scale factor is calculated to represent the largest value in the block, then the data is scaled upward so the largest value is just below full scale. This reduces the number of bits needed to represent the signal. The data block is transmitted, along with the single scale factor exponent. During decoding, the block is properly rescaled. In the example in Fig. 4-20, 16-bit words are scaled to produce blocks of 10-bit words, each with one 3-bit exponent. Because only one exponent is required for the entire data block, data rate efficiency is increased over conventional floating-point systems. On the other hand, system cost is higher because a full word A/D converter is required.

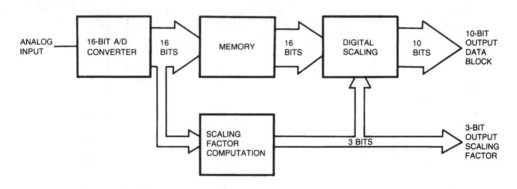

4-20 A block floating-point system uses a scaling factor, but only over a block of data.

Block floating-point systems avoid many of the audible artifacts introduced by instantaneous scaling. The noise amplitude lags the signal amplitude by the duration of the buffer memory (for example, 1 ms); because this delay is short compared to human perception time, it is not perceived. Thus, a block floating-point system can minimize any perceptual gain error.

A floating-point system works best when the audio signal has a low peak-to-average ratio for short durations. Because most acoustic music behaves in this manner, the system performance is relatively good. An instantaneous floating-point system excels when the program changes rapidly from sample to sample (as with narrow, high-amplitude peaks) yet in turn is inferior to a fixed linear system. Performance dependence on program behavior is a drawback of alternative digitization systems in general.

Nonuniform Companding Systems

With linear PCM, quantization intervals are spaced evenly throughout the amplitude range. As we have observed, the range-changing in floating-point systems provides a nonuniform quantization. Nonuniform companding systems also provide quantization steps of different sizes, but with a different approach, called companding. Although companding is not an optimal way of achieving nonuniform quantization, its ease of implementation is a benefit.

In nonuniform companding systems, quantization levels are spaced far apart for high-amplitude signals, and closer together for low-amplitude signals. This is accomplished by compressing and expanding the signal, hence the term companding. When the signal is compressed prior to quantization, small values are enhanced, and large values are diminished. This is in accord with some signals, such as speech, in which small amplitude signals occur more often than large amplitude signals.

A logarithmic function is used to accomplish companding. Within the compander, a linear PCM quantizer is used. Because the compressed signal sees quantization intervals that are uniform, the conversion is equivalent to one of nonuniform step sizes. On the output, an expander is used to inversely compensate for the nonlinearity in the reconstructed signal. In this way, quantization levels are more effectively distributed over the audio dynamic range. A companding system is shown in Fig. 4-21. This technique is similar to that used in analog noise reduction systems. However, in this case the compander is linked to the conversion logic, eliminating tracking errors. The encoded signal must be decoded before any subsequent processing. High-amplitude signals are more easily encoded, and lower amplitude signals have reduced quantization noise. This results in a higher S/N ratio for small signals, and can increase the overall dynamic range compared to fixed linear PCM systems. Noise increases with large amplitude audio signals, and is correlated; however, the signal amplitude tends to mask this noise. Noise modulation audibility might be problematic for low-frequency signals with quickly changing amplitudes.

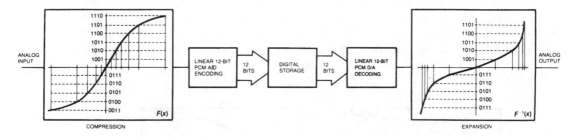

4-21 A nonlinear conversion system uses companding elements before and after signal conversion

μ-Law and A-Law Companding

The μ-law encoding system is commonly used for speech applications, particularly in North America and Japan; it is defined by the CCITT (International Telegraph and Telephone Consultative Committee) Recommendation G.711. Its nonuniform quantization step sizes increase logarithmically with signal level. Its compression characteristic has the form:

$$y = \frac{\log(1 + \mu x)}{\log(1 + \mu)} \text{ for } x \geq 0$$

where

> y is the magnitude of the output,
> x is the magnitude of the input,
> μ is a positive parameter defined to yield the desired compression characteristic.

The signal is compressed prior to quantization and the inverse function is used for expansion. The value of 0 corresponds to linear amplification—that is, no compression, or uniform quantization. Larger values result is greater companding. A μ-255 system is often used to encode speech waveforms. An 8-bit implementation can achieve a small signal S/N ratio and dynamic range equivalent to that of a 12-bit uniform PCM system.

The A-law also is a quantization characteristic that varies logarithmically; it also is specified by the CCITT. It is used throughout Europe and elsewhere. Its compression characteristic has the form:

$$y = \begin{cases} \dfrac{Ax}{1 + \log A} & \text{for } 0 \le |x| \le \dfrac{1}{A} \\[2em] \dfrac{1 + \log(Ax)}{1 + \log A} & \text{for } \dfrac{1}{A} \le |x| \le 1 \end{cases}$$

where A is the positive parameter.

Figure 4-22 shows μ-law and A-law transfer functions for several values of μ and A. Generally, logarithmic PCM methods such as these require about four fewer bits per sample for speech quality equivalent to linear PCM; for example, eight bits might be sufficient, instead of twelve. Because speech signals are typically sampled at 8 kHz, the basic standard data rate for μ-law or A-law PCM data is therefore 64,000 bits/second (or 64 kbps). The devices used to convert analog signals to/from compressed signals are often called codecs (coder/decoders).

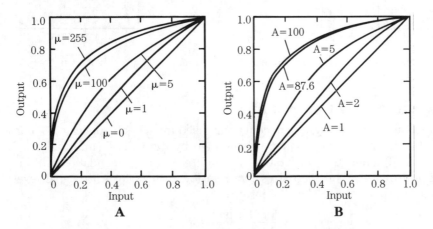

4-22 Companding characteristics determine how the quantization step size varies with signal level. A. μ-law characteristic. B. A-law characteristic.

Differential PCM Systems

Differential PCM (DPCM) systems are unlike linear, or nonuniform PCM methods. Intuitively, it is not necessary to store the entire amplitude of a waveform, only how it changes from one sample to the next. Moreover, because the differences between samples are smaller than the amplitudes of the samples, fewer bits should be required to encode them. Furthermore, a waveform's average value should change only slightly from one sample to the next, if the sampling frequency is fast enough; most sampled signals show significant correlation between successive samples. A differential system exploits the redundancy from sample to sample. Rather than code the entire amplitude of the signal, a few bits code the difference in amplitude between successive samples.

Differential coding uses a form of predictive coding; a predicted signal is subtracted from the input and the difference signal (the error) is quantized. The coded value is the difference between the prediction and the actual signal. The decoder produces the prediction from the previous data; using the prediction and the difference value, the waveform is reconstructed sample by sample. This method requires fewer bits to encode an audio signal, but performance depends on the type of function used to derive the prediction signal and its ability to anticipate the changing signal. The rate at which signal voltage can change is inherently limited in DPCM systems; the coded signal amplitude decreases at 6 dB/octave; thus S/N ratio decreases at 6 dB/octave. The frequency response of the coded signal can be filtered to improve S/N. For example, a signal with little high-frequency content can be filtered to increase high frequencies; this is reversed during decoding; noise is relatively masked by the low-frequency content. Differential PCM systems are cost effective both in hardware and data rate.

Delta Modulation

Differential systems encode the difference between the input signal and the prediction. As the sampling frequency increases, the possible amount of change between samples decreases and encoding resolution increases. Delta modulation (DM) is a form of differential PCM that carries the method to the extreme. It uses a very high sampling frequency so that only a 1-bit quantization of the difference signal is needed to encode the audio waveform. Conceptual operation of a delta modulation system is shown in Fig. 4-23. Positive or negative transitions in the quantized waveform are used to encode the audio signal. Because the staircase can move from sample to sample by only one quantization interval, a fast sampling frequency is required to track the signal's transients. In the example in Fig. 4-23, the sampling frequency is insufficient to track the signal's rise time. In this slope overload condition, the differential itself is encoded, rather than the original signal.

Delta modulation is quite efficient from a hardware standpoint, as shown in Fig. 4-24. Integrators are used as first-order predictors. The difference between the input signal and its predicted value is quantized as a 1-bit correcting word and generated at sample time. The system determines if the sign of its error is positive or negative, and applies the sign (a positive or negative pulse) to the integrator that correspondingly moves its next value up or down one increment, always closer to the

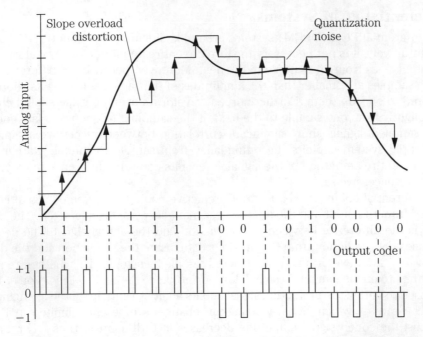

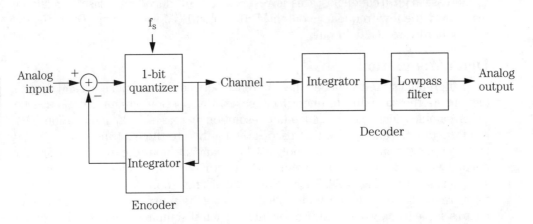

4-23 In a delta-modulation coder, one differential bit is used to encode the audio signal.

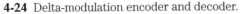

4-24 Delta-modulation encoder and decoder.

present value. The accuracy of the encoding rests on the size of the increment, or step. Also, the signal must change at each sample; it cannot be constant. At the output, the correction signal is decoded with an integrator to estimate the input signal. As with any DPCM system, coded signal amplitude decreases with frequency, so S/N ratio decreases by 6 dB/octave. Only one correction can occur per sample interval, but a very fast rate could theoretically allow tracking of even a fast-transient audio waveform. Delta modulation offers excellent error performance. In a linear PCM system, an uncorrected MSB error results in a large discontinuity in the signal. With delta modulation, there is no MSB. Each bit merely tracks the difference between samples, thus inherently limiting the amount of error to that difference. The possibility of degradation, however, necessitates error correction. Parity bits and interleaving are commonly used for this purpose.

On the practical side, DM fails to perform well in high-fidelity applications because of its inherent trade-off between sampling frequency and step size. Encoding resolution is directly dependent on step size. The smaller the steps, the better the approximation to the audio signal, and the lower the quantization error. However, when the encoding bit cannot track a complex audio waveform, slew rate limitations yield transient distortion. The sampling frequency can be increased to compensate, but the rates required for successful encoding of wide bandwidth signals are prohibitive. Perceptually, when slope overload is caused by high-frequency energy, the signal tends to mask the distortion. Quantization error is always present, and is most audible for low-amplitude signals. To make the best of the circumstances, step size can be selected to minimize the sum of the mean squares of the two distortion values from slope overload and quantization. Timothy Darling and Malcolm Hawksford have shown that the signal to quantization error ratio of a delta modulation system can be expressed as:

$$S/E \text{ (dB)} = \left[-16 + 10\log\left(\frac{f_s^3}{f_b f_i^2}\right) \right]$$

where

f_s is the sampling frequency
f_b is the noise bandwidth
f_i is the audio (sinewave) frequency

To achieve a 16-bit PCM S/N ratio of 96 dB over a 20 kHz bandwidth, a DM system requires clocking at 200 MHz. This is not exceptional performance. Although a doubling of bit rate in DM results in an increase in S/N of 9 dB, a doubling of word length in PCM produces an exponential S/N increase. From an informational standpoint, we can see that the nature of DM hampers its ability to encode audio information. A sampling frequency of 500 kHz, for example, would theoretically permit encoding of frequencies up to 250 kHz, but most of that bandwidth is wasted because of the low frequency of audio signals. In other words, the informational encoding distribution of delta modulation is poor for audio applications.

On the other hand, the high sampling frequency required for delta modulation offers at least one benefit. As observed with noise shaping, for each doubling of sampling frequency, the noise in a fixed band decreases by 3 dB. The total noise remains constant, but it is spread over a larger spectrum thus audio band noise is reduced. This helps a DM system to provide a somewhat lower noise floor. In addition, because of the high sampling frequency, brick-wall filters are not required. Very gentle filters with low-phase shift can be used to adequately roll off audio frequencies well before the half-sampling frequency. Of course, conventional A/D and D/A converters are not required. Ultimately, because of its limitations, delta modulation is not used for high-fidelity applications. However, a variation known as sigma-delta modulation offers excellent results and is widely used in oversampling A/D and D/A converters, as discussed in chapter 16.

Adaptive Delta Modulation

Adaptive delta modulation (ADM) permits quantization increment size to vary, to overcome the transient response limitations of delta modulation. At the same time, quantization error is held to a reasonable value. A block diagram of an adaptive delta modulation system encoder is shown in Fig. 4-25A. Algorithms examine input data, then determine how to best adjust step size. For example, with a simple adaptive algorithm, a series of all-positive or all-negative difference bits would indicate a rapid change from the approximation. The increment size would increase to follow the change either positively or negatively. The greater the overload condition, the larger the step size selected. Alternating positive and negative difference bits indicate good tracking, and increment size is reduced for even greater accuracy, as shown in Fig. 4-25B. The result is an increase in S/N, with no increase in sampling frequency or bit rate. As greater numbers of bits in the stream are used to diagnose signal behavior, step size selection can be improved.

ADM hardware design is complicated because the decoder must be synchronized to the step size strategy to recognize the variation. Also, it is difficult to change step size quickly and radically enough to accommodate sharp audio transients. As high-frequency and high-amplitude signals demand large increments, quantization noise is increased, producing noise modulation with a varying noise floor. In addition, it is difficult to inject a dither signal in an ADM system; since the step sizes change, a fixed amount of dither is ineffective. Error feedback can be used to reduce in-band noise. A pre-emphasis filter characteristic can be used to reduce subjective noise in small amplitude signals, mask the change in noise with changing step size, and reduce low-frequency noise in high-amplitude, high-frequency signals. As the audio slope increases, a control signal from the delta modulator, the same signal used to control step size, raises the frequency of the highpass filter and attenuates low frequencies. Another variation of ADM is continuously variable slope delta modulation (CVSDM), in which step size is continuously variable, rather than incremental.

Companded Predictive Delta Modulation

Companded predictive delta modulation (CPDM) rejects adaptive delta modulation in favor of a compander delta modulation scheme. Instead of varying the step size in relation to the signal, the signal's amplitude is varied prior to the constant step size delta modulator, to protect against modulator overload. To reduce the quantization floor level, a linear predictive filter is used, in which an algorithm uses many past samples to better predict the next sample.

The companding subsystem consists of a digitally controlled amplifier in both the encoder and decoder sections, for control of broadband signal gain. The bit stream itself controls both amplifiers to minimize tracking error. The digitally controlled amplifiers continually adjust the signal over a large range to best fit the fixed step size of the delta modulator. A transient "speed-up" circuit in the level sensing path allows faster gain reduction during audio transients. Strings of 1s or 0s indicate

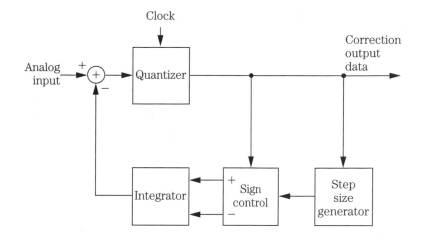

A Block diagram of an adaptive delta modulation encoder, with variable step size.

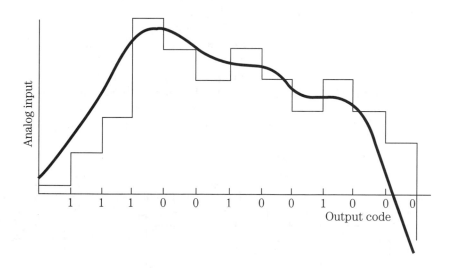

B Changes in step size are triggered by continuous 1s or 0s.

4-25 Operation of an adaptive delta modulation encoder.

the onset of an overload, and trigger compression of broadband gain to ensure that the transients are not clipped at the modulator. The speed of the gain change can be either fast or slow, depending on the musical dynamics. Spectral compression can be used to reduce variations in spectral content; the circuit could reduce high frequencies when the input spectrum contains predominantly high frequencies, and boost high frequencies when the spectrum is weighted with low frequencies. The spectrum at the A/D converter is thus more nearly constant.

Adaptive Differential Pulse-Code Modulation

Adaptive differential pulse-code modulation (ADPCM) uses predictive coding to achieve data reduction. ADPCM combines the adaptive difference signal of ADM with the binary code of PCM. Although methods vary, in many cases the difference signal to be coded is first scaled by an adaptive scale factor, then quantized according to a fixed quantization curve. An ADPCM encoder and decoder are shown in Fig. 4-26. The scale factor is selected according to the signal's properties; for example, the quantizer step size can be varied in proportion to the signal's average amplitude. Signals with large variations cause rapid changes in the scale factor whereas more stable signals cause slow adaptation. Step size can be effectively varied by either directly varying the step size, or by scaling the signal with a gain factor. A linear predictor optimized according to the type of signal to be coded is used to output a signal estimate of each sample. This signal is subtracted from the actual input signal to yield a difference signal; it is the difference signal that is coded with a short PCM word (perhaps 4 or 8 bits) and output from the encoder. In this way, the signal can be adaptively equalized, and the quantization noise adaptively shaped, to help mask the noise floor for a particular application. For example, the noise can be shaped so that its spectrum is white after decoding. Noise shaping is described in chapter 16. The decoder performs the same operations as the encoder; by reading the incoming data stream, the correct step size is selected, and the difference signal is used to generate the output samples. The benefit of ADPCM is bit rate reduction based on the tendency for amplitude and spectrum distribution of audio signals to be concentrated in a specific region. The scale factors and other design elements in an ADPCM algorithm take advantage of these statistical properties of the audio signal. In speech

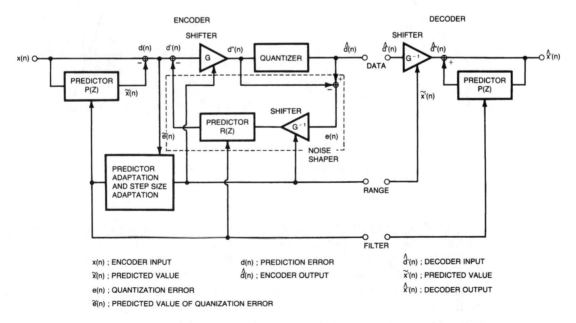

4-26 ADPCM encoder and decoder.

transmission applications, a bit rate of 32 kbps (kilobits per second) is easily achieved; ADPCM is widely used in the telecommunications industry.

ADPCM's performance is competitive, or relatively superior to that of fixed linear PCM. When the audio signal remains near its maximum frequency, ADPCM's performance is similar to PCM's. However, this is rarely the case with audio signals. Instead, the instantaneous audio frequency is relatively low, thus the signal changes more slowly, and amplitude changes are smaller. As a result, ADPCM's quantization error is less than that of PCM. In theory, given the same number of quantization bits, ADPCM can achieve better signal resolution. In other words, relatively fewer bits are needed to achieve good performance. In practice, a 4-bit ADPCM signal might provide fidelity subjectively similar to an 8-bit PCM signal. In practice, because of the overriding need for data reduction, ADPCM coding fidelity is lower than a PCM signal.

The CD-I (compact-disc interactive) and CD-ROM/XA formats use several AD-PCM coding levels to deliver fidelity according to need. An 8-bit ADPCM quality level can yield an S/N ratio of 90 dB, and bandwidth of 17 kHz. The two 4-bit levels yield an S/N of 60 dB, and bandwidths of 17 kHz and 8.5 kHz. During encoding, the original audio data frequency (44.1 kHz) is reduced by a sampling rate converter to a lower frequency (37.8 kHz or 18.9 kHz) depending on the quality level selected. The original word length (16 bits) is reduced (4 or 8 bits) per sample with ADPCM encoding. Four different prediction filters can be selected; a filter is selected for a block of 28 samples depending on the spectral content of the signal. Straight PCM is used for high-frequency passages, and some combination of first-order and two kinds of second-order differential PCM modes are selected for low- and middle-frequency passages; this optimizes instantaneous S/N ratio. Companding and noise shaping are also used to increase dynamic range. Data describing the filter type is conveyed once in a block along with the range data. During ADPCM decoding, in addition to other reproduction processing, the ADPCM audio data is block-decoded and expanded to linear 16-bit form. D/A conversion and lowpass filtering complete the audio reproduction processing. Depending on audio quality level, this ADPCM encoder can output from 80 to 309 kbps/channel, a considerable reduction in data rate.

ADPCM with a 4:1 compression ratio also is often used in computer applications; for example, current QuickTime and Windows software both use ADPCM coding; however, the processor must devote overhead to decode audio signals in real time. ADPCM also appears in many video game platforms. ADPCM, as well as other specialized designs, offer alternatives to classic linear PCM design. They adhere to the same principles of sampling, quantization, and digital storage; however, their implementations are quite different. Perceptual coding systems are increasingly used to code audio signals when bit rate is the primary concern; these systems are discussed in chapter 11.

Time-Base Correction

As we observed in chapter 3, modulation coding is used in storage and transmission channels to make the data self-clocking. However, successful recovery of data is limited by the time-base accuracy of the received clock. For example, speed variations in a digital tape recorder, jitter imposed on a data stream's embedded clock, and inaccuracies in the oscillator used to clock an A/D or D/A converter can all lead to degraded performance in the form of noise and modulation artifacts. Phase-locked loops are often used to re-synchronize a receiver with the channel code's clock. Because of jitter, a receiver using a clock with fixed frequency could not re-synchronize the signal, even if its rate was equal to the signal's clock rate. For successful recovery of data, receiver circuits must minimize time-base errors that occur in the storage medium, during transmission, or within regeneration and conversion circuitry itself. This is challenging in the digital environment, because of the considerable noise and interference that is present; moreover, tolerances needed for time-base control increase with word length; for example, 20-bit conversion requires much greater time-base accuracy than 16-bit conversion. Above all, jitter is troublesome because of the tolerances it demands. A clock might require jitter accuracy of 20 ps. Note that a picosecond is the reciprocal of 1 THz, which is 1000 GHz (gigahertz), which is 1,000,000 MHz.

Jitter

Any time-axis variation in a digital signal can be characterized as jitter. In particular, it is the time displacement of a clock signal measured against an ideal reference with no jitter. Jitter manifests itself as variations in the transition times of the signal, as shown in Fig. 4-27. Around each ideal transition is a period of uncertainty in arrival time; this range is called the peak-to-peak jitter. Jitter occurs in data in a storage medium, transmission channel, or processing or regeneration circuits such as A/D and D/A converters. Jitter can occur as random variations in clock edges (white phase jitter), it can be related to the width of a clock pulse (white FM jitter), or it can be related to other events (correlated jitter), sometimes periodically.

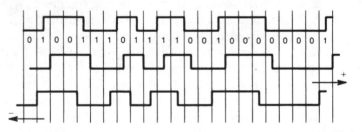

4-27 A time variation in the medium, or regeneration or processing circuits results in a time-base jitter error.

Jitter is best described by its spectral characteristics; this shows the amplitude and frequency of the jitter signal. Random jitter will show a broadband spectrum; when the data is reconstructed as an analog waveform it will have an increased noise floor. Periodic jitter will appear as a single spectral line; FM sidebands or modulated noise could appear in the reconstructed signal, spaced on either side of the signal frequency. Jitter at frequencies less than the sampling frequency causes a timing error to accumulate; the error depends on the amplitude and frequency of the modulation waveform. Generally, peak-to-peak jitter is a valid measure; however, when the jitter is random, a root mean square (rms) jitter measure is valid. Care must be taken when specifying jitter; for example, if the deviation in a clock signal's period width is averaged over time, the average can converge to zero, resulting in no measured jitter.

Interface Jitter Versus Sampling Jitter

It is important to distinguish between interface jitter and sampling jitter. Interface jitter occurs in transmitted data clocks, when conveying data from one device to another. Interface jitter is not a concern unless it causes uncorrected errors in the recovered signal. The quality of transmitted data can be monitored by error detection circuits at the receiver. Other static or slowly-varying deviations (drift) can cause synchronization problems between connected devices, but should not produce errors in the interface data. Simply stated, if the recovered data is free of errors, jitter has not affected it. However, if subsequent reclocking circuits do not remove jitter from the recovered data, potentially audible artifacts can result from sampling jitter at the D/A converter.

Specifically, interface timing errors are distinct from those caused by sampling jitter. Sampling jitter can affect quality of an audio signal as it is sampled or resampled with this timing error. Sampling jitter occurs in sampling clocks, and affects the quality of the reproduced signal. These tolerances must be very tight, so that timing errors in a recovered clock are minimized. The clock generating circuits used in a sampling device derive a timing reference from the interface signal. A phase-locked loop (PLL) circuit might be needed to remove interface jitter to yield a sample clock that is pure enough to avoid potentially audible jitter modulation products. An interface PLL, as shown in Fig. 4-28, accepts the channel signal as a timing reference, measures the phase error between the reference and its own output and uses the error to control a voltage-controlled oscillator within the loop. Once locked, the oscillator will run at the reference frequency, yet be decoupled from the reference, preventing jitter from passing through the PLL on the output data or output clock.

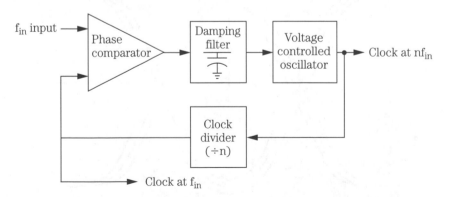

4-28 An example of an interface phase-locked loop. The oscillator prevents jitter from passing through the PLL on the output data or output clock.

Jitter can occur throughout the signal chain so that precautions must be taken at each stage to decouple the bit stream from the jitter, so data can be passed along without error. This is particularly important in a chain of connected devices because jitter will accumulate in the throughput signal. Each device might contribute a small amount of jitter, as will the interface connections, eventually leading to data errors or conversion artifacts. Even a badly jittered signal can be cleaned by retiming it through jitter attenuation. With proper means, the output data is correct in frequency and phase, with propagated jitter within tolerance.

Eye Pattern

An oscilloscope triggered in synchronization with the bit clock will display noise as the waveform's amplitude variations become indistinct, and jitter as the transitions shift about time intervals of the code period. Peak shift, dc offset, and other faults can be observed as well. This display of superimposed successive transitions, known as the eye pattern, can be used to interpret the quality of the received signal. The success in regeneration can similarly be evaluated by examining the eye pattern after processing. Noise in the channel will tend to close the pattern vertically (noise margin), and jitter closes it horizontally (sampling time margin), as shown in Fig. 4-29, possibly degrading performance to the point where pulse shaping can no longer accurately retrieve the signal. The amount of deterioration can be gauged by measuring the extent of amplitude variations, and forming an eye opening ratio:

$$E = \frac{a_2}{a_1} = \frac{(a_1 - 2\Delta a)}{a_1}$$

where

a_1 is the outside amplitude,
a_2 is the inside amplitude, and
Δa is the amplitude variation

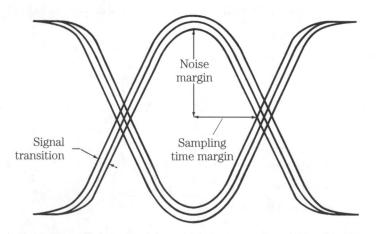

4-29 The eye pattern can be used to interpret the quality of an RF data signal.

Both variations are measured from the center of the opening in the eye pattern. The eye height is specified in volts, and eye width in bit time or percent of cell period. The width of the eye gives the percentage of the data period available to ascertain its logical value, and the height shows the maximum difference between these levels during the available time. The receiver generally is able to determine the binary state of the signal if the eye opening is maintained at coded intervals; the center of the eye effectively shows the amplitude level decision threshold and the sampling time. However, jitter introduced into the receiver's clock recovery circuits will cause the receiver to sample the data further from the center of the data cell.

Jitter observed on an oscilloscope shows the dynamic variations in the signal, but a more careful method applies the data signal to an FM demodulator, which is connected to a spectrum analyzer. With correlated jitter with a slow clock variation, for example, a low-frequency spectral component is observed, but a fast variation yields a high-frequency component on the display.

Jitter in Storage Media, Transmission, and Converters

Jitter must be controlled throughout the audio digitization chain. In particular, jitter must be minimized in the clocks used for both A/D and D/A converter circuits; faults can result in degradation of the output analog waveform. Audio samples must be acquired particularly carefully at the A/D converter. Simply put, clock jitter at the A/D converter results in the wrong samples at the wrong time. Moreover, even if these samples are presented to a D/A converter with a jitter-free clock, the result will be the wrong samples at the right time. In that respect, jitter is most critical in the A/D converter clock. Crystal oscillators typically have jitter of less than 10 ps rms; they must be used as reference for the entire digital system. Good circuit design and board layout are mandated.

The effects of jitter on the sampling clock of an A/D converter are quite similar to FM modulation; the input frequency acts as the carrier, and clock jitter acts as the modulation frequency. Low-frequency periodic jitter reduces the amplitude of the input signal, and adds sideband components equally spaced at either side of the input frequency at a distance equal to multiples of the jitter frequency. As jitter increases, the amplitude of the sidebands increases. The effect of jitter increases as the input signal frequency increases; specifically, jitter amplitude error increases with input signal slew rate. In A/D converters, jitter must not interfere with correct sampling of the LSB. A 2-ns white-noise clock jitter applied to a successive approximation 16-bit converter will degrade its theoretical dynamic range of 98 dB to 91 dB, as shown in Fig. 4-30.

The timing accuracy required for A/D conversion is considerable: the maximum rate of change of a sinusoidal waveform occurs at the zero crossing and can be calculated as: $2\pi A f$ where A is peak signal amplitude and f is frequency in Hz. By one estimation, a jitter specification of 250 ps would allow 16-bit accuracy from a full amplitude, 20-kHz sinewave. Only then would the jitter components fall below the quantization noise floor. Steve Harris has shown that oversampling sigma-delta A/D converters are equally susceptible to sinusoidal clock jitter as Nyquist nonoversampling successive approximation A/D converters. Oversampling sigma-delta A/D con-

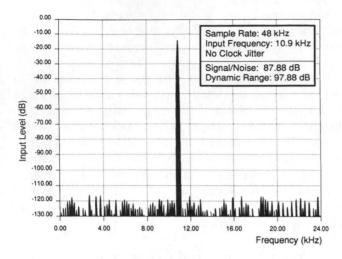

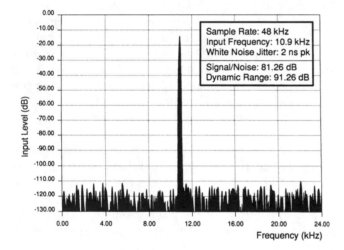

4-30
Simulations showing the spectrum output of nonoversampling A/D conversion. A. No clock jitter. B. White noise clock jitter with 2-ns peak value.
Harris

verters are less susceptible to random clock jitter than Nyquist sampling A/D converters because the jitter is extended over the oversampling range, and lowpass filtered.

Storage media such as magnetic tape and optical disk can impose time-base errors on the output data signal because of speed variations in the mechanical drives they use. Accurate clocks and servo systems must be designed to limit mechanical speed variations, and input and output data must be buffered to absorb the effects of data irregularities. Because magnetic tape is a flexible medium, it is more prone to jitter than an optical disk; however, both require jitter control. Speed variations in the transport caused by eccentricities in the rotation of capstan and spindle motors will cause the data rate to vary; the transport's speed can slowly drift about the proper speed, or fluctuate rapidly. If the amount of variation is within tolerance, that is, if the proper value of the recorded data can be recovered, then no error in the signal results.

Servo control circuits are used to read timing information from the output data and generate a transport correction signal. In many cases, a phase-locked loop (PLL) circuit is used to control the servo, as shown in Fig. 4-31. Speed control can be achieved with a PLL by comparing the synchronization words in the output bit stream (coded at a known rate) to a reference, and directing a speed control servo voltage to the spindle motor to dynamically minimize the difference. Fine speed control can use a second PLL, for example, to achieve constant linear velocity in a CD drive.

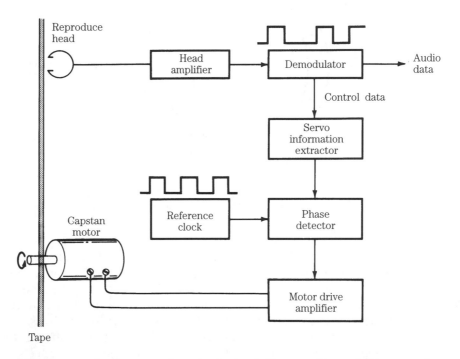

4-31 An example of a servo-pulse extractor/control loop used to control tape speed.

Although phase-locked servo systems act to maintain correct accurate and constant speed of the storage medium, time-base errors can still exist in the data. Likewise, jitter might be encountered whenever data is transmitted through an electrical or optical interconnection. To minimize the effect of time-base variations, data is often reclocked through a buffer. A buffer memory effectively increases the capture range for a data signal; for example, sampling frequency variations can be absorbed by the buffer. However, the longer the buffer, the greater the absolute time delay experienced by the throughput signal; delays greater than a few milliseconds can be problematic in real-time applications such as radio broadcasting where off the air monitoring is needed.

A buffer can be designed using RAM such that its address counter periodically overflows, resulting in a virtual ring structure, as shown in Fig. 4-32. Because data

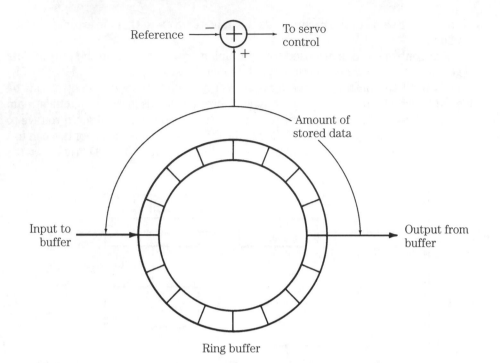

4-32 A ring buffer is a memory designed so that its addressing periodically overflows.

output from the memory is independent from data being written, an inconsistent data input from the medium does not affect a precise data output. Clearly, the clock controlling the data readout from memory must be decoupled from the input clock. The amount of data in the buffer at any time can be used to control a transport's speed. For example, the difference between the input and output address, relative to buffer capacity, can be converted to an analog servo signal. If the buffer's level differs from the optimal half-full condition, the servo is instructed to either speed up or slow down the transport's speed. In this way, the audio data in the buffer neither overflows nor underflows.

Alternatively a buffer can be constructed using a FIFO (first in first out) memory. Input data is clocked into the top of the memory as it is received from the medium, and output data is clocked from the bottom of the memory. In addition to their application in reducing jitter, such time-base correction circuits are required whenever a discontinuous storage medium such as a hard disk is used. The buffer must begin filling when a sector is read from the disk, and continue to output data between sector read cycles. Likewise, when writing to memory, a continuous data stream can be supplied to the disk drive for each sector.

Interface jitter must be minimized during data transmission. No matter what jitter errors are introduced by the transmitting circuit and cable, the receiver has two tasks: data recovery and clock recovery. Jitter in the signal can affect the recovery of both, but the effect of jitter depends on the application. When data is transferred but will not be regenerated (converted to analog) at the receiver, only data recovery is necessary. The interface jitter is only a factor if it causes data errors at the receiver. The jitter tolerance is relatively low; for example, data with 5 to 10 ns of jitter could be recovered without error. However, when the data is to be regenerated, requantized and data recovery and particularly clock recovery are needed. Depending on the D/A converter design, clock jitter levels as low as 20 ps might be required.

For example, when transferring data from a CD player, to DAT recorder, to workstation, to DAT recorder, only interface jitter is relevant to the data recovery. Jitter attenuation might be required at points in the signal path so that data errors do not occur. However, when the data is converted to an analog signal at a D/A converter, jitter attenuation is essential. Clock jitter is detrimental to the clock recovery process because it might compromise the receiver's ability to derive a stable clock reference needed for conversion.

A receiving circuit separates the received clock from the received data, uses the received clock to recover the data, then regenerates the clock (attenuating jitter), using it as the internal time-base to reclock the data. For example, Fig. 4-33 shows a receiver that reads the synchronizing signal from input data, places the data in a buffer, then regenerates the clock and outputs the data with the frequency and phase appropriate to the destination. The buffer must be large enough to prevent underflow or overflow; in the former, samples must be repeated at the output, and with the latter, samples must be dropped (in both cases, ideally, during silences). The method of synchronizing from the embedded transmission clock is sometimes called genlock; it works well in most point to point transmission chains. When the data sampling frequency is different from the local system sampling frequency, a sample rate converter is needed to convert the incoming time-base; this is described in chapter 10. Sample rate converters can also be used as receivers for jitter attenuation.

Many receivers used in regeneration devices use a two stage clock recovery process, as shown in Fig. 4-34. The first step is clock extraction; the received em-

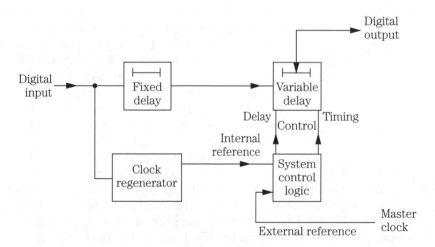

4-33 An example of a sample clock genlock synchronizer in which synchronization is derived from the embedded transmission clock. Shelton

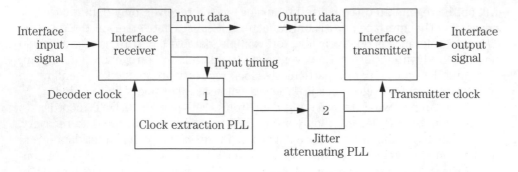

Note: A different clock is used for data
decoding and output timing.

4-34 An example of dual-clock transceiver architecture, providing clock extraction and jitter attenuation.

bedded clock is synchronized so the data can be decoded error-free in the presence of jitter. An initial PLL uses data transitions as its reference; the PLL is designed to track jitter well, but not attenuate it. At this stage, the sample clock might have jitter. The recovered data is placed in a FIFO buffer. A buffer is not needed if the jitter at this stage is considerably less than one bit period. The second step is jitter attenuation: A PLL with low-jitter clock characteristics locks to the sample clock and retimes it with an accurate reference. The new, accurate clock is used to read data from the FIFO. In other words, the second PLL is not required to track incoming jitter, but is designed for jitter attenuation. Overall, a receiver must decouple the digital interface from the conversion circuitry before regeneration. Looked at in another way, poor sound from a converter due to clock jitter might not be the converter's fault—it might be the receiver's.

Levels of transmission jitter often depend on cable characteristics. One type of cable-induced jitter, called pattern-dependent jitter, is a modulation that depends on the data values themselves. For example, patterns of 0s might produce more delay in transitions than patterns of 1s. The amount of modulation is a function of the high-frequency loss (bandwidth) of the cable. For example, jitter might be less than 1 ns if the cable has a 3-dB bandwidth of more than 4 MHz, but jitter increases to 9 ns if bandwidth is halved. For this reason, many transmission protocols use a fixed synchronization pattern or preamble; because the pattern is static, this cause of pattern-dependent jitter is removed. However, pattern-dependent jitter can be caused by other factors. For example, pattern-dependent jitter can be correlated to the polarity and frequency of the audio signal. When the coded audio signal level is low and at a single frequency, the more significant bits change together to reflect signal polarity, and pattern-dependent jitter can occur at that frequency. Any serial format that does not scramble its data word is prone to this phenomenon; with scrambling, this pattern-dependent jitter would be decorrelated and thus would be benign.

In more complex installations, with many devices, jitter protection is more sophisticated. Data must be transmitted accurately between pieces of sampling equipment, and each piece of equipment must be frequency locked to a star-configuration distributed master clock. Devices must have both data inputs, as well as external clock inputs. The use of an external clock is sometimes called master clock synchronization; it is recommended when numerous devices are interconnected. Interconnection synchronization issues are discussed in chapter 10.

As we have seen, D/A converters are particularly susceptible to jitter. The quality of samples taken from a perfectly clocked A/D converter will be degraded if the D/A converter's clock is nonuniform, creating the scenario of the right samples at the wrong time. Even though the data values are numerically accurate, the time deviations introduced by jitter will result in increased noise and distortion in the output analog signal. Fortunately, the distortion in the output waveform is a playback-only problem; the data itself might be correct, and awaits only a more accurate conversion clock. The samples are not wrong, they are only being converted at the wrong times. Not all data receivers (such as some S/PDIF receivers discussed in chapter 10) provide sufficiently low jitter. As noted, in improved designs, data from a digital interconnection or hardware source is re-synchronized to a new and accurate clock to remove jitter from the data signal prior to D/A conversion; phase-locked loops or other circuits are used to achieve this.

The effect of jitter on the output of a resistor ladder D/A converter can be observed by subtracting an output staircase affected with jitter from an ideal, jitter-free output. The difference signal contains spikes corresponding to the timing differences between samples; the difference widths correspond to the differences in arrival time between the ideal and jittered clocks. The heights of the error pulses correspond to the differences in amplitude from the previous sample to the present; large step sizes yield large error. The signal modulates the amplitudes, yielding smaller values at signal peaks. The error noise spectrum is white because there is no statistical relationship between error values. The noise amplitude is a function of step size, specifically, the absolute value of the average slope of the signal. Thus, the worse case for white phase jitter on a resistor ladder D/A converter occurs with a full-amplitude signal at the Nyquist half-sampling frequency (e.g., 20 kHz). Depending on converter design (and other factors) a jitter level of at least 1 ns is necessary to obtain 16-bit performance from a resistor ladder converter. A tolerance of half that level, 500 ps, is not unreasonable. Unfortunately, consumer devices might contain clocks with poor stability; jitter error can cause artifact peaks to appear 70 or 80 dB below the maximum level. When an oversampling filter is used prior to resistor ladder conversion, the converter's sensitivity to random (white phase) jitter is reduced in proportion to the oversampling rate; for example, an eight-times oversampling D/A converter is four times less sensitive to jitter as a two-times converter. Low-frequency correlated jitter is not affected by oversampling.

Low-bit D/A converters, discussed in more detail in chapter 16, can be very sensitive to clock jitter, or not particularly, depending on their architecture. When a true 1-bit signal is output, jitter pulses have constant amplitude. In a 1-bit converter in which the output is applied to a continuous-time filter, random jitter is signal independent, and in fact jitter pulses will be output even when no signal is present. A jitter sensitivity of 20 ps might be required to achieve 16-bit noise performance in a 1-bit converter with a continuous-time filter. As Robert Adams notes, this is because phase modulation causes the out-of-band shaped noise to fold down into the audio band, increasing the in-band noise level. Some low-bit converters use a switched-capacitor (discrete-time) output filter; because a switched capacitor will settle to an output value regardless of when a clock edge occurs, it is inherently less sensitive to jitter. The jitter performance of this type of converter is similar to that of a resistor ladder converter operating at the same oversampling rate. However, to achieve this, the switch-capacitor circuit must remove all out-of-band noise. Newer multiplying D/A converter topologies might greatly reduce the converter's susceptibility to jitter.

Clearly, jitter must be controlled at every stage of the audio digitization chain. Although designers must specially measure clock jitter in their circuits, traditional analog measurements such as THD+N and spectrum analysis can be used to evaluate the quality of the output signal, and will include effects caused by jitter. For example, if THD+N measured at 0 dB, 20 kHz is not greater than THD+N measured at 1 kHz, then jitter is not significant in the converter. As noted, if a receiving circuit can recover a data signal without error, interface jitter is not a factor. This is why data can be easily copied from one point to another without error. However, because of sampling jitter, an A/D converter must be accurately clocked, and clock recovery is important prior to D/A conversion. Ultimately, jitter is one of several causes of distortion in an output audio signal that must be minimized through good design practices.

5
CHAPTER

Error Correction

The advent of digital audio changed audio engineering forever and introduced entirely new techniques; error correction was probably the most revolutionary of them all. With analog audio, there is no opportunity for error correction. If the recorded signal is disrupted or distorted, then the signal is irrevocably damaged. With digital audio, the nature of binary data lends itself to recovery in the event of damage. When audio data is transmitted or stored, it can be specially coded and accompanied by redundancy. This enables the reproduced data to be checked for errors. When an error is detected, further processing can be performed to absolutely correct the error, or the error can be concealed by synthesizing new data. In either case, error correction makes digital data transmission and storage much more robust. For example, strong error-correction techniques relax the manufacturing tolerances for mass media such as the compact disc.

However, error correction is more than a fortuitous opportunity; it also is an obligation. Because of high data densities in audio storage media, for example, a petty defect in the manufactured medium or a particle of dust can cause the loss of hundreds or thousands of bits. Compared to absolute numerical data stored digitally, where a bad bit might mean the difference between adding or subtracting figures from a bank account, digital audio data is relatively forgiving of errors; enjoyment of music is not necessarily ruined because of occasional defects in the output waveform. However, error correction is mandatory for a digital audio system because uncorrected errors can be audible and these can easily occur because of the relatively harsh environment to which most audio media are subjected.

Error correction for digital audio is thus an opportunity to preserve data integrity, an opportunity not available with analog audio, and it is absolutely necessary to ensure the success of digital audio transmission and storage, because errors surely occur. With proper design, digital audio systems such as the compact disc system can approach the computer industry standard, which specifies an error rate of 10^{-12}—that is, less than one uncorrectable error in 10^{12} (one trillion) bits. However, much less stringent error performance is fully adequate for most audio applications. Without such protection, digital audio recording would not be viable. Indeed, the evolution of digital audio technology can be measured by the prerequisite advances in error correction.

Sources of Errors

Degradation can occur at every stage of the digital audio recording chain. Quantization error, converter nonlinearity, jitter and peak shift can all limit system performance. Use of high-quality components, careful circuit design, and strict manufacturing procedures minimizes these degradations. For example, a high-quality A/D converter can exhibit satisfactory low-level linearity, and phase-locked loops overcome jitter.

However, the science of error correction mainly attends to transmitted and stored data, because it is errors presented by those media that are most severe and least subject to control. For example, magnetic tape can be affected by dust, scratches, fingerprints, tape stretching or abuse, impure oxide or binder, irregular tape slitting, and physical editing. Likewise, optical media can be affected by pit asymmetry, bubbles or defects in substrate, and coating defects. In addition, transmitted data is subject to errors from multipath interference, atmospheric conditions, and other interfering signals.

Barring design defects or a malfunctioning device, the most severe types of errors occur in the recording or transmission medium. Such errors result in corrupted data, and hence a defective audio signal. The most significant cause of errors in digital media are dropouts. In analog systems, a defect in the medium causes a momentary drop in signal strength called a dropout. Dropouts can occur in any digital audio magnetic tape or optical disk, and can be traced to two causes: a manufactured defect in the medium or a defect introduced during use. For example, magnetic tape and optical disks are manufactured under clean conditions; however, microscopic particles of dust and other foreign particles can enter into the manufacturing materials. These might produce dropout errors. Defects in the medium cause signal transitions that are misrepresented as erroneous data. A loss of data or invalid data can provoke a click or pop, as the D/A converter's output jumps to a new amplitude while accepting invalid data. The severity of the error depends on the nature of the error. An error in the least significant bit of a PCM word might pass unnoticed, but an error in the most significant bit would create a drastic change in amplitude.

Errors occur in several modes; thus, classifications have been developed to better identify them. Errors that have no relation to each other are called random-bit errors. They occur singly and are generally easily corrected. A burst error is a large error, disrupting perhaps thousands of bits, caused by a manufacturing defect or a foreign particle on a tape or disk, or noise spikes, crosstalk, or connector problems in a transmission cable. An important characteristic of any error-correction system is the burst length—that is, the maximum number of adjacent erroneous bits that can be corrected. Both random and burst errors can occur within a single medium; therefore, an error-correction system must be designed to correct both error types simultaneously. In addition, because the nature of errors depends on the medium, error-correction techniques must be optimized for the application at hand. Thus, both magnetic and optical media errors as well as transmission errors must be considered separately. Finally, error-correction design is influenced by the kind of modulation code used to convey the data.

Several error conditions are encountered in digital magnetic media. As noted, dropouts are most problematic. With normal wear and tear, oxide particles will come loose from the backing and might become misplaced on the tape; other foreign particles, such as dust, dirt, and oil from fingerprints, as well as tape guides scratching the tape oxide, can contribute to the number of dropouts. Although physically small to bulky humans, foreign objects such as those shown in Fig. 5-1 are large when it is considered that the recorded bit size can be smaller than 1 micron. A dropout might occur at a fixed spot on the tape, or might travel to various spots on the tape as the errant particle moves, creating a phantom dropout. Manufactured tape dropouts usually occur more frequently at the beginning and end of a tape, in part because the slitting process produces a greater likelihood of variations in the cut tape width at the ends. During recording or playback, a particle could cause the tape to lift away from the head, causing the recorded or playback signal strength to fail momentarily; this error is known as spacing loss. Tape splicing causes errors around an edit point. Interpolation must provide a smooth output waveform to conceal this type of disrupted data.

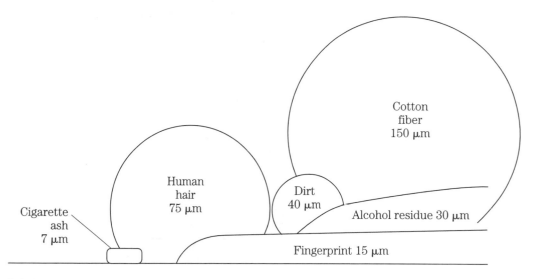

5-1 Small physical objects are large in the context of 1-μm recorded bit size.

Optical disks suffer from dropouts; however, they result from different manufacturing and handling problems. When a master disk is manufactured, an incorrect intensity of laser light, incorrect developing time, or a defect in the photoresist can create badly formed pits on the disk. Dust or scratches incurred during the plating or pressing processes, or pinholes or other defects in the disk reflective coating can all create dropouts. As is the case with magnetic tape, stringent manufacturing conditions and quality control can prevent many of these dropouts from leaving the factory. Optical disks become dirty or damaged with use. Dust, dirt, and oil can be wiped clean from the disk; however, scratches might interfere with the pickup's ability to read data. When cleaning optical media, such as a compact disc, a clean, soft cloth should be used to wipe the compact disc radially, that is, across the width of the disc and not around its circumference. Any scratches that result will be perpendicular to tracks and thus easier to correct, but a single scratch along one track could be impossible to correct, as shown in Fig. 5-2, because of the sustained consecutive loss of data.

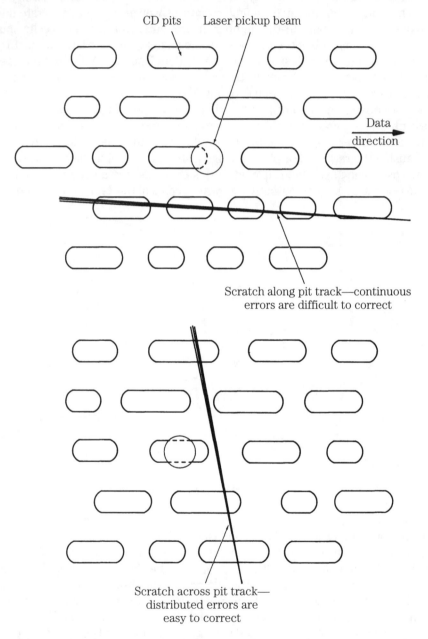

5-2 Severity of a scratch on an optical disk is determined by its geometry relative to the pit track.

A number of factors conspire to degrade quality of transmitted data including limited bandwidth and intersymbol interference, attenuation, noise, ringing, and reflection. For example, as data travels down a length of cable, the cable acts as a low-pass filter, reducing bandwidth and adding group delay. A square wave signal will show a gradual rise and fall time, and if the data rate is too high, the signal might not reach its full logical 1 and 0 levels. In other words, the level actually representing one bit can partly depend on the level of the previous bit; this is intersymbol interference. Similarly, interference can be caused by signal reflection, echoes from the terminating circuits that can reinforce, or cancel signal levels. Reflections can be caused by impedance mismatches between cables and terminating circuits. Other error sources include external low-frequency noise that can shift data transitions, causing jitter. High-frequency RF interference must be prevented with proper shielding and grounding. Fiber-optic cables are largely immune to radio-frequency interference and other problems that plague copper cables. The quality of a digital signal can be evaluated from its eye pattern, as discussed in chapter 4.

A number of parameters have been devised to quantify the integrity of data. The bit-error rate (BER) is the number of bits received in error divided by the total number of bits received. For example, a BER of 10^{-9} specifies one bit error for 10^9 (one billion) bits transmitted. In other words, BER is an error count. An optical disk system, for example, can contain error-correction algorithms able to handle a BER of 10^{-5} to 10^{-4}. The BER specifies the number of errors, but not their distribution. For example, a BER value might be the same for a single large error burst, as for several smaller bursts. Thus the BER is not a good indicator for an otherwise reliable channel subject to burst errors. For example, over 80% of the errors in an optical disk might be burst errors. Taking a different approach, the block error rate (BLER) measures the number of blocks or frames of data per second that have at least one occurrence of uncorrected data. The burst-error length (BERL) counts the number of consecutive blocks in error. BLER and BERL are often specified as the rate of errors per second; for example, a CD might exhibit 20 BLER errors per second. These values do not reflect the literal number of errors, but gauge their relative severity. BLER is discussed in more detail in the context of Cross-Interleave Reed-Solomon code error correction algorithm.

Similarly, because burst errors can occur intermittently, they are difficult to quantify with a bit error rate; in some cases, the errored second is measured; this tallies each second of data that contains an error. Errors can be described as the number of errored seconds over a period of time, or the time since the last errored second. As with BLER and BERL, it does not indicate how many bits are in error, but rather counts the occasions of error. No matter how errors are tabulated, it is the job of any system to detect and correct errors, keeping uncorrected errors to a minimum.

Objectives of Error Correction

Any practical storage or transmission channel will introduce errors in the stored or transmitted data; for accurate recovery it is thus necessary for the data to include a redundancy that overcomes the error. However, redundancy alone will not ensure accuracy of the recovered information; appropriate error detection and correction coding must be used.

Although a perfect error-correction system is theoretically possible, in which every error is detected and corrected, such a system would create an unreasonably high data overhead because of the amount of redundant data required to accomplish it. Thus, an efficient audio error-correction system should aim to provide a low audible error rate after correction and concealment, while minimizing the amount of redundant data and data processing required for successful operation. An error-correction system comprises three operations:

1. Error detection uses redundancy to permit data to be checked for validity
2. Error correction uses redundancy to replace erroneous data with newly calculated valid data
3. In the event of large errors or insufficient data for correction, error concealment techniques substitute approximately correct data for invalid data

In the worst case, when not even error concealment is possible, digital audio systems mute the output signal rather than let the output circuitry attempt to decode severely incorrect data, and produce severely incorrect sounds.

Error Detection

All error-detection and correction techniques are based on the redundancy of data. The data is said to be redundant because it is entirely derived from existing data, and thus conveys no additional information. In general, the greater the likelihood of errors, the greater the redundancy required. Information systems rely heavily on redundancy to achieve reliable communication; for example, spoken and written language contains redundancy. If a garbled telegraph message "AJL IS FIR-GIVRN. PLEAOE COMW HOME," is received, the message could be recovered. In fact, Claude Shannon estimated that 50% of written English is redundant.

Similarly, redundancy is required for reliable data communication. If a data value alone is generated, transmitted once, and received, there is no absolute way to check its validity at the receiving end. We might examine the data word by word, and question, for example, a word that unexpectedly differs from its neighbors. With digital audio, in which there is some sample correlation from one forty-thousandth of a second to the next, such an algorithm might be reasonable. However, we could not absolutely detect errors, or begin to correct them. Clearly, additional information is required to reliably detect errors in received data. Moreover, such information must originate from the same point as the original data so that it is subject to the same error-creating conditions as the data itself. The task of error detection is to properly code transmitted or stored information, so that when data is lost or made invalid, the presence of the error can be detected.

In an effort to detect errors, the original message could simply be repeated. For example, each data word could be transmitted twice. A conflict between repeated words would reveal that one is in error, but it would be impossible to identify the correct word. If each word was repeated three times, probability would suggest that the two in agreement were correct while the differing third was in error. Yet all three words could agree and all be in error, unknown to us. Given enough repetition, the probability of correctly detecting an error would be high; however, the data overhead would be enormous. Also, the increased data load can itself introduce additional errors. More efficient methods are required.

One-Bit Parity

Practical error detection uses techniques in which redundant data is coded such that it can be used to efficiently check for errors. Parity is one such method. One early error detection method was devised by Islamic mathematicians in the ninth century; it is known as "casting out 9s." In this technique, numbers are divided by 9, leaving a remainder or residue. Calculations can be checked for errors by comparing residues. For example, the residue of the sum (or product) of two numbers equals the sum (or product) of the residues. It is important to compare residues, and sometimes the residue of a sum or product residue must be taken. If the residues are not equal, an error has occurred in the calculation, as shown in Fig. 5-3. An insider's trick makes the method even more efficient; the sum of digits in a number always has the same 9s residue as the number itself. The technique of casting out 9s can be used to cast out any number, and forms the basis for a binary error detection method called parity.

Casting out 9s:

$240 + 578 \underset{?}{=} 818 \rightarrow$
$(2 + 4 + 0 = 6)$
$(5 + 7 + 8 = 20, 2 + 0 = 2)$
$(8 + 1 + 8 = 17, 1 + 7 = 8)$

$6 + 2 \overset{\checkmark}{=} 8$ Casting out 9s sum agrees, thus no error

$227 \times 67 \underset{?}{=} 15209$
$2 \times 4 \overset{\checkmark}{=} 8$ Casting out 9s product agrees, thus no error

5-3
Casting out of 9s and 2s provides simple error detection.

$154 \times 95 \underset{?}{=} 14613$
$1 \times 5 \neq 6$ Casting out 9s product does not agree calculation is in error

Casting out 2s:

Sum of 11001011 is 5, which is odd.
Cast out 2s to get 1 and append to word:110010111. In this way, the number of 1s is always even.

Given a binary number, a residue bit can be formed by casting out 2s. This extra bit is formed when the word is transmitted or stored, and is carried along with the data word. This extra bit, known as a parity bit, permits error detection, but not correction. Rather than cast out 2s, a more efficient algorithm can be used. An even parity bit is formed with a simple rule: if the number of 1s in the data word is even (or 0), the parity bit is a 0; if the number of 1s in the word is odd, the parity bit is a 1. In other words, with even parity, there is always an even number of 1s. To accomplish this, the data bits are added together with modulo 2 addition, as shown in Fig. 5-4. Thus, an 8-bit data word, made into a 9-bit word with an even parity bit,

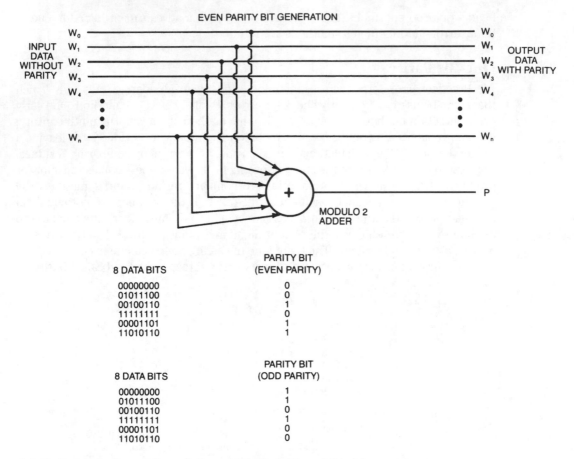

EVEN PARITY BIT GENERATION

INPUT DATA WITHOUT PARITY — W_0, W_1, W_2, W_3, W_4 ... W_n

OUTPUT DATA WITH PARITY — W_0, W_1, W_2, W_3, W_4 ... W_n

MODULO 2 ADDER

P

8 DATA BITS	PARITY BIT (EVEN PARITY)
00000000	0
01011100	0
00100110	1
11111111	0
00001101	1
11010110	1

8 DATA BITS	PARITY BIT (ODD PARITY)
00000000	1
01011100	1
00100110	0
11111111	1
00001101	0
11010110	0

5-4 Parity can be formed through the modulo 2 addition of data bits.

will always have an even number of 1s (or none). This parity method results in even parity. By forcing an odd number of 1s, odd parity results. Both methods are functionally identical.

At playback, the validity of the received data word is tested using the parity bit; that is, the received data bits are added together to calculate parity of received data. If the received parity bit and the calculated parity bit are in conflict, then an error has occurred. We can say that it is a 1-bit detector with no correction ability. With even parity, for example, the function can determine when an odd number of errors (1, 3, 5, etc.) are present in the received data; an even number of errors will not be detected, as shown in Fig. 5-5. Probability dictates that the error is in the data word, rather than the parity bit itself. However, the reverse could be true, and the parity bit error could be detected. As noted, errors tend to occur as burst errors. Thus, many errors could occur within each word and 1-bit parity would not provide reliable detection. By itself, a 1-bit parity check code is not suitable for error detection in a digital audio storage or transmission system.

Transmitted word		Received word		Parity calculated from received data word	
Data	Parity	Data	Parity		
00011001	1	00001001	1	0	Error detected
10101011	1	11001011	1	1	Errors not detected
01110100	0	01110100	1	0	Parity error detected
01101011	1	00000011	0	0	Errors not detected

5-5 Examples of one-bit parity error detection.

ISBN

In practice, simple 1-bit parity is not particularly useful in many applications. More sophisticated error detection codes have been devised to make more efficient use of redundancy. One example of coded information is the International Standard Book Number (ISBN) code found on virtually every book published. No two books and no two editions of the same book have the same ISBN. Even soft and hard cover editions of a book have different ISBNs.

An ISBN number is more than just a series of numbers. For example, consider the ISBN number, 0-14-044118-2 (the hyphens are extraneous). The first digit (0) is a country code; for example, 0 is for the U.S. and some other English-speaking countries. The next two digits (14) is a publisher code. The next six digits (044118) is the book number code. The last digit (2) is particularly interesting; it is a check digit. It can be used to verify that the other digits are correct. The check digit is a modulo 11 weighted checksum of the previous digits. In other words, when the digits are added together in modulo 11 the weighted sum must equal the number's checksum. (To maintain uniform length of ten digits per ISBN, the Roman numeral X is used to represent the check digit 10.) Given this code, with its checksum, we can check the validity of any ISBN by adding together the series of digits, and comparing them to the last digit.

Consider an example of the verification of an ISBN code. To form the weighted checksum of a ten-digit number abcdefghij, compute the weighted sum of the numbers by multiplying each digit by its digit position, starting with the leftmost digit:

$$10a + 9b + 8c + 7d + 6e + 5f + 4g + 3h + 2i + 1j.$$

For the ISBN number 0-14-044118-2, the weighted sum is:

$$10 \times 0 + 9 \times 1 + 8 \times 4 + 7 \times 0 + 6 \times 4 + 5 \times 4 + 4 \times 1 + 3 \times 1 + 2 \times 8 + 1 \times 2 = 110.$$

The weighted checksum modulo 11 is found by taking the remainder after dividing by 11:

$$\frac{110}{11} = 10, \text{ with a 0 remainder}$$

The 0 remainder suggests that the ISBN is correct. In this way, ISBNs can be accurately checked for errors. The use of a weighted checksum, compared to the calculated remainder with modulo arithmetic, provides a very powerful way of detecting errors. In fact, error detection codes in general are based on this principle.

Cyclic Redundancy Check Code

The cyclic redundancy check code (CRCC) is an error detection method preferred in audio applications because of its ability to detect burst errors in the recording medium. The CRCC is a cyclic block code that generates a parity check word. For example, the bits of a data word can be added together to form a sum of the bits; this forms a parity check word. In 1011011010, the six binary 1s are added together to form binary 0110 (6 in base 10), and this check word is appended to the data word to form the code word for transmission or storage. As with 1-bit parity, any disagreement between the received checksum and that formed from the received data would indicate with high probability that an error has occurred.

The CRCC works similarly, but with a more sophisticated calculation. Simply stated, each data block is divided by an arbitrary and constant number. The remainder of the division is appended to the stored or transmitted data block. Upon reproduction, division is performed on the received word; a zero remainder is taken to indicate an error-free signal, as shown in Fig. 5-6. A more detailed examination of the encoding and decoding steps in the CRCC algorithm is shown in Fig. 5-7. A message m in a k-bit data block is operated upon to form an $n–k$ bit CRCC detection block, where n is the length of the complete block. The original k-bit

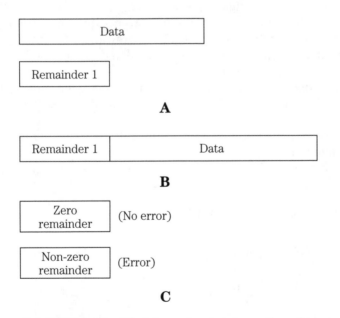

5-6 CRCC in simplified form showing generation of remainder. A. Original block of data is divided to produce a remainder. The quotient is discarded. B. The remainder is appended to the data word and both words are transmitted or stored. C. The received data is again divided to produce a remainder, used to check for errors.

$\longleftarrow$ *k* bits $\longrightarrow$

message *m*

$\mathbf{m} = (m_0, m_1, m_2 \cdots m_{k-1})$
in polynomial form,
$\mathbf{m}(X) = m_0 + m_1 X + m_2 X^2 + \cdots + m_{k-1} X^{k-1}$
multiplying $\mathbf{m}(X)$ by X^{n-k}
$X^{n-k} \mathbf{m}(X) = m_0 X^{n-k} + m_1 X^{n-k-1} + \cdots + m_{k-1} X^{n-1}$
dividing $X^{n-k} \mathbf{m}(X)$ by $\mathbf{g}(X)$, the generation polynomial,
$X^{n-k} \mathbf{m}(X) = \mathbf{q}(X) \mathbf{g}(X) + \mathbf{r}(X)$
where $\mathbf{q}(X)$ and $\mathbf{r}(X)$ are quotient and remainder respectively,
where $\mathbf{r}(X) = r_0 + r_1 X + r_2 X^2 + \cdots + r_{n-k-1} X^{n-k-1}$
arranging previous equation and adding $\mathbf{r}(X)$,
$\mathbf{r}(X) + X r^{n-k} \mathbf{m}(X) = \mathbf{q}(X) \mathbf{g}(X) + \mathbf{r}(X) + \mathbf{r}(X)$
however $\mathbf{r}(X) + \mathbf{r}(X) = 0$ thus,
$\mathbf{r}(X) + X^{n-k} \mathbf{m}(X) = \mathbf{q}(X) \mathbf{g}(X)$
thus $\mathbf{r}(X) + X^{n-k} \mathbf{m}(X)$ is a multiple of $\mathbf{g}(X)$.
$\mathbf{r}(X) + X^{n-k} \mathbf{m}(X)$ is the transmitted code polynomial $\mathbf{v}(X)$:
$\mathbf{v}(X) = \mathbf{r}(X) + X^{n-k} \mathbf{m}(X) = r_0 + r_1 X + r_2 X^2 + \cdots + r_{n-k-1} X^{n-k-1}$
$\qquad\qquad\qquad + m_0 X^{n-k} + m_1 X^{n-k-1} + \cdots m_{k-1} X^{n-1}$

this corresponds to the transmitted code word:
$(r_0, r_1, r_2, \cdots r_{n-k-1}, m_0, m_1, m_2 \cdots m_{k-1})$

$\longleftarrow$ *n* – *k* $\longrightarrow$ $\longleftarrow$ *k* bits $\longrightarrow$

parity *r*	message *m*

A

$\longleftarrow$ *n* bits $\longrightarrow$

received data

$\mathbf{u} = (u_1, u_2, u_3, u_4, \cdots u_{n-1})$
in polynomial form:
$\mathbf{u}(X) = u_0 + u_1 X + u_2 X^2 + \cdots + u_{n-1} X^{n-1}$
where $u_0, u_1, u_2, \cdots u_{n-k-1}$ are parity check bits and u_{n-k},
$\cdots u_{n-1}$ are information bits. The syndrome $\mathbf{s}$ is calculated
by taking the mod 2 sum of the received parity bits and
the parity bits formed from the received information.
Thus, syndrome $\mathbf{s}(X)$ is equal to remainder of $\mathbf{u}(X)$
divided by $\mathbf{g}(X)$:
$\mathbf{u}(X) = \mathbf{p}(X) \mathbf{g}(X) + \mathbf{s}(X)$
a nonzero value for $\mathbf{s}$ detects an error. The difference
between received ($\mathbf{u}$) and transmitted ($\mathbf{v}$) information is an
error pattern $\mathbf{e}$. From $\mathbf{e}$, we can recover $\mathbf{v}$, by using the
syndrome for error correction
$\qquad \mathbf{u}(X) = \mathbf{v}(X) + \mathbf{e}(X)$
since $\mathbf{v}(X) = \mathbf{m}(X) \mathbf{g}(X)$,
$\qquad \mathbf{u}(X) = \mathbf{m}(X) \mathbf{g}(X) + \mathbf{e}(X) = \mathbf{p}(X) \mathbf{g}(X) + \mathbf{s}(X)$
thus $\mathbf{e}(X) = [\mathbf{p}(X) + \mathbf{m}(X)] \mathbf{g}(X) + \mathbf{s}(X)$

Thus when the error pattern is divided by the generation
polynomial, the remainder is the syndrome, which can be
used to correct errors. Note that the generation
polynomial was chosen so that the error polynomial
consists of an error pattern not divisible by $\mathbf{g}$. The above derivations
utilize the properties of modulo 2 arithmetic.

B

5-7
CRCC encoding and
decoding algorithms. A.
CRCC encoding. B. CRCC
decoding and syndrome
calculation.

data block is multiplied by X^{n-k} to shift the data in preparation to appending the
check bits. It is then divided by the generation polynomial g to form the quotient
q and remainder r. The transmission polynomial v is formed from the original
message m and the remainder r; it is thus a multiple of the generation polynomial

g. The transmission polynomial *v* is then transmitted or stored. The received data *u* undergoes error detection by calculating a syndrome, in the sense that an error is sign of malfunction or disease. Specifically, the operation creates a syndrome *c* with modulo 2 addition of received parity bits and parity newly calculated from the received message. A zero syndrome shows an error-free condition. A nonzero syndrome denotes an error.

Error correction can be accomplished by forming an error pattern that is the difference between the received data and the original data to be recovered. This is mathematically possible because the error polynomial *e* divided by the original generation polynomial produces the syndrome as a remainder. Thus the syndrome can be used to form the error pattern and hence recover the original data. It is important to select *g* so that error patterns in the error polynomial *e* are not exactly divisible by *g*. CRCC will fail to detect an error if the error is exactly divisible by the generation polynomial.

In practice, CRCC and other detection and correction code words are described in mathematical terms, where the data bits are treated as the coefficients of a binary polynomial. As we observed in chapter 1, the binary number system is one of positional notation such that each place represents a power of 2. Thus we can write binary numbers in power of two notation. For example, the number 1001011 (MSB leading) can be expressed as:

$$1 \times 2^6 + 0 \times 2^5 + 0 \times 2^4 + 1 \times 2^3 + 0 \times 2^2 + 1 \times 2^1 + 1 \times 2^0$$

or:

$$2^6 + 2^3 + 2^1 + 2^0$$

In general, the number can be expressed as:

$$x^6 + x^3 + x + 1$$

With LSB leading, the notation would be reversed. This polynomial notation is the standard terminology in the field of error correction. In the same way that use of modulo arithmetic ensures that all possible numbers will fall in the modulus, polynomials are used to ensure that all values fall within a given range. In modulo arithmetic, all numbers are divided by the modulus and the remainder is used as the number. Similarly, all polynomials are divided by a modulus polynomial of degree *n*. The remainder has *n* coefficients, and is recognizable as a code symbol. Further, just as we desire a modulus that is a prime number (so that when a product is zero, at least one factor is 0), we desire a prime polynomial—one that cannot be represented as the product of two polynomials. The benefit is added structure to devised codes, resulting in more efficient implementation.

Using this notation, we can see how CRCC works. An example of cyclic code encoding is shown in Fig. 5-8. The message 1001 is written as the polynomial $x^3 + 1$. So that three parity check bits can be appended, the message is multiplied by x^3 to shift the data to the left. The message is then divided by the generation polynomial $x^3 + x^2 + 1$. The remainder $x+1$ is appended to create the polynomial $x^6 + x^3 + x + 1$. A shift register implementation of this encoder is shown in Fig. 5-9. The register is initially loaded with 0s, and the four message bits are sequentially shifted into the register, and appear at the output. When the last message bit has been output, the encoder's switches are switched, 0s enter the register, and three parity bits are output. Modulo 2 adders are used. This example points up an advantage of this type of error detection encoding: the implementation can be quite simple.

Given a message m = (1001) to be encoded, message polynomial $m(x) = x^3 + 1$. Multiplying by x^{n-k}, $x^3 m(x) = x^6 + x^3$.

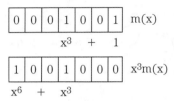

| 0 | 0 | 0 | 1 | 0 | 0 | 1 | m(x) |

$$x^3 + 1$$

| 1 | 0 | 0 | 1 | 0 | 0 | 0 | $x^3 m(x)$ |

$$x^6 + x^3$$

Given a generation polynomial $g(x) = x^3 + x^2 + 1$ division by g(x) is performed:

$$
\begin{array}{r}
x^3 + x^2 + x + 1 \\
x^3 + x^2 + 1 \ \overline{\smash{)}\ x^6 \qquad\quad x^3} \\
\underline{x^6 + x^5 \quad + x^3} \\
x^5 \\
\underline{x^5 + x^4 \qquad + x^2} \\
x^4 \qquad + x^2 \\
\underline{x^4 + x^3 \qquad + x} \\
x^3 + x^2 + x \\
\underline{x^3 + x^2 \qquad + 1} \\
x + 1
\end{array}
$$

Remainder = r(x)

The code word polynomial
$$(x) = x^3\, m(x) + r(x)$$
$$= x^6 + x^3 + x + 1$$

| 1 | 0 | 0 | 1 | 0 | 1 | 1 |

$$\underbrace{x^6 \quad + \quad x^3}_{\text{Message}} + \underbrace{x+1}_{\text{Parity}}$$

5-8
An example of cyclic code encoding, with message 1001 written as the polynomial $X^3 + 1$. The encoder outputs the original message and parity word.

The larger the data block, the less redundancy results, yet mathematical analysis shows that the same error detection capability remains. However, if random or short duration burst errors tend to occur frequently, then the integrity of the detection is decreased and shorter blocks might be necessitated. The extent of error detectability of a CRCC code can be summarized. Given a k-bit data word with m ($m = n - k$) bits of CRCC, a code word of n bits is formed, and the following are true:

1. Burst errors less than or equal to m bits are always detectable
2. Detection probability of burst errors of $m + 1$ bits is $1 - 2^{-m+1}$
3. Detection probability of burst errors longer than m+1 bits is $1 - 2^{-m}$. (Items 1–3 are not affected by the length n of the code word)
4. Random errors up to three consecutive bits long can be detected

CRCC is quite reliable. For example, if 16 parity check bits are generated, the probability of error detection is $1 - 2^{-16}$ or about 99.99%. Ultimately the medium determines the design of the CRCC and the rest of the error-correction system. Magnetic tape, for example, might call for longer CRCC blocks, but optical disks might require shorter blocks. The power of the error-correction processing following the

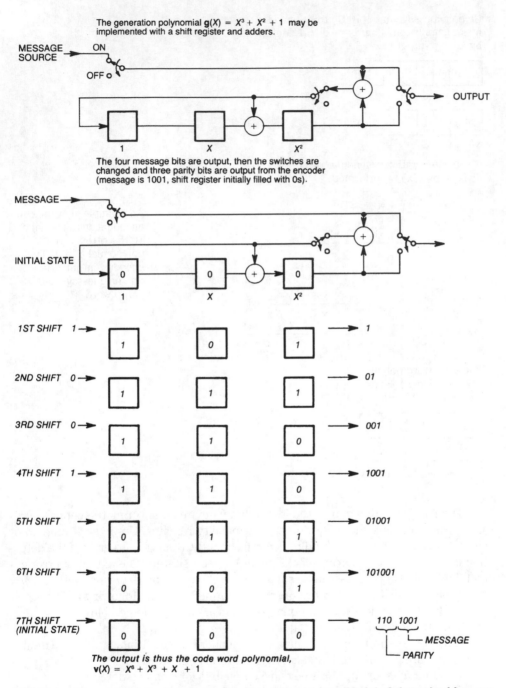

The generation polynomial $g(X) = X^3 + X^2 + 1$ may be implemented with a shift register and adders.

The four message bits are output, then the switches are changed and three parity bits are output from the encoder (message is 1001, shift register initially filled with 0s).

The output is thus the code word polynomial,
$$v(X) = X^6 + X^3 + X + 1$$

5-9 An implementation of a cyclic encoder using shift registers. Modulo 2 (EX OR) adders are used.

CRCC also influences how accurate the CRCC detection must be. The CRCC is typically used as an error pointer to identify the number and extent of errors prior to other error-correction processing.

Error-Correction Codes

With the use of redundant data, it is possible to correct errors that occur during transmission or storage of digital audio data. In the simplest case, data is simply duplicated. For example, instead of writing only one data track to recorded tape, two tracks of identical data could be written. The first track would normally be used for playback, but if an error were detected through parity or other means, data could be taken from the second track. To alleviate the problem of simultaneously erroneous data, redundant samples could be displaced with respect to each other in time.

In addition, channel coding can be used beneficially. For example, three-bit sequences could be coded as 7-bit words, selected from 2^7 possible combinations to be as mutually different as possible. The receiver examines the 7-bit words and compares them to the eight allowed code words. Errors could be detected, and the words changed to the nearest allowed code word, before the code word is decoded to the original three-bit sequence. Four correction bits are required for every 3 data bits; the method can correct a single error in a 7-bit block. This minimum length concept is important in more sophisticated error-correction codes.

Although such simple methods are workable, they are inefficient because of the data overhead they require. A more enlightened approach is that of error correcting codes, which can achieve more reliable transmission or storage with less redundancy. In the same way that redundant data in the form of parity check bits is used for error detection, redundant data is used to form codes for error correction. Digital audio is encoded with related detection and correction algorithms. On playback, errors are identified and corrected by the detection and correction decoder. Coded redundant data is the essence of all correction codes; however, there are many types of codes, different in their designs and functions.

The field of error-correction codes is a highly mathematical one. Many types of codes, developed for different applications, have been developed. In general, two approaches are used: block codes using algebraic methods, and convolutional codes using probabilistic methods. Block codes form a coded message based solely on the message parsed into a data block. In a convolutional code, the coded message is formed from the message present in the encoder at that time as well as previous message data. In many cases, algorithms use a block code in a convolutional structure known as a cross-interleave code. Such codes are used in the DASH and CD formats.

Block Codes

Block error-correction encoders assemble a number of data words to form a block and, operating over that block, generate one or more parity words and append them to the block. During decoding, an algorithm forms a syndrome word that detects errors and, given sufficient redundancy, corrects them. Such algorithms are effective against errors encountered in digital audio applications. Error correction is enhanced by interleaving consecutive words. Block codes base their parity calculations on an entire block of information to form parity words. In addition, parity can be formed from individual words in the block, using 1-bit parity or a cyclic code. In this way, greater redundancy is achieved and correction is improved. For example, CRCC could be used to detect an error, then block parity used to correct the error.

A block code can be conceived as a binary message consolidated into a block, with row and column parity. Any single word error will cause one row and one column to be in error; thus the erroneous data can be corrected. For example, a message might be grouped into four 8-bit words (called symbols). A parity bit is added to each row and a parity word added to each column, as shown in Fig. 5-10. At the decoder, the data is checked for correct parity, and any single symbol error is corrected. In this example, bit parity shows that word three is in error, and word parity is used to correct the symbol. A double word error can be detected, but not corrected. Larger numbers of errors might result in misdetection or miscorrection.

```
Transmitted          Transmitted
data block           single bit parity

00010111                  0
01101010                  0
10010111                  1
11010110                  1
00111100 ──────────────────── Transmitted parity word


Received             Received
data block           parity bit

00010111                  0
01101010                  0
11100100                  1
11010110                  1
00111100 ──────────────── Received parity word
01110011 ──────────────── Parity word calculated from
                          received data and parity word
```

5-10
An example of block parity with row parity bits and column parity word.

```
Parity calculated
on received data block

    0
    0
    0 ───────── Indicates error in word 3
    1


    01110011 ──────── Calculated parity word
  + 11100100 ──────── Incorrect word 3
    10010111 ──────── Corrected word 3
```

Block correction codes use many methods to generate the transmitted code word and its parity; however, they are fundamentally identical in that only information from the block itself is used to generate the code. The extent of the correction capabilities of block correction codes can be simply illustrated with decimal number examples. Given a block of six data words, a seventh parity word can be calculated by adding the six data words. To check for an error, a syndrome is created by comparing (subtracting in the example) the parity (sum) of the received data with the received parity value. If the result is zero, then most probably no error has occurred, as shown in Fig. 5-11A. If one data word is detected and the word is set to zero, a condition called a single erasure, a nonzero syndrome indicates that; furthermore, the erasure value can be obtained from the syndrome, as shown in Fig. 5-11B. If CRCC or 1-bit parity is used, it points out the erroneous word, and the correct value can be calculated using the syndrome, as shown in Fig. 5-11C. Even if detection itself is in error and falsely creates an error pointer, the syndrome yields the correct result, as shown in Fig. 5-11D. Such a block correction code is capable of detecting a one-word error, or making one erasure correction, or correcting one error with a pointer. The correction ability depends on the detection ability of pointers. In this case, unless the error is identified with a pointer, erasure, or CRCC detection, the error cannot be corrected, as shown in Fig. 5-11E.

For enhanced performance, two parity words can be formed to protect the data block. For example, one parity word might be the sum of the data and the second parity word the weighted sum as shown in Fig. 5-12A. If any two words are erroneous and marked with pointers, the code provides correction, as shown in Fig. 5-12B. Similarly, if any two words are marked with erasure, the code can use the two syndromes to correct the data. Unlike the single parity example, this double parity code also can correct any one-word error, even if it is not identified with a pointer, as shown in Fig. 5-12C. This type of error correction is well suited for audio applications.

Cyclic codes, such as CRCC, are a subclass of linear block codes, which can be used for error correction. Special block codes, known as Hamming codes, create syndromes that point to the location of the error. Multiple parity bits are formed for each data word, with unique encoding. For example, three parity check bits (4, 5, and 6) might be added to a 4-bit data word (0, 1, 2, and 3); seven bits are then transmitted. For example, suppose that the three parity bits are uniquely defined as follows: parity bit four is formed from modulo 2 addition of data bits 1, 2, and 3; parity bit 5 is formed from data bits 0, 2, and 3; and parity bit 6 is formed from data bits 0, 1, and 3. Thus, the data word 1100, appended with parity bits 110, is transmitted as the 7-bit code word 1100110. A table of data and parity bits is shown in Fig. 5-13A.

This algorithm for calculating parity bits is summarized in Fig. 5-13B. An error in a received data word can be located by examining which of the parity bits detects an error. The received data must be correctly decoded; therefore, parity check decoding equations must be written. These equations are computationally represented as a parity check matrix H, as shown in Fig. 5-13C. Each row of H represents one of the original encoding equations. By testing the received data against the values in H, the location of the error can be identified. Specifically, a syndrome is calculated from the modulo 2 addition of the parity calculated from the received data and the received parity. An error generates a 1; otherwise a 0 is generated. The resulting error pattern is matched in the H matrix to locate the erroneous bit. For example, if the code word 1100110 is transmitted, but 1000110 is received, the syndromes will detect the error and generate a 101 error pattern. Matching this against the H matrix, we see that it corresponds to the second column; thus, bit 1 is in error, as shown in Fig. 5-13D. This algorithm is a single error correcting code; therefore, it can correctly identify and correct any 1-bit error.

Returning to the design of this particular code, we can observe another of its interesting properties. Referring again to Fig. 5-13A, recall that the seven-bit data words are each comprising four data bits and three parity bits. These seven bits pro-

Original data words and parity

W_1 10
W_2 30
W_3 20
W_4 25
W_5 30
W_6 15
P $130 = W_1 + W_2 + W_3 + W_4 + W_5 + W_6$

Received data words and parity

W_1 10
W_2 30
W_3 20   Syndrome $S = W_1 + W_2 + W_3 + W_4 + W_5 + W_6 - P$
W_4 25 $= 10 + 30 + 20 + 25 + 30 + 15 - 130 = 0$
W_5 30
W_6 15   Thus no error is indicated
P 130

A Block correction code showing no error condition

Received data and parity word

W_1 10
W_2 30
W_3 —   Syndrome $S = 10 + 30 + 0 + 25 + 30 + 15 - 130 = -20$
W_4 25
W_5 30   Erasure correction: $W_3 = W_3' - S$
W_6 15 $= 0 - (-20) = 20$
P 130

B Block correction code showing single erasure correction

Received data and parity word

W_1 10   CRCC error pointer
W_2 30
W_3 20
W_4 15
W_5 30
W_6 15
P 130   Syndrome $S = 10 + 30 + 20 + 15 + 30 + 15 - 130 = -10$

              Error correction: $W_4 = W_4' - S$
                            $= 15 - (-10)$
                            $= 25$

C Block correction code showing correction with pointer

5-11 Examples of single-parity block coding.

Received data and parity word

W_1	10
W_2	30
W_3	20
W_4	25
W_5	30
W_6	15
P	130

False error pointer

Syndrome $S = 10 + 30 + 20 + 25 + 30 + 15 - 130 = 0$

Error correction: $W_5 = W_5' - S$
$= 30 - 0$
$= 30$

D Block correction code showing false pointer

Received data and parity word

W_1	10
W_2	30
W_3	20
W_4	15
W_5	30
W_6	15
P	130

Syndrome $S = 10 + 30 + 20 + 15 + 30 + 15 - 130 = -10$

Error correction: Not possible

E Block correction code showing uncorrectable error correction

5-11 Continued.

vide 128 different encoding possibilities, but we use only 16 of them; thus, 112 patterns are clearly illegal, and their presence would denote an error. In this way, the patterns of bits themselves are useful. We also may ask the question: How many bits must change value for one word in the table to become another word in the table? For example, we can see that three bits in the word 0101010 must change for it to become 0110011. Similarly, we observe that any word in the table would require at least three bit changes to become any other word. This is important because this dissimilarity in data corresponds to the code's error-correction ability. For example, if we receive a word 1110101, which differs from a legal word 1010101 by one bit, the correct word can be determined. In other words, any single bit error leaves the received word closer to the correct word than any other.

The number of bits that one legal word must change to become another legal word is known as the Hamming distance, or minimum distance. In this example, the Hamming distance is three. Hamming distance thus defines the potential error correctability of a code. A distance of one determines simple uniqueness of a code. A distance of two provides single error detectability. A distance of three provides single error correctability or double error detection. A distance of four provides both single error correction and double error detection, or triple error detection alone. A distance of five provides double error correction. As the distance increases, so does the correctability of the code. The greater the correctability required, the greater

Received data and two parity words

W_1 10
W_2 30
W_3 20
W_4 25
W_5 30
W_6 15
P $130 = W_1 + W_2 + W_3 + W_4 + W_5 + W_6$
Q $440 = 6W_1 + 5W_2 + 4W_3 + 3W_4 + 2W_5 + W_6$

Syndrome $S_1 = W_1 + W_2 + W_3 + W_4 + W_5 + W_6 - P = 10 + 30 + 20 + 25 + 30 + 15 - 130 = 0$
$S_2 = 6W_1 + 5W_2 + 4W_3 + 3W_4 + 2W_5 + W_6 - Q = 60 + 150 + 80 + 75 + 60 + 15 - 440 = 0$

A Block correction code with double parity showing no error condition

Received data and two parity words

W_1 10 ⟋ Error pointer
W_2 20
W_3 20
W_4 25
W_5 30 ⟋ Error pointer
W_6 10
P 130
Q 440

Syndrome $S_1 = 10 + 20 + 20 + 25 + 30 + 10 - 130 = -15$
$S_2 = 60 + 100 + 80 + 75 + 60 + 10 - 440 = -55$

$W_2' = W_2 + E_2$
$W_6' = W_6 + E_6$

$S_1 = E_2 + E_6 = -15$
$S_2 = 5E_2 + E_6 = -55$

$E_2 = S_1 - E_6$ ⟋ $E_6 = S_1 - E_2$
$5E_2 = S_2 - E_6$ ⟋ $E_6 = S_2 - 5E_2$

$E_2 = \dfrac{1}{4}S_2 - \dfrac{1}{4}S_1 = -10$

$E_6 = \dfrac{5}{4}S_1 - \dfrac{1}{4}S_2 = -5$

Correction:

$W_2 = W_2' - E_2 = 20 - (-10) = 30$
$W_6 = W_6' - E_6 = 10 - (-5) = 15$

B Block correction code with double parity showing

5-12 Examples of double-parity block coding.

Received data and two parity words

W_1	10		
W_2	30		
W_3	20	$S_1 = -20$	
W_4	25	$S_2 = -40$	
W_5	10		
W_6	15		
P	130		
Q	440		

Algebraically we see that

If $6S_1 = S_2$ then W_1 is erroneous
If $5S_1 = S_2$ then W_2 is erroneous
If $4S_1 = S_2$ then W_3 is erroneous
If $3S_1 = S_2$ then W_4 is erroneous
If $2S_1 = S_2$ then W_5 is erroneous
If $S_1 = S_2$ then W_6 is erroneous
If $S_1 \neq 0$ and $S_2 = 0$ then P is erroneous
If $S_1 = 0$ and $S_2 \neq 0$ then Q is erroneous

In this case $2S_1 = S_2$, W5 is erroneous, thus (as in single erasure case):

$$S_1 = 10 + 30 + 20 + 25 + 0 + 15 - 130 = -30$$

$$
\begin{aligned}
W_5 = W_5' - S \\
= 0 - (-30) \\
= 30 \qquad \text{Corrected}
\end{aligned}
$$

C Block correction code with double parity
showing single error without pointer

5-12 Continued.

the distance the code must possess. In general, to detect t_d number of errors, the minimum distance required is greater than or equal to $t_d + 1$. In the case of an erasure e (when an error location is known and set to zero), the minimum distance is greater than or equal to $e + 1$. To correct all combinations of t_c or fewer errors, the minimum distance required is greater than or equal to $2t_c + 1$. For a combination of error correction, the minimum distance is greater than or equal to $t_d + e + 2t_c + 1$. These hold true for both bit-oriented and word-oriented codes. If m parity blocks are included in a block code, the minimum distance is less than or equal to $m + 1$. For the maximum-distance separable (MDS) codes such as B-adjacent and Reed-Solomon codes, the minimum distance is equal to $m + 1$.

Block codes are notated in terms of the input relative to the output data. Data is grouped in symbols; the smallest symbol is one bit long. A message of k symbols is used to generate a larger n-bit symbol. Such a code is notated as (n, k). For example, if 12 symbols are input to an encoder and 20 symbols are output, the code would be (20,12). In other words $n - k$, or 8 parity symbols are generated. The source rate R is defined as k/n; in this example, $R = 12/20$.

X_0	X_1	X_2	X_3	X_4	X_5	X_6
0	0	0	0	0	0	0
0	0	0	1	1	1	1
0	0	1	0	1	1	0
0	0	1	1	0	0	1
0	1	0	0	1	0	1
0	1	0	1	0	1	0
0	1	1	0	0	1	1
0	1	1	1	1	0	0
1	0	0	0	0	1	1
1	0	0	1	1	0	0
1	0	1	0	1	0	1
1	0	1	1	0	1	0
1	1	0	0	1	1	0
1	1	0	1	0	0	1
1	1	1	0	0	0	0
1	1	1	1	1	1	1

A

5-13
With Hamming codes, the syndrome points to the error location. A. In this example with 4 data bits and 3 parity bits, the code has a Hamming distance of 3. B. Parity bits are formed in the encoder. C. Parity check matrix in the decoder. D. Single-error correction using a syndrome to point to error location.

X_0, X_1, X_2, X_3 — Data bits
$X_4 = X_1 + X_2 + X_3$ — (Mod 2) parity check bits
$X_5 = X_0 + X_2 + X_3$ — (Mod 2)
$X_6 = X_0 + X_1 + X_3$ — (Mod 2)
$X_0, X_1, X_2, X_3, X_4, X_5, X_6$ — Transmitted code word

B

$$\begin{aligned} X_1 + X_2 + X_3 + X_4 &= 0 \\ X_0 + X_2 + X_3 + X_5 &= 0 \\ X_0 + X_1 + X_3 + X_6 &= 0 \end{aligned}$$ Decoding algorithm

$$\begin{bmatrix} 0 & 1 & 1 & 1 & 1 & 0 & 0 \\ 1 & 0 & 1 & 1 & 0 & 1 & 0 \\ 1 & 1 & 0 & 1 & 0 & 0 & 1 \end{bmatrix} = H$$ Parity-check matrix

C

Example: 1100110 Transmitted word
1000110 Received word

$P_4 = X_1 + X_2 + X_3 = 0 + 0 + 0 = 0$ Parity of received data
$P_5 = X_0 + X_2 + X_3 = 1 + 0 + 0 = 1$
$P_6 = X_0 + X_1 + X_3 = 1 + 0 + 0 = 1$

Syndromes are calculated with mod 2 addition of parity of received data and received parity bits:

$P_4 = 0, \quad X_4 = 1, \quad 0 + 1 = 1$ (Error)
$P_5 = 1, \quad X_5 = 1, \quad 1 + 1 = 0$ (Correct)
$P_6 = 1, \quad X_6 = 0, \quad 1 + 0 = 1$ (Error)

The resulting syndromes form the error pattern $\begin{bmatrix} 1 \\ 0 \\ 1 \end{bmatrix}$ which corresponds to the second column of H

$$H = \begin{bmatrix} 0 & 1 & 1 & 1 & 1 & 0 & 0 \\ 1 & 0 & 1 & 1 & 0 & 1 & 0 \\ 1 & 1 & 0 & 1 & 0 & 0 & 1 \end{bmatrix}$$ Thus bit X_1, is in error

D

Convolutional Codes

Convolutional codes, sometimes called recurrent codes, differ from block codes in the way data is grouped for coding. Instead of dividing the message data into blocks of k digits and generating a block of n code digits, convolutional codes do not partition data into blocks. Instead, message digits k are taken a few at a time and used to generate coded digits n, formed not only from those k message digits, but from many previous k digits as well, saved in delay memories. In this way, the coded output contains a history of the previous input data. Such a code is called an (n, k) convolutional code. It uses $(N - 1)$ message blocks with k digits. It has constraint length N blocks (or nN digits) equal to $n(m + 1)$, where m is the number of delays. Its rate R is k/n. Parameters k and n typically are small integers.

As with linear block codes, encoding is performed and code words are transmitted or stored. Upon retrieval, the correction decoder uses syndromes to check code words for errors. Shift registers can be used to implement the delay memories required in the encoder and decoder. The amount of delay determines the code's constraint length, which is analogous to the block length of a block code. An example of a convolutional encoder is shown in Fig. 5-14. There are six delays, thus the constraint length is 14. The other parameters are $q = 2$, $R = \frac{1}{2}$, $k = 1$, $n = 2$, and the polynomial is $x^6 + x^5 + x^2 + 1$. As shown in the diagram, message data is continually circulated through the encoder, and many previous bits affect the current coded output.

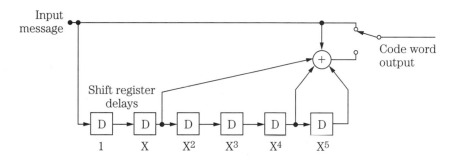

5-14 A convolutional code encoder with six delay blocks.

Another example of a convolutional encoder, demonstrated by Andrew Viterbi, is shown in Fig. 5-15A. The upper code is formed from input data with the polynomial $x^2 + x + 1$, and the lower with $x^2 + 1$. The data sequence enters the circuit from the left and is shifted to the right one bit at a time. The two sequences generated from the original sequence with modulo 2 addition are multiplexed to again form a single coded data stream. The resultant code has a memory of two because, in addition to the current input bit, it also acts on the preceding two bits. For every input bit, there are two output bits; hence the code's rate is $\frac{1}{2}$. The constraint length of this code is $k = 3$.

A convolutional code can be analyzed with a tree diagram as shown in Fig. 5-15B. It represents the first four sequences of an infinite tree, with nodes spaced n digits apart and with $2k$ branches leaving each node. Each branch is an n-digit code block that corresponds to a specific k-digit message block. Any code word sequence is represented as a path through the tree. For example, the encoded sequence for the previous

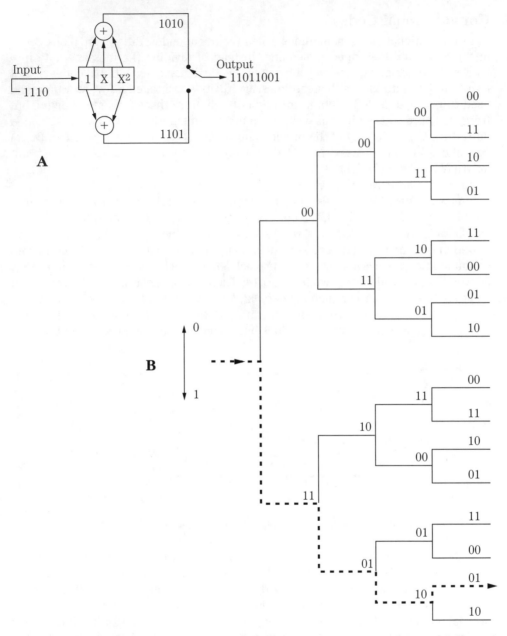

5-15 An example of convolutional encoding. A. Convolutional encoder with $k = 3$ and $r = \frac{1}{2}$. B. Convolutional code tree diagram. _{Viterbi}

encoder example can be traced through the tree. If the input bit is a 0, the code symbol is obtained by going up to the next tree branch; if the input is a 1, the code symbol is obtained by going down. The input message thus dictates the path through the tree, each input digit giving one instruction. The sequence of selections at the nodes forms the output code word. From the previous example, the input 1110 generates the output path 11011001. Upon playback, the data is sequentially decoded and errors can be detected and recovered by comparing all possible transmitted sequences to those actually received. The received sequence is compared to transmitted sequences, branch by branch. The decoding path through the tree is guided by the algorithm, to find the transmitted sequence that most likely gave rise to the received sequence.

Another convolutional code, suggested by Toshi Doi, is shown in Fig. 5-16. Here, the encoder uses four delays, each with a duration of one word. Parity words are generated after every four data words, and each parity word has encoded information derived from the previous eight data words. The constraint length of the code is 14. Convolutional codes are often inexpensive to implement, and perform well under high error conditions. One disadvantage of convolutional codes is error propagation; an error that cannot be fully corrected generates syndromes reflecting this error, and this can introduce errors in subsequent decoding.

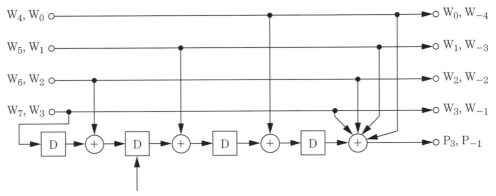

$$P_0 = W_0 + W_1 + W_2 + W_3 + W_{-4} + W_{-7} + W_{-10} + W_{-13}$$
$$P_4 = W_4 + W_5 + W_6 + W_7 + W_0 + W_{-3} + W_{-6} + W_{-9}$$
$$P_8 = W_8 + W_9 + W_{10} + W_{11} + W_4 + W_1 + W_{-2} + W_{-5}$$
$$P_{12} = W_{12} + W_{13} + W_{14} + W_{15} + W_8 + W_5 + W_2 + W_{-1}$$
$$P_{18} = W_{16} + W_{17} + W_{18} + W_{19} + W_{12} + W_9 + W_6 + W_3$$

5-16 An example of a convolutional code encoder, generating one check word for every four data words. Doi

Interleaving

Error correction depends on an algorithm's ability to efficiently use redundant data to reconstruct invalid data. When the error is sustained, as in the case of a burst error, both the data and the redundant data are lost, and correction becomes difficult or impossible. To overcome this, data is interleaved or dispersed through the data stream prior to storage or transmission. If a burst error occurs, it damages a continuous section of data. However, upon playback the bit stream is de-interleaved; thus, the data is returned to its original sequence and the errors are distributed through the bit stream. With valid data and parity now surrounding the damaged data, the algorithm is better able to reconstruct the damaged data, using valid data. Figure 5-17 shows an example of interleaving and de-interleaving, with a burst error occurring during storage or transmission. Following de-interleaving, the errors have been dispersed, facilitating error correction.

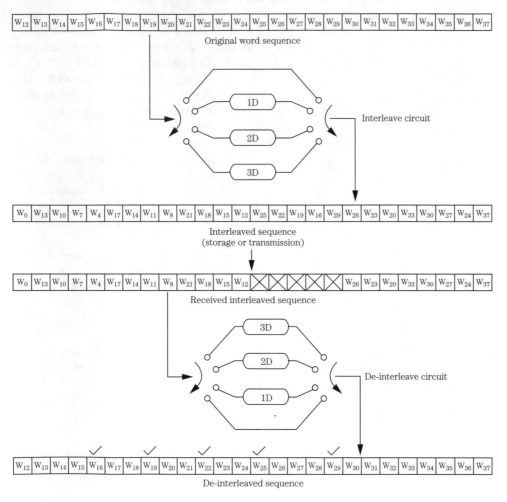

5-17 Zero-, one-, two-, and three-word delays perform interleaving and de-interleaving for error dispersion prior to correction. Doi

Interleaving provides an important advantage. Without interleaving, the amount of redundancy would be dictated by the size of the largest correctable burst error. With interleaving, the largest error that can occur in any block is limited to the size of the interleaved sections. Thus, the amount of redundancy is determined not by burst size, but by the size of the interleaved section. Simple delay interleaving effectively disperses data. Many block checksums work properly if there is only one word error per block. A burst error violates this rule; however, interleaved and de-interleaved data can very well result in one erroneous word in a given block. Thus, interleaving greatly increases burst error correctability of block codes. Bit interleaving accomplishes much the same purpose as block interleaving: it permits burst errors to be handled as shorter burst errors or random errors. Any interleaving process requires a buffer long enough to hold the distributed data during both interleaving and de-interleaving.

Cross-Interleaving

Interleaving might be inadequate when burst errors are accompanied by random errors. Although the burst is scattered, the random errors add additional errors in a given word, perhaps overloading the correction algorithm. One solution is to generate two correction codes, separated by an interleave and delay. When block codes are arranged in rows and columns two-dimensionally, the code is called a product code (or cross word code). The minimum distance is the product of the distances of each code. When two block codes are separated by both interleaving and delay, cross-interleaving results. In other words, a cross-interleave code comprises two (or more) block codes assembled with a convolutional structure, as shown in Fig. 5-18. The method is extremely efficient because the syndromes from one code can be used to point to errors, which are corrected by the other code. Because error location is known, correctability is enhanced. For example, a random error is corrected by the interleaved code, and a burst error is corrected after de-interleaving. When

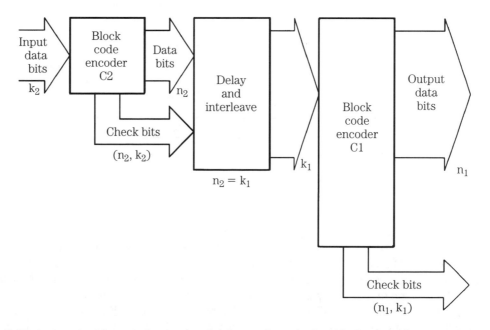

5-18 A cross-interleave code encoder. Syndromes from the first block are used as error pointers in the second block. In the CD format, $k_2 = 24$, $n_2 = 28$, $k_1 = 28$, and $n_1 = 32$. In the DASH format, $k_2 = 6$, $n_2 = 7$, $k_1 = 7$, and $n_1 = 8$. In both cases, the C_1 and C_2 codes are Reed-Solomon codes.

both codes are single erasure correcting codes, the resulting code is known as a cross-interleave code (CIC). For compact discs, Reed-Solomon codes are used and the algorithm is known as the Cross-Interleave Reed-Solomon code (CIRC).

An example of a CIC encoder suggested by Toshi Doi is shown in Fig. 5-19. The delay units produce interleaving, and the modulo 2 adders generate single erasure correcting codes. Two parity words (P and Q) are generated, and with two single erasure codes, errors are efficiently corrected. Triple-word errors can be corrected; however, four-word errors produce double-word errors in all four of the generated sequences, and correction is impossible. The CIC enjoys the high performance of a convolutional code but without error propagation, because any uncorrectable error in one sequence always becomes a one-word error in the next sequence and thus can be easily corrected. The stationary head DASH format uses a CIC code.

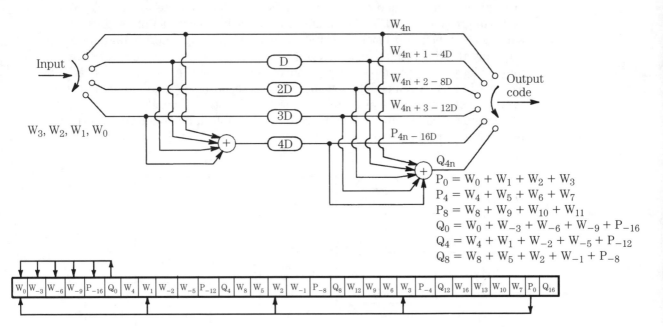

$$P_0 = W_0 + W_1 + W_2 + W_3$$
$$P_4 = W_4 + W_5 + W_6 + W_7$$
$$P_8 = W_8 + W_9 + W_{10} + W_{11}$$
$$Q_0 = W_0 + W_{-3} + W_{-6} + W_{-9} + P_{-16}$$
$$Q_4 = W_4 + W_1 + W_{-2} + W_{-5} + P_{-12}$$
$$Q_8 = W_8 + W_5 + W_2 + W_{-1} + P_{-8}$$

5-19 An example of a CIC encoder and its output sequence. Doi

The cross-interleave encoder selected for the EIAJ video rotary head format, shown in Fig. 5-20, uses a double erasure correction code, interleaving, and CRCC for pointers. The correction code used is the B-adjacent code with a minimum distance of three. The B-adjacent code is a maximum distance separable code; its Hamming distance is defined to be $m + 1$, where m is the number of parity words in the block code. The P and Q parity words are generated for every six data words. P is the modulo 2 addition of all data words and Q is a weighted summation. Following interleaving, CRCC is encoded for the resultant eight words; this forms data blocks for each horizontal video line. The double erasure code can correct two words per block prior to delay. The recorded code can be corrected for burst errors up to thirty-two blocks long. This algorithm can correct up to 4096 bits in a rotary head tape recording.

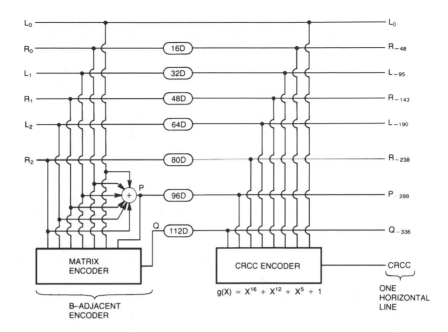

5-20 The EIAJ encoder used in rotary head recorders showing interleaving and dual code structure.

Reed-Solomon Codes

Reed-Solomon codes were devised by Irving Reed and Gustave Solomon in 1960, in MIT's Lincoln Laboratories. They are an example of an important subclass of codes known as q-ary *BCH* (Bose-Chaudhuri-Hocquenghem) codes. BCH codes are a subclass of Hamming codes. Reed-Solomon codes are cyclic codes that are multiple-error correcting codes. They define code symbols from n-bit bytes, with code words consisting of $2^n - 1$ of the n-bit bytes. If the error pattern affects s bytes in a code word, $2s$ bytes are required for error correction. Thus $2^n - 1 - 2s$ bytes are available for data. When combined with cross-interleaving, Reed-Solomon codes are very effective for audio applications.

Reed-Solomon codes exclusively use polynomials derived using finite field mathematics known as Galois Fields to encode and decode block data. Galois Fields, named in honor of the extraordinary and tormented mathematical genius Evariste Galois (who devised them before his death in a duel at age 20), comprise a finite number of elements with special properties. Either multiplication or addition can be used to combine elements, and the result of adding or multiplying two elements is always a third element contained in the field. For example, when an element is raised to higher powers, the result is always another element in the field. Such fields generally only exist when the number of elements is a prime number or a power of a prime number. In addition, there exists at least one element called a primitive such that every other element can be expressed as a power of this element.

For error correction, Galois Fields yield a highly structured code, which ultimately simplifies implementation of the code. In Reed-Solomon codes, data is formed into symbols that are members of the Galois Field used by the code; RS codes are thus nonbinary BCH codes. They achieve the greatest possible minimum distance for the specified input and output block lengths. The minimum distance, the number of nonbinary symbols in which the sequences differ, is given by: $d = n - k + 1$. The size of the Galois Field, which determines the number of symbols in the code, is based on the number of bits comprising a symbol; 8-bit symbols are commonly used. The code thus contains $2^8 - 1$ or 255 eight-bit symbols. A primitive polynomial often used in $GF(2^8)$ systems is $x^8 + x^4 + x^3 + x^2 + 1$.

As with some other codes, Reed-Solomon codes yield polynomials with roots that locate errors, and provide syndromes to correct errors. For example, the code can use the input word to generate two types of parity, P and Q. The P parity can be a modulo 2 sum of the symbols. The Q parity multiplies each input word by a different power of the GF primitive element. If one symbol is erroneous, the P parity gives a nonzero syndrome S_1. The Q parity yields a syndrome S_2; its value is S_1, raised to a power—the value depending on the position of the error. By checking this relationship between S_1 and S_2, the RS code can locate the error. When a placed symbol is in error, S_2 would equal S_1 multiplied by the element raised to the placed power. Correction is performed by adding S_1 to the designated location. This correction is shown in the example below. Alternatively, if the position of two errors is already known through detection pointers, then two errors in the input can be corrected. For example, if the second and third symbols are flagged, then S_1 is the modulo 2 sum of both errors, and S_2 is the sum of the errors multiplied by the second and third powers.

To illustrate the operation of a Reed-Solomon code, consider a $GF(2^3)$ code comprising 3-bit symbols. In this code, α is the primitive element and is the solution to the equation:

$$F(x) = x^3 + x + 1 = 0$$

such that an irreducible polynomial can be written:

$$\alpha^3 + \alpha + 1 = 0$$

where + indicates modulo 2 addition. The elements can be represented as ordinary polynomials:

$$
\begin{aligned}
0\,0\,0 &= &&= 0 \\
0\,0\,1 &= &+ 1 &= 1 \\
0\,1\,0 &= &+ x\quad &= x \\
0\,1\,1 &= &+ x + 1 &= x + 1 \\
1\,0\,0 &= x^2 &&= x^2 \\
1\,0\,1 &= x^2 &+ 1 &= x^2 + 1 \\
1\,1\,0 &= x^2 + x &&= x^2 + x \\
1\,1\,1 &= x^2 + x + 1 &&= x^2 + x + 1
\end{aligned}
$$

Because $\alpha = x$, using the properties of the Galois Field and modulo 2 (where $1 + 1 = \alpha + \alpha = \alpha^2 + \alpha^2 = 0$) we can create a logarithmic representation of the irreducible polynomial elements in the field where the bit positions indicate polynomial positions:

$$0 \qquad\qquad\qquad\qquad = 000$$
$$1 \qquad\qquad\qquad\qquad = 001$$
$$\alpha \qquad\qquad\qquad\qquad = 010$$
$$\alpha^2 \qquad\qquad\qquad\qquad = 100$$
$$\alpha^3 = \alpha + 1 \qquad\qquad\qquad = 011$$
$$\alpha^4 = \alpha \cdot \alpha^3 = \alpha(\alpha + 1) = \alpha^2 + \alpha \qquad = 110$$
$$\alpha^5 = \alpha^2 + \alpha + 1 \qquad\qquad = 111$$
$$\alpha^6 = \alpha \cdot \alpha^5 = \alpha(\alpha^2 + \alpha + 1) = \alpha^3 + \alpha^2 + \alpha$$
$$\qquad = \alpha + 1 + \alpha^2 + \alpha = \alpha^2 + 1 \qquad = 101$$
$$\alpha^7 = \alpha(\alpha^2 + 1) = \alpha^2 + \alpha = \alpha + 1 + \alpha = 1 = 001 = 1$$

In this way, all possible 3-bit symbols can be expressed as elements of the field $(0, 1 = \alpha^7, \alpha, \alpha^2, \alpha^3, \alpha^4, \alpha^5,$ and $\alpha^6)$ where α is the primitive element (010). Elements can be multiplied by simply adding exponents, always resulting in another element in the Galois Field. For example:

$$\alpha \cdot \alpha \quad = \alpha^2 = (010)(010) = 100$$
$$1 \cdot \alpha^2 \quad = \alpha^2 = (001)(100) = 100$$
$$\alpha^2 \cdot \alpha^3 = \alpha^5 = (100)(011) = 111$$

The complete product table for this example GF(2^3) code is shown in Fig. 5-21; the modulo α^7 results can be seen. For example, $\alpha^4 \cdot \alpha^6$ is α^{10}, or α^3. Using the irreducible polynomials and product table, the correction code can be constructed. Suppose that A, B, C, and D are data symbols and P and Q are parity symbols. The RS code will satisfy the following equations:

$$A + B + C + D + P + Q = 0$$
$$\alpha^6 A + \alpha^5 B + \alpha^4 C + \alpha^3 D + \alpha^2 P + \alpha^1 Q = 0$$

Using the devised product laws, we can solve these equations to yield:

$$P = \alpha^1 A + \alpha^2 B + \alpha^5 C + \alpha^3 D$$
$$Q = \alpha^3 A + \alpha^6 B + \alpha^4 C + \alpha^1 D$$

For example, given the irreducible polynomial table, if:

$$A = 001 = 1$$
$$B = 101 = \alpha^6$$
$$C = 011 = \alpha^3$$
$$D = 100 = \alpha^2$$

we can solve for P and Q using the product table:

$$P = \alpha^1 \cdot 1 + \alpha^2 \cdot \alpha^6 + \alpha^5 \cdot \alpha^3 + \alpha^3 \cdot \alpha^2 = \alpha + \alpha + \alpha + \alpha^5$$
$$= \alpha + \alpha + \alpha + (\alpha^2 + \alpha + 1) = \alpha^2 + 1 = 101$$
$$Q = \alpha^3 \cdot 1 + \alpha^6 \cdot \alpha^6 + \alpha^4 \cdot \alpha^3 + \alpha^1 \cdot \alpha^2 = \alpha^3 + \alpha^5 + 1 + \alpha^3$$
$$= (\alpha + 1) + (\alpha^2 + \alpha + 1) + 1 + (\alpha + 1) = \alpha^2 + \alpha = 110$$

Bits		000	001	010	011	100	101	110	111
Elements		0	1	α	α^3	α^2	α^6	α^4	α^5
000	0	0	0	0	0	0	0	0	0
001	$\alpha^7 = 1$	0	1	α	α^3	α^2	α^6	α^4	α^5
010	α	0	α	α^2	α^6	α^3	1	α^5	α^6
011	α^3	0	α^3	α^4	α^6	α^5	α^2	1	α
100	α^2	0	α^2	α^3	α^5	α^4	α	α^6	1
101	α^6	0	α^6	1	α^2	α	α^5	α^3	α^4
110	α^4	0	α^4	α^5	1	α^6	α^3	α	α^2
111	α^5	0	α^5	α^6	α	1	α^4	α^2	α^3

5-21 The product table for a GF(2^3) code with F(x) = $x^3 + x + 1$ and primitive element 010.

Thus:

$$P = 101 = \alpha^6$$
$$Q = 110 = \alpha^4$$

Errors in received data can be corrected using syndromes, where a prime (') indicates received data:

$$S_1 = A' + B' + C' + D' + P' + Q'$$
$$S_2 = \alpha^6 A' + \alpha^5 B' + \alpha^4 C' + \alpha^3 D' + \alpha^2 P' + \alpha^1 Q'$$

If each possible error pattern is expressed by E_i, we write the following:

$$S_1 = E_A + E_B + E_C + E_D + E_P + E_Q$$

$$S_2 = \alpha^6 E_A + \alpha^5 E_B + \alpha^4 E_C + \alpha^3 E_D + \alpha^2 E_P + \alpha^1 E_Q$$

If there is no error, then $S_1 = S_2 = 0$.
If symbol A' is erroneous, $S_1 = E_A$ and $S_2 = \alpha^6 S_1$.
If symbol B' is erroneous, $S_1 = E_B$ and $S_2 = \alpha^5 S_1$.
If symbol C' is erroneous, $S_1 = E_C$ and $S_2 = \alpha^4 S_1$.
If symbol D' is erroneous, $S_1 = E_D$ and $S_2 = \alpha^3 S_1$.

If symbol P' is erroneous, $S_1 = E_P$ and $S_2 = \alpha^2 S_1$.
If symbol Q' is erroneous, $S_1 = E_Q$ and $S_2 = \alpha^1 S_1$.

In other words, an error results in nonzero syndromes; the value of the erroneous symbols can be determined by the difference of the weighting between S_1 and S_2. The ratio of weighting for each word is different thus single word error correction is possible. Double erasures can be corrected because there are two equations with two unknowns. For example, if this data is received:

$$A' = 001 = 1$$

$$B' = 101 = \alpha^6$$

$$C' = 001 = 1 \text{ (erroneous)}$$

$$D' = 100 = \alpha^2$$

$$P' = 101 = \alpha^6$$

$$Q' = 110 = \alpha^4$$

We can calculate the syndromes (recalling that $1 + 1 = \alpha + \alpha = \alpha^2 + \alpha^2 = 0$):

$$S_1 = 1 + \alpha^6 + 1 + \alpha^2 + \alpha^6 + \alpha^4 = 1 + (\alpha^2 + 1) + 1 + \alpha^2 + (\alpha^2 + 1) + (\alpha^2 + \alpha)$$
$$= \alpha = 010$$

$$S_2 = \alpha^6 \cdot 1 + \alpha^5 \cdot \alpha^6 + \alpha^4 \cdot 1 + \alpha^3 \cdot \alpha^2 + \alpha^2 \cdot \alpha^6 + \alpha^1 \cdot \alpha^4 = \alpha^6 + \alpha^4 + \alpha^4 + \alpha^5 + \alpha + \alpha^5$$
$$= (\alpha^2 + 1) + (\alpha^2 + \alpha) + (\alpha^2 + \alpha) + (\alpha^2 + \alpha + 1) + \alpha + (\alpha^2 + \alpha + 1)$$
$$= \alpha^2 + \alpha + 1 = \alpha^5 = 111$$

Because $S_2 = \alpha^4 S_1$ (that is, $\alpha^5 = \alpha^4 \cdot \alpha$), symbol C' must be erroneous and because $S_1 = E_C = 010$, $C = C' + E_C = 001 + 010 = 011$, thus correcting the error.

In practice, the polynomials used in CIRC are:

$$P = \alpha^6 A + \alpha^1 B + \alpha^2 C + \alpha^5 D + \alpha^3 E$$

$$Q = \alpha^2 A + \alpha^3 B + \alpha^6 C + \alpha^4 D + \alpha^1 E$$

and the syndromes are:

$$S_1 = A' + B' + C' + D' + E' + P' + Q'$$

$$S_2 = \alpha^7 A' + \alpha^6 B' + \alpha^5 C' + \alpha^4 D' + \alpha^3 E' + \alpha^2 P' + \alpha^1 Q'$$

Because Reed-Solomon codes are particularly effective in correcting burst errors, they are highly successful in digital audio applications when coupled with error detection pointers such as CRCC, and interleaving. For example, a double erasure correction RS code (minimum distance of three) with CRCC pointers is used in the PD stationary head tape format.

Cross-Interleave Reed-Solomon Code

A quadruple erasure (double error) correction RS code (minimum distance of five), known as the cross-interleave Reed-Solomon code (CIRC) has been adopted for the compact disc. CIRC applies Reed-Solomon codes sequentially, with an interleaving process between C2 and C1 encoding. Encoding carries data through the C2 encoder, then the C1 encoder. Decoding reverses the process.

C2 is a (28,24) code, that is, the encoder inputs 24 symbols, and outputs 28 symbols (including four parity symbols). C1 is a (32,28) code; the encoder inputs 28 symbols, and 32 symbols (with four parity symbols) are output. In both cases, because 8-bit bytes are used, the size of the Galois Field is $GF(2^8)$; the calculation is based on the primitive polynomial: $x^8 + x^4 + x^3 + x^2 + 1$. Minimum distance is five. Up to four symbols can be corrected if the error location is known, and two symbols can be corrected if the location is not known.

Using a combination of interleaving and parity to make the data more robust against errors encountered during storage, the data is encoded before being placed on the disc, then decoded upon playback. The CIRC encoding algorithm is shown in Fig. 5-22; the similarity to the general structure shown in Fig. 5-18 is evident. Using this encoding algorithm, symbols from the audio signal are cross-interleaved, and RS encoding stages generate P and Q parity symbols.

The CIRC encoder accepts 24 eight-bit symbols. An interleaving stage assists interpolation. A two-symbol delay is placed between even and odd samples. Because even samples are delayed by two blocks, interpolation is possible where two uncorrectable blocks occur. The symbols are scrambled to separate even and odd-numbered symbols; this process assists concealment. The 24-byte parallel word is input to the C2 encoder that produces four symbols of Q parity. Q parity is designed to correct one erroneous symbol, or up to four erasures in one word. By placing the parity symbols in the center of the block, the odd/even distance is increased. This permits interpolation over the largest possible burst error.

In cross-interleaving, 28 symbols are delayed by differing periods. These periods are integer multiples of four blocks. This convolutional interleave stores one C2 word in 28 different blocks, stored over a distance of 109 blocks. In this way, the data array is crossed in two directions. Because the delays are long and of unequal duration, correction of burst errors is facilitated. Twenty-eight symbols (from 28 different C2 words) are input to the C1 encoder, producing four P parity symbols. P parity is designed to correct single-symbol errors and detect and flag double and triple errors for Q correction.

An interleave stage delays alternate symbols by one symbol. This odd/even delay spreads the output symbols over two data blocks. In this way, random errors cannot corrupt more than one symbol in one word even if there are two erroneous adjacent symbols in one block. The P and Q parity symbols are inverted to provide nonzero P and Q symbols with zero data. Thirty-two 8-bit symbols leave the CIRC encoder.

The error processing must be decoded each time the disc is played to de-interleave the data, and perform error detection and correction. When a Reed-Solomon decoder receives a data block (consisting of the original data symbols plus the parity symbols) it uses the received data to recalculate the parity symbols. If the recalculated parity symbols match the received parity symbols, the block is assumed to be error free. If they differ, the difference syndromes are used to locate the error. Erroneous words are flagged, for example, as being correctable, uncorrectable, or possibly correctable. Analysis of the flags determines whether the errors are to be corrected by the correction code, or passed on for interpolation. The complete CIRC decoding process is shown in Fig. 5-23.

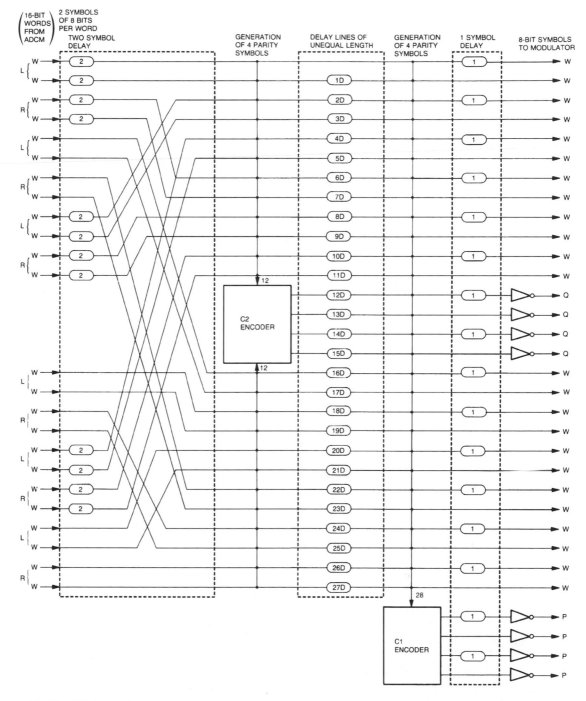

5-22 The CIRC encoding algorithm.

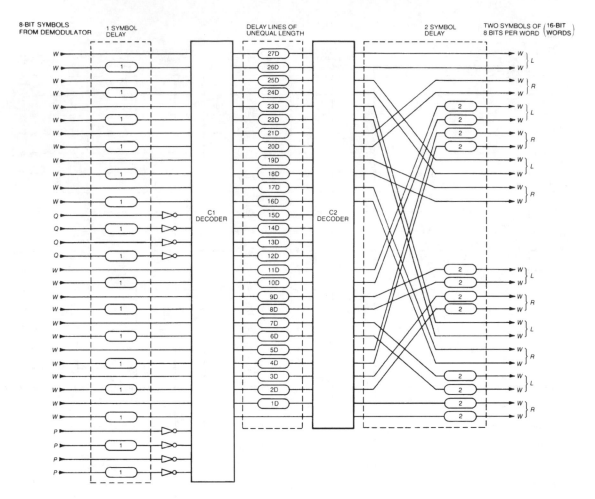

5-23 The CIRC decoding algorithm.

A frame of thirty-two 8-bit symbols is input to the CIRC decoder; twenty-four are audio symbols, and eight are parity symbols. Odd-numbered symbols are passed through a one-symbol delay. In this way, even-numbered symbols in a frame are de-interleaved with the odd-numbered symbols in the next frame. Audio symbols are restored to their original order and disc errors are scattered. This benefits C1 correction, especially for small errors in adjoining symbols. Following this de-interleaving, parity symbols are inverted.

Using four P parity symbols, the C1 decoder corrects random errors and detects burst errors. The C1 decoder can correct one erroneous symbol in each frame. If there is more than one erroneous symbol, the 28 data symbols are marked with an erasure flag and passed to the C2 decoder. Valid symbols are passed along unprocessed. The convolutional de-interleave between the decoders enables the C2 decoder to correct long burst errors. The frame input to C2 contains symbols from C1 decoded at different times; thus, symbols marked with an erasure flag are scattered. This assists the C2 decoder in correcting burst errors. Symbols without a flag are assumed error free, and are passed through unprocessed.

Given precorrected data, and help from de-interleaving, C2 can correct burst errors as well as random errors that C1 was unable to correct. Using four Q parity symbols, C2 can detect and correct single symbol errors and correct up to four symbols, as well as any symbols miscorrected by C1 decoding. C2 also can correct errors that might occur in the encoding process itself, rather than on the disc. When C2 cannot accomplish correction, for example, when more than four symbols are flagged, the 24 data symbols are flagged and passed on for interpolation. Final descrambling and delay completes CIRC decoding.

The success of CIRC error correction ultimately depends on the implementation of the algorithm. Generally, CIRC might provide correction of up to 3874 bits, corresponding to a track-length defect of 2.5 mm. Good concealment can extend to 13,282 bits, corresponding to an 8.7-mm defect, and marginal concealment can extend to approximately 15,500 bits.

The integrity of data stored on a CD and passing through a CIRC algorithm can be assessed through a number of error counts. A two-digit nomenclature specifies the number of erroneous symbols, and at which decoder they occur, respectively. Three error counts are measured at the output of the C1 decoder. The E11 count specifies the frequency of occurrence of single symbol (correctable) errors per second in the C1 decoder; E21 indicates the frequency of occurrence of double-symbol (correctable) errors in the C1 decoder; and E31 indicates the frequency of triple-symbol (uncorrectable) errors in the C1 decoder.

The block error rate (BLER) measures the number of frames of data that have at least one occurrence of uncorrected data at the C1 decoder input (E11 + E21 + E31); it is thus a measure of both correctable and uncorrectable errors at that decoding stage. BLER is specified as rate of errors per second. The CD standard sets a maximum of 220 BLER errors per second for audio discs; however, a well-manufactured disc will have a BLER of less than 50 (10 is often measured). A high BLER count often indicates poor pit geometry that disrupts the pickup's ability to read data, resulting in many random bit errors. The CD block rate is 7350 blocks per second; hence the maximum BLER value of 220 counts per second shows that 3% of frames contain a defect. This defines the acceptable (correctable) error limit; greater frequency might lead to audible faults. The BLER does not provide information on individual defects between 100 to 300 μm, because the BLER responds to defects the size of one pit. BLER is often quoted as a one-second actual value or as a sliding 10-second average across the disc, as well as the maximum BLER encountered during a single 10-second interval during the test.

There are three error counts at the C2 decoder. The E12 count indicates the frequency of occurrence of a single symbol (correctable) error in the C2 decoder measured in counts per second. A high E12 count is not problematic because one E31 error can generate up to 30 E12 errors due to interleaving. The E22 count indicates the frequency of double-symbol (correctable) errors in the C2 decoder. E22 errors are the worst correctable errors; the E22 count indicates that the system is close to producing an uncorrectable error; a CD-ROM with 15 E22 errors would be unacceptable even though the errors are correctable. A high E22 count can indicate localized damage to the disc, from manufacturing defect or usage damage. The E32 count indicates triple-symbol (uncorrectable) errors in the C2 decoder, or unreadable data in general; ideally, an E32 count should never occur on a disc. E32 errors are sometimes classified as noise interpolation (NI) errors; when an E32 error occurs, interpolation must be performed. If a disc has no E32 errors, all data is output accurately.

The E21 and E22 signals can be combined to form a burst error (BST) count. It counts the number of consecutive C2 block errors exceeding a specified threshold number. It generally indicates a large physical defect on the disc such as a scratch, affecting more than one block of data. For example, if there are 14 consecutive block errors and the threshold is set at seven blocks, two BST errors would be indicated. This count is often tabulated as a total number over an entire disc. A good quality control specification would not allow any burst errors (seven frames) to occur. In practice, a factory-fresh disc might yield BLER = 5, E11 = 5, E22 = 0, and E31 = 0. E32 uncorrectable errors are rarely found even in well-used discs.

Error-Correction Summary

Many types of error correction exist for many types of applications. Designers must judge correctability of random and burst errors, redundancy overhead, probability of misdetection, and maximum burst error lengths to be corrected or concealed, and cost of encoder and decoder. For digital audio, errors that cannot be corrected are concealed. However, a misdetected error often cannot be concealed, and this can result in a click in the audio output of the system. Error-correction designers must ensure that this does not happen under normal worst-case conditions. Other design criteria are set by the particular application; for example, open-reel digital tape recorders are susceptible to burst errors from fingerprints, but the compact disc is relatively tolerant of fingerprints because the transparent substrate places them out of focus to the optical pickup. Because of the varied nature of errors—some predictable and some, such as those produced by misaligned recorders and players, unpredictable—error-correction systems ultimately must use various techniques to guard against them. Delay, interleaving, parity, and cross-interleaving are all used to successfully correct most types of errors found in digital audio recordings.

Error Concealment

As noted, a theoretically perfect error detection and correction method could be devised in which all errors are completely supplanted with redundant data or calculated with complete accuracy. However, such a scheme would be impractical because of the data overhead and the cost of the encoder and decoder. A practical error-correction method balances those limitations against the probability of uncorrected errors, and allows severe errors to remain uncorrected. However, a subsequent circuit—an error-concealment system—compensates for those errors and ensures that they are not audible. Several error-concealment techniques, such as interpolation and muting, have been devised to accomplish this.

Generally, there are two kinds of uncorrectable errors output from correction algorithms. Some errors can be properly detected; however, the algorithm is unable to correct them. Other errors are not detected at all, or are miscorrected. The first type of error, detected but not corrected, can usually be concealed with properly designed concealment methods. However, undetected and miscorrected errors often cannot be concealed and might result in an audible click in the audio output. These types of error, often caused by simultaneous random and burst errors, must be minimized. Thus, the design strategy of the error-correction system aims to reduce undetected errors in the error-correction algorithm, then rely on the error-concealment methods to resolve detected but not corrected errors.

Interpolation

Following de-interleaving, most errors, even burst errors, are interspersed with valid data words. It is thus reasonable to use techniques in which surrounding valid data is used to calculate new data to replace the missing or uncorrected data. This technique works well, provided that errors are sufficiently dispersed and there is some correlation between data values. Fortunately, digital data comprising a musical selection can often undergo interpolation without it becoming audible. Interpolation techniques perform concealment with great success in digital audio recording because of the high correlation between sample points. Although it is nonintuitive, studies have shown that the time duration of an error does not overly affect perception of the error, as long as the interpolated samples are surrounded by valid data.

In its simplest form, interpolation holds the previous sample value and repeats it to cover the missing or incorrect sample. This is called zero-order or previous-value interpolation. In first-order interpolation, sometimes called linear-order interpolation, the erroneous sample is replaced with a new sample derived from the mean value of the previous and subsequent samples. In many digital audio systems, a combination of zero- and first-order interpolation is used. If consecutive sample errors occur in spite of interleaving, then previous-value interpolation is used to replace consecutive errors, but the final held sample's value is calculated from the mean value of the held and subsequent sample. If the errors are random, that is, valid samples surround the errors, then mean value calculations are used. One interpolation strategy is shown in Fig. 5-24. Other higher-order interpolation is sometimes used; nth-order interpolation uses a higher-order polynomial to calculate substituted data. In practice, third- and fifth-order interpolation are sometimes used. Clearly, any interpolation calculations must be accomplished quickly enough to maintain the data rate. The relative values of interpolation noise, as demonstrated by Toshi Doi, are shown in Fig. 5-25.

Muting

Muting is the simple process of setting the value of missing or uncorrected words to zero. This silence is preferable to the unpredictable sounds that can result from decoding incorrect data. Muting might be used in the case of uncorrected errors, which would otherwise cause an audible click at the output. The momentary increase

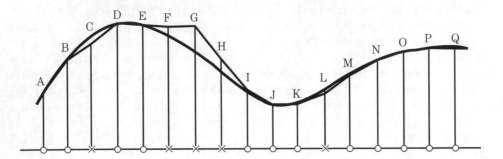

(Thick lines for analog input data. × is for error data)

Interpolation by maintenance of previous value

G = F(=E)

Interpolation by maintenance of mean value

$$C = \frac{1}{2}(B + D)$$

$$H = \frac{1}{2}(G + I) = \frac{1}{2}(E + I)$$

$$L = \frac{1}{2}(K + M)$$

5-24 Interpolation is used to conceal errors. For example, a previous value can be held, followed by calculation of the mean value.

in distortion from a brief mute might be imperceptible, but a click would typically be audible. Also, in the case of severe data damage or player malfunction, it is preferable to mute the data output. To minimize audibility of a mute, muting circuitry gradually attenuates the output signal's amplitude prior to a mute, and then gradually restores the amplitude afterward. For example, gain can be adjusted by multiplying successive samples by attenuation coefficients over a few milliseconds. Of course, gain reduction must begin prior to the error itself, to allow time for a smooth fade. This is easily accomplished by delaying all audio samples briefly and feeding the mute flag forward. Such muting for 1- to 4-ms durations cannot be perceived by the human ear. Concealment strategies are assisted when audio channels are processed independently, for example, by muting only one channel rather than both.

Duplication

One of the benefits of digital audio recording is the opportunity to copy recordings without the inevitable degradation of analog duplication. Although digital audio duplication can be lossless, its success depends on the success of error correction. Although error-correction methods provide completely correct data, error concealment does not. Under marginal circumstances, error-concealment techniques do in-

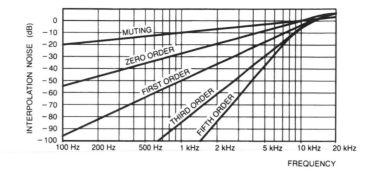

5-25 Noise characteristics for different interpolation methods (for 100-bit burst length, pure tone signals, and uncorrectable errors).

troduce audible errors into copied data. Thus, subsequent generations of digital copies could contain an accumulation of concealed errors not present in the original. As a result, errors must be corrected at their origin. Routine precautions of clean media, clean machine mechanisms, and proper interfacing are important with digital audio duplication, particularly when many generations of copying are anticipated. In practice, digital audio data can be copied with high reliability.

CHAPTER

Magnetic Tape Storage

Magnetic recording has been a mainstay for analog storage of audio signals for over 50 years. Its ability to read, write, and erase has made it unique among storage media. With the proliferation of computers and the parallel development of magnetic media for data storage, it is logical for digital audio data to be stored magnetically, using techniques pioneered by the computer industry. With digital storage (both magnetic and optical) the storage medium is no longer the limiting performance factor, as in analog systems. However, the large amount of data contained in even a short musical selection places great demands on even the most sophisticated data storage system. Magnetic tape is a highly effective form of digital audio storage, as exemplified by stationary and rotary head tape recorders. The DAT format is discussed in detail in chapter 7.

Recording Bandwidth

The bandwidth of a device measures the range of frequencies it is able to accommodate with an acceptable amplitude loss. In the case of an analog tape recorder, a bandwidth of 20 kHz (0 to 20 kHz) is adequate, because those audio frequencies are recorded directly on the tape, aided by a high-frequency bias signal. However, a digital tape recorder requires a much larger bandwidth; the highest frequency to be recorded on tape is much higher than the 20-kHz audio frequency. Specifically, a 20-kHz audio signal demands a sampling rate of 44.1 kHz, and when quantized with 16-bit words, the recorded signal consumes 44.1 kHz × 16 bits, or about 705 kbps (kilobits per second). With overhead for data such as synchronization and error correction, the highest frequency to be recorded might be 1 Mbps (megabits per second) for a monaural audio channel. (Error correction data increases the overall volume of data stored, but permits increased data density.) Thus, the recording bandwidth required of a digital tape recorder might be 50 times the bandwidth required of an analog recorder. Clearly, even with a high linear recording density, a lengthy magnetic tape is required for even modest digital audio recording time. Given professional digital multitrack recorders with 24, 32, or 48 audio channels, the problem is considerable. However, an analog tape recorder must attempt to linearly record a signal, but a digital recorder need not linearize the recording process. This allows a distorted recorded waveform, and greater storage density for digital audio data, but the mere problem of storing so many transitions remains difficult.

Digital Magnetic Tape

A magnetic tape is comprised of a plastic backing, such as polyester, coated with a thin layer of magnetic material, such as gamma ferric oxide (Fe_2O_3) or chromium dioxide (CrO_2). These materials are comprised of particles that are acicular (cigar-shaped); the former measures about 0.3×0.03 μm (micrometer), and the latter 0.5×0.04 μm. When tape is manufactured, the particles are physically aligned along the direction of tape travel; this increases packing density. Each particle exhibits a permanent magnetic pole structure that produces a constant magnetic field. The orientation of the magnetic field can be switched back and forth. When a tape is unrecorded, the magnetic fields of the particles have no net orientation, as shown in Fig. 6-1A. To record information, an external magnetic field orients the particles' magnetic fields according to the alignment of the applied field. The coercivity of the particles describes the strength of the external field that is needed to affect their orientation; further, the coercivity of the particles exhibits a Gaussian distribution in which a few particles are oriented by a weak applied field, and the number increases as the field is increased, until the tape saturates and an increase in the external field will no longer change net magnetization. In analog recording, the relative net alignment of the magnetic fields of the particles continuously represents the magnitude of the recorded signal; thus a continuously variable change in analog amplitude can be stored, as shown in Fig. 6-1B.

Saturation recording is used when storing binary data. The force of the external field is increased so that the magnetic fields in all the particles are oriented. When a bipolar waveform is applied, a saturated tape thus has two states of equal magnitude but opposite polarity. The write signal is a current that changes polarity at transitions in the channel bit stream. Signals from the write (record) head cause entire regions of particles to be oriented either positively or negatively, as shown in Fig. 6-1C. These transitions in magnetic polarity can represent transitions between 0 or 1 binary values. Unlike analog recording, a bias signal is not needed. During playback, the magnetic medium with its different pole-oriented regions passes before a read (reproduce) head, which detects the changes in orientation, as shown in Fig. 6-2. Each transition in recorded polarity causes the flux field in the read head to reverse, generating an output signal that reconstructs the write waveform. The physical spacing between transitions ultimately determines the recorded bandwidth. The strength of the net magnetic changes recorded on the medium determines the medium's robustness. A strong recorded signal is desired because it can be read with less chance of error. Saturation recording ensures the greatest possible net variation in orientation of domains; hence, it is robust.

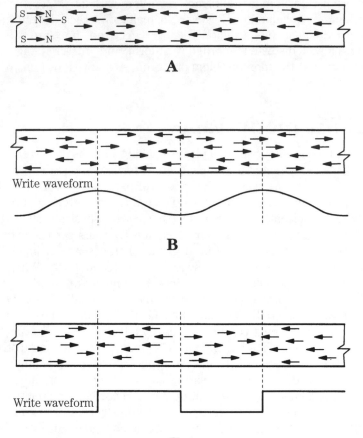

6-1 In magnetic tape recording, the polarity of magnetic fields of oxide particles are oriented relative to the amplitude and frequency of the recorded signal. A. Prior to recording, polarity of the magnetic fields is oriented with no net magnetization. B. Analog recording continuously varies the magnetic polarity of particles. C. In digital recording, data is represented with saturation recording.

Digital magnetic recording tape differs in several respects from that used in analog recording. Base thickness for professional analog tape is about 35 μm, and the oxide thickness is about 15 μm. (One micrometer equals 1 micron. Tape is sometimes specified in mils. One mil equals 0.001 inch, and 1 mil equals 25.40 micrometers.) A thick base is required to minimize print-through of an analog recorded signal across tape layers while it is wound. With digital tape, higher track densities and their short wavelengths require precise tape-to-head contact. Because print-through is nonexistent, this is achieved with more flexible and thus thinner tape, with base thickness of 20 μm and oxide thickness of 5 μm. For ana-

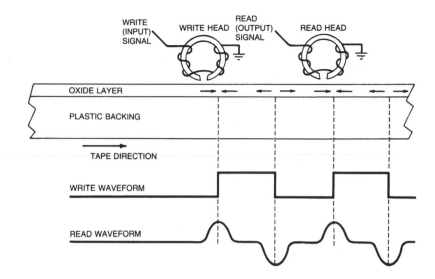

6-2 Magnetic recording and reproduction of binary signals is accomplished by simple flux reversals. The output pulses in the read waveform represent transitions in the recorded data.

log tape, magnetic particle type is selected for noise, print-through, and distortion characteristics. Coercivity, a measure of magnetic field strength needed to return a saturated tape to zero magnetization, is typically 300 to 400 oersteds. With digital tape, linear density, the number of bits that can be recorded linearly on tape, as measured in kbpi (kilobits per inch), is the overriding concern. To permit this density, digital audio tape uses particle types with higher magnetic energy levels, which accommodate higher packing densities. Cobalt is often used to modify the ferric oxide particles to achieve coercivity levels of 800 to 1000 oersteds. Metal particle tapes used in DAT, digital video, and some analog cassettes have a coercivity of 1500 oersteds. The binder used in digital audio tape is much more durable than that in analog tapes. This durability permits better adhesion of oxide to the backing, reducing rub-off and debris generation. This minimizes dropout, a major concern in digital tape recording.

Intersymbol Interference

Intersymbol interference, sometimes called peak shift, is a form of distortion generated by closely spaced flux transitions in a magnetic medium. If the bandwidth of the recording system is insufficient or the recording density is too great, interference between adjacent waveforms causes asymmetry in the reproduced waveform. Reproduction of data becomes difficult because timing errors are created. Intersymbol interference is due to a combination of limitations in the recording chain, both in heads and tape. Peak shift is shown in Fig. 6-3. In a recording system with sufficient bandwidth, the peaks of reproduced waveforms can be correctly identified. With insufficient bandwidth, adjacent waveforms are crowded and mutually interfere; the asymmetry shifts the waveform peaks apart. These broadened, incorrect waveforms

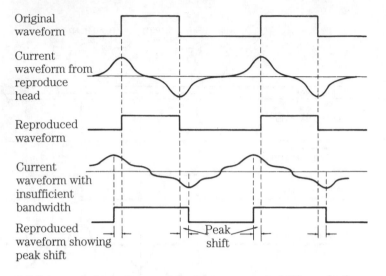

Original waveform

Current waveform from reproduce head

Reproduced waveform

Current waveform with insufficient bandwidth

Reproduced waveform showing peak shift

Peak shift

6-3 Intersymbol interference (also known as peak shift) results from insufficient recording bandwidth, and causes timing errors in playback.

cause data errors in playback. Peak shift can be addressed by filtering and precompensating the write waveform, but it ultimately dictates the maximum recording data density on a medium.

Longitudinal Magnetic Recording

Longitudinal recording is conventionally used in digital tape recording. With this method, the magnetic particles are aligned along the length of tape travel. Thus, the polarity transitions in the magnetically recorded waveform are longitudinal with tape travel (see Fig. 6-1). As data density increases, the recorded wavelength decreases; as the magnetic transitions come closer together, intersymbol interference might result, thus limiting data density for a given tape formulation. To obtain the high bandwidth required by digital recording, higher tape speeds can be used. Because of the resulting drawback of high tape consumption and short recording times, multiple tracks are often used. In other words, digital data from one audio channel can be written to multiple data tracks on the tape to achieve higher data density per area. The more tracks available for a signal, the greater the area density of the recording, as measured in kbpi^2. However, if many narrow tracks are created, the problem of tape defects becomes relatively greater. As the area density of the recording increases, error correction measures such as error-correction codes and interleaving must become more sophisticated. The designer's challenge is to maximize area density: too low a density dictates high tape consumption; too high a density requires additional error-correction data, which decreases the space available for audio data. A balance between the two must be achieved.

Thin-film heads can be used to increase the linear and area recording density of longitudinal tape recordings. These heads are made with the same techniques used

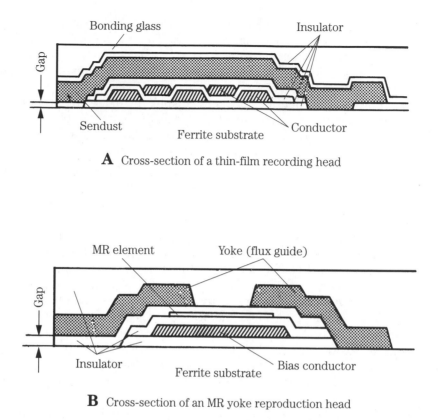

A Cross-section of a thin-film recording head

B Cross-section of an MR yoke reproduction head

6-4 Digital audio magnetic heads can use hybrid integrated circuit fabrication techniques for high track density with low crosstalk.

to manufacture hybrid integrated circuits, as shown in Fig. 6-4. Multiturn thin-film inductive record heads (IRH) are used for recording, and thin-film magneto-resistive heads (MRH) are used for playback. For recording efficiency, the IRH head uses a thick pole piece with good magnetic properties. To achieve desirable track density, a guard band of 15 microns or less can be used. Quartz insulators, permalloy flux guides, and gold conductors are deposited on a substrate. Following the wafer fabrication, the substrate is bonded to a top layer of glass and cut and lapped appropriately. At slow tape speeds, an inductive thin-film head does not have adequate playback ability. An MR read head is used because its output is independent of tape speed. The electrical resistance of the permalloy sensor varies according to the recorded signal; a bias current applied near the sensor is needed to linearize the effect. In a yoke-type head, the MR element is never exposed to the tape, thus promoting longer life and reliability. Crosstalk between tracks is extremely low, so the tracks can be placed closer together. Signal-to-noise ratio is better than for conventional heads. The head's dimensions are precise because of the photolithography technique used to produce it.

Even with technical improvements, there is a limit to the linear density achievable by longitudinal magnetic recording techniques. The amount of information that can be stored on a track is limited by the number of magnetic particles that can be placed along the magnetic coating. Because the particles are laid longitudinally, data density is limited by the length of the acicular particles, which in turn is limited by the particles' thickness. At densities of about 50 kbpi, the oxide layer coating is so thin that the net magnetic output is quite low. Hence, the signal-to-noise ratio of the medium, its ability to output an electrical signal above the background noise, is diminished. The only means to increase recording density per area is to increase the number of tracks recorded across an area. More sophisticated recording techniques, such as vertical recording, are used to increase data density.

Vertical Magnetic Recording

Vertical magnetic recording, sometimes called VR or perpendicular recording, provides high-density data recording. It differs from longitudinal recording in that the medium is magnetized perpendicularly to the surface, instead of along the surface, permitting greater density; this is shown in Fig. 6-5. To accomplish this, the particles are placed vertically in the magnetic medium, perpendicular to the surface. With longitudinal recording, the limiting factor for density is the length of the particles; however, with vertical recording, thinner particles yield greater densities. This is advantageous because greater density and thinner particles improve the length-to-thickness ratio, thus increasing the magnetic strength of the medium. In other words, higher densities are effectively more robust. Research has suggested that vertical recording might be capable of a density of 500 kbpi, ultimately limited by the thickness of the particles themselves. Adjacent dipole fields defeat self-demagnetization, thus permitting short wavelength recording.

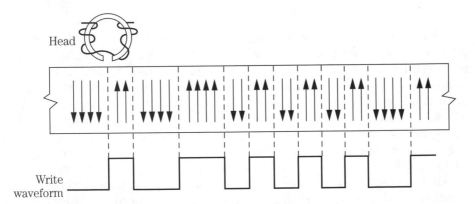

6-5 In vertical recording, the medium is magnetized perpendicularly to the magnetic surface, increasing data density.

To realize vertical recording, a suitable magnetic recording medium must be found. Media might use an alloy of chromium and cobalt, or barium ferrite producing crystals in the form of flat hexagonal plates. The crystals might measure 0.06 μm across the flat plate, with a thickness of 0.01 μm. The magnetic axis is perpendicular to the flat plate. Sputtering can be used to place the layer on the medium. This process places the medium in a vacuum chamber; the alloy such as chromium cobalt is used as a cathode and struck with positive ions, and molecules of chromium cobalt are transferred to the medium. Even more elaborate vertical mixed mode recording techniques use media with two layers. The first layer uses a high coercivity cobalt and chromium material to cause a polarization in the vertical direction. The second layer uses a highly permeable iron and nickel material, and provides a return path for the flux. Vertical recording systems can use a ring-head, monopole-head, or a double-head design. In this design, the secondary pole and Fe-Ni sublayer increase the longitudinal field gradient in the Co-Cr layer, as recorded by the primary pole.

Isotropic Recording

Isotropic recording takes advantage of the fact that an oxide layer can be magnetized in all directions. It records in longitudinal and vertical modes simultaneously. This is difficult to achieve because the two recorded fields might combine out of phase and thus produce an attenuated output signal. By matching head specifications to the properties of a tape formulation, it is possible to record those components in phase. The isotropic head is designed so that the vertical record field erases longitudinal fields near the tape surface. The tape is recorded internally with longitudinal fields, and with vertical fields at the tape surface. Longitudinal components within the magnetic coating and vertical components near the surface comprise the recorded signal. When the tape is played back, the fields are balanced so that the longitudinal field is dominant at low frequencies and reinforced by the vertical field at higher recorded frequencies. The small head gaps used in isotropic recording limit the recording region to a small area at the trailing edge of the gap; therefore, there is essentially no intersymbol interference.

Stationary Head Tape Recorders

Analog audio tape recorders have primarily used stationary head designs. Simplicity and low cost of design, long head life, ease of editing, and compact and rugged construction are inherent advantages for stationary head recorders. However, analog recorders traditionally were the weak link in the studio chain, inferior to microphones and mixing consoles, and particularly poor in generation copying. Stationary head digital recorders were introduced as plug-in replacements, immediately upgrading the weakest link into one of the strongest. However, digital audio recorders using stationary heads are challenged by the density of storage required. High tape speeds or multiple data tracks are mandated. Rotary head digital audio recorders (discussed in the next section), using transports derived from videotape recorders, provide greater bandwidth at the expense of more complicated mechanical design.

Stationary head recorders offer several important features. Stationary head tapes can be physically edited, allow punch-in and punch-out, and record and playback of separate channels for synchronous recording. These are all important functions in professional multichannel recording applications. The recording engineer often uses synchronous recording techniques; some channels are recorded while others are simultaneously replayed in time synchronization. This overdubbing technique is used extensively in multitrack recordings. Analog recorders uniquely use the record head to permit synchronous recording; previously recorded tracks are played back on some record head tracks while new tracks are simultaneously recorded on different record head tracks. If this was not the case, the performer would listen to the previous tracks from the reproduction head, and record new tracks at the record head. Because of the physical displacement between those heads, the new tracks would be delayed in relation to the previous tracks.

With digital tape recorders, it is difficult to combine record and reproduce functions in the same head. Thus, a digital tape recorder typically has two write (record) heads: one preceding the read (reproduce) head and used as a regular write head, and another following the read head, used for synchronous recording, as shown in Fig. 6-6. The write-1 and read heads provide read-after-write, and the read and write-2 heads are used for synchronous recording. The tracks played in synchronization are taken from the read head and delayed to coincide in time with the write head, as shown in Fig. 6-7. In this example, signals from previously recorded tracks 1, 2, and 3 are taken from the read head and delayed to coincide with the writing of track 4.

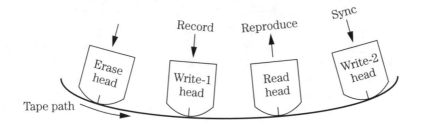

6-6 Head block for multichannel stationary-head digital tape recorder.

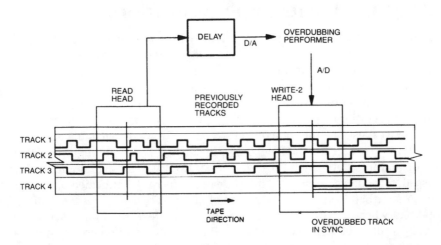

6-7 Synchronous overdub recording using delay element. Previously recorded tracks are delayed relative to the physical head spacing.

Individual audio channels are often modified within the context of a recording by punching in and punching out; that is, as a channel is played back it is placed in the record mode at a certain point in the music to record new material, then taken out of the record mode. The punch-in procedure for a digital tape recorder is shown in Fig. 6-8. Punch-out follows the reverse procedure. Crossfading is used to provide a smooth transition between the amplitudes of the two signals.

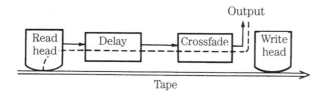

A Playback mode

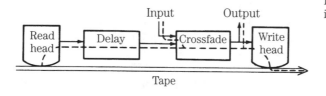

B Playback-record mode

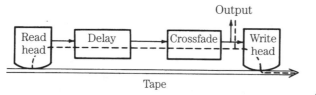

C Crossfade mode

6-8
A punch-in procedure with a digital audio recorder requires four intermediate steps including crossfading.

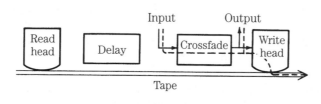

D Record mode

The recording engineer can manually edit analog tape with a razor blade and splicing tape. Razor blade splicing can be similarly accomplished on a stationary head digital tape recorder because crossfade and interpolation circuits form a signal bridge across the area of disrupted data. This interpolation is difficult because of the large interleaving times used in tape formats to add robustness to the data; interleaving distributes errors, but also distributes the damage caused by splicing. To help overcome this, samples are shuffled so that even-numbered and odd-numbered samples are separated further than the interleave length. During playback, the splice appears as two burst errors at different times, one affecting even samples, the other affecting odd samples, where they are more easily corrected and interpolated.

The DASH Format

The Digital Audio Stationary Head (DASH) format is an example of a reel-to-reel, stationary head, longitudinal digital audio recording format. It is used for 16-bit professional 24- and 48-channel tape recorders, as well as two-channel recorders. DASH provides high audio quality, robustness of recorded data, reasonable tape consumption, and interchangeability of tapes between recorders from different manufacturers. DASH supports synchronous and punch-in recording, read-after-write monitoring, and electronic and manual editing. In addition, DASH establishes a framework that accommodates recorders with different numbers of channels and recorded tracks, and tape speeds; as such, its specification is quite sophisticated.

The DASH standard covers a wide range of formats, from 2-channel to 48-channel tape recorders, using ¼ or ½-inch tape, respectively. In practice, the 24- and 48-channel recorders are the most widely used. Twenty-four channel recorders write 24 parallel data tracks in the normal-density DASH I format. Forty-eight channel recorders write 48 tracks in the double-density recording DASH II format. In the double-density configuration, the normal digital track pitch of 0.44 mm is halved to 0.22 mm; in either case, track width remains 0.17 mm. In this way, 24 additional tracks are layered between 24 existing audio tracks. Because the additional tracks are physically interleaved across the tape width, 48-channel recorders also can read tapes recorded on 24-channel recorders. In any case, four auxiliary tracks are always recorded; two on the outer tape edges, and two in the center. Pitch of auxiliary tracks is the same in both DASH I and II. Although ferrite heads can be used on 24-channel recorders, thin-film heads must be used for 48-track recorders. This reduces crosstalk, permitting higher track density.

The DASH format has three versions, based on tape speed: fast (F), medium (M), and slow (S). The actual tape speeds for these versions depend on the selection of a 48 or 44.1 kHz sampling rate. Specifically, at 48 kHz, the F, M, and S speeds are: 76.20 cm/s (30 ips), 38.10 cm/s (15 ips) and 19.05 cm/s (7.5 ips) respectively, and at 44.1 kHz the speeds are: 70.01 cm/s, 35.00 cm/s, and 17.50 cm/s. The number of tracks on the tape required to record one audio channel depends on the tape speed. For example, the 48-channel recorder can record 48 channels on 48 tracks at fast speed, or 24 channels on 48 tracks at medium speed. The 24-channel recorder always uses the fast speed with 24 channels on 24 tracks.

A two-channel recording on ¼-inch tape records 12 tracks on the tape: eight digital audio tracks and four auxiliary tracks placed on the outer tape edges. In the slow-speed version, all eight tracks are used for two audio channels. Each channel is divided into four subchannels at one-fourth the sampling frequency and recorded on four tracks. Rather than periodically subsample the data, the sequence of words is split, preserving the pattern of even/odd samples. This preserves manual editability while improving data recovery in case of a single track loss. A two-channel, medium-speed "Twin Recording" version of the ¼-inch DASH format provides improved cueing and editing performance, afforded by the higher tape speed compared to the low-speed version. In the twin version, because density and track format are unchanged, each audio channel is recorded twice on separate tracks; the odd/even shuffle of the first track is supplemented in the second track by an even/odd shuffle. In this way, each sample is recorded twice, separated on the tape by a distance of 1.53 inches (204 blocks). Splices can be played without interpolation. This also improves data reliability in the case of tape edge damage; however, errors occurring simultaneously on the tracks would negate this advantage. Playing time is cut in half, compared to the low-speed version.

As noted, all DASH tapes carry four auxiliary tracks. The control (CTL) track is a reference track for all digital audio tracks and is synchronous with the sampling rate; one sector corresponds to 48 audio samples. The CTL track contains a 4-bit synchronization pattern marking the beginning of sectors (groups of four data blocks). A 16-bit control word describes the sampling rate and type of format. A 28-bit sequential sector address provides an internal timecode; its word length is 28 bits, allowing encoding of a time duration beyond the duration of any tape. It can be used for autolocating or for locking recorders together. After the control track is recorded, all subsequent audio tracks are recorded synchronously to it. A 16-bit cyclic redundancy check code (CRCC) block provides sector error detection. The three other auxiliary tracks are used for stereo or mono cueing, auxiliary data, or conventional timecode.

A linear packing density is common to all versions and is independent of tape speed: 38.4 kbits/inch are recorded with 25.6 thousand flux reversals per inch, with a minimum wavelength of 78.2 mils and a maximum wavelength of 235 mils. The High-Density Modulation-1 (HDM-1) code is used throughout the DASH format; it is a run-length code, but does not use group coding. According to its encoding rules, the output waveform is defined as two periods per input bit. Transitions in the output waveform encode all data, and the output waveform is polarity free. The encoding rules ensure a minimum distance of three periods between transitions, and a maximum distance (which cannot occur twice in a row) of nine periods. Thus T_{min} is $1.5T$ and T_{max} is $4.5T$. The minimum wavelength is 50% longer than conventional codes such as MFM; density ratio is 1.5, thus greater recording density is permitted. The code has dc content.

Audio data is written as 18-word data blocks. Blocks consist of an 11-bit synchronization pattern, five auxiliary bits, twelve 16-bit audio words, four parity words, and a 16-bit CRCC word for error detection. The synchronization pattern is formed with a violation of the HDM-1 coding rules. At a 48-kHz sampling rate and fast tape speed, one block corresponds to 0.25 ms of audio. Consecutive blocks are written continuously on tape, without an interblock gap; when overdubbing, new blocks can partially overwrite old ones; error correction conceals this.

The Cross Interleave code (CIC) provides error correction in the DASH format. The theory of CIC is discussed in chapter 5. In the DASH format, even and odd input samples are separated, and given an odd/even delay of 204 blocks. All audio data is in 16-bit, two's complement form, MSB leading. Each channel is processed identically. An EXCLUSIVE-OR checksum P is derived from six audio samples. An EXCLUSIVE-OR checksum Q is derived from six interleaved audio samples and checksum P, using a cross-interleave delay of two blocks. Another interleaving delay is performed on six audio samples, and both checksums, using an interleave delay of seventeen blocks. A CRCC generation polynomial $x^{16} + x^{12} + x^5 + 1$ is computed. As a result, parity checks are made in two directions across a data matrix, and CRCC is made in a third direction.

During reproduction, retrieved data is checked against the CRCC word; a mismatch is interpreted as a high probability of an error. Blocks marked as erroneous, scattered because of interleaving, are de-interleaved and corrected with the Q checksum. Words are then re-interleaved to bring the P codewords into alignment, and then corrected with the P checksum, and de-interleaved. Full correction is obtained for errors up to 8640 consecutive bits, good concealment for 33,982 bits, and marginal concealment for 83,232 bits. Error correction in each version is independent of each track; if one of the tracks is damaged, the error-correction performance on the other tracks is not affected. Crossfading and interpolation are provided for punch-in and punch-out, tape splicing, and electronic editing.

DASH recorders have analog inputs and outputs, as well as AES3 digital input and output. An AES3 block structure with 16-bit words is preserved throughout the recorder so that 16-bit AES3 blocks enter and leave the recorder. Several proprietary DASH formats have been developed to record 20- and 24-bit audio samples. One variation of the DASH format can record 24-bit samples; a 48-track/16-bit machine is modified to record in 24-track/24-bit mode by placing additional data on alternate tracks. The most significant 16-bit tracks can be played (with truncation) on conventional machines. Another variation provides a 16-track/24-bit mode using a 24-track machine; tapes are not compatible with conventional DASH machines.

The DASH PCM-3324S Recorder

The PCM-3324S is an example of a digital 24-channel tape recorder using the DASH format. The recorder uses the DASH-F (fast speed) format in which normal track density permits recording of 24 digital tracks on a ½-inch tape, one track per channel. A PCM-3348 recorder can additionally record tracks 25–48 to an existing 24-track tape. Cue tracks use pulse-width modulation recording for a dynamic range of 60 dB. Electronic editing can be performed between two recorders; a built-in timecode generator provides SMPTE/EBU and standard film timecodes. Each track can have its own edit point and crossfade.

High-speed prestriping is permitted; prestriping is the open reel equivalent of formatting a computer disk or black bursting a videotape. It provides continuous timecode and an unbroken control track. Subsequent recording is done in an insert mode instead of assemble mode, as in video recording. The recorder will lock within one bit of timecode data—one eightieth of a video frame. With DASH sync, the machines synchronize to the sample clocks themselves.

With digital ping-pong, any or all of the 24 channels of digital audio can be copied simultaneously in real time to any other track position. This allows the user to take tapes recorded elsewhere and reassign tracks for easier grouping at the console or for conformity to other tapes used in assembling a project, thus simplifying the mix process. This bouncing is done with zero timing error and zero phase error. A 60-Mbit sound memory board stores 20 seconds of stereo audio (or 40 seconds of mono) in memory; start and end points can be trimmed and then dropped into selected tracks at selected cue points. It also can be triggered manually via the remote or with an audio signal. The sound memory also can be played in reverse. This memory also can be used on other recorders that are locked to the multitrack because the signal can appear on any analog or digital output even in input mode.

The PD Format

The ProDigi (PD) format is another example of a stationary head tape format for professional audio applications, supporting both 2-track and multichannel tape recorders. The PD format uses two tape widths: ¼ inch and 1 inch. The ¼-inch format has three modes: mode 1 records 16-bit words at high speed (15 ips with 48 kHz sampling); mode 2 records 16-bit words at low speed (7.5 ips with 48 kHz sampling); and mode 3 records 20-bit words so that longer AES3 blocks can be recorded. Sampling rates of both 44.1 and 48 kHz are supported, at corresponding tape speeds. Eight digital audio tracks and four auxiliary tracks are recorded in the two-channel PD format.

In the 1-inch format, 32 audio channels of 16-bit words are recorded. The 32 channels are divided into four groups and the eight channels in each group are recorded to eight tracks. Error correction redundancy is collected from each group and recorded to two additional P and Q tracks. Thus, 40 digital audio tracks are recorded, interleaved across the tape width. The tape also contains two cue tracks, two auxiliary data tracks, and a timecode track, for a total of 45 tracks. The cue tracks are recorded with pulse-width modulation to allow replay over a wide range of speeds.

A convolutional 2/4M channel code is used in the ¼-inch PD format; two data bits are modulated to four bits in which there are always two 0s between 1s, except where run length violations prevent it. The multitrack format uses a 4/6M block code; input groups of four or eight bits are modulated to six or nine bits. A Cross-Interleave Reed-Solomon code is used for error correction in both PD versions. The PD format supports punch-in and punch-out, manual and electronic editing, with interpolation and crossfading.

Note that digital tape is cheaper than analog tape and routine alignment is not necessary with a digital machine. With the introduction of mature technology stationary head multichannel digital recorders, it is possible to muse that the science of open reel audio tape recorders has reached its zenith, and will only be superseded by entirely different forms of data storage.

Rotary Head Tape Recorders

A digital audio signal requires storage of 1 Mbps per audio channel. A video recorder can achieve data transfer rates well beyond this using appropriate modulation and rotary head recording methods. Using digital audio processing, a stereo audio signal can be converted to a synchronized pseudo-video signal and recorded with a helical scan video transport. Upon playback, the signal is returned to a continuous digital audio bit stream and then to an analog waveform. Proprietary video-type transports or video recorders can be used to store the stereo digital audio data. In modular digital multitracks, video-type transports are used to record multiple channels of digital audio signals using proprietary track formats; binary channel codes are written directly to tape thus pseudo-video converters are not used. Multiple recorders can be synchronized to create large multichannel formats.

Operation of a Videotape Recorder

The information normally recorded on videotape represents pixels, the points that comprise a video image. However, a processor can be used to encode audio signals into a video format, so that a videotape recorder (VTR) can store digital audio signals. In addition, video-type transports can be used for multichannel audio recording. To understand the limitations and opportunities of these methods, the operation of video viewing and recording must first be examined. As shown in Fig. 6-9, a television picture is drawn on a cathode ray tube by a scanning process. Hundreds of scan lines constitute the video image—525 in the NTSC (National Television Systems Committee) standard and 625 in the PAL/SECAM (phase-alteration line/sequential-and-memory) standard. Starting in the upper left corner of the screen, the scanning spot moves horizontally across the screen, illuminating each of the pixels of red, blue, and green phosphorus with correct brightness and color information. Then in horizontal flyback mode, the spot returns in a blanked fashion to begin another scanning line. To reduce flicker, interlacing is used to trace alternate scanning lines; that is, the odd field is illuminated, then the spot returns to the top of the screen in the vertical blanking interval, and the even field is illuminated. Two fields make one complete video picture. Depending on the standard, this process repeats 29.97 (NTSC) or 25 (PAL/SECAM) times per second. As the information controlling the brightness and color changes, the display on the screen changes to effect a moving image. The time needed to scan one line (and return) is called a horizontal interval (H), and the time to scan from the top of the screen to the bottom (and return) is called a vertical interval (V). The actual video signal recorded on tape closely follows this format and is grouped in discontinuous parts, separated by horizontal and vertical retrace points, as shown in Fig. 6-10.

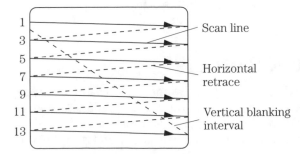

6-9
Television screen picture scanning. Even/odd horizontal lines are interlaced.

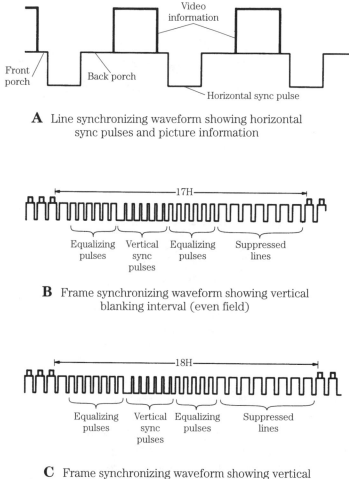

A Line synchronizing waveform showing horizontal
sync pulses and picture information

B Frame synchronizing waveform showing vertical
blanking interval (even field)

C Frame synchronizing waveform showing vertical
blanking interval (odd field)

6-10 Television frame synchronization waveforms.

A video signal requires a high-bandwidth recording medium. Video recorders meet the bandwidth requirement with a high head-to-tape speed. A rotary drum is used with a technique called helical scanning. Two or more video heads are positioned oppositely on a cylindrical drum; because the cylinder rotates at high speed (for example, 1800 rpm), linear tape speed can be slow (for example, ½ ips). The tape is wrapped across the drum, as shown in Fig. 6-11A. Using this relatively simple device, analog and digital video signals can be recorded, and data transfer rates can easily exceed the bandwidth required for a stereo digital audio recording, and can support eight (or more) channels of digital audio. Because the tape is guided past the heads at an angle, each recorded track is placed diagonally across the tape width, as shown in Fig. 6-11B. Each head lays down a track on the tape, alternating between even and odd fields. The discontinuities between tracks mark the vertical re-

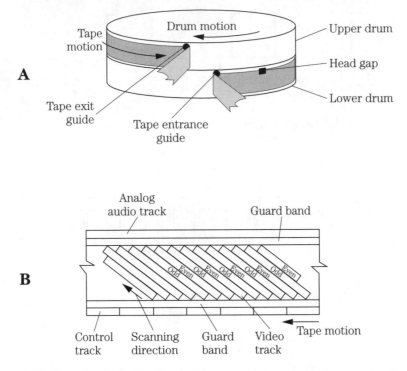

6-11 View of helical scan drum with wrapped tape, and video scan tracks recorded to tape. A. Tape transport for helical scanning in videocassette recorder. B. Recorded pattern of videocassette recorder.

trace points. Thus, the video signal for one vertical period is recorded on each video track. The fields are recorded discontinuously, but the tape is wrapped around the drum so the fields are recorded with the same synchronization as they appear on the screen. There is a guard track between video tracks in the ¾-inch format; however, tracks are recorded side by side in other formats such as ½-inch consumer videocassette recorders. This necessitates the use of a tracking control for proper alignment. Both the guard band and tracking control minimize the effects of variations in the manufacturing specifications of tape, which can cause misalignment between tape head and recorded tracks. A separate fixed head can record a longitudinal track for analog audio accompanying video. A control track also can be used to phase lock the rotation of the head cylinder and the capstan servo, the electromechanical transport controller, to ensure accurate tape speed.

Analog FM modulation is used to record signals in many analog VTRs; it reduces the bandwidth of the signal that must be recorded to tape. Consider that a luminance signal can range from 30 Hz to 4.5 MHz, a range of 17 octaves; this large ratio of long to short wavelengths could not be linearly recorded; a dynamic range of 100 dB would be needed. This problem is solved in video recorders by modulating the signals onto carriers with frequency modulation. When a video signal modulates the carrier, the resulting sidebands determine the required recording bandwidth. Thus, selection of an appropriate carrier frequency moderates bandwidth requirements. With frequency modulation, a constant amplitude carrier is varied in frequency, depending on the amplitude of the modulation signal, and the rate of variation similarly reflects the frequency of the modulating signal. For example, in the VHS (Video Home System) format, the luminance (brightness) signal is FM modulated with a deviation from 3.4 to 4.4 MHz, and the chrominance (color) signal is modulated on a carrier centered at 629 kHz. The bandwidth of the signal is reduced, and the high frequency can be successfully recorded with a helical scan method. In addition, high frequencies can be boosted with a pre-emphasis circuit before recording, then equal but opposite de-emphasis is applied upon playback. This improves the signal-to-noise ratio in the recorded signal. The signals used to identify the end of a video horizontal or vertical line, called synchronization pulses, are represented with an independent frequency. Proprietary multichannel rotary head recorders support binary coded data recording.

The Digital Audio Processor

To use an analog videotape recorder for digital audio storage, the digital audio signal must be processed to conform to the video signal format. Thus, the audio signal is transformed into a pseudo-video composite signal and bits are stored as black-and-white levels. To accomplish this, audio data is coded with analog FM modulation, and synchronization pulses appropriate for the television format are added to the signal. In other words, the video recorder records what appears to it to be a television signal. For example, the EIAJ digital audio processor format emulates NTSC or PAL/SECAM television signals, so consumer digital audio processors can be connected to videocassette recorders, such as the VHS format. Similarly, professional digital audio processors convert audio data to a standard video format, to be recorded on professional U-matic videocassette recorders.

An audio processor functions in much the same way as the record and reproduce electronics of a stationary head digital tape recorder. The components of a PCM recorder—input lowpass filter, S/H circuit, A/D converter, error correction circuits, multiplexer, demultiplexer, digital filters, D/A converter, and output filter—are all also present in an audio processor. However, an audio processor also must create the simulated video signal, to permit storage on a video recorder. Several important operations take place. The pseudo-video signal is given horizontal and vertical sync pulses, and head switching periods. This can be readily accomplished with the FM processing used in video recording; however, the resulting discontinuity in the signal necessitates further processing.

Video is recorded frame by frame in discrete lines, but audio comprises continuous data. A video recorder divides the data into separate blocks. During the vertical sync pulse, there is a gap, equivalent in duration to 17 (odd tracks) or 18 (even tracks) scanning lines, during which no data is recorded. Therefore, for audio recording, data time compression before recording and data time expansion at playback must be used. The audio signal is directed through a record buffer memory to pack data so it is recorded discontinuously onto video tape. Similarly, on the output side, a reproduction buffer outputs continuous audio data even though recorded data is replayed discontinuously. In addition, because a video recorder only records one track of data, all audio channels must be multiplexed into one channel. Buffers are used to store samples from alternate channels as the counterpart sample is being recorded on the video track.

Because only one videotape recorder track is recorded at a time, a defect in the tape oxide or an obstruction, such as a dust particle, could destroy a large number of successive samples. Thus, data is recorded with interleaving between samples using a buffer memory. Interleaving ensures that time-adjacent samples are not destroyed. Instead, the errors are distributed in time, where they are more easily corrected. Also, CRCC and correction codes are used for error detection and correction. During playback, errors are detected by monitoring check bits and the amplitude of the playback FM signal. When an error is discovered, error correction is used to restore the original data. For more severe errors, linear interpolation is used to average the values of the preceding and succeeding words, to approximate the value of the missing samples.

The video scan rate determines how the audio data is fitted into the video frame. Because a video frame occupies approximately $\frac{1}{30}$ of a second for a standard NTSC video signal, the data for $\frac{1}{30}$ of a second of audio must fit into one video frame—that is, two video tracks. For example, in the EIAJ/NTSC format, a sampling rate of 44.05594 kHz (rounded off to 44.056 kHz) with 14-bit quantization permits a stereo audio signal with full error correction to be placed in one NTSC video frame. This is compatible with a 44.1-kHz sampling rate. Using the video format, quantized audio data is placed on each horizontal scanning line instead of a video signal. Specifically, three 14-bit samples of audio data are recorded, along with a 16-bit CRCC word for dropout detection, and double 14-bit parities for error correction, for a total of 168 bits per horizontal scanning line. Alternatively, a 16-bit sample can be placed in a video frame, with bits given to error correction. In the 16-bit mode, six 16-bit data words are recorded, along with a 16-bit CRCC word. However, there is room for only one 16-bit parity word in the remaining interval; thus some error correction capability is lost. In the EIAJ/NTSC format, 262.5 H intervals comprise one vertical interval. The first H block contains control information.

Professional digital audio processors also convert digital audio signals into a pseudo-video composite signal. However, they offer design features not included in their lower-priced cousins. Professional processors are used to create tape masters for compact disc replication. One example of a professional processor is the PCM-1630. It places PCM digital audio data within the NTSC video format with 17 H or 18 H vertical banking intervals (for even and odd tracks) placed every 245 H intervals. Each horizontal synchronizing pulse of pseudo-video signal contains six 32-bit data words. The PCM-1630 audio processor can use pre-emphasis; it provides a 10 dB lift at 20 kHz. A code in the bit stream indicates pre-emphasis on/off, so that de-emphasis circuitry can be automatically activated when appropriate.

The A/D converters output serial two's complement words, which are interleaved and error-protected by a crossword code with 100% redundancy. Error detection is provided by a CRCC generation polynomial of $x^{16} + x^{12} + x^5 + 1$. Following detection, the crossword code can correct burst errors as large as 2258 bits (11.7 H) in one interleaved block of 6720 bits (35 H). Linear interpolation is used for errors as large as 4480 bits (23.3 H). Audio reconstruction is performed through oversampling filters and D/A converters.

The PCM-1630 composite digital interface is used to convey data between the digital audio processor and the videotape recorder. Within the processor, a 25-bit word is output from the A/D converter section. Audio data is sent MSB first; therefore the last nine bits in the word are packed with 0s. Interleaving circuits process the PCM data at 105-word intervals producing an interleave block spacing. Following interleaving, CRCC is generated for error detection and parity is generated for error correction. In all, one interleave block (420 words) is comprised of 105 channel-1 samples, 105 channel-2 samples, 105 parity words, and 105 CRCC words. Following this processing, the signal is combined with a video signal to produce a composite digital signal. Thirty-five horizontal lines equal one interleave block; one field (245 H) equals 7×35 H; and one frame equals two fields (490 H). Although PCM data occupies 490 horizontal lines in one frame, there are 525 lines per frame in the NTSC standard. In the PCM-1630 format, 17.5 H is blanked in the even field, and 17.5 H in the odd field.

Separate digital audio inputs and outputs are provided for direct interconnection via the AES3 interface. Interface methods are discussed in chapter 10. Using the processor's dubbing mode, direct copies can be made between two U-matic tape recorders. The playback signal is error detected and corrected before it is encoded for recording on the second transport. Read-after-write, or confidence monitoring, is possible when using transports with additional play-only heads. In addition, read-after-read is possible when an optional board is used in the processor. During playback, the U-matic machine outputs two signals from the A and B heads, which are decoded independently in the processor. A comparator checks the CRCC codes and in real-time selects the signal with the least errors. When the A channel is selected, it is appropriately delayed by 75 lines to make it coincident with the B channel. The processor also can be specially configured for mastering CD-ROM and CD-I compact disc formats. Among other things, error correction performance is augmented to correct a 31,523-bit loss.

Professional Digital Video Formats

A variety of professional videotape recorders use digital audio recording in addition to their video recording capabilities. This represents a great improvement over previous professional video formats that used longitudinal analog audio tracks. Because of slow tape speed, and inherently high wow and flutter, the audio quality was often inadequate.

The type C format analog video format has been modified to record digital audio yet maintain backward compatibility with existing recorders. To accomplish this, digital heads are placed in the rotary drum, and data is recorded on an area of tape previously used for video synchronization. One-inch, open reel videotape is used. Five audio channels are supported: two PCM channels, two analog channels, and one timecode channel. Both 44.1 and 48 kHz sampling rates are supported and a dynamic range of 90 dB is achieved. Sixteen-bit audio data is error corrected with a Cross-Interleaved Reed-Solomon code; however, interleaving is limited to one drum revolution to facilitate editing. A total of 800 samples are recorded per field per audio channel. An 8/10 channel code is used, the same as in the DAT format. Pre-read, record, and confidence PCM heads are used so that lip-sync is maintained, and simultaneous playback is possible during recording or editing. Recorders also feature an AES3 digital audio interface.

Professional digital videotape recorders (DVTRs) also permit high-quality digital audio recording. Because the bit rate for an audio channel is about 1 Mbps, only one-hundredth of that required for digital video, it is easy to combine four audio tracks into the video RF signal, and record the audio signal within the video signal. However, the audio data must be time compressed to raise its data rate to fit into that of the video signal. In addition, the audio data must be locked to a video synchronizing signal. As with their analog predecessors, digital videotape recorders use helical scan techniques to achieve extremely high-bandwidth recording. Composite formats combine color and luminance data; component formats store luminance and two color difference signals to achieve higher picture quality.

The D-1 or 4:2:2 format was the first component digital video recording standard, developed in the 1980s. Because it is a digital video format (using the CCIR-601 standard), D-1 can be used in both 525/60 and 625/50 video environments thus creating a worldwide system. In a component video signal, 8-bit color-difference (R-Y and B-Y) and 8-bit luminance (Y) data are kept separate. 4:2:2 refers to the ratios of frequencies used to record different video components; Y is sampled at 13.5 MHz, and R-Y and B-Y at 6.75 MHz, all based on a standard reference frequency of 3.375 MHz. The overall data rate is approximately 2×10^5 kbps. NRZ modulation is used with oxide tape. The ¾-inch (19 mm) D-1 tape is contained in a cassette shell; its specification provides for one digital video signal, four digital audio channels, and three analog longitudinal tracks for timecode, cue, and control. Audio signals are sampled at 48 kHz, with provision for 16- to 24-bit word lengths as outlined by AES3. The recording mode can be selected from eight available modes; this specifies the number of audio bits per sample and defines the type and quantity of associated auxiliary data. This ensures transparency to AES3 digital audio sources. There is 100% redundancy between audio sectors. Moreover, odd/even samples are separated and recorded in different locations to reduce the effect of tape errors. A product code with Reed-Solomon parity is used for error correction.

The D-2 format was developed concurrently with the D-1 format, and is similar; however, it uses a composite video standard. Single 8-bit samples represent each element in the composite video signal; the sampling rate is 14.318 MHz with 910 samples per video line; 768 samples correspond to the active digital line, with 142 for blanking. The overall data rate is approximately 1×10^5 kbps. The video signal and four 16-bit PCM digital audio channels are recorded with helical scan, with cue, control, and timecode on longitudinal tracks. Audio is recorded with 100% redundancy. The 19-mm D-2 tape is contained in a cassette shell. Miller-squared code is used, with metal particle tape. A product code is used with Reed-Solomon redundancy. The AES3 standard is supported.

The D-3 composite format is similar to D-2, but uses ½-inch metal particle tape rather than ¾ inch, permitting a smaller camcorder size. The D-3 uses 10 heads. As in D-2, video signals are sampled at four times the color subcarrier at 14.318 MHz with 8-bit quantization. Playing times of four hours can be achieved. An 8-14 modulation is used. Four 20-bit audio channels are recorded. There is no D-4 format.

The D-5 format is a component video version of the D-3 format; it uses ½-inch tape. A D-5 recorder can record an SMPTE 259M 4:2:2 signal at 270 Mbps. Both 18-MHz/8-bit, and 13.5-MHz/10-bit video signals can be input. In a 16:9 recording mode, 10-bit video words are reformatted into 8-bit words from the aggregated two-bit difference in word length and stored at 18 MHz. This extended mode operates at a rate of 360 Mbps. The D-5 uses 18 heads to record four scan tracks per segment, as shown in Fig. 6-12. Four audio channels are recorded, with data shuffled and reallocated over the four tracks to increase reliability. Because the track pitch is identical to that of D-3, and the digital signal compatible, D-3 tapes can be played on a D-5 machine. Because tape speed is double that of D-3, playing time is halved to two hours.

DB (Digital Betacam) is a camcorder format and specifically a composite digital implementation of the analog Betacam SP format; some Digital Betacam machines

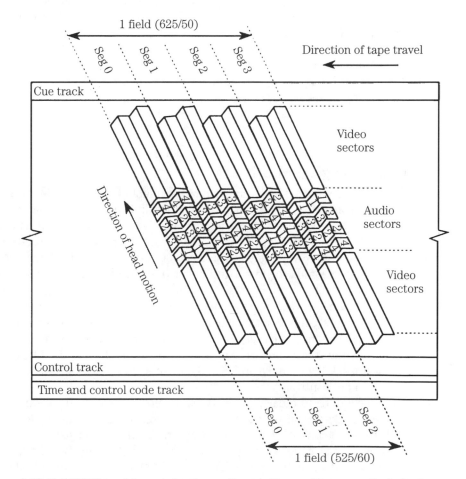

6-12 D-5 DVTR track layout showing audio and video sectors across the helical scan tracks. Suesada, et al.

will play analog Betacam SP tapes. Mild data reduction is used in the DB format; a picture-dependent intrafield compression algorithm achieves 2:1 reduction to provide input and output of a 10-bit 4:2:2 signal. The DCT (Digital Component Technology) cassette format also uses a mild 2:1 data reduction, and 19-mm tape. Up to three hours of composite program can be recorded; 16:9 ratio is supported. The D-6 format records uncompressed high-definition (HDTV) video signals at a rate of 1.2 Gbps over eight data channels. With confidence replay and other applications, a total of 32 video heads can be used. Sampling frequency is 72 MHz for luminance and 36 MHz for chrominance. Up to 12 digital audio channels can be recorded. A cassette holds a 64-minute program, storing a total of 500 Gbytes. Many DVTRs use the SDI (Serial Digital Interface) to convey 8- or 10-bit video data with four audio channels, nominally at a rate of 270 Mbps, over a coaxial cable.

The SMPTE 259M standard is often used to distribute serial digital video signals at 270 Mbps; composite and component digital video as well as digital audio can be conveyed. Data is coded with NRZI modulation, with a peak to peak voltage of 0.8 V; rise time (20% to 80%) must occur within 0.75 to 1.5 ns; jitter must be less than 0.5 ns peak to peak; 75-Ω (ohm) terminations are used; a typical S/N ratio at the receiver is 40 dB or greater. As with any high-frequency distribution system using coaxial cable, bit errors increase significantly with cable length. As with many aspects of digital technology, cable runs exhibit a cliff effect, in which failure is swift and catastrophic; the margin of performance can be gauged by adding extra cable to determine when failure occurs. Interconnection is discussed in more detail in chapter 10.

ADAT Modular Digital Multitrack

Low-cost modular multitrack recorders can record eight channels of 16-bit digital audio on videotape; in addition, multiple recorders can be linked with sample-accurate synchronization. The ADAT (Alesis Digital Audio Tape) system uses ½-inch-wide S-VHS (Super-Video Home System) tape running at 95.76 mm/s or 3¾ ips, or three-times standard-play video speed; rewind time is less than 100 seconds. Standard VHS tapes should not be used. Tapes must be formatted either prior to recording, or during an initial recording by writing a proprietary 32-bit timecode to the tape; the timecode permits sample-accurate ($\frac{1}{48,000}$ second) synchronization, as well as time counter readings, autolocate and editing functions. When formatting begins, the recorder writes a 15-second leader, followed by 2 minutes of initialization data, then writes timecode to a special synchronization area. Initialization data such as punch-in and -out points, start times, song titles, MIDI tempo maps, SMPTE offsets, and pre/post roll times are interpreted by a remote controller.

Up to 16 recorders can be daisy chained, using nine-pin cables, providing 128 tracks; no audio tracks must be sacrificed for synchronization timecode. One recorder is selected to act as the master, and the others function as slaves. All synchronized recorders must have the same software version (to identify the version, hold the Set Locate button and press Fast Forward); if mixed, the recorder with the oldest software version should act as the master. Together, the recorders function as a single machine under one controller; however, a separate tape must be used in each eight-track recorder. Two recorders can be used efficiently by placing basic tracks on the master recorder, then using as many slave tapes as needed with the slave recorder; all tapes can then be digitally edited and compiled into a master tape. In addition, a recorder could be interfaced to a multichannel hard disk workstation for editing and mixing.

Using a remote controller, tracks can be digitally bounced from one machine to another, to either the same section of a recording or to another section with sample-accuracy; for example, background vocals can be placed in every chorus of a song. In addition, each copied track is software assignable; for example, channel 1 can be copied to channel 5 without repatching. Both punch-in and -out are available, each with selectable crossfade times from 10 to 40 ms. In addition, independent delays can be added to any number of tracks. Maximum recording time is 40 minutes with a 120-minute S-VHS tape at a 48-kHz sampling rate; playing time is 53 minutes from a 160-minute tape; the rate is variable from approximately 40.4 to 50.8 kHz (+1, –3 semitones). Conventional analog inputs and outputs provide both professional balanced +4 dBm and consumer unbalanced –10 dBV interfacing. In addition, each recorder uses an ADI (Alesis Digital Interface) that conveys eight audio channels; dubbing can be performed without degradation. The ADI interface is described in more detail in chapter 10. Using an optional converter, pairs of tracks can be configured according to the AES3 or S/PDIF formats. The system can be programmed to provide overlap between recorders so that one begins recording just before the other finishes; this can be continued indefinitely, then later played back seamlessly. Session configuration information can be recorded to a header area on a tape, then quickly reloaded when work begins again.

As with any S-VHS video recorder, the multichannel format uses a rotary head with helical scan; there are two read heads and two write heads placed at 90° intervals around the drum. Read-before-write is supported such that data is read into a RAM buffer even if the data is immediately overwritten; this permits digital crossfading, used during punch-in and punch-out. Head wrap is about 180°. Drum diameter is 62 mm, and drum rotation speed is 3000 rpm; relative head-to-tape speed is 9739 mm/s. Clock speed is 13.788 MHz with 137,880 clock pulses per track. Two tracks are scanned during each drum rotation; azimuth recording is used. A summary of track data contents is shown in Fig. 6-13. The recorded track width is 100 μm, and the read head is 30 μm wide; this provides a tolerance of tracking error caused, for example, by positioning error between the control track head and the record or playback head, or servo error. The recorded track is 96.437 mm in length, placed at an angle of 5° 59' 39.2" with a bit density of 1430 bits per millimeter. Minimum wavelength is 0.699 μm. Eight-to-ten modulation is used.

Audio data from each of the eight channels is stored in discrete data blocks along the scan track length and separated by interblock gaps. Each audio channel is divided into odd and even samples and divided between two helical tape tracks. Odd and even samples are accompanied by sector guards, synchronization blocks, error-correction data, and a timecode block. Included in the half-channel synchronization block is an overdub ID word that enables punch-in and -out operations. In addition, each half channel is given a unique timecode word that facilitates high-speed scan and searching. Also, write timing sectors placed at the end of each scan track are

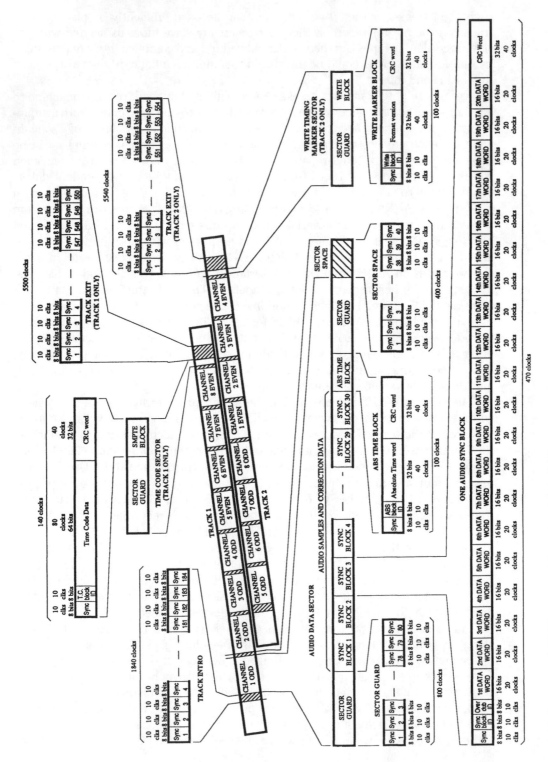

6-13 Summary of ADAT scan-track layout and data fields. Alesis Corporation

used as absolute location markers, to determine precise head alignment with the tape tracks. In addition, the system uses a longitudinal servo control track.

Reed-Solomon error correction is used in the error-correction fields. Typically, rotating heads require replacement after 2000 hours of use. An error indicator lights when a tape exhibits wear, or when the heads require cleaning. As with any rotary system, a cleaning cassette must be used; cleaning the heads with a cotton swab or rubbing them in the wrong direction might damage them. The ADAT format was developed by Alesis Corporation; it is supported by Matsushita.

DA-88 Modular Digital Multitrack

The DA-88 modular recorder uses Hi-8 videocassettes to record eight tracks of 16-bit digital audio. The Hi-8 format was developed as a successor to the VHS format, using a smaller tape width (8 mm) and a metal particle tape formulation with higher coercivity and retentivity than Fe_2O_3 VHS tapes; Hi-8 tape enables greater data density. Standard 8-mm tapes cannot be used in this recorder. Maximum recording time is 108 minutes, with a typical rewind time of 80 seconds, using 120-minute NTSC tape; 90-minute tapes also can be used. Up to 16 recorders can be linked using 15-pin D-sub connectors for synchronization to form a 128-track recording system. Individual tapes are used for each modular recorder. Individual recorders must be identified with rear panel ID switches; the master machine is designated as recorder #0. Sampling rates of 44.1 and 48 kHz can be selected.

Features include variable speed tape shuttling, selectable crossfade time from 10 to 90 ms, track slipping, automated punch-in and -out, in/out edit point trimming, variable pitch, timecode synchronization, and advance/delay playback for time correction. Both unbalanced –10 dBV and balanced +4 dBm analog inputs and outputs are supported, as is digital input/output. Data is transferred between recorders via the TDIF-1 (Tascam Digital InterFace); this is a bidirectional 25-pin port using a D-sub connector. Using special converters, this data can be linked to AES3, S/PDIF and SDIF-2 interfaces. With a chase synchronization board, the recorder will generate all SMPTE timecode formats; SMPTE timecode can be written into a subcode area on the tape tracks. Other options include RS-422 port and MIDI ports.

The recorder uses a 40-mm diameter head revolving at 2000 rpm; relative head-to-tape speed is 4189 mm/s. Physical track layout is shown in Fig. 6-14. Data fields are shown in Fig. 6-15. Four heads are spaced along the drum circumference to provide a read-after-write function. Head wrap is 226°. Linear tape speed is 15.939 mm/s. A recorded track is approximately 63 mm long, track angle is 4° 54' 13.2" and track width is 20.5 μm. Minimum wavelength is 0.67 μm. Clock frequency is 12.608 MHz. Azimuth recording is used. Servo control signals are embedded in the center of the helical scan track to enable use of automatic track following. Using this method, the width of the playback head equals the width of the recorded scan track; automatic track following is described in more detail in chapter 7.

Double Reed-Solomon code provides error correction. Sixteen bit samples are divided into even and odd data fields, and stored on two scan tracks. Specifically, eight channels of audio data are stored as four sets of track pairs placed along the

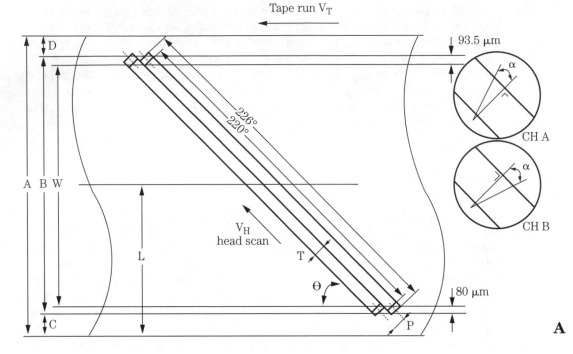

	Item	Spec.	Detail
A	Tape width	8 mm	
V_T	Tape speed	15.939 mm/sec	14.345 mm (NTSC) × 2000 rpm/1800 rpm
∅	Drum diameter	40 mm	
V_H	Writing speed	4.2 m/sec	
P	Track pitch	20.5 μm	
T	Track width	20.5 μm	
B	Effective wrap area (VTR)	6.72 mm	(6.7179 mm) 226°
C	Edge guard	0.6 mm	(0.567 mm)
D	Edge guard	0.7 mm	(0.715 mm)
W	Effective R/W area	6.54 mm	(6.5445 mm) 220° (220.167°)
L	Track center	3.92 mm	(3.91925 mm)
Θs	Track angle (tape stop)	4° 53' 6"	
ΘR	Track angle (tape run)	4° 54' 13.2"	
α	Head gap azimuth angle	±10°	

B

6-14 DA-88 track pattern showing layout and dimensions. A. Scan track layout viewed from magnetic coating side. B. Dimensions in DA-88 format. Teac Tascam Corporation

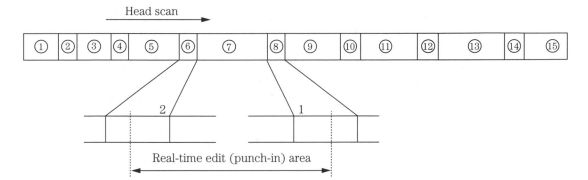

	Area name	Classification	Signal	Angle (degree)	Number of blocks	Length (µs)
①	Marginal area	Gap	1/4 fch	5.482	16	456.853
②	Inter block gap	Gap	1/4 fch	1.371	4	114.213
③	Sub data area	Preamble	1/2 fch	0.685	2	57.107
		Sub data		2.741	8	228.426
		Postamble 1	1/2 fch	0.343	1	28.553
		Postamble 2	1/4 fch	1.713	5	142.766
④	Inter block gap	Gap	1/4 fch	2.056	6	171.320
⑤	CH1/2 PCM data	Preamble	1/2 fch	0.685	2	57.107
		Main data		43.858	128	3654.822
⑥	Inter block gap	Gap	1/4 fch	2.056	6	171.320
⑦	CH3/4 PCM data	Preamble	1/2 fch	0.685	2	57.107
		Main data		43.858	128	3654.822
⑧	Inter block gap	Gap	1/4 fch	1.371	4	114.213
⑨	ATF area	ATF		13.706	40	1142.132
⑩	Inter block gap	Gap	1/4 fch	1.371	4	114.213
⑪	CH5/6 PCM data	Preamble	1/2 fch	0.685	2	57.107
		Main data		43.858	128	3654.822
⑫	Inter block gap	Gap	1/4 fch	2.056	6	171.320
⑬	CH7/8 PCM data	Preamble	1/2 fch	0.685	2	57.107
		Main data		43.858	128	3654.822
⑭	Inter block gap	Gap	1/4 fch	1.371	4	114.213
⑮	Marginal area	Gap	1/4 fch	5.482	16	456.853
Total				219.975	642	18331.218

(fch = 12.608 MHz)

6-15 Layout of data fields along the DA-88 scan track. _{Teac Tascam Corporation}

recorded track; if only one track is recorded, data from the nonrecording track is read and copied along with new data. Eight-to-ten modulation is used. Like most cassette formats, Hi-8 cassettes use a write-protect tab to prevent accidental recording or erasure; other sensing holes describe tape type and thickness. Tapes previously recorded with video information should not be formatted for digital audio use. The DA-88 format was developed by Teac Tascam Corporation; it is supported by Fostex and Sony Corporation.

Advantages and Disadvantages of Rotary Head Design

Rotary head recorders readily achieve the high bandwidth required for digital audio storage. The narrow track width and high head-to-tape speed of rotary head designs yields high recording density with low tape consumption. The electronics required are relatively simple; because all data is multiplexed to a single recorded track, redundancy of recording circuitry is greatly reduced. Data synchronization is easy to obtain when using a video signal format, because the video synchronization pulses are an inherent part of the format. Mass production also allows video transports to be manufactured at low cost. Thus, a highly efficient storage medium is widely available to both consumers and professionals.

Disadvantages of rotary head designs are related mainly to specialized applications. Razor blade editing is not possible with a rotary head data track; therefore, electronic editing must be used using multiple tape recorders or buffer memory circuitry. Standard video editors are often not adequate, because more precise subframe editing is often required in audio, so digital audio editors have been developed. Although it is more difficult to overdub multiplexed audio channels, newer methods have overcome this.

Professional audio applications that require physical editing and extremely robust reliability will retain the stationary head design for digital audio recorders. However, rotary head designs are highly successful for low-cost semiprofessional and professional multitrack applications. From an engineering standpoint, the rotary design lends itself to the high densities required for multichannel recording. The rotary head design has already proven itself for consumer applications in the home video recorder market and is similarly efficient for consumer digital audio tape formats. The Digital Audio Tape (DAT) digital audio cassette format is discussed in chapter 7, and the DCC format is discussed in chapter 11.

7
CHAPTER

Digital Audio Tape (DAT)

Digital Audio Tape (DAT) was the first mass-market digital audio tape recorder. Because it borrows technical solutions such as a rotary head from videotape technologies, DAT provides the wide recording bandwidth needed for PCM digital audio storage. The technical specifications of the format were standardized by the EIAJ, ensuring compatibility among manufacturers. Work on DAT began in 1981, soon followed by demonstrations of prototypes. Eighty-one companies participated in the DAT Conference in June 1983, during which R-DAT (rotary head) and S-DAT (stationary head) formats were examined. In August 1986, a conference announced the completion of the R-DAT standard. Since its introduction in March 1987, the R-DAT format has become known simply as DAT.

In the DAT format, the audio signal is recorded and played back using helical-scan tape storage. The DAT format supports three sampling frequencies: 32, 44.1, and 48 kHz. Because DAT recorders have digital inputs and outputs, two decks can be interconnected for high-quality tape copying; subcode information is conveyed along with digital audio data. As with many digital audio tape formats, wide dynamic range, low distortion, high signal-to-noise ratio, and low wow and flutter are facilitated. However, the operation of DAT is a great deal more sophisticated than that of other recording mediums. In fact, several of its features are unprecedented in audio recording technology.

DAT Cassette

The DAT cassette was developed and standardized exclusively for the DAT format. Cassette size is $73 \times 54 \times 10.5$ mm, slightly more than half the size of an analog cassette, as shown in Fig. 7-1. The cassette weighs approximately 20 grams. It uses tape that is 3.81 mm wide (often referred to as 4-mm tape), equal to the ⅛-inch tape used in analog cassettes. The tape typically has a total thickness of 13 μm (the oxide coating accounts for about 3 μm), equal to that used in analog C-90s. DAT tapes can record up to two hours of audio, on a tape about 60 meters long. By slowing tape

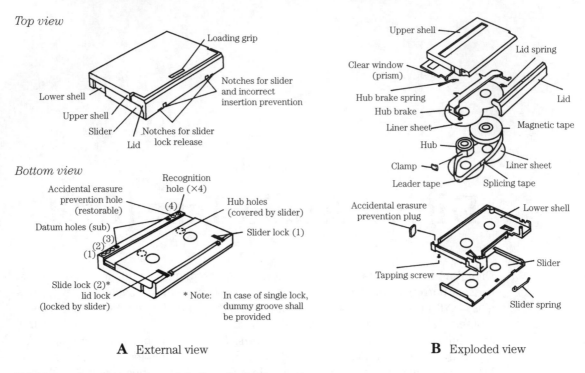

Top view

Loading grip

Notches for slider and incorrect insertion prevention

Lower shell

Upper shell

Slider

Lid

Notches for slider lock release

Bottom view

Recognition hole (×4)

Accidental erasure prevention hole (restorable)

(4)

Datum holes (sub)

(3)
(2)
(1)

Hub holes (covered by slider)

Slider lock (1)

Slide lock (2)*
lid lock
(locked by slider)

* Note: In case of single lock, dummy groove shall be provided

A External view

Upper shell

Lid spring

Clear window (prism)

Hub brake spring

Hub brake

Liner sheet

Hub

Clamp

Leader tape

Lid

Magnetic tape

Liner sheet

Splicing tape

Accidental erasure prevention plug

Lower shell

Tapping screw

Slider

Slider spring

B Exploded view

7-1 External and internal construction of a DAT cassette. Sony Corporation

speed, reducing sampling frequency, reducing hub diameter, or using thinner tape, recording times of four to six hours can be achieved. Blank tapes use a high-coercivity metal particle oxide with coercivity of 1500 oersteds.

DAT cassettes are designed to physically protect the tape inside. Only when a tape is loaded into a DAT deck is a slider retracted to reveal tape hubs, and a lid opened to allow access to tape. Tape guides draw the tape from the cassette and wrap the tape around the rotary drum, as shown in Fig. 7-2. A hub brake mechanism inside the cassette is provided to minimize tape slackness. In addition, there is provision for either transmitted-light or reflected-light optical detection for identifying the end (or beginning) of a tape. The former method might shine light across the corner of a cassette, and the latter might use a prism molded into the cassette's transparent window.

There are four recognition holes in every DAT cassette, located in standard positions. These holes are used by the recorder to identify the kind of cassette inserted. The first three holes form a code with four states defined for tape thickness and track pitch. Given holes 1, 2, and 3, the following codes apply: 000 (standard pitch, 13-μm tape), 010 (standard pitch, thin tape), 001 (wide pitch, 13-μm tape), 011 (wide pitch, thin tape) where 1 = open and 0 = closed. The fourth hole identifies a prerecorded (1), or nonprerecorded (0) tape. DAT cassettes contain a safety tab on one end. To prevent recording or accidental erasure, the tab can be slid toward the center of the cassette, opening a copy-prohibit hole (1) on the cassette's underside. To make a recording, the tab must be slid out (0) to the edge of the cassette.

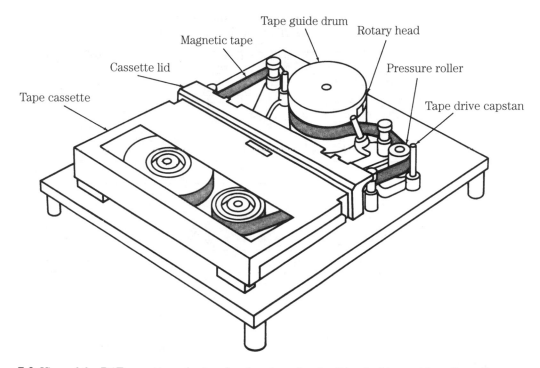

7-2 View of the DAT cassette and rotary head system showing lid unlocking and tape threading.

Two other datum holes toward the center of the cassette are used for alignment. A notch on the top of the cassette is used as a loading grip.

DAT Modes

As summarized in Table 7-1, the DAT standard calls for four record/playback modes and two playback-only modes. The standard record/playback, and both playback-only modes (called wide and normal) are implemented on every DAT recorder. The standard mode offers 16-bit linear quantization and 44.1- or 48-kHz sampling frequency. Most recorders have both analog and digital inputs and outputs. Consumer DAT recorders contain an SCMS circuit that prevents second-generation recording if the copy-inhibit flag in the bit stream of any digital source has been enabled. CDs and DATs can be recorded via an analog connection without consequence.

Three other record/playback modes, called options 1, 2, and 3, all use a 32-kHz sampling frequency. Option 1 provides two-hour recording time with 16-bit linear quantization. Option 2 provides four hours of recording time with 12-bit nonlinear quantization. In addition, the linear tape speed and drum rotating speed are halved. Option 3 provides four-channel recording and playback, also using 12-bit nonlinear quantization. These options are compatible with some direct broadcast satellite (DBS) transmissions, beamed earthward at 32 kHz in some countries. Some manufacturers have introduced DAT recorders operating at a 96-kHz sampling frequency;

Table 7-1. Specifications for the various record/playback modes of DAT for both blank and prerecorded tapes.

ITEM \ MODE	DAT (REC/PB MODE)				PRERECORDED TAPE (PB ONLY)	
	STANDARD	OPTION 1	OPTION 2	OPTION 3	NORMAL TRACK	WIDE TRACK
CHANNEL NUMBER [CH]	2	2	2	4	2	2
SAMPLING FREQUENCY [kHz]	48	32	32	32	44.1	
QUANTIZATION BIT NUMBER [BIT]	16 (LINEAR)	16 (LINEAR)	12 (NONLINEAR)	12 (NONLINEAR)	16 (LINEAR)	16 (LINEAR)
LINEAR RECORDING DENSITY [kBPI]	61.0	61.0			61.0	61.1
SURFACE RECORDING DENSITY [MBPI²]	114	114			114	76
TRANSMISSION RATE [MBPS]	2.46	2.46	1.23	2.46	2.46	
SUBCODE CAPACITY [KBPS]	273.1	273.1	136.5	273.1	273.1	
MODULATION SYSTEM	8-10 MODULATION					
CORRECTION SYSTEM	DOUBLE REED-SOLOMON CODE					
TRACKING SYSTEM	AREA SHARING ATF					
CASSETTE SIZE [mm]	73×54×10.5					
RECORDING TIME [MIN]	120	120	240	120	120	80
TAPE WIDTH [mm]	3.81					
TAPE TYPE	METAL PARTICLE					OXIDE TAPE
TAPE THICKNESS [μm]	13±1 μ					
TAPE SPEED [mm/s]	8.15	8.15	4.075	8.15	8.15	12.225
TRACK PITCH [μm]	13.591				13.591	20.41
TRACK ANGLE	6° 22'59.5"					6°23'29.4"
STANDARD DRUM SPECIFICATIONS	φ30 90° WRAP					
DRUM ROTATIONS [rpm]	2000		1000	2000	2000	
RELATIVE SPEED [m/s]	3.133		1.567	3.133	3.133	3.129
HEAD AZIMUTH ANGLE	±20°					

tape speed is doubled, thus playing time is halved. A modified version of this recorder provides 24-bit recording at a 48-kHz sampling frequency. In either case, tapes are incompatible with conventional DAT recorders.

Although DAT was designed for audio storage, its reliability has led to the development of the Digital Data Storage (DDS) format. A tape holds 1300 Mbytes, with an error rate of 10^{-15}. The same transport is used. However, a third layer of error correction is added, and a standard I/O port such as SCSI is used for transferring data (for example, for data back-up applications).

DAT Hardware Design

The DAT format is an original design, thus many unique technical solutions were devised. Still, DAT borrows from both rotary-head video technology and compact-disc technology. The tremendous data density recorded to tape necessitates a number of sophisticated recording techniques for track format. In addition, user features such as subcode overwrite require flexibility in data recording. As with any digital audio system, modulation code and error correction play an important role in determining system performance.

From a hardware point of view, a DAT recorder utilizes many of the same building blocks as a CD player, with the addition of encoding circuits. Elements such as A/D and D/A converters, modulators and demodulators, error-correction encoding and decoding are all used, as shown in Fig. 7-3. Audio input is received in digital form, or is converted to digital form by an A/D converter. Error-correction encoding and interleaving are performed. As with any helical scan system, time compression must be used to separate the continuous input analog signal into discrete fields prior to

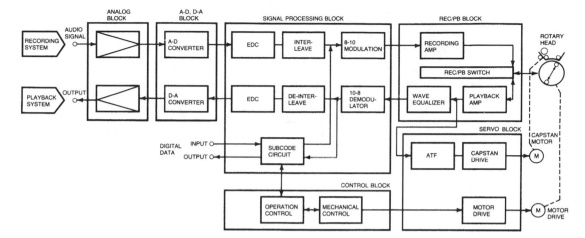

7-3 Hardware design of a DAT recorder/player.

recording, then to rejoin them upon playback with time expansion to form a continuous audio output signal. On the recording side, the output of a buffer memory is clocked faster than the input data is entered thus achieving the time compression required. Subcode information is added to the bit stream, and data is converted from parallel to serial form. The digital signal is coded with eight-to-ten (8/10) modulation to aid recording on magnetic tape. This signal is recorded via a recording amplifier and rotary transformer and head.

During playback, the transitions on the tape induce signal in the head that regenerates the record waveform. Track-finding signals are derived from the tape and used to automatically adjust tracking. Eight-to-ten demodulation is performed and data is returned to a parallel bit stream. Subcode data is separated and used for operator and servo control. A memory permits de-interleaving as well as time expansion, and also eliminates wow and flutter. De-interleaving is accomplished in the context of error correction. Finally, the audio signal is output as a digital signal, or through D/A converters as an analog signal.

The data density achieved by DAT is truly remarkable. Each channel bit of data occupies only 0.67 μm, with an overall recording data density of 114 Mbits/inch^2. With a sampling frequency of 48 kHz and 16-bit quantization, the audio data rate is 1.536 Mbps. Error correction encoding adds extra information amounting to 37.5% of the original, increasing the data rate to about 2.46 Mbps. Finally, subcode raises the overall data rate to 2.77 Mbps.

Rotary Head

The DAT rotary head permits slow linear tape speed while achieving high recording bandwidth. Each track is discontinuously recorded as the tape runs past the angled head drum, which spins rapidly in the same direction as tape travel. A DAT drum rotates at 2000 rpm, and has two or four heads placed 180° or 90° apart; four heads allow off-tape simultaneous monitoring. Tape wrap is 90° with a 30-mm drum. Thus, the record/playback signal is recorded (or played back) 50% of the time, and for the other 50% is interrupted, as shown in Fig. 7-4. The same head gap can be used for recording and playback.

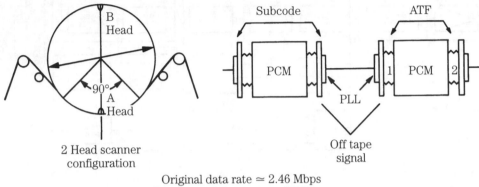

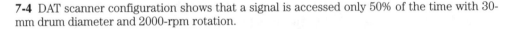

2 Head scanner configuration

Off tape signal

Original data rate ≃ 2.46 Mbps
Compressed data rate ≃ 7.5 Mbps

7-4 DAT scanner configuration shows that a signal is accessed only 50% of the time with 30-mm drum diameter and 2000-rpm rotation.

Because the output RF signal from the rotary head is dependent on frequency and is reduced at lower frequencies, and because the rotary transformer has a poor low-frequency characteristic, the output frequency must be converted to a higher frequency. The 2.46-Mbps signal (30-mm drum, 90° wrap) is compressed by a factor of three and converted to a rate of 7.5 Mbps. This process allows discontinuous recording, facilitates a small drum diameter and small size of the rotary transformer, and increases the head's S/N ratio. Because the rotary head performs all read/write and tracking functions, other fixed control heads are not needed.

In most cases, the drum diameter is 30 mm. However, other diameter drums can be used. Smaller-diameter 15-mm rotating drums have been developed for use in portable DAT decks; with these, the tape makes contact with a 180° portion of the drum. A professional 60-mm diameter drum, in which the tape wrap angle is only 45°, can be used to facilitate high-speed tape handling while the tape is loaded, thus providing quick access. In either case, different head diameters produce identical track lengths, ensuring compatibility.

The tape mechanical running system is shown in Fig. 7-5. Both roller guides lean forward slightly and are lowered in the tape path; this maintains the tape height against the action of the rotating drum. The entrance and exit slant guides place the tape parallel to the drum surface. Tracking stability is improved over M-wrap and U-wrap video systems. Because of low wrap, only a short length of tape is in contact with the drum. This lower contact reduces tape and head wear, and permits high-speed transport and search while the head is in contact with the drum. In addition, lower tape tension can be used to promote longer head life. A tape can be replayed more than 200 times before signal deterioration begins. Despite the slow tape speed of 8.15 mm/s (about ¼ ips), a high relative tape speed of about 3 m/s is obtained,

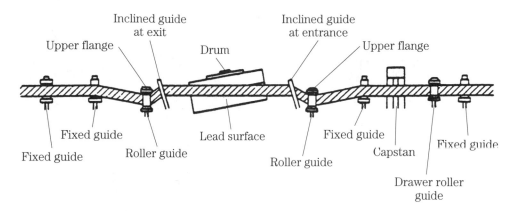

Upper flange
Inclined guide at exit
Drum
Inclined guide at entrance
Upper flange

Fixed guide
Fixed guide
Roller guide
Lead surface
Fixed guide
Roller guide
Capstan
Fixed guide
Drawer roller guide

7-5 Simplified drawing of the tape path showing drum, capstan, roller, and fixed guides.

making it possible to record 2.2 Gbyte of information (two hours of audio) on a single tape. The fundamentals of rotary head storage are discussed in chapter 6.

Track Format

Rotary head recording produces diagonal tracks at an angle of approximately 6.5° from horizontal, as shown in Fig. 7-6. The width of each track is 13.591 μm (perhaps ⅒₀ the thickness of a human hair) and the length of each track is 23.501 mm. Data is recorded over helical scan track pairs, one track from each head. In addition to these tracks, the tape contains two additional longitudinal areas, one at each edge of the tape. They are not used for signal recording, but protect the scan tracks against edge damage. Each helical track is divided into a series of data fields. PCM audio data constitutes the majority of data on a track and is recorded in the center of each track. However, substantial fields are given to pairs of subcode, ATF, and other data fields are defined, as described below.

The DAT track format is shown in Fig. 7-7. Each recorded scan track contains 196 audio blocks, contained in 16 fields. Audio data is contained in 128 blocks recorded in the center of the track. Subcode data is written into two fields (redundantly written to increase reliability) each with eight data blocks, each followed by a postamble field. In addition, phase-locked loop (PLL) preambles are recorded prior to the subcode and PCM data areas; these addresses label the fields and assist in phase locking the data in the fields. In this way, subcode data can be written independently. For example, when overwriting new subcode data, the preamble, subcode, and postamble are all updated; the PLL locates and locks data, and the postamble moves the head turn-off pulse away from the subcode data. Each track is further divided into different data areas. Inter-Block Gap (IBG) signals of 1.568 MHz are used to ensure full overwriting of old tracks, and prevent interference between data areas. When new data is written over old data, data areas are rewritten in accordance with IBG positioning. In addition, timing can be derived from the ATF signals, permitting accurate rerecording.

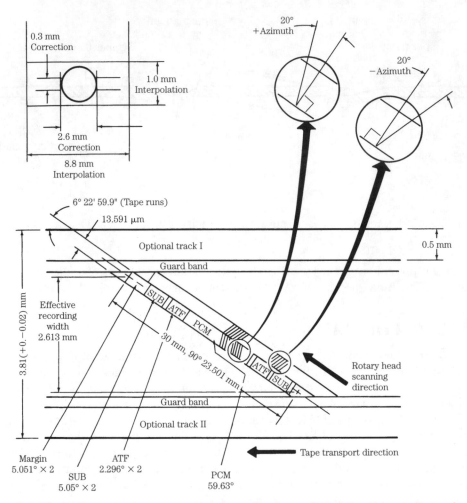

7-6 The DAT scan track pattern, using rotary head recording. Azimuth recording and error-correction capability are also shown. Sony Corporation

PCM audio and subcode data in the scan tracks are formatted in a block structure, as shown in Fig. 7-8. Each data block contains a synchronization byte, ID code (W1) byte, block address code (W2) byte, parity byte, and 32 data bytes. Blocks are considered as pairs so that alternate blocks contain 32 data (or outer Reed-Solomon code) bytes, and 24 bytes of data with eight bytes of C1 inner code redundancy. In total, there are 288 bits per data block (following eight-to-ten modulation, this is increased to 360 channel bits). Following modulation, the synchronization word consists of a unique 10-bit pattern (0100010001 or 1100010001). Synchronization occurs at the start of each block in the scan track; this ensures that synchronization can be achieved at the playback phase-locked loop. The remaining data fields are assigned differently, depending on whether the block is in a PCM or subcode track area.

In PCM track blocks, the 8-bit ID code (W1) contains PCM-ID subcode data. Unlike the independent subcode blocks written elsewhere on the scan track, it cannot

Track format

1	2	3	4	5	6	7	8	9	10	11	12	13	14	15	16

		Signal	Angle* (deg)	Number of blocks	Period* (μs)
1	Margin	½ fch	5.051	11	420.9
2	PLL(sub)	½ fch	0.918	2	76.5
3	Sub-1		3.673	8	306.1
4	Post amble	½ fch	0.459	1	38.3
5	IBG	⅙ fch	1.378	3	114.8
6	ATF		2.296	5	191.3
7	IBG	⅙ fch	1.378	3	114.8
8	PLL(PCM)	½ fch	0.918	2	76.5
9	PCM		58.776	128	4898.0
10	IBG	⅙ fch	1.378	3	114.8
11	ATF		2.296	5	191.3
12	IBG	⅙ fch	1.378	3	114.8
13	PLL(sub)	½ fch	0.918	2	76.5
14	Sub-2		3.673	8	306.1
15	Post amble	½ fch	0.459	1	38.3
16	Margin	½ fch	5.051	11	420.9
	Total		90	196	7500

Recording density = 61.0 kBPI   fch = 9.408 MHz

*Calculated under the condition that 30-mm diameter, 90° wrap
angle, 2000 rpm cylinder is used

7-7 The DAT track format signal assignment. A total of 196 blocks
are recorded over the scan track.

be edited. This PCM-ID records pre-emphasis, sampling frequency, quantization
level, tape speed, copy-inhibit flag, channel number, and other parameters. Specifically, the PCM-ID subcode creates eight 2-bit data blocks, ID-0 through ID-7, as
shown in Table 7-2. They are written one pair per block, in every other block. This 8-
block sequence (called a subframe) is repeated throughout the 128-block PCM field
(16 subframes per track, 32 per frame). ID-7 differs from the other ID codes; it can
change its content and accumulate data over 32 subframes, creating a 64-byte block.
It is used for a variety of pack data, including professional timecode. In subcode
blocks, the 8-bit ID code contains subcode-ID data, as described in the following
paragraphs.

The 8-bit block address code (W2) byte specifies whether the data block contains audio or subcode data; the MSB is 0 for audio, and 1 for subcode. In the case of
audio blocks, the remaining seven bits store the audio block address (0 to 127). For
subcode blocks, the least significant four bits store the subcode block address (0 to
15); the other three bits contain subcode-ID data as follows. The parity byte is the

1 block = 288 bits

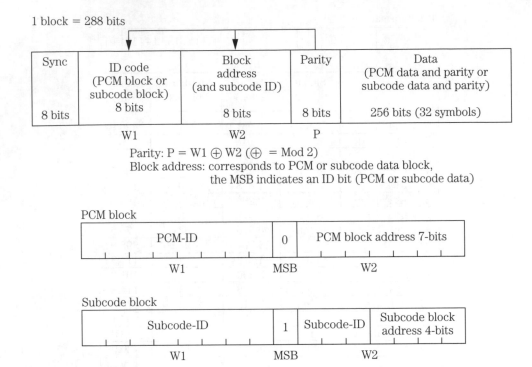

Parity: P = W1 $\oplus$ W2 ($\oplus$ = Mod 2)
Block address: corresponds to PCM or subcode data block,
the MSB indicates an ID bit (PCM or subcode data)

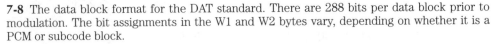

7-8 The data block format for the DAT standard. There are 288 bits per data block prior to modulation. The bit assignments in the W1 and W2 bytes vary, depending on whether it is a PCM or subcode block.

EXCLUSIVE-OR sum of the ID and block address bytes, and is used to detect errors in these header bytes. The remainder of the block holds 256 bits of data, that is, 32 bytes of audio or subcode data, and error correction data.

The majority of DAT subcode data is used for program timing and selection numbering. This primary subcode data, called subcode-ID, is written to two locations along the scan track to provide greater resistance to dropouts. (As described above, additional PCM-ID subcode data is contained in the PCM data areas.) Subcode-ID blocks are considered as pairs. The first block contains 11 bits of ID information in the header fields, and four 8-byte packs in the data field. The ID bits contain flags such as Start ID, Skip ID, and TOC-ID, as well as Data-ID data that duplicates ID-0, and Format-ID data describing the number of packs recorded. The second block contains 11 bits of Program number data in the header fields, and three packs, as well as eight bytes of C1 inner code redundancy. The Program number indicates lead-in and lead-out areas and selection numbering.

The information contained in the subcode-ID data packs is quite complex, and very flexible in its operation. These 64-bit blocks can contain data on program time, absolute time, running time, table of contents, catalog number, ISRC, professional timecode and other items, as well as control and parity data. (An example of a pack storing professional timecode is shown in Fig. 7-16.) Within each of these, other data

Table 7-2. The PCM-ID data is used to specify eight ID types; they describe basic recording parameters. ID-7 is used to create 64-byte pack data.

ID-0 (ID format)	ID-1 to ID-7	Description	
0 0 (for audio)	ID-1 (Emphasis)	00: off 10, 11: reserved	01: Pre-emp. (50/15μSec)
	ID-2 (Sampling frequency)	00: 48 kHz 10: 32 kHz	01: 44.1 kHz 11: reserved
	ID-3 (No. of channels)	00: 2 ch 10, 11: reserved	01: 4 ch
	ID-4 (No. of quantization bits)	00: 16 bits linear 10, 11: reserved	01: 12 bits nonlinear
	ID-5 (Track pitch)	00: 13.6 μm 10, 11: reserved	01: 20.4 μm
	ID-6 (Copy inhibit)	00: Digital copy permit 10: Digital copy inhibit	01: reserved 11: SCMS flag
	ID-7	Pack consists of 32 ID-7s.	

might be coded; for example, a program time pack might contain information on program number, index number, hours, minutes, second, and frames. The specification is considerable.

Because the subcode-ID data format is written in the subcode scan tracks, it can be recorded independently of PCM data. The user can write and erase nonaudio information either during recording or playback, manually or automatically. This capability permits various user functions. For example, desired points on the tape, such as the beginning of selections, can be searched for at high speed by detecting ID codes. The start ID codes from the current position can be detected in sequence, or a specific program number can be searched for directly. During playback, if the skip ID is marked, playback skips to the point at which the next start ID is marked, and playback begins again. Overall, the subcode capacity is 273.1 kbps, or about 4.5 times that of the 60 kbps rate of the CD.

The scan-track pattern is designed so that data needed for control purposes, such as subcode, can be read during high-speed search, as shown in Fig. 7-9. During high-speed shuttling, track following is not engaged, and instead the heads cross over many data tracks. Some synchronization blocks can be read, as well as some PCM and error correction data, thus bursts of audio data can be recovered and played. In addition, subcode as well as timecode (when recorded) can be recovered. Because subcode is repeated over many tracks, the recorder can perform a high-speed search for specific program addresses by specifying an address within the block format.

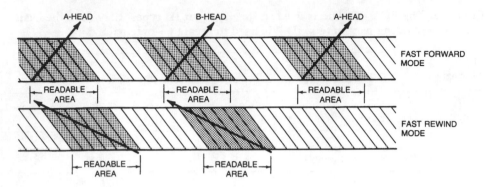

7-9 The head trace in fast forward and rewind mode is designed to read subcode (and limited audio) during high speed search.

The recorded area is distinguished from a blank section of tape with no recorded signal, even if the recorded area does not contain an audio signal. Unlike blank areas, the track format is always encoded on the tape even if no signal is present. If these sections are mixed on a tape, search operations might be slowed; hence, blank sections should be avoided.

Azimuth Recording

DAT scan tracks are recorded with azimuth recording, sometimes referred to as guard-bandless, or chevron recording. With azimuth recording, tracks can be recorded adjacent to one another, without a spacing; this increases recorded density. Moreover, the read head gap might be wider than the recorded track (1.5 times the track pitch) so the read head overscans the track; this simplifies tracking requirements. With this system, the drum's head pairs are angled differently from each other with respect to the tape. This creates two track types, sometimes referred to as A and B, with azimuth angles of ±20° between successively recorded tracks (see Fig. 7-6). This azimuth angle means that the A head, for example, reads track A and also adjacent B tracks at a greatly attenuated level due to phase cancellation. This reduces crosstalk between adjacent tracks, eliminates the need for a guardband between tracks, and promotes high-density recording.

The signals from the adjacent tracks are used for automatic track following (ATF) tracking control. In addition, selection of a channel code with minimal low-frequency content reduces the problem of phase reinforcement at long wavelengths. A greater angle would result in lower crosstalk, but the effective writing speed (calculated as the head-to-tape speed multiplied by the cosine of the azimuth angle) would be reduced as well. The angle of ±20° reduces crosstalk to a level comparable to tape noise, yet reduces signal level by only 1 dB as a result of lower writing speed. Moreover, some tolerance to tracking error is assured because as crosstalk from one track increases, it is offset by a decreasing crosstalk level from the opposite track.

Erasure is accomplished by simply overwriting new data to tape. By reducing the linear speed of the tape relative to the drum rotating speed, successive tracks partially write over previous tracks. Thus the head gaps (20.4 µm) are approximately 50% wider than the tracks (13.59 µm) recorded to tape. As noted, the resulting crosstalk from adjacent tracks is attenuated by azimuth recording, and permits automatic track following (ATF).

Automatic Track Following

To assist tape tracking and hence maintain a good quality playback signal, a sophisticated tracking correction system is used. Each scan track contains two bursts of an automatic track following (ATF) tracking signal. Its job is to control the capstan to ensure correct tracking. The ATF signals recorded on adjacent tracks permit this. The A head, for example, can follow an A track, using ATF signals recorded on adjacent B tracks. Likewise, the B head follows B tracks, using ATF signals on track A.

As shown in Fig. 7-10, ATF uses a pilot signal (f_1) at 130.67 kHz, sync signal 1 (f_2) at 522.67 kHz for A tracks, sync signal 2 (f_3) at 784.00 kHz for B tracks, and IBG erase signal (f_4) at 1.568 MHz. As each track is read, ATF of adjacent tracks is detected according to timing from either the f_2 or f_3 sync signals. The pilot signal occurs early in an A track, and late in a B track. Moreover, the ATF pattern repeats over four tracks with changes in the time of the synchronization signals to prevent the heads from following an incorrect track. The head overscans the track width to read a small

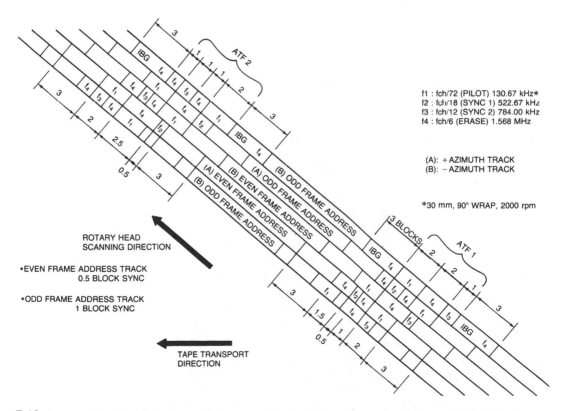

f1 : fch/72 (PILOT) 130.67 kHz*
f2 : fch/18 (SYNC 1) 522.67 kHz
f3 : fch/12 (SYNC 2) 784.00 kHz
f4 : fch/6 (ERASE) 1.568 MHz

(A): + AZIMUTH TRACK
(B): − AZIMUTH TRACK

*30 mm, 90° WRAP, 2000 rpm

ROTARY HEAD
SCANNING DIRECTION

•EVEN FRAME ADDRESS TRACK
0.5 BLOCK SYNC

•ODD FRAME ADDRESS TRACK
1 BLOCK SYNC

TAPE TRANSPORT
DIRECTION

7-10 Automatic track following (ATF) fields are located in two areas on the scan track; ATF helps ensure accurate tape tracking. Sony Corporation

part of the f_1 pilot signals on the adjacent tracks. The pilot signals on adjacent tracks do not occur simultaneously with respect to the following head thus the signals are delayed for comparison.

The intensity of the adjacent pilot signals is compared using analog means to generate a tracking-error signal. The RF signal from the tape is amplified and fed to a low-pass filter to extract the pilot signals from the current track and adjacent tracks. These signals are envelope-detected and applied to two sample-and-hold circuits to obtain the ATF error signal. Through this error signal, a servo system seeks to equalize the levels of the adjacent pilot signals, by causing the tracking-correction servo system to adjust tape-to-head positioning accordingly.

To accomplish this process, linear tape speed is varied so that the head is properly centered on the diagonally aligned track. The recorder output-data buffer removes all time variations from the signal. The wider tracks on prerecorded tapes automatically cause the linear tape speed to increase; the operation of the servo correction system is not altered.

The f_1 pilot signal uses a low-frequency (130.67 kHz) burst that is not affected by the head's azimuth setting; thus, the signal can be detected from both adjacent tracks. On the other hand, this low frequency is difficult to erase. After overwriting, remnants of the previous pilot signal could affect ATF, limiting tracking performance. The head and its recording current must be designed to overcome this. The ATF area is divided into two parts in the track format and moved inward along the track, so small amounts of track curvature do not yield tracking errors. Furthermore, automatic gain control in the servo system compensates for changes in playback gain because of head variations. Compatibility is easily achieved. The tracking control CTL head used in video recorders is not needed.

Eight-to-Ten Modulation

The 8/10 modulation group code used in DAT provides efficient operation in an azimuth recording system. Azimuth recording does not sufficiently attenuate crosstalk at low frequencies, thus the 8/10 code is designed to eliminate dc content and provide reduced low-frequency content in general. In addition, to facilitate overwriting, because erasure is optimized for short wavelengths, 8/10 provides a small ratio between the shortest and longest wavelengths, by limiting the maximum run length. Finally, 8/10 supports high-data density. In this code, a conversion is used in which an 8-bit information word is converted to a 10-bit channel word. Encoded codewords are written to tape with NRZI modulation.

The ideal 8/10 codeword would have no net dc content, with equal durations at high and low amplitudes in its modulated waveform. However, there are an insufficient number of such 10-bit channel words to represent the 256 states needed to encode the 8-bit data input. Moreover, given the maximum run length limitation, only 153 channel codes satisfy both requirements. Thus 103 codewords must have dc content, or nonzero digital sum value (DSV). DSV is used to monitor dc component. Simply put, the DSV tallies the high-amplitude channel bit periods versus the low-amplitude channel bit periods as encoded with NRZI. Two patterns are defined for each of the 103 non-zero DSV codewords, one with a +2 DSV and one with a −2 DSV;

to achieve this, the first channel bit is inverted. Either of these codewords can be selected based on the cumulative DSV. For example, if DSV ranges negatively, a +2 word is selected to tend toward a zero dc condition. Figure 7-11 shows a portion of the 8/10 lookup table, and a codeword that does not require an alternate, and a codeword that does.

Dataword	Codeword	DSV	Alternate codeword	DSV
MSB	MSB		MSB	
01110000	0010010010	0	0010010010	0
01110001	1011010010	2	0011010010	−2
01110010	1010010010	0	1010010010	0
01110011	1010110010	0	1010110010	0
01110100	0010110001	2	1010110001	−2
01110101	0010110011	2	1010110011	−2
01110110	0010110110	2	1010110110	−2
01110111	0010110010	0	0010110010	0

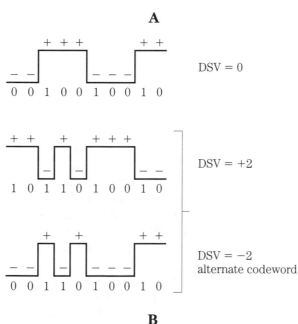

A

B

7-11
With 8/10 modulation, a digital sum value (DSV) is used to constrain the signal dc component. A. A portion of the 8/10 lookup table showing that codewords with +2 DSV are given alternate codewords with −2 DSV. B. DSV is determined from the polarity levels of the NRZI signal.

To facilitate conversion, the 8/10 relationship was prepared via computer optimization. A programmed logic array can be used to generate the 8/10 code in real time. The decoding process is relatively easy to implement because DSV need not be computed. A single-channel bit error in an 8/10 channel word can result in another valid channel word; this increases the need for error correction. The 8/10 code permits adjacent channel 1s, and there are no more than three channel 0s between 1s. The density ratio is 0.8 and FoM (figure of merit) is 0.64. Bit synchronization and block synchronization are provided with a $3.2T + 3.2T$ synchronization signal, a prohibited 8/10 pattern. Also, at the start of each data area, up to two blocks of a 4.7-MHz signal are recorded to assist PLL operation. Modulation codes are discussed in chapter 3.

DAT Error Correction

Because the tape is always in contact with the rotating heads during record, playback, and search modes, tape wear necessitates sophisticated error correction. In addition, tape is prone to manufacturing defects and environmental factors. DAT is thus designed to correct random and burst errors; the former caused by crosstalk from an adjacent track, traces of an imperfectly erased signal, or mechanical instability; the latter from dropouts caused by dust, scratches on the tape, or head clogging with dirt. DAT error correction, however, must permit editing. Therefore, data cannot be interleaved over many tracks; it must be limited to pairs of tracks. In this way, new material can be recorded over old. The DAT format requires a large data buffer to achieve the time compression needed for rotary head storage, and to perform interleaving; in practice, a DAT recorder may use a RAM memory that is eight times that used in a CD player for de-interleaving and jitter absorption. Two DAT tracks (one drum rotation) are required to start playback (128 blocks × 32 symbols × 8 bits × 2 tracks = 65,536 bits); in practice, a buffer twice this size (128k bits) is used.

The DAT format assumes a symbol error rate of 10^{-5} (at 48 kHz, two errors every second); this is a reasonable value, given the data density. Clearly, particularly robust error correction processing is needed. To facilitate error correction, each data track is split into halves, between left and right channels. In addition, data for each channel is interleaved into even and odd data blocks, one for each head. The interleave process completes every two tracks. (In addition, a C2 error correction code is inserted between the first and second half of a track.) The data interleaving format is shown in Fig. 7-12A. Interleaving guards against burst errors such as caused by a dirty head, because half of each channel's samples are recorded by each head. For example, one head records the right channel's even samples and the left channel's odd samples, and the other head records the left channel's even samples and right channel's odd samples. With a dirty head, only half of each channel's samples will be lost. This can be concealed by interpolation, as shown in Fig. 7-12B. Similarly, a tape defect could cause losses in both channels, but only even or odd samples would be lost simultaneously. The interleaving maps for 48-, 44.1-, and 32-kHz sampling frequencies are shown in Fig. 7-13.

All the data is encoded with a doubly encoded Reed-Solomon error correction code over a Galois field GF(2^8) using the polynomial: $x^8 + x^4 + x^3 + x^2 + 1$. The inner code C1 is a (32,28) Reed-Solomon code with a minimum distance of five. Four bytes of redundancy are added to the 28 data bytes. The outer code C2 is a (32,26) Reed-Solomon code with a minimum distance of seven. Six bytes of redundancy are added to the 26 data bytes. Both C1 and C2 codes are composed of 32 symbols (a symbol is comprised of eight bits) and are orthogonal with each other. C1 is interleaved over two blocks, and C1 is interleaved across an entire PCM data track, every four blocks. As with the com-

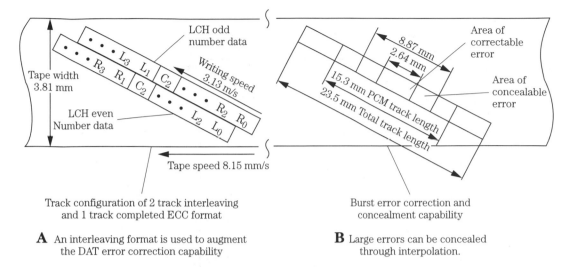

A An interleaving format is used to augment the DAT error correction capability

B Large errors can be concealed through interpolation.

7-12 DAT error-correction configuration showing even/odd writing and interleaving.

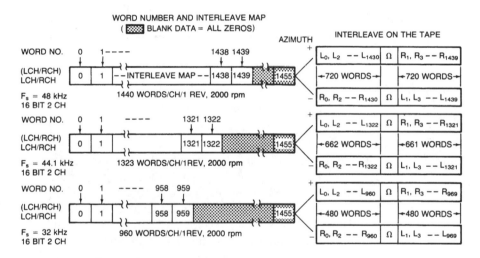

7-13 DAT interleaving is provided for 48-, 44.1-, and 32-kHz sampling rates.

pact disc, the error correction code used in DAT endeavors to detect and correct random errors (using the inner code) and eliminate them prior to de-interleaving; burst errors are detected and flagged. Following de-interleaving, burst errors are scattered and more easily corrected. Using the error flags, the outer code can correct remaining errors. Uncorrected errors must be concealed.

The code configuration of a data frame is shown in Fig. 7-14. Two blocks of data are assembled, one from each head, and placed in a memory arranged as 128 columns by 32 bytes. Samples are split into two bytes to form 8-bit symbols. Symbols are placed in memory, reserving a 24-byte wide area in the middle columns. Rows of data

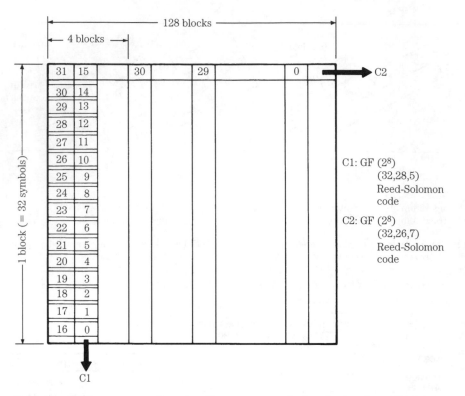

7-14 The DAT error-correction algorithm uses a product code structured from inner and outer Reed-Solomon codes across an array.

are applied to the first (outer C2 code) Reed-Solomon encoder, selecting every fourth column, finishing at column 124, yielding 26 bytes. The Reed-Solomon encoder generates six bytes of parity yielding 32 bytes. These are placed in the middle (empty) columns, at every fourth location (52, 56, 60, etc.). The encoder repeats its operation with the second column, taking every fourth byte, finishing at column 125. Six parity bytes are generated and placed in every fourth column (53, 57, 61, etc.). Similarly, the memory is filled with 112 outer codewords. (The final eight rows require only two passes because odd-numbered columns have bytes only to row 23.)

Memory is next read by columns. Sixteen even-numbered bytes from the first column and the first twelve even-numbered bytes from the second column are applied to the second (inner C1 code) encoder, yielding four parity bytes for a total codeword of 32 bytes. This word forms one recorded synchronization block. A second pass reads the odd-numbered row samples from the first two columns of memory, again yielding four parity bytes and another synchronization block. Similarly, the process repeats until 128 blocks have been recorded on tape.

The decoding procedure, flow-charted in Fig. 7-15, utilizes first the C1 code, then the C2 code. In C1 decoding, a syndrome is calculated to identify data errors as erroneous symbols. The number of errors in the C1 code is determined using the syndrome; in addition, the position of the errors can be determined. Depending on

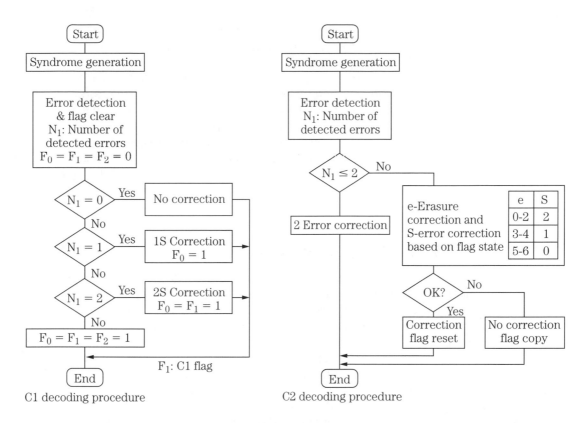

7-15 A flow chart of the error correction decoding strategy, showing the correction capability of the C1 and C2 codes.

the number of errors, C1 either corrects the errors, or flags the erroneous symbols. In C2 decoding, a syndrome is again calculated, and the number and position of errors determined, and correction is carried out. During C1 decoding, error correction is performed on one or two erroneous bytes due to random errors. For more than two errors, erasure correction is performed using C1 flags attached to all bytes in the block prior to de-interleaving. After de-interleaving these errors are distributed, and appear as single byte errors, with flags. The probability of uncorrectable or misdetected errors increases along with the number of errors in C1 decoding. It is negligible for a single error because all four syndromes will agree on the error. A double error increases the probability.

The C2 decoding procedure is selected to reduce the probability of misdetection. For example, the optimal combination of error correction and erasure correction can be selected based on error conditions. In addition, C2 carries out syndrome computation even when no error flags are received from C1. Because C1 has corrected random errors, C2's burst error correction is not compromised. C2 independently corrects one- or two-byte errors in the outer codeword. For two to six erroneous bytes in the outer codeword, C2 uses flags supplied by C1 for erasure correcting. Because the outer code undergoes four-way interleaving, four erroneous synchronization blocks result in only one erroneous byte in an outer codeword. Because C2 can correct up to six erroneous bytes, burst errors up to 24 synchronization blocks in duration can thus be corrected.

Overall, the system can completely correct burst errors of up to 792 symbols long (22 blocks × 36 symbols/block × 8 bits/symbol) = 6336 bits) and random errors up to two symbols per block. Generally, a block error rate of 50 to 100 is normal; rates higher than 200 would indicate a problem in tape playback. Physically, the error-correction system can correct a vertical defect up to 2.6 mm in diameter, or a horizontal defect up to 0.3 mm high (see Fig. 7-6). Dropouts up to 8.8 mm long and 1.0 mm high can be concealed with interpolation. In practice, mechanical tracking problems, for example, caused by transport misalignment, rather than tape defects, lead to greater error problems. Error correction is discussed in detail in chapter 5.

Serial Copy Management System

Consumer DAT recorders contain a Serial Copy Management System (SCMS) circuit to prevent multiple-generation digital copying of protected material, as described in chapter 10. In particular, data entering the recorder via an S/PDIF interface (for example via a phono cable or fiber-optic cable) is examined for copyright information. The recorder examines the C-bit, category code, and L-bit, and writes the appropriate SCMS code to tape. Internally, SCMS information is stored in two PCM-ID subcode bits identified as ID-6, within the main ID data area. The status of ID-6 can change throughout a tape. When ID-6 is set to 00, no copy protection is in effect for that portion of the tape. When ID-6 is set to 10, the data is copied (not original) and becomes copy protected. If ID-6 is 11, the data is original and copy protected. During playback, the recorder examines ID-6 and outputs the appropriate C-bit, category code, and L-bit in its bit stream. SCMS signals do not appear on AES3 connectors, thus data is not copy protected, and can be indefinitely copied.

Prerecorded DAT

As with any audio source hardware, DAT will play back prerecorded digital tapes. However, the DAT prerecorded format differs from the recording format. The prerecorded DAT tape format provides for normal and wide modes, depending on the method of duplication. (Specifications for prerecorded DATs are included in Table 7-1.) In the normal mode, prerecorded DAT tapes are duplicated in real time; as with the record/playback modes, metal particle tape is used. In the wide playback mode, tapes can be duplicated at high speed. However, because the resulting signal level is lower than that from real-time dubbing, the wide mode requires a wider track width to compensate for the decrease in output level. Track pitch (width) is increased from 13.591 μm to 20.4 μm by increasing linear tape speed 1.5 times, from 8.15 mm/s to 12.225 mm/s. The 50% difference in track pitch gives a 3.5-dB margin in playback output level; however, playing time is reduced to 80 minutes.

In addition, the ATF pattern is modified slightly in the wide track pitch format to maintain playback compatibility of the ATF circuit between the normal mode and the wide track pitch mode. In practice, prerecorded DAT tapes have found little favor with consumers.

Professional DAT

Although DAT was originally designed as a consumer digital audio recording format, it has applications for the professional recording industry in areas such as studio and portable recording, TV and radio broadcast, editing, timecode video, and CD mastering. Its high audio performance, data integrity, ease of handling, and long playing time make it useful for these and other tasks, but only if certain professional requirements are met.

To promote widespread use and take advantage of the cost reduction enabled by its consumer origins, professional DAT recorders must retain compatibility with the consumer format. In this way, professional recorders can play back tapes made on consumer recorders, and professional tapes can be played back on consumer decks. To ensure compatibility, all tape formats and ATF must be identical, as defined in the consumer DAT specification. Similarly, professional DAT recorders must adhere to other DAT parameters, such as a 16-bit word length, to ensure compatibility. Moreover, professional subcode must be defined within the context of consumer subcode; however, professional DAT recorders can implement subcode features reserved but unspecified for consumer decks. In this way, professional features can be added without violating the DAT specification.

DAT Interfacing

Many professional digital audio recorders are interconnected via the AES3 (or AES/EBU) serial transmission interface, in which digital audio data is conveyed along with information such as auxiliary bits, channel status and user data. The data capacity required to store all the data in the AES3 interface is considerable; for example, total capacity for two-channel auxiliary data (user data and channel status) is 192 kbps without compression, blocking structure or error correction. By consolidating left and right channel auxiliary data, discarding some channel status information, and using an internal blocking structure related to the DAT track structure (and independent of the AES3 interface) pertinent interface information can be economically recorded on DAT. The AES3 interface is discussed in detail in chapter 10.

DAT Timecode

SMPTE/EBU timecode is important in applications such as film and video recording and posting, audio sweetening, and CD premastering where synchronization of sources is paramount. The original consumer DAT standard was not designed to support timecode. An SMPTE timecode signal can be coded with a data rate of 2.4 kbps. However, the task of adding timecode while retaining compatibility with the existing DAT standard was challenging because SMPTE/EBU timecode clocking has no integral relationship whatsoever with the DAT recording format.

One simple design approach is not workable. The DAT tape format has optional longitudinal tracks along both outer tape edges, without compulsory function. However, the slow linear tape speed makes it difficult to record full timecode data. Moreover, the short recorded wavelength (less than a μm) and the need to provide correspondence between record and playback would make the alignment of a stationary record/playback head extremely critical.

Instead, timecode is recorded in the helical scan tracks. Although it is not possible to reduce the amount of audio, track following, and error-correction data recorded, the subcode area on these tracks can accommodate timecode data because only a small portion of DAT subcode is assigned. However, the solution is not simple because the frame rate of DAT (33.333 frames/second) is incompatible with timecode rates (24, 25, 29.97, and 30 frames/second).

As noted, scan tracks are recorded as blocks, each of which contains 360 channel bits. A track contains 196 blocks, of which 16 are devoted to subcode. The subcode-ID area is divided into two areas, each with 8 blocks. In addition to ID marks such as skip ID and start ID, subcode data is divided into seven divisions known as packs. Each pack contains 64 bits (52 bits of user data) and can be used for a variety of purposes. For example, in the consumer DAT standard, some packs contain a running time that continuously increases. Other packs contain program time, absolute time, TOC, catalog number, ISRC, etc. In all, 16 types of packs are possible, but only a maximum of seven can be recorded within any two-block group. This is where SMPTE/EBU timecode is placed into the DAT standard.

In the pro DAT format, the consumer R-Time (running time) pack is modified to form a Pro R-Time pack. In addition, an entirely new pack, Pro Binary, is established. Incoming timecode, of any rate, is converted to pro DAT timecode (or pro-running time as it is known) according to defined frame rate conversion algorithms. Pro R-Time is then recorded in the same pack structure as R-Time at 33.333 Hz, with 11-bit timecode marker in hours, minutes, seconds, and frames, as shown in Fig. 7-16. The Pack item identifies this as a Pro R-Time pack; the SPI0/SPI1 bits designate IEC timecode, AES3 sample address code or AES3 time of day code; the F1/F0 bits designate input sampling frequency; and T2/T1/T0 indicate original timecode rate. The pro-running time is converted back to timecode upon playback. In addition to the frame number conversion, the absolute phase relationship between the DAT frame edge and the incoming timecode frame edge must be maintained. The difference is expressed as a number of samples and is recorded along with the Pro R-Time as the 11-bit timecode marker. In this way, during playback, phase accuracy between audio and timecode can be recreated to sample accuracy.

The system essentially converts real time to real time. This approach is a more complex approach, but highly beneficial. The Pro DAT code that is recorded is unique. Every professional machine can read and convert it back to SMPTE/EBU frame rates. The original timecode frame rate can be ignored. The playback timecode frame rate can be selected by the playback hardware thus a universal timecode conversion method is inherent in the pro DAT system. Using standard algorithms defined in the pro DAT format, various SMPTE/EBU timecodes can be successfully transcribed and recorded onto DAT. In other words, in theory, any type of timecode could be converted to pro DAT time. In addition, timecode and interface standards include auxiliary data. For example, the AES3 interface contains information in the channel status blocks and the SMPTE/EBU interface contains user bits as well. The pro DAT standard can record

	B7	B6	B5	B4	B3	B2	B1	B0
	Pack item							
PC1	0	0	1	1	1	0	SP0	SP1
PC2	F1	F0	T2	T1	T0	(MSB)		
PC3	11-bit timecode marker					(LSB)		
PC4	Hours (RH)							
PC5	Minutes (RM)							
PC6	Seconds (RS)							
PC7	Frames (RF)							
PC8	Pack parity							

7-16
The Pro R-time pack structure is used to record timecode in professional recorders. Data includes designation of the original timecode, sampling frequency, 11-bit timecode differential marker, and timecode recorded at 33.333 Hz.

this data using a Pro-binary pack. The IEC has ratified this timecode modification to the original R-DAT standard.

Professional DAT Features

All professional recorders are compatible with the consumer DAT standard. Professional recorders use the standard DAT helical scan; however, a four-head format is typically used. During recording and dubbing, a read-after-write function provides off-tape audio monitoring. In editing, either the recorder or player can be monitored. Audio data and timecode can be recorded either simultaneously in the assemble mode or individually in the insert mode. Start IDs and program numbers can be added using read-modify-write functions; accuracy of 1 frame can be obtained. Playback speed can be varied over a ±12.5% range. Cueing is performed at higher or lower than normal speed using a search dial in a shuttle mode. Digital I/O includes the AES3, S/PDIF, and SDIF-2 interfaces. Analog connections are provided through balanced XLR-type connectors. Timecode and word synchronization input/output connectors are used for external synchronization.

An SMPTE/EBU timecode reader/generator enables the recorder to operate synchronously with an external video synchronization signal. The recorder can perform timecode chase synchronization. In normal mode, playback starts automatically when locked to the received timecode. In the rechase mode, the recorder continually chases, maintaining synchronization despite variations in the master clock. The recorders can be locked to reference signals such as SMPTE/EBU drop or nondrop frame, EBU timecodes, and video synchronization. When video machines are not used, synchronization can be achieved via word clock from a digital audio system. Recorders can have a 4 Mbit memory so the recorder can start with zero rise time; this instant start feature is used for on-air and sweetening applications. An RS-232C computer interface allows the recorder to be placed under computer control.

Two properly equipped recorders form a complete editing system, allowing both assemble editing and insert editing. In the latter, insert in/out points are placed in a large (for example, 16 Mbit) memory using a search dial, and specified for the player and recorder. Insert audio recording can occur only in the context of the track block structure. Synchronization is required prior to the edit point, necessitating a preroll. Memory rehearsal is used to modify the points before automatic editing. The editor provides memory search/rehearsal, and crossfading, and editing accuracy to 1 ms. Crossfading is required at the end of an insert edit point, because the last over-written track results in a half-width track of previously written data. Pro DATs can record only in the 16-bit linear mode, and cannot use the wide track pitch established for consumer prerecorded tapes. Otherwise, the PCM data area is identical to that in consumer DAT.

Although the DAT format failed in its attempt to supplant the analog cassette, it has found many important applications in consumer and professional audio. Like the CD, it provides high fidelity, long playing time, and conveniences such as programmability and indexing. The DAT format is useful as a low-cost, highly portable, linear 16-bit recording system.

8
CHAPTER

Optical Storage
and Transmission

Optical media can provide about 100 times the storage capacity of the same size magnetic media; the storage cost of optical media is a fraction of the cost per byte of magnetic media. Erasable optical drives hold over 1 Gbyte, and development of blue lasers in the 460- to 500-nm range will further increase optical disk capacity. The life expectancy of optical disks is much longer than that of magnetic media, they are much less susceptible to damage from heat and humidity, and they are essentially impervious to magnetic fields and head crashes. Conservatively, a magneto-optical disk should last 10 years, and a compact disc for 100 years.

In the same way that digital audio technology's voracious appetite for data has made optical storage critical in technological development, new technologies have been developed to move this vast quantity of data over both long and short distances. Increasingly, to reliably handle high data rates, fiber-optic communication is used; this high-bandwidth technology is very effective with multimedia data, particularly when it is directed over long distances. Although audio engineers have always been proficient with audio, and even radio-frequency phenomena, it is increasingly useful to understand the physics occurring at somewhat higher, perhaps visible, frequencies.

Optical Phenomena

Light is an electromagnetic vibration that can be characterized by wavelength, frequency, propagation velocity, propagation direction, vibration direction, and intensity. The optical spectrum, within the context of the electromagnetic spectrum, is shown in Fig. 8-1. Generally, light ranges from 7.5×10^{10} to 6.0×10^{16} Hz. Because light occupies a higher frequency than other communications methods, it provides a higher bandwidth.

Wavelength is the distance between identical points on a waveform; the wavelengths of visible light extend from about 400 to 800 nm. Wavelength equals velocity

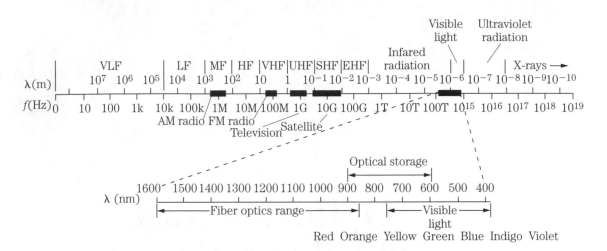

8-1 The electromagnetic spectrum, showing the wavelengths used in optical storage and fiber-optic systems.

of propagation divided by frequency. Likewise, velocity of propagation is the product of wavelength and frequency. The velocity of light in a vacuum is 3×10^8 m/s; light travels slower in other materials. Frequency measures the number of vibrations per second; the frequency of an electromagnetic wave is constant, and does not change in matter, but its velocity and wavelength are reduced. Light at different wavelengths travels at different velocities in the same medium. Light can exist at a single wavelength (monochromatic light) or a mixture of various wavelengths (for example, natural light). The intensity of a light wave is the amount of energy that flows per second across a unit area perpendicular to the direction of propagation. It is proportional to the square of the amplitude, and to the square of the frequency.

Refraction takes place when light passes into a medium with a different index of refraction; light changes speed, which causes a deflection in path. For example, when light in air strikes a glass prism, the velocity of propagation is decreased, the wavelength in the denser medium is shorter, thus the light travels through the receiving medium at a different angle, as shown in Fig. 8-2. When light leaves the prism, refraction occurs again. When white light (comprising many wavelengths) strikes a prism, each wavelength changes speed differently, and is refracted at a different angle. Light emerges from the prism dispersed into colors of the visible spectrum. The index of refraction is smallest for red light, and increasingly larger for smaller wavelengths.

A medium's index of refraction (n) is the ratio of the light's velocity (c) in a vacuum, to its velocity (v) in a medium; in other words, $n = c/v$. The index of refraction of light in a vacuum is 1.00; in air is 1.0003 (rounded to 1.0); in water is 1.33; in glass is 1.5. The indexes of refraction of the incident and receiving mediums determine the angle of the refracted beam relative to the incident beam. The angle of incidence is the angle between the incident ray and the normal, an imaginary line perpendicular to the materials' interface; the angle of refraction is the angle between the refracted ray and the normal.

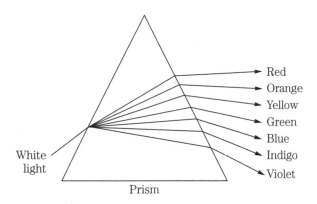

8-2
When white light passes through a prism, refraction occurs at both surfaces. Refraction disperses the beam into its component wavelengths. Similarly, water droplets in the air act as prisms, creating rainbows.

When light passes into a medium with higher index of refraction, it is refracted toward the normal, as shown in Fig. 8-3A. However, when light passes into a material with a lower index of refraction, it refracts away from the normal, as shown in Fig. 8-3B. As the angle of incidence increases, the angle of refraction approaches 90°; this is the critical angle, as shown in Fig. 8-3C. At any incident angle greater than this critical angle, no refraction takes place, and all light is reflected back into the first medium at an angle identical to that of the incident angle, as shown in Fig. 8-3D. Specifically, when the angle of incidence is greater than the critical angle, the result is total internal reflection. This phenomenon is essential for light propagation in fiber optics.

More specifically, Snell's law states:

$$\frac{n_1}{n_2} = \frac{\sin \theta_2}{\sin \theta_1}$$

where

n_1 = index of refraction of incident medium (such as a fiber-optic core)
θ_1 = the angle of incidence
n_2 = index of refraction of receiving medium (such as a fiber-optic cladding)
θ_2 = the angle of refraction

The critical angle of incidence is $\theta_{critical}$ where $\theta_2 = 90°$:

$$\theta_{critical} = \sin^{-1}\left(\frac{n_2}{n_1}\right)$$

Light is totally reflected at angles greater than $\theta_{critical}$, and the angle of total reflection equals the angle of incidence.

Diffraction

Light can be modelled to propagate via rays (which exist only in theory) in the direction of propagation. Surfaces perpendicular to the rays are called wavefronts (which exist in actuality). Wavefront normals, similar to rays, indicate the direction of propagation. The advance of light can be viewed as a summed collection of an infinite number of spherical waves emitted by point sources; this is described in Huygen's principle. They are in phase, thus creating a wavefront. However, destructive interference occurs between the spherical waves at all other angles.

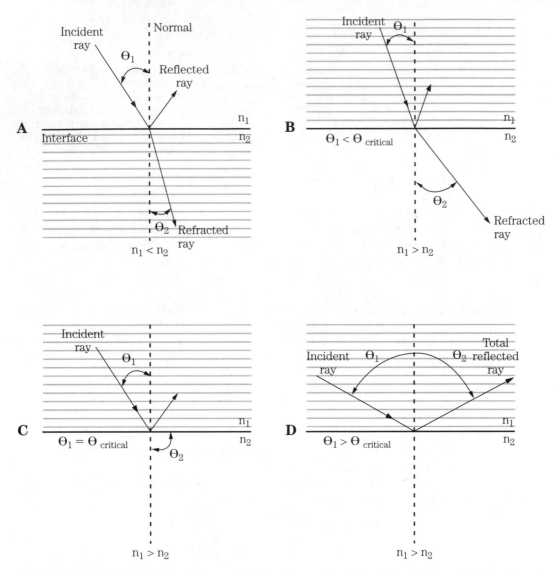

8-3 Light refracts when it passes from one medium to another with different indexes of refraction. A. When n_1 is less than n_2 the refracted ray is bent toward the normal. B. When n_1 is greater than n_2 the refracted ray is bent away from the normal. C. When n_1 is greater than n_2 and the incident angle equals the critical angle, light does not enter n_2. D. When n_1 is greater than n_2 and the incident angle is greater than the critical angle, all light is reflected back into n_1; this is total internal reflection.

When a wavefront passes through an aperture that is small relative to the wavelength (an order of a half wavelength), diffraction occurs, and the wavefront emerges as a point source. For example, diffraction occurs when a single slit is placed in a barrier (as first observed by Joseph von Fraunhofer). A diffraction grating contains a series of identical equidistant slits. Because of interference, a wavefront will only leave the grating in directions where light from all the slits is in phase. This happens straight ahead, and at certain other angles. The angle of the first oblique wave is a function of the wavelength of the light, and the spacing of the slits. If the spacing of the slits is reduced (the spatial frequency is increased), the oblique ray will leave at a greater angle to the center line. Similarly, the smaller a physical object, the larger the angle over which light must be collected to view the object; fine detail can be resolved only if the diffraction wavefront is collected by the lens. As described in the following sections, this angle is specified as the numerical aperture of the lens. A diffraction pattern shows the maxima and minima intensities corresponding to the phase differences resulting from different path lengths. The central maximum is the zero order maxima. Other light is diffracted into a series of higher-order maxima. The diffraction pattern formed behind a circular aperture is known as the Airy pattern, proposed by British astronomer George Airy in 1835.

Specifically, even if a lens is perfectly free of aberration, a laser beam, for example, cannot be focused to a point with a circular lens of finite aperture. The focused laser spot is actually an area where the intensity of light varies as a function called the Airy pattern, as shown in Fig. 8-4. This is a circular diffraction pattern of maximum and minimum light intensities corresponding to phase differences. The central spot is the zero-order maximum, and the surrounding rings are higher-order maxima. About 83% of the total light falls in the central spot, and the brightest intensity in the first ring is only ⅟₆₀ that of the central spot.

The size of the Airy pattern is a function of the light wavelength and the numerical aperture of the lens (described in the following text). Laser pickup optics are

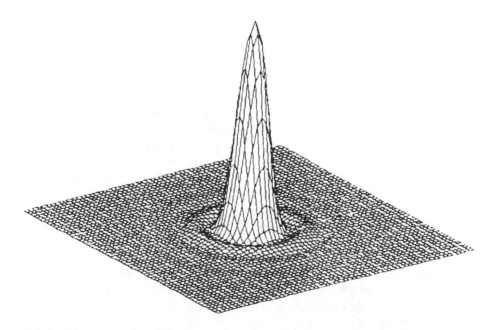

8-4 An Airy pattern is a diffraction pattern for a point source emerging from an aperture. Robert Dunn

said to be diffraction-limited as opposed to tolerance-limited. This dictates a higher-quality lens would still result in the same spot size. As a result, for example, an optical microscope cannot image the diffraction-limited pit spiral on an optical disk; a scanning electron microscope is needed. More important, a high-density CD with smaller pit size would demand a laser pickup operating at a shorter wavelength.

A simple hands-on experiment suggested by Christian Nöldeke can be used to demonstrate diffraction. In particular, we can show that the CD data surface causes diffraction, and we can use the result to calculate a CD's track pitch. Fetch a CD and a ruler, and seat yourself with a light bulb—60 W or so—about a meter behind you. Hold the CD about a foot from your face (reflective side facing you) and angle it so the light bulb's reflection disappears in the disc center hole. Now slowly move the disc toward your face, keeping the bulb's reflection centered in the hole. The bright display is a result of the diffraction created by the pit track.

Now move the disc away from you until the violet ring is located on the edge of the CD. If you measure this, you will find it to be about 20 cm from your eye. Now you can calculate the track pitch using the equation:

$$d = \lambda \left(1 + \frac{a^2}{r^2}\right)^{1/2}$$

where

    d = the track pitch
    λ = the wavelength of the violet light (450 nm)
    a = the distance away (20 cm)
    r = the radius of the violet ring (5.5 cm)

Calculating, you obtain a track pitch value of 1.7 µm—only $\frac{1}{10,000,000}$ of a meter away from the actual pitch (on most CDs) of 1.6 µm.

Resolution of Optical Systems

As described in previous sections, whenever parallel light passes through a circular aperture, it cannot be focused to a point image, but yields a diffraction pattern in which the central maximum has a finite width—an Airy pattern. The aperture of an objective lens system is circular. Consider the images of two equally bright point sources of light. Now, consider each point as an Airy pattern. If the points are close, the diffraction patterns will overlap. When the separation is such that it is just possible to determine that there are two points and not one, the points are said to be resolved, as shown in Fig. 8-5. This is the case when the center of one diffraction pattern coincides with the first minimum of the other. The distance between the two diffraction pattern maxima equals the radius of the first dark ring. This condition is called the Rayleigh criterion.

Similarly, the smaller the object that is viewed, the greater the angle over which light must be collected. In other words, the diffracted wave front must be collected. The resolving power of the lens is determined by its numerical aperture (NA). The numerical aperture of a lens is the diameter of the lens in relation to its focal length and describes the angle over which it collects light. NA is calculated as the sine of the angle between the optic axis and the diffracted wave front determined by the high-

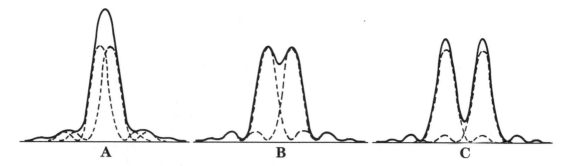

8-5 The Rayleigh Criterion determines the resolution of an optical system. A. Overlapping diffraction patterns cannot be resolved. B. Partially overlapping patterns are resolved (Rayleigh Criterion). C. Nonoverlapping patterns are resolved.

est spatial frequency. A lens is a spatial filter and the cutoff of the spatial frequency is determined by the numerical aperture; the modulation transfer function (MTF) describes the response of the lens. This defines the minimum size of a resolved object for a given wavelength. Because the finite numerical aperture results in a cutoff of spatial frequency, the Airy pattern is analogous to the impulse response of a low-pass filter.

The spot size (d) is often defined as the half-intensity diameter of the Airy pattern such that $d = 0.61\lambda/NA$ where λ is the wavelength of the laser light in a vacuum. For high data density on an optical disk, d must be small. In a CD, λ is fixed at 780 nm; thus NA must be as large as possible. However, as NA is increased, tolerances become severe: the depth of focus tolerance is proportional to NA^{-2}, skew tolerance is proportional to NA^{-3}, and disc thickness tolerance is proportional to NA^{-4}. Clearly, for system stability, NA should be as low as possible. Balancing these factors, the CD designers selected $NA = 0.45$. Thus, spot size is approximately 1.0 μm.

Similarly, NA and λ determine many other specifications; track pitch, cutoff frequency, track velocity and ultimately, disc playing time are deduced. For example, the spatial cutoff frequency can be determined:

$$f_{co} = \frac{2NA}{\lambda} = \frac{2(0.45)}{780 \times 10^{-9}} = 1.15 \times 10^6$$

Thus formations with a higher spatial frequency (for example, lines smaller than 1.15 lines per micrometer) cannot be resolved. Optical systems must be designed to operate within this constraint. For example, in the CD system, the shortest pit/land length is 0.833 μm. A series of short pit/lands would thus yield a spatial frequency of $1/(2)(0.833 \times 10^{-6}) = 0.600 \times 10^6$, or about half the cutoff frequency and hence easily readable. Furthermore, given a CD with a track velocity of 1.2 m/s, the cutoff temporal frequency is:

$$f_c = \frac{2(NAv)}{\lambda} = \frac{2(0.45)(1.2)}{780 \times 10^{-9}} = 1.38 \text{ MHz}$$

In terms of an optical channel, the amplitude of the modulated signal is maximum at 0 Hz and linearly decreases to zero at 1.38 MHz.

Polarization

Electromagnetic waves such as light waves (and radio waves) consist of electric and magnetic fields that are perpendicular to each other, and both oscillating transversely to the direction of propagation. (The reader will recall that sound propagates longitudinally.) Either field can be used to characterize light, but the electric field is generally used. The transverse electric field can oscillate with vertical, horizontal, diagonal, or other more complex geometry, but is always perpendicular to the direction of travel. Light from a light bulb is said to be unpolarized because an infinite number of electric fields exist and are randomly perpendicular to the direction of travel. Any one of these electric (E) fields, at any angle, can be considered as a vector represented by two orthogonal components E_x and E_y. Examination shows that the component waves are phase incoherent.

However, when only one electric field is allowed to oscillate, in a single direction that is perpendicular to the direction of travel, the light is said to be linearly polarized or plane polarized. A polarizer accomplishes this, as shown in Fig. 8-6. The electric field lies in one plane, and does not change direction; moreover, one plane contains the electric vector and the direction of propagation. When the orthogonal components representing the E field are examined, we observe that each of them represent linearly polarized light, and are in phase with each other, as shown in Fig. 8-7A. Combined, they produce a single linearly polarized wave. In addition, the linearly polarized E_x and E_y components can be combined with a relative phase shift. In particular,

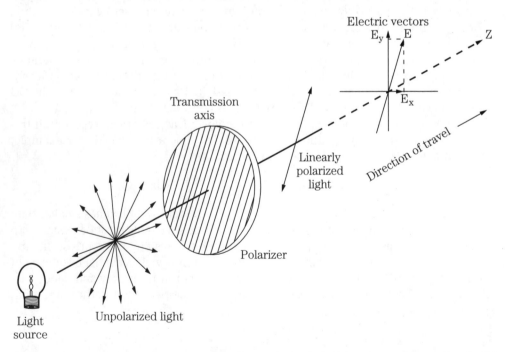

8-6 A polarizer is used to create linearly polarized light. Only light waves with an electric (E) field vector parallel to the transmission axis can pass through. The E vector can be represented by two components E_x and E_y.

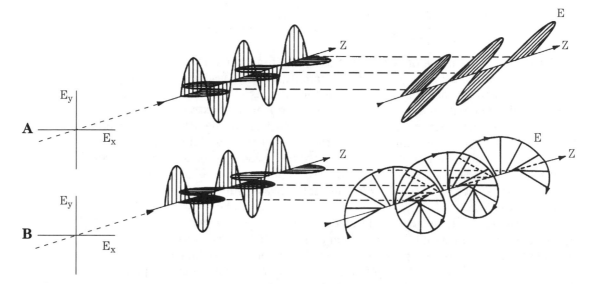

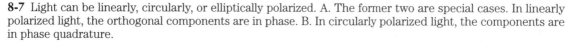

8-7 Light can be linearly, circularly, or elliptically polarized. A. The former two are special cases. In linearly polarized light, the orthogonal components are in phase. B. In circularly polarized light, the components are in phase quadrature.

when the phase difference is 90° (phase quadrature) the light is circularly polarized, as shown in Fig. 8-7B. The magnitude of the resulting electric vector is constant, but instead of remaining in one plane, it varies from point to point and from time to time. Specifically, it rotates through a helix once per wavelength; viewed from the direction of propagation, it traces a circle. At other component phase shifts, the light is elliptically polarized; the electric vector varies as it rotates, and traces out an ellipse. In any case, the wave can be resolved into its linearly polarized components.

Isotropic materials have one velocity of transmission independent of the plane of propagation. A material is anisotropic when the light entering it does not have the same velocity in all planes; in other words, the index of refraction depends on the direction of travel through it. Anisotropic materials such as calcite can be used to create polarized light. When unpolarized light enters an anisotropic medium, light rays are split into two part rays. One ray passes through the object as in an isotropic medium, diffracting normally; the second ray is refracted more strongly and is thus displaced from the first as it emerges. The first ray is called the ordinary ray, and the second is called the extraordinary ray. The two rays are linearly polarized, in mutually perpendicular planes. This is known as double refraction, or birefringence. The direction along which no birefringence occurs, where the material behaves exactly like an isotropic medium, is called the optic axis.

The plastic used in optical disk substrates can exhibit birefringence after it is subjected to the stress of melting and injection molding during disk manufacture. This birefringence is an unwelcome effect of anisotropy. A wave front (perhaps emitted from a laser pickup) travelling through the substrate is distorted because the two orthogonal components travel at different velocities, creating a birefringent image. The velocity difference depends on the direction of the light ray passing through the bire-fringence material. In practice, birefringence is minimized through careful manufacturing technique.

A rotation in the plane of polarization, resulting from different velocities in different planes, can be usefully employed. A retardation plate is a slice cut from a crystal in such a manner that the slice contains the optic axis. A beam of unpolarized light normally incident on the plate will create an ordinary and extraordinary beam. The phase difference between these beams is proportional to the distance travelled within the plate. When the beams emerge, they are not separated, but they are out of phase. If the thickness of the plate is such that the phase difference at emergence between the superimposed ordinary and extraordinary beam is λ/4, the plate is called a quarter-wave plate (QWP). Similarly, if the phase difference is λ/2, the plate is a half-wave plate.

By passing linearly polarized light through a QWP, it can be converted to circularly or elliptically polarized light, depending on the angle between the incident vibration plane and the optic axis. If the angle between the plane of linear polarization and the optic axis is exactly 45°, light is transformed from linear to circular polarization (or vice versa), as shown in Fig. 8-8. For other angles, the transformation is from linear to elliptical (or vice versa).

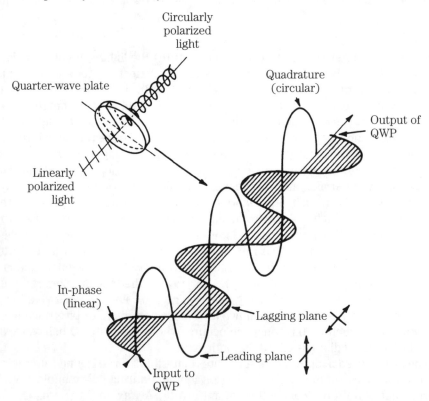

8-8 Linearly polarized light passing through a quarter-wave plate is converted to circularly polarized light. The angle between the plane of linear polarization and the optical axis must be 45°.

This rotation in the plane of polarization can be used to distinguish between light beams in an optical pickup. For example, a linearly polarized light beam might pass through the QWP to become circularly polarized, strike an optical disk, return through the QWP again, becoming linearly polarized. Because the resulting plane of polarization is perpendicular to the incident linearly polarized beam, it can be separated from the incident light by a polarizing prism, acting transparently to the incident light, but as a mirror to the reflected light. Many CD pickups use this technique, as described in chapter 9. A half-wave plate operates similarly, but the plane rotates at twice the angle of the plane of polarization of the incident beam.

Design of Optical Media

Most optical storage systems store data across the surface of a flat disk. This allows for fast random access of data, as well as ease of manufacturing replication. In most designs, because data is written and read via optical means, there is no physical contact between the media and the pickup. This ensures long media and pickup life and minimizes damage through head crashes or other catastrophes. In addition, because there is no need for physical contact between the data surface and pickup, data can be embedded within a protective layer to promote long media and pickup life, and to minimize the effect of surface contamination and damage on data readout. However, stored data must undergo both modulation and error correction encoding to maximize data density, and guard against the effect of reading errors.

Data can be stored either along a spiral, or concentric tracks. Most optical disk pickups shine a laser on the medium, and the reflected light is detected by a sensor and decoded to recover the carried data. To accomplish this, the medium must present two states so the change between them varies the reflected light, and thus the data can be recognized in much the same way that the black characters on this page stand in contrast to the white paper. Data can be represented as a change in the phase, change in the polarization, or change in the intensity of reflected light. For example, pits in a reflective surface produce diffraction in the reflected light beam, decreasing its intensity. The resulting variation in intensity, from high intensity in reflecting areas, to low intensity in pit areas, can be converted to a varying electrical signal for data recovery.

To expedite data writing and recovery, a laser beam is used. This permits a higher information density (10^9 to 10^{11} bytes per disk) to be achieved. The 1.5 Mbyte text of this book, for example, would occupy a small portion of an optical disk. As noted, track pitch, minimum spot size and other dimensions are defined by the wavelength of the laser used. Disks are thus diffraction-limited. Only shorter wavelength laser light would yield greater storage density. A laser light source also is required to provide a sufficient signal-to-noise ratio for a high bit rate, given an illumination of an area as small as 1 μm^2, for a period of 1 ms or less. Either analog or digital signals can be encoded and stored on a disk, within the bandwidth constraints of the medium.

Any optical media must be supported by a sophisticated servo system to provide positioning, tracking, and focusing of the pickup, as well as accurate disk rotation.

Focus tolerance, for example, can be on the order of 1 μm, and ideally should be maintained in spite of mechanical shock and vibration. The pickup must generate a set of correction signals derived from the signal from the optical media itself and use a set of actuators to maintain proper conditions. Radial tracking correction signals can be derived using methods such as twin spot, which uses a diffraction grating to create additional scanning spots, or wobble, in which the scanning spot is given a sinusoidal movement. Similarly, focus correction signals can be generated through methods such as Foucault knife edge, using unequal distribution of illumination in a split beam; astigmatism, using a cylindrical lens to create spot asymmetry; or critical angle, using angle of incidence and a split beam. Laser pickup design is discussed in more detail in chapter 9.

Performance of Optical Media

Optical media typically provide about 100 times the storage capacity of the same size magnetic media. For example, a hard disk can store 40 Mbits/in.^{2}, but an erasable optical disk can store 300 Mbits/in.^{2}. Although the theoretical storage density of magnetic media can be 100 Mbits/in.^{2}, that of optical media is 30 times more. An optical disk can contain several gigabytes of data (1 gigabyte is 1024 megabytes). Current-generation 5¼-in. erasable optical drives hold 1.2 Gbytes; over the coming years, their capacity will increase more than tenfold. Data transfer rates achieve 5 Mbps, but faster rotational speeds and systems using multiple laser heads placed on parallel tracks will boost the rate to 500 Mbps or more.

Unlike most hard disks, optical disks are removable from the drive. In addition, their shelf life is much longer than that of magnetic media, they are much less susceptible to damage from heat and humidity, and they are essentially impervious to magnetic fields, fingerprints, and head crashes. The corrected bit error rate of optical media is comparable to that of hard disks, about 10^{-13}. A floppy disk, by comparison, has a corrected error rate of about 10^{-6}. The raw (uncorrected) error rate of an optical disk can be 10^{-6}; perhaps 10 to 30% of the disk capacity can be required for error correction coding to bring the corrected rate to 10^{-13}.

Any optical recording material must exhibit long-term stability, high absorptivity at the recording wavelength, low writing energy, high signal-to-noise ratio, good forming characteristics, low thermal conductivity, and low manufacturing cost. Although any magnetic medium can be recorded, read and erased with relative ease, optical media accomplishing the same tasks are more complex. Thus it is advantageous to design optical storage with specific applications in mind. Specifically, three separate systems, read-only, write-once, and erasable mediums have been developed for various applications.

Nonerasable Optical Storage

In nonerasable optical disk systems, a laser light shines on the data surface, and the reflected light is detected by a pickup and decoded to recover the carried data. To accomplish this, the surface presents two states, for example, to vary the intensity of the reflected light. In this way, data can be recognized by the pickup. For example, a reflective disc might have holes burned into its surface to vary reflected intensity. The actual technology used depends on whether the media is read only, or write once. Several mechanisms are available to achieve both of these results, but questions of durability, density, and feasibility of mass production ultimately define the most appropriate method.

Read-Only Optical Storage

The standard compact disc is an example of a read-only optical format. Whether a compact disc (spelled with the letter *c*) holds audio or software data, the data is permanently formed on the medium during manufacture; it is a playback-only format. A plastic disc is impressed with a spiral track of pits cut to a depth calculated to decrease the intensity of the laser light of the reading pickup. To provide reflectivity, the data surface is metalized. The reflective surface of the disc and the data pits are embedded between the transparent plastic substrate and a protective layer. The effect of scratches and dust particles on the reading surface are minimized because they are separated from the data surface and thus made out of focus with respect to the laser beam focused on the inner reflective data surface.

In a read-only optical medium such as the compact disc, the pit surface and laser readout forms a very sophisticated optical device. The numerical aperture of the lens, wavelength of the laser light, thickness and refractive index of the disc substrate, and size and height of the pits all interact to form an optical system. As noted, when a laser beam is focused, on the data surface, an Airy pattern results, as shown in Fig. 8-9. The spot diameter can be specified at half-intensity (for example, 1.0 μm) or at the first dark ring (for example, 2.1 μm). Allowable crosstalk between tracks determines track pitch (for example, 1.6 μm). Crosstalk must be acceptable even in the worst case of a slightly defocused beam and slight tracking error. In any case, the beam is focused so that approximately half its center area falls on a pit, and half falls on the surrounding reflective land.

An optical storage surface that uses a phase structure (such as a CD) is a reflection grating, and acts similarly to a diffraction grating. Specifically, the pits cause diffraction. The smaller the pits in relation to the light wavelength, the greater is the angle at which light leaves. Light diffracted by the grating consists of a single zero-order and multiple first-order beams, as shown in Fig. 8-10. They will partly overlap each other resulting in cancellation due to interference. The area of light striking a pit is about equal to that striking the surrounding land, and the pit is about one-quarter wavelength in height. Light striking the pit is out of phase by a half wavelength with that striking the land. This results in destructive interference between the zero- and first-order beams in the light ray returning to the lens. For good contrast, the power in the two beams with different phases should be equal. Effectively, a pit reduces the intensity of light returning to the lens. Pit depth does not require great accuracy. Equality of pit/land areas is more important.

The system is diffraction-limited because it operates at dimensions that are as small as permitted by the wave nature of light at that wavelength. With a spot diameter of 1.0 μm, details this size would give diffracted rays that only just fall within the

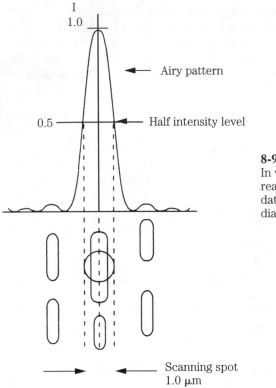

8-9
In write-once optical disk systems, the reading laser forms an Airy pattern on the data surface. The half intensity spot diameter covers the pit track.

lens aperture. Finer details yield greater convergence thus rays diffracted by the pits must fall outside the lens aperture. This is in fact the case with the pits on the data surface because they are narrower than the diameter of the spot. Rays diffracted by the pits must consequently fall outside the lens aperture, decreasing intensity reflected back into the lens.

This type of diffraction medium, using physical pits to store data, is attractive because it can be economically mass produced. Furthermore, a disc can store 650 Mbytes of formatted data on its 12-cm diameter. The medium is open-ended with respect to the type of data to be encoded. The CD-DA audio standard has already been joined by CD-ROM, CD-I, Video-CD, and other formats. The CD remains an open-ended format, with ongoing improvements. Manufacturers have developed high density CDs (such as DVD) with many times the storage capacity of a CD-DA disc; this is accomplished with a short wavelength red laser, which permits smaller pit and track dimensions. The CD family is discussed in detail in chapter 9.

Write-Once Optical Storage

Recordability is essential for many professional applications; the simplest recordable optical systems are write-once (WO). The user records data permanently, until the disk capacity is filled. Perhaps at first uncomfortable to magnetically inclined minds, a write-once system is very workable for many applications;

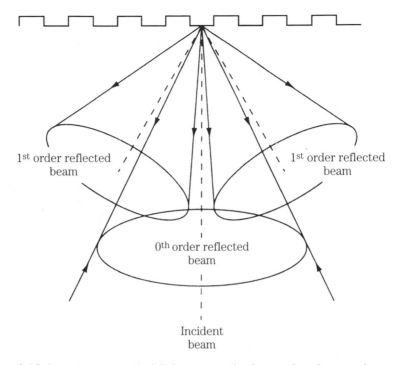

8-10 In write-once optical disk systems, the data surface forms a phase structure that acts like a reflective grating. Diffraction causes cancellation through interference in the reflected beams.

it is certainly true that in many cases, magnetic tape is recorded only once. When only a few CD-DA or CD-ROM compatible discs are needed, a write-once CD-WO system is ideal. Write-once disks are widely used throughout the audio and computer industries.

A write-once optical disk can be implemented in a variety of ways, as described in Fig. 8-11. Dye-polymer recording uses a recording layer containing a heat-absorptive organic dye; the dye is absorptive at the wavelength of a writing laser. When the layer is heated, it melts and forms a depression. Simultaneously, a reflective layer is deformed. Data is read by shining a laser light on the surface; the physical formations decrease the intensity of the reflected beam. CD-WO recorders use a dye-polymer method; the CD-WO format is discussed in detail in chapter 9.

In some systems, an irreversible phase change is used to alter the reflectivity of the medium at the point where a writing laser is focused. In this way, a reading laser can differentiate between data. Some systems use a thin metallic recording layer that varies its physical property from crystalline (high reflectivity) to amorphous (low reflectivity) when it is heated (to perhaps 170°C) by a writing laser. The phase transition can triple the reflectivity of the recording layer at written spots, thus allowing laser reading of the data. The recording layer can use an antimony selenium (Sb-Se) metallic film and the heat absorbing layer can be a bismuth-tellurium (Bi-Te) metallic film.

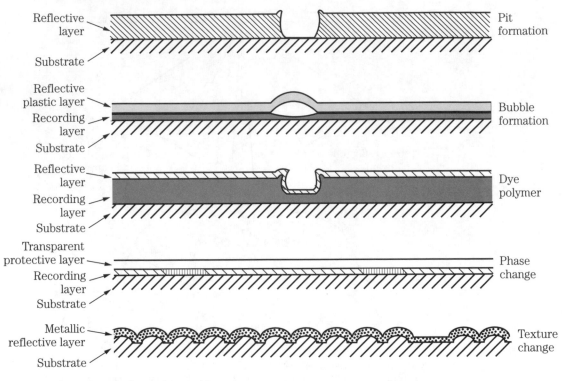

8-11 A variety of methods can be used in write-once storage.

Other methods include pit formation, bubble formation, and texture change. With pit formation, a mechanism called ablation uses a laser writer of approximately 10 mW to burn holes in a reflective layer; the material is melted or vaporized by the heated spot. Melting is preferred because no residue is created around the pit. In either case, data can be read by monitoring the change in intensity. Similarly, bubble formation uses a laser to vaporize a recording layer, causing a bubble to form in an adjacent reflective layer. The bubble can be read with a laser, by monitoring reflecting light levels. The texture change method uses a reflective surface with small aberrations with dimensions and spacing designed to diffract a reading laser. When the layer is heated and melted, it forms a smooth face that increases reflectivity at that point.

All WO disks are nonerasable and this limits their applicability to digital audio applications. However, WO can be a highly economical form of storage. A WO disk can store several gigabytes of data. Because of their low cost and ease of handling, many disks can be used together. Some changer/recorder systems provide access to hundreds of WO disks. With such large amounts of storage capacity, the need to erase and record over unwanted data is alleviated. A user can simply keep recording new data, ignoring the unwanted. For final editing, the required data is accessed from the recorded library.

Erasable Optical Storage

Erasable optical disk systems provide completely versatile data storage. Data can be written, read, erased, and written again. In most cases, the number of erasures is essentially unlimited. Several recordable/erasable optical media technologies have been introduced in a variety of formats, varying broadly in cost. These erasable technologies include magneto-optical, phase-change, and dye-polymer recording. Magneto-optic recording uses a laser beam and magnetic bias field to record and erase data, and a laser beam alone to read data. Phase-change media use a reversible change in the index of reflectivity of materials. Dye-polymer media use reversible changes in physical formations induced by heating the recording layer.

Magneto-Optical Recording

Magneto-optical (MO) recording (sometimes known as optically assisted magnetic recording) technology combines magnetic recording and laser optics, utilizing the record/erase benefits of magnetic materials with the high density of optical materials. Magneto-optical recording uses a vertical magnetic medium in which magnetic particles are placed perpendicularly to the surface of a pregrooved disk. Vertical recording provides greater particle density, and shorter recorded wavelengths; however, the high recording density is not fully utilized by conventional magnetic heads because their flux fields cannot be narrowed sufficiently. The recorded area is thus a far larger area than necessary. Optical assistance increases the recording density.

With magneto-optics, a magnetic field is used to record data, but the applied magnetic field is much weaker than conventional recording fields. It is not strong enough to orient the magnetic fields of the particles, thus a unique property of magnetic materials is used. As the oxide particles are heated to their Curie temperature, their coercivity (the minimum magnetic field strength required to reverse an induced magnetization), decreases radically. In other words, when heated, a magnetic material loses its resistance to change in its magnetic orientation; its orientation can be affected by a small applied magnetic field. (Similarly, variations in the earth's magnetic field over time can be traced by studying the magnetic fields imprinted in ancient volcanic rocks.)

In the case of MO recording, this allows data to be written with a weak field. For example, coercivity falls almost to zero as the temperature rises to 150°C. A laser beam focused through an objective lens heats a spot of magnetic material to its Curie temperature. At that temperature, only the particles in that spot are affected by the magnetic field from the recording coil, as shown in Fig. 8-12A. When the beam is turned off, or the area moves away from the beam, it cools below the Curie temperature as the absorbed energy is dissipated to the substrate by thermal conduction. The applied magnetic field is withdrawn, and the magnetic orientation of the field is "frozen" and retained as data. In this way, the laser beam creates a recorded spot much smaller than otherwise possible thus increasing recording density.

The Kerr effect is used to read data; it describes the slight rotation of the plane of polarization of polarized light as it reflects from a magnetized material. (The Fara-

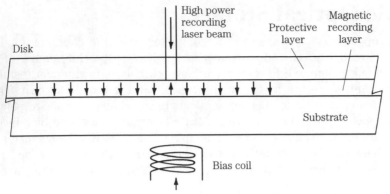

A In magneto-optical recording, a high power laser beam heats the medium, and magnetic recording is induced by the bias coil.

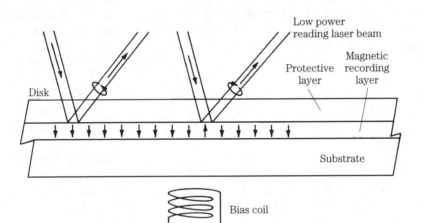

B Data is read by reflecting a low power laser beam from the surface and observing the rotation in the plane of polarization of the reflected light.

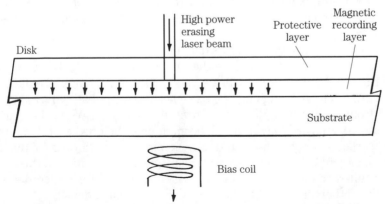

C Data is erased by heating the medium and reapplying the bias field.

8-12 Principles of magneto-optical recording, reading, and erasing.

day effect describes the same phenomenon as light passes through a medium.) The rotation of the plane of polarization of light reflected from the reverse-oriented regions differs slightly from that reflected from unreversed regions. To read the disk, a laser is focused on the data surface, and the angle of rotation of reflected light is monitored, as shown in Fig. 8-12B. An analyzer distinguishes between rotated and unrotated light, and converts that information into a beam with varying light intensity. For example, by passing the polarized light through a polarizing prism, the light with a plane parallel to that of the prism will pass through, while relatively rotated light will be blocked, resulting in an intensity difference. Data is then recovered from that modulated signal. The power of the reading laser is much lower than the recording laser (perhaps by a factor of 10) so the recorded magnetic information is not affected. To erase data, a magnetic field is applied to the disk, along with the laser heating spot, and new data is written, as shown in Fig. 8-12C. New data can be rerecorded.

The magneto-optical recording layer can be placed between a transparent substrate and a protective layer. The laser light can shine through either the substrate or the protective layer, placing surface dust and scratches out of focus with respect to the data surface. A coil can be wrapped about the laser lens structure to produce the magnetic field. In some cases its perpendicular alignment is assisted by a metal plate located on the opposite side of the disk. A variety of magnetic materials can be used. Selection is on the basis of signal-to-noise ratio, orientation properties, and long term stability. In general, amorphous, thin-film magnetic materials are used. Some applications use a material such as terbium ferrite cobalt. At room temperatures, the coercivity of the recording layer can be more than 10,000 oersteds, effectively eliminating the possibility of accidental erasure.

Tests indicate that data can be erased and rewritten 10 million times or more, equivalent to conventional magnetic media. Accelerated life measurements suggest MO disks will last at least 10 years. In one test, when exposing disks to 95°C at 95% humidity for 1000 hours, magneto-optical disks survived better than conventional hard or floppy disks; it is generally agreed the latter are reliable for only a few years. Because the coercivity required to write or erase data is very high at room temperature, it is virtually impossible to alter data accidentally. Magneto-optics is thus a great deal more stable and reliable than other magnetic media.

To achieve mechanical compatibility from one recorder to another within the high tolerances of a magneto-optical medium, blank disks can be manufactured with prerecorded and nonerasable addressing. One method, called hardware address sectoring, uses a disk with spiral or concentric grooves, in which address information is physically formed in the groove and detected by light beam reflection. Using this system, a magneto-optical player can automatically track both address and data information contained on a magneto-optical disk. Storage capacity is not reduced because the recorded data signal is superimposed on the hardware addressing information.

One magneto-optical disk system uses a 5.25-inch diameter disk (the same size as a compact disc) to record over an hour of music. A photopolymer layer with a pre-grooved surface is deposited on a glass substrate; a dielectric layer separates it from the recording layer of terbium, gadolinium, and iron. A top protective layer completes the disk construction, and the data surface is accessed through the glass substrate. The light source in this system is an AlGaAs laser with 850-nm wavelength.

The beam is pulsed during recording for a duration of 50-ns at 250-ns intervals. Oxide particles within the groove are oriented within the spot of the light pulse. To read the disk, the pulsed laser light reflects from the disk and the difference in rotation of the plane of polarization of the reflected light is read as intensity modulation. Erasure is accomplished by uniformly magnetizing data to be overwritten, then rerecording. With minor modifications, such an erasable recorder could be used to read standard compact discs as well.

MO Applications

Many MO drive manufacturers adhere to an ISO and ANSI disk format in which a two-sided, preformatted, 5.25-inch constant angular velocity (CAV) disk holds 650 Mbytes of data (with 325 Mbytes of data per side), when formatted for 1024 byte sectors. This yields about ½ hour of digital audio per side; however, the user must turn over the disc to access both sides. Widely used double-density versions of this format use a 5.25-inch double-sided MO disk with either 1.0- or 1.3-Gbyte storage; these formats are backward compatible with 650-Mbyte ISO formats. Other MO formats include a single-sided 256-Mbyte 3.5-inch disk as well as a 20-Mbyte floptical disk. In zoned CAV disks, bit densities increase on the outer tracks; with a track pitch of 1.39 μm, linear density is 0.86 μm per bit. A disk rotational speed of 3000 rpm provides a data transfer rate of 2 to 4 Mbytes per second with an average seek time of 20 to 40 ms. Drives also can incorporate a 1-Mbyte buffer. Data reduction techniques can be used to increase playing time and effectively increase the transfer rate. With current trends, industry standard 3.5-inch MO disks should achieve a 2.6-Gbyte capacity and 10-Mbyte per second transfer rate, and 5.25-inch MO discs should achieve 10.4-Gbyte capacity and 10-Mbyte per second transfer rate as well. Larger-capacity MO disks (greater than 1 Gbyte) and drives with multibeam heads (transfer rates greater than 15 Mbytes per second) are available, but these formats cannot conform to industry standards because of the proprietary media used. MO drives such as these supply the missing link between general computer applications and a dedicated audio studio recorder.

Stand-alone optical disk recorders using a 650-Mbyte magneto-optical drive provide full recording, replaying and erasing/rerecording of audio data. One unit is a 4-track recorder manipulating tracks as stereo pairs; pairs of tracks are recorded together; however, either one or both pairs can be replayed together. The dual-sided disk holds 25 minutes of stereo track time per side at a sampling frequency of 48 kHz, 30 minutes at 44.1 kHz, and 45 minutes at 32 kHz. Additional drives can be slaved to the recorder. The disk is a standard 5.25-inch size (not CD compatible) enclosed in a protective plastic sleeve. It is completely removable at any point during a session without any downloading delay.

An optical recorder operates much like a hard disk recorder, with bar graph VU meters, level adjustment pots, and RAM scrubber. Sound files are created and named. Waveforms are displayed, and their time-base scale can be varied. Edit points can be entered on the fly or entered as timecode numbers via a keypad. General purpose marks can be dropped into a file to serve as synchronization points, for example, to lay in sound effects. Sound files can be sequentially combined to create an entire song. A number of songs can be assembled into an edited master with fade up and down, crossfades, intertrack gaps, etc. Alternatively, an edit list can be used to assemble a track from timecode. In addition, these recordings can be called up by their timecode addresses.

Magneto-optical technology also has appeared in the mastering studio. The Sony PCM-9000 is an MO disk recorder that can record up to 80 minutes of 20-bit linear, 44.1-kHz sampled digital audio data on a single-sided 5.25-inch disc storing 1.3 Gbyte. The disk is housed in a removable cartridge. Alternatively, the recorder can be configured for 24-bit recording (with 65 minutes of recording time) or 16-bit recording (100 minutes). The two channels can be recorded independently, along with ±12.5% varispeed recording. Both destructive and nondestructive editing and real-time jump editing (ability to skip over unwanted data areas) are available; a disk can store TOC and editing information. Disks are pregrooved, with fixed address marks for block sectoring; the format also stores auxiliary data such as timecode and subcode. The recorder does not require an erase pass before recording over old material; this permits read-after-write (confidence replay), and synchronous drop-in read-write-read recording. The recorder is equipped with an AES3 interface, RS-422 port, SCSI interface (allowing double-speed data transfer), and proprietary editor interface.

The MiniDisc format uses a small MO disc; it is designed to provide recordability and portability. To provide 74 minutes of recording time on the 2.5-inch disc, the ATRAC data-reduction algorithm is used. The MD format is discussed in detail in chapter 12.

Phase-Change Optical Recording

Erasable phase-change systems use technology similar to that used in write-once systems. They use materials that exhibit a reversible crystalline/amorphous phase change when recorded at one temperature and erased at another. For erasable media, a crystalline (high reflectivity) to amorphous (low reflectivity) phase change is typically used to record data and the reverse to erase. Information is recorded by heating an area of the crystalline layer to a temperature slightly above its melting point. When the area solidifies, it is amorphous, and the change in reflectivity can be detected. Because the crystalline form is more stable, the material will tend to change back to this form. Thus, when the area is heated to a point just below its melting temperature, it will return to a crystalline state, erasing the data.

A number of materials have been devised for the recording layer. For example, layers comprised of gallium antimonide and indium antimonide have been developed. Some systems use tellurium alloyed with elements such as germanium and indium. Permanent recording can be achieved by simply increasing the power of the writing laser; this burns holes in the recording layer rather than change its phase. Phase-change media have a long shelf life, and are not affected by ambient temperatures and humidity. A large number of erasures can be achieved.

In one phase-change erasable system, writing and reading are accomplished with an 830-nm wavelength laser, writing at 8 mW and reading at 1 mW of power. A 780-nm wavelength laser with 10-mW power is used for erasing. The recorded spot is about 1 by 10 μm in size. A single lens structure is used for both erasing and recording, which can be done in a single pass. The 8-inch diameter disc revolves at 1800 rpm, with a capacity of 700 Mbyte per side, and over 1 million erase-rewrite cycles can be performed. Both erasable and write-once disks can be used in the recorder.

Dye-Polymer Optical Recording

In dye-polymer recording, light-absorbing dyes are placed in a bi-layer disk structure. The two layers, an expansion layer and retention layer, are sensitive to different wavelengths. The physical deformation that the polymer layers undergo results in bumps; in this way, data can be written and read. For example, the top expansion layer can be composed of an elastomer containing a dye sensitive to light with an 840-nm wavelength. The inner retention layer can be sensitive to 780-nm wavelength light. During recording, infrared laser light of 840-nm wavelength is absorbed in the top recording layer, causing its temperature to rise; the bottom layer is transparent to this light. The top layer's heat causes it to expand, pushing against the bottom layer to form a bump. When the temperature cools, the bump is retained. This formation can be read by a low-power laser beam through diffraction. To overwrite new data, light of a 780-nm wavelength is absorbed by the bottom layer, but not the top layer. The retention layer is softened, reducing its modulus of elasticity. The expansion layer pulls itself back to its original condition, restoring the surface to a flat condition, ready for new data.

The system is efficient because the recording surface changes state each time laser light with the correct wavelength and power strikes the surface. One wavelength creates a bump; another wavelength flattens it. In addition, the wavelength that flattens a bump does not affect an already smooth surface. Data can thus be overwritten on a single revolution of the medium, with data passing under the smoothing laser just before it passes under the forming laser.

Other types of optical disk storage, still exotic, are copper sulfate in glass technology, cryogenic frequency domain storage, surface texturing techniques, and spectral-hole burning in crystals.

Disk Standards

Although standardization has assisted growth of the optical disk industry, incompatibility remains an obstacle. The CD-ROM industry has addressed standardization with the development of a file structure, ISO-9660. When a compact disc adheres to this format (as well as other Yellow Book standards) it can be used on different types of computers (IBM, Apple, etc.). However, executable software programs cannot be universal thus most compact discs will only play in one computer environment. On the other hand, hybrid compact discs can be authored to operate on both IBM and Apple computers. The lack of standards plagues the recordable optical disk industry. There are numerous disk formats available, incompatible in disk diameter, construction, recording and playing method, and file format. This is inevitable because of competition among developing manufacturers, and the need to address individual application demands, as opposed to generic universality. Despite standardization efforts, the audio industry will never enjoy a universal optical disk format. CD standards are discussed in chapter 9.

Digital Audio for Theatrical Film

Several theatrical film formats have been developed to provide conventional optical storage of frame images, as well as multichannel digital audio storage. In double systems, external audio playback devices are synchronized to the picture using a timecode stripe added to conventional motion picture film. Single systems use optically encoded digital audio data on the film itself to produce a modulated signal. The latter approach, although technically more difficult, is preferred. Motion pictures generally use a stereo optical soundtrack (often matrixed for four channels), called the stereo variable area (SVA) printed along the frame edge; some digital systems retain this track for compatibility with existing motion picture projection systems. In addition, in the event of catastrophic damage to the digital soundtrack, the system can automatically and momentarily switch to the analog soundtracks. New digital audio cinema systems have supplanted the older 70-mm six-track analog audio format, using magnetic striping.

Any theatrical film audio system must be multichannel, minimally with left, right, and center channels, two surround channels for ambience, as well as a subwoofer channel. Other channels can encode foreign language dialogue, or nonaudio data for timecode, control of theater curtains, etc. Of the six (or more) audio channels, five must provide wide audio bandwidth, with the subwoofer channel reproducing signals below 100 Hz; all must provide a high dynamic range. Optical tracks must be robust, able to withstand hundreds or thousands of trips through the projector; raw error rates of 10^{-3} are typical for a worn film. Reliable error correction is mandated. In addition, the method must support high-speed copying for mass replication of films.

Several imaging dye methods have been developed in which binary data is recorded as a series of transparent and opaque dots, using conventional film dyes and layers. The mosaic pattern is placed in the 0.1-inch wide area now used to hold analog soundtracks on 35- and 70-mm film. Alternatively, data can be placed along the film edges, between the sprocket holes, as shown in Fig. 8-13. During playback, light from a source is focused on the tracks, and read with a sensor array on the opposite side. To encode sufficient data on the film, data reduction methods must be used, as described in chapter 11. Film using this method can be copied at high speed using conventional methods.

The DTS format is a double system using external storage. The DTS debuted with the film *Jurassic Park*; a 30 fps timecode track is placed between the picture and the standard analog sound track; this code is used to synchronize external CD-ROM drives. As with other double systems, timecode is read in advance of the picture so that any edits in the picture (such as missing footage or reel changes) can be anticipated and compensated for by the sound source. DTS discs contain six data-compressed audio channels that are output on a SCSI bus to external compression decoders that plug into movie house sound systems. Discs are placed in shipping containers that fit within the standard cases used to ship 2000-foot projection pancakes to theaters. The DTS system was developed by Digital Theater Systems.

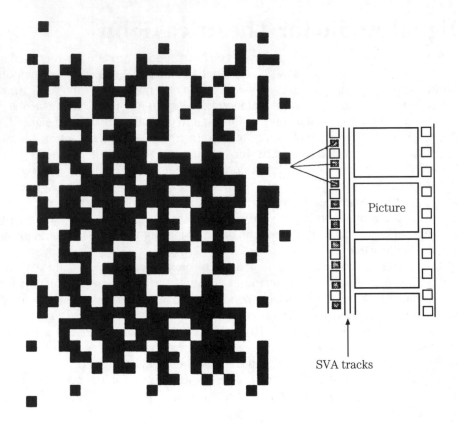

8-13 In some digital-audio optical film systems, bit patterns are placed between sprocket holes; analog SVA tracks are not affected.

The LC Digital format also is a double system. A 24-fps timecode track is placed on the outside edge of the film on the soundtrack side; the sound sources are magneto-optical drives. The system allows recording of dual-language dialogue mixes, as well as subtitle text data. As with other double systems, to prevent a disk mix-up, the system will not play back from the digital source unless serial numbers on film and disk match; the analog soundtracks are played instead. The LC digital format, used mainly in Europe, was developed by the LC Concept Company.

The SR-D system retains analog soundtracks for compatibility, and adds an optical data track between sprocket holes, on the same side as the analog tracks. Six audio channels (left/center/right in front, left/right stereo surround in rear, and subwoofer) are sampled at 48 kHz, encoded through AC-3 data reduction, multiplexed together and with a 9.6 kbps data channel, and written to film as 96 data blocks. Data blocks are formed from a 76 × 76 pixel array matrix. The composite bit rate is 320 kbps, excluding error-correction data. A CCD scanner reads the optical information, then it is demultiplexed, decoded, and output to the theater sound system. Audio data is recorded 2.5 seconds prior to picture to allow time for processing, and so the time base can be adjusted to achieve subjectively correct synchronization of sound to picture for a given theater size. Printing laboratories are able to perform high-speed duplication using special heads. AC-3 is discussed in chapter 11. This SR-D system was developed by Dolby.

In the SDDS system, eight audio channels are encoded and placed in two data tracks running outside the perforation holes, one stripe on each side of the film. Existing optical analog tracks are retained. Five loudspeakers are placed behind the screen, along with one subwoofer loudspeaker, also usually placed behind the screen, and two surround sound loudspeakers; smaller playback configurations are supported as well. The ATRAC data reduction algorithm, originally devised for the MiniDisc format, is used to code the audio channels. The Sony Dynamic Digital Sound system was developed by Sony Corporation.

In the single-system CDS format, six audio channels are recorded and multiplexed to form one optical bit stream that replaces analog soundtracks; five channels use 16-bit words compressed to 12 bits, sampled at 44.1 kHz, and a subwoofer channel is sampled at 1.4 kHz. In addition, three control tracks are recorded. The overall data rate is 5.8 Mbps, with a bit size of 14 µm; Reed-Solomon and CRCC codes are used for error correction. The optical track is printed as 180 narrow, parallel tracks. It is read by a CCD scanner with 512 light sensitive regions lying across the optical track width; the sensor is stationary, but designed to continually read the track despite film weave as it moves through the projector. Conventional film stock can be used for release prints. This CDS system was developed by Kodak and Optical Radiation Corporation.

Another method was developed in which a clear fluorescent layer is applied across the film stock. The layer is colorless and clear under visible light, but fluoresces under ultraviolet light, emitting visible light that can be detected by scanners. Digital audio data is written on the fluorescent layer across the film images. However, sophisticated chemical processing is needed to manufacture and record to such a medium.

Holostore

One limitation of most existing audio storage systems, analog or digital, is that of moving media. The mechanical task of rotating disks and positioning a pickup, or moving tape past stationary or rotary heads places an inherent limit on size, power consumption, and cost. The next great step in audio technology will be a solid-state storage medium, in which the digitized audio signal is recorded and read directly from memory. Many devices use memory to hold audio data but even with data reduction, the volume of data and the high price of memory prohibits its application to high-fidelity music. One storage technology, now being researched, is photorefractive volume holographic storage (PVHS), sometimes called holostore; its capacity is measured in hundreds of gigabytes. This random-access memory stores data as three-dimensional optical holograms, and data is written and retrieved as two-dimensional patterns of laser light. A light-sensitive crystal serves as the medium for holostore.

A laser beam is directed to a memory location by a stack selector, and the beam is split into two subbeams by a beam splitter; one is the data beam, and the other is a reference beam. The data beam strikes the holostore's page composer; this spatial light modulator is illuminated to create a pattern of light and dark spots dictated by the data being read into the holostore. This data pattern is superimposed on the laser beam, and along with the reference beam, enters an array of light-sensitive crystal rods made of strontium barium niobate doped with cerbium. Inside the crystal, the reference beam crosses the data beam to create an interference pattern in the crystal. The holostore converts the interference pattern, modifying the optical characteristics of the photorefractive crystal, to store the data pattern as electronic charges. As new data enters the composer, the holostore shifts the reference beam slightly to access new physical portions of the crystals. The data in the beam is thus preserved as a three-dimensional holographic bit pattern image in the crystals.

To read data, the data beam is turned off, the holostore directs the reference beam to the correct portion of the crystal, the beam illuminates the interference pattern, and the original bit pattern reappears in the beam. This image strikes a detector array such as a charge-coupled device (CCD) that converts the light and dark patterns into electrical signals. Conventional digital audio processing and D/A conversion complete the path. The crystal memory is nonvolatile, and removable.

A data transfer rate of 1 Tbyte (terabyte) per second is possible; today's fastest magnetic disk system would take five hours to deliver the same amount of data that a holostore could deliver in one second. Tests have shown that a holostore could be read a billion times without S/N degradation. A removable holostore module measuring $10 \times 10 \times 0.5$ cm would store 100 Gbytes. Using mild data reduction, stereo playing time would be 760 hours—about a month. Alternatively, such a large-capacity medium could be used to store multimedia programs.

Whatever the format, optical storage promises to surpass the performance levels of both magnetic tape and disk. Optical disk technology provides data reliability and longevity, large storage capacity, low cost per bit, removability, recordability, no medium wear, and ability to mix digital audio data with video, control and timecode. Certainly optical storage is an excellent option for both professional and consumer applications, for playback-only, write-once, and erasable applications. Over the coming decade, all users of magnetic media will have to evaluate their recording technology in light of optical recording.

Fiber-Optic Transmission

Over the past 100 years or so audio engineering has become synonymous with copper wires. It is copper that connects electrical components to make audio devices, copper that connects audio devices to make audio systems, and copper that connects audio systems to make audio networks. That great of rite of passage, that first test of audio maturity is the soldering together of copper wires. From the first telegraph to the latest 48-track digital recorder, it was copper wire that conveyed the signal.

Today, the environment is one of high-speed computing and software intensive transmission. Because the information capacity of a signal increases with frequency, fiber-optic cable eclipses the data capacity of copper wires. Large scale networks have abandoned copper conductors and turned to fiber optics to convey their information; fiber is literally the backbone of the information highway. For the same reasons, the alternative of fiber optics presents itself to the audio environment. Both off-the-shelf systems, and proprietary designs assembled from discrete components can be used to build an audio fiber-optic system offering a number of advantages over copper wire. Whether it is used to convey microphone signals from a concert hall to a remote truck, to form a workstation network, or carry telephone calls between continents, fiber optics is increasingly the preferred technology.

Advantages of Fiber Optics

Fiber optics offer advantages in almost any respect important to signal transmission: complete electromagnetic interference immunity, low attenuation, high bandwidth, low propagation delay, low bit error rates, small size, light weight, and ruggedness. Because fiber-optic cables are nonmetallic insulators, ground loops are avoided. A fiber is safe because it cannot cause electrical shock or spark. In particular, bandwidth is fiber optic's forte; transmission rates of 1 Gbps are common, and experimental systems have achieved rates of 30 Gbps over a long-distance fiber. Put into perspective, that is the equivalent of 500,000 simultaneous telephone transmissions over a single, thin strand.

As with electrical systems, the transmission loss of fiber-optic cable necessitates repeaters to boost the signal; however, the transmission distance is much greater with fiber optics—100 miles or more. New fluoride fiber can extend the range to thousands of miles before a repeater is needed. In any case, because fiber losses do not depend on modulation bandwidth, there is no need for equalization. Although its bandwidth is very high, the physical dimensions of the fibers are small. Fiber size is measured in micrometers, with a typical fiber diameter ranging from 10 to 200 μm. Moreover, many individual fibers might be housed in a thin cable. For example, there can be 6 independent fibers in a tube, with 144 tubes within one cable.

Fiber-Optic Systems

With electrical wire, information is transmitted by means of electrons. With fiber optics, photons are the carrier, and a signal is conveyed by sending pulses of light down an optically clear fiber. Although the signal can be either analog or digital, digital is preferred because modulation coding, multiplexing, routing, signal quality and other factors are improved. Either glass or plastic fiber can be used; plastic fiber is limited to short distances (perhaps 150 feet) and is thicker in diameter than glass fiber; communications systems use glass fiber. The purity of a glass fiber is such that light can pass through 15 miles of it before the light's intensity is halved. In comparison, one inch of window glass will halve light intensity. Fibers are pure to within one part per billion, yielding absorption losses less than 0.2 dB/km. Fiber-optic communication is not affected by electromagnetic and radio frequency interference, lightning strikes or other high voltage, and other conditions hostile to electrical signals. For example, fiber-optic cable can be run in the same conduit as high-power cables, or along the third rail of an electric railroad. Moreover, because a fiber-optic cable does not generate a flux signal, it causes no interference of its own.

Any fiber-optic system, whether linking stereos, cities, or continents, consists of three parts: an optical source acting as an optical modulator to convert an electrical signal to a light pulse; a transmission medium to convey the light; and an optical receiver to detect and demodulate the signal. The source can be a light-emitting diode (LED), laser diode, or other component. Fiber optics provide the medium. Positive-intrinsic-negative (PIN) photodiodes or avalanche (APD) photodiodes can serve as receivers. As with any data transmission line, other components such as encoding and decoding circuits are required. A complete fiber-optic data link is shown in Fig. 8-14.

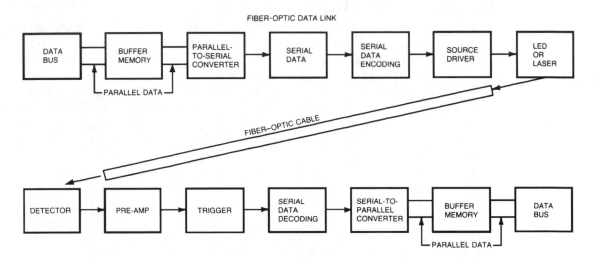

8-14 A complete fiber-optic data link requires encoding and decoding of data, as well as electrical/optical converters.

In general, low-bandwidth systems use LEDs and PINs with TTL interfaces and multimode fiber, but high-bandwidth systems use lasers, single-mode fiber, and APDs, with emitter coupled logic (ECL) interfaces. Laser sources are used for long-distance applications. The laser sources can be communication laser diodes, distributed feedback lasers, or lasers similar to those used in compact disc player pickups. Although the low-power delivery available from LEDs limits their applications, they are easy to fabricate, and useful for short-distance, low-bandwidth transmission, when coupled with PIN photodiodes. Over longer distances, LEDs can be used with single-mode fiber and avalanche photodiodes. Similarly, selection of the type of detector often depends on the application. Data rate, detectivity, crosstalk, wavelength, and available optical power are all factors.

Fiber-Optic Operation

The fiber itself is simply a light pipe that traps entering light. The glass or plastic rod, called the core, is surrounded by a reflective covering, called the cladding, to reflect light back toward the center of the fiber, and hence to the destination. A protective buffer sleeve surrounds the cladding. A fiber-optic cable is shown in Fig. 8-15. The cladding is comprised of a glass or plastic material with an index of refraction lower than that of the core. This boundary creates a highly efficient reflector. When light travelling through the core reaches the cladding, the light is either partly or wholly reflected back into the core. If the angle of the ray with the boundary is less than the critical angle (determined from the refractive indexes of the core and the cladding) the ray is partly refracted into the cladding, and partly reflected into the core. If the ray is incident on the boundary at an angle greater than the critical angle, the ray is totally reflected back into the core. This is known as total internal reflection (TIR). Thus, all rays at incident angles greater than the critical angle are guided by the core, affected only by absorption and connector losses. TIR is shown in Fig. 8-16 (see also Fig. 8-3). For the record, the principle of TIR is credited to British physicist John Tyndall, when in 1870, with a candle and two beakers of water, he demonstrated that light could travel contained within a stream of flowing water.

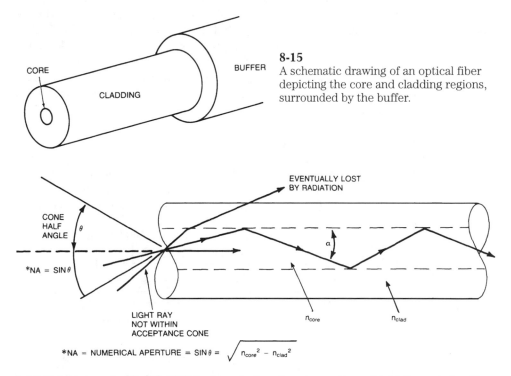

8-15
A schematic drawing of an optical fiber depicting the core and cladding regions, surrounded by the buffer.

8-16 Total internal reflection (TIR) characterizes the propagation of light through the fiber. The numerical aperture (NA) of an optical fiber is a measure of its light acceptance and is determined by the refractive indexes of the core and the cladding.

In 1873, James Clerk Maxwell proved that the equations describing the behavior of electric waves apply equally to light. Moreover, he showed that light travels in modes—mathematically, eigenvalue solutions to his electromagnetic field equations that characterize wave guides. In the case of optical fiber, this represents one or more paths along the light wave guide. Multimode fiber-optic cable has a core diameter (perhaps 50 to 500 μm) that is large compared to the wavelength of the light source; this allows multiple propagation modes. The result is multiple path lengths for different modes of the optical signal; simply put, most rays of light are not parallel to the fiber axis. Multimode fiber is specified according to the reflective properties of the boundary: stepped index, and graded index. In stepped index fiber, the boundary between core and cladding is sharply defined, causing light to reflect angularly. Light with an angle of incidence less than the critical angle will pass into the cladding. With graded index fiber, the index of refraction decreases gradually from the central axis outward. This gradual interface results in smoother reflection characteristics. In either case, in a multimode fiber, most light travels within the core.

Performance of multimode fiber is degraded by pulse broadening caused by intermodal and intramodal dispersion, both of which decrease the bandwidth of the fiber. Stepped index fiber is inferior to graded index in this respect. With intermodal dispersion (also called modal dispersion) some light reaches the end of a multimode fiber earlier than other light due to path length differences in the internal reflective angles. This results in multiple modes. In stepped index cable, there is delay between the lowest order modes, those modes that travel parallel to the fiber axis, and the highest order modes, those propagating at the critical angle. In other words, reflections at steeper angles follow a longer path length, and leave the cable after light travelling at shallow angles. A stepped index fiber can exhibit a delay of 60 ns/km. This modal dispersion significantly reduces the fiber's available bandwidth per km, and is a limiting factor. This dispersion is shown in Fig. 8-17A.

Multimode graded index fiber has reduced intermodal dispersion. This is achieved by compensating for high order mode delay, to ensure that these modes travel through a lower refractive index material than the low-order modes, as shown in Fig. 8-17B. The high order modes travel at a greater speed than the lower order modes, compen-

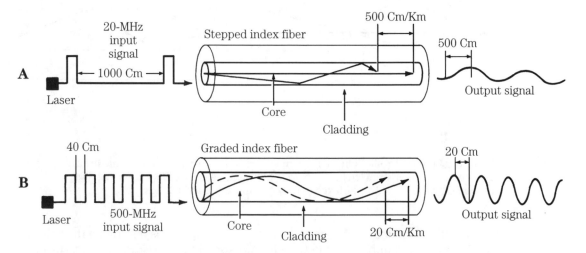

8-17 Both stepped and graded index fibers can be used. A. Stepped index fiber suffers from modal dispersion. B. Graded index fiber provides a higher transmission bandwidth.

sating for their longer path lengths. Specifically, light travels faster near the cladding, away from the center axis where the index of refraction is higher. The velocity of higher mode light travelling farther from the core more nearly equals that of lower mode light in the optically dense center. Pulse broadening is reduced, hence data rate can be boosted. By selecting an optimal refractive index profile, this delay can be reduced to 0.5 ns/km.

Intramodal dispersion is caused by irregularities in the index of refraction of the core and cladding; these are wavelength dependent thus the delay varies according to the wavelength of the light source. Fibers are thus manufactured to operate at preferred light wavelengths.

In stepped- and graded-index multimode fibers, the degree of spreading is a function of cable length; bandwidth specification is proportional to distance. For example, a fiber can be specified at 500 kbps for 1 km. It could thus achieve a 500-kbps rate over 1 km or, for example, a 5-Mbps rate over 100 meters. In a multimode system, using either stepped or graded index fiber, wide core fibers carry several light waves simultaneously, often emitted from an LED source. However, dispersion and attenuation limit applications. Multimode systems are thus most useful in applications with short to medium distances, and lower data rates.

Single-mode fiber was developed to eliminate modal dispersion. In single-mode systems, the diameter of the stepped index fiber core is small (perhaps 2 to 10 μm) and approaches the wavelength of the light source. Thus only one mode, the fundamental mode, exists through the fiber; there is only one light path so rays travel parallel to the fiber axis. For example, a wide band 9/125-μm single-mode fiber contains a 9-μm diameter light guide inside a 125-μm cladding. Because there is only one mode, modal dispersion is eliminated. In single-mode fibers, a significant portion of the light is carried in the cladding. Single-mode systems often use laser drivers; the narrow beam of light propagates with low dispersion and attenuation, providing higher data rates and longer transmission distances. For example, high-performance digital and RF applications such as CATV would use single-mode fiber and laser sources. Tables 8-1 and 8-2 summarize the differences between types of sources and fibers.

The amount of optical power loss due to absorption and scattering is specified at a fixed wavelength over a length of cable, typically 1 km, and is expressed as decibels of optical power loss per km (dB/km). For example, a 50/125-μm multimode

Table 8-1. Typical specifications for optical sources.

Type	Output Power (μW)	Peak Wavelength (nm)	Spectral Width (nm)	Rise Time (ns)
LED	250	820	35	12
	700	820	35	6
	1500	820	35	6
LASER	4000	820	4	1
	6000	1300	2	1

AMP Incorporated

**Table 8-2. Typical specifications
for optical fibers.**

Type	Core	Cladding	Buffer	NA	Band-width MHz/km	Attn. dB/km
		—Diameter— (μm)				
Single mode @ 1300 nm	8	125	250		6ps/km*	0.5
	5	125	250		4ps/km*	0.4
	50	125	250	0.20	400	3
Graded index @ 850 nm	62.5	125	250	0.275	150	3
	85	125	250	0.26	200	3
	100	140	250	0.30	150	4
Step index @ 850 nm	200	380	600	0.27	25	6
	300	440	650	0.27	20	6
PCS** @ 790 nm	200	350	-	0.30	20	10
	400	450	-	0.30	15	10
	600	900	-	0.40	20	6
Plastic @ 650 nm		750	-	0.50	20	400
		1000	-	0.50	20	400

*Dispersion per nanometer of source width.
**PCS (Plastic-clad silica: plastic cladding and glass core.)
AMP Incorporated

fiber has attenuation of 2.5 dB/km at 1300 nm, and 4 dB/km at 850 nm. (Because light is measured as power, 3 dB represents a doubling or halving of power.) Generally, a premium glass cable can have attenuation of 0.5 dB/km, and a plastic cable can exhibit 1000 dB/km.

Most fibers are best suited for operation in visible and near infrared wavelength regions. Fibers are optimized for operation in certain wavelength regions called windows where loss is minimized. Three commonly used wavelengths are: approximately 850, 1300, and 1550 nm (353,000, 230,000, and 194,000 GHz respectively). Generally, 1300 nm is used for long-distance communication; small fiber diameter (less than 10 μm) and a laser source must be used. Short distances, such as LANs (local-area networks), use 850 nm; LED sources can be used. The 1550-nm wavelength is often used with wavelength multiplexers so that a 1550-nm carrier can be piggy-backed on a fiber operating at 850 or 1300 nm, running either in a reverse direction or as additional capacity.

Single-mode systems can operate in the 1310- and 1550-nm wavelength ranges. Multimode systems use fiber optimized in the 800- to 900-nm range. Generally, multimode plastic fibers operate optimally at 650 nm. In general, light with longer wavelengths passes through fiber with less attenuation. Most fibers exhibit medium losses (3 to 5 dB/km) in the 800- to 900-nm range, low loss (0.5 to 1.5 dB/km) at 1150- to 1350-nm region, and very low loss (less than 0.5 dB/km) at 1550 nm.

Fiber optics lends itself to traditional time-division multiplexing, in which multiple independent signals can be transmitted simultaneously. One digital bit stream operating, for example, at 45 MHz, can be interleaved with others to achieve an overall rate of 1 GHz. This signal is transmitted along a fiber at an operating wavelength. With wavelength division multiplexing (WDM), multiple optical signals can be simultaneously conveyed on a fiber at different wavelengths. For example, transmission windows at 840, 1310, and 1550 nm could be used simultaneously. Independent laser sources are tuned to different wavelengths and multiplexed, and the optical signal consisting of the input wavelengths is transmitted over a single fiber. At the receiving end, the wavelengths are demultiplexed and directed to separate receivers or other fibers. Passive wavelength selective devices operate as optical filters; using dielectric materials of high and low refractive indexes, they create a cutoff frequency that depends on the angle at which the light strikes the filter. These wavelength-dependent devices can be used for multiplexing and demultiplexing. For example, four lasers can be multiplexed by shining the beams through a wavelength selective device to combine the beams, and transmitted through a fiber. At the output, another device breaks the light into its original components, and independent channels. Simultaneously, four channels, on different wavelengths, convey information in the opposite direction. Wavelength dispersive devices, containing prisms and gratings, also can be used to separate light into the spectral components, thus performing demultiplexing.

Glass Fiber Fabrication

Glass fibers are fabricated using vapor deposition methods, in which layers of chemical vapor are deposited onto a glass rod before it is drawn into a fiber; by adjusting the deposition processes, the index of refraction can be varied. The glass rod itself is made of ultra pure silica. Two manufacturing methods are the inside, or modified chemical vapor deposition (MCVD), and outside vapor deposition (OVD) process. In the MCVD process, a glass preform structure is made by spinning a quartz tube on an optical lathe. As the tube is spun, gas vapors of a reactive composition are fed into the tube and heated. A soot is produced and is deposited on the inside walls of the tube, gradually building the core and cladding with the desired refractive index profile (stepped or graded). Following deposition, the soot is sintered and the tube is collapsed to create the fiber.

In the OVD process, the glass rod is heated as dopants are introduced to yield the desired index of refraction (either stepped or graded). The dopants form a fine soot that is deposited onto the core material, building up outside layers prior to sintering into a preform. In both MCVD and OVD, the preform is placed vertically in a drawing tower, heated, pulled to create an optical fiber, and coated with a protective layer. The steps in fiber manufacture are shown in Fig. 8-18. Although fibers are prone to breakage from bending, their tensile strength is quite good. The pull strength of a fiber-optic cable can be 200–300 pounds, and the pull strength of a similar copper cable might be 25 pounds.

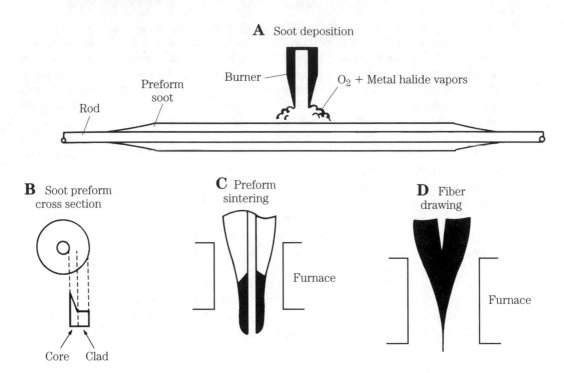

A Soot deposition

Burner

O_2 + Metal halide vapors

Preform soot

Rod

B Soot preform cross section

Core   Clad

C Preform sintering

Furnace

D Fiber drawing

Furnace

8-18 Four steps are involved in the manufacture of optical fibers.

Interconnection and Installation

Fiber-optic interconnection provides a number of interesting challenges. Although the electrons in an electrical wire can pass through any secure mechanical splice, the light in a fiber-optic cable is more fickle through a transition. Fiber ends must be clean, planar, smooth, and touching—a not inconsiderable task considering that the fibers can be 10 μm in diameter. (In some cases, rounded fiber ends yield a more satisfactory transmission.) Similarly, the interfacing of fiber to connectors requires special consideration and tools. Fundamentally, fiber and connectors must be aligned and mechanically held together.

Fibers can be joined with a variety of mechanical splices. Generally, fiber ends are ground and polished and butted together using various devices. A V-groove strip holds together fiber ends, where they are secured with an adhesive and a metal clip. Ribbon splice and chip array splicers are used to join multifiber multimode fibers. A rotary splicer is used for single-mode fibers; fibers are placed in ferrules that allow the fibers to be independently positioned until they are aligned and held by adhesive. However, a microscope must be used to see the small fibers. Many mechanical splices are considered temporary, and are later replaced by permanent fusion splicing; it is preferred because it reduces connector loss. With fusion splicing, fiber ends are heated to the fiber melting point, and fused together to form a continuous fiber. Specialized equipment is needed to perform the splice; in some cases an automated system uses small electrodes to create an electric arc across the fiber ends; cameras and computers are used to accomplish and monitor the work. Losses as low as 0.01 dB can be achieved.

Some fiber maintenance is simple: for example, to test continuity, a worker can shine a flashlight on one cable end, while another worker watches for light on the other end. Other measures are more sophisticated. An optical time-domain reflector (OTDR) is used to locate the position of poor connections or a break in a very long cable run. Light pulses are directed along a cable and the OTDR measures the delay and strength of the returning pulse. With short runs, a visual fault inspection can be best; a bright visible light source is used, and the cable and connectors are examined for light leaks. An optical power meter and a light source are used to measure cable attenuation and output levels. An inspection microscope (approximately 200×) is used to examine fiber ends for scratches and contamination. Although light disperses after leaving a fiber, workers should use eye protection near lasers and fiber ends. A fiber link does not require periodic maintenance. Perhaps the primary cause of failure is a "back hoe fade," which happens when a cable is accidentally cut during digging.

Various connectors and couplers are used in fiber installations; the purpose of an optical connector is to mechanically align one fiber with another, or with a transmitting or receiving port. Simple connectors allow fibers to be connected and disconnected; they properly align fiber ends; however, connector loss is typically between 0.5 and 2.0 dB, using butt-type connectors. Directional couplers connect three or more ports to combine or separate signals. Star couplers are used at central distribution points to distribute signals evenly to several outputs. Receivers, and transmitters such as shown in Fig. 8-19, integrate several elements into modules, simplifying installation. Subsystem integration provides data links in which the complete path from one buffer memory to another is integrated, making fiber optics as simple to install as copper wire.

Generally, the principal design criteria of a fiber installation are not complex. Consider an example suggested by Brent Karley, of a system with a 300-foot fiber run from a microphone panel to a recording console; in addition, midway in the cable, a split runs to a house mixing console. Design might begin by specifying the fiber's S/N ratio (as opposed to the audio signal's S/N) to determine the bit error rate (BER). For example, to achieve a BER of 10^{-10} (1 error for every 10^{10} transmitted bits), an S/N of 22 dB would be needed. A multimode graded index fiber would be appropriate in terms of bandwidth and attenuation. For example, the manufacturer's bandwidth length product (band factor) might be 400 MHz. For a fiber length of 300 feet (0.09 km) the cable's optical bandwidth is the band factor divided by its length, yielding 4.4 GHz. Dividing this by 1.41 yields the cable's electrical bandwidth of 3.1 GHz. The total system bandwidth is determined by:

$$\frac{1}{BW_{\text{total}}{}^2} = \frac{1}{BW_{\text{trans}}{}^2} + \frac{1}{BW_{\text{rec}}{}^2} + \frac{1}{BW_{\text{cable}}{}^2}$$

where the transmitter, receiver, and cable bandwidths are all considered. If BW_{trans} is 40 MHz, BW_{rec} is 44 MHz, and BW_{cable} is 3.1 GHz, total bandwidth is 30 MHz.

If the cable's attenuation is specified as 5.5 dB/km, this 0.09-km length would have 0.5 dB of attenuation. The splitter has 3-dB loss. Total coupling loss at the con-

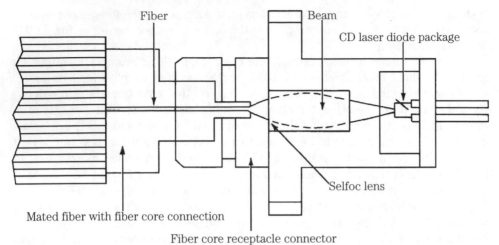

8-19 Laser-diode packages consolidate a laser diode, lens, and receptacle connector.

nection points is 5.5 dB, and temperature and aging loss is another 6 dB. Total loss is 15 dB. The system's efficiency can be determined: The adjusted output power is the difference between the transmitter output power and the detector sensitivity. For example, selected parts might yield figures of –8 dBm and –26 dBm respectively, yielding adjusted output power of 18 dB. Received signal level is –8 dBm –(–15 dB) = 23 dBm; this would yield an acceptable S/N ratio of 56 dB. The power margin is the difference between the adjusted power output and the total loss. In this case, 18 dB minus 15 dB yields 3 dB, a sufficient power margin, indicating good choice of cable, transmit and receive parts with respect to system loss.

As with any technology involving data protocol, standards are required. In the case of fiber optics, FDDI (Fiber Distributed Data Interface) and FDDI II are two standards governing fiber-optic data communications networks. They interconnect processors and can form the basis for a high-speed network, for example, linking workstations and a file server. FDDI uses LED drivers transmitting at a nominal wavelength of 1310 nm over multimode fiber with a 62.5-μm core and 125-μm cladding, with numerical aperture of 0.275. Connections are made with a dual-fiber cable (separate send and receive) using a polarized duplex connector. FDDI offers data bandwidths of 100 MHz with up to 500 station connections. The FDDI II standard adds greater flexibility to fiber-optic networking; for example, it allows a time-division multiplexed mode providing individual routes with a variety of data rates.

The SONET (Synchronous Optical NETwork) provides wideband optical transmission for commercial users. The lowest bandwidth optical SONET protocol is OC-1 with a bandwidth of 51.84 Mbps; a 45-Mbps T-3 signal can be converted to an STS-1 (synchronous transport signal level 1) signal for transmission over an OC-1 cable. Other protocols include OC-3 (155.52 Mbps) for uncompressed NTSC digital video, and OC-12 (622.08 Mbps) for high-resolution television. SONET is defined in the ANSI T1.105-1991 standard. Telecommunications is discussed in more detail in chapter 10.

Economics of Fiber Optics

Clearly, over long distances such as several miles or more, fiber is cheaper than wire cable. That was quickly discovered during the Vietnam war when the high price of copper (and increasing bandwidth demands) inspired telecommunications companies to decommission their copper cables, and replace them with fiber optics. Although audio studios are not always concerned with long distances, fiber optics is viable, for example, when RF or other interference is problematic. The question of transmission method is often determined by data rate. As rate requirements are increased, the case for fiber optics becomes convincing. A single 500-Mbps-km cable could carry a studio's digital audio data. Of course, the hidden cost effectiveness of fiber optics is its quality of transmission. In that respect, there might be no choice. As recording studios run data lines of 50 MHz or more, fiber optics will be the only practical means of interconnection. Similarly, many remote systems now use fiber; but 3000 feet of multichannel copper wiring can weigh 1.5 tons, 3000 feet of equivalent fiber can weigh only 50 pounds, an important cost advantage in a mobile environment. For many companies, the question is not whether to install fiber cables, but how many. Telephone companies generally install three times more capacity than initially needed, to allow for future increases in data traffic.

Many companies are aggressively developing active optical technology. For example, integrated optical components (IOCs) are optical devices that provide both wave guide capabilities, and interaction with the light carrier to provide signal processing. That is made possible by changing the optical path length of the guided light or by separating various modes of the guided light. Phase and amplitude modulation, mode conversion, polarization, and switching are some examples of optical signal processing. IOCs made with lithium niobate, coupled to single-mode fiber, are already used for a variety of sensors. According to some researchers, optical computing might one day replace electronic computing.

9
CHAPTER

The Compact Disc

The compact disc system is perhaps the most remarkable development in audio technology since the birth of the technology in 1877 with Edison's invention of the tinfoil recorder. It embodies many revolutionary steps in design, such as digital signal storage, optical scanning, error correction, and new manufacturing processes; altogether it establishes a new fidelity standard for the consumer. In addition, compact disc music playback is only one aspect of the many CD applications now available.

The compact disc system contains several unique technologies original to the audio field; when combined, they form an unprecedented means of storage. A compact disc contains digitally encoded data that is read by a laser beam. Because the laser is focused on a reflective layer embedded within the disc, dust and fingerprints on the reading surface do not normally affect reproduction. The effect of most errors that normally occur can be minimized by error correction circuitry. Because no stylus touches the disc surface, there is no disc wear, no matter how often the disc is played. Thus, digital storage, error correction, and disc longevity result in a robust digital storage medium.

Origins of the Compact Disc

The chronology of events in the development of the compact disc spans almost a decade from inception to introduction. The compact disc incorporates many technologies pioneered by many individuals and corporations; however, Philips Corporation of the Netherlands and Sony Corporation of Japan must be credited with its primary development. Optical disc technology developed by Philips and error-correction techniques developed by Sony, when merged, resulted in the successful compact disc format. The original standard established by these two companies guarantees that discs and players made by different manufacturers are compatible.

Philips first announced the technique of storing audio material optically in 1972. Analog modulation methods used for video storage were deemed unsuitable, and the possibility of digital signal encoding was examined. Furthermore, Philips established small disc diameter as a design prerequisite. Sony similarly had explored the possibility of an optical, large-diameter audio disc, and had extensively researched the error-processing requirements for a practical realization of the system. Other manufacturers such as Mitsubishi, Hitachi, Matsushita, JVC, Sanyo, Toshiba, and Pioneer advanced proposals for a digital audio disc. By 1977, numerous manufacturers had shown prototype optical disc audio players. In 1978, Philips and Sony designated signal format and error-correction methods, and in 1979 reached an agreement in principle to collaborate, with decisions on signal format and disc material. In June 1980, they jointly proposed the Compact Disc Digital Audio system, which was adopted by the Digital Audio Disc Committee, a group representing over 25 manufacturers.

Following development of a semiconductor laser pickup and LSI (large-scale integration) circuits for signal processing and D/A conversion, the compact disc system was introduced in October of 1982 in Japan and Europe. In March 1983, the compact disc was made available in the United States. Over 350,000 players and 5.5 million discs were sold worldwide in 1983, and 900,000 players and 17 million discs in 1984, making the CD one of the most successful electronic products ever introduced. Starting with the original CD-DA format, the compact disc family has been expanded to include CD-ROM (1984), CD-I (1986), CD-WO (1988), Video-CD (1994) and DVD (1996), with a host of applications in audio, video, and beyond. Today, well over a billion discs are sold annually.

Compact Disc Overview

The compact disc system is a highly efficient information storage system. Each audio disc stores a stereo audio signal comprised of two 16-bit data words sampled at 44.1 kHz; thus 1.41 million bits/second of audio data are output from the player. Other data overhead such as error correction, synchronization, and modulation are required, which triple the number of bits stored on a disc. Altogether, the channel bit rate, the rate at which data is read from the disc, is 4.3218 Mbps. A disc containing an hour of music thus holds about 15.5 billion channel bits—an impressive number for a disk that measures 12 cm in diameter, and costs a few cents to manufacture. Apart from modulation and error correction overhead, a CD-DA disc holds a maximum of 6.3 billion bits, or 783 million bytes (8-bit bytes) of user information (1.41 million bits per second, for 74 minutes).

Maximum disc playing time (strictly according to legend) was determined after Philips consulted conductor Herbert von Karajan. He advised them that a disc should be able to hold his performance of the Beethoven Ninth Symphony without interruption. A compact disc has a maximum playing time of 74 minutes, 33 seconds. By varying the CD standards slightly, playing times of over 80 minutes can be achieved. For example, a track pitch of 1.5 μm and linear velocity of 1.2 m/s would yield about 82 minutes of playing time.

Information is contained in pits impressed into the disc's plastic substrate. That surface is metalized to reflect the laser beam used to read the data from underneath the disc. A pit is about 0.6 μm wide, and a disc might hold about two billion of them. If a disc were enlarged so that its pits were the size of grains of rice, the disc would be half a mile in diameter. Each pit edge represents a binary 1; flat areas between pits or areas within pits are decoded as binary 0. Data is read from the disc as a change in intensity of reflected laser light; reading a CD causes no more wear to the recording than your reading causes to the words printed on this page.

The pits are aligned in a spiral track running from the inside diameter of the disc to the outside. CDs with shorter playing time thus provide a greater manufacturing yield. If unwound, a CD track would run for three miles. The pitch of the CD spiral, that is, how close together tracks are, is 1.6 μm; the period at the end of this sentence would cover more than 200 tracks. There are 22,188 revolutions across the disc's signal surface of 35.5 mm.

An optical pickup retrieves data. A laser beam is emitted and is guided through optics to the disc surface. The reflected light is detected by the pickup, and the data from the disc conveyed on the beam is converted to a digital electrical signal. Because nothing touches the disc except light, light itself and electrical servo circuits are used to keep the laser beam properly focused on the disc surface, and properly aligned with the spiral track. The pits are encoded with eight-to-fourteen modulation (EFM) for greater storage density, and Cross-Interleave Reed-Solomon code (CIRC) for error correction; circuits in players provide demodulation and error correction. When the audio data has been properly recovered from the disc and converted into a binary signal, it is input to digital oversampling filters and D/A converters for reconstruction of the analog signal.

Music CDs delivers high fidelity sound with outstanding performance specifications. With 16-bit quantization sampled at 44.1 kHz, players typically exhibit a frequency response of 5 Hz to 20 kHz with a deviation of ±0.2 dB. Dynamic range exceeds 100 dB, signal-to-noise ratio exceeds 100 dB, and channel separation exceeds 100 dB at 1 kHz. Harmonic distortion at 1 kHz is less than 0.002%. Wow and flutter are limited to the tolerances of quartz accuracy, which is essentially unmeasurable. With digital filtering, phase shifts are less than 0.5°. D/A converters provide linearity to within 0.5 dB at –90 dB. Excluding unreasonable abuse, a disc will remain in satisfactory playing condition indefinitely, as the pickup does not touch the disc, and the medium does not significantly age. The CD-Audio or CD-DA format, sometimes called the Red Book standard, is specified in the IEC 908 standard. Other nonaudio CD formats are discussed subsequently.

Disc Encoding

The CD's high data density results from a combination of the optical design of the disc and the method of coding the data impressed on it. For example, the wavelength of the reading laser and numerical aperature of the objective lens are selected to achieve a small spot size. This allows small pit/land dimensions. In addition, the pit/land track uses a constant linear velocity, and that velocity is set low, to increase the track's linear data density. Also, EFM modulation is used to encode the stored data. Although it creates more channel bits to be stored, the net result is a 25% increase in audio data capacity.

Disc Specifications

The physical characteristics of the compact disc are shown in Fig. 9-1. Disc diameter is 120 mm, hole diameter is 15 mm, and thickness is 1.2 mm. The innermost part of the disc does not hold data; it provides a clamping area for the player to hold the disc firmly to the spindle motor shaft. Data is recorded on an area 35.5 mm wide. A lead-in area rings the innermost data area, and a lead-out area rings the outermost area. The lead-in and lead-out areas contain nonaudio data used to control the player.

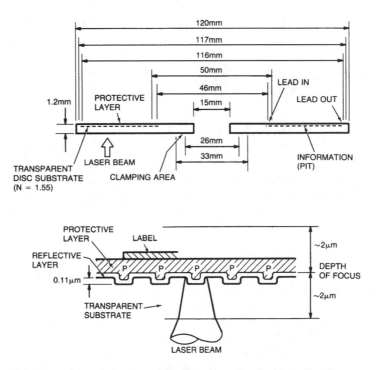

9-1 Physical specification of the compact disc showing disc dimensions and relief structure of data pits. Sony Corporation

A transparent plastic substrate forms most of a disc's 1.2-mm thickness. Data is physically contained in pits that are impressed along its top surface and are covered with a very thin (50 to 100 nm) metal (for example, aluminum or gold) layer. Another thin (10 to 30 μm) plastic layer protects the metalized pit surface, on top of which the identifying label (5 μm) is printed. A laser beam is used to read the data. It is applied from below and passes through the transparent substrate and back again.

The fact that the laser beam travels through the disc substrate provides a significant asset. The velocity of light decreases when it passes from air to the substrate. The plastic substrate has a refractive index of 1.55 (as opposed to 1.0 for air); the velocity of light slows from 3×10^5 km/s to 1.9×10^5 km/s. When the velocity of light slows, the beam is refracted, and focusing occurs. Because of the refractive index, the thickness of the disc, and the numerical aperture of the laser's lens, the size of the laser beam on the disc surface is approximately 800 μm, but is focused to approximately 1.0 μm (Airy pattern half-intensity level) at the pit surface. The laser beam is thus focused to a point slightly larger than the 0.6 micron pit width, as shown in Fig. 9-2. Moreover, the effects of any dust or scratches on the substrate's outer surface are minimized because their size (and importance) at the data surface are effectively reduced along with the laser beam. Specifically, any obstruction less than 0.5 mm becomes insignificant and causes no error in the readout.

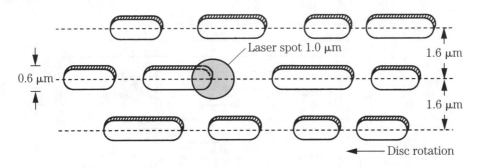

9-2 Data pits are aligned along a spiral track. The laser spot on the data surface has a diameter of approximately 1.0 μm (half-power level of the Airy pattern), covering the 0.6-μm pit width.

Data is physically stored as a phase structure. The data reference surface, as noted, is metalized. The reflective flat surface, called land, typically causes 90% of the laser light to be reflected back into the pickup. The construction of the CD is diffraction-limited, that is, the wavelength of the laser light would not permit smaller formations. When viewed from the laser's perspective (underneath), the pits appear as bumps. The height of each bump is between 0.11 to 0.13 μm. This dimension is slightly smaller than a specific dimension: the laser beam's wavelength in air is 780 nm. Inside the polycarbonate substrate, with a refractive index of 1.55, the laser's wavelength is about 500 nm. The height of the bumps is thus approximately ¼ of the laser's wavelength in the substrate.

A pit height equal to ¼ the laser's wavelength creates a phase difference of ½ wavelength (¼ + ¼ wavelength path differences) between the part of the beam reflected from the bump and the part reflected from the surrounding land, as shown in Fig. 9-3. The phase difference forms a diffraction pattern in the reflected light; this causes destructive interference in the main reflecting beam. A pit thus reduces the intensity of the reflected light. Pit diffraction is discussed in chapter 8.

In theory, when the beam strikes the land between pits, virtually all of its light is reflected, and when it strikes a pit, virtually all of its light is canceled, so that virtually none is reflected. In practice, the laser spot is larger than is required for complete cancellation between pit and land reflections, and pits are made slightly shallower than the theoretical figure of ¼ wavelength; this yields a better tracking signal, among other things. About 25% of the power of the incident light is reflected from a long bump. In any case, the presence of pits and land is thus read by the laser

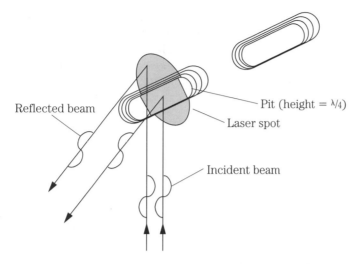

9-3
The laser spot reads data as an intensity modulation of its reflected beam. The phase structure of the data surface places the pit height about λ/4 over the land surface; this creates destructive interference in the reflected beam.

Reflected beam

Pit (height = λ/4)

Laser spot

Incident beam

beam; specifically, the disc surface modulates the intensity of the light beam. Thus the data physically encoded on the disc can be recovered by the laser and later converted to an electrical signal.

Examination of a pit track reveals that the linear dimensions of the track are the same at the beginning of its spiral as at the end. Specifically, a CD rotates with constant linear velocity (CLV), a condition in which a uniform relative velocity is maintained between the disc and the pickup. The player must adjust the disc's rotational speed to maintain a constant velocity as the spiral diameter changes. Because each outer track revolution contains more pits than each inner track revolution, the disc must be slowed down as it plays. The disc rotates at a speed of 500 rpm when the pickup is reading the inner circumference, and as the pickup moves outward, the rotational speed gradually decreases to 200 rpm. Thus a constant linear velocity is maintained. In other words, all of the pits are read at the same speed, regardless of the circumference of that part of the spiral. This is accomplished by a CLV servo system; the player reads frame synchronization words from the data and adjusts the disc speed to maintain a constant data rate.

Although the CLV of any particular compact disc is fixed, the CLVs used on different discs can range from 1.2 to 1.4 m/s. In general, discs with playing times of less than 60 minutes are recorded at 1.4 m/s, and discs with longer playing times use a slower velocity, to a minimum of 1.2 m/s. The CD player is indifferent to the actual CLV; it automatically regulates the disc rotational speed to maintain a constant channel bit rate of 4.3218 MHz.

Data Encoding

The channel bits, the data actually encoded on the disc, are the end product of a coding process accomplished prior to disc mastering, then decoded as a disc is played. Whether the original is an analog or digital recording, the audio program is coded as two's complement, 16-bit PCM data. The data stream must undergo CIRC error correction encoding and EFM modulation, and subcode and synchronization words must be incorporated as well.

All data on a CD is formatted by frames. By definition, a frame is the smallest complete section of recognizable data on a disc. The frame provides a means to distinguish between audio data and its parity, the synchronization word, and the subcode. Frame construction prior to EFM modulation is shown in Fig. 9-4. All of the required data is placed into the frame format during encoding. The end result of encoding and modulation is a bit stream of frames, each frame consisting of 588 channel bits.

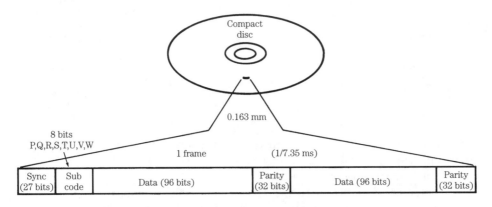

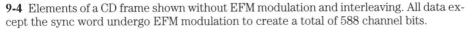

9-4 Elements of a CD frame shown without EFM modulation and interleaving. All data except the sync word undergo EFM modulation to create a total of 588 channel bits.

To begin assembly of a frame, six 32-bit PCM audio sampling periods (alternating between left and right channel) are grouped in a frame. Although this places 192 audio bits in the frame, it is a small segment of the recorded waveform. The 32-bit sampling periods are divided to yield four 8-bit audio symbols. To scatter possible errors, the symbols from different frames are interleaved so that the audio signals in one frame originate from different frames. In addition, eight 8-bit parity symbols are generated per frame, four in the middle of the frame and four at the end. The interleaving and generation of parity bits constitute the error correction encoding based on the Cross-Interleave Reed-Solomon code. CIRC is discussed in chapter 5.

One subcode symbol is added per frame; two of these subcode bits (P and Q) contain information detailing total number of selections on the disc, their beginning and ending points, index points within a selection, and other information. Six of these subcode bits (R, S, T, U, V, and W) are available for other applications, such as encoding text or graphics information on audio CDs. Subcode is discussed in more detail later in this chapter.

After the audio, parity, and subcode data is assembled, the data is modulated using eight to fourteen modulation (EFM). This gives the bit stream specific patterns of 1s and 0s, thus defining the lengths of pits and lands to facilitate optical reading of the disc. EFM permits a high number of channel bit transitions for arbitrary pit and land lengths. This increases data density and helps facilitate control of the spindle motor speed. To accomplish EFM, blocks of 8 data bits are translated into blocks of 14 channel bits using a dictionary that assigns an arbitrary and unambiguous word of

14 channel bits to each 8-bit word. The 8-bit symbols require $2^8 = 256$ unique patterns, and of the possible $2^{14} = 16,384$ patterns in the 14-bit system, 267 meet the pattern requirements; therefore, 256 are used and 11 discarded. A portion of the conversion table is shown in Table 9-1. EFM is discussed in chapter 3.

8-bit data	14-bit EFM
01100100	01000100100010
01100101	00000000100010
01100110	01000000100100
01100111	00100100100010
01101000	01001001000010
01101001	10000001000010
01101010	10010001000010
01101011	10001001000010
01101100	01000001000010
01101101	00000001000010
01101110	00010001000010
01101111	00100001000010
01110000	10000000100010

Table 9-1. Excerpt from the EFM conversion table. Data bits are translated into channel bits.

Blocks of 14 channel bits are linked by three merging bits primarily to maintain the proper run length between words, as well as suppress dc content, and aid clock synchronization. Successive EFM words cannot simply be concatenated; this might violate the run length of the code by placing binary 1s closer than three periods, or further than eleven periods. To prevent the former, a 0 merging bit is used, and the latter is prevented with a 1 merging bit. Two merging bits are sufficient to maintain proper run length. A third merging bit is added to more effectively control low frequency content of the output signal. A 1 can be used to invert the signal and minimize accumulating dc offset in the signal's polarity. This is monitored by the digital sum value (DSV); it tallies the number of 1s by adding a +1 to its count, and the number of 0s by adding a –1. An example of a merging bit determination, observing run length and DSV criteria, is shown in Fig. 9-5.

With the addition of merging bits, the ratio of bits before and after modulation is 8:17. The resultant channel stream produces pits and lands that are at least two but no more than ten successive 0s long; the pit/land family portrait is shown in Fig. 9-6. These pit/land lengths are described at 3T, 4T, 5T, . . . 11T where T is one channel bit period. Physically, pit and land length vary incrementally from 0.833 to 3.054 μm at a track velocity of 1.2 m/s, and from 0.972 to 3.56 μm at a velocity of 1.4 m/s.

That collection of pit (and land) lengths is used to encode all EFM channel bits on the CD surface. This is accomplished by coding the channel bits as NRZ, and then NRZI data. Each logical transition in the NRZI stream represents a pit edge, as shown in Fig. 9-7. The code is invertable; pits and lands represent channel bits equally; inversions caused by merging bits do not affect the data content. When the signal is decoded, the merging bits are discarded. After EFM, there are more channel bits to accommodate, but acceptable pit and land patterns become available. With this modulation, the highest frequency in the signal is decreased;

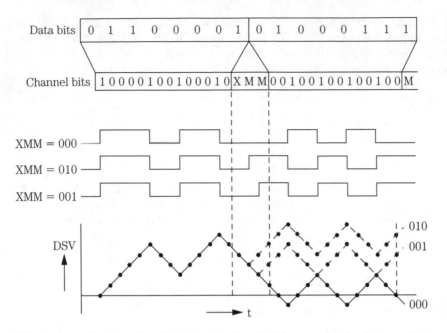

9-5 An example of merging bit determination. In this example, the first merging bit is set to 0 to satisfy EFM run length rules; the two remaining bits are set to 00 to minimize DSV. <small>Heemskerk and Schouhamer Immink</small>

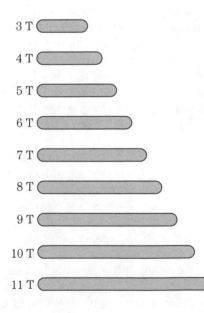

9-6
The complete collection of pit (and land) lengths created by EFM ranges from 3T to 11T. Minimum pit length is 0.833 to 0.972 μm; maximum pit length is 3.054 to 3.56 μm, depending on velocity (1.2 to 1.4 m/s).

therefore, a lower track velocity can be utilized. One benefit is conservation of disc real estate.

The resulting EFM data must be delineated, so a synchronization pattern is placed at the beginning of each frame. The synchronization word is uniquely identifiable from

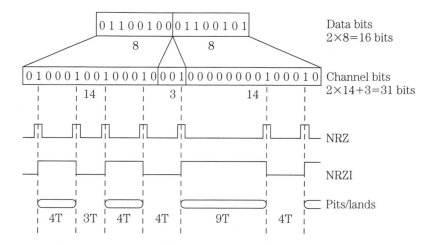

9-7 Each 8-bit half-sample undergoes EFM, three merging bits concatenate 14-bit words, the NRZ representation is converted to NRZI, and transitions are represented as pit edges on the disc.

any other possible data configuration (specifically, the 24-channel bit synchronization word is 100000000001000000000010 plus three merging bits). With the synchronization pattern, the player can identify the start of data frames. A complete frame contains one 24-bit synchronization word, 14 channel bits of subcode, 24 words of 14-channel bit audio data, eight words of 14-channel bit parity, and 102 merging bits, for a total of 588 channel bits per frame. Because each 588-bit frame contains twelve 16-bit audio samples, the result is 49 channel bits per audio sample. Thus when the data manipulation is completed, the original audio bit rate of 1.41 million bits/second is augmented to 4.3218 million channel bits/second. This resulting channel bit stream is physically stored on the disc. The entire encoding process is summarized in Fig. 9-8.

Player Optical Design

The CD player's function is to recover the data encoded on compact discs. That job begins at the laser pickup used to read data. In addition, automatic optical tracking and focusing systems must be used. Players generally use either three-beam or one-beam pickup designs. Consider the more common three-beam design first.

Optical Pickup

The data is recovered from the compact disc with an optical pickup, which moves across the surface of the rotating disc. A disc might contain two billion pits precisely arranged on a spiral track; the optical pickup must focus, track, and read that data track. The entire lens structure, laser source, and reader must be small enough to move laterally across the disc, underneath the disc surface, moving in response to tracking information or user random access programming. Although particulars vary among manufacturers, pickups are similar in design and operation. A

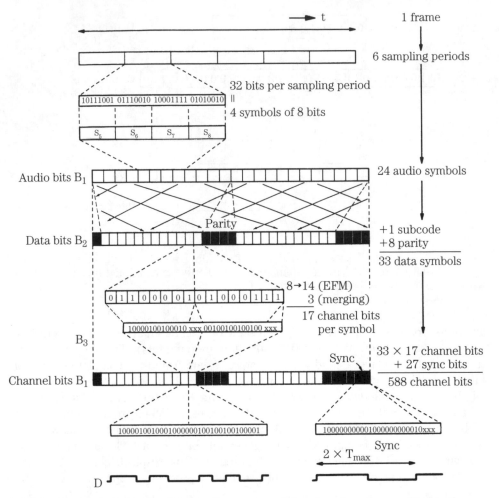

9-8 The algorithm used in the CD encoding process. Subcode and parity are added to the audio data, the data undergoes interleaving and modulation, and a synchronization word is added. Heemskerk and Schouhamer Immink

three-beam optical pickup contains a laser diode, diffraction grating, polarization beam splitter, quarter-wave plate, and several lens systems, as shown in Fig. 9-9.

The laser beam originates from a laser diode. A CD pickup uses a semiconductor laser with approximately a 0.5-mW optical output irradiating a coherent AlGaAs beam with a 780-nm wavelength. The light emitting properties of semiconductors have been utilized for many years. By adding forward bias to a PN junction, the injected part of the carrier is recombined to emit light; light emitting diodes (LEDs) use this phenomenon. However, laser light is significantly different from ordinary light in that it is comprised of a single wavelength and is coherent with respect to phase. Thus, a modified device is required.

The injection laser diode used in CD players uses a double heterojunction structure. It contains a thin (perhaps 0.1 μm) active layer of GaAs semiconductor, sand-

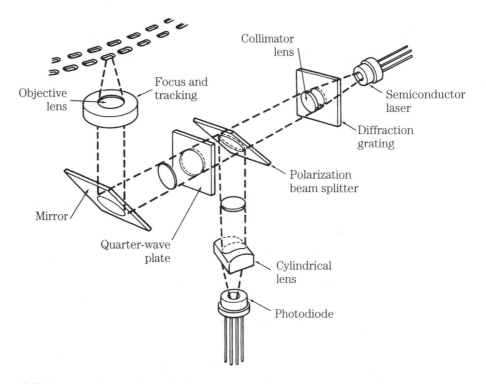

Collimator
lens

Objective
lens

Focus and
tracking

Semiconductor
laser

Diffraction
grating

Polarization
beam splitter

Mirror

Quarter-wave
plate

Cylindrical
lens

Photodiode

9-9 Diagram showing the optical elements in a three-beam optical pickup. Sony Corporation

wiched between heavily doped P- and N-type AlGaAs materials, sometimes called cladding layers. Forward bias creates a high concentration of electrons (from the N layer) and holes (from the P layer) in the active layer. An inverted population condition is created with many electrons in a high energy state band and many holes in a low energy band. Electrons fall to a lower energy band, releasing a photon; this reaches equilibrium with the input energy pumping rate. Stimulated light emission is thus induced. However, the light must be amplified, so several steps are taken. Both sides of the activating layer are sandwiched within materials with a large band gap to enclose the carrier, and the refraction ratio at both boundaries of the activating layer is different to effect enclosure. Also, for amplification within the layer, the crystal surface in the direction of the light emission is made reflective, and acts as a light resonator for continuous wave emission. A monitor photodiode is placed next to the laser diode to control power to the laser, compensating for temperature changes. The monitor diode conducts current proportionally to the laser's light output. If the monitor diode's current output is low with respect to a reference, current to the laser's drive transistors is increased to increase the laser's light output. Similarly, if monitor current is too high, supply current to the laser is decreased to compensate. Laser diodes have a very long life expectancy, from hundreds of thousands, to millions of operating hours.

In a three-beam pickup, the light from the laser point source passes through a diffraction grating, as shown in Fig. 9-10. This is a screen with slits spaced only a few laser wavelengths apart. As the beam passes through the grating, it diffracts at different angles. When the resulting collection is again focused, it appears as a bright center beam with successively less intense beams on either side. In a three-beam pickup design, the center beam is used for reading data and focusing, and two secondary beams, the first order beams, are used for tracking.

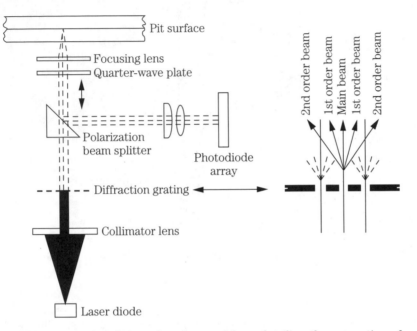

9-10 The optical path in a three-beam pickup, detailing the generation of secondary beams at the diffraction grating.

The polarization beam splitter (PBS) directs laser light to the disc surface, then angles the reflecting light to the photodiode. For the light approaching the polarization beam splitter, it acts as a transparent window, but for reflected light with rotated plane of polarization, it is a prism redirecting the beam. The PBS is comprised of two orthogonal prisms with a common face with a dielectric membrane between them. A collimator lens follows the PBS (in some designs it precedes it). Its purpose is to take the divergent light rays and make them parallel. The light then passes through a quarter-wave plate (QWP), a crystal material with anisotropic properties of double refraction. It rotates the plane of polarization of the incident and reflected laser light; plane of polarization is rotated 45° as light passes through the plate, then rotates another 45° as reflected light returns through it. The reflected light is thus polarized in a plane at a right angle relative to that of the incoming light, thus allowing the PBS to properly deflect the reflected light.

The final piece of optics in the path to the disc is the objective lens with a numerical aperture of 0.45; it is used to focus the beam to about 1.0 μm (half-intensity level) at the reflective surface, slightly wider than the pit width of 0.6 µm. The objective lens is attached to a two-axis actuator and servo system for up/down focusing motion and lateral tracking motion.

As noted, when the spot strikes a land interval between two pits, the light is almost totally reflected. When it strikes a pit (a bump from the reading side) a lower intensity light is returned. Ultimately, a change in intensity is deciphered as a 1 and unchanged intensity as 0. The varying intensity light returns through the objective lens, the QWP (to further rotate plane of polarization), and the collimator lens, and strikes the angled surface of the PBS. The light is deflected and passes through a collective lens and cylindrical lens. These optics are used to direct the operation of the focusing servo system to keep the objective lens at the proper depth of focus. The beam's main function, however, is to carry the data via reflected light to a four-quadrant photodiode. The electrical signals derived from that device are decoded into an audio waveform.

Autofocus Design

To properly distinguish between reflective surface and pits, the laser beam must rely on interference in the reflected beam created by the height of the bumps, a mere 110-nm difference. The focus of the beam on the data surface is therefore critical; an unfocused condition might result in inaccurate data. Specifically, the laser must stay focused within ±0.5 µm. A disc can contain deviations approaching ±0.4 mm. Thus, the objective lens must be able to refocus as the disc surface deviates. This is accomplished by a servo-driven autofocus system, which utilizes the center laser beam, a four-quadrant photodiode, control electronics, and a servo motor to move the objective lens. An operational diagram of the autofocus system is shown in Fig. 9-11.

The optical property of astigmatism creates distorted images and is used to achieve autofocus in many pickups. The cylindrical lens performs the essential trick needed to detect an out-of-focus condition. As the distance between the objective lens and the disc reflective surface varies, the focal point of the system changes, and the image projected by the cylindrical lens changes its shape. The change in the image on the photodiode generates the focus correction signal.

When the disc surface lies at the focal point of the objective lens, the reflected image through the intermediate convex lens and the cylindrical lens is unaffected by the astigmatism of the cylindrical lens, and a circular spot strikes the center of the photodiode. When the distance between the disc and the objective lens decreases, the focal points of the objective lens, convex lens, and cylindrical lens move farther from the cylindrical lens, and the pattern becomes elliptical. Similarly, when the distance between the disc and the objective lens increases, the focal points are closer to the lens, and an elliptical pattern again results, but rotated 90° from the first elliptical pattern.

The four-quadrant photodiode reads an intensity level from each of the quadrants to generate four voltages. The value $(A + B + C + D)$ creates an audio data signal. If a focus correction signal is mathematically created to be $(A + C) - (B + D)$, the output error voltage is a bipolar S curve, centered about zero. Its value is zero when the beam

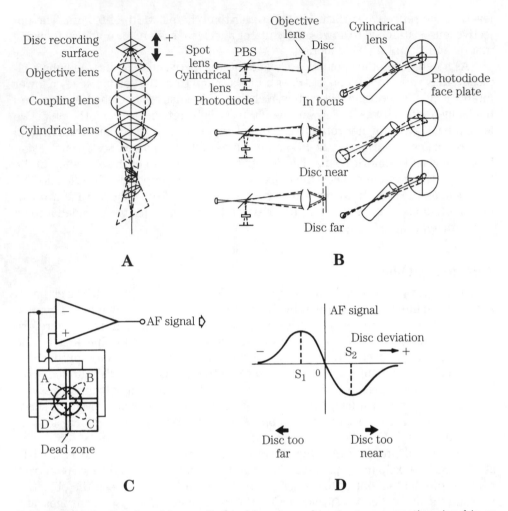

9-11 Astigmatism produced by a cylindrical lens is used to create a correction signal in an autofocus system. A. The main beam passes through a cylindrical lens; the image distorts and rotates relative to path length. B. Astigmatism creates an asymmetrical optical pattern because of path-length errors. C. A four-quadrant photodiode converts the optical pattern into an auto-focus correction signal. D. The AF signal represents disc position and controls a servo to dynamically maintain focus.

is precisely focused on the disc; a positive-going focus correction signal is generated as the disc moves away, and a negative-going signal is generated as the disc moves closer. Using a closed loop system, the difference signal continually corrects the mechanism to achieve a zero difference signal—in this case, a focused laser beam.

A servo system is used to move the objective lens up and down, to maintain a depth of focus within tolerance. A circuit deciphers the focus correction signal and generates a servo control voltage, which in turn controls the actuator to move the objective lens. The objective lens is displaced in the direction of its optical axis by a coil and a permanent magnet structure, similar to that used in a loudspeaker except that the objective lens takes the place of the speaker cone. A two-axis actuator is used to accomplish this. The top assembly of the pickup is mounted on a base with a circular magnet ringing it. A circular yoke supports a bobbin with both the focus and tracking coils inside. Control voltages from the focus drive circuit are applied to the bobbin focus coil; this moves up and down with respect to the magnet. The objective lens thus maintains its proper depth of focus. The other axis of movement, from side to side, is used to achieve tracking accuracy.

Autotracking Design

Nothing except laser light touches the data surface. That poses the engineering challenge of tracking a spiral pit sequence with nothing tangible to guide the pickup. The result is the autotracking system found in all CD players. The spiral pit track has a 1.6-μm pitch. An off-center disc might exhibit track eccentricity of over 100 μm. Vibration further challenges the pickup's ability to track within a ±0.1-μm tolerance. The laser beam system is appropriately used for tracking; it would be impossible for any purely mechanical system to track as well. In a three-beam pickup, the center beam is split by a diffraction grating to create a series of secondary beams of diminishing intensity. The first-order beams are conveyed to the disc surface along with the central beam. The central beam spot covers the pit track, while the two tracking beams are aligned above and below and offset to either side of the center beam. During proper tracking, part of each tracking beam is focused on the pit, while the other part covers the land between pit tracks. The three beams are reflected back through the QWP and PBS; the main beam strikes the four-quadrant photodiode and the two tracking beams strike two separate photodiodes mounted to either side of the main photodiode. The complete photodiode assembly for data, tracking, and focusing is shown in Fig. 9-12.

As the three spots drift to either side of the pit track, the amount of light reflected from the tracking beams varies as one of the beams encounters more pit area; this results in less average light intensity. Meanwhile, the other beam encounters less pit area, returning greater reflected intensity. The relative voltage outputs from the two tracking photodiodes thus form a correction signal, as shown in Fig. 9-13. If tracking is precisely aligned, the difference between the tracking signals is zero. If the beams drift, a difference signal is generated, for example, varying positively for a left drift and negatively for a right drift, to create a tracking correction signal. That signal is applied to the two-axis actuator assembly containing the permanent magnet and focus/tracking coil. To correct for a tracking error, the correction voltage is applied to the coil; the bobbin swings around a shaft to laterally move the objective lens so that the main laser spot is again centered, and the tracking correction signal is again zeroed.

One-Beam Pickup

The optical components of a one-beam pickup are shown in Fig. 9-14A, along with the photodiode array used to generate tracking and focusing signals, and read the data signal. A semitransparent mirror is used to direct light from the laser diode

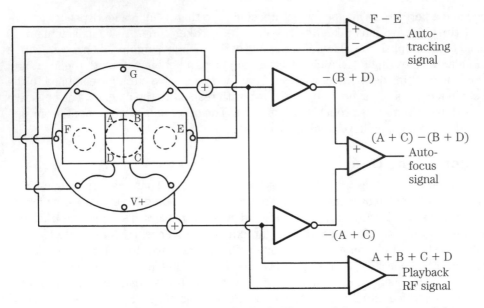

9-12 The four-quadrant photodiode (A, B, C, D) is used for autofocus and data playback. Photodiodes E and F are used for autotracking.

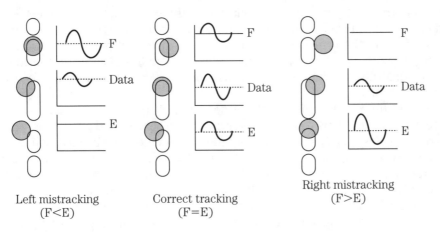

Left mistracking
(F<E)

Correct tracking
(F=E)

Right mistracking
(F>E)

9-13 A tracking-correction signal is generated from an intensity imbalance in the two secondary beams. A servo system dynamically maintains tracking.

to the disc surface. Light reflected from the disc passes through the mirror and is directed through a wedge lens. The wedge lens splits the beam into two beams, adjusted to strike an array of four horizontally-arranged photodiodes. The outputs of all the photodiodes are summed to provide the data signal ($D_1 + D_2 + D_3 + D_4$), which is demodulated to yield both audio data and control signals for the laser servo system.

Autotracking uses a push-pull technique. A symmetrical beam is reflected when the laser spot is centered on the pit track. When the laser beam deviates from the pit

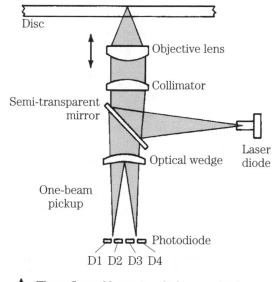

A The reflected beam is split by a wedge lens and directed to four photodiodes.

9-14
A one-beam optical pickup.
Philips

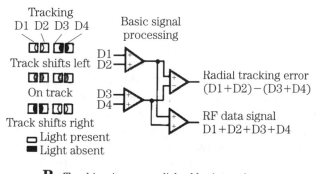

B Tracking is accomplished by intensity asymmetry in the beam.

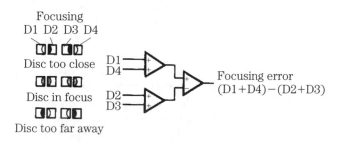

C Focusing is maintained through the angle of deflection between the split beams.

track, interference creates intensity asymmetry in the beam. This results in an intensity difference between the split beams. When the beam is off-track, one side of the beam encounters more pit area; hence, greater interference occurs on that side of the beam, and reflected light is less intense there, as shown in Fig. 9-14B. As a result, the split beam derived from that side of the beam is less intense, and the photodiode's output is decreased. The difference between the pairs $(D_1 + D_2) - (D_3 + D_4)$ is used to generate an error signal to correct the pickup's tracking.

The intensity of the reflected beam could become asymmetrical from dirt in the optical system. This would create an offset in the tracking correction signal, causing the pickup to remain slightly off track. To prevent this, a second tracking error signal is generated. A low-frequency (for example, 600 Hz) signal is applied to the tracking servo. This signal modulates the output signal from the four photodiodes. As the pickup mistracks, a deviation occurs in the modulated signal. This signal is rectified and used to correct the primary tracking signal with a direct voltage. In this way, the effect of an offset is negated.

Autofocusing uses a Foucault technique. As shown in Fig. 9-14C, when correct focus is achieved, two images are centered between photodiode pairs. When focus varies, the focal point of the system is shifted. When the disc is too far, the split beams draw together, and when the disc is too near, the beams move apart. The difference in intensity between diode pairs D1/D4 and D2/D3 forms a focus error signal $(D_1 + D_4) - (D_2 + D_3)$ that maintains focus of the servo-driven objective lens.

Pickup Control

Aside from the tracking accuracy needed to keep the laser beam on track, a motor must precisely move the pickup across the disc surface to track the entire pit spiral. The pickup must be able to jump from one place on the disc to another, find the desired place on the spiral, and resume tracking. These functions are handled by separate circuits, primarily using previously generated control signals. Three-beam pickups are mounted on a sled, which moves radially across the disc surface. Linear motors are used to position the pickup according to user commands, and bring the pickup within capture range of the autotracking circuit. Most one-beam pickups are mounted on a pivoting arm, which describes an arc across the disc surface. A coil and magnet are placed around the pivot point of the arm. When the coil is energized, the pickup can be positioned anywhere across the pit track and its precise position corrected by the autotracking circuit. In both three- and one-beam designs, tracking in a CD player is similar to that of a conventional record player. In the same way that a record groove pulls the stylus across an LP, the autotracking system pulls the pickup across a CD, keeping the pickup on track.

For fast forward or reverse, the microprocessor assumes control of the tracking servo to provide faster motion than is possible during normal tracking. When the correct location is reached, the S curve generated by the tracking correction signal is referenced to a microprocessor-generated control signal, and a signal signifies that proper tracking alignment is imminent. Just prior to alignment, a brake pulse is generated to compensate for the inertia of the pickup. The actuator comes to rest on the correct track, and normal autotracking is resumed.

The reflectivity of discs can vary because of manufacturing process differences, soiling of the player optics, etc. It is important to maintain a constant voltage level for proper data recovery; thus, the gain of the output control amplifier is variable, depending on the intensity of the reflected laser beam. This gain adjustment is automatically accomplished during the initial reading of the disc table of contents and is maintained while the disc is played. This occurs under control of a microprocessor. For example, resistors can be switched into the amplifier's circuit, varying gain by about ±10 dB. A control signal might come from the detection circuit, to alert the focus servo system to defective or damaged discs. In scvcrc cases, the objective lens is pulled away from the disc to prevent damage to the pickup.

Player Electrical Design

A CD player's task of reproducing the audio signal requires demodulation and error correction processing, as well as filtering and digital-to-analog conversion. Only then is the signal recovered from the disc suitable for playback. In addition, controls and displays are required to interface the player with the human user. To simplify operation, and control the many subsystems, players incorporate one or more microprocessors in their design. A block diagram of a CD player is shown in Fig. 9-15.

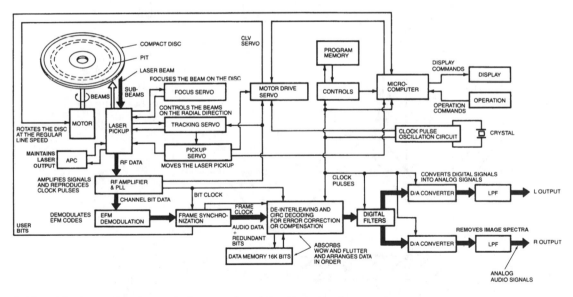

9-15 A CD player, showing optical processing and output signal processing.

EFM Demodulation

Voltage from the photodiode array is ultimately transformed into the analog audio signal output from the player. Following amplification of this RF signal, the first signal processing is EFM demodulation. The signal encoded on the disc uses EFM, which specifies that the signal be comprised of not less than two nor more than ten successive 0s between 0-to-1 transitions. This results in nine different incremental pit lengths, from three channel bits long to 11 channel bits long. This sets the frequency limits of the EFM signal, ranging from 196 kHz (11T) to 720 kHz (3T). This range is sometimes referred to as a 3T-11T signal, with T referring to the period of 1 channel bit. The large range of pit length values, a range of nearly 400% of the smallest length, allows a substantial tolerance for jitter error (45 nm) during data playback.

The photodiode and its processing circuits produce a data signal resembling a high-frequency sinusoid called the EFM signal; this is an RF signal. A collection of EFM waveforms is called the eye pattern. The information contained in the eye pattern is shown in Fig. 9-16. Whenever a player is tracking data, the eye pattern is always present, and the quality of the signal can be observed from the pattern. Although this signal is made up of sinusoids, it is truly digital. It undergoes processing to convert it into an NRZI signal, in which the preceding polarity is reversed whenever there is a binary 1. This does not affect the encoded data because the width of the EFM periods holds the pertinent values. The NRZI signal is further converted to NRZ.

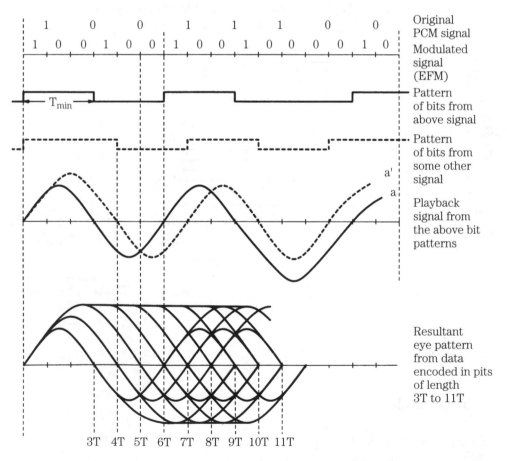

9-16 The modulated EFM data is read from the disc as an RF signal. The RF signal can be monitored through an eye pattern by simultaneously displaying successive waveform transitions.

Synchronization words are first recovered from the NRZ signal. Frame synchronization bits that were added to each frame during encoding are extracted, and symbol synchronization is generated to synchronize the thirty-three symbols of channel data in each frame. Merging bits are discarded, and the individual channel bits are used to generate a synchronization pulse. The EFM code is demodulated so that every 14-bit EFM word is converted to eight bits. Demodulation is accomplished by logic circuitry or a lookup table, that is, a list stored in memory, which uses the recorded data to reference back to the original patterns of eight bits. The process from eye pattern to demodulated data is summarized in Fig. 9-17.

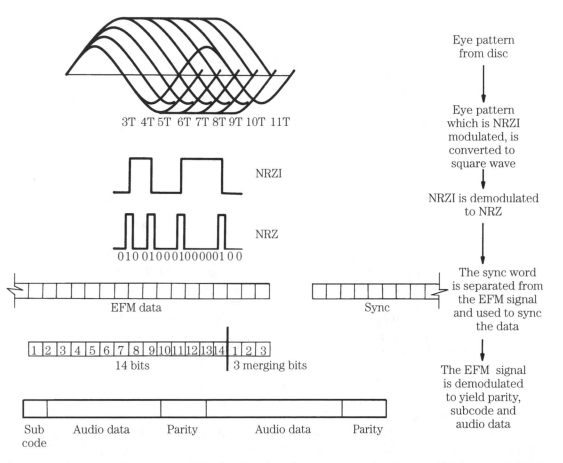

9-17 Demodulation of the output RF signal permits recovery of synchronization, subcode, audio, and error-correction data.

During decoding, data is applied to a buffer memory. Disc rotational irregularities might make data input irregular, but clocking ensures that the buffer output is precise. To guarantee that the buffer neither overflows nor underflows, a control signal is generated according to the buffer's current filled level. This is used to control the disc rotating speed. By varying the rate of data from the disc, the buffer is maintained at 50% capacity. Time-base correction is discussed in chapter 4.

Error Detection and Correction

Following demodulation, data is sent to a Cross-Interleave Reed-Solomon code circuit for error detection and correction. The CIRC error correction decoding strategy uses a combination of two Reed-Solomon code decoders, C1 and C2. The CIRC is based on the use of parity bits and an interleaving of the digital audio samples. Depending on implementation, CIRC can enable complete correction of burst errors up to 3874 bits (a 2.5-mm section of pit track).

Theoretically, the raw-bit error rate (BER) on a CD is between 10^{-5} and 10^{-6}; that is, there is 1 incorrectly recorded bit for every 10^5 (100,000) to 10^6 (1 million) bits on a disc. Following CIRC error correction, the bit error rate is reduced to 10^{-10} or 10^{-11}, or less than one bad bit in 10 to 100 billion. In practice, because of the data density, even a mildly defective disc can exhibit a much higher bit error rate. As discussed in chapter 5, data is corrected through two CIRC decoders, C1 and C2. The C1 decoder corrects minor errors and flags uncorrectable errors. The C2 decoder corrects larger errors, aided by the error flags. Uncorrected errors leaving C2 are flagged as well. Error correction flags generated from the CIRC circuitry during CD playback can represent the error rate (from sources such as pit structure, birefringence, and pinholes) present on a disc.

If the CIRC decoder cannot correct all errors, it outputs the data symbols uncorrected (the parity symbols have been dropped), but marked with an erasure flag. Most of these symbols can be reconstructed by linear interpolation, using the combination of error flags to aid interpolation. The function of these error concealment circuits is to reduce such errors to inaudibility. Only uncorrected symbols, marked with erasure flags, are processed. All valid audio data passes through the concealment circuitry unaffected, except in the case of data surrounding a mute point, which is attenuated to minimize audibility of the mute. Concealment methods vary according to the degree of error encountered, and from player to player. In its simplest form, when a single sample is flagged between two correct samples, mean value interpolation is used to replace the erroneous sample. For longer consecutive errors, the last valid sample value is held, then the mean value is taken between the final held value and the next sample value. The system might permit recovery through adjacent sample interpolation of losses of up to 13,282 bits (8.7 mm track length).

If large numbers of adjacent samples are flagged, the concealment circuitry performs muting. Using delay lines, a number of previous valid samples (perhaps thirty) are gradually attenuated with a cosine function to avoid the introduction of high frequency components. Gain is kept at zero for the duration of the error, then gain is gradually restored. Errors that have escaped the CIRC decoder without being flagged are not detected by the concealment circuitry, therefore do not undergo concealment and might produce an audible click in the audio reproduction. Not all CD players are alike in error correction. Any CD player's error correction ability is determined by the success of the strategy devised to decode the CIRC, as well as the concealment algorithm.

Output Processing

Following error correction, the digital data is processed to recover subcode information. During encoding, eight bits of subcode information per frame are placed in the bit stream. During decoding, subcode data from 98 frames is read and grouped together to form one block, then assigned eight different channels to provide control and (optionally) video information.

Output anti-imaging filtering is accomplished in the digital domain with oversampling filters. In oversampling, data is demultiplexed into left and right channels, and applied to an FIR transversal filter. Through interpolation, additional samples are inserted between disc samples, thus raising the sampling rate. Rates of four, eight times or more are commonly used. As a result of oversampling, the output image spectra are raised to the corresponding multiple of the sampling frequency. When shifted to this high frequency range, they can be easily removed by a low order analog filter, free of phase distortion. Oversampling filters are discussed in chapter 4.

Following this processing, the data is converted into two's complement or offset binary, depending on the type of D/A converter used in the player. The output stage of a compact disc player contains output sample-and-hold circuits, lowpass filters, and output amplifiers. These circuits are described in chapter 4. Alternatively, low-bit conversion can be used, as described in chapter 16.

Compact Disc Subcode

Each CD frame contains eight subcode bits, containing information describing where tracks begin and end, track numbers, disc timing, index points, and other parameters. During playback, the subcode bits are used by the player to properly interpret the information on the disc, and facilitate user control of the player in accessing disc contents.

Eight subcode bits are contained in every frame and are designated as P, Q , R, S, T, U, V, and W as shown in Fig. 9-18A. Only the P and Q subcode bits are used in the audio format. (There is no relation to the P and Q codes in CIRC.) A subcode block is constructed sequentially from 98 successive frames. Thus the eight subcode bits (P through W) are used as eight different channels, with each frame containing 1 P bit, 1 Q bit, and so forth. This interleaving minimizes the effect of disc errors on subcode data. The subcode block rate can be determined: A CD codes 44,100 left and right 16-bit audio samples per second, so the byte (8 bit) rate is $44,100 \times 4$, or 176.4 kbytes per second. With 24 audio symbols in every frame, the frame rate is 176.4/24 or 7350 Hz. Because 98 frames form one subcode block, the subcode block rate is 7350/98 or 75 Hz; that is, 75 subcode blocks per second. Parenthetically, 7350 frames per second multiplied by the number of channel bits, 588, results in 4.3218 MHz, the overall channel bit rate.

A subcode block is complete with its own synchronization word, instruction, data, commands, and parity. The start of each subcode block is denoted by the presence of S_0 and S_1 synchronization bits in the first symbol positions of two successive blocks. On most audio discs, only the P and Q subcode channels contain information; the others are recorded with 0s.

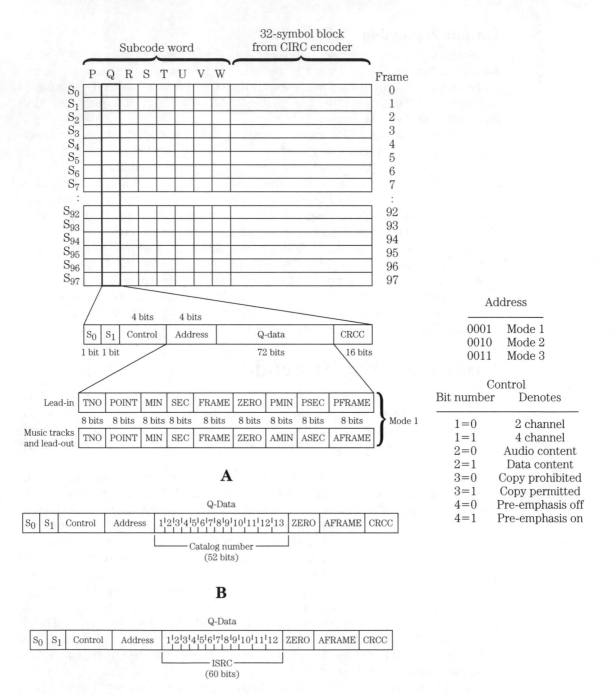

9-18 The data structure of the CD subcode block, showing detail of the Q subcode channel. A. Mode 1 has provisions for a lead-in, and program format. B. Mode 2 format stores UPC codes. C. Mode 3 format stores ISRC code.

The P channel contains a flag bit. It designates the start of a track, as well as the lead-in and lead-out areas on a disc, as shown in Fig. 9-19. The music data is denoted by 0, and the start flag as 1. The length of a start flag is a minimum of two seconds, but equals the pause length between two tracks if this length exceeds two seconds. Lead-in and lead-out signals tell the player where the music program on the disc begins and ends. A lead-in signal consists of all 0s appearing just prior to the beginning of the music data. At the end of the lead-in, a start flag two to three seconds long appears just prior to the start of music. During the last music track, preceding the lead-out, a start flag of two to three seconds appears. The end of that flag designates the start of lead-out and the flag remains at 0 for two to three seconds. Following that time, a signal consisting of alternating 1s and 0s (at a 2-Hz rate) appears. These various signals can be used by players of basic design to control the optical pickup. For example, a player could count start flags placed in the blank interval between tracks to locate any particular track on a disc. In practice, players use only the more sophisticated Q code.

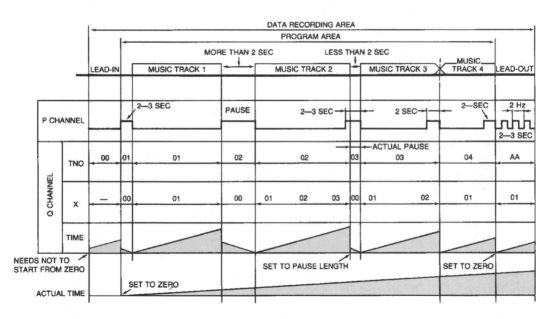

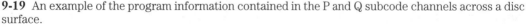

9-19 An example of the program information contained in the P and Q subcode channels across a disc surface.

The Q channel (see Fig. 9-18) contains four basic kinds of information: control, address, Q data, and an error detection code. The control information (four bits) handles several player functions. The number of audio channels (two or four) is indicated; this distinguishes between two- and four-channel CD recordings (the latter not implemented). The digital copy (permit/deny) bit regulates the ability of other digital recorders to record the CD's data digitally. Pre-emphasis (on/off) is also indicated. The player reads the code and automatically switches to the appropriate de-emphasis circuit.

The address information consists of four bits designating the three modes for the Q data bits. Primarily, mode 1 contains number and start times of tracks, mode 2 contains a catalog number, and mode 3 contains the International Standard Recording Code (ISRC) code. Each subcode block contains 72 bits of Q data, as described below, and 16 bits for the CRCC generation polynomial $x^{16} + x^{12} + x^5 + 1$, used for error detection on the control, address and Q data information in each block.

As noted, there are three modes of Q data. Mode 1 stores information in the disc lead-in area, program area, and lead-out area. The data content in the lead-in area (see Fig. 9-18A) differs from that in the other areas. Mode 1 lead-in information is contained in the table of contents (TOC). The TOC stores data indicating the number of music selections (up to 99) as a track number (TNO) and the starting times (P times) of the tracks. The TOC is read during disc initialization, before the disc begins playing, so that the player can respond to any programming or program searching that is requested by the user. In addition, most players can display this information.

In the lead-in area, the TNO is set to 00, indicating that the data is part of a TOC. The TOC is assembled from the point field; it designates a track number and the absolute starting time of that point in minutes, seconds, and frames (75 frames per second). The times of a multiple disc set can also be designated in the point field. When the point field is set to A0 (instead of a track number) the minute field shows the number of the first track on the disc. When the point field is set to A1, the minute field shows the number of the last track on the disc. When set to A2, the absolute running time of the start of the lead-out track is designated. During lead in, running time is counted in minutes, seconds, and frames. The TOC is repeated continuously in the lead-in area, and the point data is repeated in three successive subcode blocks.

In the program and lead-out area (see Fig. 9-18A) mode 1 contains track numbers, index numbers (X) within a track, time within a track, and absolute time (A-time). TNO designates individual tracks and is set to AA during lead-out. Running time is set to zero at the beginning of each track (including lead-in and lead-out areas) and increases to the end of the track. At the beginning of a pause, time decreases ending with zero at the end of the pause. The absolute time is set to zero at the beginning of the program area (the start of the first music track) and increases to the start of the lead-out area. Program time and absolute time are expressed in minutes, seconds, and frames. Index numbers both separate and subdivide tracks. When set to 00, X designates a pause between tracks, and countdown occurs. Nonzero X values set index points inside tracks. A 01 value designates a lead-out area. Using indexing, up to 99 locations within tracks can be indexed. Mode 1 information occupies at least 9 out of 10 successive subcode blocks. Figure 9-19 summarizes the timing relationships contained in mode 1 Q channel information.

In Q data modes 2 and 3 (see Fig. 9-18B and C) the program and time information is replaced by other kinds of data. Mode 2 contains a catalog number of the disc, such as the bar code of the universal product code (UPC). Mode 2 also continues absolute time count from adjacent blocks. Mode 3 provides an ISRC number for each track. The ISRC number includes the country code, owner code, year of recording, and serial number. Mode 3 also continues absolute time.

Modes 2 and 3 can be deleted from the subcode if they are not required. If they are used, mode 2 and mode 3 must occupy at least 1 out of 100 successive subcode blocks, with identical contents in each block. In addition, mode 2 and 3 data can be present only in the program area. The remaining six subcode bits (R, S, T, U, V, and W) are packed with zeros on most CDs. However, they are available for CD+G/M data as described below.

Disc Manufacturing

The compact disc manufacturing process enjoys the advantages of the disc medium, in which the information is placed on the disc simultaneously with its creation. However, the compact disc requires high-cost manufacturing processes and stringent quality control to guarantee a satisfactory yield. Although manufacturers use different techniques to produce compact discs, the manufacturing process always involves three general steps: tape mastering, disc mastering, and disc replication. Tape mastering can be accomplished in a properly outfitted recording studio; however, the latter steps require specialized equipment found only in CD manufacturing plants.

Tape Mastering

The tape mastering process is the culmination of the recording process, in which the master audio tape has been edited and recorded on a ¾-inch format video recorder via a digital audio processor. Most audio CDs are manufactured from the video PCM format; however, it is possible to transfer from an incompatible digital recording format. Although the digital recording could be converted to analog and then to the PCM format, degradation would result; hence, a sampling frequency converter can be used for a digital-to-digital transfer without deterioration in signal quality. The PCM format is recorded using a digital audio processor and a videocassette recorder. The master tape contains the following information: 1) video format tracks with digital audio data; 2) analog audio channel 1 with PQ subcode; 3) analog audio channel 2 with continuous SMPTE (nondrop frame) timecode. During mastering, the PQ subcode is uniquely created for the master using a subcode editor. The subcode is entered on the video PCM tape and along with the music data is later modulated into the CD format during disc mastering.

Disc Mastering

Compact disc mastering is the first process in disc manufacturing; the entire process is shown in Fig. 9-20. A glass plate about 240 mm in diameter and 6 mm thick, comprised of simple float glass, is washed in alkali and freon, lapped, and polished with a CeO_2 optical polisher. The plate is prepared in a clean room with extremely stringent dust filtering. After inspection and cleaning, the plate is tested for optical dropouts with a laser; any burst dropouts in reflected intensity are cause for rejection of the plate. To prepare the plate for photoresist mastering, an adhesive is applied, followed by a coat of photoresist applied by a spinning developer machine. The depth of the photoresist coating is critical; it ultimately determines the pit

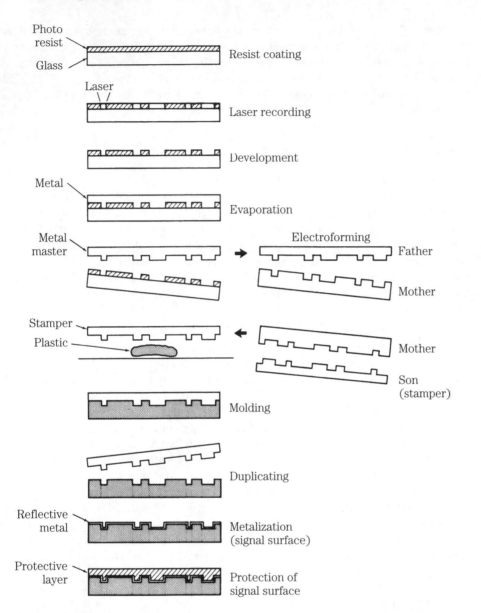

Photo resist

Glass

Resist coating

Laser

Laser recording

Development

Metal

Evaporation

Metal master

Electroforming

Father

Mother

Stamper

Plastic

Mother

Son (stamper)

Molding

Duplicating

Reflective metal

Metalization (signal surface)

Protective layer

Protection of signal surface

9-20 A summary of the principal steps in the CD disc manufacturing process.

depth. The plate is cured in an oven and stored, with a shelf life of several weeks. The plate is ready for mastering.

The mastering lathe is a device that photographically exposes the data spiral into the photoresist on the master glass disc. The mastering machine has a control rack consisting of a minicomputer with video terminal and floppy disk drive, video transport, PCM audio processor, and diagnostic equipment. The lathe may use a 15-mW, 460-nm wavelength, argon gas laser, with NA of 0.9. The laser is intensity modulated by an acousto-optical modulator to create the exposing signal corresponding to the encoded data. Another laser, which does not affect the master disc photoresist, is used for focusing and tracking. The master glass plate coated with photoresist is placed on the lathe and exposed with the laser to create the spiral track, creating the disc contents in real time as the master tape is played through the PCM processor and CD-encoded.

Quality of the production discs depends directly on the master lathe's signal characteristics, such as eye pattern symmetry, signal modulation amplitude, and track following. To guard against disc contamination, stringent air filtering is used inside the mastering lathe. Although the optics are similar to those found inside consumer CD players (polarization beam splitter, objective lens, laser source), the mechanisms are built on a grander scale, especially for isolation from vibration. For example, the stylus block may be supported and moved by an air-float slider. The entire mastering process is accomplished automatically, under computer control.

After exposure in the lathe, the glass master is developed by an automatic developing machine. Developing fluid washes the rotating disc surface, etching away the exposed areas of photoresist. During development, a laser monitors photoresist depth and stops development when proper engraving depth has been reached—that is, when the etching reaches the glass substrate. In theory, the optimum signal from the finished CD results when the pit depth equals one-quarter the wavelength in the transparent substrate of the 780-nm laser used in CD players. Pit depth (one-fourth of 780 nm, divided by the refraction index of 1.55) is theoretically 126 nm. Given equal spot areas so that the intensity of the light reflected from the pit bottom equals the intensity of the light reflected from the surface; this pit depth creates destructive interference causing an absence of reflected light wherever there is a pit, distinguishing it from the almost total reflection when the spot strikes the land surrounding pits. In practice, a compromise must be made to balance the need for zero reflected pit light against that conducive for signal tracking, which requires a one-eighth wavelength pit depth. A production pit depth of 110 nm is typical. Following etching, a metal coating, usually of silver, is evaporated onto the photoresist layer. The master glass plate is ready for electroforming.

In some cases, a nonphotoresist mastering technique is used. Using a glass plate coated with a proprietary recording layer, the lathe directs the input signal to an acousto-optical modulator that controls the recording laser. Pits are physically cut directly into the recording layer on the master disc using an ablative process. The system provides a direct-read-after-write (DRAW) function so the recorded signal can be continuously monitored during mastering. A trailing laser is focused on the disc just behind the recording laser, but does not affect the recording. Instead, it reads data so that analysis equipment can dynamically control cutting laser power and other critical parameters to assure optimum pit geometry, and decode the EFM signal to evaluate data error rates; this decreases production time.

Electroforming

The metalized master disc is transferred to an electroplating room, where the plating process produces metal stampers. The master electroplating process imparts a nickel coating on the metalized glass master. The metal part is separated from the glass master, and any photoresist is removed. This metal disc is called the metal master, or father. Using the same electroplating process, the resulting metal father is used to generate a number of positive nickel impressions, called mothers. The process is repeated to produce a number of negative impression stampers, or sons. Discs are replicated from these stampers.

Disc Replication

Mass production of discs can be accomplished with injection molding to produce disc substrates. A polycarbonate material is used, chiefly because of its low vapor absorption coefficient, about 70% less than that of a PMMA material. Polycarbonate material has an inferior birefringence specification, especially when produced by injection molding; however, injection molding is a more efficient production method. After experimentation with different kinds of mold shapes and molding conditions, techniques for producing a single piece polycarbonate disc were achieved. CD birefringence is specified to be less than 100 nm (measured double pass through the substrate). Molten polycarbonate is injected into the mold cavity, and the disc substrate (with pits) is produced; the process takes less than five seconds. The center hole is typically formed simultaneously. In some cases the center hole is punched later, in a separate operation.

After molding, a layer of aluminum, silver, or gold (about 50–100 nm thick) is placed over the pit surface to provide reflectivity. In most cases, aluminum is used. The reflection coefficient of this layer, including the polycarbonate substrate (note that the CD player laser must pass through the substrate to the metal layer), is specified to be at least 70%. Aluminum evaporation can be accomplished with vapor deposition in a vacuum. Alternatively, high voltage magnetron sputtering can be used to deposit the reflective layer. A cold solid target is bombarded with ions, releasing metal molecules that coat the disc. Using high voltages, a discharge is formed between a cathode target and an anode. Permanent magnets behind the cathode form a concentrated plasma discharge above the target area. Argon ions are extracted from the plasma; they bombard the target surface, thus sputtering it; the disc is placed opposite the target and outside the plasma region. Metalization may take three seconds. The metal layer is covered by an acrylic layer with a spin coating machine, and cured with an ultraviolet light. This layer protects the metal layer from scratches and oxidation. The label is printed directly upon this layer.

The final step in CD manufacturing is inspection and packaging. Finished discs are inspected for continuous and random defects, using both automated and human checking. A number of optical, mechanical, and electrical criteria have been established. Molded discs are checked for correct dimensions, lack of flash and burrs, birefringence, reflectivity, flatness (skew angle), and general appearance. The pit surface is checked for correct pit depth, correct pit volume or pit form and dimensions. The metallized coating is checked for pinholes and uneven thickness; reflectivity is tested. Birefringence can be checked with a circularly polarized light used to convert the phase change to an intensity variation measured with a photodiode. The disc can be scanned, creating a map of birefringence versus radius.

Angle deviation measures the angle formed by the normal to the disc in the radial direction. This angle is critical because any deviation causes the reflected laser beam to deviate from its return path through the objective lens. This angle deviation could result from an improper manufacturing method; specifications call for a maximum angle of ±0.6°. Disc eccentricity measures the deviation from circularity of the pit track and the positioning of the center hole. The electroforming and molding processes introduce some eccentricity in the shape of the pit track. In addition, the player's positioning of the disc in the drive might introduce eccentricity. If it is excessive, it could exceed the ability of the radial tracking servo of the player. Tolerances for deviation from circularity call for maximum eccentricity of ±70 μm. Disc eccentricity must also account for alignment of the center hole. Specifications call for a center hole tolerance of 0.1 mm. A hole that is off center would lead to disc imbalance and noise and resonance errors. Following packaging and wrapping, compact discs are ready for distribution. In most cases, the injection machine, sputtering machine, spin coater, and label printer are consolidated into one production unit; it might take a disc two minutes to travel from injection machine to labelling; one unit can produce two million discs per year. Equipment used for disc replication is shown in Fig. 9-21.

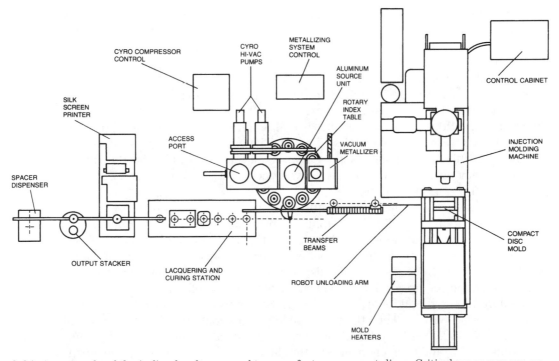

9-21 An example of the in-line hardware used to manufacture compact discs. Critical processes are enclosed in small clean enclosures. Musitech

Alternative CD Formats

The compact disc is a remarkable digital storage medium. Over 15 billion channel bits of data can be reliably stored on a disc thanks to EFM modulation and CIRC error correction techniques. Fortuitously, that medium is available to other types of data not restricted to audio applications, as in the CD-Audio format (sometimes called CD-Digital-Audio, or CD-DA). In place of audio data, computer software or other published material can be stored in a read-only format, and delivered as a data or video signal rather than an audio signal. This is the CD-ROM format. The CD-I format is an interactive, multimedia format storing audio, video, text, graphics, and software. The CD-WO format permits users to record their own data permanently on disc, and erasable optical media permit fully erasable recording. CD+G adds graphics and other types of data, stored in the subcode field. As with many families, the interrelationships between members of the CD family are somewhat complicated, as shown in Fig. 9-22. Together, these alternative CD formats demonstrate the remarkable range of applications open to the compact disc.

CD+G and CD+MIDI

The CD+G and CD+MIDI formats encode graphics or MIDI software on CDs, in addition to regular audio data. A special player is required to access this data. As noted, eight subcode channels are accumulated over 98 frames; thus each 98-bit subcode word is output at a 75-Hz rate. Subcode synchronization occupies the first two frames, thus a subcode block contains 8 channels with 96 data bits. This data block is called a packet, and each quarter of a packet is called a pack. A pack is generated every 3.3 ms. Only P and Q are reserved for audio control information. Over the length of a CD, the remaining channels, R to W, provide about 25 Mbytes of 8-bit data. Utilization of that capacity has been promoted as CD+G, or CD+Graphics, and CD+MIDI, sometimes known as CD+G/M. The use of a plus sign reminds consumers that this data capacity is in addition to all the audio and subcode data already present on an audio CD. The player decodes the graphics or MIDI data separately from the audio data.

Within the pack structure, five different 3-bit mode/items are presently defined. Mode1/Item1 specifies TV graphics information, and Mode3/Item0 defines MIDI information. "Instruction" further defines the nature of the "Data Field," and P and Q are error detection and correction codes independent of the audio data's CIRC code. The TV graphics mode displays text and graphics with image units called fonts; they comprise 6×12 pixel character units. A full screen consists of 50 vertical by 18 horizontal fonts. Outer rows and columns are intended for scroll action and are not visible. Thus the total visible picture contains $(50 - 2) \times 6 = 288$ vertical by $(18 - 2) \times 12 = 192$ horizontal pixels. Font data is given a channel number from 0 to 15, and each channel can store individual images, for example: channel 1 might show English lyrics and channel 2 show French lyrics.

Color is obtained through the use of CLUT (color look-up table) and each screen can display 16 colors from among 4096 colors, with 4-bit gradations for each primary RGB (red-green-blue) color. In addition, CD+G instructions can preset a memory

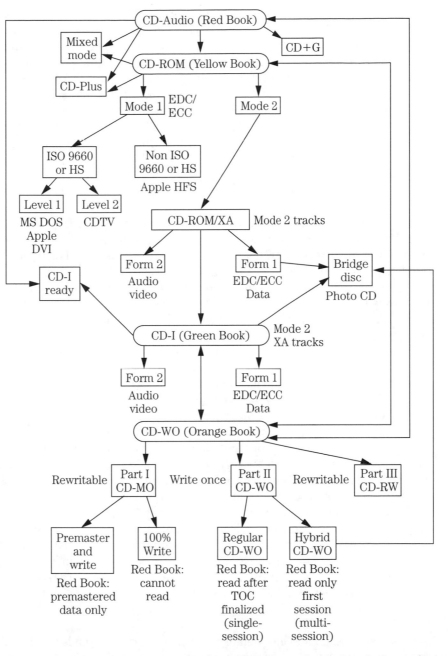

9-22 A simplified road map showing the complex interrelationships between CD formats.

with color, preset the border with color, write a font using two colors for foreground/background, EXCLUSIVE-OR a font with two colors, load the CLUT, and soft scroll the screen.

In CD+G discs, data is collected over thousands of CD frames to form video images or other data fields. For example, a CD+G audio disc can contain video images relating directly or conceptually to the music, or liner notes, librettos, or other alphanumeric information. Either video camera images or computer generated graphics can be displayed. Because video images require a large amount of data for storage, CD+G images provide limited resolution. Data reduction algorithms can be used.

In another CD application, MIDI (Musical Instrument Digital Interface) information can be stored in the subcode field. Known as CD+MIDI, this format allows a MIDI data stream to be stored, and output synchronously with the audio playback. External MIDI instruments can synchronize to the melody, pitch, rhythm, or other musical parameters of an encoded disc. Using their own processing, instruments can be revoiced and new arrangements created. The subcode capacity is sufficient to store up to 16 channels of MIDI information.

MIDI messages are sent over any of 16 channels, adhering to MIDI protocol. The hardware MIDI interface operates asynchronously at 31.25 ($\pm$1%) k-baud, using a start bit, eight data bits (D0 to D7), and a stop bit. This yields a total of 10 bits for a period of 320 μs per serial byte. The start bit is a logical 0 and the stop bit is a logical 1. Bytes are sent LSB first. Communication uses multibyte messages consisting of one status byte followed by one or two data bytes (real time and exclusive messages excepted). All common MIDI messages such as note off, note on, polyphonic key pressure, pitch bend, and system common messages and system real time messages are supported. MIDI data is recorded into CD subcode using the same data packs as in CD+G, with MIDI data arranged in bytes 0 through 12 within packs. To maintain the baud rate specified by the MIDI standard, 12 consecutive packs can contain no more than 125 MIDI bytes. If playback on equipment with up to +12.5% pitch bend is used, it is recommended that the data be limited to a maximum of 110 bytes in any 12 consecutive packs. MIDI information could be supplemented with graphics information; for example, music notation, fingering positions, and other data relating to the music could be supplied. Still another variation could encode music notation in the subcode area, permitting external computer systems to print out sheet music.

Although CD+G/M discs are compatible with any CD player, only players equipped with CD+G/M output ports or CD-I players are able to retrieve and decode the information from the disc. Alternatively, an external decoder could be connected to any CD player with a digital output port, provided that subcode data is available from the port. Because CD+G/M data is stored digitally, it provides a universal format that is independent of television format. Thus the graphics on a CD+G/M disc is playable on any NTSC or PAL/SECAM television.

CD-ROM

The Compact Disc Read-Only Memory (CD-ROM) format extends the digital audio CD format to the broader application of information storage in general. Rather than store only music, the CD-ROM format is intended for diverse program material. It serves mainly as a mass storage medium for computer applications, and for information distribution. CD-Audio is a specific application of compact disc technology; it is a standard for recording PCM audio. The CD-ROM standard is derived from the CD-Audio standard, but defines a format for general data storage. Unlike CD-Audio,

CD-ROM is not tied to any specific application. Both formats use the 120-mm-diameter disc, but with different data formats. The CD-ROM format, sometimes called the Yellow Book, is specified in the ISO/IEC 10149 standard (International Standards Organization/International Electrotechnical Commission).

A Mode 1 CD-ROM holds 682 million bytes of user information (333,000 blocks × 2048 bytes). This is a large storage area, equivalent to 470 1.44-Mbyte floppy disks, 275,000 pages of alphanumerics, 18,000 pieces of computer graphics, or 3600 still video pictures. A CD-ROM can efficiently store information such as computer applications software, operating systems, on-line databases, published reference materials, directories, encyclopedias, libraries of still pictures, parts catalogs, or other type of information not requiring frequent updating. CD-ROM is, in fact, an entirely new publishing medium. Anything publishable is a candidate for CD-ROM. CD-ROM is much more efficient than paper. For example, the U.S. Navy investigated the use of CD-ROM to reduce the paperwork on naval ships. They found that a cruiser carries about 5.32 million pages of documentation, weighing almost 36 tons. The amount of paper stored above the main deck impacted the ship's stability. In theory, that mass of paperwork could be reduced to about 20 CD-ROM discs, weighing 280 grams.

A CD-ROM disc uses a data format modified from the audio CD format. Ninety-eight CD frames are summed (as in CD subcode) to form a data block 2352 bytes (24 bytes × 98 frames) in length. Each disc is divided into a maximum of 330,000 blocks; a 60-minute disc holds 283,500 blocks. The first 12 bytes of a block form a synchronization pattern, and the next four bytes make up a header field for time and address flags. The remaining 2336 bytes can store user data, or data plus extended error correction, depending on the mode selected. The header contains three address bytes and a mode byte. Addresses are stored as a disc playing time. One address byte stores minutes, the second byte stores seconds, and the third stores block number within the second. For example, an address of 47-15-30 identifies the 30th block in the 15th second of the 47th minute on the disc.

The mode byte identifies three modes, used for two different types of data. There are two data modes, as shown in Fig. 9-23. The Mode 1 format assigns 2048 bytes of each block to user data. Each block contains 2 Kbytes (2 × 1024) of user data; 280 bytes are given to extended error detection and correction (EDC/ECC). The Mode 2 format allows for the full 2336 bytes to be used for user data (14% more data), but in practice is rarely used except when coded in CD-ROM/XA mode (described in the following paragraphs). There is also a null mode, Mode 0.

Because of extended error correction, Mode 1 has the greatest applications. The EDC/ECC field is essential for high-density numerical data storage, which is more demanding than audio data. A $GF(2^8)$ Reed-Solomon product code (RSPC) is used to encode each block. It produces P and Q parity bytes with (26,24) and (45,43) code words respectively. Because the EDC/ECC field is independent and supplements the CIRC error correction code applied to the frame structure, the error rate is improved over that of CD-DA. In Mode 1, the typical CD-ROM bit error rate is approximately 10^{-15}, or one uncorrectable bit in every 10^{15} bits.

CD-ROM/XA (eXtended Architecture) is an extension to the Yellow Book Mode 2 standard and defines a new type of data track; computer data, compressed audio data, and video and picture data can all be contained on one XA track. CD-ROM/XA

Mode 1   (153.6 kbytes/s)

Sync	Header (4)			User data	Auxiliary data (288)			
	Block address (3)		Mode		EDC	Space	ECC (276)	
	Min	Sec	Block	1				P parity	Q parity
(12)	(1)	(1)	(1)	(1)	(2048)	(4)	(8)	(172)	(104)

EDC—error detection code;
ECC—error correction code

Mode 2   (175.2 kbytes/s)

Sync	Header (4)			All user data
	Block address (3)		Mode	
	Min	Sec	Block	2	
(12)	(1)	(1)	(1)	(1)	(2336)

Scrambled area
2352 bytes/CD block

This area is equivalent to 1/75 s in CD audio, i.e., 16 bits × 2 channel × 44.1 kHz × 1/75 • 18,816 bits • 2352 bytes

1 mode per track
1—99 tracks per disc

9-23 The CD-ROM specification contains two modes of data block structures. Mode 1 allows for extended error detection and correction, and Mode 2 provides capacity for additional user data.

Mode 2 differs from CD-ROM Mode 2 because it provides a subheader that defines the block type, as shown in Fig. 9-24. In this way, the XA track can interleave Form 1 and 2 blocks, as in the CD-I format; this is extremely useful and used in many applications. For this reason, CD-ROM/XA is often called a bridge format between CD-ROM and CD-I. Specifically, XA defines two types of blocks: Form 1 for computer data and Form 2 for compressed audio/video data. The former provides a 2048-byte user area, and the latter provides 2324 bytes; this follows the CD-I format described below. The XA format can use the CD-I ADPCM audio levels (A, B, C,) as well as 8-bit/22-kHz and 8-bit/11-kHz coding. CD-DA Red Book data cannot be placed on an XA track. The XA data rate is 1.4 Mbps; double-speed drives read discs at about 2.5 Mbps. Clearly, special hardware is needed to decode the various data types found on an XA disc. Some players are dedicated to specific types of CD-ROM/XA discs; the Video CD, and Photo CD are types of CD-ROM/XA. The CD-ROM/XA format is defined in the White Book. CD-ROM/XA discs can be played in CD-I players. Not all CD-ROM drives support CD-ROM/XA; in some cases a special interface board must be used.

A mixed-mode CD format, sometimes called Enhanced CD, CD Plus or Stamped Multisession, combines several different format types (such as CD-DA and CD-ROM/XA) on a single disc; however, each session must be the same data type. For example, a CD Plus disc has Red Book audio data in the first session, with Yellow Book ROM data in the second session. A CD-DA player plays the first session, but

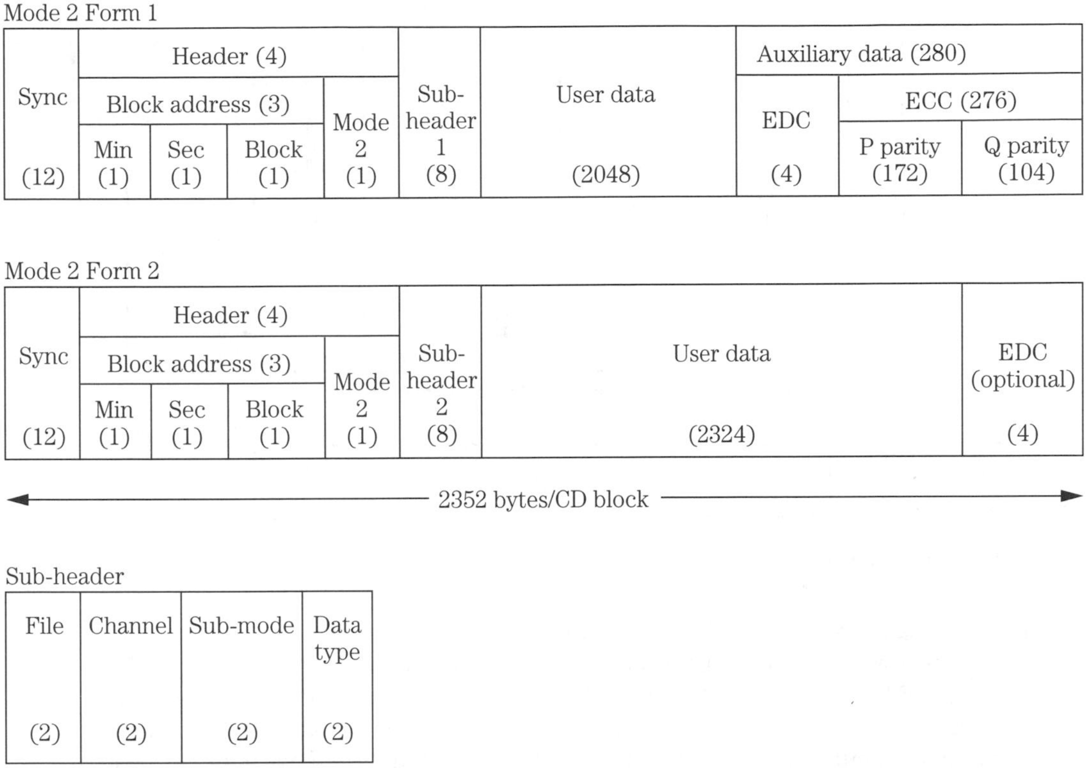

Mode 2 Form 1

Sync	Header (4)				Sub-header 1	User data	Auxiliary data (280)		
	Block address (3)			Mode 2			EDC	ECC (276)	
	Min	Sec	Block					P parity	Q parity
(12)	(1)	(1)	(1)	(1)	(8)	(2048)	(4)	(172)	(104)

Mode 2 Form 2

Sync	Header (4)				Sub-header 2	User data	EDC (optional)
	Block address (3)			Mode 2			
	Min	Sec	Block				
(12)	(1)	(1)	(1)	(1)	(8)	(2324)	(4)

←——————————— 2352 bytes/CD block ———————————→

Sub-header

File	Channel	Sub-mode	Data type
(2)	(2)	(2)	(2)

9-24 The CD-ROM/XA data format is based on the CD-ROM Mode 2 format. It provides two forms: extended error detection and correction, or increased user data capacity. These structures also apply to CD-I and Bridge discs.

would not play the second. A CD-ROM drive reads the second session (as well as the audio session), containing, for example, programming relating to the audio session. An Enhanced CD disc is essentially a replicated multisession Orange Book disc, in which each session has lead-in and lead-out areas. Enhanced CD is supported in the Windows 95 operating system. In some cases, ROM data is placed after the disc TOC, but before the first track (containing music). An audio player thus skips over the data, starting playback at the first music track.

As noted, the CD-ROM data format is similar to that of music CDs; music discs can be played on ROM players, but ROM discs are not playable on audio players. A CD-ROM drive dispenses with D/A conversion, output filtering, and audio output stages, but requires an interface, and an external computer for output, as shown in Fig. 9-25. Because a CD-ROM drive alone costs less than an audio CD player, the consolidation of both functions into one player is ideally cost effective. To permit this, a CD-ROM disc automatically identifies itself as differing from an audio CD (through the Q subcode channel).

Unlike the audio CD standard, the CD-ROM standard does not stipulate how data is to be defined. In an effort to provide compatibility, the ad hoc High Sierra

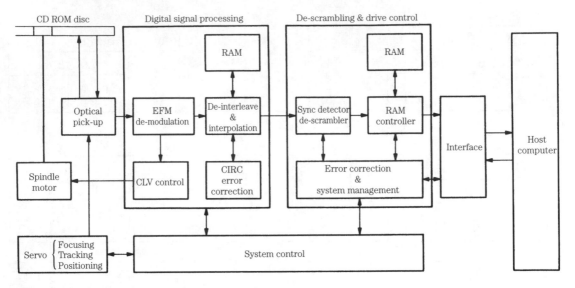

9-25 The primary subsystems in a CD-ROM drive. Sony Corporation

group (meeting at Del Webb's High Sierra Hotel and Casino in Nevada) developed a standard logical file structure. It was adopted by the ISO as standard ISO/DIS 9660, "Volume and File Structure of CD-ROM for Information Exchange." It universally specifies how computer data is placed on a CD-ROM; to read the data, the computer operating system must be able to read the ISO 9660 file structure. Level One 9660 is similar to an MS-DOS file system; Level Two allows longer file names, and is not usable in MS-DOS systems. MSCDEX.EXE is an MS-DOS Extension available from Microsoft; it contains extension programming and drivers so that an MS-DOS program can access a CD-ROM. The computer requires both Microsoft Extensions and the device driver for the MPC ROM drive. MSCDEX.EXE is often placed in the AUTOEXEC.BAT file, and the device driver is loaded from CONFIG.SYS. The computer can then read 9660 file directories and files from disc. Microsoft Windows 95 contains an AutoPlay feature that installs and runs CD-ROM titles automatically; when an AutoPlay-coded CD-ROM is loaded, the system checks for a text file called AUTORUN.INF in the root directory containing directions for running the application.

The extension of ISO 9660 for the Unix platform is sometimes called the Rock Ridge extension. Using these and other programs, 9660 directories and files can be accessed from diverse platforms. HFS is Macintosh's native Hierarchical Filing System; most CD-ROMs authored for the Macintosh adhere to this format; it is unrelated to ISO 9660. CD-ROM discs can be authored for multiple platforms; however, executable files can only be run on the appropriate platform. Until recently, the IBM and Macintosh platforms were incompatible; some compatibility now exists with PowerPC computers. Additional incompatibility, such as file formats, file headers, bit resolutions, and sampling rates exists within each platform, with competing CD-ROM systems. In some cases, cross-platform compatibility can be achieved, for example, hybrid CD-ROM titles can be played on IBM and Macintosh platforms. The different data types are physically partitioned on the disc surface.

CD-ROM thus forms the basis for a new electronic publishing medium applicable to book publishing, dictionaries, technical manuals, business catalogs, computer storage, and so on. It represents an entirely new technology of information dissemination.

CD-I

The Compact Disc Interactive (CD-I) format further extends the applications of the compact disc. CD-I is a product-specific application of the CD-ROM format. Although both CD-ROM and CD-I permit storage of a simultaneous combination of audio, video, graphics, text, and data, the CD-I format provides specific data formats for all these data. In addition, through data reduction, and by interleaving data types on a track, discs can function in a real-time interactive manner. CD-I is thus a multimedia extension of CD-ROM. CD-I has rigidly defined implementations, as in the CD-DA format. The CD-I standard, sometimes called the Green Book, defines how various types of information (for example, video, audio, text, executable code, and graphics) are identified on the media. It identifies how each type of information is encoded, including specifications for several grades of resolution for data types. It specifies the logical layout of files on the disc. It also specifies how hardware reads discs and decodes information. CD-I hardware can read CD-I discs, all CD-DA discs, and some compatible CD-ROM discs.

The CD-I data format is derived from the CD-ROM Mode 2 format. CD-I data is arranged in 2352 byte blocks, as in the CD-ROM/XA format. Blocks are output at a rate of 75 blocks per second. A subheader, placed after the regular 16 byte CD-ROM sync/address/mode header, contains coding information, and is used to identify CD-I data types (audio, video, or programming) and two data formats. These formats, referred to as forms (see Fig. 9-24), define two levels of data integrity. Form 1 is used for text, computer software, and compressed visual data. It uses the same extended error detection and correction code (EDC/ECC) as for CD-ROM Mode 1; user data occupies 2048 bytes, and 280 bytes are occupied by EDC/ECC. Form 2 is used for real time audio and video. User data occupies 2324 bytes; ECC is omitted for this noncritical data. Audio data comprises 2304 bytes (with 20 spare bytes) divided into 18 groups of 128 bytes each. Each group contains 16 bytes of audio parameters (such as ADPCM range and filter values) and 112 bytes of sound data.

The CD-I format provides five levels of audio quality. These levels can be selected by disc software designers according to the fidelity required and availability of storage space on the disc. A CD-DA mode uses linear 16-bit PCM encoding for the same stereo fidelity as Red Book CDs. An 8- or 4-bit adaptive differential pulse-code modulation (ADPCM) code can be used. Three levels of fidelity are defined: Hi-Fi *A* level (8-bit/37.8 kHz); Mid-Fi *B* level (4-bit/37.8 kHz); and Speech *C* level (4-bit/18.9 kHz). CD-I also calls for a special text-to-speech mode using phonetic coding to yield a quality level similar to synthesized speech. MPEG-1 audio data reduction is used for full-motion video (FMV) coding.

The varying audio quality levels allow CD-I to combine audio with video, and text. Obviously, a full-fidelity, full-length audio program as found on a CD-DA disc consumes the entire storage area. By using data reduction on the audio information, storage capacity for other types of information is provided. ADPCM is much more efficient than PCM; for example, an audio-only CD-I disc with speech mode ADPCM could contain over 19 hours of program. Of course, a price is paid in fidelity.

Because of ADPCM's data efficiency, a CD-I's music program is divided into channels. Up to sixteen channels can be stored in parallel across a disc surface, each with a playing time of about 74 minutes. The 16-bit PCM channel is stereo. The three ADPCM modes can be recorded in either stereo or monaural. There are always twice as many monaural channels as stereo channels. In Speech mode a disc can have up to sixteen monaural channels, each 74 minutes long.

A CD-I disc stores video material with varying quality levels for resolution and pixel coding. Three standards of video resolution are supported: normal, double, and high resolution. Thirty-two video channels are available. The specification for picture pixel coding provides three picture qualities: natural picture quality, and two graphics levels. A wide range of visual effects are defined, including cuts, overlays, scrolls, dissolves, fades, etc. Because CD-I stores video information in digital form, it is compatible with both the NTSC and PAL/SECAM television systems. The CD-I format specifies scanning of both 525 and 625 lines. A disc in either format can be viewed over a television adhering to the other format with only slight visual distortion. Alternatively, the CD-I format provides a 525/625 compatible standard, yielding slight distortion in both television formats.

To ensure universal compatibility between discs and drives, dedicated hardware and interfaces are defined. A CD-I player contains a disc drive as the system's input, decoder chips for text, graphics, video, and audio, and microprocessor controllers; the player is interfaced to a television, and stereo. A CD-I player can play regular CD-DA discs; however, an audio CD player cannot play CD-I discs. CD-ROM Mode 1 discs adhering to the 9660 standard can play on CD-I systems. However, a CD-ROM drive cannot always process the multimedia information on a CD-I disc. The CD-Bridge format defines a way to add additional information to a CD-ROM/XA disc so it can be played on a CD-I player; the disc must be compatible with both CD-ROM/XA drives and CD-I players. Bridge tracks use Mode 2 data, tracks are listed in the TOC as a CD-ROM/XA track, and block layout is identical to CD-I and CD-ROM/XA. The Photo CD is an example of a bridge disc.

The full-motion video (FMV) extension to the CD-I standard allows 74 minutes of full-motion digital video and stereo audio to be placed on a disc; two CDs thus hold a feature film. Discs are compatible in both NTSC and PAL/SECAM environments. The MPEG-1 coding standard is used to reduce the video bit rate to 1.15 Mbps, and the audio rate to 0.22 Mbps; lower rates can also be used. FMV also allows very high video bit rates (up to 5 Mbps) for playback from memory. The FMV manager is part of the CD-RTOS operating system. The video bit stream can be joined with other CD-I applications data to provide interactivity. The multiplexed MPEG-1 bit stream is placed in specially defined CD-I video blocks as well as a special audio block; they are all Form 2 blocks with a user field of 2324 bytes. Any FMV application programs are stored in normal data blocks. A full-motion digital video program provides VHS quality. CD-I players can also play Video CDs coded with the MPEG-1 algorithm. MPEG-1 is described in chapter 11.

CD-I Ready discs are Red Book audio discs with added CD-I information that can only be played on CD-I players. Red Book discs use index points 0 and 1 to mark the start of the first track, and the start of the music in the first track; there is usually a two- to three-second gap; Red Book players automatically skip over this gap. A CD-I Ready disc can increase the gap to 182 seconds, and place CD-I data there, where it is only read by a CD-I player. The data can be read and stored for use later during audio playback.

The CD-I specification, summarized in Table 9-2, is considerable. A CD-I disc might contain over 19 hours of audio, 7000 color pictures, 275,000 typed pages, or any combination of the three. A single CD-I disc might contain recorded music or speech, color pictures, animation, graphics, text, or any combination of these. For example, a CD-I dictionary might contain a word and its definitions, as well as spoken pronunciation, pictures, and additional cataloguing to synonyms, antonyms, word relationships, origins, or translations into foreign languages.

DVI

Digital Video Interactive (DVI) is a coding algorithm that stores full-motion video and audio on a CD-ROM disc, with high resolution and long playing time. The all-digital system works interactively with a personal computer to allow user control of video, text, and audio information. Storage of video information requires considerable capacity, and a high data transfer rate. Assuming 24 bits per pixel, an analog video picture of 320 pixels by 200 lines would require 192 Kbytes of data per frame for digital storage. With the NTSC standard of 30 frames per second, a CD could hold 90 seconds of digital video. A CD would have to play for an hour, outputting 150 Kbytes per second, to display that 90 seconds of video. Storage of raw video data is thus not feasible. DVI solves this problem with data reduction prior to storage and reconstruction during playback. Although nonreal-time reduction can be used, reconstruction of video frames must be done in real time. Computation is done prior to mastering; the algorithm uses a pyramid delta method, in which a video frame is compressed to only 5 Kbytes (the first frame of a new scene requires 15 Kbytes). The result is an hour of video storage, at 30 frames per second.

The data must be reconstructed when the CD is played. This is accomplished by the video display processor. A pixel processor runs the decompression algorithm in software. An output display processor determines the resolution modes and pixel formats. Its resolution ranges from 256 to 768 pixels horizontally and up to 512 pixels vertically. The DVI pixel format uses 8, 16, or 24 bits per pixel. Audio is encoded via ADPCM. As with CD-I, DVI offers various audio bandwidth and dynamic ranges.

One DVI CD can hold a CD's worth of video playing time (a maximum of 74 minutes). Storage capacity is divided between audio quality and video playing time. DVI hardware is designed to be compatible with several personal computer architectures. As with CD-ROM and CD-I, a player with disc drive is required. The result is a computer application that integrates software programs, text, graphics, sound, and full-motion video.

CD-WO (CD-R)

The Compact Disc Write Once (CD-WO) format allows users to record their own audio or other digital data to a compact disc; it is often called the CD-R format. It is

Table 9-2. CD-Interactive primary specifications.

1. Physical format
   Total data capacity   Approximately 650 Mbyte
   Reading speed   75 sectors/second
   Sector capacity   2352 bytes
      Sync   12 bytes
      Header   4 bytes
      Subheader   8 bytes
      User data   2048 bytes in mode 2, form 1 (with EDC/ECC)
                           2324 bytes in mode 2, form 2 (without EDC/ECC)

2. Stored data
   Audio and video information, and computer data (text and binary);
   sector interleavable

3. Audio

	S/N	Stereo/ mono	Sampling rate/bits	Number of channels
CD-Digital audio (PCM)	98	Stereo	44.1/16	1
Hi-Fi mode (ADPCM) "A"	90	Stereo	37.8/8	2
		Mono		4
Mid-Fi mode (ADPCM) "B"	60	Stereo	37.8/4	4
		Mono		8
Speech mode (ADPCM) "C"	60	Stereo	18.9/4	8
		Mono		16

   Playing time per channel: 74 minutes

4. Video
   Maximum number of channels: 32

   Resolution:

	NTSC monitor	PAL/SECAM monitor
Normal	360 × 240	384 × 280
Double	720 × 240	768 × 280
High	720 × 480	768 × 560

   Pixel coding:
   Type of picture   Natural/still, graphics, animation
   Natural picure   Delta YUV (4:2:2)
                                          4-bit quantization
   RGB graphics   15 bits/pixel
   CLUT (Color lookup table) graphics   8-bit (256 colors) mode
                                          7-bit (128 colors) mode
                                          4-bit (16 colors) mode
   Animation (run length/CLUT)   7-bit (128 colors) mode
                                          3-bit (8 colors) mode
   Visual effects, such as wipes and dissolves, overlays, scrolling,
   partial updating, etc.

5. Single media system with:
   68000 family CPU and CD-RTOS (CD real-time operating system) for handling
   real-time files/records, file protection, compatible system extensions, standard
   graphics functions, real-time audio, and video manipulations.

6. File structure
   Hierarchical, but able to open a file in one seek.

Philips

a write-once format, the recording is permanent, and can be read indefinitely, but can never be erased and written with new data. Text, audio, video, multimedia and other executable data can be recorded and applications for CD-R are diverse. For example, the monthly phone bill for a large corporation might run 50,000 pages or more, but can be recorded on one CD-R disc. CD-R is ideal for distributing a lot of data to a few users. CD-R discs that are used to carry audio and nonaudio data prior to CD replication are written with the PMCD (premastered CD) format; the disc contains index and other information normally found on a CD master tape. CD-R discs with up to 74 minutes (or about 650 Mbytes) of playing time are available. A complete subcode table is written in the disc table of contents, and appropriate flags are placed across the playing surface.

The CD-WO standard is defined in the Orange Book Part II. Although most CD-R discs can be played on Red Book players, they differ from Red Book CDs. All user data is recorded as a reflectivity change in a pregrooved track. Two areas are written to the inner portion (22.35 to 23 mm radius) of the disc before the Red Book lead-in diameter, as shown in Fig. 9-26. The PMA (program memory area) contains data describing the recorded tracks, a temporary table of contents, as well as track skip information. When the disc is finalized, this data is transferred to the table of contents.

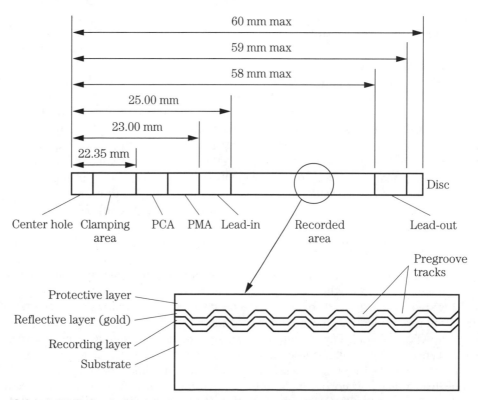

9-26 A CD-R disc holds data in pregrooved tracks, permanently written into an organic dye recording layer. The PCA area is used to calibrate the writing laser, and the PMA holds a temporary table of contents.

In addition, the PCA (power calibration area) allows the laser to automatically make test recordings to determine optimum laser power for data recording; this is performed initially, then the information is stored on the disc. The pregrooved program area holds user-recorded information. A recording is complete when a lead-in area (with table of contents), user data, and lead-out area have been written. A maximum of 99 tracks can be recorded on a disc.

As with regular CDs, CD-R discs are built on a polycarbonate substrate, and contain a reflective layer and a protective top layer. Sandwiched between the substrate and reflective layer, however, is a recording layer comprised of an organic dye (see Fig. 9-26). Together with the reflective layer it provides a typical in-groove reflectivity of 73%, and CNR of 47 dB. To achieve the minimum 70% reflectivity standard of CD, a gold reflective layer must be used. A CD-R disc looks like a regular CD, but is distinguished by its top gold layer, and the green or yellow-green dye recording layer.

Unlike regular CDs, CD-R discs are manufactured with a pregrooved 1.6-μm pitch spiral track, used to guide the recording laser along the spiral track; this greatly simplifies recorder hardware design and ensures disc compatibility. The 0.6-μm wide track is physically modulated with a ±0.03-μm sinusoidal wobble with a frequency of 22.05 kHz; this allows the recorder to control disc CLV rotation speed (a task accomplished with Red Book discs from the recorded data). Also, the groove wobble excursion is frequency modulated with a ±1-kHz signal; this is used to create an absolute time clocking signal (called ATIP for absolute time in pregroove). Sixty-three-minute discs use a 1.4 m/s track velocity, and 74-minute discs use 1.2 m/s.

The recording mechanism itself can be described as heat-mode memory. The recording layer is actually a photo-absorption surface in that it absorbs energy from the recording laser as heat. A writing laser with 4 to 8 mW of power passes through the polycarbonate substrate, and heats the organic dye recording layer to approximately 250°C. This causes the substrate layer to expand into the absorption layer and mix with the dye materials there. Together, the polymer mixed with decomposed (from heat) dye acts to form a pit in the substrate. These pits create the change in reflectivity (for example, 75% to 25% for an 11T pit) required by standard CD player pickups. During readout, the same laser, reduced to 0.5 mW of power, is reflected from the pit (bump from underneath) and its changing intensity is monitored. The result is an eye pattern and modulation amplitude essentially identical to that of conventional CDs. Generally, two types of organic dye polymers are used to form the recording layer: cyanine, or phthalocyanine. Cyanine-based media are usually recognized by a bright green color and are typically used in lower power, low writing speed recorders. Phthalocyanine-based media have a yellow-green color, and are often used in higher power, higher speed recorders.

The Orange Book Part II defines both single session (regular) and multisession (hybrid) recording; a session is defined as a recording with lead-in, data, and lead-out areas. With single session recording, sometimes called disc-at-once recording, a disc is recorded in its entirety, without pause. The recorder records a table of contents (TOC) in the lead-in portion of the disc, data tracks, and a lead-out area, so a standard player can read the disc. Alternatively, with track-at-once recording, tracks are written one at a time; recording can be stopped after each track. A partially recorded disc can be played on the CD-R recorder, but cannot be played on a CD-DA player until the session ends when the final TOC and lead-out areas are recorded. Most recorders permit an unwanted track (such as a false start) to be marked and deleted from the TOC so the CD-R player (and CD-DA players recognizing skip-ID flags) will skip over it. A recorder using track-at-once can also write a single-session CD-R. A PMCD recording is an example of a disc-at-once application.

The Orange Book Part II also specifies multisession recording. Multisession (sometimes called hybrid) recording allows sessions to be recorded one or a few at a time. Separate recording sessions are permitted, each with its own lead-in TOC, data, and lead-out areas, as shown in Fig. 9-27. Track-at-once recorders allow multisession recording, in addition to single-session recording. Older CD-ROM drives and all CD-DA players can read only the first session on a multisession disc. Thus multisession recording typically is not used for CD-R audio discs. Photo CD, and some CD-ROM titles, are examples of multisession hybrid discs.

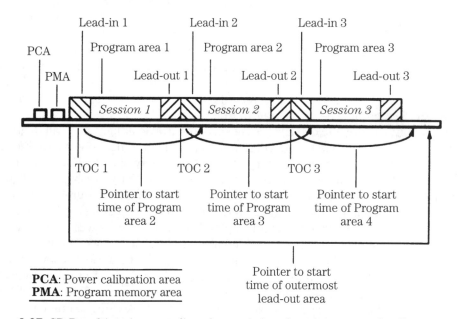

9-27 CD-R multisession recordings form a series of sessions across the disc surface, each with its own lead-in, program, and lead-out areas.

Both stand-alone and peripheral CD-R recorders have been developed. Stand-alone recorders are best described as being a cross between a DAT recorder and a CD player; users can record discs and perform simple editing of tracks and subcode. These are intended for audio use, and apply SCMS data to the recorded program. Peripheral recorders interface to a host computer via a SCSI interface; some recorders are packaged as half-height drives. The recorders operate in real-time (or faster), generating all synchronization, header, EDC, ECC, CIRC, and EFM processing required by the CD standard. Depending on the software package, various degrees of data manipulation are possible; for example, a software application can consolidate fragmented files and specify the physical location of CD-ROM data on a disc so that retrieval time is shorter. When a CD-R is authored according to the ISO 9660 file format, the disc can be read on multiple platforms.

Real-time recorders operate at a 150-kbps rate, however two, four and six times (and higher) recorders are available. It has been reported that higher-speed recorders provide lower error rates because of their increased rotational stability. Discs suitable for high-speed recording are specially approved for reliability. It has been reported that cyanine discs provide better performance over a wider range of writing speeds. Many systems can transfer data from either tape or hard disks to the recorder, and can produce CD-DA, CD-ROM (including CD-ROM/XA and CD-I) and Photo CD discs. Generally, a large SCSI hard drive (1.2 Gbyte) with fast access (10-ms seek time) and transfer rate of at least 1 Mbyte per second is required for single-speed recording. During recording, any interruption in the data stream will render a disc unusable. Some CD-R recorders have a large (1.2 Mbyte) cache memory on board; this helps prevent data stream problems. It is also important to avoid physically fragmented data on the hard disk. Many users recommend hard drives with embedded servo tracks so that automatic thermal recalibration will not interrupt the data stream; alternatively hard drives with unobtrusive recalibration procedures can be used. In addition, network services, sound utilities, screen savers, and TSR (terminate and stay resident) programs should be turned off during recording to prevent glitches. It is often wise to emulate a CD recording before actually burning a disc.

Generally, the organic dye layer is sensitive to ultraviolet light and will degrade; cyanine dye is more prone to degradation than phthalocyanine. To evaluate life expectancy of CD-R discs, engineers subject discs to a variety of tests. For example, in one test, read cycle durability showed no change in reflectivity or CNR over 20,000 playback cycles with a read power of 2.1 mW. However, read power greater than 2.1 mW can cause spontaneous recording on the disc. Discs were subjected to bending tests, bending discs 10,000 times at an amplitude of 20 mm; there was no increase in BLER until, eventually, the discs broke in half. Scratch tests showed no increase in BLER up to a load of 375 grams—the same as with regular CDs. Heat tests revealed no change in performance after 1000 hours at 70°C. Shelf life of cyanine media is said to be from 10 to 100 years at 25°C and 65% relative humidity. Typical BLER error rate is less than 20 per second, well below the Red Book CIRC tolerance of 220. In another accelerated aging test, the life expectancy of phthalocyanine discs was calculated to be 240 years.

CD-MO

The Orange Book Part I defines a Compact Disc-Magneto-Optical (CD-MO) standard; data can be written, erased, and rewritten. Two types of discs are defined: a disc with a premastered area (recorded with pits) containing CD-ROM data plus a writable area, and a disc that is completely writable. Because writable data is read via changes in light polarization rather than intensity, CD-MO discs are not playable in CD-DA or CD-WO drives (however, CD-MO drives can play CD-DA and CD-WO discs). A CD-DA player can read the premastered area on a CD-MO disc. In many ways the MiniDisc is an evolution of the CD-MO specification.

Other erasable disc formats have been developed, using a variety of optical technologies. One erasable disc system uses dye-polymer technology, wherein a layer is physically changed when recorded, and changed again when erased. The disc is made of two layers coated with a light-absorbing dye. Data writing and reading is done by laser. When the surface is heated with a laser, the inner surface contracts, forming a pit on the surface. In this way data is written to the surface. As in the CD-DA format, the data pits are recognized by the read laser. To erase data, pits are heated again and the outer surface contracts, smoothing the surface. It is now ready to be written with new data.

Because the data surface is physically changed (with pits), the disc can be read by a CD-DA player. Likewise, because the recorder is designed to read these data formations, a CD-DA disc can be played in the recorder. There is a limit to how many times the recording surface can be erased and re-recorded (perhaps a hundred or less) before the layers become fatigued. This is acceptable for most consumer audio applications, but hinders use in computer storage applications. Erasable optical technologies are discussed in detail in chapter 8; the MiniDisc is discussed in chapter 12.

Photo CD

The Photo CD uses digital imaging technology to store, manipulate, and display photographic pictures. Standard camera photographs can be viewed on televisions or computers and reproduced as high-quality prints of images using color printers. Up to 100 photographs can be stored on a Photo CD, with resolution that is 16 times the resolution capability of conventional NTSC or PAL/SECAM televisions. In addition, a Photo CD player will also play back audio CDs. Discs are compatible with any Photo CD, CD-I, or CD-ROM/XA player. Individual Photo CD players conform to local television standards such as NTSC or PAL/SECAM. HDTV (high-definition television) Photo CD players can make use of higher resolution image data; the 35-mm version of Photo CD provides three to four times the resolution required in any HDTV standard.

Images from a conventional photographic camera are processed with standard photographic techniques and any slide or negative, black and white or color film can be used, as well as hardcopy photographs. Images are scanned by a Photo CD authoring system to produce a digitized image, and the image is processed to correct for exposure and color balance. Images are scanned with 2048 scan lines across the short dimension of a 35-mm frame, with 3072 pixels on each line. This yields a 3:2 aspect ratio, the same used in the 35-mm format. For each of the 6.3 million pixels, the scanner measures red, green, and blue colors with 12-bit quantization. This RGB data then undergoes processing with the Photo-YCC algorithm that applies a nonlinear transformation to the image data. The resulting values are encoded such that each color pixel is separated into one 8-bit luma component and two 8-bit chroma components. The luma and chroma encoding equations used in the Photo-YCC format follow the CCIR Recommendation 601-1 standards document, and the RGB values and nonlinear transformation coding follow the CCIR 709 video standards document.

A full-resolution image with 2048 lines by 3072 pixels by 24-bit coding would require 18 Mbytes of storage; because the data transfer rate is 153.6 Kbytes/second, it would take two minutes to display an image. Thus the Photo CD system uses data compression and decomposition of the image signal to increase storage efficiency and decrease data transfer time. During authoring, high resolution image files are subjected to 4:1 data reduction. This quadruples the number of images that can be stored, and likewise decreases transfer time. In addition, file sizes can be reduced without significant visual loss by using chroma subsampling to take advantage of limitations in human visual perception. In each image component (except in the 4Base file that contains only luma values) the two chroma channels are two-times subsampled in both the vertical and horizontal directions so there is only one chroma value for every four luma values from each of the channels. With chroma subsampling, a high-resolution file is reduced to 9 Mbytes.

Data is stored in a hierarchical form; data placed in a low-resolution file is omitted from a medium-resolution file, which in turn is omitted from a high-resolution file. This method is known as data decomposition. Three low-resolution image types (Base/16, Base/4 and Base) are stored uncompressed. However high-resolution image types (4Base and 16Base) are formed by successively interpolating and correcting high-resolution residuals (differences from pixels at the previous level of resolution) relative to the Base file. The Base image consists of 512 lines of 768 pixels; it is used to produce images on consumer televisions. The 4Base file consists of 1024 lines by 1536 pixels, and the 16Base file consists of 2048 lines by 3072 pixels; they are used to produce higher resolution images. The Base/4 file consists of 256 lines by 384 pixels, and the Base/16 file consists of 128 lines by 192 pixels; they are used to produce indexing photographs as well as picture-in-picture. Decomposition permits both rapid image access, and ability to efficiently store higher resolution files.

Photographic images are written to a Photo CD disc using the authoring system's CD-WO recorder. Photo CD discs conform to the Orange Book Part II standard and are physically identical to CD-WO audio discs however different data headers make them incompatible. Data blocks are written according to the CD-ROM/XA, Mode 2, Form 1 standard (see Fig. 9-24). Because discs use the CD-Bridge format, they are playable on CD-I and CD-ROM/XA players. Because the Orange Book II permits additional multisession recording to a disc, images can be added over time (see Fig. 9-27). Pacs initially recorded on a disc are structured as a file using the ISO 9660 structure. Subsequently recorded Pacs use a CD-WO Volume and File Structures format, using the multisession method. All Pacs are addressed through the block-addressing method used by CD-ROM discs and defined by the ISO/IEC 10149 standard.

A CD-I or Photo CD player, and television set are used to convert the digital signal into an analog signal for viewing. Users are able to view, zoom in and out, and pan across images stored on disc. Because the images are compatible with the CD-ROM/XA format, a CD-ROM drive (supporting a Mode 2 data transfer) can be used to digitally enter images into a computer system to perform digital image processing. For example, the system could adjust colors, remove unwanted blemishes, add text, rotate images, reduce exposure errors, crop and enlarge images, and create special effects. Because Photo CD adheres to the CD-ROM/XA format, audio and video data can be interleaved; in this way, a soundtrack can accompany visuals. To summarize: a Photo CD disc is coded with Mode 2 Form 1 blocks according to the CD-ROM/XA specifications; the disc is physically written according to the Orange Book Part II hybrid disc specifications, allowing multiple sessions; finally, because the disc uses a bridge format, it is playable on both CD-ROM/XA drives and CD-I players, as well as dedicated Photo CD players.

CD-3

In addition to regular 120-mm diameter CDs, the CD-3 format describes 80-mm diameter discs. The name derives from the approximately 3-inch diameter. This small size promotes greater portability through the use of players specially designed to handle the small discs. In addition, the format is useful for short audio programs. A CD-3 disc holds a maximum of 20 minutes of music. Because a CD data track begins at the innermost diameter, CD-3 discs are fully compatible with regular discs and players. Many players have concentric rings in their disc drawers to center both diameter discs over the spindle. In some cases, an adaptor is needed to center the CD-3 properly. The CD-3 format is also used to hold over 200 Mbytes of CD-ROM data, the equivalent of 100,000 pages of text.

Video CD

The Video-CD format uses the MPEG-1 coding standard for audio and video. The audio signal is coded with the Layer II standard at 44.1 kHz. A disc stores about 74 minutes of full-motion digital video and audio; a feature film is placed on two discs. The video decoder chip permits full-motion video to be shown at either 29.97 (NTSC) or 25 (PAL/SECAM) frames per second at 352 pixels by 240 lines and 352 pixels by 288 lines respectively. Video bit rate is 1.15 Mbps and audio bit rate is 0.22 Mbps. The video-CD format is sometimes called the White Book standard. From a disc standards standpoint, the Video-CD format is a CD-ROM/XA bridge disc, Mode 2, Form 2; this allows a Video CD to play on a CD-ROM drive. A Video CD disc will play on a CD-I player, but will not play on a CD-DA audio player. Video CD and the MPEG-1 algorithm are discussed in chapter 11.

DVD

The success of the compact disc encouraged the video industry to develop a small optical disc holding a motion picture coded with digital audio and digital video. In early 1995 two proposals emerged: Toshiba's Super Density Digital Video Disc (SD-DVD) and the Sony/Philips MultiMedia Compact Disc (MMCD). The formats were similar but incompatible, and at the urging of the computer industry the two sides produced a unified standard. In January 1996 the preliminary DVD format was announced. The DVD family includes formats for video, audio, and computer applications. Because the scope of the applications far exceeded digital video, the name Digital Versatile Disc was proposed. In fact, DVD itself is the official name. Whatever the jargon, DVD supercedes the CD family in the music and computer software markets, and supercedes VHS tape in the video market.

DVD-Video was the first DVD format to be launched; one disc digitally stores a feature film with 5.1 channel soundtracks. As with CD, DVD uses a pit/land structure to store data. The DVD track pitch is 0.74 µm. The CLV track velocity is 3.49 m/s on a single layer and 3.84 m/s on a dual layer. The pits and lands that store binary data are as short as 0.4 µm. These small dimensions are possible because the laser beam used to read DVD-Video discs uses a visible red wavelength of 635 or 650 nm (both wavelengths are supported) compared to 780 nm in a CD. The standard specifies a lens with a numerical aperture of 0.6. These specifications provide a large storage capacity; one DVD-Video layer can store 4.7 Gbytes of data (about seven times the capacity of a CD) and multiple data layers provide greater capacity.

A DVD-Video disc appears similar to a CD and is the same diameter (120 mm) and thickness (1.2 mm). Whereas a CD uses a single polycarbonate substrate, a DVD-Video disc employs two 0.6-mm substrates, bonded together with the data layers placed near the internal interface. Thinner substrates are advantageous because they are inherently more resistant to tracking errors that result when a disc is slightly tilted relative to the laser pickup. A single-layer, single-sided DVD-Video disc uses one substrate with a data surface and one blank substrate; the disc holds 4.7 Gbytes of data. Two substrates with data surfaces can be bonded together to form a single-layer, double-sided disc holding 9.4 Gbytes of data; the disc is turned over to access the opposite layer. The DVD-Video standard also allows data to be placed on two layers in a substrate, one embedded beneath the other to create a dual-layer disc that is read from one side. The layers are separated by a semi-transparent (semi-reflective) layer of aluminum. Both layers can be read from one disc side by simply focusing the reading laser on either layer. The beam either reflects from the lower semi-reflective layer or passes through it and reflects from the top reflective layer. The laser light can be switched to either data layer in a few milliseconds (they are only about 40 µm apart) by simply moving the objective lens; a buffer memory makes the transition indiscernible. Because its reflectivity is slightly reduced, for reliable playback the embedded layer is formed with a faster linear velocity and thus holds somewhat less data than the top data layer. Together, the layers hold 8.5 Gbytes of data. The dual-layer design is manufactured with a photopolymerization method in which a molded single-layer substrate is coated with a semi-transparent layer followed by a layer of liquid plastic that is molded by a second stamper and hardened by exposure to ultraviolet light; a fully reflective metal layer is applied and the substrate is ready for bonding. The DVD-Video standard allows for a double-sided, double-layer disc in which two dual-layer substrates are bonded together, creating a capacity of 17 Gbytes. In addition, the DVD-Video standard calls for 8-cm discs holding 1.4 and 2.6 Gbytes.

DVD-Video uses a Reed-Solomon code; the code is known as RS-PC (Reed Solomon—Product Code) and differs from the CD's CIRC code. DVD-Video uses two interleaved correction codes, C1 and C2, which can be decoded multiple times to improve performance. Error correction is more challenging on a DVD disc because the pit size is smaller; the thin substrate places the data surface closer to the laser lens, thus surface defects are less out of focus than on a CD substrate and can more readily obscure the data surface. RSPC can correct a burst error along a track length of 6 mm, compared to a 2.5-mm correction length for CIRC. RSPC also is more powerful than the double error correction used in the CD-ROM format. RSPC is more efficient than CIRC, thus increasing data density by 16 percent. The DVD-Video format uses a variation on the CD's EFM modulation code, called EFM-Plus. Compared to EFM, EFM-Plus uses 6 percent fewer pits and lands to convey the same data. The DVD-Video data structure is similar to that of a CD-ROM in which data is stored in files within directories; this increases data density.

Although a DVD-Video data layer can hold 4.7 Gbytes, it is woefully insufficient to store a motion picture, which may comprise 200 Gbytes of data; to fit this program on a 4.7-Gbyte disc, data reduction must be employed. In particular, the DVD-Video standard uses the MPEG-2 data compression algorithm to encode its video program. The MPEG-2 algorithm uses psychovisual models to analyze the video signal to determine how it will be perceived by the human viewer. Image data that is deemed redundant, not perceived, or marginally perceived is not coded. This analysis is carried out for both individual video frames and series of frames (it is similar in principle to the MPEG-1 algorithm summarized in chapter 11). Over time, as much as 95% of the video data can be omitted without significant degradation of the picture. Because some pictures are more difficult to code than others, MPEG-2 allows for a variable bit rate. Simple pictures are given a low bit rate, while complex pictures are given a high bit rate. The DVD-Video maximum output bit rate (video, audio, and auxiliary data) is 10.08 Mbps, and the average bit rate is about 3.5 Mbps. Using MPEG-2, a single-layer DVD-Video disc can store up to 133 minutes of digital video with digital audio soundtracks. This will accommodate over 90% of all feature films; longer titles can use the dual-layer disc design (a four-layer disc can hold 482 minutes of program). The video program is stored as 4:2:0 component video (Y, R-Y, B-Y) with progressive scan, and picture resolution is 720 by 480 pixels. The MPEG-2 algorithm is specifically engineered so that improvements can be made in the encoding algorithm while retaining complete compatibility with existing decoders. Thus the look of video software titles can improve, and the improvement will be seen on current and future players. The picture quality of a particular DVD-Video title is primarily determined by the expertise of the picture encoding.

The audio portion of the DVD-Video standard provides both multichannel and stereo soundtracks. DVD-Video titles can accommodate three independent 5.1-channel (five main channels plus a low-frequency effects channel) soundtracks. The DVD-Video standard recognizes two 5.1 channel formats: the Dolby Digital (also known as AC-3) surround sound format and the MPEG-2 AAC surround sound format. The Dolby Digital sampling frequency is 48 kHz, the nominal output bit rate is 384 kbps, and the maximum bit rate is 448 kbps. Nominally, NTSC titles use Dolby Digital, and PAL titles use MPEG-2 audio coding; however, PAL titles can opt for Dolby Digital instead of MPEG audio. For compatibility, all movies also carry a redundant linear PCM digital stereo soundtrack. These linear PCM audio tracks can employ sampling rates of either 48 or 96 kHz, and word lengths of 16, 20 or 24 bits. Up to eight independent PCM channels are permitted; in this way, for example, movies can be released in different languages. The maximum linear PCM bit rate is 6.144 Mbps.

A home DVD-Video player is connected to a home theater system and is used to play motion pictures. In addition, a DVD-Video player can play audio CDs (not all players can play CD-R discs). DVD-Video discs cannot be played in CD players. Some DVD players provide a component video output, a professional video standard that avoids the carrier frequencies used in composite video signals. The DVD-Video standard provides a parental lock-out; movies can be coded to play different versions, skipping potentially offensive scenes or using alternate scenes and dialogue tracks. DVD-Video also supports both normal (4:3) and widescreen (16:9) aspect ratios, an automatic pan-scan feature, chapter division, forward and reverse scanning, up to nine camera angles and interactive story lines, and up to 32 sets of subtitles (each at a bit rate of 10 kbps). These features are options, and implementation is left to the content provider. The DVD-Video format uses copy protection; the Copy Generation Management System (GCMS) blocks digital dubbing of discs, and a version of Macrovision prevents analog dubbing. Discs and players contain regional coding flags so that, for example, a Region 2 (Europe and Japan) player will not play discs intended for the North American (Region 1) market.

In addition to the DVD-Video format (known as Book B), the DVD family includes DVD—Read Only (Book A), DVD-Audio (Book C), DVD—Write Once (Book D) and DVD-Rewritable (Book E). DVD Books A, B, and C use a UDF bridge file format (M-UDF+ISO 9660) and Books D and E use the UDF format. The DVD-Audio format is similar to the DVD-Video format, but is used for stereo and multichannel music programs. Its specification uses many scalable parameters. For example, it permits up to six PCM channels with 48/96 kHz, 44.1/88.2 kHz, and 16/20/24 bits, as well as up to two channels with 176.4 kHz or 192 kHz and 16/20/24 bits. Within the maximum bit rate of 9.216 Mbps, many permutations are possible. For example, a disc may contain a 96-kHz/24-bit/2-channel mix as well as a 96/24/3 front channel +48/24/2 rear channel mix, with total playing time of 78 minutes on two layers. Multichannel programs may be down-mixed to stereo using mix coefficients. The format also supports Dolby Digital, MPEG-1 or -2, and DTS, and has provisions for lossless compressed coding and 1-bit coding.

The other DVD formats are employed in computer applications; Books A and E are often called DVD-ROM and DVD-RAM (random access memory). A DVD-RAM disc may hold 2.6 Gbytes (or more) per side with phase change technology; the disc is held in a protective cartridge. DVD-ROM and DVD-RAM drives are connected to personal computers, and function much like CD-ROM drives. With appropriate software, DVD-ROM and -RAM drives can play DVD-Video discs. DVD-ROM and -RAM drives can play a CD-ROM disc, but CD-ROM drives cannot play DVD discs.

Postscript: Existential Comment

Finally, an interesting analogy. Just how much information can be stored on a CD? It has been estimated that the capacity of a single disc is one or two percent of that of the human brain. In other words, the equivalent of a year of human experience could be stored on a single disc. This remarkably illustrates the storage potential of the CD or the shallowness of human existence, depending on your point of view.

10
CHAPTER

Interconnection

Although analog signals can be conveyed from one device to another with relative ease, the transfer of audio signals in the digital domain is a good deal more complex. Sampling frequency, word length, control and synchronization words, and coding must all be precisely defined to permit successful interfacing. Above all, the file format itself takes precedence over the physical medium or interconnect line it happens to currently occupy. Numerous data formats have been devised to interconnect digital audio devices, both between equipment of the same manufacture, and between equipment of different manufacturers. Using appropriate interconnection protocols, data can be conveyed over local network, telephone, or other transmission systems that might span a room, or the entire globe, and operate in either non-real time, or real time. However, specialized technology is needed to preserve the integrity of a digital audio signal as the data transfer takes place.

Real-Time Audio Interfaces

Perhaps the most fundamental interconnection in a digital studio is the connection of one hardware device to another, so that digital audio data can be conveyed between them in real time. Clearly, a digital connection is preferred over an analog connection; the former can be transparent, but the latter imposes degradation from conversion. To convey digital data, there must be both a data communications channel, and a common clock synchronization. One hardwired point to point connection can provide both functions, but as the number of devices increases, a separate master clock signal is recommended. In addition, the interconnection requires an audio format recognized by both the transmitting and receiving device. Data flow is usually unidirectional, directed point to point (as opposed to a networked or bus distribution), and runs continuously without handshaking. Perhaps two, or many audio channels, as well as auxiliary data, can be conveyed, usually in serial fashion. The data rate is determined by the signal's sampling frequency, word length, number of channels, amount of auxiliary data, and modulation code. When the receiving device is a recorder, it can be placed in record mode, and in real time can copy the received data stream; given correct operation, the received data will be a clone of the transmitted data.

An important criterion for successful transmission of serial data over a coaxial cable is the cable's attenuation at one-half the clock frequency of the transmitted signal. Very generally, the maximum length of a cable can be gauged by the length at which the cable attenuates the frequency of half the clock frequency by 30 dB. Professional interfaces can permit cable runs of 100 to 300 meters, but consumer cables might be limited to less than 10 meters. Fiber cables are much less affected by length loss and permit much longer cable runs. Examples of digital audio interfaces are: SDIF-2, PD, Yamaha Interconnect, ADI, AES3 (AES/EBU), S/PDIF, and AES10 (MADI).

SDIF-2 Interconnection

The SDIF-2 (Sony Digital InterFace) protocol is an interconnection used in some professional digital products. For example, it allows digital transfer from recorder to recorder. It uses two separate unbalanced BNC coaxial connections, one for each audio channel. In addition, there is a separate BNC connection for word clock synchronization, a symmetrical square wave at the sampling frequency, common to both channels. The word clock period is 22.676 μs at a 44.1-kHz sampling frequency—the same period as one transmitted 32-bit word. Any sampling frequency can be used. The signal is structured as a 32-bit word, as shown in Fig. 10-1. The MSB through bit 20 are used for digital audio data, with MSB transmitted first, with NRZ coding. When 16-bit samples are used, the remaining four bits are packed with 0s. Bits 21 through 29 form a control (or user) word. Bits 21 through 25 are held for future expansion; bits 26 and 27 hold an emphasis ID determined at the point of A/D conversion; bit 28 is the dubbing prohibition bit; and bit 29 is a block flag bit, which signifies the beginning of an SDIF-2 block. Bits 30 through 32 form a synchronization pattern. This field is uniquely divided into two equal parts of $1.5T$ (one and one-half bit cell) forming a block synchronization signal. The first word of a block contains a high-to-low pulse and the remaining 255 words have a low-to-high pulse.

This word structure is reserved for the first 32-bit word of each 256-word block. The digital audio data and synchronization pattern in subsequent words in a block are structured identically; however, the control field is replaced by user bits, nominally set to 0. The block flag bit is set to 1 at the start of each 256-word block. Internally, data is processed in parallel; however, it is transmitted and received serially through digital input/output (DI/O) ports. For two-channel operation, SDIF-2 is carried on single-ended 75-Ω coaxial cable, as a TTL-compatible (transistor-transistor logic) signal. To ensure proper operation, all three coaxial cables should be the same length. Some multitrack recorders use a balanced/differential version of SDIF-2 with RS-422-compatible signals. A twisted pair ribbon cable is used, with 50-pin D-sub type connectors, in addition to a BNC word clock cable. The SDIF-2 interface was introduced by Sony Corporation.

ProDigi Interface Format

The PD (ProDigi) format uses a serial interconnection to transmit data between tape recorders; data is conveyed in two's complement form, MSB first. In this format,

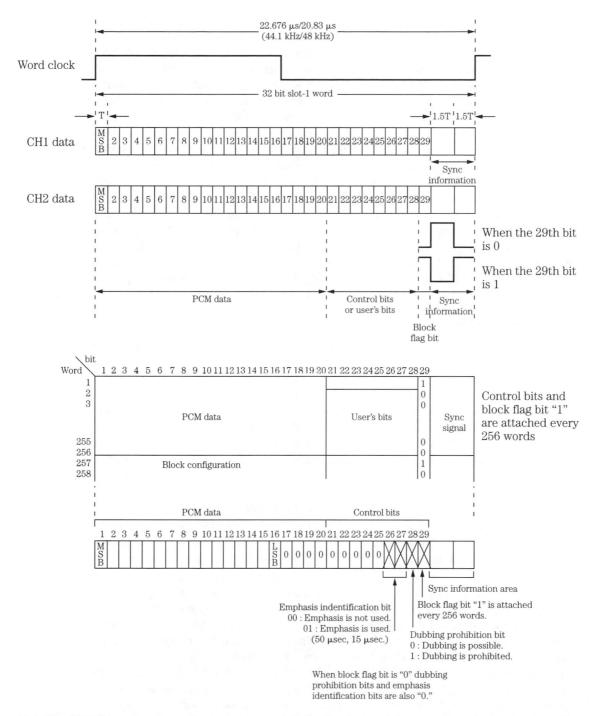

10-1 The SDIF-2 interface is used to interconnect digital audio devices. The control word conveys nonaudio data in the interface.

Dub-A and Dub-B connectors provide interfacing between multitrack recorders, and a Dub-C connector provides a two-channel interface; word lengths and connector pin assignments differ between two-channel and multichannel interfaces. All three types are provided as input and output connectors. Dub-A and Dub-B use balanced/differential lines. Thirty-two-bit length words are transmitted, along with a single pulse word clock operating at the sampling frequency, and a 1.536-MHz bit clock at a sampling frequency of 48 kHz. Sixteen channels are conveyed on each multipin connector; each audio channel is transmitted along separate electrical conductors. In Dub-A, two additional channels indicate recording status of the multichannel recorder; the Rec. A signal serves the first 16 channels, and Rec. B serves channels 17–32. These status channels are formatted the same as the audio channels. The appropriate bits are placed in a logical 0 state if the corresponding channel is in the record mode. The Dub-C format conveys two audio signals, single pulse word clock (at the sampling frequency) at the start of each sample, and bit clock (at 24 times the word clock frequency). With Dub-C, 24 data slots are placed in a word clock interval, and the bit clock is 1.152 MHz at a 48-kHz sampling frequency. Dub-C also conveys a master clock signal of 2.304 MHz at 48-kHz sampling frequency. Recorders manufactured by Mitsubishi and Otari adhere to the PD format.

Yamaha Digital Cascade

The Yamaha two-track digital interconnection uses a multipin cable to transmit stereo signals. Stereo audio data is transmitted LSB and left channel first, with up to 24 audio bits per channel. A separate word clock operating at the sampling frequency identifies the start of each left/right data word. A total of 64 time slots are transmitted with each word clock cycle. This format allows devices such as mixers to be daisy-chained with input and output connectors. The format uses a single 8-pin DIN connector; two balanced pins carry the multiplexed audio signal, two balanced pins carry word clock, and the remaining pins are used for remote control; signals are RS-422-compatible.

Alesis Multichannel Optical Digital Interface

The Alesis multichannel optical digital interface, often called the ADI interface, conveys eight channels of digital audio serial information along a single optical fiber over short distances. The proprietary protocol supports 24-bit samples, and is self-clocking with NRZI modulation, over a range of sampling frequencies. A group of 192 bits (8 channels of 24 bits each) are transmitted with 256 channel clocks, constituting a single data frame. Each frame of 256 slots contains a synchronization pattern (ten 0s), a synchronization period terminator (one 1), four user bits, a 1 marking the end of the user sequence, and 192 data bits. The binary 1s surrounding the user bits act as clocking information; this allows the receiver to lock onto the sample rate of the data stream without other explicit sample rate information. The 192 data bits are divided into 48 groups of four bits each, with a binary 1 appended to the end of each group; this occupies the remaining 240 slots of the frame. Groups are serially transmitted, with data 1s represented by a channel transition, and data 0s represented by an absence of a transition, as in NRZI. The nominal clock frequency is 12.288 MHz at a 48-kHz audio sampling frequency. Multiple recorders are connected via the ADI optical loop; using software control, channels can be reassigned providing a digital patch bay function; for example, channel 3 on one recorder can be copied to channel 1 on another recorder. ADI is also used to interconnect modular recorders as well as digital audio workstations, keyboards, effects processors, and other devices.

AES3 (AES/EBU) Professional Interface Format

The Audio Engineering Society (AES) has established a standard interconnection generally known as the AES3 or AES/EBU digital interface. It is a serial transmission format for linearly represented digital audio data. It permits transmission of two-channel digital audio information, including both audio and nonaudio data, from one professional audio device to another. In addition, it provides flexibility within the defined standard for specialized applications. The format has been codified as the AES3-1992 standard; this is a revised version of the original AES3-1985 standard. In addition, other standards organizations have published substantially similar interface specifications. The International Electrotechnical Commission (IEC) developed the IEC-958 professional or broadcast use (known as type I) format. The International Radio Consultative Committee (CCIR) provides Rec. 647 (1990). The Electronic Industries Association of Japan specifies an EIAJ CP-340-type I format. The American National Standards Institute has ratified the ANSI S4.40-1985 standard. The European Broadcasting Union has established EBU Tech. 3250-E; because of the cooperation between the AES and EBU, and substantial similarity of standards, the interface is often called the AES/EBU interface.

The AES3 format establishes a standard for conveying two channels of periodically sampled and uniformly quantized audio signals on a single twisted wire pair. The format is intended to convey data over distances of up to 100 meters without equalization. Longer distances are possible with equalization. Left and right audio channels are multiplexed, and the channel is self-clocking and self-synchronizing. Because it is independent of sampling frequency, the format can be used with any sampling frequency. Typically, sampling frequencies of 32 kHz, 44.1 kHz, and 48 kHz are used; these are recommended by the AES for PCM applications in standards document AES5-1984. Sixty-four bits are conveyed in one sampling period; the period is thus 22.7 μs with a 44.1-kHz sampling frequency. AES3 alleviates polarity shift between channels, channel imbalances, absolute polarity inversion, gain shifts, as well as analog transmission problems such as hum and noise pickups, and high frequency loss. Furthermore, an AES3 data stream can identify mono/stereo, use of pre-emphasis, and the sampling frequency of the signal.

The biphase mark code, a self-clocking code, is the binary frequency modulation channel code used to convey data over the AES3 interconnection. There is always a transition (high to low, or low to high) at the beginning of a bit interval; a 1 places another transition in the center of the interval; a 0 has no transition in the center. A transition at the start of every bit ensures that the bit clock rate can be recovered by the receiver. The code also minimizes low-frequency content, and is polarity free (information lies in the timing of transitions, not their direction). All information is contained in the code's transitions. Using the code, a properly encoded data stream will have no transition lengths greater than one data period (two cells), and no transition lengths shorter than one-half coding period (one cell). This kind of differential code can tolerate about twice as much noise as channels using threshold detection. However, its bandwidth is large, limiting channel rate; logical 1 message bits cause the channel frequency to equal the message bit rate. The overall bit rate is 64 times the sampling frequency; for example, it is 3.072 Mbps at a 48-kHz sampling frequency. Channel codes are discussed in chapter 3.

The AES3 format defines a number of terms. An audio sample is a signal that has been periodically sampled, quantized, and digitally represented in a two's complement manner. A subframe is a set of audio sample data with other auxiliary information. Two subframes, one for each channel, are transmitted within the sampling period; the first subframe is labelled 1, and second is labelled 2. A frame is a sequence of two subframes; the rate of transmission of frames corresponds exactly to the sampling rate of the source. With stereo transmissions, subframe 1 contains left A-channel data and subframe 2 contains right B-channel data, as shown in Fig. 10-2A. For

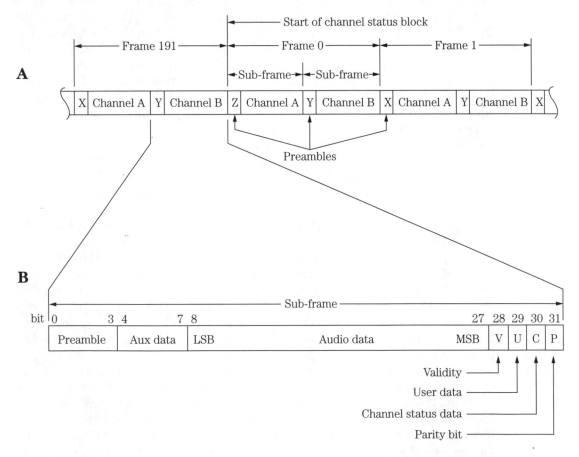

10-2 The AES3 interface is structured in frames and subframes as well as channel status blocks formed over 192 frames. A. There are two subframes per frame; each subframe is identified with a preamble. B. The interface uses a subframe of 32 bits.

mono, the rate remains at the 2-channel rate, and audio data is placed in subframe 1. A block is a group of channel status data bits and an optional group of user bits, one per subframe, collected over 192 source sample periods. A subframe preamble designates the starts of subframes and channel status blocks, and synchronizes and identifies audio channels. There are three types of preambles. Preamble Z identifies the start of subframe 1 and frame 0, which is also the start of a channel status block. Preamble X identifies the start of subframe 1 otherwise, and Preamble Y identifies the start of subframe 2. Preambles occupy four bits; they are formed by violating the biphase mark coding in specific ways.

The format specifies that a subframe has a length of 32 bits, with fields that are defined as shown in Fig. 10-2B. Audio data might occupy 24 bits. Data is linearly represented in two's complement form, with the least significant bit (LSB) transmitted first. If the audio data does not require 24 bits, then the first four bits can be used as an auxiliary data sample, as defined in the channel status data. Because most devices use 16-bit words, the last 16 bits in the data field are typically used, with the others set to 0. Four bits conclude the subframe: An audio sample validity bit is 0 if the transmitted audio sample is error free, and 1 if the sample is defective and not suitable for conversion to an analog signal. A user data bit can optionally be used to convey blocks of user data. A recommended format for user data is described in the AES18-1992 standard, as described below. The audio channel status bit is used to form blocks describing information about the interconnection channel and other system parameters, as described below. A subframe parity bit provides even parity for the subframe; the bit can detect when an odd number of errors have occurred in the transmission.

The audio channel status bit is used to convey a block of data 192 bits in length. An overview of the block is shown in Fig. 10-3. Received blocks of channel status data are accumulated from each of the subframes to yield two independent channel status data blocks, one for each channel. At a sampling frequency of 48 kHz, the blocks repeat at 4-ms intervals. Each channel status data block consists of 192 bits of data in 24 bytes, transmitted as one bit in each subframe, and collected from 192 successive frames. The block rate is 250 Hz at a 48-kHz sampling frequency. The channel status block is synchronized by using the alternate subframe preamble every 192 blocks.

There are 24 bytes of channel status data. Details on the first six bytes are shown in Fig. 10-4. Byte 0 of the channel status block contains information that identifies the data for professional use, as well as information on sampling rate and use of pre-emphasis; with any AES3 communication, bit 0 in byte 0 must be set to 1 signifying professional use of the channel status block. Byte 1 specifies signal mode such as stereo, or mono. Byte 2 specifies maximum audio word length and number of bits used in the word; an auxiliary coordination signal can be specified. Byte 3 is reserved for multichannel functions. Byte 4 identifies type of digital audio reference signal (Grade 1 or 2). Byte 5 is reserved. Bytes 6 through 9 contain alphanumeric channel origin code, and bytes 10 through 13 contain alphanumeric destination code; these can be used to route a data stream to a destination, then display its origin at the receiver. Bytes 14 through 17 specify a 32-bit sample address. Bytes 18 through 21 specify a 32-bit time-of-day timecode with 4-ms intervals at 48-kHz sampling fre-

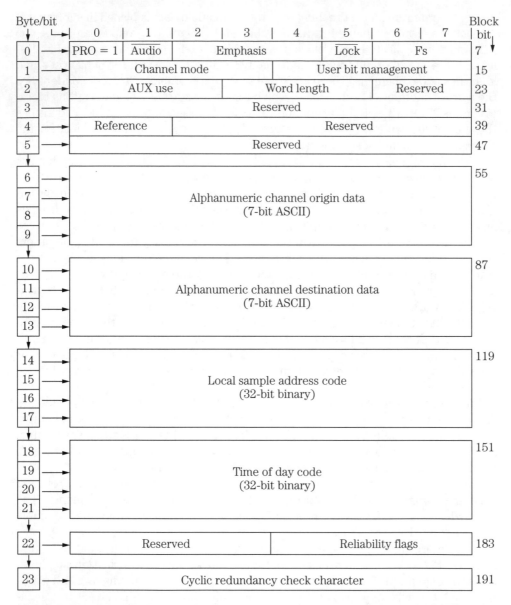

Byte/bit

Byte	0	1	2	3	4	5	6	7	Block bit
0	PRO = 1	$\overline{\text{Audio}}$	Emphasis			$\overline{\text{Lock}}$	Fs		7
1	Channel mode				User bit management				15
2	AUX use			Word length			Reserved		23
3	Reserved								31
4	Reference			Reserved					39
5	Reserved								47

6	Alphanumeric channel origin data (7-bit ASCII)	55
7		
8		
9		

10	Alphanumeric channel destination data (7-bit ASCII)	87
11		
12		
13		

14	Local sample address code (32-bit binary)	119
15		
16		
17		

18	Time of day code (32-bit binary)	151
19		
20		
21		

22	Reserved	Reliability flags	183

23	Cyclic redundancy check character	191

10-3 Specification of the 24-byte channel status block used in the professional AES3 serial interface.

quency; this timecode can be divided to obtain video frames. Byte 22 contains data reliability flags for the channel status block, and indicates when an incomplete block is transmitted. The final byte, byte 23, contains a CRCC codeword with generation polynomial $x^8 + x^4 + x^3 + x^2 + 1$ across the channel status block for error detection.

Three levels of channel status implementation are defined in the AES3 standards document: minimum, standard, and enhanced; these establish the nature of the data directed to receiving units. With the minimum level, the first bit of the channel status block is set to 1 to indicate professional status, and all other channel status bits are set to 0. With standard implementation, all channel status bits in bytes 0, 1, and 2 (used for sampling frequency, pre-emphasis, mono/stereo, audio resolution, etc.) and CRCC data in byte 23 must be transmitted; this level is the most commonly used. With enhanced implementation, all channel status bits are used.

As noted, audio data can occupy 24 bits per sample. Because most audio data occupies 20 bits or less, the four remaining bits can be optionally used as an auxiliary

BYTE 0	Bit 0	PRO = 1 (Professional)
	0	Consumer use of channel status block
	1	Professional use of channel status block
	Bit 1	$\overline{\text{Audio}}$
	0	Digital audio
	1	Non-audio
	Bit 234	Emphasis
	000	Emphasis not indicated
	100	No emphasis
	110	50/15 μs emphasis
	111	CCITT J.17 emphasis
	Bit 5	$\overline{\text{Lock}}$
	0	Sampling frequency locked
	1	Sampling frequency unlocked
	Bit 67	Encoded sampling frequency
	00	Not indicated
	01	48 kHz
	10	44.1 kHz
	11	32 kHz

BYTE 1	Bit 0123	Encoded channel mode
	0000	Not indicated
	0001	Two-channel
	0010	Single-channel
	0011	Primary/Secondary
	0100	Stereophonic
	0101	Reserved
	0110	Reserved
	1111	Vector to byte 3
	Bit 4567	User bits management
	0000	Default
	0001	192-bit block
	0010	AES18
	0011	User defined

10-4 Description of the data contained in bytes 0–5 in the 24-byte channel status block used in the professional AES3 serial interface.

BYTE 2	Bit 012	Auxiliary sample bits	
	000	Maximum 20 bits	
	001	Maximum 24 bits	
	010	Maximum 20 bits (single coordination)	
	011	Reserved	
	Bit 345	Sample wordlength (24)	Sample wordlength (20)
	000	Default	Default
	001	23 bits	19 bits
	010	22 bits	18 bits
	011	21 bits	17 bits
	100	20 bits	16 bits
	101	24 bits	20 bits
	Bit 67	Reserved	

3	Bit 0-7	Vector from byte 1 (multichannel reserved)
BYTE 4	Bit 01	Digital audio reference signal (AES11)
	00	Default
	01	Grade 1
	10	Grade 2
	11	Reserved
	Bit 2-7	Reserved
5	Bit 0-7	Reserved

10-4 Continued.

speech-quality coordination channel, providing a path so that verbal communication can accompany the audio data signal. Such a channel could use a sampling rate that is one-third that of the main data rate, and use 12-bit coding; one 4-bit nibble is transmitted in each subframe. Complete words would be collected over three frames, providing two independent speech channels. The resolution of the main audio data must be identified by information in byte 2 of the channel status block.

In many ways, an AES3 signal can be treated similarly to a video signal in its practical usage. The electrical parameters of the format follow those for balanced-voltage digital circuits as defined by the International Telegraph and Telephone Consultative Committee (CCITT) of the International Telecommunication Union (ITU) in Recommendation V.11. Driver and receiver chips used for RS-422 communications, as defined by the Electronic Industries Association (EIA), are typically used; the EBU specification dictates use of a transformer. The line driver has a balanced output with internal impedance of 110 Ω from 0.1 to 6.0 MHz. Similarly, the interconnecting cable's characteristic impedance is 110 Ω at frequencies from 0.1 to 6.0 MHz. The transmission circuit uses a symmetrical differential source and twisted pair cable, typically shielded, with runs of 100 meters. Runs of 500 meters are possible when adaptive equalization is used. The waveform's amplitude (measured with a 110-Ω resistor across a disconnected line) should lie between 2 to 7 V peak-to-peak. The signal conforms to RS-422 guidelines. Jitter tolerance in AES3 can be specified with respect to unit intervals (UI), the shortest nominal time interval in the coding scheme; there are 128 UIs in a sample frame. Output jitter is the jitter intrinsic to the device as well as jitter passed through from the device's timing reference. Peak-to-peak output jitter from an AES3 transmitter should be less than 0.04 UI when measured with a jitter highpass weighting filter. An AES3 receiver requires a jitter tolerance of 0.25 UI peak-to-peak at high frequencies above 8 kHz, increasing to 10 UI at frequencies below 200 Hz. Some manufacturers use an interface with unbalanced 75-Ω coaxial cable (such as 5C2V type), signal level of 1 V peak-to-peak, and BNC connectors. This can be preferable in a video-based environment, where switchers are used to route and distribute digital audio signals, or where long cable runs (up to 1 kilometer) are required. This is described in the AES3-ID document.

The receiver should provide both common-mode interference and direct current rejection, using either transformers or capacitors. The receiver should present a nominal resistive impedance of 110 Ω to the cable over a frequency range from 0.1 to 6.0 MHz. More than one receiver on a line can cause transmission errors. Receiver circuitry must be designed with phase-lock loops to reduce jitter. The receiver must also synchronize the input data to an accurate clock reference with low jitter; these tolerances are further defined in the AES11 standard. Input (female) and output (male) connectors use an XLR type connector with pin 1 carrying signal ground, and pins 2 and 3 carrying the unpolarized signal.

AES10 (MADI) Multichannel Interface Format

The Multichannel Audio Digital Interface (MADI) extends the AES3 protocol to provide a standard means of interconnecting multichannel digital audio equipment. MADI, as specified in the AES10 standard, allows up to 56 channels of linearly-represented, serial data to be conveyed along a single length of BNC-terminated cable for distances of up to 50 meters. Audio samples of up to 24 bits are permitted. In addition, the AES3 validity, user, channel status, and parity bits are all conveyed. Using this interconnection, it is possible to perform a single analog-to-digital conversion on the original audio signal, then perform all subsequent processing through recording consoles, multichannel recorders, and mix-down recorders without leaving the digital domain. Although an interconnection between console and multichannel recorder with the AES3 format requires two cables for every two audio channels (for send and return), a MADI interconnection requires only two audio cables (plus a master synchronization signal) for up to 56 audio channels. The MADI protocol is documented as the AES10-1991, and ANSI S4.43-1991 standards.

To reduce bandwidth requirements, designers of the MADI protocol did not use the biphase mark code; instead, an NRZI code is used, with a 4/5 encoding format (this is based on the FDDI protocol). The link transmission rate is fixed at 125 Mbps regardless of the sampling rate or number of active channels. Because of the encoding scheme, the data transfer rate is thus 100 Mbps. Although AES3 is self-clocking, MADI is designed to run asynchronously. To operate asynchronously, a MADI receiver must extract timing information from the transmitted data so the receiver's clock can be synchronized. To ensure this, the MADI protocol stipulates that a 10-bit synchronization symbol is transmitted at least once per frame. Moreover, a dedicated master synchronization signal (such as defined by AES11) must be applied to all interconnected MADI transmitters and receivers.

The MADI channel format is based on the AES3 subframe format; a MADI channel differs from a subframe only in the first four bits, as shown in Fig. 10-5. Each channel therefore consists of 32 bits, with four mode identification bits, up to 24 audio bits, as well as the V, U, C, and P bits. The mode identification bits provide frame synchronization, identify channel active/inactive status, identify A and B subframes, and identify a block start. The 56 MADI channels are transmitted serially, starting with channel 0 and ending with channel 55, with all channels transmitted within one sampling period; the frame begins with bit 0 of channel 0. Because biphase coding is not used in the MADI format, preambles cannot be used to identify the start of each channel. Thus in MADI a 1 setting in bit 0 in channel 0 is used as a frame synchronization bit identifying channel 0, the first to be transmitted in a frame. Bit 0 is set to 0 in all other channels. Bit 1 indicates the active status of the channel. If the channel is active it is set to 1, and if inactive it is set to 0. Further, all inactive channels must have a higher channel number than the highest numbered active channel. The bit is not dynamic, and remains fixed after power is applied. Bit 2 identifies whether a channel is A or B in a stereo signal; this also replaces the function of the preambles in AES3. Bit 3 is set when the user data and status data carried within a channel falls at the start of a 192-frame block. The remainder of the MADI channel is identical to an AES3 subframe. This is useful because MADI and AES3 are thus compatible, allowing free exchange of data.

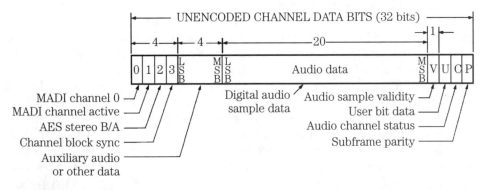

10-5 The AES10 (MADI) interface is used to connect multichannel digital audio equipment. The MADI channel format differs from the AES3 subframe format only in the first four bits.

Although the AES3 can use a twisted pair wire to convey 3 Mbps, MADI must use coaxial cable to support 100 Mbps. The interconnection is designed as a transmitter to receiver single-point to single-point link; in the case of a console and recorder, two cables for sends and returns are required. Standard 75-Ω video coaxial cable with BNC connector terminations is specified; peak-to-peak transmitter output voltage should lie between 0.3 and 0.6 V. Fiber-optic cable can also be used; for example, an FDDI interface could be used for distances of up to 2 kilometers. Alternatively, the synchronous optical network (SONET) could be used. As noted, a distributed master synchronizing signal must be applied to all interconnected MADI transmitters and receivers. Because of the asynchronous operation, buffers are placed at both the transmitter and receiver, so that data can be reclocked from the buffers according to the master synchronization signal.

The audio data frequency can range from 32 kHz to 48 kHz, a ±12% variation is permitted. Higher sampling frequencies could be supported by transmitting at a lower rate, and using two consecutive MADI channels to achieve the desired sampling rate.

S/PDIF Consumer Interconnection

Consumer applications usually use the S/PDIF (Sony/Philips Digital InterFace) format. The IEC-958 consumer format (known as type II) is a substantially identical standard; in some applications, the EIAJ CP-340 type II format is used. These consumer standards are very similar to the AES3 standard, and in some cases professional and consumer equipment can be directly connected. However, this is not recommended because important differences exist in the electrical specification, and in the channel status bits, so unpredictable results can occur.

The overall structure of the consumer channel status block is shown in Fig. 10-6. It differs from the professional channel status block (see Fig. 10-3). The serial bits are arranged as twenty-four 8-bit bytes; only the first four bytes are defined. Fig. 10-7 provides specific details on bytes 0–3. They differ from the professional AES3 channel status block (see Fig. 10-4). Byte 0, bit 0 is set to 0, indicating consumer use; bit 1 specifies whether the data is audio (0) or nonaudio (1); bit 2 is the copyright or C bit, and indicates copy protected (0) or unprotected (1); bit 3 shows use of pre-emphasis (if bit 1 shows audio data and bits 4 and 5 show two-channel audio); bits 6 and 7 set the mode, that defines bytes 1 through 3. Presently, only mode 00 is specified.

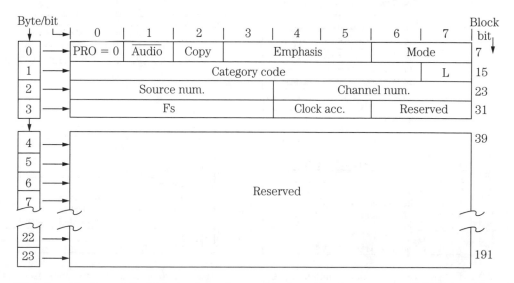

10-6 Specification of the 24-byte channel status block used in the consumer S/PDIF serial interface. Sanchez

BYTE 0

bit 0	PRO = 0 (consumer)
0	Consumer use of channel status block
1	Professional use of channel status block
bit 1	Audio
0	Digital Audio
1	Non-Audio
bit 2	Copy / Copyright
0	Copy inhibited / copyright asserted
1	Copy permitted / copyright not asserted
bit 3 4 5	Pre-emphasis - if bit 1 is 0 (dig. audio)
0 0 0	None - 2 channel audio
1 0 0	50/15 us - 2 channel audio
x x 1	Reserved - 4 channel audio
bit 3 4 5	if bit 1 is 1 (non-audio)
0 0 0	Digital data
bit 6 7	Mode
0 0	Mode 0 (defines bytes 1-3 as listed below)

BYTE 1

bit 0 1 2 3 4 5 6	Category Code
0000000	General
0000001	Experimental
0001xxx	Solid state memory
001xxxx	Broadcast reception of digital audio
010xxxx	Digital/digital Converters
01100xx	A/D converters w/o copy info
01101xx	A/D converters w/ copy info (using Copy and L bits)
0111xxx	Broadcast reception of digital audio
100xxxx	Laser-Optical
101xxxx	Musical Instruments, Mics, etc.
110xxxx	Magnetic Tape or Disk
111xxxx	Reserved
bit 7	L: Generation Status
	Only Category Codes: 100xxxx 001xxxx 0111xxx
0	Original/Commercially pre-recorded
1	No indication/1st generaltion or higher
	All other category codes
0	No indication/1st generaltion or higher
1	Original/Commercially pre-recorded

BYTE 2

bit 0 1 2 3	Source Number
0 0 0 0	Unspecified
1 0 0 0	1
0 1 0 0	2
	to
1 1 1 1	15 (binary - 0 is LSB, 3 is MSB)
bit 4 5 6 7	Channel Number
0 0 0 0	Unspecified
1 0 0 0	A (Left in 2 channel format)
0 1 0 0	B (Right in 2 channel format)
1 1 0 0	C
	to
1 1 1 1	O (binary - 4 is LSB, 7 is MSB)

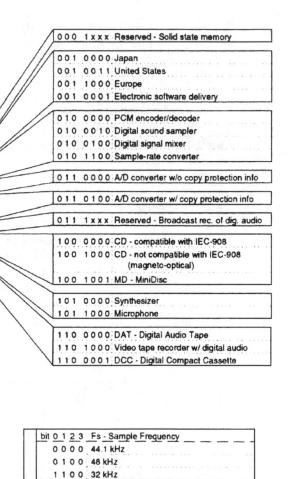

0 0 0	1 x x x	Reserved - Solid state memory
0 0 1	0 0 0 0	Japan
0 0 1	0 0 1 1	United States
0 0 1	1 0 0 0	Europe
0 0 1	0 0 0 1	Electronic software delivery
0 1 0	0 0 0 0	PCM encoder/decoder
0 1 0	0 0 1 0	Digital sound sampler
0 1 0	0 1 0 0	Digital signal mixer
0 1 0	1 1 0 0	Sample-rate converter
0 1 1	0 0 0 0	A/D converter w/o copy protection info
0 1 1	0 1 0 0	A/D converter w/ copy protection info
0 1 1	1 x x x	Reserved - Broadcast rec. of dig. audio
1 0 0	0 0 0 0	CD - compatible with IEC-908
1 0 0	1 0 0 0	CD - not compatible with IEC-908 (magneto-optical)
1 0 0	1 0 0 1	MD - MiniDisc
1 0 1	0 0 0 0	Synthesizer
1 0 1	1 0 0 0	Microphone
1 1 0	0 0 0 0	DAT - Digital Audio Tape
1 1 0	1 0 0 0	Video tape recorder w/ digital audio
1 1 0	0 0 0 1	DCC - Digital Compact Cassette

BYTE 3

bit 0 1 2 3	Fs - Sample Frequency
0 0 0 0	44.1 kHz
0 1 0 0	48 kHz
1 1 0 0	32 kHz
bit 4 5	Clock Accuracy
0 0	Level II, ± 1000 ppm (default)
0 1	Level III, variable pitch
1 0	Level I, ± 50 ppm - high accuracy
bit 6 7	
0 0	Reserved

10-7 Description of the data contained in bytes 0–3 in the 24-byte channel status block used in the consumer S/PDIF serial interface. Sanchez

Byte 1, bits 0–6, define a category code that identifies the type of equipment transmitting the data stream; byte 1 bit 7 (the 15th bit in the block) is the generation or L bit, and indicates when the data is original or copied. If a recorder with an S/PDIF input receives an AES3 signal, it can read the professional pre-emphasis indicator as a copy prohibit instruction, and thus refuse to record the data stream. Likewise, a professional recorder can correctly identify a consumer data stream by examining bit 0 (set to 0), but misinterpret a consumer copy inhibit bit as a sign that emphasis is not indicated. In mode 00, the category code in byte 1 defines a variety of transmitting formats including CD, MiniDisc, DAT, DCC, synthesizer, sample rate converter, and broadcast reception. Byte 2 specifies source number, and channel number, and byte 3 specifies sampling frequency, and clock accuracy.

The category code, as noted, defines different types of digital equipment; this in turn defines the subframe structure. For example, the category code for CD players (100 0000) defines the subframe structure with 16 bits per sample, a sampling frequency of 44.1 kHz, control bits derived from the CD's Q subcode, and places the CD's subcode itself in the user bits. Subcode is transmitted as it is derived from the disc, one subcode channel bit at a time, over 98 CD frames. However, the P subcode, used to identify different data areas on a disc, is not transmitted. The start of subcode data is designated by a minimum of sixteen 0s, followed by a high start bit. Seven subcode bits (Q–W) follow. Up to eight 0s can follow for timing purposes, or the next start bit and subcode field can follow immediately. The process repeats 98 times until the subcode is transmitted. Subcode blocks from a CD have a data rate of 75 Hz. There is one user bit per audio sample, but there are fewer subcode bits than audio samples ($12 \times 98 = 1176$) so the remaining bits are packed with 0s.

The category code (110 0000) defining use of DAT recorders conveys conventional information as well as track number. The same 24-bit audio data word is transmitted, LSB leading; bits 12 to 27 carry audio data; and subcode is placed in bits 4 to 11. In addition, synchronizing information used for editing purposes can be transmitted. When the first sample of a DAT interleave block is present, a high user bit is transmitted for each drum revolution. A start ID bit will be transmitted when a recorder has located a recorded code, a skip ID bit is transmitted when a recorder locates a skip-begin code, and a skip-end bit is transmitted when the end-of-skip code is found. In this way, DAT recorders can be synchronized for editing.

The consumer interface does not require a low impedance balanced line, as does the professional standard. Instead, a single-ended 75-Ω coaxial cable is used, with 0.5 V peak-to-peak amplitude, over a maximum distance of 10 meters. To ensure adequate transmission bandwidth, video-type phono cables are recommended. Alternatively, some consumer equipment uses an optical Toslink connector and plastic fiber-optic cable over distances less than 15 meters. Glass fiber cables and appropriate code/decode circuits can be used for distances over 1 kilometer.

Serial Copy Management System

A Serial Copy Management System (SCMS) circuit is used on many consumer recorders to limit the number of copies that can be derived from a recording. A user can make digital copies of a prerecorded, copyrighted work, but the copy itself cannot be copied; first generation copying is permissible, but not second generation copying. For example, a user can digitally copy from CD to a DAT, but a copy-inhibit flag is set in the DAT tape's subcode so that it is impossible to digitally copy from the DAT copy to another DAT tape. However, a SCMS-equipped DAT recorder can record any number of digital copies from an original source. SCMS does not affect analog copying in any way. SCMS is a fair solution because it allows a user to make a digital copy of purchased software, for example, for compilation of favorite songs, but helps prevent a second party from copying music that was not paid for. On the other hand, SCMS might prohibit the recopying of original recordings, a legitimate use. Use of SCMS is mandated in the U.S. by the Audio Home Recording Act of 1992, as passed by Congress to protect copyrighted works.

The SCMS circuit is found in consumer-grade recorders with S/PDIF (IEC-958 type II) interfaces; it is not present in professional AES3 (IEC-958 type I) interfaces. In particular, SCMS resides in the channel status bits as defined in IEC-958 type II, Amendment No. 1 standard; this data is used to determine whether the data is copyrighted, and whether it is original, or copied. The SCMS circuit first examines the channel status block (see Fig. 10-7) in the incoming digital data to determine whether it is a professional bit stream, or a consumer bit stream. In particular, when byte 0 bit 0 is a 1 the bit stream is assumed to adhere to the AES3 standard; SCMS takes no action. SCMS signals do not appear on AES3 interfaces, and the AES3 standard does not recognize nor carry SCMS information; thus, audio data is not copy-protected, and can be indefinitely copied. When bit 0 is set to 0, the SCMS identifies the data as consumer data. It examines byte 0 bit 2, the copyright or C bit; it is set to 0 when copyright is enabled, and set to 1 when copyright is not enabled. Byte 1 bit 7 (the 15th bit in the block) is the generation or L bit; it is used to indicate the generation of the recording. For most category codes, an L bit of 0 indicates that the transmitted signal is a copy and a 1 means the signal is original. However, the meaning is reversed for laser optical products, and broadcast reception: 0 indicates an original, and 1 indicates a copy. The L bit is thus interpreted by the category code contained in byte 1 bits 0–6 that indicates the type of transmitting device. In the case of the compact disc, because the L bit is not defined in the CD standard (IEC 908), the copy bit designates both copyright and generation. The disc is not copyrighted if the C bit is 0; the disc is copyrighted and original if C is 1; if C alternates between 0 and 1 at a 4–10-Hz rate, the disc is copyrighted for the first generation or higher. Also, because the general category and A/D converter category without copyrighting cannot carry C or L information, these bits are ignored and the receiver sets C for copyright, and L to original.

Generally, the following recording scenario exists when bit 0 is set to 0, indicating a consumer bit stream: When bit C is 1, incoming audio data will be recorded no matter what is written in the category code or L bit, and the new copy can in turn be copied an unlimited number of times. When bit C is 0, the L bit is examined; if the incoming signal is a copy, no recording is permitted. If the incoming signal is original, it will be recorded, but the recording is marked as a copy by setting bits in the recording's subcode; it cannot be copied. When no defined category code is present, one generation of copying is permitted. When there is a defined category code but no copyright information, two generations are permitted. However, different types of equipment respond differently to SCMS. For example, equipment that does not store, decode, or interpret the transmitted data is considered transparent and ignores SCMS flags. Digital mixers, filters, optical disk recorders and tape recorders require different interpretations of SCMS; the general algorithm used to interpret SCMS code is thus rather complicated.

By law, the SCMS circuit must be present in consumer recorders with the S/PDIF or IEC-958 type II interconnection; however, some professional recorders, essentially upgraded consumer models, also contain an SCMS circuit. If recordists use the S/PDIF interface, copy-inhibit flags are sometimes inadvertently set, leading to problems when subsequent copying is needed.

AES11 Digital Audio Reference Signal

The AES11-1990 standard specifies criteria for synchronization of digital audio equipment in studio operations. It is important for interconnected devices to share a common timing signal so that individual samples are processed simultaneously; timing inaccuracies can lead to increased noise, and even clicks and pops in the audio signal. With a proper reference, transmitters, receivers, and D/A converters can all work in unison. Devices must be synchronized in both frequency and phase, and be SMPTE time synchronous as well. It is relatively easy to achieve frequency synchronization between two sources—they must follow a common clock, and the signals' bit periods must be equal. However, to achieve phase synchronization, the bit edges in the different signals must begin simultaneously.

When connecting one digital audio device to another, the devices must operate at a common sampling frequency, and bits in the sending and received signals must begin simultaneously. These synchronization requirements are relatively easy to achieve. Most digital audio data streams are self-clocking; the receiving circuits read the incoming modulation code, and reference the signal to an internal clock to produce stable data. In some cases, an independent synchronization signal is transmitted. In either case, in simple applications, the receiver can lock to the bit stream's sampling frequency.

However, with numerous devices, it is difficult to obtain frequency and phase synchronization. Different types of devices use different time-bases hence they exhibit noninteger relationships. For example, at 44.1 kHz, a digital audio bit stream will clock 1471.47 samples per NTSC video frame; sample edges align only once every 10 frames. Other data, such as the 192 sample channel status block, creates additional synchronization challenges; in this case, the audio sample clock, channel status, and video frame will align only once every 20 minutes. To achieve synchronization, a common clock with good frequency stability should be distributed through a studio. In addition, external synchronizers are needed to read SMPTE timecode, and provide time synchronization between devices. Figure 10-8 shows an example of synchronization for an audio/video studio; timecode is used to provide general time lock; a master oscillator (using AES11 or video sync) provides a stable clock to ensure frequency lock of primary devices (the analog multitrack is locked via an external synchronizer and synthesizers are not locked). It is important that the timecode reference is different from the frequency lock reference. In addition, most timecode sources are not sufficiently accurate to provide frequency and phase lock references through a studio.

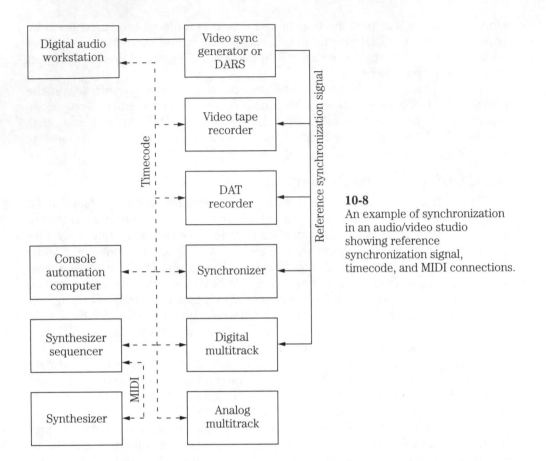

10-8
An example of synchronization in an audio/video studio showing reference synchronization signal, timecode, and MIDI connections.

Although an AES3 line could be used to distribute a very stable clock reference, a dedicated word clock is preferred. Specifically, the AES11 digital audio reference signal (DARS) has been defined, providing a clocking signal with high frequency stability for jitter regulation. Using this reference signal, any sample can be time aligned to any other sample, or with the addition of a timecode reference, aligned to a specific video frame edge. The digital audio reference signal uses the same format and electrical configuration, and connectors, as AES3; only the preamble is used as a reference clock. The AES11 signal is sometimes called AES3 black because when displayed it looks like an AES3 signal with no audio information present.

The AES11 standard defines Grade 1 long-term frequency accuracy (accurate to within ±1 ppm) and Grade 2 long-term accuracy (accurate to within ±10 ppm), where ppm is one part per million. Use of Grade 1 or 2 is identified in byte 4, bits 0 and 1 of the channel status block: Grade 1 (01), Grade 2 (10). With Grade 1, for example, a reference sampling clock of 44.1 kHz would require an accuracy of ±0.0441 Hz. A Grade 1 system would permit operation with 16- or 18-bit audio data; 20-bit resolution might require a more accurate reference clock, such as one derived from a video sync pulse generator (SPG). Timecode references lack sufficient stability. When synchronizing audio and video equipment, the DAR must be locked to the

**Table 10-1. Frequency stability of
the clocking in some audio and video interface signals.**

Digital signal	Frequency stability	Jitter performance
AES3/IEC 958 Type I	10^{-5}	Very good
S/PDIF/CP-340/IEC 958 Type II	10^{-3} to 10^{-5}	Varies
AES11 DARS	10^{-5} to 10^{-6}	Excellent
NTSC video	3×10^{-6}	Excellent
PAL video	2×10^{-7}	Excellent
Film sync	10^{-3}	Poor
SMPTE timecode	NA	Varies; usually poor
MIDI timecode	NA	Varies; usually poor
Analog tape recorder	Varies	Varies; usually poor

video synchronization reference. Frequency stability of the clocking in several audio and video interface signals is summarized in Table 10-1.

A separate word clock cable is run from the reference source to each piece of digital equipment through a star-type architecture, using a distribution amplifier as with a video sync pulse generator, to the reference (or genlock) inputs of all digital audio devices. Only a small buffer is needed to reclock data at the receiver. For example, a 5-ms buffer would accommodate 8 minutes of program that varies by ±10 ppm from the master reference. When A/D or D/A converters do not have internal clocks, and derive their clocks from the DAR, timing accuracy of the DAR must be increased; any timing errors are applied directly to the reconstructed audio signal. For 16-bit resolution at the converter, the AES11 standard recommends that peak sample clock modulation, sample to sample, be less than ±1 ns at all modulation frequencies above 40 Hz, and that random clock jitter, sample to sample, be less than ±0.1 ns per sample clock period, as shown in Fig. 10-9. Jitter is discussed in more detail in chapter 4.

AES18 Format for User Data

The AES18-1992 standard describes a method for formatting the user data channels found within the AES3 interface. This format is derived from the packet-based high-level data link control (HDLC) communications protocol. It conveys text and other message data that might be related or unrelated to the audio data. The user data channel is a transparent carrier providing a constant data rate when the AES3 interface operates at an audio sampling frequency of 48 kHz ±12.5%; justification bits are inserted at sampling frequencies greater than 42 kHz. A message is sent as one or more data packets, each with the address of its destination; a receiver reads only the messages addressed to it. Packets can be added or deleted as appro-

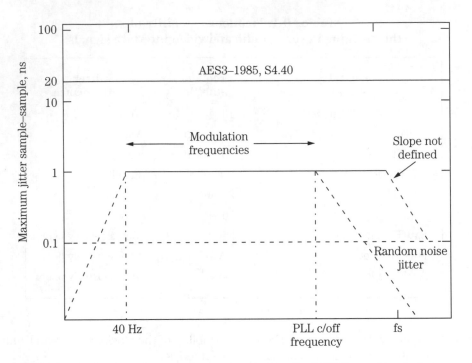

10-9 Time-base tolerances must be increased when the DARS is used to clock sample converters. Recommended jitter limits for sample clocks in 16-bit A/D and D/A converters are depicted.

priate as data is conveyed from one device to another. A packet is comprised of an address byte, control byte, address extension byte (optional), and an information field that is no more than 16 bytes. Multiple packets are placed in an HDLC frame; it contains a beginning flag field, packets, a CRCC field, and an ending flag. As described above, each AES3 subframe contains one user bit. User data is coded as an NRZ signal, LSB leading. Typical user bit applications can include messages such as scripts, subtitles, editing information, copyright, performer credits, switching instructions, and other annotations.

Sample Rate Converters

In a perfect digital world, there would be one sampling frequency. Unfortunately, the world is populated by many different sampling frequencies. Although 44.1 kHz and 48 kHz are the most common, 32 kHz is used in many broadcast applications; the AES5-1984 standard defines the use of these sampling frequencies. Soundcards use frequencies of 44.1 kHz, 22.05 kHz, and 11.025 kHz (among others), and 44.056 kHz is often used with video equipment. In addition, in many applications, varispeed is used to bend pitch, producing radically diverse sampling rates.

Many people wonder why 44.1 kHz was selected as a standard sampling frequency. Originally, the only tape recorders capable of handling the high bandwidth requirements of digital audio signals were video recorders. Because a 16-bit digital audio signal (and error correction) were encoded as a video signal, the sampling frequency had to relate to television standards' line and field rate, storing a few samples per scan line. The NTSC format uses 525 lines in 30 frames/second; only 490 are available for storage. With two samples per line, $490 \times 30 \times 2 = 29.4$ kHz, a too-low sampling frequency. With four lines, $490 \times 30 \times 4 = 58.8$ kHz, which was considered too high. With three lines, $490 \times 30 \times 3 = 44.1$ kHz—just right. Moreover, the PAL/SECAM format uses 625 lines (588 active lines) in 25 frames/second, and $588 \times 25 \times 3 = 44.1$ kHz as well. In the case of CD, because professional video recorders were used to prepare CD master tapes, 44.1 kHz became the sampling frequency for both master, and finished discs.

As noted, many different sampling rates are used; devices cannot be interconnected when their sampling rates differ. Even when sources are recorded at a common sampling frequency, their data streams can be asynchronous and thus differ by a few hertz; they must be synchronized to an exact common frequency. In addition, a signal can be degraded by jitter; this changes the accuracy of the signal's sampling rate. In some cases, sample rates can be changed with little effort. For example, a 44.1-kHz signal can be converted to 44.056 kHz by removing a sample approximately every 23 ms, or about every 1000 samples. Typically, dedicated circuits are needed.

A synchronous sample rate converter converts one rate to another using an integer ratio; the output rate is fixed in relation to the input rate—this limits applications. An asynchronous sample rate converter (ASRC) can accept a dynamically changing input sampling frequency, and output a constant and uninterrupted sampling frequency, at the same or different frequency. The input and output rates can have an irrational ratio relationship; in other words, the input and output rates are completely decoupled. In addition, the converter will follow any slow rate variations. This solves many interfacing problems.

Conceptually, sample rate conversion works like this: a digital signal is passed through a D/A converter, the analog signal is lowpass filtered, then passed through an A/D converter operating at a different sampling frequency. In practice, these functions can be performed digitally, through interpolation and decimation. The input sampling frequency is increased to a very high oversampling rate by inserting zeros in the bit stream then is digitally lowpass filtered. This interpolated signal, with a very high data rate, is then decimated by deleting output samples and digitally lowpass filtered to decrease output sampling frequency to a rate lower than the oversampling rate. The resolution of the conversion is determined by the number of samples available to the decimation filter; for example, for 16-bit accuracy, the difference between adjacent interpolated samples must be less than 1 LSB at the 16-bit level. This in turn determines the interpolation ratio; an oversampling ratio of 65,536 is required for 16-bit accuracy.

This ratio could be realized with a time-varying FIR filter of length 64 in which only nonzero data values are considered, but the required master clock signal of 3.27 GHz is impractical. Another approach uses polyphase filters. A lowpass filter highly oversampling by factor N can be decomposed into N different filters, each filter using a different subset of the original set of coefficients. If the subfilter coefficients are relatively fixed in time, their outputs can be summed to yield the original filter. They act as a parallel filter bank differing in their linear-phase group delays. This can be used for sample rate conversion; if input samples are applied to the polyphase filter bank, samples can be generated at any point between the input samples by selecting the output of a particular polyphase filter. An output sample late in the input sampling period would require a short filter delay (a large offset in the coefficient set), but an early output sample would demand a long delay (a short offset). That is, the offset of the coefficient set is proportional to the timing of the input/output sample selection. As before, accurate conversion requires 2^{16} polyphase filters; in practice, reduction methods reduce the number of coefficients.

To summarize, by adjusting the interpolation and decimation processes, arbitrary rate changes can be accommodated; these functions are effectively performed through polyphase filtering. Input data is applied to a highly oversampled digital low-pass filter; it has a passband of 0 Hz to 20 kHz, and many times the filter coefficients needed to provide this response (equivalent to thousands of polyphase filters). Depending on the instantaneous temporal relationship between the input/output frequency ratio, a selected set of these coefficients processes input samples, and computes the amplitude of output samples, at the proper output frequency.

The computation of the ratio between the input and output samples is itself digitally filtered; effectively, when the frequency of the jitter is higher than the cutoff frequency of the polyphase selection process, the jitter is attenuated; this reduces the effect of any jitter on the input clock. Short periods of sample rate conversion can thus be used to synchronize signals. An internal FIFO (first-in-first-out) buffer is used to absorb data during dynamically changing input sample rates. Input audio samples enter the buffer at the input sampling rate, and are output at the output rate. For example, a timing error of one sample period can exist at the input, but the sampling rate converter can correct this by distributing the content of 99 to 101 input samples over 100 output samples. In this way, the ASRC isolates the jittered clock recovered from the incoming signal, and synchronizes the signal with an accurate low-jitter clock. Devices such as this make sample rate conversion essentially transparent to the user, and overcome many interfacing problems such as jitter. Because rate converters mathematically alter data values, when sampling rate conversion is not specifically required, it is better to use dedicated reclocking devices to solve jitter problems.

Two examples of ASRC chips are the Analog Devices AD1890 and AD1891 devices, designed by Robert Adams. They are both 28-pin integrated circuits; the AD1890 accepts up to 20-bit input samples, and the AD1891 accepts up to 16-bit input samples; both devices output 24-bit samples. They provide clock slaves on the input and output side; the input sampling frequency is automatically sensed. The input sampling frequency can dynamically and asynchronously change over a range of an input/output ratio of 1:2 to 2:1, over an absolute range of 8 kHz to 60 kHz. The chips provide AES3 input and output ports.

Computer Networks and File Transfers

Whereas most dedicated audio interfaces operate point to point, with continuous data flow, and in real time, computer networks are typically asynchronous, transmitting data in discrete packets, and can interconnect many disparate devices. Successful communication across a network calls for arbitration to avoid usage conflicts. Although a dedicated audio interface uses a dedicated audio format, a network is not concerned with the type of data being transmitted, and uses a common file format for all data types; e-mail, graphics, audio, and video can all be conveyed. In addition, unlike dedicated audio interfaces, data delivery over a network is usually not continuous, and often not in real time; delivery depends, for example, on network data rate as well as current network traffic; transfer can occur at speeds well below, or well above real time. In some applications, a portion of the network bandwidth can be reserved to allow, for example, continuous real-time multimedia exchanges such as video conferencing. Of course, network communications are also limited by file format compatibility; for example, even after a successful file transfer, a Macintosh program will not run on a PC. In any event, networked data transfer will increasingly supplant the traditional practice of hand-carrying physical media, using the "sneaker net."

A network can link computers separated by a partition, or a continent, such that the separation is transparent to the user. Files can be downloaded from the central storage connected to a file server, processed in a local workstation, then conveyed to a distant end user. Using real-time methods, two recording studios can be bidirectionally linked so that overdub data can smoothly flow between them. The Internet is an example of a network providing both a powerful communications system, and an access gateway to vast quantities of information.

Telephone Services

Alexander Graham Bell is given credit for inventing the telephone in 1876. Bell registered his telephone patent two hours before Elisha Gray registered a caveat, an announcement of a telephone invention he intended to patent soon. It was later determined that Gray's apparatus would have worked, but Bell's would not. The litigation lasted for years. Since then, telephone technology has evolved tremendously. Today, the system's sophistication is impressive; by entering a string of digits, a user's voice is routed over copper wire, fiber and satellite to another user in a distant part of the globe. The digital transmission systems used to convey voice communications synonymously carry high bandwidth digital audio transmission. Both analog and digital signals attenuate over long distances, whereas analog signals are thus subject to increased noise, digital signals can be regenerated with great precision. Telephone companies almost exclusively use electronic switching and fiber-optic cable between telephone exchanges. As far as the telephone company is concerned, any phone call is treated simply as data; a long-distance call has the same sound quality as a local call. However, in most cases, the connection from the consumer's phone to the exchange is still analog.

Some information regarding the plain old telephone system (POTS): the telephone lines provided by the phone company are known as subscriber loops, or central office lines. They connect users with central offices via analog lines. Trunk lines connect users to a private branch exchange (PBX) where switching routing takes place. Circuit switching is used, in which a continuous connection is temporarily established between users, exchanging data at the same rate. The audio frequency response for typical subscribers is 300 Hz to 3400 Hz. Speech is coded with PCM, at a sampling frequency of 8 kHz; bandwidth is sharply limited to 3.4 kHz. Eight-bit quantization is used, and amplitude companding is used (such as μ-law) to improve dynamic range.

Before the 1960s, telephone companies used copper wires to convey analog communications between switching offices, one pair of wires per phone conversation. Bundles of wires, each with thousands of pairs each, ran through underground conduits. To increase capacity, Bell Laboratories turned to digital communications, and devised the T-carrier network. Illinois Bell installed the first T-carrier digital transmission system in 1962; today, most long-distance telephone carriers use a variety of T-carrier lines, using copper, optical fiber, microwave radio, and coaxial cables to convey digital audio, video and data.

T-1 serial digital communication circuits provide a dedicated point-to-point bandwidth of 1.544 Mbps; the signal they convey is called DS-1. Each end of a T-1 line terminates in a customer service unit (CSU), as shown in Fig. 10-10. The CSU interfaces data from the customer premises equipment (CPE) or a data service unit (DSU) and encodes it for transmission along the T-1; a multiplexer or local area network (LAN) bridge could be used. For example, long haul T-1 lines can connect a long distance provider's office in Miami with an office in Los Angeles; each office is known as a point of presence (POP). Each POP then communicates with local access networks, where the T1 line terminates with a CSU; the CSU then communicates via a DSX-1 signal that interfaces to data signals such as RS-449 or V.35. The user's view of T-1 comprises two conventional copper wire pairs, one for send, and one for receive, using an RJ-48C plug.

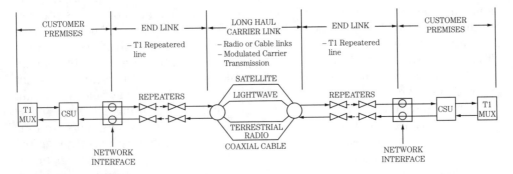

10-10 A T-1 circuit provides long-haul digital communication at a data rate of 1.544 Mbps; a CSU terminates each end of the line.

A T-1 circuit is capable of carrying compact disc data (1.41 Mbps) without data reduction, 24 voice channels, or a single video program with data reduction. A T-1 circuit is comprised of 24 subchannels (called DSOs or slots) each carrying 64 kbps (8 bits with 8-kHz sampling); everything from data to normal voice traffic runs through these subchannels. Data bytes are applied to frames, with one frame holding 24 DSOs plus one framing bit; thus a frame holds 193 bits (24 × 8 + 1); the frame rate of 8 kHz yields a 1.544-Mbps overall rate.

Many different applications, such as voice, data, or video, can share one T-1 line, with individual channels assigned to one or multiplexed DSOs, as needed. T-1 is full duplex (bidirectional) and the assignments need not be identical; a line might convey a few high-quality audio channels in one direction, with many voice channels in the other. In some cases a Fractional T-1 line can be used; only a few DSO slots are assigned, as needed. T-1 lines are very reliable, with a bit error rate (BER) of 10^{-9}. Using the digital access cross-connect system (DACS), individual DSOs can be sent to different destinations.

Other services include the T-0 (or DS-0) service. Operating at 64 kbps, a T-0 line can deliver one 56 kbps digitized voice channel, sampled at 4 kHz, with 7 bits, that is, one standard voice telephone call. Some video teleconferencing systems use six DS-0 slots (384 kbps). The T-1C service operates at 3.152 Mbps. The T-2 service operates at 6.312 Mbps; it is not offered commercially. The T-3 (or DS-3) service operates at 44.736 Mbps; it can deliver 28 T-1 channels or 672 voice channels, or one compressed television channel. The T-4 service operating at 274.760 Mbps delivers 168 T-1 channels or 4032 voice channels. The overall data rates have numerical differences from multiples of the basic 64 kbps; this is due to framing information that must be added. All DS levels use alternate mark inversion (AMI) channel coding; the signal has three levels: positive, negative, and ground reference. The T-1 through T-4 rates in Europe are: 2.048, 8.448, 34.368, and 565.000 Mbps, respectively.

ISDN

Integrated Services Digital Network (ISDN) is an advanced dial-up telephone service with full duplex operation. ISDN provides a digital connection between the consumer and the telephone exchange, and ultimately to long haul digital transmission systems. An overall rate of about 144 kbps is supported. Although ISDN uses existing telephone lines, specialized equipment is needed at the send and receive ends. Basic rate ISDN (sometimes called 2B + D) is intended for home use. It uses standard copper pair wire to provide two 64 kbps circuits (B or bearer channels) to send and receive audio or other information, and one 16 kbps (D or data channel) circuit for dialing and other signalling functions. Audio, video, fax, telephone or other data can be transmitted. Primary rate ISDN is offered to business customers. It exists as either coaxial cable or fiber cable; it can provide 23 (or more) 64 kbps channels, along with a 64 kbps D channel (23B + D), totalling 1.544 Mbps of bandwidth (equivalent to a T-1 line).

With regular switched telephone lines, communication can be briefly interrupted by concurrent signalling and call-directing data (for example, tones in the same bandwidth as the communication data); this is called in-band signalling. With ISDN, the bearer channels are independent of the signalling channel; this is called out-of-band signalling. The advantage is that the bearer channels are specifically designated for the user and are uninterrupted by any signalling data. Timecode information can be transmitted over ISDN using, for example, an RS-232 data channel. In addition, numerical data and compressed video signals are sent over ISDN, with speeds exceeding that of dial-up modems that must convert data for analog transmission through the subscriber loop.

Although simple telephones could be used in a basic voice-only ISDN hookup, to exchange audio data the user supplies an A/D and D/A converter, data reduction encoder/decoder (codec), and ISDN hook-up as shown in Fig. 10-11. Data between the user and the local telephone exchange is sent over copper wires; lines are terminated at a dedicated terminal adapter (TA) interface. The copper wire pair connecting to the user is called the user (U) interface and a network termination (NT-1) converts this to a four-wire ST interface. The outgoing data is converted to a telecommunications format where it is directed over a carrier to the receiving party, which must have corresponding ISDN service and equipment. Using an inverse multiplexer (I-MUX), multiple digital lines can be combined to create a higher data rate service. For example, a 384-kbps signal could be transmitted over six 64-kbps channels. The I-MUX resynchronizes the different lines (they might go through different long distance routing) to produce a coherent stream at the receiver. I-MUX devices are placed at the terminal adapter or the codec. Depending on the number of channels, and fidelity required, numerous data reduction methods can be used, as discussed in chapter 11. The coding delay in an ISDN system must be accounted for; for example, when recording an overdub from a remote location, the user might send the mix over ISDN and listen to a delayed mix over the monitors. The received (de-

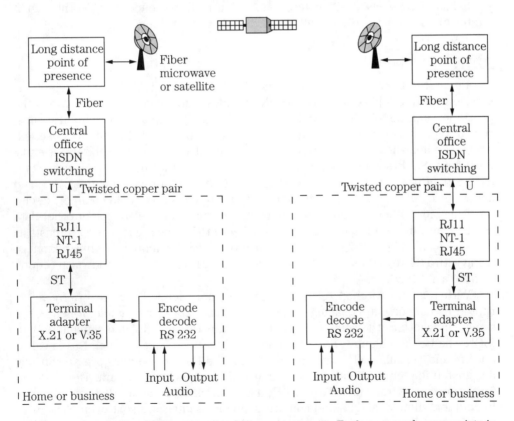

10-11 An example of an ISDN connection between two users. Each user needs appropriate interfacing equipment; the long-distance connection can be via fiber, microwave, or satellite.

layed) overdub part is then remixed and recorded. Later, the overdubbed part can be slipped back into synchronization with the mix.

Similar to ISDN, the Switched-56 dial-up service provides a bidirectional 56-kbps data channel; 56k DDS is a dedicated 56-kbps service, with long distance calls billed by the minute, at prices similar to those of regular long distance calls. Channel service units (CSU) are used to interface the user's application to a Switched-56 line; they can be purchased or leased. Units are required at both the send and receive ends of the line.

The EDNet system commercially provides multiple (2 to 12) channels of full duplex digital audio connection over reserved T-1 telephone lines. For example, an ED-NET connection might use Dolby AC-2 data reduction (discussed in chapter 11) at 256 kbps for dual mono, with timecode occupying a third channel. Alternatively, a monaural or stereo voice-over service can be provided over Switched 56 and ISDN lines using ISO/MPEG data reduction. In addition, video services are available. Timecode can be conveyed through the system, permitting synchronized overdubs.

Computer Networks

Arguably, the first network was installed by Samuel Morse, linking Washington DC to Baltimore with 35 miles of copper cable. His first transmitted telegraphic message on May 24, 1844 was: "What hath God wrought?" Today, thousands of networks interconnect millions of communications devices around the world and into outer space.

Whereas a dedicated digital audio link provides bandwidth that is sufficient to transmit a program in real time, a network is designed to interconnect multiple devices as networked nodes. For example, personal computers equipped with network interface cards, each with a unique address, can be nodes on a common network. Data is sent when a path is available, at the speed determined by the network interface. File exchange as well as random-access functions among workstations are both permitted. The task of conveying high-bandwidth data (one channel of 44.1 kHz, 16-bit samples requires 705.6 kbps) in real time (and over an extended time) without interruption requires special consideration in the network design. In addition, one workstation node can transmit multiple audio channels, or a video channel; bandwidth of 30 to 40 Mbps might be needed. It might be necessary to lock out lower priority transfers while a high priority time-sensitive transfer is in progress. A typical office LAN will not suffice. On the other hand, a multimedia network allows one major concession: data reduction. Perceptual coding of audio and video data can effectively multiply the bandwidth of the network.

A network must provide fast storing and loading of projects for editing and archiving, easily accessible directories, remote operation of system elements, background backup of files, communication among users, and multiple user access to one project as well as single user access to multiple projects. Networks can be configured in a variety of ways. Most commonly, a bus configuration places nodes along a serial bus, a ring configuration places nodes along a closed circuit, and a star configuration gives each node direct physical access to the central controller. A star configuration is preferred because a disabled node does not affect other node performance. A central concentrator unit is needed to monitor and direct bus traffic in a star configuration. When the maximum number of nodes are placed on a network, or the system's longest length is reached, it can be extended with a repeater, a device that receives signals, then resynchronizes and retransmits them. A bridge isolates network segments so that data is only transmitted across the bridge when its destination is another segment. A router is a computer with two network interfaces; it can pass data between different types of networks, for example, between AppleShare and Ethernet; moreover, it can optimize the routing for faster communication. A hybrid configuration is sometimes recommended; for example, in addition to a ring joining workstation nodes and a central storage area, nodes might be star-configured to central storage using SCSI. An example of local networks bridged to other local networks, also showing different network configurations, is shown in Fig. 10-12.

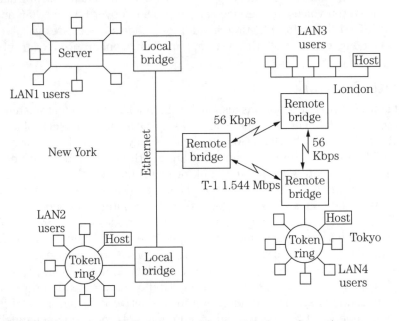

10-12 An example of star, ring, and bus network configurations, connected through long-distance bridging circuits.

Generally, it is the job of a network to break a message into data packets of uniform size and code them with a destination address and a header that describes where each packet fits within the message; the packets are transmitted, and received where they are assembled into the message. A packet that is corrupted with errors can be quickly retransmitted. Packet switching is extremely efficient at conveying bursty communication through a distributed computer environment. However, because the arrival speed of packets cannot be guaranteed, real-time transfer is not always possible. All networks must define rules for access to physical storage and terminal devices; this limits bandwidth of the network. Two common control methods are token passing, and collision detection. With token passing, when a node finishes a transmission, it sends a token (a bit pattern) to the next node; a node can transmit only when it has the token. Each token ring node has both an input and output, so that connections are passed from one node to another, forming a ring. The ARCnet, operating at 2.5 Mbps uses token passing. A Fiber Distributed Data Interface (FDDI) network configured in a ring and using token ring can achieve 100 Mbps; FDDI is defined in the ISO 9314 standard. With Carrier Sense Multiple Access with Collision Detection (CSMA/CD) transmission occurs on command, and if a collision occurs, priority is assigned, and data is retransmitted. Utilization (measuring successful transmission) of CSMA/CD networks decreases considerably with heavy use, as more collisions occur. A CSMA/CD protocol can achieve an overall efficiency of approximately 37%.

In client-server networks, most applications, data, and the network operating system, are centrally placed on a common file server. In peer-to-peer networks, data is kept locally under the control of individual workstations. For example, a user could access files, a CD-ROM drive, and a printer, all in different physical locations; any computer can act as the server. Because of the size of audio and multimedia files, emphasis on distributed storage is often most efficient, in which nodes act as peers, each serving as both client and server, each with local storage. A distributed network with modest bandwidth of 10–15 Mbps might be adequate for many applications; for example, this would allow transfer of audio data at a rate several times faster than real time. However, this cannot always be achieved when multiple users are on the network, particularly when relatively slow SCSI hard drive transfer rates limit data transfer speed. In many applications, data reduction algorithms are used to reduce size of files, speeding up communications.

A wide-area network (WAN) connects multiple stations beyond a single building, reaching up to global distances. For example, a WAN network can use an ISDN interconnection. A local-area network (LAN) distributes data through an office, building or campus. A LAN can use FDDI, CDDI, or ATM protocols.

Ethernet is a computer network used to connect personal computers, printers, disk drives, and other equipment over coaxial cable, twisted pair, and optical fiber. It uses collision detection with a typical bandwidth of 10 Mbps. AppleShare is a slower (2 Mbps) protocol. Neither are suitable for digital audio networking, but could be used to distribute control and command information between devices.

An FDDI installation uses duplex (two conductor) optical fiber cables to permit 2 kilometer runs between nodes, and up to 200 kilometers on a single ring. It uses a token ring arbitration method. The FDDI standard specifies bandwidth of 100 Mbps. FDDI uses a Token Ring protocol. Copper Distributed Data Interface (CDDI) is a copper implementation of FDDI, offering 100 Mbps performance on Class 5 twisted pair cable. It is more economical than FDDI, but does not provide the immunity to RF and magnetic interference afforded by optical fiber, and it is limited to 50–100-meter runs between nodes. CDDI and FDDI can be freely mixed using converters. Fiber-optic technology is discussed in more detail in chapter 8.

Generally, unshielded, twisted pair cable (similar to that used in telephony) is classified in five levels: Level 1 (voice), Level 2 (RS-232 low-speed data), Level 3 (10 Mbps Ethernet), Level 4 (16 Mbps Token Ring), and Level 5 (100 Mbps high-speed). For example, a 10Base-T network implementation requires Level 3 unshielded twisted pair cable. It is used in a star configuration with a multiport hub; it can be terminated with RJ-45 modular plugs. Daisy-chained Ethernet cabling is specified as 10Base2 (thin coaxial), or RG58 coaxial cable; it is limited to 185 meter segments. It is fitted with 50-Ω BNC plugs and attached to each node with a BNC T adapter. 10Base5 (thicker coaxial), also known as RG8 or RG11 cable, is used in Ethernet backbones; it is limited to 500-meter segments.

ATM

Asynchronous Transfer Mode (ATM) is a high-bandwidth network standard using low-delay switching, variable bandwidth, and multiplexing to provide flexible and efficient communications. Audio, video and data can be simultaneously delivered at a rate of 1 Gbps, or more; it is used primarily in wide area networking and local area network backbones, with many users. Traditional networks pool many channels of information, with each receiver picking its information from the stream; considerable routing data is needed, and this increases overhead. The ATM architecture uses switching and multiplexing to form a temporary dedicated, virtual channel within the transmission path bandwidth; the virtual channel is allocated a sufficient data rate, providing bandwidth on demand. Data packets, called cells, carry the name of the channel with much less routing data required. In addition, many ATM users can share a channel through multiplexing, yet maintain a fixed-time relationship between data cells. In this way, slower moving data can be efficiently combined with fast data, with every time slot of the channel packed with data. In particular, this helps ensure continuous data flow, an important criterion for real-time audio and video transfers.

Some implemented ATM channels provide transmission rates of 155, or 620 Mbps, or 2.4 Gbps along copper or fiber cables; however, data is transmitted at variable data rates, using only the rate needed at that moment. Billing is based, for example, on the number of cells transmitted. Moreover the data flow can be asymmetric; for example, a remote user can query a database with little data, but receive considerable data in return.

Specifically, ATM transmits data in fixed length data fields; it uses 53-byte (8-bit) cells each composed of 48 bytes of user (payload) data, a 5-byte routing and control header, and an 8-bit error correction header. ATM switchers can thus route cells efficiently to proper destinations where they are assembled into useful information. In addition, packets are sequentially delivered along the virtual channel. Corrupted data cells are detected by the receiver, which requests a retransmission of cells. ATM data protocol is based on the Open Systems Interconnection (OSI) model that specifies the physical medium and links.

Each ATM header is composed of six data fields. The Generic Flow Control (GFC) controls usage between several terminals using the same access connection. The Virtual Path Identifier (VPI) designates the path, or bundle of individual channels connecting two points in an ATM network. The virtual channel identifier (VCI) is a number allocated to every connection on the ATM during the call. The Payload Type (PT) defines maintenance cells, congestion conditions and other types of cells. The Cell Loss Priority (CLP) assigns a priority rating to a cell, designating which cells can be discarded if necessary. The Header Error Check (HEC) is a checksum used to detect errors in the 5-byte header.

MediaNet

The MediaNet is an example of a dedicated high speed multimedia LAN network; it allows multiple users to simultaneously access materials on central disk drives. MediaNet is implemented on CDDI and FDDI protocols, and supports the Apple Filing Protocol, Networked File System, and ATM. Using CDDI, the network can simultaneously handle multiple channels of compressed audio and video, with throughputs of 24 Mbps from node to node. With ATM, transfer rates of 120 Mbps can be achieved. Computers can be interfaced either as servers or clients; both have SCSI controllers and ports for connection to hard disk drives. Disk drives are local in node Macintosh computers; however, any node can access data on any other node hard drive in the same way that one would access a printer or other network device. Token ring is used for data traffic control. Using such networks, multimedia data can be directly manipulated remotely without copying files from place to place. MediaNet was developed by Sonic Solutions.

Sound System Control

Specialized audio networks are designed to connect and integrate computers and audio equipment. A primary application is sound system control; for example, a computer networked to equalizers and power amplifiers via a LAN might transmit a command over the network, instructing a particular amplifier to increase its volume by 3 dB. Such control/monitoring networks can use data rates of 50–100 kbps. In addition, such systems might transmit MIDI data. The AES-24ID standard describes the format and interpretation of data packets for communication.

OMF Interchange

In a perfect world, audio and video projects produced on workstations from different manufacturers could be interchanged between platforms with complete compatibility. That kind of common cross-platform interchange language is the goal of the Open Media Framework (OMF) interchange. OMF is a set of file format standards for audio, text, still graphics, images, animation, and video files. In addition, it defines editing, mixing and processing notation so that both content and description of edited audio and video programs can be interchanged. The format also contains information identifying the sources of the media as well as sampling and timecode information, and accommodates both compressed and uncompressed files. Files can be created in one format, interchanged to another platform for editing and signal processing, then returned to the original format without loss of information. In other words, an OMF file contains all the information needed to create, edit, and play digital media presentations. In most cases, files in a native format are converted to the OMF format, interchanged via direct transmission or removable physical medium, then converted to the new native format. However, to help streamline operation, OMF is structured to facilitate playback directly from an interchanged file when the playback platform has similar characteristics as the source platform. To efficiently operate with large files, OMF is able to identify and extract specific objects of information such as media source information, without reading the entire file. In addition, a file can be incrementally changed without requiring a complete recalculation and rewriting of the entire file.

OMF uses two basic types of information. "Compositions" are descriptions of all the data required to play or edit a presentation; compositions do not contain media data, but point to them and provide coordinated operation using methods such as timecode-based edit decision lists, source/destination labels, and crossfade times. "Physical sources" contain the actual media data such as audio and video, as well as identification of the sources used in the composition. Data structures called media objects (or mobs) are used to identify compositions and sources. An OMF file contains objects, information that other data can reference; for example, a composition mob is an object that contains information describing the composition; an object's data is called its values. An application programmer interface (API) is used to access object values and translate proprietary file formats into OMF-compatible files.

OMF allows file transfer via removable disk exchange and transmission on a fiber network. Common file formats included in the OMF format are: TIFF (including RGB, JPEG and YCC) for video and graphics, and AIFC and RIFF WAVE for audio. Clearly, a common transmission method must be used to link stations; for example, Ethernet, FDDI or ATM could be used. OMF can also be used in a client-server system that allows multi-user real-time access from the server to the client. OMF was developed by Avid Corporation.

Satellite Transmission

Increasingly, much information, whether it is electronic mail or recorded music, comes to us as transmitted data, to be used in real time or placed in private storage. Direct broadcast satellite, cable, and interactive systems are examples of new transmission media. However, traditional analog frequency modulation methods are not suitable to convey such data; thus digitally modulated transmission techniques are used. Moreover, a number of different communications links are required to form the entire transmission chain. Satellite broadcasting is discussed in detail in chapter 13.

The Internet

The Internet is a global collection of interconnected networks that permits transmission of diverse data in any mixture. A network is a collection of computers sharing resources between them; the Internet is a network of networks. The advantage of inter-networking is clear—the more systems on line, the greater the resources available to any single user.

The Internet was born in 1969 when the Advanced Research Projects Agency (ARPA) of the Department of Defense created ARPANET by linking four computers in California and Utah with packet-switching lines. The experiment was a success and in 1984 the MILnet was partitioned off for military use. In 1987, seeking a way to link five supercomputers as well as regional networks, the National Science Foundation founded the NSFNET; in 1990 the NSF decommissioned the ARPANET and greatly expanded its own network; today, the NSFNET is the high-speed "backbone" of the U.S. portion of the Internet. Globally, the Internet is the biggest computer network in the world.

**Table 10-2. The Department of Defense defined
the protocols used in the Internet; these are defined
in military specifications and RFC documents.**

File transfer	Electronic mail	Terminal emulation	Network management
File transfer protocol (FTP) MIL-STD-1780 RFC 959	Simple mail transfer protocol (SMTP) MIL-STD-1781 RFC 821	TELNET Protocol MIL-STD-1782 RFC 854	Simple network management protocol (SNMP) RFC 1098
Transmission control protocol (TCP) MIL-STD-1778 RFC 793		User datagram protocol (UDP) RFC 768	
Address resolution ARP RFC 826 RARP RFC 903	Internet protocol (IP) MIL-STD-1777 RFC 791	Internet control message protocol (ICMP) RFC 792	
Network interface cards: Ethernet, StarLAN, Token ring, ARCNET RFC 894, RFC 1042, RFC 1051			
Transmission media: Twisted pair, coax, or fiber optics			

The Internet operates on protocols defined by the Department of Defense; they are provided in Request for Comments (RFC) documents published by the Defense Data Network Information Center. Some of the basic specifications and documents that define implementation of the Internet are shown in Table 10-2. The communication and message routing standard that forges the links to form the Internet is a set of documents called the Transmission Control Protocol/Internet Protocol (TCP/IP). Using these protocols, networks can share information resources, thus forming the Internet. For example, the NSFNET ties together regional domestic nets such as WESTnet, SURAnet, and NEARnet, as well as wide area nets such as BITNET, FIDOnet, and USENET that provide foreign links to other nets. The result is a complicated global map of computer systems using links with data rates ranging from 56 kbps to 2.4 Gbps.

The Internet is a packet switched network. A user sends information to a local network, which is controlled by a central server computer. At the server, the Transmission Control Protocol packages the information into smaller pieces, and puts each of them in a packet according to the Internet Protocol, with the proper address on each packet. The network sends the packets to a router computer that reads the address, and sends the packets out over data lines to other routers, each determining the best path to the address. Each packet can travel a different route. This helps spread loads across the network and reduces average travel time; however, real-time transmission is difficult because packets can be delivered out of order, multiple times, or dropped altogether. When the packets arrive at the destination address, the information is assembled and acted upon; for example, a database file server might retrieve a color picture, and send it to the source of the request, using its return address.

To help illustrate the structure used to route data, the Internet Protocol (IP) header is shown in Table 10-3. This header is contained in an IP datagram, contained in every information field conveyed along the Internet, and is based on a 32-bit word. The Version specifies the current IP software used; the Internet Header Length (IHL) specifies the length of the header; Type of Service flags indicate reliability and other parameters; Total Length gives length of datagram; Identifier identifies the datagram; Flags specify if fragmentation is permitted; fragment offset specifies where a fragment is placed; Time to Live measures gateway hops; Protocol identifies the next protocol such as TCP following the IP; the Checksum can be used for error detection; Source Address identifies originating host; Destination Address identifies destination host; Options can contain a route specification and padding completes the 32-bit byte; the Data field contains the TCP header and user data, with a maximum total of 65,535 8-bit octets in the datagram.

**Table 10-3. The Internet
Protocol (IP) header field contains 32-bit
bytes to identify and route IP datagrams over the Internet.**

Version 4	IHL 4	Type of service 8	Total length 15	
Identifier 16			Flags 3	Fragment offset 13
Time to live 8		Protocol 8	Header checksum 16	
Source address 32				
Destination address 32				
Options and padding 32				
User data multiple of 8, less than 65,535 octets				

Packet networks such as the Internet operate on a first-come, first-serve basis thus throughput rate is unpredictable. There is no bandwidth reservation; the Internet cannot guarantee a percentage of the network throughput to the sender. The number of packets delivered per second is continuously variable; buffers at the receiver can smooth discontinuities due to bursty delivery, but add delay time to the throughput. Finally, traditional packet networks such as the Internet operate point to point; a message addressed to multiple receivers must be sent multiple times; this greatly increases bandwidth requirements for multicasting.

In the same way that the post office does not need a special truck to send a letter from one address to another, but rather routes it through an existing infrastructure, the Internet sends information over its infrastructure according to standardized addresses. For example, a user at UC Berkeley sending a message to Dartmouth would log onto the University of California Berkeley campus network, and a router may direct it to BARRNet, the Bay Area Regional Research Network, which may route it to the NSFnet backbone, which may route it to NEARnet, the New England Academic and Research Network, which may route it to the Dartmouth campus network, and to the individual account.

Each Internet address is governed by the Domain System Structure, a method that uniquely identifies host computers and individual users. When the Internet was first created, six high-level domains were created to distinguish between types of users: com (commercial), edu (education), gov (government), mil (military), org (other), and net (network). Many other domains have since been created; for example, fr designates France.

Access to the Internet requires a computer, a communications link such as LAN connection or a modem, and a gateway. Historically, universities, corporations and governments have provided Internet access to their students and employees via in-house computer systems. More recently, the Internet has been made available through networks such as CompuServe and America Online, as well as e-mail providers such as AT&T Mail; users use dial-up modems, which convert data into modulated sound signals for transmission over voice telephone lines. Modem speeds generally range from 1200 bps to 57,600 bps, with rates over 9600 accomplished with data compression.

Like the true electronic organism it is, the Internet thrives on complexity, and tends toward greater complexity as it evolves. Very generally, the Internet has three applications: e-mail, news groups, and file transfer. The ability to send electronic mail has changed the way people work and play, and saves time and money. Using e-mail is quite easy. For example, you might log onto the Internet, type "mail" and "send" and enter the address "president@whitehouse.gov". It is possible to convert addresses between different e-mail service providers. For example, a CompuServe address might read: 12345,123; its Internet equivalent would be 12345.123@compuserve.com. There is no comprehensive address book of Internet users. To locate an individual, you might try the "finger" command to find out who's using the Internet on a particular system.

Access to news groups is an interesting Internet feature. News groups are the running bulletin board collection of messages, soliloquy, and debate. Whatever your interest (or perversion) there's certain to be a news group for you. Many news groups are part of USENET, a worldwide, free collection of groups. USENET is not part of the Internet, and in fact predates the Internet; USENET is a set of rules for creating and passing along news groups. USENET has seven major categories of news: comp (computer science), news (news networks), rec (recreational activities and hobbies), sci (scientific disciplines), soc (social issues), talk (debate forums) and misc (everything else). In addition to these, there are many other news groups. News groups consist of postings and are not engaged in real time. Commands can be used to subscribe to certain groups. To avoid wasting bandwidth, a new subscriber should read the group's Frequently Asked Questions (FAQ) file to avoid asking redundant questions.

If you prefer real-time interactivity, you can directly "talk" to another user in real time, from one network to another, on a one-to-one basis, or you can "chat" with multiple people at multiple sites. The Internet Relay Chat (IRC) contains a number of chat channels, each with a directed topic. You can talk and listen to multiple channels at once. Some systems provide high quality multimedia transmission over long haul packet networks for video conferencing and other applications. Users can initiate a real-time video conference with another dedicated site; these systems use bandwidth reservation and multicasting over T-1 circuits using, for example, the ST-II Internet stream protocol. Because of heavy network demands, multiple T-1, or a T-3 link may be used.

Remote login is one of the Internet's greatest assets. The web of networks on the Internet contains thousands of databases and services, many of them accessible through the Internet; they contain vast quantities of data, pictures, sound files, and software programs. Access begins with telnet, a remote login application that lets users access another computer system's database, connecting interactively at the remote computer. For example, if you wanted to read Hamlet from the Shakespeare database at Dartmouth, you would type: "telnet lib.dartmouth.edu" and enter "select file" and "shakespeare plays" and "Hamlet."

The File Transfer Protocol (FTP) is used to move files from one computer to another. For example, to download MS-DOS games from the f.ms.uky.edu site, type in "ftp f.ms.uky.edu" and use ftp commands such as "dir" (directory) and "cd" (change directory) to browse the archive. Because this is a public archive, login as an "anonymous" user; some sites are privileged, and require a password for clearance. Other interesting ftp sites include vmd.cso.uiuc.edu (satellite pictures of North America updated hourly), oak.oakland.edu and wuarchive.wustl.edu (software database), ames.arc.nasa.gov (space photos), and mrcnext.cso.uiuc.edu (Project Gutenberg's texts of many books).

Some ftp files are in binary form, others are in ASCII, some are compressed, others are not, and so on. Fortunately, many utility programs (such as compress, zmodem, tar, and zip) are available from ftp sites to help untangle files. Numerous file sites contain libraries of music selections, often encoded with MPEG data reduction to diminish file size; a four-minute program might occupy 5 Mbytes; it can be decoded with XING software on the PC. Any computer needs appropriate hardware and software to utilize sound files, games, and so on. A word of warning: check any downloaded files for viruses.

Several good navigating tools have been developed. Archie is a system used to search indexes of files of public servers on the Internet; Archie indexes over 1200 servers, with more than 2 million files. To use Archie, you must log onto an Archie server; for most efficient use of the Internet, find one geographically closest to you. For example, the Archie for the southeastern U.S. is archie.sura.net. One way to contact Archie is through Telnet; for example, type in "telnet archie.sura.net" and login "archie." Archie commands can be used to search for filenames or key words, and the system responds with the name of an ftp site. Although less convenient, information can also be requested from Archie via e-mail.

Gopher is a menu-based service that lets you search for Internet resources and Wide Area Information Servers (WAIS) lets you search indexed material using key words or phrases. The World Wide Web (WWW) is a collection of menu-based Internet nodes using hypertext links; WWW uses HyperText Markup Language (HTML) scripting to create multimedia documents. Using hypertext, users can easily move from one computer site to another in search of desired information. A wide variety of multimedia presentations are available for browsing or downloading from the Web. Mosaic and Netscape are Web interfaces used to send and receive multimedia (text, image and audio) programs over the Internet. Many people feel that the Web is the future of the Internet. A wide bandwidth backbone connection is needed for efficient multimedia access; protocols such as Serial Line Internet Protocol (SLIP), Point-to-Point Protocol (PPP), or The Internet Adapter (TIA) provide this to varying degrees. Newly available are "user agents"—programs that automatically and continuously roam the Internet looking for requested information, and periodically report their findings back to the human user.

Science fiction writers have always wondered what would happen if gigantic computer systems took over the world. The Internet is answering their question.

11

Perceptual Coding

Edison cylinders, like all analog formats, store acoustical waveforms with a mimicking pattern—an analog—of the original waveform. Digital media such as the compact disc do essentially the same thing, but replace the continuous mechanical pattern with a discrete series of numbers that represent the waveform's sampled amplitude. In both cases, the goal is to reconstruct a waveform that is physically identical to the original within the audio band. With perceptual coding, physical identity is waived in favor of perceived identity. Using a psychoacoustical model of the human auditory system, the coder calculates where losses can be tolerated. This reduces the quantity of data needed to code an audio signal.

In the view of many observers, compared to new perceptual coding methods, PCM is a powerful but inefficient dinosaur. Because of its gargantuan appetite for bits, PCM coding is limited in its usefulness. The desire to achieve lower bit rates through perceptual coding is intense because it opens new applications for digital audio (and video) with acceptable signal degradation. Through psychoacoustics, we can understand how much information is perceived by the ear. A perceptual coding system strives to deliver all of this information, but no more.

Data Compression

A newspaper with the headline: "Dog Bites Man" might not sell many copies. However, the headline "Man Bites Dog" might elicit considerable response. The former is commonplace, but the latter rarely happens; from an information standpoint, "Dog Bites Man" contains little information, but "Man Bites Dog" contains a large quantity of information. Generally, the lower the probability of occurrence of an event, the greater the information it contains. Looked at in another way, large amounts of information rarely occur. The average amount of information occurring over time is called entropy, denoted as H. When each event has the same probability of occurrence, entropy is maximum, and notated as H_{max}; usually, entropy is less than this maximum value. Most functions can be viewed in terms of their entropy; for example, the active commodities market has high entropy whereas CDs (certificates of deposit) have much lower entropy. Redundancy in a signal is obtained by subtracting from 1 the ratio of actual entropy to maximum entropy: $1 - (H/H_{max})$. Adding redundancy increases the data rate; decreasing redundancy decreases the rate; this is data compression, or lossless coding. An ideal compression system removes redundancy, leaving entropy unaffected; entropy determines the average number of bits needed to convey a digital signal.

An audio signal contains information; a rare audio sample contains considerable information; a frequently occurring sample has much less. The former is hard to predict, the latter is readily predictable. Similarly, a tonal (sinusoidal) sound has considerable redundancy, but a nontonal (noiselike) signal has little redundancy. For example, Fig. 11-1 shows a rather periodic violin tone, and an aperiodic cymbal crash. Further, the probability of a certain sample occurring depends on its neighboring samples; generally, a sample is likely to be close in value to the previous sample. For example, this is true of a low frequency signal. A predictive coder uses previous sample values to predict the current value; the error in the prediction (dif-

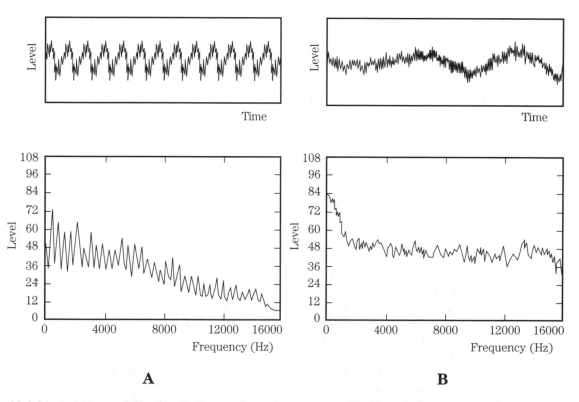

11-1 Musical tones can show periodicity or not; this can be examined in both the time domain and by the tone's spectral content in the frequency domain. A. This violin tone is periodic and shows distinct harmonic content. B. This cymbal crash is aperiodic and has an inharmonic content.

ference between the actual and predicted values) is transmitted. The decoder forms the same predicted value and adds the error value to form the correct value. Reduction can be achieved by quantizing the error signal.

The ear only perceives a portion of the information in an audio signal; this could be called the perceptual entropy. Small entropy signals can be efficiently compressed; large entropy signals cannot. For this reason, a compression coder can output a variable bit rate that is low when information is poor, and high when information is rich. The output is variable because although the sampling rate of the signal is constant, the entropy in its waveform certainly is not.

Entropy Coding

Entropy (or Huffman) coding devised by David Huffman uses probability of occurrence to code a message. For example, a signal can be analyzed and samples that occur the most often are assigned the shortest codewords; samples that occur less frequently are assigned longer codewords. The decoder contains these assignments and reverses the process. The compression is lossless because no information is lost; the process is completely reversible.

The Morse telegraph code is a simple entropy code. The most commonly used character (*e*) is assigned the shortest code (·), and less frequently used characters (such as *z*) are assigned longer codes (- - ··). In practice, telegraph operators further improved transmission efficiency by dropping characters during coding then replacing them during decoding. The information content remains unchanged. U CN RD THS SNTNCE, thanks to the fact that written English has low entropy thus its data is readily compressed. Many text and data storage systems use data compression techniques prior to storage on hard, floppy, or optical disk.

Generally, a Huffman code is a noiseless coding method that uses statistical techniques to represent a message with the shortest possible code length. It is an entropy code based on prefixes. To code the most frequent characters with the shortest code words, the code uses a nonduplicating prefix system so that shorter code words cannot form the beginning of a longer word. For example, 110 and 11011 cannot both be code words. The code can thus be uniquely decoded, without loss. Suppose we wish to transmit information about the arrival status of trains. Given four conditions, on-time, late, early, and train wreck, we could use a fixed 2-bit codeword, assigning 00, 01, 10, and 11 respectively. However, a Huffman code considers the frequency of occurrence of source words. We observe that the probability is 0.5 that the train is on-time, 0.35 that it is late, 0.125 that it is early, and 0.025 that it has wrecked. These probabilities are shown in Fig. 11-2 and used to create a tree structure, with each node the sum of its inputs. Moreover, each branch is assigned a 0 or 1 value; the choice is arbitrary but must be consistent. A unique Huffman code is derived by following the tree from the 1.0 probability branch, back to each source word. For example, the code for early arrival is 110. In this way, a Huffman code is created so that the most probable status is coded with the shortest code word and the least probable are coded with longer code words. We reduce the number of bits needed to indicate on-time arrival, even though we increase the number of bits needed for two other statuses. Also note that prefixes are not repeated in the code words.

Train status	Probability	Tree	Huffman code	Train status
On-time	0.5		0	On-time
Late	0.35		10	Late
Early	0.125		110	Early
Wrecked	0.025		111	Wrecked

11-2 A Huffman code is based on a nonduplicating prefix, assigning the shorter codewords to the more frequently occurring events. If trains were usually on-time, this code would be particularly efficient.

The success of the code is gauged by calculating its average code length; it is the summation of each code word length multiplied by its frequency of occurrence. In this example, the 1-bit word has a probability of 0.5, the 2-bit words have a probability of 0.35, and the 3-bit words have a combined probability of 0.15; thus the average code length is $1(0.5) + 2(0.35) + 3(0.15) = 1.65$ bits. This compares favorably with the 2-bit fixed code, and approaches the entropy of the message. A Huffman code is suited for some messages, but only when the frequency of occurrence is known beforehand. If the relative frequency of occurrence of the source words is approximately equal, the code is not efficient. If an infrequent source word's probability approaches 1 (becomes frequent), the code will generate coded messages longer than the original. (To overcome this, some coding systems use adaptive measures that modify the compression algorithm for more optimal operation.) The Huffman code is optimal when all symbols have a probability that is an integral power of ½.

Run-length coding also provides data compression, and is optimal for highly frequent samples. When a data value is repeated over time, it can be coded with a special code that indicates the start and stop of the string. For example, the message 6666 6666 might be coded as 86. This coding is efficient; run-length coding is used in fax machines, for example, and explains why blank sections of a page are transmitted more quickly than densely written sections. Although Huffman and run length codes are not directly efficient for music coding, they are used for compression within some perceptual algorithms.

In summary, data compression is lossless because the original source data can be restored exactly; it is said to be invertible, with average distortion of zero. Data compression algorithms require greater processing complexity with the attendant coding delay; generally compression ratios of 1.5:1 to 3.5:1 are possible, depending on the complexity of the data itself. Although data compression is used in some perceptual coders, other lossy methods are required for more significant results. In particular, irrelevant data also can be removed; this is data reduction. The original signal cannot be reconstructed exactly. A data reduction system reduces entropy; by modelling the perceptual entropy, only irrelevant information is removed, hence the reduction can be inaudible. Thus a perceptual coder must use psychoacoustics to identify irrelevant content in the audio signal.

Psychoacoustics

When you hear a plucked string, can you distinguish the fifth harmonic from the fundamental? How about the seventh harmonic? Can you tell the difference between a 1000- and a 1002-Hz tone? You are probably adept at detecting this 0.2% difference. Have you ever heard "low pitch" in which complex tones seem to have a slightly lower subjective pitch than pure tones of the same frequency? All of this and more is the domain of psychoacoustics, the study of human auditory perception, ranging from the biological design of the ear, to the brain's interpretation of aural information. Sound is only an academic concept without our perception of it. Psychoacoustics explains the subjective response to anything we hear. It is the ultimate arbitrator in acoustic concerns because it is only the response to sound that fundamentally matters. Psychoacoustics seeks to reconcile acoustic stimuli and all the scientific, objective, and physical properties that surround them, with the psychological responses evoked by them.

The ear and its associated nervous system is an enormously complex, interactive system. Over the past million years or so, the physiology of the human hearing system has evolved incredible powers of perception. At the same time, as with any complex system, it has its limitations. On one hand, the ear is astonishingly acute in its ability to detect nuance or defect in a signal; on the other hand, it is surprisingly casual with portions of the signal it deems irrelevant. The accuracy of a coded signal can be very low, but this accuracy is very frequency and time dependent.

The ear is a highly developed organ (the eye, for example, can only perceive frequencies over one octave), but the ear is useful only when coupled to the interpretative powers of the brain. Those mental judgments form the basis for everything we experience from sound and music. The left and right ears do not differ physiologically in their capacity for detecting sound, but their respective right and left brain halves do. The two halves loosely divide the brain's functions. There is some overlap, but the primary connections from the ears to the brain halves are crossed; the right ear is wired to the left brain half and the left ear to the right brain half. The left cerebral hemisphere processes most of the speech (verbal) information. Thus, theoretically the right ear is perceptually superior for spoken words. On the other hand, it is mainly the right temporal lobe that processes melodic (nonverbal) information. Therefore, we are better at perceiving melodies heard by the left ear.

The ear's response to frequency is logarithmic; this can be demonstrated through its perception of musical intervals. For example, the interval between 100 and 200 Hz is perceived as an octave, as is the interval between 1000 and 2000 Hz. In linear terms, the second octave is much larger, yet the ear hears it as the same interval. For this reason, musical notation uses a logarithmic measuring scale. Each four and one-half spaces or lines on the musical staff represent an octave, which might be only a few tens of hertz apart, or a few thousands, depending on the clef and ledger lines used.

Frequency is a literal measurement. Pitch is not. It is a subjective, complex characteristic based on frequency, as well as other physical quantities such as waveform and intensity. For example, if a 200-Hz sinewave is sounded at a soft then louder level, most listeners will agree that the louder sound has a lower pitch. In fact, a 10% increase in frequency might be necessary to maintain a listener's subjective evaluation of constant pitch at low frequencies. On the other hand, in the ear's most sensitive region, 1 to 5 kHz, there is almost no change in pitch with loudness. Also, with musical tones, the effect is much less.

Beat frequencies occur when two nearly equal frequencies are sounded together. When the difference in frequency between tones is itself an audible frequency, a difference tone can be heard. The effect is especially audible when the frequencies are high, the tones fairly loud, and separated by not much more than a fifth. Although debatable, some listeners claim to hear sum tones. An intertone also can occur, especially below 200 Hz where the ear's ability to discriminate between simultaneous tones diminishes. For example, simultaneous tones of 65 and 98 Hz will be heard not as a perfect fifth, but as an 82-Hz tone. On the other hand, when tones below 500 Hz are heard one after the other, the ear can differentiate between pitches only 2 Hz apart.

The ear can accommodate a very wide dynamic range; the threshold of feeling at 120 dB SPL has a sound intensity 1,000,000,000,000 times that of the threshold of hearing at 0 dB SPL. For convenience of expression, it is clear why the logarithmic decibel is used when dealing with that extreme range. Although the dynamic range is vast, the ear's sensitivity is frequency dependent. Maximum sensitivity occurs at 1 to 5 kHz, with relative insensitivity at low and high frequencies. Through testing, equal-loudness contours such as the Robinson-Dadson curves have been derived, as shown in Fig. 11-3. Each contour describes a range of frequencies that are perceived to be equally loud. The lowest contour describes the minimum audible field, the minimum sound pressure level across the audible frequency band that a person with normal hearing can perceive. For example, a barely audible 30-Hz tone would be 60 dB louder than a barely audible 4-kHz tone. The response varies with respect to loudness; the louder the sounds, the flatter the response. The contours are rated in phons, measuring the SPL of a contour at 1 kHz.

All characteristics of sound except one can be perceived by one ear; localization can only be accomplished with two ears. When sound originates from the side, the ear-brain uses cues such as intensity differences, waveform complexity and time delays to determine the direction of origin. When equal sound is produced from two loudspeakers, instead of localizing sound from the left and right sources, the ear-brain interprets sound coming from the empty space between the sources. Because each ear receives the same information, the sound is stubbornly decoded as coming from straight ahead. Similarly, stereo is nothing more than two different monaural channels. The rest is simply illusion.

There is probably no limit to the complexity of psychoacoustics. For example, consider the musical tones in Fig. 11-4A. A major scale is played through headphones to the right and left ears. Most listeners hear the pattern in Figure 11-4B, where the sequence of pitches is correct, but heard as two different melodies in contrary motion. The high tones appear to come from the right ear, and the lower tones from the left. When the headphones are reversed, the headphone formerly playing low tones now appears to play high tones, and vice versa. Other listeners might hear low tones to the right and high tones to the left, no matter which way the headphones are placed. Curiously, right-handed persons tend to hear high tones on the right and lows on the left; not so with lefties. Still other listeners might perceive only high tones and little or nothing of the low tones. In this case, most right handers perceive all the tones, but only half the lefties do so.

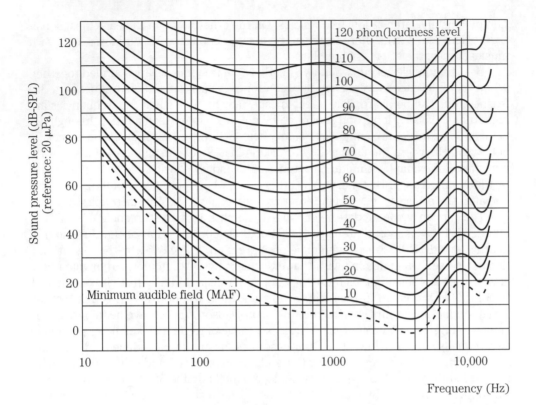

Frequency (Hz)

11-3 The Robinson-Dadson equal-loudness contours show that the ear is nonlinear with respect to frequency, and loudness. These contours are based on psychoacoustic studies, using sine tones.

Traditionally, audio recording systems have used objective parameters as their design goals—flat response, minimal noise, and so on. Perceptual coders recognize that the final receiver is the human auditory system. Following the lead of psychoacoustics, they use the ear's own performance as the design criterion. After all, any musical experience—whether created, conveyed and reproduced via analog or digital means—is purely subjective.

Physiology of the Human Ear and Critical Bands

The ear performs the transformation from acoustic energy to mechanical energy and ultimately to the electrical impulses sent to the brain, where information contained in sound is perceived. Figure 11-5 offers a simplified look at the ear's physiological design. The outer ear collects sound, and its intricate folds help us to assess directionality. The ear canal resonates at about 3 kHz, providing extra sensitivity in the frequencies critical for speech intelligibility. The eardrum transduces acoustical energy into mechanical energy; it reaches maximum excursion at about 120 dB SPL,

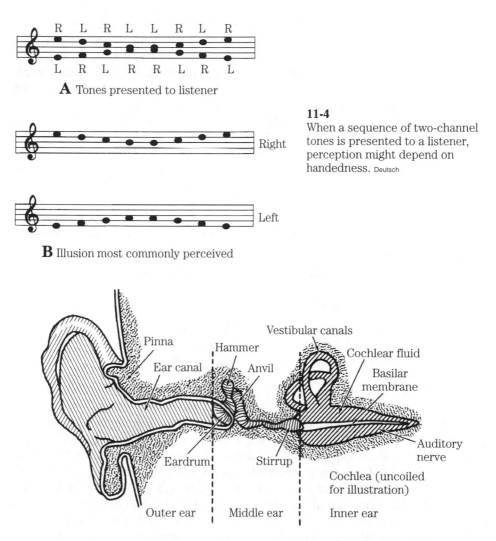

A Tones presented to listener

11-4
When a sequence of two-channel tones is presented to a listener, perception might depend on handedness. Deutsch

Right

Left

B Illusion most commonly perceived

11-5 A simplified look at the design and construction of the human ear. The coiled cochlea and basilar membrane are straightened for clarity of illustration.

above which it begins to distort the waveform. The three bones in the middle ear, the hammer, anvil, and stirrup (the three smallest bones in the body) provide impedance matching to efficiently convey sounds in air to the fluid-filled inner ear. The vestibular canals do not affect hearing, but instead are part of a motion detection system providing a sense of balance. The coiled basilar membrane detects the amplitude and frequency of sound; those vibrations are converted to electrical impulses and sent to the brain as neural information along a bundle of nerve fibers. The brain decodes the period of the stimulus and point of maximum stimulation along the basilar membrane to determine frequency; activity in local regions surrounding the stimulus is ignored.

Examination of the basilar membrane shows that the ear contains roughly 30,000 hair cells arranged in multiple rows along the basilar membrane, roughly 32 mm long; this is the Organ of Corti. The cells detect local vibrations of the basilar membrane and convey audio information to the brain via electrical impulses. Frequency discrimination dictates that at low frequencies, tones a few hertz apart can be distinguished; however, at high frequencies tones must differ by hundreds of hertz. In any case, hair cells respond to the strongest stimulation in their local region; this is called a critical band, a concept introduced by Harvey Fletcher. Experiments show that critical bands are much narrower at low frequencies than at high frequencies; three-fourths of the critical bands are below 5 kHz; the ear receives more information from low frequencies and less from high frequencies. Critical bands are approximately 100 Hz wide for frequencies from 20 to 400 Hz and approximately ⅙ octave in width for frequencies from 1 to 7 kHz. Alternatively, bands can be assumed to be ⅓ octave for frequencies from 300 Hz to 20 kHz; an error of less than 1.5 dB will occur. Still other research shows that critical bands can be approximated with the equation:

$$Critical\ bandwidth\ in\ hertz = 24.7(4.37F + 1)$$

where

F is the center frequency in kHz.

Eberhard Zwicker modelled the ear with 24 arbitrary critical bands for frequencies below 15 kHz; a 25th band occupies the region from 15 to 20 kHz. An example of critical bands is listed in Table 11-1. Physiologically, each critical band occupies a length of about 1.3 mm, with 1300 primary hair cells. The critical band for a 1-kHz sine tone is about 160 Hz in width; thus a noise or error signal that is 160 Hz wide and centered at 1 kHz is audible only if it is greater than the same level of a 1-kHz sine tone. As another example, the loudness of a band of noise at a constant SPL remains constant as the bandwidth increases; however, when the critical bandwidth is exceeded, loudness increases. Critical bands are analogous to a spectrum analyzer with variable center frequencies. Importantly, critical bands are not fixed; they are continuously variable in frequency and any audible tone will create a critical band centered on it. The critical band concept is an empirical phenomenon. Looked at in another way, a critical band is the bandwidth at which subjective responses abruptly change.

Interestingly, critical bands have been used to explain consonance and dissonance. Tone intervals with a frequency difference greater than a critical band are generally more consonant; intervals less than a critical band tend to be dissonant with intervals of about 0.2 critical band being most dissonant. Dissonance tends to increase at low frequencies; for example, musicians tend to avoid thirds at low frequencies.

The bark (named after German physicist Georg Heinrich Barkhausen) is a unit of perceptual frequency; specifically, a bark measures the critical band rate; a critical band has a width of one bark; ¹⁄₁₀₀ of a bark equals 1 mel. The bark scale relates absolute frequency (in hertz) to perceptually measured frequencies such as pitch or critical bands (in bark). Using bark, the physical spectrum can be converted to a psychological spectrum. In this way, a pure tone (a single spectrum line) can be represented as a psychological masking curve.

The pitch place theory further explains the action of the basilar membrane; carried by the surrounding fluid, a sound wave travels the length of the membrane, and

Table 11-1. An example of critical bands in the human hearing range showing increase in bandwidth with absolute frequency. A critical band will arise at an audible sound at any frequency.

Critical band number (Bark)	Center frequency (Hz)	Critical band (Hz)	Lower cutoff frequency (Hz)	Upper cutoff frequency (Hz)
1	50	–	–	100
2	150	100	100	200
3	250	100	200	300
4	350	100	300	400
5	450	110	400	510
6	570	120	510	630
7	700	140	630	770
8	840	150	770	920
9	1000	160	920	1080
10	1170	190	1080	1270
11	1370	210	1270	1480
12	1600	240	1480	1720
13	1850	280	1720	2000
14	2150	320	2000	2320
15	2500	380	2320	2700
16	2900	450	2700	3150
17	3400	550	3150	3700
18	4000	700	3700	4400
19	4800	900	4400	5300
20	5800	1100	5300	6400
21	7000	1300	6400	7700
22	8500	1800	7700	9500
23	10,500	2500	9500	12,000
24	13,500	3500	12,000	15,500
25	18,775	6550	15,500	22,050

Tobias

the wave stops at particular places along the length of the membrane, where the greatest vibration of the membrane occurs, corresponding to different frequencies. Specifically, high frequencies are sensed at the membrane near the middle ear while low frequencies are sensed at the far end. The wave excited by a high-frequency sound does not reach the far end of the basilar membrane. However, a low-frequency sound will pass through all the high frequency places to reach the far end. Because hair cells tend to vibrate at the frequency of the strongest stimulation, they will convey that frequency in a critical band, ignoring lesser stimulation. This excitation curve is described by the cochlear spreading function, an asymmetrical contour. This explains, for example, why broadband measurements cannot describe threshold phenomena, which are based on local frequency conditions. There are about 620 degrees of differentiable frequencies equally distributed along the basilar membrane; thus a resolution of $\frac{1}{25}$ Bark is reasonable. Summarizing, critical bands are important in perceptual coding because they show that the ear discriminates between energy in the band, and energy outside the band; in particular, this promotes masking.

Threshold of Hearing, and Masking

Two fundamental phenomena that govern human hearing are the minimum hearing threshold, and masking, as shown in Fig. 11-6. The threshold of hearing curve describes the minimum level (0 sone) at which the ear can detect a tone at a given frequency. The threshold is referenced to 0 dB at 1 kHz. The ear is most sensitive around 1 to 5 kHz, where we can hear signals several decibels below the 0-dB reference. Generally, two tones of equal power and different frequency will not sound equally loud. Similarly, the audibility of noise and distortion varies according to frequency. Sensitivity decreases at high and low frequencies. For example, a 20-Hz tone would have to be approximately 70 dB louder than a 1-kHz tone to be barely audible. Perceived loudness can be expressed in sones; one sone describes the loudness of a 40 dB SPL sine tone at 1 kHz. A loudness of 2 sones corresponds to 50 dB SPL; similarly, any doubling of loudness in sones results in a 10-dB increase in SPL. For example, 64 sones corresponds to 100 dB SPL. A perceptual coder compares the input signal to the minimum threshold, and discards signals that fall below the threshold, because the ear cannot hear these signals.

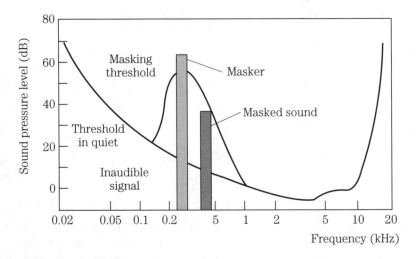

11-6 The threshold of hearing describes the softest sounds audible across the human hearing range. A masker tone or noise will raise the threshold of hearing in a local region, creating a masking curve. Masked tones or noise, perhaps otherwise audible, that fall below the masking curve during that time will not be audible.

Amplitude masking occurs when a tone shifts the threshold curve upward in a frequency region surrounding the tone. The masking threshold describes the level where a tone is barely audible. When tones are sounded simultaneously, masking occurs in which louder tones can completely obscure softer tones. In other words, the physical presence of sound certainly does not ensure audibility and conversely can ensure inaudibility of other sound. The strong sound is called the masker and the softer sound is called the maskee. Masking theory argues that the softer tone is just detectable when its energy equals the energy of the part of the louder masking signal in the critical band; this is a linear relationship with respect to amplitude. For example, a tone of 500 Hz can mask a softer tone of 600 Hz; a perceptual recording system may ignore the 600-Hz tone because it is masked, and instead code the audible 500-Hz tone as precisely as possible. Generally, depending on relative amplitude, soft (but otherwise audible) audio tones are masked by louder tones at a similar frequency (within 100 Hz at low frequencies).

The mechanics of the basilar membrane explain the phenomenon of masking. A loud response at one place on the membrane will mask softer responses in the critical band. Unless the activity from another tone rises above the masking threshold, it will be swamped by the masker. Fig. 11-7A shows four masking curves (tones masked by narrow band noise) at 60 dB SPL, on a logarithmic scale in hertz. Figure 11-7B shows seven masking curves on a bark scale; using this natural scale, the critical band rate can be seen. Masking thresholds are sometimes expressed as an exci-

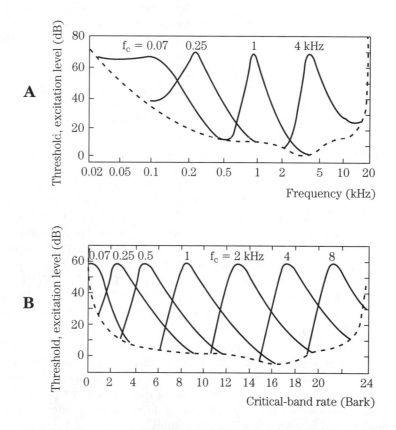

11-7 Masking curves describe the threshold where a tone or noise is just audible in the presence of a masker. Threshold width varies with frequency when plotted logarithmically. When plotted on a bark scale, the widths and slopes are similar, reflecting response along the basilar membrane. A. Masking thresholds plotted with logarithmic frequency. B. Masking thresholds plotted with critical band rate. Zwicker

tation level; this is obtained by adding a 2 to 6 dB masking index to the sound pressure level of the just-audible tone. Low frequencies can interfere with the perception of higher frequencies. Masking can overlap adjacent critical bands when a signal is loud, or contains harmonics; for example, a complex 1-kHz signal can mask a 2-kHz signal. Low amplitude signals provide little masking. Narrow band tones such as sine tones also provide relatively little masking. Likewise, louder, more complex tones provide greater masking with masking curves that are broadened, and with greater high-frequency extension.

Many masking curves have been derived from studies in which both single tones or narrow bands of noise are used as the masker stimulus. Generally, single tone maskers produce dips in the masking curve near the tone due to beat interference between the masker and maskee tones. Narrow noise bands do not show this effect. In addition, tone maskers seem to extend high frequency masking thresholds more readily than noise maskers. Generally, it is agreed that these differences are artifacts of the test itself. Tests with wide band noise show that only the frequency components of the masker that lie in the critical band of the maskee are effective at masking.

Many masking studies examine masking of a tone by another tone or by noise; in perceptual coding, it is reversed; we are concerned with quantization noise that is masked by a music tone. As noted, noise bands provide masking curves that differ from sine tone stimulus; generally, music is more tonelike in its masking properties. Sine-tone masking is used in masking models because it provides the least (worst case) masking of noise; complex tones provide greater masking. Generally, a tone is inaudible when it is about 4 dB below a ⅓ octave masking noise in a critical band. Conversely, when a ⅓ octave band of noise is masked by a pure tone, the noise must be 24 dB below the tone; it is 20 dB harder to mask noise. Ultimately, careful listening is needed to tune any masking criteria. In addition, coders presume a threshold of quiet that is below the standard curves, because it cannot be known what the listening level will be. Relatively little scientific study has been done with music as the stimulus. However, it is generally agreed that tone and noise curves are valid models for music coding. Clearly, one musical sound can mask another, but future work in the mechanics of music masking will result in better masking algorithms.

Simultaneous masking curves are asymmetrical. The slope of the shifted curve is less steep on the high-frequency side. Thus it is relatively easy for a low tone to mask a higher tone, but the reverse is more difficult. Specifically, the lower slope is about 27 dB/bark; the upper slope varies from –20 to –5 dB/bark depending on the amplitude of the masker. Low-level maskers influence a relatively narrow band of masked frequencies. However, as sound level of the masker increases, the threshold curve broadens, and in particular its upper slope decreases; its lower slope remains relatively unaffected. Figure 11-8 shows a series of masking curves produced by a narrow band of noise centered at 1 kHz, sounded at different amplitudes. Clearly, the ear is most discriminating with low amplitude signals.

Temporal masking occurs when tones are sounded close in time, but not simultaneously. A signal can be masked by a noise (or another signal) that occurs later; this is premasking (sometimes called backward masking). In addition, a signal can be masked by a noise (or another signal) that ends before the signal begins. This is post masking (sometimes called forward masking). In other words, a louder tone appear-

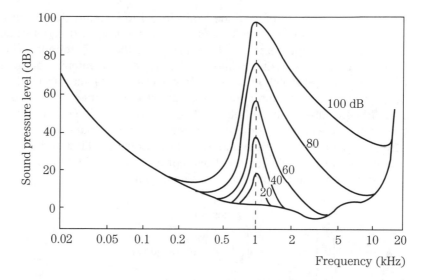

11-8 Masking thresholds vary with respect to sound pressure level; this test uses a narrow band masker noise centered at 1 kHz. The lower slope remains essentially unchanged.

ing just before (premasking), or after (post masking) a softer tone overcomes the softer tone. Just as simultaneous masking increases as frequency differences are reduced, temporal masking increases as time differences are reduced. Given an 80-dB tone, there may be 40 dB of post masking within 20 ms, and 0 dB of masking at 200 ms. Premasking can provide 60 dB of masking for 1 ms, and 0 dB at 25 ms. This is shown in Fig. 11-9. Temporal masking decreases as the duration of the masker decreases. In addition, a tone is post masked by an earlier tone when they are close in frequency or when the earlier tone is lower in frequency; post masking is slight when the masker has a higher frequency. Logically, simultaneous masking is stronger than either pre- or post masking because the sounds occur at the same time.

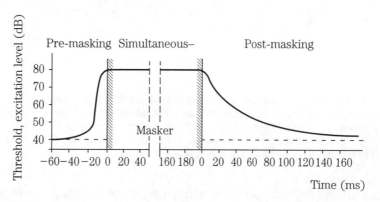

11-9 Temporal masking occurs before, and in particular, after a masker sounds; the threshold decreases with time. Dashed line indicates threshold for test tone impulse without a masker signal. zwicker

Temporal masking suggests that the brain integrates sound over a period of time, and processes the information in bursts at the auditory cortex; alternatively, perhaps the brain simply processes loud sounds faster than soft sounds. Whatever the mechanism, temporal masking is important in frequency domain coding; these coders have limited time resolution because they operate on blocks of samples, thus spreading error over time; temporal masking can prevent artifacts caused by transient signals. Ideally, filter banks should provide a time resolution of 2 to 4 ms. Acting together, amplitude and temporal masking form a contour that can be mapped in the time-frequency domain, as shown in Fig. 11-10. Sounds falling under that contour will be masked; it is the obligation of perceptual coders to identify this contour for changing signal conditions, and code the signal appropriately.

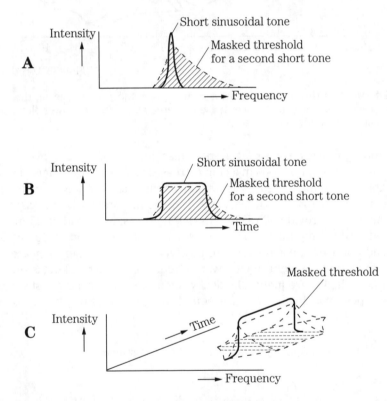

11-10 When simultaneous and temporal masking are combined, a time-frequency contour results. A perceptual coder must place quantization noise and other artifacts within this contour to ensure inaudibility. A. Simultaneous masking. B. Temporal masking. C. Combined masking effect in time-frequency. Beerends and Stemerdink

Multichannel playback presents additional opportunities for data reduction. Joint stereo coding takes advantage of interchannel redundancy between stereo (or multiple) channels to increase efficiency. The data rate of a stereo signal is double that of a mono signal, but most stereo programs are not dual-mono. Rather, the channels share some level and phase information to create phantom images. Joint stereo coding codes common information only once. A 256-kbps joint stereo coding channel will perform better than two 128-kbps channels.

Using diverse and dynamically changing psychoacoustical cues and signal analysis, inaudible components can be removed with acceptable degradation. For example, a loud sound in one channel can mask other softer sounds in other channels. Above 2 kHz, localization is achieved primarily by amplitude; because the ear cannot follow fast individual waveform cycles, it tracks the envelope of the signal, not its phase. Thus the waveform itself becomes less critical; this is intensity localization. In addition, the ear is limited in its ability to localize sounds close in frequency. To convey a multichannel surround field, the high frequencies in each channel can be divided into bands and combined band by band into a composite channel; the bands of the common channel are reproduced from each loudspeaker, or panned between loudspeakers, with the original signal band envelopes. Use of a composite channel achieves data reduction; in addition, other masking principles can be applied prior to forming the composite channel. Many multichannel systems use a 5.1 format with three front channels, two independent surround channels, and a subwoofer channel. Very generally, the number of bits required to code a multichannel signal is proportional to the square root of the number of channels. A 5.1 channel coder, for example, would theoretically require 2.26 times the number of bits needed to code one channel.

Although a maskee signal exists acoustically, it does not exist perceptually. It might seem quite radical, but aural masking is as real as visual masking. Lay your hand over this page. Can you see the page through your hand? Aural masking is just as real.

Rationale for Perceptual Coding

The purpose of any data reduction system is to decrease the data rate, the product of the sampling frequency and the word length. This can be accomplished by decreasing the sampling frequency; however, the Nyquist theorem dictates a corresponding decrease in high frequency audio bandwidth. Another approach decreases the word length; however, this reduces the dynamic range of the audio signal by 6 dB/bit, thus increasing quantization noise. A more enlightened approach uses psychoacoustics. Perceptual coders maintain sampling frequency, but decrease word length; however, the word-length reduction is done dynamically based on signal conditions. Specifically, masking and other factors are considered so that the resulting increase in quantization noise is rendered as inaudible as possible.

Perceptual coding systems analyze the frequency and amplitude content of the input signal, and compare it to a model of human auditory perception. Using the model, the encoder removes the irrelevancy and statistical redundancy of the audio signal. In theory, although the method is lossy, the human perceiver will not hear degradation in the decoded signal. Considerable data reduction is possible. For example, a perceptual coder can reduce a data rate from 1.41 Mbps to 384 kbps; data quantity has been reduced by about 75%. Table 11-2 lists various reduction ratios and resulting bit rates for 48- and 44.1-kHz signals. Moreover, a well-designed perceptually coded recording, with a conservative level of reduction, can rival the sound

Bits/sample	Comp ratio	48 kHz	44.1 kHz
16	1:1	768 kbps	705.6 kbps
8	2:1	384	352.8
4	4:1	192	176
2.67	6:1	128	117.7
2	8:1	96	88.2
1.45	11:1	69.6	64

Table 11-2. Bit-rate reduction for 48- and 44.1- kHz sampling frequencies.

quality of a conventional recording because the data is coded in a much more intelligent fashion, and quite simply, because we don't hear all of what is recorded anyway. In other words, perceptual coders are so efficient that they require only a fraction of the data needed by a conventional system.

Part of this efficiency stems from the adaptive quantization used by most perceptual coders. With PCM, all signals are given equal word lengths. Perceptual coders assign bits according to audibility. A prominent tone is given a large number of bits to ensure audible integrity. Conversely, fewer bits can be used to code soft tones. Inaudible tones are not coded at all. Together, bit rate reduction is achieved. A coder's reduction ratio (or coding gain) is the ratio of input bit rate to output bit rate. Reduction ratios of 4:1, 6:1, or 12:1 are common. Perceptual coders have achieved remarkable transparency, so that in many applications reduced data is audibly indistinguishable from linearly represented data. Tests show that ratios of 4:1 or 6:1 can be transparent.

Generally, two kinds of bit allocation strategies are used in perceptual coders. In forward adaptive allocation, all allocation is performed in the encoder and this encoding information is contained in the bit stream. Very accurate allocation is permitted, provided the encoder is sufficiently sophisticated. An important advantage of forward adaptive coding is that the psychoacoustic model is located in the encoder; the decoder does not need a psychoacoustic model because it uses the encoded data to completely reconstruct the signal. Thus as psychoacoustic models improve in encoders, the increased sonic quality can be conveyed through existing decoders. A disadvantage is that a portion of the available bit rate is needed to convey the allocation information to the decoder. In backward adaptive allocation, bit allocation information is derived from the coded audio data itself without explicit information from the encoder. The bit rate is not partly consumed by allocation information. However, because bit allocation in the decoder is calculated from limited information, accuracy may be reduced. In addition, the decoder is more complex, and the psychoacoustic model cannot be easily improved following introduction of coders.

In addition, perceptual coding is tolerant of errors. With PCM, an error introduces a broadband noise; however, with most perceptual coders, the error is limited to a narrow band corresponding to the bandwidth of the coded critical band, thus limiting its loudness. Instead of a click, an error might be perceived as a low burst of noise. Perceptual coding systems also permit targeted error correction; for example, particularly vulnerable sounds (such as pianissimo passages) may be given greater protection than less vulnerable sounds (such as forte passages). As with any coded data, perceptually coded data requires error correction appropriate to the storage or transmission medium.

Because perceptual coders tailor the coded signal to the ear's acuity, they similarly tailor the required response of the playback system itself. Live music does not pass through amplifiers and loudspeakers, it goes directly to the ear. But recorded music must pass through the playback signal chain. Much of the original signal present in a live recording merely degrades the playback system's ability to reproduce the audible signal. Because a perceptual coder removes inaudible signal content, the playback system's ability to convey audible music logically should improve. In short, a perceptual coder more properly codes an audio signal for passage through an audio system.

In many applications, perceptual coders will be cascaded. For example, a radio station may receive a coded signal, decode it to PCM for mixing, crossfading and other operations, then code it again for broadcast, where it is decoded by the consumer, who can make a coded recording of it. In all, perhaps nine different coding processes can occur. As the signal passes through this chain, coding artifacts will accumulate and can become audible. Each coder will quantize the audio signal, adding to the noise already permitted by previous encoders; because many psychoacoustic models monitor the audio masking levels and not the underlying noise, noise can be allowed to rise to the point of audibility. Further, when noise reaches audibility, the coder can allocate bits to code it, thus robbing bits needed elsewhere; this can increase noise in other areas. In addition, cascaded coders can smear the signal over time, leading to audible pre-echoes in the signal. When coders are cascaded, it is important to begin with the highest-quality coding, then step down; a low fidelity link will limit all subsequent processing. Highest quality coders have high coding margin between the masking threshold and coding noise; they tolerate more coding generations.

Data Reduction Coding

Data reduction coders attempt to represent the audio signal at a reduced data rate while minimizing quantization error. Time-domain coding methods such as delta modulation can be considered to be data-reduction coders (other time-domain methods such as PCM do not provide reduction). They use prediction methods on samples representing the full bandwidth of the audio signal and yield a quantization error spectrum that spans the audio band. Although the audibility of the error depends on the amplitude and spectrum of the signal, the quantization error generally is not masked by the signal. However, time-domain coders operating across the full bandwidth of the time-domain signal can achieve reduction ratios of up to 2.5. For example, NICAM (Near Instantaneously Companded Audio Multiplex) coders reduce blocks of 32 samples from 14 bits to 10 bits using a sliding window to determine which 10 of the 14 bits can be transmitted with minimal audible degradation. Coding is lossless with low level signals, with increasing loss at high levels. Although data reduction is achieved, and is an improvement over linear PCM coding, the bit rate is too high for many applications; primarily, reduction is limited because masking is not fully exploited. Frequency-domain encoders take a different approach. The signal is analyzed in the frequency domain and coded so that quantization error can be assigned (and masked) based on psychoacoustic characteristics of the ear. However, coder complexity is greatly increased.

The reader will recall that any periodic signal can be represented as amplitude variations in time, or as a set of frequency coefficients describing amplitude and phase. Jean Baptiste Joseph Fourier first proposed this relationship between time and frequency. Changes in a time-domain signal also appear as changes in its frequency domain spectrum; for example, a slowly-changing signal would be represented by a low frequency spectral content. If a sequence of time-based samples are thus analyzed, the signal's spectral content can be determined over that period of time. A variety of mathematical transforms can be used to convert a time domain signal into the frequency domain, and back again. For example, the fast Fourier transform (FFT) gives a spectrum with half as many frequency points as there are time samples. For example, assume that 480 samples are taken at a 48-kHz sampling frequency, plus a dc point. In this 10-ms interval, 240 frequency points are obtained over a spectrum from the highest frequency of 24 kHz to the lowest of 100 Hz, which is the period of 10 ms, with frequency points placed 100 Hz apart. In addition, a dc point is generated.

There are two types of frequency domain coders: subband and transform coders. Generally, subband coders provide good time resolution and poor frequency resolution, but transform coders provide good frequency resolution and poor time resolution. Both subband and transform coders follow the architecture shown in Fig. 11-11; either time-domain samples or frequency-domain coefficients are quantized according to a psychoacoustic model contained in the encoder. Subband coding is a

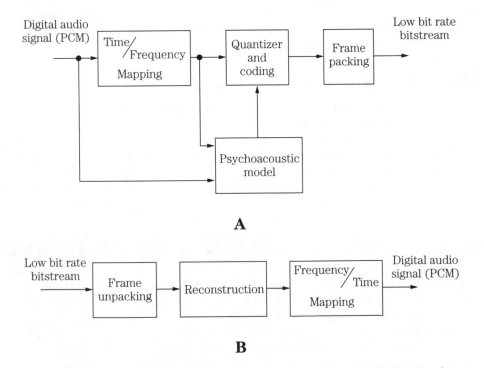

11-11 Basic structure of a frequency-domain encoder and decoder. Subband coders quantize time-based samples, and transform coders quantize frequency-based coefficients.

hybrid of time and frequency domain techniques. A short block of time-based broadband input samples are divided into a number of frequency subbands using a filter bank of bandpass filters; this determines the energy in each subband. Using a side chain transform frequency analysis, the samples in each subband are analyzed for energy content and coded according to a psychoacoustic model. In transform coding, a short block of input samples is applied to a transform to obtain the block's detailed spectrum in the frequency domain. These transform coefficients are then quantized and coded according to a psychoacoustic model. A relatively long block of data is required to obtain a high resolution spectral representation.

Both subband and transform coders operate over a block of samples. This block must be kept short to stay within the temporal resolution of the ear. Quantization noise will be spread over the frequency of the band, and over the duration of the block. If the block is too long, the noise will be heard as a pre-echo prior to the onset of the sound. This is problematic in the case of a silence followed by a transient. Transform coders are particularly affected by the problem because they require long blocks to provide greater frequency accuracy; short block length limits frequency resolution. In essence, transform coders sacrifice temporal resolution for spectral resolution. Long blocks are suitable for slowly changing signals; however, transient signals require a short block length. In some transform coders, block length dynamically adapts to signal conditions. In addition, transform coders incur longer processing delay than subband coders.

Both subband and transform methods use psychoacoustic models to adaptively quantize only the perceptually significant parts of the signal. Parts of the signal that are below the minimum threshold, or masked by more significant signals, are judged to be inaudible and are not coded. In addition, quantization resolution is dynamically adapted so that error is allowed to rise near significant parts of the spectrum, with the expectation that when the signal is reconstructed the error will be masked by the signal. This approach yields significant reduction in the data bandwidth. Frequency domain coders achieve greater reduction than time domain coders; ratios of 4:1 to 12:1 are typical.

Subband Coding

Subband coding was first developed in Bell Labs in the early 1980s, and much subsequent work was done in Europe later in the decade. Blocks of consecutive time-domain samples representing the broadband signal are collected over a short period and applied to a digital filter bank. The filter bank divides the signal into multiple (perhaps up to 32) bandlimited channels to approximate the critical band response of the human ear. The filter bank must provide a very sharp cutoff (perhaps 100 dB/octave) to emulate critical band response and limit quantization noise within that bandwidth. Only digital filters can accomplish this result. In addition, the processing delay (ideally less than 3–4 ms) must be small so that quantization error does not exceed the temporal limits of the ear. The samples in each subband are analyzed and compared to a psychoacoustic model; the coder adaptively quantizes the samples in each subband based on the masking threshold in that subband.

Each subband is coded independently with greater or fewer bits allocated to the samples in the subband. In any case, quantization noise is increased in each subband. However, when the signal is reconstructed, the quantization noise in a subband will be limited to that subband, where it is masked by the audio signal in each subband, as shown in Fig. 11-12. Otherwise intrusive quantization noise levels can be tolerated in a subband with a signal contained in it because noise will be masked by the signal. Bit allocation is determined by a psychoacoustic model and analysis of the signal itself, operations that are recalculated for every subband in every new block of data. Samples are dynamically quantized according to audibility of signals, and noise; there is great flexibility in the psychoacoustic models, and bit allocation algorithms used in coders that are otherwise compatible. The decoder uses the quantized data to re-form the samples in each block; an inverse synthesis filter bank sums the subband signals to reconstruct the output broadband signal.

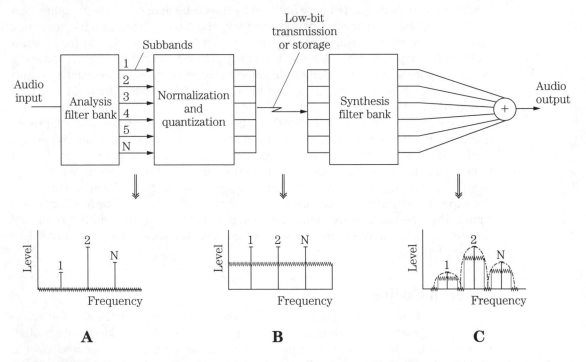

11-12 A subband coder creates narrow bands of high-resolution samples, with a low broadband noise floor. Samples in each subband are normalized and coarsely quantized, raising the broadband noise floor. When the samples are reconstructed, the filters constrain the quantization floor to each subband, where it is masked by the signal. A. High-resolution subband samples. B. Normalized and bit-rate reduced subband samples. C. Reconstructed samples with masked noise floor.

A subband perceptual coder uses a digital filter bank to split a short duration of the audio signal into multiple bands, as depicted in the example in Fig. 11-13. In some designs, a side-chain processor applies the signal to a transform such as an FFT to analyze the energy in each subband. These values are applied to a psychoacoustic model to de-

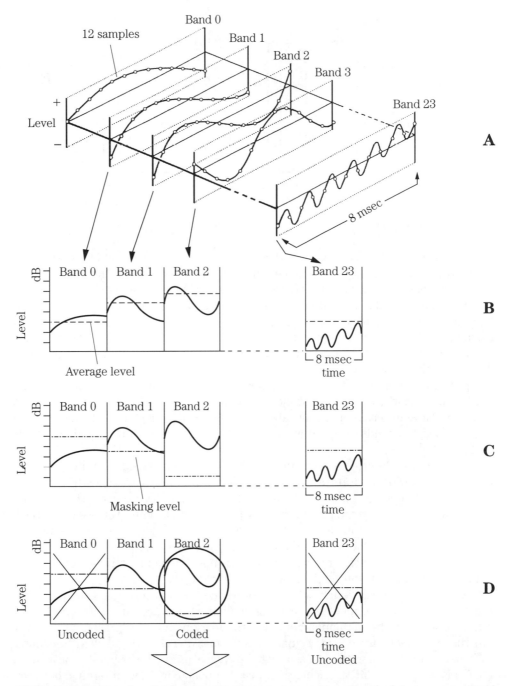

11-13 A subband coder divides the signal into narrow subbands, calculates average signal level and masking level, then quantizes the samples in each subband accordingly. A. Output of 24-band subband filter. B. Calculation of average level in each subband. C. Calculation of masking level in each subband. D. Subbands below audibility are not coded; bands above audibility are coded. E. Bits are allocated according to peak level above masking threshold.

Matsushita Electric

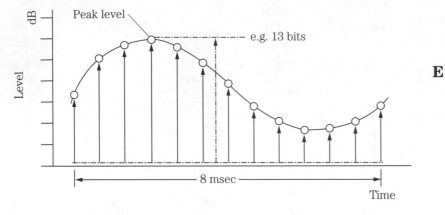

11-13 Continued.

termine the combined masking curve that applies to the signals in that block. This permits more optimal coding of the time-domain samples. Specifically, the encoder analyzes the energy in each subband to determine which subbands contain audible information. A calculation is made to determine the average power level of each subband over the block. This average level is used to calculate the masking level due to masking of signals in each subband, as well as masking from signals in adjacent subbands. Finally, minimum hearing threshold values are applied to each subband to derive its final masking level. Peak power levels present in each subband are calculated, and compared to the masking level. Subbands that do not contain audible information are not coded. Similarly, tones in a subband that are masked by louder nearby tones are not coded, and in some cases entire subbands can mask nearby subbands, which thus need not be coded. Subbands with peak levels above the masking level contain audible signals that must be coded.

Calculations determine the ratio of peak power to masking level in each subband. Quantization bits are assigned to audible program material with a priority schedule that allocates bits to each subband according to signal strength above the audibility curve. For example, Fig. 11-14 shows vertical lines representing peak power levels, and minimum and masking thresholds. The signals below the minimum or masking curves are not coded. For example, signal A is below the minimum curve and would not be coded in any event. Signal C is not coded in this frame because signal B has dynamically shifted the hearing threshold upward.

Signal B must be coded; however, its presence has created a masking curve, decreasing the relative amplitude above the minimum threshold curve. The portion of signal B between the minimum curve and the masking curve represents the fewer bits that are needed to code the signal when the masking effect is taken into account. In other words, rather than use a signal-to-noise ratio, the signal-to-mask ratio (SMR) is used. The SMR is calculated for each subband: it is the difference between the maximum signal and the masking threshold and is used to determine the number of bits assigned to a subband.

The number of bits given to any subband must be sufficient to yield a requantizing noise level that is below the masking level. The number of bits depends on this

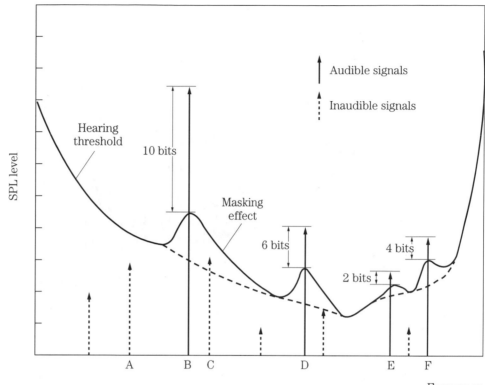

11-14 The bit allocation algorithm assigns bits according to audibility of subband signals. Inaudible tones are not assigned bits, and are not coded.

SMR ratio, with the goal of maintaining the quantization noise level below the calculated masking level for each subband. In fixed-rate coders, a bit-pool approach can be taken; a large number of subbands requiring coding and signals with large SMR ratios might exhaust the pool, resulting in less than optimal coding. On the other hand, if the pool is not empty after initial allocation, the process is repeated until all bits in the coder's data capacity have been used. Typically the iterative process continues, allocating more bits where required, with signals with the highest SMR requirements always receiving the most bits; this increases the coding margin. In some cases, subbands previously classified as inaudible might receive coding from these extra bits thus signals below the masking threshold can in practice be coded, but only on a secondary priority basis. Summarizing the concept of subband coding, Fig. 11-15 shows how a 24-subband coder might code three tones at 250 Hz, 1 kHz, and 4 kHz; note that in each case the quantization noise level is below the combined masking and threshold curve.

Transform Coding

In transform coding, a block of time-domain audio samples is converted to the frequency domain. Coders can use transforms such as the discrete Fourier trans-

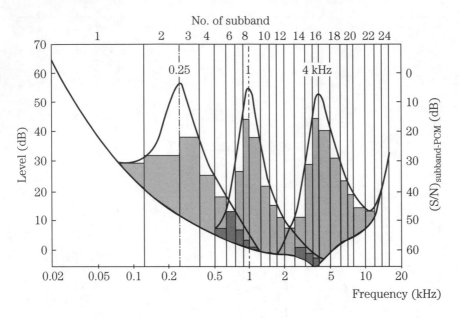

11-15 In this 24-band subband coder, three tones are coded so that quantization noise in each subband falls below the calculated composite masking curves. Thiele

form (DFT) implemented as a fast Fourier transform (FFT), or the modified discrete cosine transform (MDCT). The operation of the transform approximates how the basilar membrane analyzes the frequency content of vibrations along its length. The spectral coefficients output by the transform are quantized according to a psychoacoustic model; masked components are eliminated, and quantization decisions are made based on audibility. In contrast to a subband coder, which uses frequency analysis to code time-based samples, a transform coder codes frequency coefficients. From an information theory standpoint, the transform reduces the entropy of the signal, permitting efficient coding. Longer transform blocks provide greater spectral resolution, but thus lose temporal resolution; for example, a long block might result in a pre-echo before a transient. Most coders overlap successive blocks in time by 50% or so to improve temporal resolution; the samples in the first half of a current block are repeated from the second half of the previous block. This reduces changes in spectra from block to block. In some designs, block length is adapted according to signal conditions.

Time-domain samples are transformed to the frequency domain, yielding spectral coefficients. The coefficient numbers are sometimes called frequency bin numbers; for example, a 512 point transform can produce 256 frequency coefficients or frequency bins. The coefficients, which might number 512, 1024 or more, are grouped into about 32 bands that emulate critical band analysis. This spectrum represents the block of time-based input samples. The frequency coefficients in each band are quantized according to the coder's psychoacoustic model; quantization can be uniform, nonuniform, fixed or adaptive in each band.

In adaptive transform coders, a model is applied to uniformly and adaptively quantize each individual band, but coefficient values within a band are quantized with the same number of bits. The bit allocation algorithm calculates the optimal quantization noise in each subband to achieve a desired signal-to-noise ratio that will promote masking. Iterative allocation is used to supply additional bits as available to increase coding margin, yet maintain limited bit rate. In some cases the output bit rate can be fixed or variable for each block. Before transmission, the reduced data is often compressed with entropy coding such as Huffman coding and run length coding to perform lossless compression. The decoder inversely quantizes the coefficients and performs an inverse transform to reconstruct the signal in the time domain.

An example of an adaptive transform coder, proposed by Karlheinz Brandenburg, is shown in Fig. 11-16. A MDCT transforms the signal to the frequency domain; signal energy in each critical band is calculated using the spectral coefficients. This is used to determine the masking threshold for each critical band. Two iterative loops perform quantization and coding using an analysis-by-synthesis technique. Coefficients are initially assigned a quantizer step size and the algorithm calculates the resulting number of bits needed to code the signal in the block. If the count exceeds the bit rate allowed for the block, the loop reassigns a larger quantizer step size and the count is recalculated until the target bit rate is achieved. An outer loop calculates the quantization error as it will appear in the reconstructed signal. If the error in a band exceeds the error allowed by the masking model, the quantizer step size in the band is decreased. Iterations continue in both loops until optimal coding is achieved. Coders such as this can operate at rates as low as 2.5 bits/sample at 44.1 kHz.

Filter Banks

Frequency-domain coders often use a filter bank to partition the wide audio band into smaller subbands; the decoder uses the inverse filter bank to synthesize the subbands into a wide band. Ideally, the filters should provide ideal lowpass and

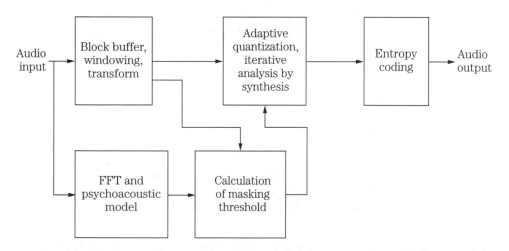

11-16 Adaptive transform coder using FFT side-chain and iterative quantization to achieve optimal reduction. Entropy coding is additionally used for data compression.

highpass characteristics with a cutoff of $f_s/2$, where f_s is the sampling frequency; however, real filters have overlapping bands. For example, in a two band system, the subband sampling rates must be decreased (2:1) to maintain an overall minimal bit rate; this decimation introduces aliasing in the subbands; in the lower band, signals above $f_s/4$ will alias to 0 to $f_s/4$; in the upper band, signals below $f_s/4$ alias up to $f_s/4$ to $f_s/2$. In the decoder, the sampling rate is restored (1:2) by adding zeros; because of interpolation, in the lower band, signals from 0 to $f_s/4$ will image around $f_s/4$ into the upper band; similarly, in the upper band, signals from $f_s/4$ to $f_s/2$ will image to the lower band.

Generally, when N subbands are created, each subband is subsampled at $1/N$ to maintain an overall sampling limit. As noted, most filter banks do not provide ideal performance because of the finite width of their transition bands; the bands overlap, and the $1/N$ subsampling causes aliasing. Clearly, bands that are spaced apart can avoid this, but will leave gaps in the signal's spectrum. Quadrature mirror filter (QMF) banks have the important property of reconstructing the original signal from N overlapping subbands without aliasing, regardless of the order of the bandpass filters; any aliasing components are exactly canceled during reconstruction. The attenuation slopes of adjacent subband filters are mirror images of each other. A QMF is shown in Fig. 11-17. Intermediate samples can be critically subsampled without loss; if the input signal is split into N equal subbands, each subband can be sampled at $1/N$; the sampling frequency for each subband filter is exactly twice the bandwidth of the filter.

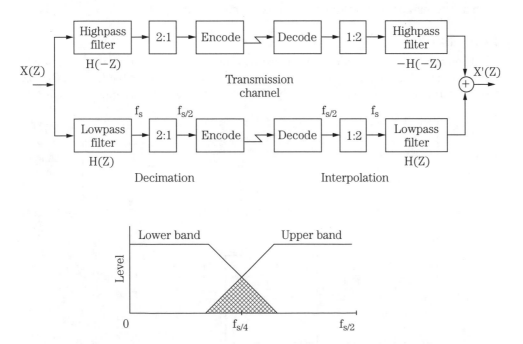

11-17 A quadrature mirror filter forms two equal subbands. Alias components introduced during decimation are exactly cancelled during reconstruction. Multiple QMF stages can be cascaded to form additional subbands.

QMF filters can be implemented as symmetrical finite impulse response filters with an even number of taps; the use of a reconstruction highpass filter with a z-transform of $-H(-z)$ instead of $H(-z)$ eliminates alias terms (when there is uniform quantizing in each subband). However, perfect reconstruction is generally limited to the case when $N = 2$, creating two equal-width subbands from one. These $f_s/2$ subbands can be further divided by repeating the QMF process, and splitting each subband into two more subbands, each with a $f_s/4$ sampling frequency. This can be accomplished with a tree structure; however, this adds delay to the processing. Other QMF architectures can be used to create multiple subbands with less delay.

A variety of other filter banks are used in perceptual coding. A polyphase filter bank is a set of equal bandwidth filters with phase interrelationships that permit efficient implementation. Polyphase filter banks provide subbands of equal width, and good frequency resolution (high stop-band attenuation) to control aliasing. MPEG-1 Layers I and II encoders can use a 32-band polyphase filter. The discrete Fourier transform (DFT), and discrete cosine transform (DCT) with sine-taper window can be used to provide many (128–512) equally spaced bands. However, the number of frequency components is greater than the number of time samples; they do not provide critical sampling. The modified discrete cosine transform (MDCT) can use time domain aliasing cancellation to allow critical sampling with good frequency resolution. Many bands (128–512) are possible with good efficiency. Hybrid filters provide different frequency resolutions at different frequencies with moderate complexity; for example, MPEG-1 Layer III encoders can use a hybrid filter using a polyphase filter bank and MDCT. Transform coders such as Layer III apply a window function to blocks prior to transformation; this helps minimize spectral leakage of spectral coefficients. A window is a time function that is multiplied by an audio block to provide a windowed audio block; the window shape governs the frequency selectivity of the filter bank. The overlap/add characteristic minimizes blocking artifacts and leakage of spectral coefficients. Digital filters and windows are discussed in chapter 15.

Many coders combine techniques from both subband and transform coding; they are known as hybrid coders. The ATRAC algorithm, examined in chapter 12, is a hybrid coder that uses QMF to divide the signal into three subbands, then each subband is transformed into the frequency domain using the MDCT.

MPEG-1 Audio Standard

The International Standards Organization and the International Electrotechnical Commission formed the Motion Picture Experts Group, which devised the ISO/IEC International Standard 11172 "Coding of Moving Pictures and Associated Audio for Digital Storage Media at up to about 1.5 Mbit/s" for reduced data rate coding of digital video and audio signals; it was finalized in November, 1992. It is commonly known as ISO/MPEG-1. The standard has three parts: system (multiplexed video and audio), video, and audio; a fourth part will define conformance testing. The maximum bit rate is set at 1.856 Mbps. The audio portion of the standard (11172-3) has found many applications such as Video CD, CD-ROM, ISDN, video games, and digital audio broadcasting. It supports coding of 32, 44.1, and 48 kHz

PCM data at bit rates of 32 to 192 kbps/channel (64 to 384 kbps for stereo). (Because data networks use data rates of 64 kbps (8 bits sampled at 8 kHz), most coders output a data channel rate that is a multiple of 64.)

The ISO/MPEG-1 standard was specifically developed to support audio and video coding for CD playback within the CD's bandwidth of 1.41 Mbps. However, the standard supports stereo bit rates ranging from 64 kbps to 448 kbps, as well as mono audio coding of 32 kbps. In addition, in the stereo modes, stereophonic irrelevance and redundancy can be optionally exploited to reduce the bit rate. Audio bit rates below 256 kbps are useful for applications requiring more than two audio channels while maintaining full screen motion video. Rates above 256 kbps are useful for applications requiring higher audio quality, and partial screen video images. In either case, the bit allocation is dynamically adaptable according to need. The MPEG-1 standard is based on a history of research and development of data reduction algorithms.

MUSICAM (Masking-pattern Universal Subband Integrated Coding And Multiplexing) was an early and successful perceptual coding algorithm. Derived from MASCAM (Masking-pattern Adapted Subband Coding And Multiplexing), MUSICAM divides the input audio signal into 32 subbands, and uses perceptual coding models of minimum hearing threshold and masking to achieve data reduction. With a sampling frequency of 48 kHz, the subbands are each 750 Hz wide. Each subband is given a 6-bit scale factor according to the peak value in the subband's 12 samples, and quantized with a variable word ranging from 0 to 15 bits. Scale factors are calculated over a 24-ms interval, corresponding to 36 samples. A subband is quantized only if it contains audible signals above the masking threshold. Subbands with signals well above the threshold are coded with more bits, yielding a high S/N ratio. In other words, within a given bit rate (for example, 128 kbps) bits are assigned where they are most needed. In addition, a side-chain Fourier spectral analysis is performed on the input signal to assist in the masking threshold calculations. In this way, the data rate is reduced, to perhaps 128 kbps per mono channel (256 kbps for stereo). Extensive tests of 128 kbps MUSICAM showed that the coder achieves fidelity that is indistinguishable from a CD source, that it is monophonically compatible, that at least two codec stages produce no audible degradation, and that it is preferred to very high quality FM signals.

The audio portion of the ISO/MPEG-1 standard can trace its origins to tests conducted by Swedish Radio in July 1990. MUSICAM coding was judged superior in complexity and coding delay; however, the ASPEC (Adaptive Spectral Perceptual Entropy Coding) transform coder provided superior sound quality at very low data rates. The architectures of these two coding methods form the basis for the ISO/MPEG-1 standard. The 11172-3 standard describes three layers of coding, each with different applications. Specifically, Layer I describes the least sophisticated method that requires relatively high data rates (approximately 192 kbps/channel). Layer II is based on Layer I but contains increased complexity and operates at somewhat lower data rates (approximately 96–128 kbps/channel). Layer IIA is a joint stereo version operating at 128 and 192 kbps per stereo pair. Layer III is somewhat conceptually different from I and II, is the most sophisticated, and operates at the lowest data rate (approximately 64 kbps/channel). The increased complexity from Layer I to III is reflected in the fact that at low data rates, Layer III will perform best for audio fidelity. Generally, Layers II, IIA and III have been judged to be acceptable for broadcast applications; in other words, the 128 kbps/channel data reduction does not impair the quality of the original audio signal.

In very general terms, all three coders operate similarly. The audio signal passes through a filter bank and is analyzed in the frequency domain. The subsampled components are regarded as subband values, or spectral coefficients. The output of a side-chain transform, or the filter bank itself, is used to estimate masking thresholds. The subband values or spectral coefficients are quantized according to the psychoacoustic model. Coded mapped samples and bit allocation information is packed into frames prior to transmission. In each case, the encoders are not defined by the ISO/MPEG-1 standard, only the decoders are specified. This forward adaptive bit allocation permits improvements in encoding methods, particularly in the psychoacoustic modelling, provided the data output from the encoder can be decoded according to the standard. In other words, existing coders will play data from improved encoders. The following describes prototypical encoder designs.

MPEG-1 Layer I

Layer I is a simplified version of the MUSICAM standard; block diagrams of a single-channel Layer I encoder and decoder (which also applies to Layer II) are shown in Fig. 11-18. Its aim is to provide high fidelity at low cost, at a somewhat high data rate. A polyphase filter is used to split the wideband signal into 32 subbands of equal width. The filter is critically sampled; there are an equal number of samples in the analyzed domain as in the time domain. Adjacent subbands overlap; a single frequency can affect two subbands. The filter and its inverse are not lossless; however, the error is small. The filter bank's bands are all equal width, but the ear's critical bands are not; this is compensated for in the bit allocation algorithm; for example, lower bands are usually assigned more bits, increasing their resolution over higher bands. This filter bank is found in all three layers.

The filter outputs 32 samples, one sample per band, for every 32 input samples. In Layer I, 12 subband samples from each of the 32 subbands are grouped to form a frame; this represents 384 wideband samples. Each subband group of 12 samples is given a bit allocation; subbands judged inaudible are given a zero allocation. Based on the calculated masking threshold (just audible noise), the bit allocation determines the number of bits used to quantize those samples. A floating point notation is used to code samples; the mantissa determines resolution and the exponent determines dynamic range. A fixed scale factor exponent is computed for each subband with a nonzero allocation; it is based on the largest sample value in the subband. Each of the 12 subband samples in a block are normalized by dividing it by the same scale factor; this optimizes quantizer resolution.

Using the scale factor information, and spectral analysis from a 512-sample FFT wideband transform, a psychoacoustic model compares the data to the minimum threshold curve; the normalized samples are quantized by the bit allocator to achieve data reduction. The subband data is coded, not the FFT spectra. Dynamic bit allocation assigns mantissa bits to the samples in each coded subband, or omits coding for inaudible subbands. Each sample is coded with one PCM codeword; the quantizer

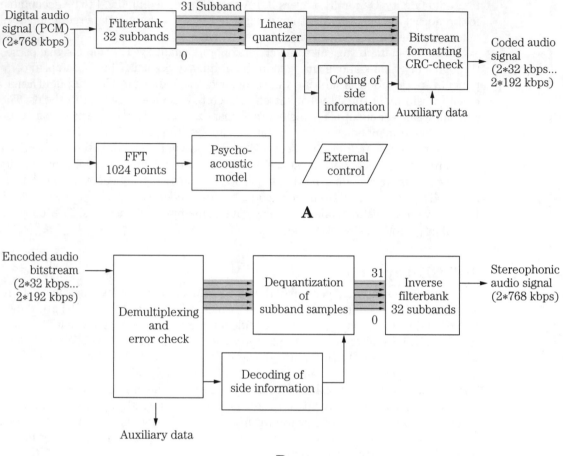

11-18 ISO/MPEG-1 Layer I or II audio encoder and decoder. The filter bank is common to all three layers. A. Layer I or II encoder (single-channel mode). B. Layer I or II decoder (two-channel mode).

provides $2^n - 1$ steps where $2 \leq n \leq 15$. Subbands with a high signal-to-mask ratio are given a long word, subbands with a low SMR ratio are given fewer bits; in other words, the SMR ratio determines the minimum signal-to-noise ratio that has to be met by the quantization of the subband samples. However, quantization is performed iteratively; when available, additional bits are added to codewords to increase the S/N ratio above the minimum. The block scale factor exponent and sample mantissas are output. Error correction and other information is added to the signal at the output of the coder.

Decoding is performed by decoding the bit allocation information, and decoding the scale factors. Samples are requantized by multiplying them with the correct scale factor. The scale factors provide all the information needed to recalculate the masking thresholds; in other words, the decoder does not need a psychoacoustic model. Samples are applied to an inverse synthesis filter to output the waveform. A version of Layer I is presently used in the DCC recording system.

MPEG-1 Layer II

Layer II is essentially identical to the original MUSICAM standard (the frame headers differ), and thus is similar to Layer I, but more sophisticated in design; it strives to provide high fidelity at moderate data rates, with somewhat higher cost. Figure 11-19 gives a more detailed look at a Layer II encoder (which also applies to Layer I). The filter creates 32 equal-width subbands, but frame size is tripled to $3 \times 12 \times 32$, corresponding to 1152 wideband samples per channel. In other words, data is coded in three groups of 12 samples for each subband (Layer I uses one group). The FFT analysis block size is increased to 1024; tonal (sinusoidal) and nontonal (noiselike) components are distinguished to better determine their effect on the masking threshold.

A single bit allocation is given to each group of 12 subband samples. Up to three scale factors are calculated for each subband, each corresponding to a group of 12 subband samples. However, to reduce the scale factor bit rate, scale factors are shared between groups when differences are small or when temporal masking will

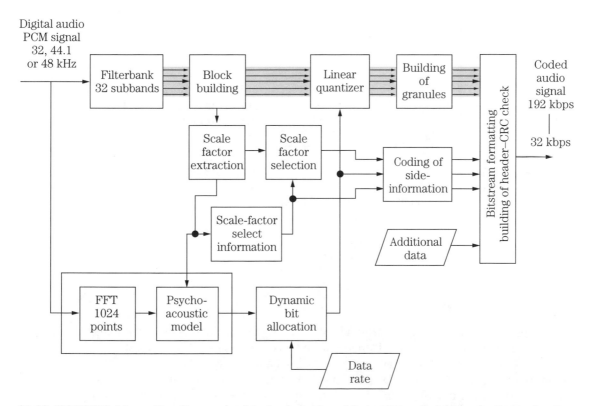

11-19 ISO/MPEG-1 Layer II audio encoder (single-channel mode) showing scale factor selection and coding of side information.

occur. Bit allocation is used to maximize both the subband and frame signal-to-mask ratios. Quantization covers a range from 3 to 65,535 (or none), but the number of available levels depends on the subband. Lower subbands can receive as many as 15 bits, middle subbands can receive seven bits, and higher subbands are limited to three bits. In each band, prominent signals are given longer codewords. It is recognized that quantization varies with subband number; higher subbands usually receive fewer bits, with larger step sizes. Thus for greater efficiency, three successive samples (for all 32 subbands) are grouped to form a granule and quantized together.

As in Layer I, decoding is relatively simple. The decoder unpacks the data frames and applies appropriate data to the reconstruction filter. Layer II coding can use stereo intensity coding. Layer II coding provides for a dynamic range control to adapt to different listening conditions, and uses a fixed-length data word. Layer II coding is used in the Eureka 147 DAB system. Minimum encoding and decoding delays are about 30 and 10 ms respectively. Layer I and II are compared in Table 11-3.

Parameter	MPEG layer–I	MPEG layer–II
Frame length (samples)	384	1152
Subbands	32	32
Subband samples	12	36
FFT (samples)	512	1024
Bit allocation (bits)	4 per	2 to 4 depending on subband
Scalefactor select information (bits)	None	2 per subband
Scalefactors (bits)	6 per subband	6 to 18 per subband (selectable)
Sample grouping	None	3 per subband (granule)

Table 11-3. Comparison of parameters in ISO/MPEG-1 Layer I and Layer II.

MPEG-1 Layer III

Layer III combines elements from MUSICAM and ASPEC, and is more complex than Layers I and II; its strength is moderate fidelity even at very low data rates, at somewhat higher cost. Block diagrams of a single-channel Layer III encoder and decoder are shown in Fig. 11-20. As in Layers I and II, the wideband signal is split into 32 subbands with a polyphase filter. Additionally, each subband is transformed into 18 spectral coefficients by a MDCT (modified discrete cosine transform) for a maximum of 576 coefficients each representing a bandwidth of 41.67 Hz at a 48-kHz sam-

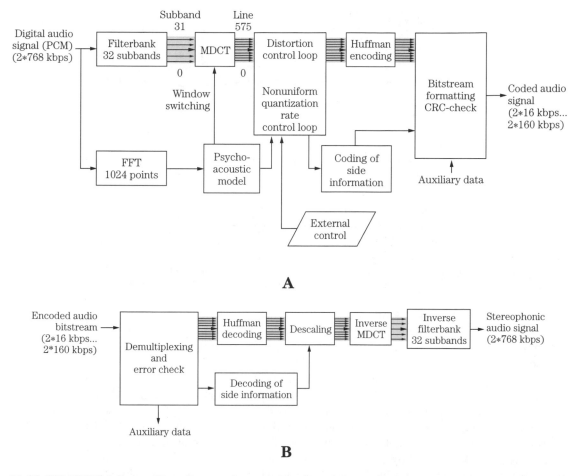

11-20 ISO/MPEG-1 Layer III audio encoder and decoder. A. Layer III encoder (single-channel mode). B. Layer III decoder (two-channel mode).

pling rate; time resolution is 24 ms. This provides good spectral resolution that is needed for steady state signals, at the expense of temporal resolution that is needed for transient signals.

As noted, quantization errors spread over a window length can produce pre-echo artifacts. Thus some or all of the MDCT window sizes can be switched between frequency or time resolution, using a threshold calculation, as shown in Fig. 11-21. A long window has a length of 36 samples (the MDCT has a 50% overlap); it is used for steady state signals. A short window has a length of 12 samples; it is used for transients; time resolution is 8 ms at a 48-kHz sampling frequency with 192 spectral lines. Because the switchover is not instantaneous, a hybrid start window is used to switch from long to short windows, and a stop window switches back. This ensures alias cancellation. There are three block modes: in two modes, the outputs of all 32 filter banks are processed through the MDCT with equal block lengths; in a mixed mode, the two lower bands use long blocks and the upper 30 bands use short blocks.

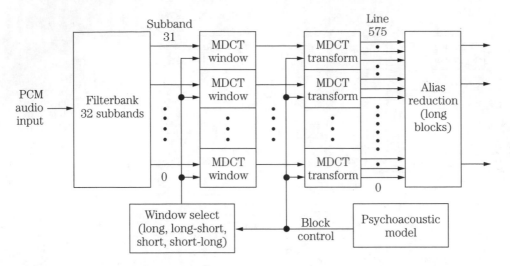

11-21 Long and short blocks can be selected for the MDCT transform used in ISO/MPEG-1 Layer III encoder. Both long and short windows, and two transitional windows, are used.

The allocation control algorithm uses dynamic quantization; a noise allocation iteration loop is used to calculate optimal quantization noise in each subband; this is referred to as noise allocation, as opposed to bit allocation. An analysis-by-synthesis method calculates a quantized spectrum that satisfies the noise requirements of the modelled masking threshold; quantization of this spectrum is iteratively adjusted so the bit rate limits are observed. Nonuniform quantization is used; values are raised to the ¾ power before quantizing to optimize S/N over a range of quantizer values (the decoder reciprocates by raising values to the ⁴⁄₃ power). Huffman and run length entropy coding exploit the statistical properties of the audio signal to achieve data compression; different coding tables are selected based on signal properties; Huffman coding is used for both scale factors and coefficients. The data rate from frame to frame can vary in Layer III; this can be used for variable rate recording. When a constant rate is required, Layer III can use an optional bit reservoir to allow more accurate coding of particularly difficult (large perceptual entropy) short window passages. In this way, the average transmitted data rate can be smaller than peak data rates. The number of bits per frame is variable, but has a constant long term average. The mean bit rate is never allowed to exceed the fixed channel capacity; in other words, there is reserve capacity in the reservoir. When additional bits are needed, they are taken from the reservoir; succeeding frames are coded with somewhat fewer bits than average to replenish the reservoir. The buffer memory adds throughput time to the coder. The decoder performs Huffman decoding, as well as decoding of bit allocation information. Coefficients are applied to an inverse MDCT transform, and 32 subbands are combined in a synthesis filter to output a broadband signal.

Psychoacoustic Models

The MPEG-1 standard suggests two psychoacoustic models. They determine the minimum masking threshold for inaudibility. The difference between the maximum signal level and the masking threshold is used by the bit allocator to set the quantization levels. Generally, model 1 is applied to Layers I and II and model 2 is applied to Layer III. In both cases, the models follow an algorithm to output the signal-to-mask ratios for each subband or group of subbands. For example, model 1 performs these nine steps:

1. Perform time to frequency mapping: A 512- or 1024-point fast Fourier transform is used, with a Hann window to reduce edge effects, to transform time domain data to the frequency domain; in this way, precise masking thresholds can be calculated.
2. Determine maximum SPL levels: This calculation is performed for each subband using spectral data and scale factors. Maxima are considered to be potential maskers, used in forming the masking threshold.
3. Determine threshold in quiet: An absolute hearing threshold is determined in the absence of any signal; this forms the lower masking bound.
4. Identify tonal and nontonal components: Tonal (sinusoidal) and nontonal (noiselike) components in the signal are identified and processed separately because they provide different masking thresholds.
5. Decimation of maskers: The number of maskers is reduced to obtain only the relevant maskers; their magnitude and distance in bark must be appropriate.
6. Calculate masking thresholds: Noise masking thresholds for each subband are determined by applying a masking function to the signal. When the subband is wide compared to the critical band, the spectral model selects minimum threshold; when it is narrow, the model averages the thresholds covering the subband.
7. Determine global masking threshold: This is the summation of the upper and lower slopes of individual subband masking curves, as well as the threshold in quiet to form a composite contour.
8. Determine minimum masking threshold: These values are determined for each subband, based on the global masking threshold.
9. Calculate signal-to-mask ratios: The difference between the maximum SPL levels and the minimum masking threshold values determines the SMR ratio in each subband; this value is supplied to the bit allocator.

MPEG-1 Features and Performance

The MPEG-1 layers support stereo joint coding using intensity coding. Left/right high frequency subband samples are summed into one channel but scale factors remain independent; the decoder forms the envelopes of the original left and right channels using the scale factors. The spectral shape of the left and right channels is the same in these upper subbands, but their amplitudes differ. The bound for joint coding is selectable at four frequencies: 3, 6, 9, and 12 kHz at a 48-kHz sampling frequency; the bound can be changed from one frame to another. Care must be taken to avoid aliasing between subbands and negative correlation between channels when joint coding. Layer III also supports MS (sum and difference) coding between channels; some subbands are coded as sum and difference signals. Joint stereo coding increases coder complexity only slightly.

MPEG-1 audio data is transmitted in frames, as shown in Fig. 11-22; the frame begins with a 32-bit ISO header with a 12-bit synchronizing pattern and 20 bits of general data on layer, bit rate index, sampling frequency, type of emphasis, etc. This is followed by an optional 16-bit CRCC check word with generation polynomial $x^{16} + x^{15} + x^2 + 1$. Subsequent fields describe bit allocation data (number of bits used to code subband samples), scale factor selection data, and scale factors themselves. This varies from layer to layer. For example, Layer I sends a fixed 6-bit scale factor for each coded subband. Layer II examines scale factors and uses dynamic scale-factor selection information (SCFSI) to avoid redundancy; this reduces the scale factor bit rate by a factor of 2.

The largest part of the frame is occupied by subband samples. Again, this varies among layers. In Layer II, for example, samples are grouped in granules. The length of the field is determined by a bit rate index, but the bit allocation determines the actual number of bits used to code the signal; if the frame length exceeds the number

ISO/MPEG/AUDIO layer I frame structure: valid for 384 PCM audio input samples
Duration: 8 ms with a sampling rate of 48 kHz

A

Header		Bit allocation	Scalefactors	Subband	Samples	AD

A) 12 bit sync
B) 20 bit system info

16 bit

4 bit linear

6 bit linear

1 subband sample corresponds to 32 PCM audio input samples.

Auxiliary data field length not specified

ISO/MPEG/AUDIO layer II frame structure: valid for 1152 PCM audio input samples
Duration: 24 ms with a sampling rate of 48 kHz

B

Header		Bit allocation	Scalefactors	Subband	Samples	AD

A) 12 bit sync
B) 20 bit system info

16 bit

Low subbands 4 bit linear — 00
Mid subbands 3 bit linear — 01
High subbands 2 bit linear — 11
10

2 bit

6 bit linear

Gr0 .... Gr11
12 granules [Gr] of 3 subband samples each.
3 subband samples correspond to 96 PCM audio input samples.

Auxiliary data field length not specified

11-22 Structure of the ISO/MPEG-1 audio Layer I, II, and III bit streams. The header and some other fields are common, but other fields differ. Higher-level coders might transcode lower-level bit streams. A. Layer I bit stream format. B. Layer II bit stream format. C. Layer III bit stream format.

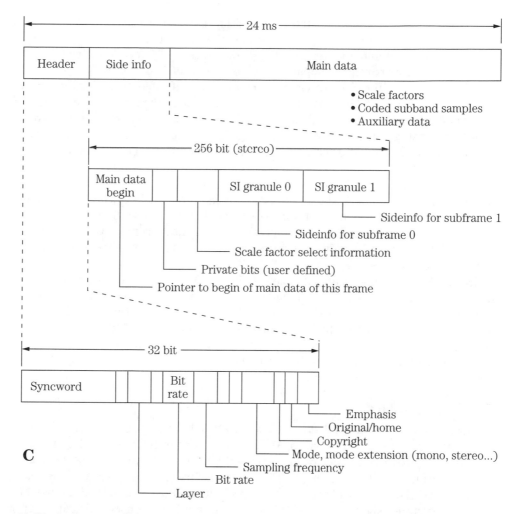

11-22 Continued.

of bits allocated, the remainder of the frame can be occupied by auxiliary data (this feature is used by MPEG-2, for example). Auxiliary data is coded similarly to primary frame data. Frames contain 384 samples in Layer I and 1152 samples in II and III (or 8 and 24 ms respectively at 48 kHz).

The similarity between the layers promotes tandem operation; for example, Layer III data can be transcoded to Layer II without returning to the analog domain (other digital processing is required however). An MPEG-1 decoder must be able to decode its layer, and all layers below it. Layer I preserves highest fidelity for acquisition and production work at high bit rates where six or more codings can take place; Layer II distributes programs efficiently where two codings can occur; Layer III is most efficient, with lowest rates, with somewhat lower fidelity, and a single coding. Radio broadcasters have recommended Layer II for applications such as contribution, distribution, and transmission of programs, and Layer III for commentary.

Extensive tests have demonstrated that either Layer II or III at 2×128 kbps or 192 kbps joint stereo can convey a stereo audio program with no audible degradation compared to a 16-bit linear system. If a higher data rate of 384 kbps is allowed, Layer I also achieves transparency compared to 16-bit linear PCM. At rates as low as 128 kbps, Layers II and III can convey stereo material that is subjectively very close to 16-bit fidelity. Tests also have studied the effects of cascading perceptual codecs. For example, in one experiment, critical audio material was passed through four Layer II codec stages at 192 kbps and two stages at 128 kbps and they were found to be transparent. On the other hand, a cascade of five codec stages at 128 kbps was not transparent for all music programs. More specifically, a source reduced to 384 kbps with MPEG-1 Layer II sustained about 15 code/decodes before noise became significant; however, at 192 kbps, only two codings were possible. These particular tests did not enjoy the benefit of joint stereo coding, and as with any perceptual coder, overall performance can be improved by substituting new psychoacoustic models in the encoder. In addition, transcoding produces no appreciable noise after multiple code/decodes.

ISO/MPEG-Surround is an extension of the ISO/MPEG standard; it encodes 5.1 channels, taking advantage of redundancy between channels. Clearly, because there is more redundancy between six channels than between two, greater coding efficiency is achieved. Overall, the 5.1 channels can be coded at 384 kbps, or about $\frac{1}{10}$ the rate needed for PCM channels. In addition, ISO/MPEG-Surround is backward compatible with ISO/MPEG such that two-channel decoders can play stereo channels from multichannel programs.

MPEG-2 Standard

In addition to the MPEG-1 standard, MPEG-2 is designed for digital HDTV television and computer-quality images; MPEG-2 meets or exceeds the full CCIR-601 resolution. The MPEG-2 standard provides multichannel 5.1 sound, using the same audio algorithms as MPEG-1, thus MPEG-2 audio is forward and backward compatible. An MPEG-2 decoder will accept an MPEG-1 bit stream and an MPEG-1 decoder can derive a stereo signal from an MPEG-2 bit stream; however, MPEG-2 also permits use of incompatible audio coders. The multichannel MPEG-2 format uses an encoder matrix that allows a two-channel decoder to decode a compatible two-channel signal that is a subset of a multichannel bit stream. The multiple channels of MPEG-2 are matrixed to form compatible MPEG-1 left/right channels, as well as other MPEG-2 channels, as shown in Fig. 11-23. These are encoded into MPEG-1 frames, and additional multichannel data is placed in the expanded auxiliary data field. Subwoofer data can be added as well. MPEG-2 uses intensity coding, crosstalk reduction, interchannel prediction coding, and center channel phantom image coding to achieve a combined bit rate of 384 kbps, using Layer II at a 48-kHz sampling frequency. The MPEG-2 decoder outputs MPEG-1 compatible left/right channels, and other MPEG-2 channels, then applies the inverse matrix to recover all five MPEG-2 channels. The video portion of MPEG-2 specifies 704 pixels by 480 lines (NTSC) and 704 pixels by 576 lines (PAL/SECAM) resolutions at data rates of 4 Mbps to 8 Mbps, 16:9 aspect ratio and interlaced fields.

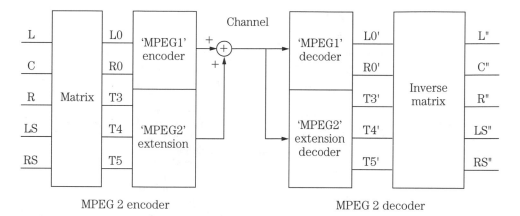

11-23 ISO/MPEG-2 audio encoder and decoder showing how a 5.1 surround format can be achieved with backward compatibility with MPEG-1.

The menu of data rates, fidelity, and layer compatibility provided by MPEG are useful in a wide variety of applications such as computer multimedia, CD-ROM, DVD, computer disks, local area networks, studio recording and editing, multichannel disk recording, ISDN transmission, digital audio broadcasting, and multichannel HDTV. An MPEG-4 committee is studying future technologies to code audio and video at very low data rates such as 4.8 to 64 kbps. For example, a voice recognition algorithm might code speech as ASCII text for transmission along with coded voice attributes. Numerous C and C++ programs performing MPEG-1 and -2 audio coding and decoding can be freely downloaded from a number of Internet file sites, and executed on personal computers. Fig. 11-24 shows a flow chart summarizing the complete Layer I and II encoding algorithm. Figure 11-25 shows details on the common subband filter bank calculation.

The Digital Compact Cassette

The Digital Compact Cassette (DCC) tape format is similar to DAT in that audio data is recorded digitally on a magnetic tape housed in a protective shell. However DCC differs considerably in technical details, and most significantly, DCC is designed to be backward compatible with existing analog cassettes. A DCC recorder records and plays DCC cassettes and plays analog cassettes. This necessitates a stationary head design, using standard ⅛-inch-width chromium dioxide tape, moving at the standard speed of 1⅞ ips. To provide sufficient recorded data density, eight parallel data tracks are required for stereo audio channels. However, this is not sufficient capacity to record linear PCM data. Thus a data reduction algorithm known as PASC (Precision Adaptive Subband Coding) is used to reduce the data flow to 384 kbps. PASC is a version of MPEG-1 Layer I.

The face of a DCC cassette is the same size as an analog cassette; however, it is somewhat slimmer. A sliding metal cover is used to protect the tape from the outside

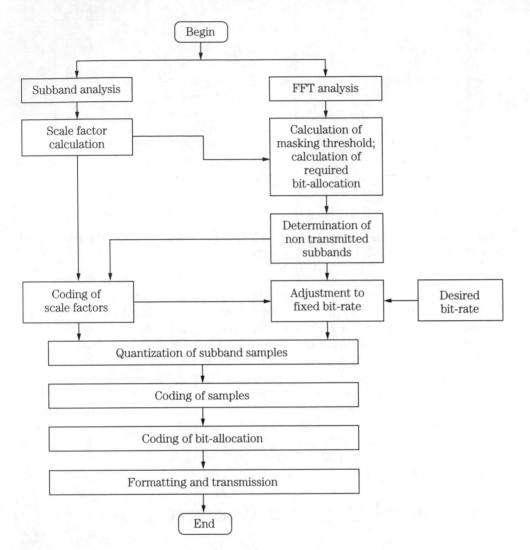

11-24 Flow chart of the entire ISO/MPEG-1 audio Layer I and II encoding algorithm.

environment. The top face does not have spindle holes, allowing maximum surface for art work. The split head design contains both digital data gaps and analog gaps, either on separate or combined heads. Thin-film magneto-resistive technology is used for the digital playback heads, and magneto-inductive technology for the digital record heads. Recording track width is 185 µm, and playback track width is 70 µm, to allow a wide tolerance in transport and cassette manufacturing. The smallest recorded wavelength is 0.96 µm; low coercivity (620 oersted) tape is used. No erase head is required; data is overwritten. A second head is required for a read-after-write function. As in the CD standard, a Reed-Solomon error correction code is used, with 47% redundancy. The modulation code, as in DAT, is an 8/10 code.

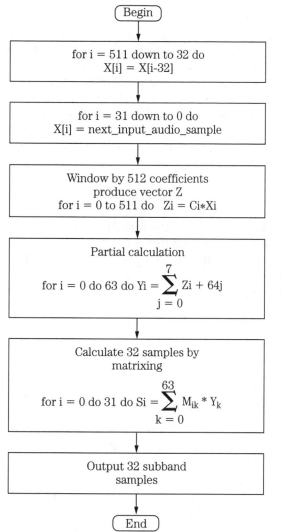

Begin

for i = 511 down to 32 do
X[i] = X[i-32]

for i = 31 down to 0 do
X[i] = next_input_audio_sample

Window by 512 coefficients
produce vector Z
for i = 0 to 511 do $Z_i = C_i * X_i$

Partial calculation

$$Y_i = \sum_{j=0}^{7} Z_{i+64j}$$
for i = 0 do 63 do

Calculate 32 samples by
matrixing

$$S_i = \sum_{k=0}^{63} M_{ik} * Y_k$$
for i = 0 do 31 do

Output 32 subband
samples

End

11-25
Flow chart of the analysis filter bank used in ISO/MPEG-1 audio Layer I and II encoding.

Subcode contained in an auxiliary track holds nonaudio information such as song titles, artist's names, and lyrics, up to a rate of 400 characters/second. A table of contents is written continuously along the length of tape. A digital tape records in two sectors (A and B) in different tape directions. However because auto-reverse is dictated by the format, a DCC digital tape is not physically turned over to switch sectors. Playing time of 90 minutes is typical. Dolby B and C noise reduction is specified as part of the analog DCC standard. DCC decks can accept digital inputs from digital sources such as CD; the DCC format stipulates that all recordings are marked with an SCMS copy-inhibit flag. Prerecorded DCC tapes can be duplicated at 64-times speed using professional equipment.

PASC Algorithm

The problem of reducing the bit rate from 1.41 Mbps to 384 kbps, without perceptually degrading the audio fidelity of the DCC medium, is solved by the PASC (Precision Adaptive Subband Coding) algorithm. As with other perceptual coding methods, PASC uses the ear's audiology performance as its model for audio encoding, relying on principles such as amplitude masking to encode a signal that is perceptually identical. PASC is a simplified but compatible version of the ISO/MPEG-1 Layer I standard. The ISO standard specifies only a decoder; PASC specifies both encoder and decoder. ISO provides an optional CRCC check code; PASC does not implement this. Generally, PASC operating at 384 kbps achieves the same quality as a Layer II coder operating at 256 kbps. Finally, PASC can be transcoded to either Layer I or II.

Signals input to a DCC recorder can be analog, or PCM digital with 32-, 44.1-, or 48-kHz sampling frequencies. At these three sampling frequencies, the subband width is 500, 689, and 750 Hz, and the frame period is 12, 8.7, and 8 ms, respectively. The following description assumes a 48-kHz sampling frequency. The stereo audio signal is passed to the first stage in a PASC encoder, as shown in Fig. 11-26. A 24-bit FIR filter with the equivalent of 512 taps divides the audio band into 32 subbands of equal 750-Hz width. The filter window is shifted by 32 points so all the 384 samples in the 8-ms frame are analyzed. The filter bank outputs 32 subbands. With this filter, the effective sampling rate of a subband is reduced by 32 to 1, for example, from a frequency of 48 kHz to 1.5 kHz. Although the channels are bandlimited, they are still in PCM representation at this point in the algorithm.

The encoder analyzes the energy in each subband to determine which subbands contain audible information. First generation PASC encoders are similar to Layer I encoders, but do not use an FFT side chain. The algorithm calculates average power

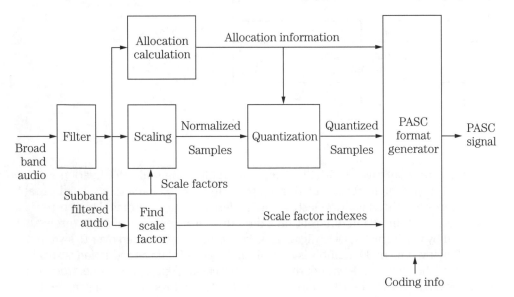

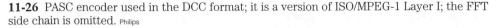

11-26 PASC encoder used in the DCC format; it is a version of ISO/MPEG-1 Layer I; the FFT side chain is omitted. Philips

levels in each subband over the 8-ms (12 sample) period. Masking levels in subbands and adjacent subbands are estimated. Minimum threshold levels are applied. Peak power levels in each subband are calculated and compared to masking levels. The SMR ratio (difference between the maximum signal and the masking threshold) is calculated for each subband and is used to determine the number of bits N assigned to a subband (i) such that $N_i \geq (SMR_i - 1.76)/6.02$. A bit pool approach is taken to optimally code signals within the given bit rate. Quantized values form a mantissa, with a possible range of 2 to 15 bits, thus a maximum resolution of 92 dB is available from this part of the coding word. In practice, in addition to signal strength, mantissa values also are affected by rate of change of the waveform pattern, and available data capacity. In any event, new mantissa values are calculated for every sample period.

Quantized values are normalized (scaled) to optimally use the dynamic range of the processor. Specifically, six exponent bits form a scale factor, which is determined by the signal's absolute amplitude. This scale factor covers the range from –118 dB to +6 dB in 2-dB steps. Because the audio signal varies slowly in relation to the sampling frequency, the masking threshold and scale factors are calculated only once for every group of 12 samples, forming a PASC frame (12 samples/subband × 32 subbands = 384 samples). For every subband, the absolute peak value of the 12 samples is compared to a table of scale factors, and the closest (next highest) constant is applied; the other sample values are normalized to that factor, and during decoding will be used as multipliers to compute the correct subband signal level.

A floating-point representation is used; one field contains a fixed length 6-bit exponent, and another field contains a variable length 2- to 15-bit mantissa. Every block of 12 subband samples may have different mantissa lengths and values, but would share the same exponent. Allocation information detailing the length of a mantissa is placed in a 4-bit field in each PASC frame. Because the total number of bits representing each sample within a subband is constant, this allocation information (like the exponent) needs to be transmitted only once every 12 samples. A "0" allocation value is conveyed when a subband is not encoded; in this case neither exponent nor mantissa values within that subband are transmitted. The 15-bit mantissa yields a maximum signal-to-noise ratio of 92 dB. The 6-bit exponent can convey 64 values; however, a pattern of all 1's is not used, and another value is used as a reference. There are thus 62 values each representing 2-dB steps for an ideal total of 124 dB. The reference is used to divide this into two ranges, one from 0 to –118 dB, and the other from 0 to +6 dB. The 6 dB of headroom is needed because a component in a single subband might have a peak amplitude 6 dB higher than the broadband composite audio signal. The broadband dynamic range is thus equivalent to 19 bits of linear coding.

A complete PASC frame contains synchronization information, sample bits, scale factors, bit allocation information, and control bits for sampling frequency information, emphasis, etc. The total number of bits in a PASC frame (with 2 channels, with 384 samples, over 8 ms, sampled at 48 kHz) is 3072. This in turns yields the 384-kbps DCC transmission rate. With the addition of error detection and correction code, and 8/10 modulation, the final bit rate to tape is 768 kbps, with 96 kbps to each of the eight main data tracks. Sampling frequencies of 32 and 44.1 kHz also are supported, and because the number of bands remains fixed at 32, the subband width becomes

689.06 Hz with a 44.1-kHz sampling frequency. Because the output bit rate is fixed at 384 kbps, and 384 samples/channel per frame is fixed, there is a reduction in frame rate at sampling frequencies of 32 and 44.1 kHz, and thus an increase in the number of bits per frame. These additional bits per frame are used by the PASC algorithm to further increase audio quality.

PASC decoding proceeds frame by frame, using the processing shown in Fig. 11-27. Following demodulation, error correction, and deinterleaving, PASC data is reformatted to linear PCM by a subband decoder, using allocation information, and scale factors. Received scale factors are placed in an array with two columns of 32 rows, each six bits wide. Each column represents an output channel, and each row represents one subband. The subband samples are multiplied by the scale factors to restore them to their quantized values; empty subbands are automatically assigned a zero value. A synthesis reconstruction filter recombines the 32 subbands into one broadband audio signal. This subband filter operates identically (but inversely) to the input filter. As in the encoder, 384 samples/channel represent 8 ms of audio signal (at a sampling frequency of 48 kHz). Following this subband filtering, the signal is ready for reproduction through D/A converters.

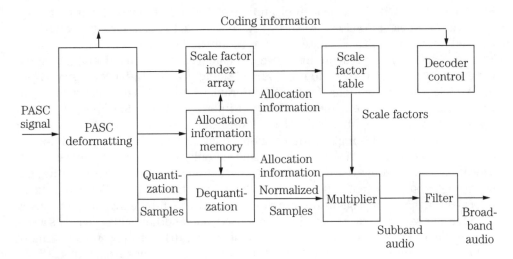

11-27 PASC decoder used in the DCC format; it is a version of ISO/MPEG-1 Layer I. Philips

Because psychoacoustic processing, bit allocation, and other operations are not used in the decoder, its cost is quite low. More importantly, the decoder is transparent to improvements in encoder technology. If the psychoacoustic models used in PASC encoders are improved, the resulting fidelity would improve as well. Because the PASC encoding algorithm is a function of digital signal processing, more sophisticated coding is possible. For example, because the number of bits per frame varies according to sample rate, it might be expedient to create different allocation tables for different sampling rates. FFT side-chains can be used to permit better analysis of the spectral content of subbands. For example, knowledge of where signals are placed within bands can be useful in more precisely assigning masking curves to adjacent bands. The first generation PASC algorithm assumes signals are at band edges, the most conservative approach. DCC recorders claim 18-bit performance. Subjectively, most listeners are unable to differentiate between a PASC recording and an original CD recording.

AC-1, AC-2, and AC-3 Coders

Many data reduction codecs have been designed for a variety of applications. The AC-1 stereo coder uses adaptive delta modulation, as described in chapter 4, combined with analog companding; it is not a perceptual coder. An AC-1 coder can code a 20-kHz bandwidth stereo audio signal into a 512-kbps bit stream (approximately a 3:1 reduction). AC-1 is used in satellite relays of television and FM programming, as well as cable radio services.

The AC-2 stereo coder is a perceptual coder using a low complexity block transform. It divides a wideband signal into multiple subbands using a 512-point 50% overlapping FFT algorithm performing a MDCT/MDST calculation. Coefficients are grouped into subbands containing from 1 to 15 coefficients to model critical bandwidths. Subbands have pre-allocated bits, with the lower subbands receiving a greater share; additional bits are adaptively drawn from a pool and assigned according to the logarithm of peak energy levels in subbands. Coefficients are quantized according to bit allocation calculations, and blocks are formed. Algorithm parameters vary according to sampling frequency. At sampling frequencies of 48, 44.1 and 32 kHz, the following apply: bytes/block: 168, 184, 190; total bits: 1344, 1472, 1520; subbands: 40, 43, 42; adaptive bits: 225, 239, 183.

The AC-2 coder provides high audio quality with a data rate of 256 kbps; with 16-bit input, reduction ratios include 6.1:1, 5.6:1, and 5.4:1 for sample rates of 48, 44.1 and 32 kHz respectively. AC-2 is also used at 120 and 192 kbps. AC-2 is a registered .WAV type so that AC-2 files are interchangeable between computer platforms. The AC-2 .WAV header contains an auxiliary data field at the end of each block selectable from 0 to 32 bits. For example, peak levels can be stored to facilitate viewing and editing of .WAV files. AC-2 coder applications include PC soundcards, studio/transmitter links, and ISDN linking of recording studios for long distance recording sessions. AC-2A is a multirate, adaptive block coder, designed for higher reduction ratios.

The AC-3 algorithm is an outgrowth of the AC-2 encoding format. It is a perceptual coder providing a 5.1 multichannel surround format with left, center right, left-surround, right-surround, and a subwoofer channel. These six channels can be coded at a rate of 384 kbps, using much less bandwidth than a CD. The AC-3 coder is backward compatible with matrix surround sound formats, two-channel stereo, and monaural reproduction; all of these can be decoded from the AC-3 data stream. Significantly, AC-3 does not use 5.1 matrixing in its bit stream; this ensures that quantization noise is not directed to an incorrect channel, where it is unmasked. AC-3 transmits a discrete multichannel coded bit stream, with digital down-mixing in the decoder to create the appropriate number (mono, stereo, matrix surround or full multichannel) of reproduction channels.

In addition, AC-3 contains a dialogue level control so that the reproduced level of dialogue is uniform for all programs and channels. AC-3 also contains a dynamic range control feature; control data can be placed in the bit stream so that a program's dynamic range can be decreased. However, the decoder can be optionally used to alter the dynamic range of a program to suit the user's preference. Additional services can be embedded in the bit stream including verbal description for the visually impaired, dialogue with enhanced intelligibility for the hearing impaired, commentary, and a second stereo program. All services may be tagged to indicate language.

AC-3 uses hybrid backward/forward adaptive bit allocation in which an adaptive allocation routine operates in both the encoder and decoder. The model defines the spectral envelope, which is encoded in the bit stream. The encoder contains a core psychoacoustic model, but can employ a different model and compare results. If desirable, the encoder can use the data syntax to code parameter variations in the core model, or convey explicit delta bit allocation information, to improve results. Block diagrams of an AC-3 encoder and decoder are shown in Fig. 11-28.

In the AC-3 encoder, blocks of 512 samples are collected and highpass filtered at 3 Hz to eliminate dc offset and analyzed with a bandpass filter to detect transients. Blocks are windowed and processed with an adaptive transform coder using a critically sampled filter bank with time domain alias cancellation (TDAC) described by Princen and Bradley. An FFT is employed to implement an MDCT/MDST algorithm; time resolution is 10.66 ms at 48 kHz. Because there is a 50% window overlap, each PCM sample is represented in two sequential transform blocks; coefficients are decimated by a factor of two to provide 256 coefficients per block. The block length can be dynamically reduced to 256 for wideband transient signals; resolution increases to 5.33 ms. The 512 sample block is split in two, and each half-block is transformed separately to produce 128 unique coefficients for a total of 512; this is the same number of coefficients as with a long block, but temporal resolution is doubled to 2.67 ms.

Each frequency coefficient is processed with floating point representation with mantissa and exponent to maintain dynamic range. The coded exponents represent the signal spectrum and their representation is referred to as the spectral envelope. The spectral envelope is coded as the difference between adjacent filters; because the filter response falls off at 12 dB/octave, deltas of +2 (+1 represents a +6-dB difference) are needed. The first dc term is coded as an absolute, and other exponents are coded as one of five changes from the previous lower frequency exponent. Groups of three differentials are coded in a 7-bit word. This is known as D15 exponent coding of the spectral envelope (2.33 bits per exponent); it provides fine frequency resolution, and is used when the audio signal envelope is relatively constant over many audio blocks. Because D15 is conveyed when the spectrum is stable, the estimate is coded only occasionally, for example, once every six blocks (32 ms) yielding 0.39 bits per audio sample.

The spectral estimate must be updated more frequently when the signal spectrum is less stable; this estimate is coded with less frequency resolution. Two methods are used. D25 provides medium frequency resolution; a delta is coded for every other frequency coefficient; the data rate is 1.16 bits per exponent. D25 is used when the spectrum is stable over 2–3 blocks, then significantly changes. In the D45 coding, one delta is coded for every four coefficients; the data rate is 0.58 bits per exponent.

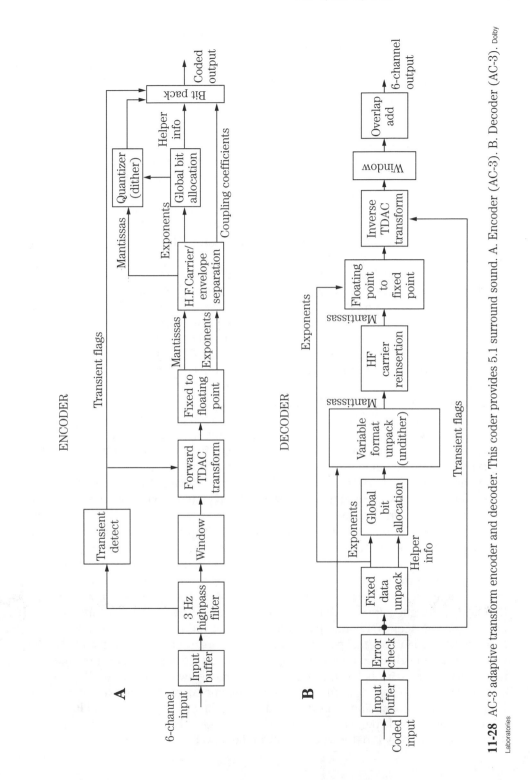

11-28 AC-3 adaptive transform encoder and decoder. This coder provides 5.1 surround sound. A. Encoder (AC-3). B. Decoder (AC-3). Dolby Laboratories

D45 provides good time and frequency resolution, and is used when transients occur within single audio blocks. The encoder selects the exponent coding method (D15, D25, D45 or REUSE) for every audio block and places this in a 2-bit exponent strategy field. In most cases, D15 is coded in the first block in a frame, and reused for the next five blocks. Because the exponent selection is coded in the bit stream, the decoder tracks the results of any encoder methodology.

The core bit allocation algorithm considers the decoded spectral envelope to be the power spectral density (psd) of the signal. This signal is convolved with a simplified spreading function that represents the ear's masking response. As many as 256 psd exponent values may be created, but these are grouped into bands that emulate critical bands and reduced in number to form 64 banded psd values. The spreading function is approximated by two masking curves: fast-decaying upwards curve and slow-decaying upwards curve, which is offset downwards in level. The curves are referred to as fast leak and slow leak. Convolution is performed starting at the lowest frequency psd; each new psd is compared to current leak values and judged to be significant or not; this yields the predicted masking value for each band.

This predicted curve is compared to a hearing threshold, and the larger of the values is used. The resulting predicted masking curve is subtracted from the original unbanded psd to determine the SMR ratio for each transform coefficient; these are used to quantize each coefficient mantissa. Bits are taken iteratively from a common bit pool available to all channels; mantissa quantization is adjusted to use the available bit rate. Pre-allocated bits are not used; the effect of interchannel masking is relatively slight. Quantized mantissas are scaled and offset; subtractive dither is optionally employed using a pseudo-random number generator; a mode bit indicates when dither is used and provides synchronization to the decoder's subtractive dither circuit. In addition, the carrier portion of high frequency localization information is removed, and the envelope is coded instead; high-frequency multichannel carrier content may be combined into a coupling channel.

Coupling may be performed at low bit rates, when signal conditions exceed the bit rate. It efficiently codes a multichannel signal, taking into account high-frequency directionality limitations in human hearing, without reducing audio bandwidth. Because the ear is unable to distinguish individual cycles of high-frequency sounds (above 2 kHz) and instead relies on envelope detection, directionality is determined by interaural time delay of the envelope and by perceived frequency response based on head shadowing. As a result, the ear cannot independently detect direction of two high-frequency sounds that are close in frequency. The AC-3 coder can couple channels at high frequencies; care is taken to avoid phase cancellation of the common channels. Coupling coordinates for each individual channel code the ratio of original signal power in a band to the coupling channel power in each band. Coupling channels are encoded in the same way as individual channels with a spectral envelope comprised of exponents, and mantissas; frequencies below a certain coupling frequency (typically 10 kHz) are encoded as individual channels, and encoded as coupling coordinates above the coupling frequency. During decoding, individual channel coupling coordinates are multiplied by the coupling channel coefficients to regenerate individual high-frequency coefficients. The coupling strategy is determined wholly in the encoder.

An AC-3 frame contains a synchronization field, header, audio data as quantized frequency coefficients, and CRCC error detection data; frame period is 32 ms at a 48-kHz sampling frequency. The synchronization information (SI) field contains a 16-bit synchronization word, 2-bit sampling rate code, and 6-bit frame size code. The bit stream information (BSI) header field describes the audio data with information such as coding mode, timecode, copyright, normalized dialogue level, and language code. Audio blocks are variable length, but six coded blocks, with 256 samples per block, must fit in one frame; these blocks mainly comprise quantized mantissas, differential exponents, coupling data, and bit allocation side chain data. One 16-bit CRCC word is contained at the end of each frame, and an additional 16-bit CRCC word may be optionally placed in the SI header. In each case, the generating polynomial is $x^{16} + x^{15} + x^2 + 1$. Error detection and the response to errors varies in different AC-3 applications. The first block always contains a complete refresh of all decoding information. Unused block area may be used for auxiliary data.

The decoder receives blocks of data, and performs error correction as necessary. Bit reallocation is performed based on exponents and allocation side chain data conveyed with the bit stream; the encoder may send bit allocation override information so that improved encoders are compatible with existing decoders. Coefficients are returned to fixed point representation, dither is subtracted, carrier and envelope information reconstructed, and the inverse transform, window, and overlap operations produce output data. Subwoofer data is padded with zeros before the inverse transform so the output sampling frequency is compatible with the other channels.

Because AC-3 eliminates redundancies between channels, greater coding efficiency is achieved relative to AC-2; a stereo version of AC-3 provides high quality with a data rate of 192 kbps. The AC-3 format also delivers data describing a program's original production format (monaural, stereo, matrix, etc.), can encode selectable dynamic range compression, can route low bass only to those speakers with subwoofers, and provide gain control of a program. AC-3 can process 24-bit digital audio signals over 20-Hz to 20-kHz bandwidth; the bass channel extends from 20 to 120 Hz. Sampling frequencies of 32, 44.1 and 48 kHz are supported. Data rates range from as low as 32 kbps for a single monaural channel to as high as 640 kbps for 5.1 channels, providing a wide range of applications. AC-3 facilitates editing on a block level, and blocks can be rocked back and forth at the decoder, and read as forward and reverse audio.

When used for film coding, AC-3 is known as Dolby Stereo Digital film sound, providing 5.1 audio channels. Data is optically printed between the sprocket holes, with a data rate of approximately 320 kbps. Existing analog soundtracks remain unaffected, providing compatibility. AC-3 is also used to code 5.1 audio for cable and satellite distribution and home theater products such as video laser discs and DVD-Video discs; this is known as Dolby Digital. AC-3 is also used to code the audio portion of the high definition television HDTV standard devised by a "Grand Alliance" of manufacturers. These coding algorithms were developed by Dolby Laboratories.

APT-X Subband Coder

The APT-X system is an example of subband coder providing 4:1 reduction; however, it does not explicitly reply on psychoacoustic modelling. It operates entirely in the time domain, and uses adaptive bit allocation with adaptive differential pulse code modulation. The audio signal is split into four subbands using QMF filters and analyzed in the time domain; linear prediction ADPCM is used to quantize each band according to content. Backward adaptive quantization is used in which accuracy of the current sample is compared to the previous sample, and correction is applied with adaption multipliers taken from lookup tables in the encoder. This codes the difference in audio signal levels from one sample to the next; the added noise is white. A 4-bit word is output for every 16-bit input word. The decoder demultiplexes the signal, applies ADPCM decoding, and inverse filtering. A primary asset is low coding delay; for example, at 32-kHz sampling frequency, coding delay is a constant 3.8 ms. A range of sampling frequencies and reduction ratios can be used. APT-X was developed by Audio Processing Technology.

Perceptual Coding Performance Evaluation

An interesting question for perceptual coders is how to objectively measure their performance. Linear measurements might reveal gross errors, but cannot penetrate the question of the algorithm's perceptual accuracy. A narrow band of noise introduced around a tone might not be audible; broadband white noise at the same energy would be plainly audible, but both would provide the same S/N measurement. A series of sine tones might provide a flat frequency response in a perceptual coder because the tones are easily coded; however, a broadband complex tone might be coded with a signal-dependent response. Traditional audio devices are measured according to their small deviations from linearity; perceptual coders are highly nonlinear, as is the human ear. Exactly how to determine the audibility of coding artifacts is not trivial.

It is possible to nonquantitatively evaluate reduction artifacts using simple test equipment. A sinewave oscillator can output test tones at a variety of frequencies; a dual-trace oscilloscope can display both the uncompressed and compressed waveforms. The waveforms should be time aligned to compensate for processing delay in the coder. With a 16-bit system, viewed at 2 V peak to peak, one bit represents 30 µv. Any errors, including wideband noise and harmonic distortion at the 1-bit level, can be observed. The idle channel signal performance can be observed with the coded output of a zero input signal; noise, error patterns, or glitches might appear. It also might be instructive to examine a low level signal (0.1 V). In addition, a maximum level signal can be used to evaluate headroom at a variety of frequencies. More sophisticated evaluation can be performed with distortion and spectrum analyzers, but analysis is difficult. For example, Fig. 11-29 shows the spectral analysis of a 16-bit linear recorder and a 384-kbps perceptual recorder. Although the perceptual coder has added noise within its masking curve around the tone, it is easily able to code the signal with low distortion.

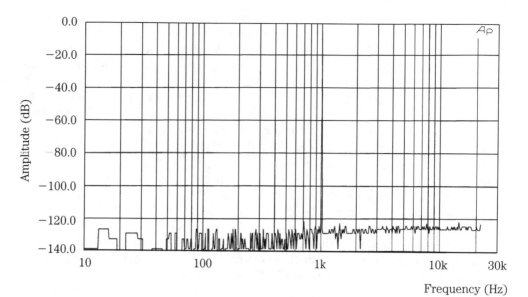

A

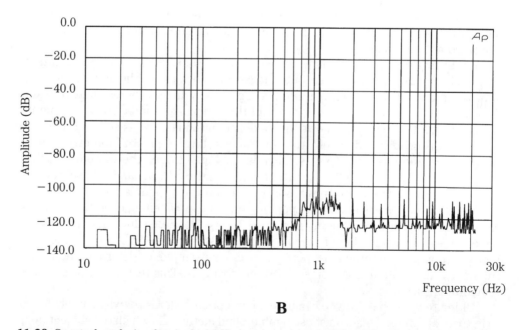

B

11-29 Spectral analysis of a single 1-kHz test tone reveals little about the performance of a perceptual coder. A. Analysis of a 16-bit linear PCM recorder shows a noise floor 120 dB below signal. B. Analysis of a 384-kbps perceptual codec shows a noise floor 110 dB below signal with slightly increased noise within the masking curve. Audio Precision

The best objective testing means for a perceptual coder is an artificial ear. To measure perceived accuracy, the algorithm contains a model that emulates the human hearing response. The measuring model can identify defects in the coder under test. Karlheinz Brandenburg has devised a noise-to-mask ratio (NMR) to estimate coding margin. The original signal (appropriately delayed) and the error signal (the difference between the original and coded signals) are independently subjected to FFT analysis, and the resulting spectra are divided into subbands. The masking threshold (maximum masked error energy) in each original signal subband is estimated; the actual error energy in each coded signal subband is determined and compared to the masking threshold; the ratio of error energy to masking threshold is the NMR in each subband. A positive NMR would indicate an audible artifact. The NMR values can be linearly averaged and expressed in dB; this mean NMR measures remaining audibility headroom in the coded signal. NMR can be plotted over time to identify areas of coding difficulty. A masking flag, generated when the NMR exceeds 0 dB in a subband (artifact assumed to be audible) can be used to measure the number of impairments in a coded signal. A relative masking flag counts the number of impairments normalized over a number of blocks and subbands.

Richard Cabot has devised a test that perceptually compares the codec output with a known steady state test signal. A multitone signal is applied to the codec, the output is transformed into the frequency domain with FFT, and applied to an auditory model to estimate masking effects of the signal. Because the spectrum of the test signal is known, any error products can be identified and measured. In particular, the error signal can be compared to internally modelled masking curves to estimate audibility. The NMR ratio of the error signal level and masking threshold can be displayed as a function of frequency.

For example, Fig. 11-30A shows a steady state test of a codec. The multitone signal consists of 26 sinewaves distributed logarithmically across the audio spectrum, approximately one per critical band with a gap to allow analysis of residual noise and distortion; it is designed to maximally load the coder's subbands, and consume its available bit rate. The figure shows the modelled masking curve based on the multitone, and distortion produced by the coder, consisting of quantization error, intermodulation products, and noise sidebands. In Fig. 11-30B, the system also has integrated the distortion and noise products across the critical bandwidth of the human ear to simulate perceived distortion level. Distortion products above the model's masking curve might be audible, depending on ambient listening conditions. In this case, some distortion might be audible at low levels. Clearly, evaluation of results depends on the sophistication of the analyzer's masking model. Stereo test tones can be used to analyze interchannel performance, for example, to determine how high frequency information is combined between channels. This test does not evaluate temporal artifacts.

Ultimately, the best way to evaluate a perceptual coder is to exhaustively listen to it. Critical listening tests must use double-blind methods in which the subject does not know the identities of the selections. For example, in a "triple-stimulus, hidden-reference, double-blind" test the listener is presented with a known reference signal and two unknown signals. One of the unknown signals is identical to the known reference and the other is the signal under test; the listener must assign a score to both

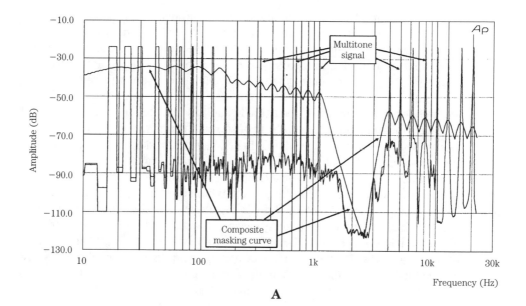

A

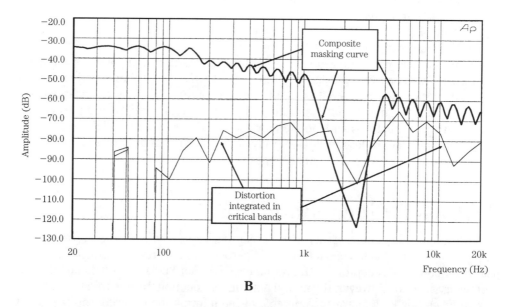

B

11-30 A multitone test signal is designed to deplete the bit capacity of a perceptual coder, emulating the action of a complex musical tone. A. Analysis shows the output test tone, and the composite masking curve calculated by the testing device. B. The testing device computes the composite distortion in critical bands; distortion above the calculated masking threshold might be audible. Audio Precision

unknown signals, rating them against the known reference. Short music examples (perhaps 10 to 20 seconds) can be auditioned repeatedly to identify artifacts. Particularly challenging examples such as glockenspiel, castanets, triangle, harpsichord, tambourine, speech, trumpet, and bass guitar are used. Generally, music with transient, complex tones, rich in content around the ear's most sensitive region, 1 to 5 kHz, are useful.

When a coder is not transparent, artifacts such as changes in timbre, bursts of noise, granular ambient sound, and shifting of stereo imaging can be used to identify the "signature" of the coder. Subband coders can have unmasked quantization noise that appears as a burst of noise in a processing block. In transform coders, errors are reconstructed as basis functions (for example, a windowed cosine) of the coder's transform; a coder with a long block length can exhibit a pre-echo burst of noise just before a transient, or there might be a tinkling sound; transform coders tend to be more audible at high frequencies. In many cases, artifacts are discerned only after repeated listening trials. Expert listeners are preferred over average listeners because they are more familiar with peculiar artifacts; alternatively, listeners might be trained with very low bit-rate examples or left-minus-right signals that expose artifacts. It is generally felt that a 16-bit recording is not an adequate reference when testing high quality perceptual coders because many coders can outperform the reference.

The International Radio Consultative Committee (CCIR) has devised a five-point impairment scale for subjection evaluation of reduction algorithms:

    5 Imperceptible
    4 Perceptible, but not annoying
    3 Slightly annoying
    2 Annoying
    1 Very annoying

Panels of listeners rate algorithms on this scale. Original, uncompressed material may receive an averaged score of 4.8 on the CCIR scale. When a coder also obtains an average score of 4.8 it is said to be transparent. Lower scores assess how far from transparency a coder is; numerous statistical analysis techniques can be used. Perhaps 50 listeners are needed for good statistical results. Higher reduction ratios generally score less well. Generally, a monaural channel coded at 128 kbps (245 kbps for stereo) can be transparent.

MPEG-1 Video Standard

Although this chapter deals with perceptual audio, many of the concepts also apply to perceptual video coding so a brief detour is appropriate. In normal daylight, the color sensitive receptors of the retina collect about 800 Mbits of visual information every second; However, the neural network connecting the eye to the visual cortex reduces this by a factor of 100; most of the information entering the eye is not needed by the brain. Similarly, video reduction algorithms such as MPEG-1 can achieve reduction ratios of 100 and beyond using spatial and temporal coding.

The magnitude of data required to code a video program is enormous. American homes receive an analog composite video NTSC signal with a bandwidth of 4.2 MHz;

to digitize this, the Nyquist theorem demands a sampling frequency of 8.4 MHz; at 8 bits/sample, this yields 67.2 Mbps. Because a color image is comprised of red, green, and blue components, this rate must be multiplied by three, yielding 201.6 Mbps. A 650-Mbyte CD could store about 26 seconds of this digital video program, and it would take 72 minutes to play back the 26-second program. Data requirements can be reduced by dropping the frame rate, the size of the image can be reduced to a quarter-screen or smaller, and the number of bits used to code colors can be reduced. More subtly, file size can be reduced by examining the file for irrelevancy within a frame and over a series of frames, and redundant data can be subjected to data reduction. The latter techniques can be very efficient at preserving good picture quality, with a low bit rate.

One goal of MPEG-1 is the reduction of audio/video data rates to within the 1.41-Mbps data transfer rate of the compact disc; this also allows transmission over computer networks and other applications. Using the MPEG-1 video coding algorithm, natural pictures coded at 165 Mbps (the CCIR 601 standard for natural quality pictures specifies 165 Mbps) can be reduced to approximately 1.15 Mbps, a reduction ratio of 140:1; audio data at 1.41 Mbps can be reduced to about 0.22 Mbps, a ratio of 7:1. The video and audio data are combined into a single data stream with a total rate of 1.41 Mbps; this provides the basis for the Video CD, CD-ROM, and other formats.

The MPEG-1 video algorithm also can perform over a wide range of bit rates and picture resolution levels. Encoding algorithms are not fixed, thus allowing optimization for particular visual phenomena, and overall improvements in encoding technique. Video reduction exploits spatial and temporal correlation between pixels that are adjacent in space and time. Highly random pictures, with high entropy, are more difficult to reduce. Most pictures contain redundancy that can be accurately predicted. MPEG-1 exploits redundancy in individual frames as well as redundancy in sequences of frames; in either case, psychovisual principles are applied to take advantage of limitations in the human visual system; in other words, perceptual coding is used.

Audio engineers are accustomed to frequency, the number of waveform periods over time. Spatial frequency describes the rate of change in visual information, without reference to time. (The way a picture changes over time is referred to as temporal frequency.) The eye's contrast sensitivity peaks at spatial frequencies of about 5 cycles/degree, and falls to zero at 100 cycles/degree. The former corresponds to viewing objects 2 mm in size at a distance of 1 meter; the latter corresponds to objects 0.1 mm in size. The contrast in a picture can thus be described in horizontal and vertical spatial frequency.

The eye can perceive about 1000 levels of grey; this would require 10 bits to quantize; in practice, 8 bits is usually sufficient. Brightness (luminance) uses one set of receptors in the retina, and color (chrominance) uses three. Peak sensitivity of chrominance change occurs at 1 cycle/degree and is zero at 12 cycles/degree. Clearly, because color resolution is less, it can be coded with fewer bits.

A color video signal can be represented as individually coded red, green and blue signals. MPEG-1 video reduction begins by converting RGB triplets into component video YCrCb triplets (Y is luminance, Cr is red chrominance difference, and Cb is blue chrominance difference); this allows more efficient coding. Because the eye is less sensitive to color, the Cr and Cb values are subsampled to reduce color bandwidth. Vertical and horizontal resolution can be halved to 352 pixels by 240 lines (NTSC). The image is divided into blocks each corresponding to an 8-×-8 pixel area. Blocks are transformed with DCT, coefficients quantized, run length coded, and entropy coded. Further, data is assembled into macroblocks containing six 8-×-8 pixel blocks, four of Y values and a number (1,2 or 4) each of Cr and Cb values. Macroblock coding is used to create highly reduced motion compensated frames. For simplicity, we will consider only luminance coding.

A static image can be represented as a two-dimensional distribution of amplitude values, or a set of two-dimensional frequency coefficients. The MPEG-1 video algorithm uses the discrete cosine transform (DCT) to convert the former to the latter. In other words, the spatial information comprising a picture is transformed into its spatial frequencies. The DCT transform requires the summation of $i{\times}j$ multiplicative blocks where $i{\times}j$ is pixel amplitude at a row i and column j position to generate the value of the transform coefficient at each point. Following the DCT, the spatial frequency coefficients are arranged with dc value in the upper-left corner, increasing horizontal frequency from left to right and increasing vertical frequency from top to bottom, as represented in Fig. 11-31. The output values are no longer pixels; they are coefficients representing the level of energy in the frequency components. For example, an image of finely spaced stripes would produce a large value at the pattern repetition frequency, with other components at zero. Figure 11-32 shows the amplitudes of pixels in a complicated image, and its transform coefficients; the latter are highly ordered. The transform does not provide reduction. However, after it is transformed, the relative importance of signal content can be analyzed. For most images, the important information is concentrated in a few number of coefficients (usually the dc and low spatial frequency coefficients).

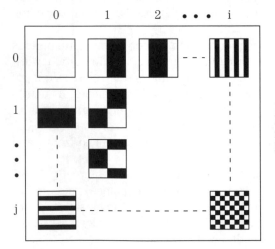

11-31
DCT transform coefficients can be represented as a block showing increasing horizontal and vertical spatial frequency.

Figure 11-33 illustrates MPEG-1 coding of an image; each pixel in the 8 × 8 matrix has an 8-bit value from 0 (black) to 255 (white) representing brightness. Observe, for example, that the lower pixels in the block (at the top of the locomotive's

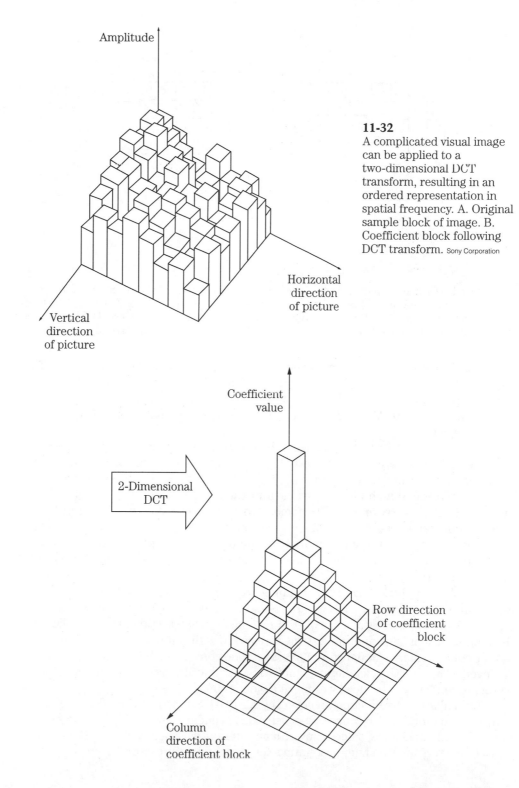

Amplitude

Vertical
direction
of picture

Horizontal
direction
of picture

2-Dimensional
DCT

Coefficient
value

Row direction
of coefficient
block

Column
direction of
coefficient block

11-32
A complicated visual image
can be applied to a
two-dimensional DCT
transform, resulting in an
ordered representation in
spatial frequency. A. Original
sample block of image. B.
Coefficient block following
DCT transform. Sony Corporation

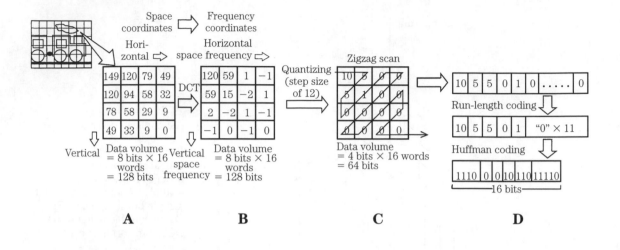

11-33 Intraframe encoding of an image using the ISO/MPEG-1 video algorithm. A. An 8-x-8 block of pixels represent luminance values. B. A DCT transform presents the frequency coefficients of the block. C. The coefficients are quantized to achieve reduction and scanned with a zig-zag pattern. D. The data sequence is applied to run-length and Huffman coding to achieve data compression. Matsushita Electric

smokestack) have low values, representing a dark picture area. Following the DCT, the spatial frequency coefficients are presented, and the dc value takes the proportional average value of all pixels in the block; in this example, the proportional average brightness is 120. Also observe that the block does not contain significant high spatial frequencies.

Reduction is achieved by quantizing the coefficients and discarding low energy coefficients by truncating them to zero. In this example, a step size of 12 is applied; it is selected according to the average brightness value. In practice, the important dc value is often coded with high precision (for example, a value of 8) and higher frequencies in the matrix are quantized more coarsely (for example, a value of 80). Quantization can be varied from block to block. In this way, the algorithm exploits the visual characteristics and limitations of human vision to place coding impairments in frequencies and regions where they are perceptually minimal. Data is reduced by a factor of 2.

Variable-Length Coding (VLC) is applied to the transform coefficients; coefficients are scanned with a zig-zag pattern and sequenced; high frequency detail is truncated and appears as a series of 0s. Run length coding is applied to consolidate the long strings of data, and these strings are coded with Huffman coding tables; the most frequent value is assigned the shortest codeword. A further reduction of 4 is achieved. The JPEG video format similarly uses intraframe reduction; in other words, redundancy is reduced within each video frame.

The majority of reduction achieved by MPEG-1 comes from temporal redundancy in sequential video frames. Because video sequences are highly correlated in time it is only necessary to code interframe differences. Specifically, motion-compensated interframe coding, accounting for past and future correlation in video frames, is used to reduce the data rate. For example, the macroblocks in the current frame are searched and compared to regions in the previous frames; if a match is made within an error criteria, a displacement vector is coded describing how many pixels the current image has moved from the previous frame. Because frame-to-frame correlation is often high, predictive strategies are used to estimate the macroblock motion from past (and future) frames. In other words, only the differences in vectors from the previous frame are coded.

Data in the current frame not found in other frames is considered as a residual error in the prediction, as shown in Fig. 11-34. Given the previous frame in memory, the displacement vectors are applied to create a motion-compensated frame. This predicted intermediate frame is subtracted from the actual current frame being coded; the additional detail is the residual prediction error that is coded with DCT as described above. During decoding, this error signal is added to the motion-compensated detail in the previous frame to obtain the current frame.

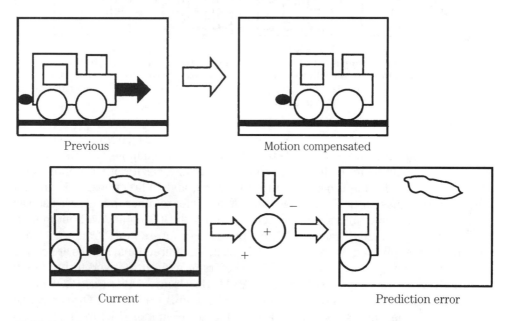

Previous   Motion compensated

Current   Prediction error

11-34 Interframe coding offers opportunity for efficient data reduction. Displacement vectors are applied to a previous frame to create a motion-compensated frame. Other residual data is coded as a prediction error. Matsushita Electric

Figure 11-35 shows complete motion compensation and coding. The current frame (A) is compared to the previous frame (B) to create intermediate motion-compensated frame (C) and displacement vectors. The prediction error (D) between the intermediate frame and the current frame is input to the DCT for coding. Feedforward and feedback control paths use the frame error produced by applying the reverse quantized data and reverse DCT as input to reduce quantization error. Macroblocks that are new to the current frame also are coded with DCT and combined with the motion vectors.

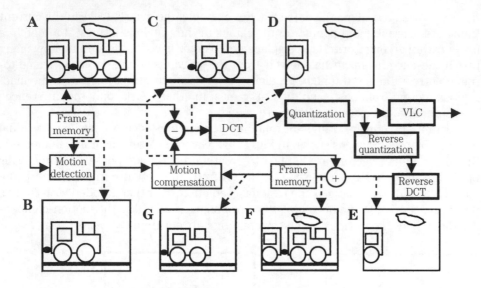

11-35 Summary of interframe coding showing how motion-compensation frames are created, and data is coded with DCT and VLC. A. Current frame to be coded. B. Previous frame. C. Intermediate motion compensated frame. D. Prediction error frame. E., F., G. Frames within the coding loop. Matsushita Electric

MPEG-1 codes three frame types; they provide key reference frames so that artifacts do not accumulate, yet provide bit rate savings. For example, accurate frames must appear regularly in the bit stream to serve as references for other motion-compensated frames. Frame types are Intra, Predicted, and Bidirectional (I,P, and B) frames. Intraframes are self-contained; they do not refer to other frames, are used as reference frames, and are moderately compressed with DCT coding without motion compensation. Predicted frames refer to a previous or future I or P frame; they are more highly compressed using motion compensation. Bidirectional frames are coded with interpolation prediction using motion vectors from both past and future I or P frames; they are very highly compressed. An MPEG Group of Pictures (GOP) consists of an I frame followed by some number of P and B frames. A GOP can range from 10–15 frames for fast motion, and 30–60 for slower motion. Picture quality suffers with GOPs less than 10 frames. I frames use more bytes, but are used for random access, still frame, etc.

A rectangular spatial format is typically used, with a maximum picture area of noninterlaced 352 pixels by 240 lines (NTSC) or 352 pixels by 288 lines (PAL/SECAM), but the picture area can be used flexibly. For example, a low and wide area of 768 pixels by 132 lines, or a high and narrow area of 176 pixels by 576 lines could be coded. During playback, the entire decoded picture, or other defined parts of it, can be displayed, with the window's size and shape under program control. Audio and video synchronization is ensured by the MPEG-1 multiplexed bit stream. The video quality of MPEG-1 coding is similar to that of the VHS format. The Video CD and CD-I FMV formats use MPEG-1 coding; they are described in chapter 9.

The similar MPEG-2 video format provides a variety of interlaced resolutions: High (less than 80 Mbps), High-1440 (less than 60 Mbps), Main (less than 15 Mbps), and Low (less than 4 Mbps). For example, using MPEG-2, an HDTV data rate of 1.2 Gbps could be delivered to homes via CATV. The DVD digital video disc uses MPEG-2 coding. Any MPEG-2 decoder can decode MPEG-1 signals.

Conclusion

Whereas traditional audio coding is often a question of specifications and measurements, perceptual coding is one of physiology and perception. Traditional audio technology occupies the physical world around us, but perceptual coders inhabit the more inaccessible world of psychoacoustics. It is only now, with the advent of digital signal processing, that audio engineers can design hardware and software that "hears" sound the same way that humans hear sound. In either case, as John William Rayleigh said in 1877 (the year in which Thomas Edison first shouted into his tinfoil recorder), "All questions connected with this subject must come for decision to the ear, as the organ of hearing; and from it there can be no appeal."

12

CHAPTER

The MiniDisc

The MiniDisc is a recording format that encompasses many aspects of contemporary digital audio technology. Conversion, magneto-optical recording, laser pickup, error correction, perceptual coding, and many subtle compact-disc technologies are contained in the MD. Yet the MiniDisc is a unique format that brings a number of desirable characteristics to both consumer and professional audio applications, as well as nonaudio data applications. Primarily, MD is designed as a low-cost, highly portable audio recorder/player that is promoted to succeed the analog cassette. In radio broadcasting, the MD is supplanting the analog cartridge.

System Overview

Development of the MiniDisc began in 1986, and the format was announced in 1991, with product launch a year later. The MD is designed to be the first recordable, erasable optical-disc audio format for consumer applications. It incorporates many aspects of CD technology, as well as existing optical media technology used in computer applications, and introduces numerous other innovations to create an original format. This disc format provides random access to data, its small size and shock memory promote portability, and its data reduction system preserves high sound quality.

The MiniDisc uses a 64-mm-diameter optical disc permanently housed in a rigid plastic cartridge measuring $72 \times 68 \times 5$ mm. Both prerecorded and recordable disc types are available. Prerecorded MD discs are quite similar to compact discs in design, using impressed pits against a reflective layer, with a single shutter on one side of the cartridge to permit access by the reading optical pickup. Prerecorded discs are playback-only, and cannot be recorded, hence accidental erasure is impossible. Recordable discs use magneto-optical technology, and the cartridge has two shutters, one on each side of the cartridge, for the optical pickup, and the magnetic head. The magnetic head physically touches the disc surface during recording, but head and disc wear are quite low. In either case, discs contain a maximum of 74 minutes of stereo audio program, along with subcode data information (serving much the same function as the CD's subcode). Prerecorded discs contain about four times more subcode data than recordable discs; however, both disc types permit value-added features such as stored text information.

A block diagram of a MiniDisc recorder/player is shown in Fig. 12-1. The servo, control, and user interface systems are similar to those found in CD players. The optical pickup functions similarly as well when reading prerecorded discs, but when writing data the laser's power is increased to heat the data surface, momentarily changing the magnetic properties of the data layer. The magnetic head is used to bathe the disc in a flux field, and in conjunction with the heating laser, writes data to the disc. In addition, the process of reading magnetically stored data from a recordable disc differs significantly from optically reading pits on a prerecorded disc. As in the CD, the MD uses eight-to-fourteen modulation (EFM). Also as in CD, a Cross-Interleave Reed-Solomon code (CIRC) is used during encoding and decoding; C1 is a (32,28) code and C2 is a (28,24) code; minimum distance is five. C1 is executed up to two errors, and C2 is executed up to four errors. A large memory buffer, holding perhaps 4 Mbits or more, gives the player great immunity over physical shock; even if the input flow is disrupted during playback, data can leave the buffer without interruption. The ATRAC (Adaptive TRansform Acoustic Coding) data reduction algorithm uses a modified discrete cosine transform and psychoacoustic masking principles to diminish data throughput to about ⅕ of its original volume, with minimal audio degradation. A/D and D/A converters are used to input and output analog audio signals, in addition to 44.1 kHz S/PDIF input/output with SCMS copy protection.

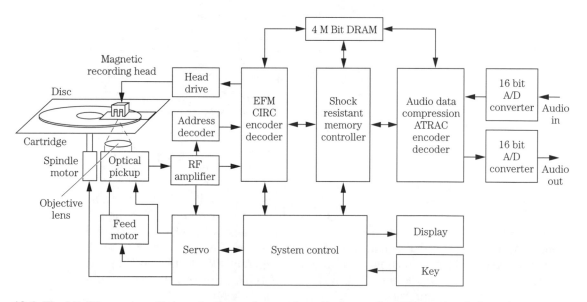

12-1 The MiniDisc system. Data reduction and magneto-optical recording differentiate it from the compact disc. Sony Corporation

Signal Format

The MiniDisc data format, shown in Fig. 12-2, is very similar to that used in the CD-ROM Mode 2 format. In the Mode 2 format, 98 CD frames comprise one sector (2352 total bytes), which is equivalent to 13.3 ms of playing time. During recording, following ATRAC, EFM and CIRC encoding, data is grouped into blocks. CIRC interleave length is 108 frames, or 14.5 ms. To use CIRC, three sectors must be used as linking sectors, and their area is called a link area. A link area greater than 108 frames (one sector) must be filled before writing begins (and after data ends) to perform proper interleaving. To utilize disc area efficiently, data can be written piecemeal across a disc; however, a random scattering would require many link areas on the disc, thus reducing capacity. To overcome this, data is written only after being grouped into substantial recording units called clusters, each containing 36 sectors. Rewriting is also performed in integer multiples of one cluster. Pending writing to disc in a cluster, data is temporarily saved in RAM, the same memory that serves as a shock buffer during playback.

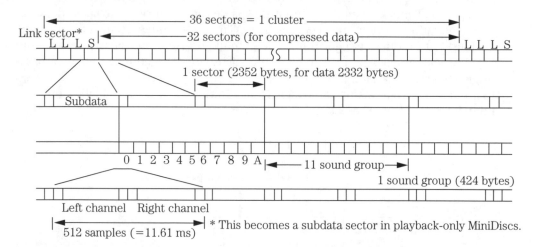

12-2 The MiniDisc data format is similar to that used in the CD-ROM Mode 2 format. However, sectors are grouped into clusters. Sony Corporation

The first three sectors of a 36-sector cluster serve as link sectors during recording; the fourth sector is reserved for subcode data. ATRAC-reduced audio data is stored in the remaining 32 sectors. After the last cluster sector is written, error correction data is written in the first link sector and half of the second sector in the following cluster. The data on master discs of playback-only MDs is recorded continuously along the data spiral thus the three sectors are not needed in a link area. As a result, all of the first four sectors can be used for subcode data holding text or other information. In addition, clearly, it is impossible to record the entire subcode data contents of a prerecorded MD onto a recordable MD.

During ATRAC encoding, following data reduction, audio data is grouped into 424-byte units called sound groups, with 212 bytes each for the left and right audio channels. Eleven sound groups are distributed into two sectors with left and right channels of five sound groups in the first sector, along with the left channel of a sixth sound group. The second sector contains the right channel of the sixth group and the left and right channels of another five sound groups. In other words, each of the two sectors contains $424 \times 5 + 212 \times 1 = 2332$ bytes of compressed audio data. In this way, eleven sound groups are written per two sectors in each 32-sector cluster. During playback, this data is decompressed with one sound group being equivalent to 512 samples ($512 \times 16 \times 2/8 = 2048$ bytes) for both channels with a playing time of 11.6 ms. Although perceptual coding is used by the ATRAC algorithm to reduce the data volume, the signal recording format itself is quite flexible.

As in the CD-ROM format, a variety of data types, with or without data reduction methods, can be placed on a MiniDisc. In one implementation, an MD-DATA disc holds 140 Mbytes of nonaudio data producing, for example, storage for personal computer applications. One disc can hold 2000 frames of still-color images; its data transfer rate is 150 kbytes/second and average seek time is 300 ms. The format is transparent to the computer platform; once the MD software is installed, information written on an MD can be retrieved or modified regardless of the differences in the computer's CPU (central processing unit) or operating system.

Disc Design

Both prerecorded and recordable MiniDisc formats have been developed to meet specific needs. The prerecorded disc format is designed to disseminate music from record companies; high-volume production at low manufacturing cost is essential. To provide this, the prerecorded format borrows many techniques from the Red Book CD format, in both concept and manufacturing method. In fact, a prerecorded MD disc is very similar to a CD. Data is recorded on a spiral from inner diameter to outer, with a lead-in area prefacing the program area, and a lead-out area following it. The lead-in area contains a table of contents (TOC). This is shown in Fig. 12-3A. As in CD, prerecorded MD data is represented as pits impressed in a polycarbonate substrate, and thus can be manufactured by injection molding techniques at CD pressing plants. Also as in CDs, the pit surface is covered by an aluminum reflective layer, as well as a protective layer. The disc cartridge has only one back shutter; the front of the cartridge can thus contain full graphics.

The recordable disc format differs considerably from the prerecorded CD and MD formats, and employs MO (magneto-optical) disc technology used in computer applications. Disc layout is similar in that lead-in, program, and lead-out areas are present. A user table of contents (UTOC) area is inserted between the lead-in and program areas; it is used to store information on data that is written to a disc. Furthermore, the table of contents in the lead-in area of a recordable disc contains information on recording power, disc recording time, and time of the UTOC. The TOC in a recordable disc is stored as pits and cannot be recorded. The UTOC, program area, and lead-out areas are all recordable. This is shown in Fig. 12-3B. Because magneto-optical recording requires both a magnetic head and laser pickup for operation, one on each side of the disc, shutters are placed on the front and back of the disc cartridge.

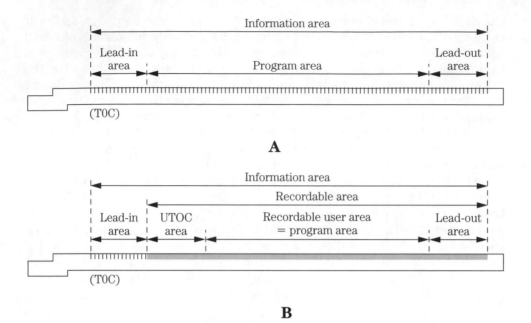

12-3 A MiniDisc recorder can play back prerecorded discs and record and play back magneto-optical discs. A. Prerecorded discs contain a lead-in area with TOC, program area, and lead-out area. B. Recordable discs contain a nonrecordable lead-in area with TOC, and a recordable UTOC, program area, and lead-out area.

To help ensure compatibility between discs and players, recordable discs are manufactured with a pregroove configuration, as shown in Fig. 12-4. Using the tracking and spindle servo control circuits, this groove guides the writing and reading laser within a spiral track that is 1.1 μm in width, separated from adjacent tracks by 0.5-μm guard bands. Although the groove is imprinted on the top of the disc, the laser beam is applied from underneath the disc substrate. The groove is 70 nm deep. Data is stored in a terbium-ferrite cobalt magnetic layer, and sandwiched by two silicon-nitride dielectric layers, which are used to concentrate laser heat into the interior recording layer. In addition, an aluminum reflective layer placed over these layers is designed to reflect the reading and writing laser beams. This entire structure is built on a polycarbonate substrate and covered by a protective layer.

Both prerecorded and recordable MD discs have an outer diameter of 64 mm, inner diameter of 11 mm, and substrate thickness of 1.2 mm. A magnetic center clamping plate covers the interior area and is used to stabilize the disc in the drive, through magnetic contact performed on one side of the disc. As with CDs, the inner circumference edge of the disc substrate is used to center the disc on the drive's spindle.

Random access to stored data is an important feature of the MiniDisc system. As in the CD, prerecorded MDs have addresses for each program selection, stored in the subcode data area. The pregrooves on recordable MDs cover the entire recordable surface and are specially formed to create addressing data, promoting quick ac-

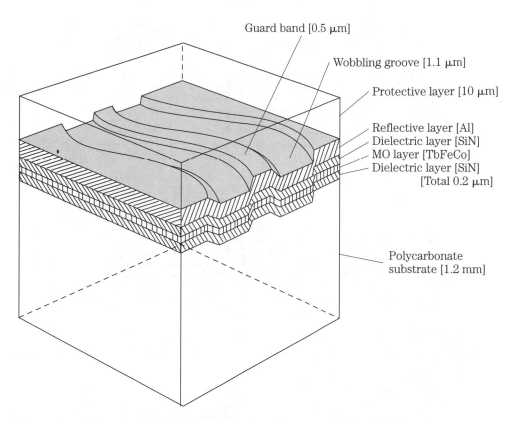

Guard band [0.5 μm]

Wobbling groove [1.1 μm]

Protective layer [10 μm]

Reflective layer [Al]
Dielectric layer [SiN]
MO layer [TbFeCo]
Dielectric layer [SiN]
[Total 0.2 μm]

Polycarbonate
substrate [1.2 mm]

12-4 Recordable discs are manufactured with a pregroove configuration to guide the writing and reading laser within a spiral track. The MO recording layer is contained within dielectric layers. Sony Corporation

cess. Specifically, the grooves contain a wobble to create addresses in 13.3-ms intervals, effectively controlling both absolute address time, and the constant linear velocity (CLV) speed. Both the program area and UTOC grooves contain a wobble. The user table of contents contains track number addresses (start and finish); because the UTOC uses the same MO technology as the recordable program area, track addresses can be edited to reflect changes in the recorded contents of a disc.

For example, Fig. 12-5 shows contents of a UTOC; in the first case, six tracks are marked with sequentially incremented start and stop addresses A through L. In the second case, an unwanted track has been erased; track 3 is removed from the UTOC, track numbers 4 through 6 are incremented upward, and addresses E and F become available. In the third case, two tracks have been combined into one; tracks 4 and 5 become track 4, track 6 becomes track 5, and start/stop address pairs G/H and I/J are rewritten to show G/J.

Although the prerecorded and recordable MD formats were developed as separate yet compatible media, a hybrid MD format combines prerecorded and recordable areas on one disc. With this format, for example, a student could listen to a pronounced phrase, repeat the phrase while recording, then listen to the result,

Before Editing

LEAD IN	UTOC	1	2	3	4	5	6	◄─Track Number	LEAD OUT

A   BC   DE   FG   HI   JK   L ◄─ Addresses

|← ─── Music data ─── →|

Contents

Track Number	Addresses
1	A B
2	C D
3	E F
4	G H
5	I J
6	K L

The UTOC contains both the Track Numbers and their associated address locations.

Editing out a Particular Track

LEAD IN	UTOC	1	2		3	4	5	◄─Track Number	LEAD OUT

A   BC   DE   FG   HI   JK   L ◄─ Addresses

Contents

Track Number	Addresses
1	A B
2	C D
3 → Blank	E F → Available
4 → 3	G H
5 → 4	I J
6 → 5	K L

When Track 3 is edited out, track numbers 4,5,6 simply move up to 3,4,5, Address EF becomes available for re-recording.

Combining Two Tracks into One

LEAD IN	UTOC	1	2	3	4	5	◄─Track Number	LEAD OUT

A   BC   DE   FG   HI   JK   L ◄─ Addresses

Contents

Track Number	Addresses
1	A B
2	C D
3	E F
4 → 4	G H → G J
5	I J
6 → 5	K L

When Tracks 4 and 5 are combined, their track number is 4 and Track 6 moves up to 5. Their addresses as well are combined to form GJ.

12-5 Two examples of track renumbering in the user table of contents in which a track is removed, and two tracks are combined. In both cases, other tracks are correspondingly renumbered in the UTOC. Sony Corporation

comparing it to the original phrase. This hybrid format remains compatible with other MD hardware players and recorders. Hybrid discs contain prerecorded program areas coded with optical pits, along with recordable MO program areas. In addition, a UTOC is necessary to log recorded tracks.

All types of MiniDiscs benefit from a particular forte of the format, namely its portability, and carefully designed ability to resist the effects of shock and vibration. Larger diameter discs, such as CDs, are inherently more sensitive to physical motion than the smaller diameter MD. Moreover, all MD players are equipped with a buffer memory that provides continuous data flow even when data reading from the disc is interrupted. This technique can be applied to CD players, but the large volume of output data necessitates a very large memory and a high-speed drive would also be preferred. In the MD, because of data reduction, the required data rate is about ⅕ that of CD, thus a correspondingly smaller memory can be used. During recording, the buffer fills continuously but empties discontinuously; during playback, the buffer fills discontinuously, but empties continuously.

Specifically, an MD player can contain a 4-Mbit FIFO memory that acts as a buffer, holding about 10 seconds of stereo playing time; it is positioned prior to data decompression and conversion stages. If the laser pickup mistracks, data will continue to output from the buffer, allowing time (10 seconds) for the pickup to resume proper tracking with the aid of address locations along the data track. The pickup reads data from the disc at a rate of 1.4 Mbps; however, through data reduction, the required output rate from the buffer is only 292 kbps (the ATRAC decoder accepts the 292-kbps rate and outputs data at a 1.4-Mbps rate). After tracking resumes, the buffer is quickly refilled (in less than a second) at a rate of 1.4 Mbps. Clearly, during normal operation, the data rate from the pickup is about five times faster than required for playback; thus data is read from the disc in intervals, as opposed to the continuous 1.4-Mbps rate from CDs. The duration of these intervals can be adjusted to replenish the buffer memory as necessary, avoiding both memory underflow and overflow. Of course, continuous pickup mistracking from sustained interruption, or intermittent interruptions that do not permit buffer refilling, would result in muted audio output.

The buffer offers another unique advantage. When adding material to a previously recorded disc, the system is able to move from one place on the disc to another, fitting the data noncontiguously into available disc space. The buffer permits continuous data input while discontinuously recording, and during playback provides continuous output.

Optical Pickup

The MiniDisc format is designed to play back two types of discs: Prerecorded discs with a pit structure, and recordable discs with a magneto-optical layer. Because these two disc types are quite different, they cannot be read with the same method. However, one pickup, with one laser, is used to read both prerecorded and user-recorded discs, and to write discs as well; for the latter, the laser's power is increased. An MD pickup is thus more sophisticated than a playback CD pickup because additional elements are placed in the optical path; in addition, as in CD, an MD pickup must supply focus and tracking signals.

Prerecorded MD discs are read similarly to compact discs; pits are detected by monitoring varying light intensity that is reflected from the pit surface. A laser beam (780-nm wavelength) of approximately 0.5 mW of power is focused on the pit surface. The objective lens has an NA of 0.45. Smooth land between pits largely reflects the light, resulting in high intensity at the receiving photodiode. A pit largely diffracts the light, resulting in low intensity at the photodiode. As in the CD format, the varying voltage output from the photodiode is processed to form a binary signal.

Recordable MiniDiscs can be read with the same pickup, but the pickup must be modified because the data encoded on the magneto-optical surface does not present variations in the intensity of reflected light. The pickup must convert the stored magnetic signal into variations in light intensity. Specifically, a polarized beam splitter (PBS) must be included to detect differences in the plane of polarization of light reflected from the MO surface. The PBS redirects the light into two paths, to two photodiodes.

The power of the reading laser is the same whether a prerecorded or user-recorded disc is being played. However, the light reflected from an MO disc is analyzed according to the Kerr effect; the plane of polarization of the reflected light is rotated slightly differently, depending on the contents of the perpendicularly magnetized data. The PBS consists of two glass prisms combined to create a multilayer structure; an optical component of incident light passes straight through the PBS and another component is redirected through another facet because of the effect of the multilayer. The determining factor is the plane of polarization of the components in the incident light. The polarization beam splitter thus varies the distribution ratio of the reflected light to two photodiodes according to the polarization angle. If the polarization of the light is in a forward angle, more light is directed to one photodiode, and if in a backward angle, more light is directed to a second photodiode. Because the signal detected by the PBS is quite small, differential detection must be used to cancel common mode noise. Thus a difference signal from the two photodiodes is used to create a binary signal output.

The polarization beam splitter is designed as a three-beam Wollaston prism; it combines two prisms with the optical axis of the first prism inclined at an angle of 45° in relation to the optical axis of the second. Incident light is split into two beams at the emergence plane of the first prism, and each of these beams is split into two beams at the plane of incidence of the second prism, as shown in Fig. 12-6A. The 1st and 2nd beams comprise the parallel component of incident light and together are one-half the intensity of the incident light. The 3rd and 4th beams comprise the perpendicular component of incident light and together are one-half the intensity of the incident light. However, the 2nd and 3rd beams are combined, thus three beams emerge from the PBS.

These three beams of analyzed light are directed at targets labelled *I*, *M*, and *J* in Fig. 12-6B. Beams *I* and *J* correspond to the reflected and passing light. Beam *M* is the summation of *I* and *J* and forms a central beam. The Kerr angle can be used to read data. In the case of prerecorded discs, the Kerr angle is 0°; the pickup can directly read differences in reflected light intensity. In the case of recordable discs, the Kerr angle is about 0.3°; the analyzer detects this difference in the angle of rotation of polarization plane according to direction of the magnetic domain and redirects light to photodiodes *I* or *J*.

As with any optical pickup, a number of mechanical functions must be performed to properly read data from a disc. In a MiniDisc, a servo actuator system is used to provide autofocusing via an astigmatic detection method, and autotracking via three-spot detection method (other methods could be used). A two-axis actuator is used for both of these functions. Any optical disc contains vertical deviations in the focus direction and radial deviations in the tracking direction. A two-axis actuator physically moves the pickup's objective lens to maintain proper lens-to-disc distance, and to track the data spiral. To accomplish this automatically, the pickup creates two servo error signals that vary in proportion to the deviations of the disc. The autofocus system must maintain a depth of focus that

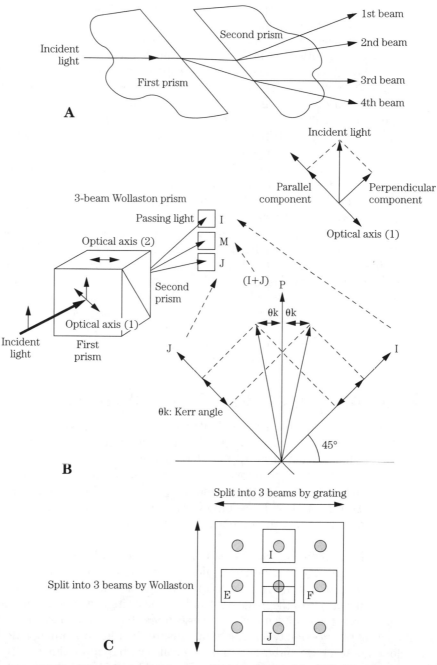

12-6 An example of the polarization beam-splitter optics used in a MiniDisc player. A. A Wollaston prism is used to create four beams from the primary beam. B. Two beams are internally combined so that three beams emerge from the prism, and are directed to three targets. Either intensity or the Kerr effect can be used to read data. C. Three beams are further split to create nine beams which are directed to a 3-x-3 photodiode; five beams are used for reading, focusing, or tracking.

deviates less than ±1 μm, and the autotracking system must track the 1.6-μm track pitch to within ±0.1 μm.

Autofocusing can be accomplished as in many CD pickups, by using a cylindrical lens to introduce astigmatism into the central beam (M). The beam is directed to a four-quadrant photodiode; a round beam falling equally on all four photodiodes indicates an in-focus condition, an elliptical beam that falls more fully on two photodiodes indicates an out-of-focus condition. Whether the disc is too near or too far is determined by the physical rotation angle of the elliptical beam. In either case, a correction signal is generated and directed to the servo system; it mechanically moves the objective lens up or down, much like a voice coil moves within a loudspeaker.

Light entering the three-beam Wollaston prism has already been split into three beams to form error tracking signals. Each of these three beams is further split into three beams as they pass through the prism. Thus nine beams ultimately reach a three-by-three photodiode, which both reads the prerecorded or recorded signal (and forms an autofocus signal), and forms an autotracking signal. The nine beams, five of them used for reading, focusing, or tracking, are shown in Fig. 12-6C. Two beams, on either side of the central beam, labelled *E* and *F*, are reflected from the opposite edges of the pit track or pregroove. When the main beam is tracking properly, the intensity of these tracking beams is equal. However, when the central beam mistracks, the intensity of the tracking beams is unequal; this inequality is used to generate a tracking correction signal that causes the servo system to laterally move the objective lens to the center of the data track or groove. The complete optical system is shown in Fig. 12-7.

MO Recording and Field Modulation

Data can be written to recordable MiniDiscs on the magneto-optical layer. Essentially, this is performed by bathing the data surface with the appropriately oriented magnetic field while heating the data surface. Heating is achieved by increasing power to the laser to approximately 4.5 mW; when the heating laser is withdrawn, the data is "frozen" in the magneto-optical layer. Moreover, this recording surface can be reheated, and new data written over the old. Importantly, these requirements are achieved with components with low power consumption, small size, and low cost.

To permit this, a highly stable magnetic layer of terbium ferrite cobalt was developed; it allows flux reversals with a magnetic field as low as 80 oersteds (approximately one-third that of conventional MO media) at the Curie temperature. This reduces the required size of the magnetic head as well as its power consumption. At room temperatures, the coercivity of the layer is more than 10,000 oersteds, practically eliminating the possibility of accidental erasure. In addition, a magnetic head was developed that allows fairly rapid flux reversals (within approximately 100 ns) at low power levels. This overcomes the potential problem of temperature increases within the recording medium, and also reduces power consumption.

In magneto-optical recording, a small area of the magnetic recording layer is heated with a focused laser beam. Coercivity is inversely proportional to applied temperature. When the material's Curie temperature (approximately 180°C) is

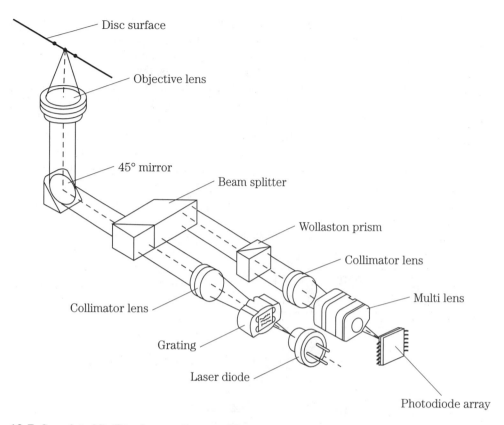

12-7 Complete MiniDisc laser-optic assembly. Sony Corporation

reached, the coercivity of the material is so diminished that only a very weak field is needed to magnetically orient the material. When a weak magnetic field is applied to the material, the small heated spot magnetically responds by orienting perpendicularly with either the north or south polarity of the applied data signal. As the area moves away from the beam, the area cools below the Curie temperature, the applied magnetic field is withdrawn, and the data is retained in chevron-shaped magnetized areas. The magnetic field is applied with a magnetic head on a slider placed over the top surface of the disc, directly over the laser writer applied from underneath the disc. The head contacts the disc surface to maintain a close and unvarying distance from the MO layer, about 10 μm within the disc.

In some MO systems, data must be erased prior to writing new data; effectively, the data surface must be heated and all areas uniformly aligned (erasing old data) before new data is written. Data is first erased by a continuous laser, then recorded with a pulsed laser. In practice, this can be performed with two lasers, one for erasing, and one for writing. Alternatively, one laser can be used; the discs makes two revolutions, one for erasing and one for writing. The former method adds cost, and the latter slows writing time. Both methods are relatively complex to implement.

In the MiniDisc system, magnetic-field modulation overwrite (MMO) method is used that directly writes new data over old, by modulating the magnetic field at high speed, creating specific orientations to represent the applied data signal. In some MO systems, the laser is modulated; with MD, the laser is always on during recording. This direct overwrite method is illustrated in Fig. 12-8. As noted, the system uses a magnetic head on one side of the disc, and a laser beam on the other side. The size of the recorded magnetic areas is determined by the magnetic flux reversal, not by switching the laser on and off. Thermal diffusion and other problems encountered by laser modulation are avoided, and short wavelengths can be recorded. Because the laser beam is continually radiating during both reading and writing (at different power output levels) optical head design is simplified.

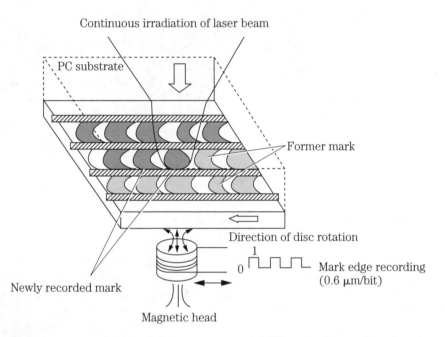

12-8 A magnetic-field modulation overwrite (MMO) method is used to directly write new data over old, by modulating the magnetic field at high speed; the laser is always on during recording.

The MMO method provides the same linear velocity as in the compact disc format (1.2 to 1.4 m/s), provides the same density as in compact disc (0.6 μm/bit), and is compatible with the 13.3-ms wobble addressing used in recordable MDs. CD recording (during mastering) uses a 460-nm wavelength argon gas laser directed through a lens with NA of 0.9. However, consumer MD recorders use a semiconductor laser of 780-nm wavelength, and lens with NA of 0.45, yielding a spot diameter of approximatley 1.0 μm. Experiments showed that this type of optical system resulted in block error rates of 200 per second, marginal relative to the CIRC minimum of 220. Conventional modulation would not permit CD density in the MD format. With MMO however, experiments showed that block-error rates dropped below 20 per second at a linear velocity of 1.2 m/s. In other words, it was demonstrated that MMO could successfully perform direct overwriting, at CD density and velocity, with consumer optics.

This success can be observed in the differences in the recording patterns between conventional laser modulation, and MMO. In conventional laser modulation, laser power is varied; the magnetic field can only be oriented in one direction with the heated area corresponding to a 1, and the unheated area corresponding to a 0. Pattern shapes are often irregular, and CD-like signals recorded with such patterns will exhibit jitter; pit length varies with respect to the EFM code, and a long pit recorded at slow linear velocity (1.2 m/s) will become tear-drop shaped because of heat accumulation as the shape is written, thus increasing jitter. Pulsed laser methods are needed to overcome this, but also increase cost and complexity. Fluctuations in laser power in conventional laser modulation result in variations in the start and stop points in recorded patterns, further leading to jitter. In addition, a laser modulation system can only tolerate a ±10% variation in recording power before the block error rate threshold is exceeded. Finally, laser modulation is sensitive to disc tilt; an off-center disc causes the laser spot to be distorted. Because the shape of the recorded pattern is determined by the shape of the spot, tilt can increase block errors.

In MMO, because the heating laser is always on, the heating and cooling process above and below the Curie temperature isothermal line determines the shape and length of the recorded 1 or 0 pattern. If the magnetic field is inverted quickly, it is possible to write patterns at a pitch of only 0.3 μm, with a 780-nm laser and a lens with NA of 0.45. Furthermore, the recorded pattern is highly symmetrical, jitter is reduced, thus promoting accuracy in data reading. With MMO, a ±20% variation in recording power is permitted before the block error rate is exceeded. MMO has also demonstrated a resistance to the effects of disc tilt; an off-axis disc causes the spot to become distorted but the laser is only used to raise the temperature and does not determine the shape of the recorded pattern. The effect of disc tilt is thus reduced.

Although the magnetic head, as in other magnetic media, touches the disc surface during recording, the MO record/erase cycle is long-lived. Estimates based on accelerated age tests projected the write/read cycle to be 1 million times; for example, a three-minute song could be written and read continuously for 12 years. The read cycle is projected to be 10 million times; the same song could be continuously replayed for 60 years. These tests used a laser write power of 4.5 mW to write EFM coded random data over a 1-second segment (7350 frames). In both cases, the block error rate started and ended the aging test at about 15 block errors/second, well under the CIRC threshold of 220 errors/second.

ATRAC Data Reduction

To achieve a small disc diameter, the MiniDisc system uses data reduction based on psychoacoustic principles. Prior to storage, the audio data rate of 1.41 Mbps (16-bit stereo samples at 44.1 kHz) is compressed using a perceptual coder to a rate of 292 kbps, approximately ⅕ that of the original. Following retrieval from disc storage, the data rate is again restored to its original rate. The proprietary ATRAC (Adaptive TRansform Acoustic Coding) algorithm was developed to perform the encoding and decoding operations. ATRAC provides a high-fidelity signal, and permits 74 minutes of recording and playing time on a MiniDisc. Without ATRAC, an MD would hold only 15 minutes of audio program.

As noted in chapter 11, the aim of a perceptual coding system is to reduce the volume of data required to code a signal; psychoacoustic principles are applied to minimize audible degradation. In the case of MD, the sampling rate remains unchanged, thus the word length must be decreased. As word length is reduced, however, quantization noise increases. ATRAC must conceal the increased noise floor, using perceptual coding.

ATRAC transform coding is based on nonuniform frequency and time splitting concepts, and assigns bits according to rules fixed by a bit allocation algorithm. The algorithm both observes the fixed threshold of hearing curve, and dynamically analyzes the audio program to take advantage of psychoacoustic effects such as masking. In other words, ATRAC changes the recorded signal according to the ear's dynamic sensitivity. ATRAC can perform coarse quantizing in areas where quantization noise is inaudible, that is, where there is strong musical activity. Looked at in another way, this method is more efficient than linear coding hence less data is required to code high-fidelity signals.

An ATRAC encoder accepts a standard digital audio input and parses it into blocks of time. It analyzes the signal in each block to determine the content in different frequency bands. Exposed regions are given long word lengths, yielding low quantization noise. Masked regions are quantized with shorter words, with the expectation that the quantization noise will be masked. More specifically, ATRAC divides the audio signal into three subbands, which are then transformed into the frequency domain using a variable block length. Transform coefficients are grouped into 512 nonuniform frequency divisions modeled on the ear's critical bands, with particular resolution given to lower frequencies. Data in these bands is quantized according to dynamic sensitivity and masking characteristics, again based on a human auditory model. During decoding, the quantized spectra are reconstructed according to the bit allocation method, and synthesized into the output audio signal. ATRAC differs from some other methods in that psychoacoustic principles are applied to both the bit allocation and the time-frequency splitting. In that respect, a combination of subband and transform coding techniques are used. In addition, the transform block length adapts to the audio signal's characteristics so that amplitude and time resolution can be varied between static and transient musical passages. Through this processing, the data rate is reduced by ⅕. The ATRAC encoding algorithm can be considered in three parts: time-frequency analysis, bit allocation, and quantization of spectral components; this is shown in Fig. 12-9A. The analysis portion of the algorithm decomposes the signal into spectral coefficients grouped into block floating units (BFU). The bit allocation portion of the algorithm divides available bits between the BFUs, allocating more bits to sensitive units. The quantization portion of the algorithm quantizes each spectral coefficient to the specified word length.

The time-frequency analysis, shown in greater detail in Fig. 12-9B, uses subband and transform coding techniques. Two quadrature mirror filters (QMF) divide the input signal into three subbands: low (0 Hz to 5.5125 kHz), medium (5.5125 kHz to 11.025

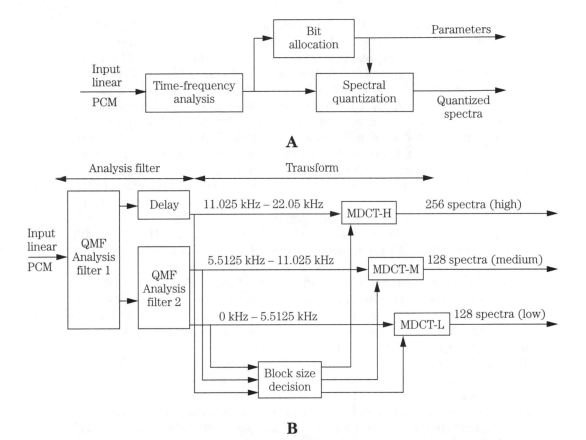

A

B

12-9 The ATRAC data-reduction algorithm is used to reduce the bit rate by coding the audio signal as spectral coefficients. A. Block diagram of an ATRAC encoder. B. Detail of time-frequency analysis block showing QMF filters and MDCT transforms used to analyze the signal.

kHz), and high (11.025 kHz to 22.05 kHz). The QMF filters ensure that time domain aliasing caused by the subband decomposition will be canceled during reconstruction. Following splitting, contents are examined to determine length of block durations. Signals in each of these bands are then placed in the frequency domain with the MDCT (modified discrete cosine transform) algorithm. The MDCT allows up to 50% overlap between adjacent time domain windows; this maintains frequency resolution at critical sampling. The coefficients are formed into 512 nonuniform frequency groups, with 128 spectra in the low band, 128 spectra in the mid band, and 256 spectra in the high band.

A transform coder must balance frequency resolution with temporal resolution. A long block size achieves high frequency resolution and quantization noise is readily masked by simultaneous masking; this is appropriate for a steady state signal. However, transient signals require temporal resolution, otherwise quantization noise will be spread in time (over the entire block of samples) beyond the limits of temporal masking, and hence might not be masked. Specifically, a pre-echo can be audible prior to the onset of the transient masker.

To address this impasse, instead of a fixed transform block length, the ATRAC algorithm adaptively performs nonuniform time splitting, with blocks that vary according to the audio program content. Two modes are used: long mode (11.6 ms in the high, medium, and low bands) and short mode (1.45 ms in the high-frequency band, and 2.9 ms in the mid and low bands). The long block mode yields a narrow frequency band, and the short block mode yields wider frequency bands, trading time and frequency resolution as required by the audio signal. Specifically, transient attacks will prompt a decrease in block duration (to 1.45 or 2.9 ms), and a more slowly changing program will promote an increase in block duration (to 11.6 ms). Block duration is interactive with frequency bandwidth; longer block durations permit selection of narrower frequency bands and greater resolution. This time splitting is based on the effect of temporal premasking (backward masking) in which tones sounding close in time exhibit masking properties.

Normally, the long mode provides good frequency resolution. However, with transients, quantization noise is spread over the entire signal block and the initial quantization noise is not masked, as shown in Fig. 12-10A. Thus, when a transient is detected the algorithm switches to the short mode as shown in Fig. 12-10B. Because the noise is limited to a short duration before the onset of the transient, it is now masked by premasking. Because of its greater extent, post masking (forward masking) can be relied on to mask any signal decay in the long mode. Finally, the block size mode can be selected independently for each band.

The MDCT frequency domain coefficients are then grouped into 52 BFUs; each contains a fixed number of coefficients. As noted, in the long mode, the units convey 11.6 ms of a narrow frequency band, and in the short mode each block conveys 1.45 or 2.9 ms, but a wider frequency band. An example of a mode selection is shown in Fig. 12-11; a long mode has been selected in the low band, and short modes in the mid and high bands. In any case, 52 nonuniform BFUs are present across the frequency range; there are more BFUs at low frequencies, and less at high frequencies. This nonlinear division is based on the concept of critical bands and reflects the way the human ear analyzes sound. Lower-frequency bands are relatively narrow, and high-frequency bands are wider. For example, in the ATRAC model, the band centered at 150 Hz is 100 Hz wide, the band at 1 kHz is 160 Hz wide, and the band at 10.5 kHz is 2500 Hz wide. These widths reflect the ear's decreasing sensitivity to high frequencies.

Each of the 512 spectral coefficients is quantized according to scale factor and word length. The scale factor defines the full-scale range of the quantization; it is selected from a list of possibilities and describes the magnitude of the spectral coefficients in each BFU. The word length defines the precision within each scale; it is calculated by the bit allocation algorithm (described below). Each of the 52 BFUs is given the same scale factor and word length because of the psychoacoustic similarity within each group. Thus the following information is coded and recorded to disc for each frame of 512 values: MDCT block size mode (long or short), word length for each BFU, scale factor for each BFU, and quantized spectral coefficients.

The bit allocation algorithm considers the minimum threshold curve and simultaneous masking conditions applicable to the BFUs, operating to yield a reduced data rate; available bits must be divided optimally between the block floating units. BFUs coded with many bits will have low quantization noise, but BFUs with few or

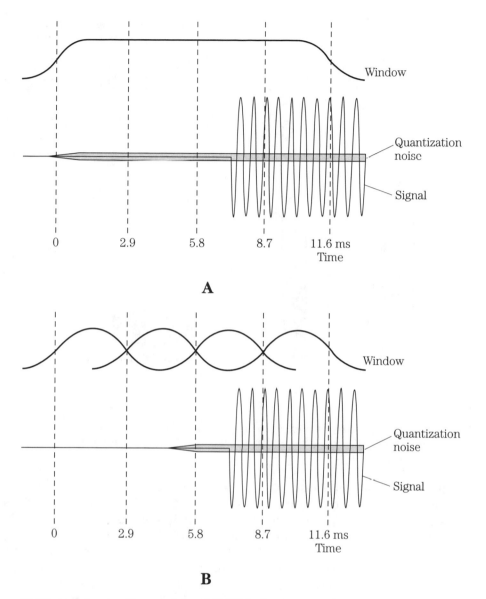

12-10 An example of long and short MDCT block size modes. In this case, a short mode is selected to overcome pre-echo artifacts. A. The long mode extends the transform over a 11.6-ms interval. B. The short mode decreases block size to 2.9 ms. Tsutsui, et al.

no bits will have greater noise. ATRAC does not specify an arbitrary bit allocation algorithm; this allows improvement in future encoder versions. The decoder is completely independent of any allocation algorithm, also allowing future improvement. To some extent, because the time-frequency splitting relies on critical band and pre-masking considerations, the choice of the bit allocation algorithm is less critical; however, any algorithm must minimize perceptual error.

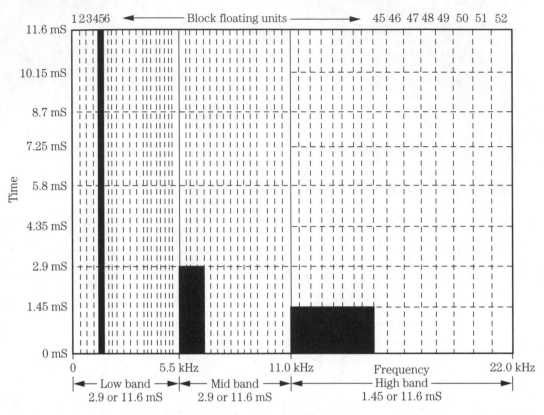

12-11 An example of mode selection in each of the three bands. A long mode has been selected in the low band, and short modes in the mid and high bands. Coefficients are grouped into 52 nonuniform BFUs across the frequency range.

One example of a bit allocation model declares both fixed and variable bits, as shown in Fig. 12-12. Fixed bits are allocated mainly to low frequency BFU regions, emphasizing their perceptual importance. Variable bits are assigned according to the logarithm of the spectral coefficients in each BFU. The total bit allocation b_{total} for each BFU is the weighted sum of the fixed bits $b_{fixed}(k)$ and the variable bits $b_{variable}(k)$ in each BFU. Thus, for each BFU k: $b_{total}(k) = Tb_{variable} + (1 - T)b_{fixed}$.

The weight T describes the tonality of the signal, taking a value close to 0 for white noise, and a value close to 1 for pure tones. Thus the proportion of fixed bits to variable bits is itself variable. For example, for noiselike signals the allocation emphasizes fixed bits, thus decreasing the number of bits devoted to insensitive high frequencies. For pure tones the allocation emphasizes variable bits, concentrating available bits to a few sensitive BFUs.

However, the allocation method must observe the overall bit rate; the previous equation does not account for this and will generally allocate more bits than available. To maintain a fixed and limited bit rate, an offset b_{offset} is devised, and set equal for all BFUs. The offset is subtracted from $b_{total}(k)$ for each BFU, yielding the final bit allocation $b_{final}(k)$: $b_{final}(k) = $ integer$[b_{total}(k) - b_{offset}]$.

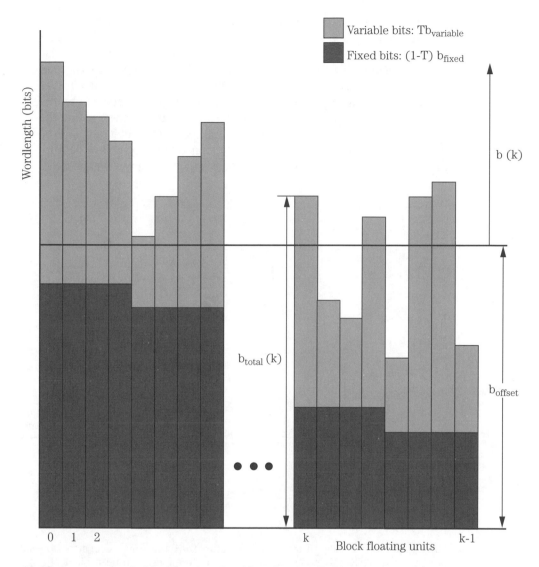

12-12 An example of a bit-allocation algorithm showing the bit assignment, using both fixed and variable bits. Fixed bits are weighted toward low-frequency BFU regions; variable bits are assigned according to the logarithm of the spectral coefficients in each BFU. Tsutsui, et al.

If the final value describes a negative word length, that BFU is given 0 bits. Because low frequencies are given a greater number of fixed bits, they generally need fewer variable bits to achieve the offset threshold, and become coded (see Fig. 12-12). As noted, ATRAC does not specify this, or any other arbitrary allocation algorithm. Following ATRAC coding, CIRC and EFM operations are performed, and compressed audio data (along with overhead data) is stored to disc at a 44.1 kHz sampling frequency.

Data played from a disc undergoes EFM demodulation, CIRC error correction, and ATRAC decoding. The ATRAC decoder essentially reverses the encoding process, performing spectral reconstruction and time-frequency synthesis, as shown in Fig. 12-13A. Time-frequency synthesis is shown in more detail in Fig. 12-13B. The decoder first accepts the quantized spectral coefficients, and uses the word length and scale factor parameters to reconstruct the MDCT spectral coefficients. To reconstruct the audio signal, these coefficients are first transformed back into the time domain by the inverse MDCT (IMDCT), using either long or short mode blocks as specified by the recorded parameters. The three time domain subband signals are synthesized into the output signal using QMF synthesis filters, obtaining a full spectrum, 16-bit digital audio signal. Wideband quantization noise introduced during encoding (to achieve data reduction) is limited to critical bands, where it is masked by signal energy in each band.

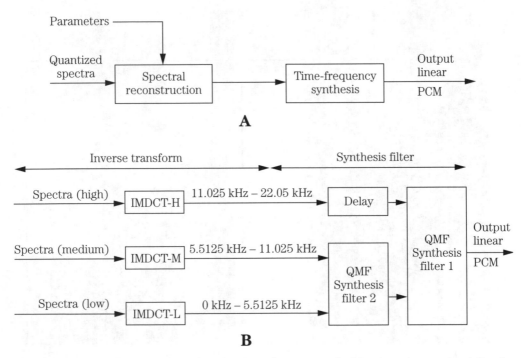

12-13 The ATRAC data reduction algorithm is used to restore the bit rate and reconstruct the signal. A. Block diagram of an ATRAC decoder. B. Detail of time-frequency synthesis block showing QMF filters and MDCT transforms used to reconstruct the signal.

In addition to smaller disc size, ATRAC also permits use of a buffer memory, an important feature in a portable medium. The ATRAC encoder is placed prior to the input buffer memory, and after the output buffer memory so that only reduced data flows through the buffer, minimizing the required memory length. In a complete MD signal path, the ATRAC encoder is placed just after the A/D converter (or digital input) and just before the D/A converter (or digital output).

Disc Mastering and Manufacture

As in CDs, prerecorded MDs contain both audio program and subcode data material, thus there are similarities between the two premastering processes. With proper modification, existing CD mastering systems using a ¾-inch U-matic tape recorder can be used to master MDs. To minimize capital investment needed to add MD premastering and mastering, manufacturers have devised a signal chain that uses much existing CD equipment. MD premastering can take place in a recording studio, or MD pressing plant.

MD premastering begins with an audio source; a format conversion process is used to prepare a ¾-inch U-matic tape containing MD ATRAC-encoded material. A ¾-inch U-matic tape source is preferred for MD mastering; it can be the same tape used for CD production; digital audio data is coded as a video signal, and the two analog longitudinal tracks contain TOC, ISRC and other subcode data on track 1, and timecode on track 2. The ¾-inch tape is played back through a PCM-1630 digital audio processor while the playback signal is checked for errors.

Corrected 16-bit signals are input to a format converter to accomplish data reduction; an ATRAC encoder in the converter performs this operation. ATRAC-encoded data is then written to a hard disk storage system. Simultaneously, the converter decompresses data from the ATRAC format to 16-bit PCM and this bit stream is input to a digital audio processor so the audio program can be monitored in real time for quality. Subcode data recorded on analog longitudinal track 1 of the master tape is passed through the format converter, converted to MD format subcode data, then stored on hard disk; text information such as song titles can be entered via a personal computer. Subcode data is combined with audio data in the MD format, and downloaded to another ¾-inch tape that becomes the MD master tape. On this tape, all audio data is contained in the video tracks, and longitudinal track 2 contains timecode. Final quality checks monitor error count, subcode data text contents, and other parameters, and review printed documentation as well.

MD replication occurs at an MD pressing plant, typically a CD pressing plant that has undergone necessary modifications. In CD mastering, the master tape is played on a master recorder; the video signal is decoded into a 16-bit audio signal by a processor, checked for errors, and the corrected 16-bit digital signal is input to a code processor. The subcode data from analog track 1, along with timecode from track 2, is directed to a cue editor/generator and converted into PQ subcode data, then input to the code processor. The code processor generates the error correction code, and combines it with the audio and subcode data, and performs EFM modulation. A sync word is added to complete the frame format, and these data packets are output to the glass disc mastering machine.

MD mastering proceeds similarly, however the PQ generator is replaced by a new address generator. The MD ¾-inch master tape is played on a master recorder, converted to a digital audio signal by the processor, and checked for errors. The digital audio signal and subcode data (located in the tape pre-roll at 01:58:30:00 in

SMPTE time) are output through an SDIF-2 interface to the address generator. The MD format of cluster and sector time units is generated and written in the Q subcode channel and applied to the code generator. Audio data is also applied to the code generator, which creates error correction code, and performs modulation. The combined CD-like data is subsequently directed to the CD glass disc mastering machine. Because of the data reduction used, a 60-minute program can be mastered in 12 minutes. Because the MD's physical dimensions are smaller than a CD's, the glass mastering machine must be modified for a lead-in starting at 29 mm, program start and stop at 32 and 61 mm, and lead-out stop at 62 mm. Following disc mastering and generation of stampers using electroforming methods, other prerecorded MD replication processes proceed as in CD replication. A metal clamping disc is ultrasonically welded to the substrate at the center opening, and prerecorded MDs are placed in single-shuttered cartridges.

As with any blank recordable medium, recordable MDs do not require any premastering or mastering processes; however, production of any MO medium is more sophisticated than that of CDs or prerecorded MDs. The creation of individual recordable MDs begins with the injection molding of the pregrooved polycarbonate substrate; the groove wobble enables tracking and rotational servos as well as addressing. Permanent information is stored in pits on the disc inner radius; information on optimum laser writing power and disc playing time is placed here. All blank MDs are identical, except for the playing time coding. The first dielectric, magnetic MO recording, second dielectric, and aluminum layers are sputtered onto the pregrooved surface. These layers are covered by a protective acrylic layer; this curable resin is applied with spin coating, and hardened with UV light. The completed discs are placed in double-shuttered cartridges.

The MiniDisc specification is contained in the Rainbow Book; it is an evolution of the CD-DA Red Book, CD-ROM Yellow Book, and CD-MO Orange Book Part I. The Rainbow Book contains details on the structure, mechanical dimensions, and optical characteristics of discs, quality of electrical signal readout, and signal processing methods for recording and playback. The MiniDisc was developed by Sony Corporation.

13
CHAPTER

Digital Audio Broadcasting

Although wired communications will remain vital, there is growing consensus that wireless methods will play an increasingly important role. In the past, broadcast frequencies were given away by the government, but companies today eagerly bid billions of dollars for spectral rights—a sure sign of the bullish attitude about the future of wireless. Wireless broadcasting can be accommodated from terrestrial towers and satellites. Local radio relies on towers, but satellites are the workhorses of the telecommunications industry. From their perches high above the equator, they look down on the earth, relaying audio, video, and data transmissions from one point to another, across oceans and continents. This chapter surveys wireless broadcasting technology and some of its applications, with attention to satellite technology and digital audio radio.

Satellite Operation

With satellite transmission, information is conveyed thousands of miles, to one receiver or to millions of receivers, using telecommunications satellites as unmanned orbiting relay stations. They use a unique orbit, rotating from west to east over the equator, moving synchronously with the earth's rotation. From the earth, they appear to be fixed in the sky; this is a geostationary orbit. Objects orbiting close to the earth rotate faster than the earth, and objects farther away rotate slower. The space shuttle (150 to 200 miles high) orbits in 90 minutes. The moon (221,000 to 253,000 miles away) orbits in 27.3 days. At 22,300 miles above the earth, geostationary orbit (one orbit per day) is achieved, as shown in Fig. 13-1; this is where telecommunications satellites are parked. International law dictates a separation of 2° between vehicles.

The signal has a line-of-sight characteristic similar to that of visible light, thus it is highly directional. From their high altitude, telecommunications satellites have a direct line of sight to almost half the earth's surface; three satellites would encompass the entire globe except for small polar regions. A satellite's footprint describes

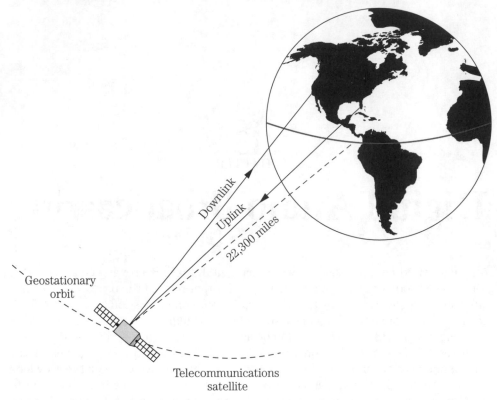

13-1 A satellite in geostationary orbit appears fixed in the sky over a particular position.

the area over which its receiving and transmitting antennas are focused; the footprint can cover an entire hemisphere, or a smaller region, with gradual reduction in sensitivity away from the footprint's center area, as shown in Fig. 13-2. In this example, the footprint is characterized as EIRP (effective isotropic radiated power). Both earth stations must lie within the satellite's footprint. Generally, C-band footprints cover larger geographical areas than Ku-band footprints. Because of the high orbit, a communications delay of 270 ms is incurred.

Satellite communications operate at microwave frequencies; specifically they take place in the SHF (super high frequency) band extending from 3 GHz to 30 GHz; the broadcast spectrum is shown in Fig. 13-3. A 12-GHz signal's wavelength is 2.5 cm long (its frequency band is often called the quasi-millimeter wave). Two FSS (Fixed Satellite Services) bands are in common domestic use: the C-band (3.4 to 7.075 GHz) and the Ku-band (10.7 to 18.1 GHz). In either case, several higher-frequency subbands (C-band: 5.725 to 7.075 GHz; Ku-band: 12.7 to 18.1 GHz) are used for uplink signals, and several lower-frequency subbands (C-band: 3.4 to 4.8 GHz; Ku-band: 10.7 to 12.7 GHz) are used for downlink signals. All telecommunications satellites share the same spectral space, and ground stations must rely on physical satellite spacing and antenna directionality to differentiate between satellites.

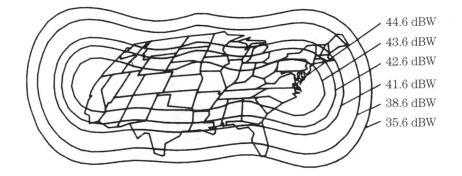

	44.6 dBW
	43.6 dBW
	42.6 dBW
	41.6 dBW
	38.6 dBW
	35.6 dBW

EIRP (dBW)

Atlanta	43.2
Boston	41.7
Chicago	42.9
Dallas	43.2
Houston	41.3
Los Angeles	43.0
New York	43.4
Orlando	39.8
San Francisco	44.1
Seattle	42.0

13-2 Satellite downlink footprints are contoured to cover a specific geographic location, and for example, minimize interference with neighboring countries.

Most C-band transponders use a 36-MHz bandwidth placed on 40-MHz centers, although in some cases 72-MHz transponders are used. Ku-band transponder bandwidths are either 36 MHz or 72 MHz wide. The C-band affords superior propagation characteristics; however, Ku-band satellites can offset this with greater transponder antenna gain. Some satellites operate in both bands. Because the C-band must share its spectral space with other terrestrial applications, it suffers from the possibility of terrestrial microwave interference such as terrestrial microwave links. This necessitates a lower transmitting power and larger antenna diameter. C-band dishes are typically 2 meters in diameter or larger, and downlink stations must properly shield their antennas. The shorter Ku-band wavelengths are more easily absorbed by moisture, thus the signal can be degraded by snow, rain, and fog. In particular, heavy rainfall might significantly degrade Ku-band signals. However, because the Ku-band is not shared with other terrestrial applications, it does not suffer from microwave interference, thus higher power can be applied. In addition, for a given size, Ku-band dishes provide higher gain than C-band dishes. Although Ku-band dishes are typically 1.8 meters in diameter, much smaller dishes are used in direct broadcast satellite applications. In some cases, a combination of bands is used. The Ku-band can be accessed via portable uplinks; the downlinked signal is converted to the C-band at a ground station, and uplinked via the C-band for distribution.

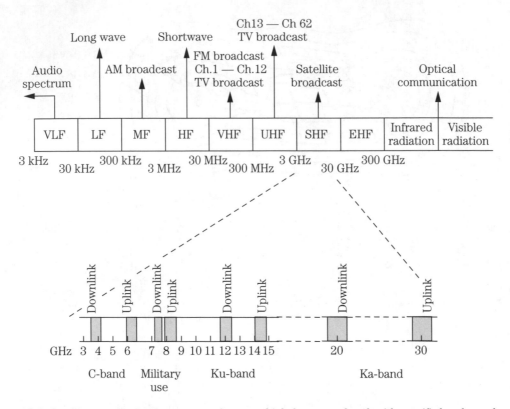

13-3 Satellite communications occupy the super high-frequency band, with specific bands used for uplink and downlink transmissions. Only a few of the uplink and downlink bands are shown.

A satellite's transponders receive the ground station's uplink signal and retransmit it back to earth where a downlink receives the signal. A communications satellite might have 48 transponders each capable of receiving multiple (8 to 12) data channels from an uplink, or transmitting those channels to a receiving downlink. Horizontally, vertically, and circularly polarized signals are broadcast, to increase capacity in a frequency band. Depending on the transmitting power of the satellite, the signal can be received by equipment of greater or lesser sophistication. For example, a 20-W satellite transmitter would require a receiving dish several meters in diameter, and a 200-W transmitter would require a dish diameter of less than a meter. Transponder reliability rate exceeds 99% over years of service.

Satellites use solar cells to derive power from solar energy. So that correct attitude stabilization is maintained (the antennas must stay pointed at the earth) the satellite must rotate once every 24 hours as it circles the earth; this action is provided by thrusters that create spin when the satellite is first orbited. In addition, in the case of cube-shaped, body-stabilized 3-D satellites, three internal gyroscopes control position about three axes, providing correction when necessary; solar cells are mounted on large solar sails, motors move the sails to face the sun. Cylindrically shaped satellites, called spinners, achieve stabilization by spinning the entire satellite body about an axis; solar cells are mounted directly on the satellite's body; antennas must be despun. Hydrazine fuel thrusters are used to maintain absolute position within a 40-mile square in the geostationary orbit, compensating for the pull of the sun and moon. Most satellite failures are due to fuel depletion, and the resulting drifting of the vehicle due to space mechanics. A satellite might measure 20 feet in height and weight 15,000 pounds at launch. A satellite's weight determines its launch cost; cost of launching a geostationary satellite is about $20,000 per pound.

Interestingly, twice each year all satellite downlink terminals undergo solar outages (for five minutes or so) when the sun, the relaying satellite, and the earth station are all in a straight line. The outage occurs when the shadow of the antenna's feed element is in the center of the dish; solar interference (noise power from the sun) degrades reception. Solar transit outages occur in the spring and fall; beginning in late February, outages occur at the U.S.-Canada border and slowly move southward at 3° latitude per day, and beginning in early October outages begin at the U.S.-Mexico border and move northward at the same rate. In addition, eclipses of geostationary satellites occur about 90 evenings a year in the spring and fall when the earth blocks the sun's light to the satellite; on-board batteries provide continuous power while the solar sails go dead for 70 minutes.

Digital Transmission

Both analog and digital transmissions are used in audio and video satellite communications. Television signals are generally transmitted with analog FM modulation because it is immune to AM noise, supports multiplexing, and provides a good carrier-to-noise (C/N) ratio. However, satellites also are widely used for digital data transmission, increasingly including audio and video data. Compressed digital video signals are often coded with the D-2 and DS-3 formats, providing 112 Mbps and 45 Mbps respectively. In addition, the U.S. radio networks (such as ABC, CBS, NBC, and United Stations) use satellite digital audio distribution of programming. Digital audio is typically transmitted with voice grade, 7.5-kHz audio, 15-kHz audio, or other data formats. The voice-grade format is coded with continuously variable slope delta (CVSD) modulation to attain a data rate of 32 kbps. The 7.5-kHz format is sampled at 16 kHz, and the 15-kHz format is sampled at 32 kHz; both use 15-bit quantization followed by μ-law companding to yield 11 bits plus parity bit. Multiple channels are multiplexed into a T-1 (1.544 Mbps) stream and sent to the uplink station. The individual audio channels are multiplexed into a 7.68-MHz bit stream, modulated to a 70-MHz IF (intermediate frequency) carrier, upconverted and uplinked for satellite distribution. A single 15-kHz PCM channel requires a bit rate of 512 kbps; companding decreases this to 384 kbps; data reduction decreases this to 128 kbps.

Radio signals are broadcast as an analog or digital baseband signal that modulates a high-frequency carrier signal to convey information. For example, an AM radio station might broadcast a 980-kHz carrier frequency, which is amplitude modulated by important baseband information such as a lite beer commercial. The receiver is tuned to the carrier frequency, and demodulates it to output the original baseband signal; IF modulation techniques are used. Digital transmissions use a digital baseband signal, often in a PCM or data reduction format. The digital data modulates a carrier signal (a high-frequency sinusoid) by digitally manipulating a property of the carrier (such as amplitude, frequency, or phase); the modulated carrier signal is then transmitted. In addition, prior to modulation, multiple baseband signals can be multiplexed to form a digital composite baseband signal. An example of a transmit/receive signal chain is shown in Fig. 13-4.

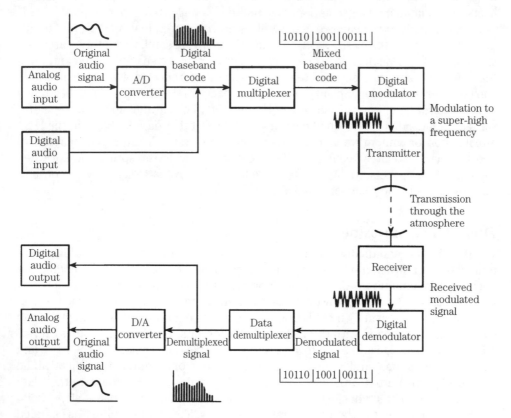

13-4 An example of signal processing in a transmit/receive signal path.

In any digital audio broadcasting system, it is important to distinguish between the source coder and the channel coder. The source coder performs data reduction coding so the wideband signal can be efficiently carried over reduced spectral space. The channel coder prepares the rate-reduced signal for modulation onto RF carriers, the actual broadcasting medium; this is needed for efficient, robust transmission. One important consideration of channel coding is diversity to reduce multipath interference that causes flat or frequency-selective interference, called a fade, in the received signal. Channel coders can use frequency diversity in which the source coder data is encoded on several carrier frequencies spread across a spectral band; a fade will not affect all of the received carriers. Using adaptive equalization, the receiver might use a "training" sequence placed at the head of each transmitted data block to recognize multipath interference and adjust its receive sensitivity across the channel spectrum to minimize interference. In addition, because multipath interference can change over time (particularly in a mobile receiver) time diversity transmits redundant data over a time interval to help ensure proper reception; a cancellation at one moment might not exist a moment later. With space diversity, two or more antennas are used at the receiver (for example, on windshield and rear bumper of a car) so the receiver can choose the stronger received signal; a fade at one spectral point at one antenna might not be present at the other antenna. Finally, in some systems, space diversity can be used in the transmission chain; multiple transmission antennas are used and the receiver selects the stronger signal.

Direct-Broadcast Satellites

In many applications, satellites are used to convey programs from one point to a few others. For example, a television channel provider can beam programming to local cable companies across the country, which in turn convey the programs to subscribers via coaxial cable. Direct-broadcast satellite (DBS) is a point-to-multipoint system in which individual households equipped with a small parabolic antenna and tuner receive broadcasts directly from a geostationary satellite. The satellite receives digital audio and video transmissions from ground stations and relays them directly to individuals. The receiving system is comprised of an offset parabolic antenna designed to collect the microwave signals sent by the satellite, and a converter mounted at the antenna's focal point to convert the microwave signal to a lower frequency signal. Because of the high sensitivity of these devices and relatively high satellite transmitting power, the parabolic antenna can be 0.5 meter in diameter. The dishes are mounted outside the home with a southern exposure and are manually aligned with a diagnostic display showing received signal strength. Inside the home, a phase-lock loop tuner demodulates the signal from the converter into video and audio signals suitable for a home television or stereo. For areas not centrally located in the satellite's footprint, larger antennas of a meter or more in diameter can be used for favorable reception. Direct-broadcast satellite systems transmit in the Ku-band, a higher frequency region than the VHF and UHF channels used for conventional television broadcasting. Bandwidth is set at 27 MHz per channel.

The Digital Satellite System (DSS) is an example of a direct-broadcast satellite system providing digital audio and video programming to consumers. With DSS and affiliated programming services, subscribers purchase a 0.5-meter-diameter satellite dish and receiver, pay a monthly fee, and receive 175 channels of programming. Three co-located, body-stabilized HS 601 satellites orbit at 101° west longitude, each providing 16 high-power (120 W) transponders in the Ku-band (uplink: 17.2–17.7 GHz, downlink: 12.2–12.7 GHz). They beam their high-power signals over the continental United States, lower Canada and upper Mexico. Signals originate from broadcast centers and are digitally delivered over the satellite link using ISO/MPEG-2 data reduction, then converted into conventional analog signals in the home, providing audio and video output. Some receivers have a serial data port so that programming and other information from the satellites can be passed directly to the consumer's home computer.

DirecPC is a satellite service that allows personal computers to receive information at high data rates; it is often used to distribute software updates or training videos to business customers. Receiving PCs are equipped with a plug-in card and a 0.6-meter dish; customers are charged by the volume of data downloaded. Although land-line services can operate at 9600 baud, DirecPC can operate at 12 Mbps; a 400-page book could be transmitted in 60 seconds. The service also provides high-speed access to other on-line services. Clearly, with the advent of low-cost satellite-based distribution technology, the way in which society receives radio and television signals is irrevocably changing. Commercial broadcasters, cable operators, and direct broadcasters will all compete for their share of the audience.

Digital Audio Radio

Audio media such as tape and disc have undergone tremendous change in recent years, with the introduction of compact disc and other technologies. Meanwhile, radio has remained static. AM and FM broadcasting harken back to the earliest days of audio, and the last substantial evolutionary step, FM stereo, occurred 40 years ago. However, on August 1, 1986, WGBH-FM in Boston simulcast its programming over sister station WGBX-TV using a pseudo-video PCM (F1) processor, coding the stereo digital audio signal as a television signal, thus experimentally delivering the first digital audio broadcast.

Following this experiment, the broadcasting industry has developed digital audio radio (DAR) technologies, also known as digital audio broadcasting (DAB). Instead of using analog modulation methods such as AM or FM, DAR transmits audio signals digitally. DAR is designed to replace analog AM and FM broadcasting, providing audio that is free from reception problems such as multipath interference, with fidelity comparable to that of CD. In addition to audio data, a DAR system supports auxiliary data transmission; for example, text, graphics, or still video images ("radio with pictures") can all be conveyed.

The evolution of a DAR standard is complicated because it is regulated by governments, and swayed by lobbies. Two principal DAR technologies have been developed: Eureka 147, and in-band broadcasting. The way to DAR is labyrinthine, and it appears that each country will choose one method or another; there will not be a worldwide standard.

Transmission Methods

DAR can be broadcast in a variety of ways. Like analog radio, DAR can be transmitted from transmission towers, but DAR is much more efficient. An analog radio station can broadcast with 100,000 W of power; however, a DAR station might require only 1000 W, providing a significant savings in energy costs. Terrestrial transmission continues the tradition of locally originated stations in which independent stations provide local programming. To its advantage, terrestrial DAR systems can be implemented rather quickly, at low overall cost.

DAR also can be broadcast directly from satellites, using a system in which programs are uplinked to satellites then downlinked directly to consumers equipped with digital radios. The resulting national radio broadcasting networks particularly benefit rural areas unable to sustain independent stations, they would be ideal for motorists traveling away from urban areas, and a satellite system could extend the effective range of terrestrial stations. In some proposed satellite radio systems, the transmitting satellite would have multiple (perhaps 28) spot beams, each aimed at a major metropolitan area, as well as a national beam; in this way, both regional and national programming could be accommodated. Each beam could convey 16 separate stereo audio programs; listeners in a metropolitan area would receive 32 channels (16 local and 16 national). Receivers would use low-gain, nondirectional antennas, for example, allowing automotive installation as small flush-mounted modules in the car roof.

The use of spot beams has been pioneered by NASA; the TDRS (Tracking Data and Relay System) geostationary satellites use space-to-earth spot beam transponders. Although TDRS is used to track low-orbit spacecraft (replacing the ground-tracking stations previously used) it approximates operation of a direct radio broadcast system. NASA and the Voice of America demonstrated a direct broadcast system in the S-band (at 2050 MHz) using ISO/MPEG-1 Layer II coding to deliver a 20-kHz stereo signal at a rate of 256 kbps. The experimental receiver used a short whip antenna, with reasonable indoor performance. The geostationary satellite used a 7-W transmitter.

Implementation of any commercial satellite system requires great capital investment, and to ensure good signal strength in difficult areas such as urban canyons and tunnels, local supplemental transmitters known as gap fillers are needed. Using a system known as single-frequency networking, these transmitters broadcast the same information and operate on the same frequency with contiguous coverage zones. The receiver automatically selects the stronger signal without interference from overlapping zones. In addition, because of limited satellite life span of 15 years or less, any satellite system must budget for periodic renewal of its spacecraft.

Alternatively, digital audio programs can be broadcast over home cable systems. For example, digital audio programming originating from a broadcast center can be delivered via satellite to local cable providers. Time-division multiplexing is used to efficiently combine many digital audio channels into one wide-band signal. At the cable head-end, the channels are demultiplexed, encrypted, and remodulated for distribution to cable subscribers over an unused television channel. At the consumer's home, a tuner is used to select a channel, the channel is decoded, unencrypted, and converted to analog form for playback. Digital radio channels could flourish in much the same way as cable television channels, with a hundred stations to choose from. In practice, a combination of all three systems, terrestrial, satellite, and cable, will be used to convey digital audio (and video) signals. Figure 13-5 shows an example of transmission routing originating from an event such as a football game, conveyed over various paths, to consumers. Today, these paths use both analog and digital technologies; increasingly, the latter is replacing the former.

Spectral Space

A significant complication for any DAR broadcast system is where to locate the DAR band (perhaps 50 MHz wide) in the electromagnetic spectrum. Spectral space is a limited resource that has already been substantially allocated. Furthermore, the

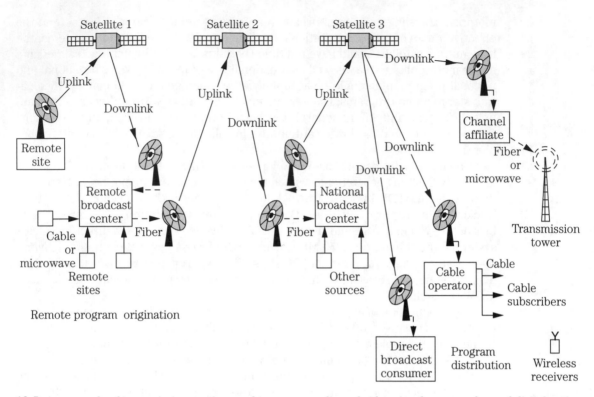

13-5 An example of transmission routing used to convey audio and video signals over analog and digital paths. Consider that a football fan seated in a stadium could use a portable television to receive signals originating in the stadium and returning over the path illustrated.

frequency of the DAR transmission band will impact the technology's quality, cost, and worldwide compatibility. Any band from 100 to 1700 MHz could be used for terrestrial DAR, but the spectrum is already crowded with applications. In general, lower bands are preferable (because RF attenuation increases with frequency) but are hard to obtain. The S-Band (2310–2360 MHz) is not suitable for terrestrial DAR because it is prone to interference. However, the S-band is suitable for satellite delivery. In general, the upper UHF-TV band is not available because it will be used by advanced television applications. Likewise the 728- to 788-MHz band, now home to 100 UHF stations, has been pledged to future television systems.

A worldwide allocation would assist manufacturers, and would ultimately lower cost, but such a consensus is impossible to obtain. The World Administrative Radio Conference (WARC) allocated 40 MHz at 1500 MHz (L-band) for digital audio broadcasting via satellite, but ultimately deferred selection for regional solution. Similarly, the CCIR (International Radio Consultative Committee) conference proposed a worldwide 60-MHz band at 1500 MHz for both terrestrial and satellite DAR, however terrestrial broadcasting at 1500 MHz is prone to absorption and obstruction, and satellite broadcasting requires repeaters. There is no realistic possibility of a worldwide satellite standard. In the United States, in 1995, the FCC allocated the S-band

(2310–2360 MHz) spectrum to establish satellite-delivered digital audio broadcasting services. Neighboring Canada and Mexico have allocated space at 1500 MHz. In Europe, both 1500-MHz and 2600-MHz regions have been proposed. Ideally, whether using adjacent or separated bands, DAR would permit compatibility between terrestrial and satellite channels. In practice, there is not a mutually ideal band space, and any allocation will involve compromises.

Alternatively, new DAR systems could cohabit spectral space with existing applications. Specifically, DAR could use a shared-spectrum technique to locate the digital signal in the FM and AM bands. By using an "in-band" approach, power multiplexing can provide compatibility with the analog transmissions, with the digital broadcast signal coexisting with the analog carriers. Because of its greater efficiency, the DAR signal transmits at lower power relative to the analog station. An analog receiver rejects the weaker digital signal as noise, but DAR receivers can receive both DAR and analog broadcasts. No matter how DAR is implemented, the eventual disposition of AM and FM is a concern. Most likely, a transition period will be required, lasting until AM and FM gradually disappear.

Data Reduction

Digital audio signals cannot be practically transmitted in a linear PCM format because the bandwidth requirements would be extreme. A stereo DAB signal might occupy 2 MHz of bandwidth, compared to the approximately 200 kHz required by an analog FM broadcast. Thus, DAR must use data reduction to reduce the spectral requirement. For example, instead of a digital signal transmitted at a 2-Mbps rate, a data-reduced signal might be transmitted at 256 kbps. There are numerous perceptual coding methods suitable for broadcasting. For example, the ISO/MPEG-1 algorithms use subband and transform coding with numerous data rates. Similarly, the Dolby AC-2 system uses transform coding. Such systems can reduce an audio signal to a 256-, 128-, 96-, or 64-kbps rate. Although telephony has used data reduction for years, this technology has only recently entered the domain of commercial radio broadcasting where transmission demands are more challenging. In addition, an audio signal passing through a broadcast chain undergoes multiple data compression/decompression; this increases distortion and artifacts. Data reduction is discussed in detail in chapter 11.

Technical Considerations

The performance of a digital audio broadcasting system can be evaluated with a number of criteria including: delivered sound quality, coverage range for reliable reception, interference between analog and digital signals at the same or adjacent frequencies, resistance to signal loss in mountains or tunnels, error correction in the presence of noise or interference, immunity to multipath distortion, receiver complexity, and capacity for auxiliary data services. In addition, ideally, the same receiver can be used for both terrestrial and satellite reception.

The designer of a DAR system must balance many variables to produce a system with low error rate, moderate transmitted power levels, and sufficient data rate, all within the smallest possible bandwidth. As with any digital data system, a broadcasting system must minimize errors; the bit error rate (BER) must be reduced through error correction data accompanying the audio data, and is monitored for a given carrier-to-noise (C/N) power of the received signal. Transmitted digital signals are received successfully with low C/N, but analog signals are not. Generally, a BER of 10^{-4} at the receiver might be nominal, but rates of 10^{-3} and 10^{-2} can be expected to occur, in addition to burst errors.

Receiver performance also can be gauged by measuring the ratio between the energy per bit received to the power spectral density of the input noise in a 1-Hz bandwidth; this is notated as E_b/N_o. Designers strive to achieve a low BER for a given C/N or E_b/N_o. Digital transmission tends to have brick-wall coverage; the system operates well with a low BER within a certain range, then BER increases dramatically (yielding total system failure) when there is an additional small decrease in signal strength.

Most digital communications systems use pulse shaping prior to modulation to limit bandwidth requirements. Pulse shaping performs lowpass filtering to reduce high-frequency content of the digital signal. Because this spreads the bit width, resulting in intersymbol interference, raised cosine filters are used so that the interference from each bit is nulled at the center of other bit intervals, eliminating interference.

Multipath interference occurs when a direct signal and one or more strongly reflected and delayed signals (perhaps 5-μs delay), for example, signals reflected from a building, destructively combine at the receiver. The result is a comb filter with 10- to 50-dB dips in signal strength, as shown in Fig. 13-6. In addition, other weak reflected signals might persist for up to 20 μs. This type of RF multipath is a frequency-selective problem, and short wavelengths, for example, in FM broadcasting, are more vulnerable. When the receiver is moving, multipath interference results in the amplitude modulation "picket fence" effect familiar to mobile FM listeners. Even worse, in a stoplight fade, when the receiver is stopped in a signal null, the signal is continuously degraded; a single, strong specular reflection completely cancels the transmitted signal's bandwidth. FM signals can become noisy, but because digital signals operate with a small C/N ratio, they can be lost altogether. Increasing power is not a remedy because both the direct and reflected signal will increase proportionally, preserving the interference nulls.

Another effect of multipath interference, caused by short delays, occurs in the demodulated bit stream. This is delay spread in which multiple reflections arrive at the receiver over a time interval of perhaps 15 μs. The result is intersymbol interference in the received data; bits arrive at multiple times. This can be overcome with bit periods longer than the spread time; however, with conventional modulation this would limit bit rate to less than 100 kbps, thus data reduction also must be used. Frequency diversity techniques are very good at combatting multipath interference; by placing the data signal on multiple carriers, interference on one carrier frequency can be overcome.

Two types of multiplexing are commonly used. The most common method is time-division multiplexing (TDM) in which multiple channels share a single carrier by time interleaving their data streams on a bit or word basis; different bit rates can be time multiplexed. Frequency-division multiplexing (FDM) divides a band into

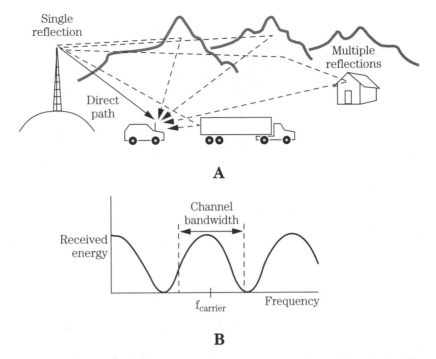

A

B

13-6 Multipath interference degrades signal quality at the receiver. A. A radio receives the direct transmission path, as well as delayed single and multiple reflection paths. B. The combined path lengths produce nulls in signal strength in the received channel bandwidth.

subbands, and individual channels modulate individual carriers within the available bandwidth. A single channel can be frequency multiplexed; this lowers the bit rate on each carrier, and lowers bit errors as well. Because different carriers are used, multipath interference is reduced because only one carrier frequency is affected; on the other hand, more spectral space is needed.

Phase-shift keying (PSK) modulation methods are commonly used, because they yield the lowest BER for a given signal strength. In binary phase-shift keying (BPSK), two phase shifts represent two binary states. For example, a binary 0 places the carrier in phase, and a binary 1 places it 180° out of phase, as shown in Fig. 13-7A. This phase change codes the binary signal, as shown in Fig. 13-7B. The symbol rate equals the data rate. In quadrature phase-shift keying (QPSK), four phase shifts are used thus two bits per symbol are represented; for example, 11 places the carrier at 0°, 10 at 90°, 00 at 180°, and 01 at 270°, as shown in Fig. 13-7C. The symbol rate is half the transmission rate. QPSK is the most widely used method, especially for data rates above 100 Mbps. Higher-order PSK can be used (for example, 8-PSK, 16-PSK), but as the number of phases increases, higher E_b/N_o is required to achieve satisfactory BER. Other modulation methods include amplitude shift keying (ASK) in which different carrier powers represent binary values, frequency-shift keying (FSK) in which the carrier frequency is varied (FSK is used in modems), and quadrature amplitude modulation (QAM) in which both amplitude and phase are varied.

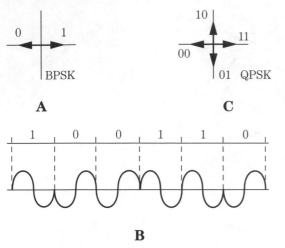

13-7
Phase-shift keying (PSK) is used to modulate a carrier, improving efficiency, for example, decreasing bit error rates. A. Phasor diagram of binary phase shift keying (BPSK). B. An example of a BPSK waveform. C. Phasor diagram of quadrature phase shift keying (QPSK).

The bandwidth (BW) for an M-PSK signal is given by:

$$\frac{D}{\log_2 M} < BW < \frac{2D}{\log_2 M}$$

where D is the data rate in bps. For example, a QPSK signal transmitting a 400-kbps signal would require a bandwidth of between 200 to 400 kHz. A 16-PSK could transmit the same data rate in half the bandwidth, but would require 8 dB more power (E_b/N_o) for a satisfactory BER. Given the inherently high bandwidth of digital audio signals, data reduction must be used to conserve spectral space, and provide low BER for a reasonable transmission power level. As Kenneth Springer has noted, a 4,000,000 level PSK modulation would be needed to make a transmitted signal's bandwidth equal its original analog baseband; the required power would be prohibitive. But with a 4:1 data reduction, 256-PSK provides the same baseband. In practice, an error-corrected, data-reduced signal, with QPSK modulation, can be transmitted with lower power than an analog signal.

One of the great strengths of a digital system is its transmission power efficiency. This can be seen by relating coverage area to the C/N ratio at the receiver. A digital system might need a C/N of only 6 dB, but an FM receiver needs a C/N of 30 dB, a difference of 24 dB, to provide the same coverage area. Kenneth Springer has shown that the field strength for a DAR system can be estimated from:

$$E = V_i + NF + C/N - \frac{96.5}{F_{\text{MHz}}}$$

where: E = minimum acceptable field strength at the receiver in dBu

V_i = thermal noise of receiver into 300 Ω in dBu

where:

$$V_i = 20 \log \left(\frac{kTRB}{10^{-6}} \right)^{1/2}$$

where:

k = 1.38×10^{-23} W/kHz

T = temperature in degrees Kelvin (290 at room temperature)

R = input impedance of the receiver

B = bandwidth of the digital signal

NF = noise figure of the receiver

C/N = carrier-to-noise ratio for a given BER

F_{MHz} = transmission frequency.

For example, if a DAR signal is broadcast at 100 MHz, with 200-kHz bandwidth, into a receiver with 6-dB noise figure, with C/N of 6 dB, then E = 5.5 dBu. In contrast, an FM receiver might require a field strength of 60 dBu for good reception, and about 30 dBu for noisy reception.

Eureka 147/DAB

Several European countries, Canada, Mexico, and Australia have tentatively approved the wideband Eureka 147 system for broadcast of DAR signals, through direct satellite broadcasting and terrestrial methods. Eureka is a research and development consortium of European governments, corporations, and universities, established in 1985 to develop new technologies. By 1990 over 7.5 billion dollars had been invested in over 300 projects ranging from biotechnology to transportation. Project number 147, begun in 1986, aimed to develop a wideband digital audio broadcasting system (formally known as DAB, as opposed to DAR). A prototype Eureka 147/DAB system was first demonstrated in September 1988, and many improvements have followed.

Eureka 147's most innovative feature is its method of transmission coding. In traditional radio broadcasting, a single carrier frequency is used to transmit a mono or stereo audio program, with one carrier per radio station. This method allows complete independence of stations, but poses a number of problems. For example, reception conditions at the receiver might produce multipath interference at the desired carrier frequency, in part because the station's bandwidth is narrow (e.g., approximately 200 kHz for analog FM radio). In addition, wide guardbands must be placed around each carrier to prevent adjacent interference. In short, independent carrier transmission methods are not particularly robust, and are relatively inefficient from a spectral standpoint.

Eureka 147 digitally combines multiple perceptually coded audio signals, and the combined signal is interleaved in both frequency and time across a wide broadcast band. More specifically, the channel coding method used is coded orthogonal frequency division multiplexing (COFDM) with quadrature phase shift keying (QPSK) modulation on each carrier. This method splits several audio data channels among many overlapping 15-kHz-wide carriers, spreading any given audio signal across a transmission band of 1.5 MHz or more. Carrier centers are separated by the inverse of the time interval between bits, and separately modulated within their fractional spectral space, with a portion of the overall signal. For example, 16 stereo channels could be transmitted over one 7-MHz band, using 512 carriers, from one antenna. This reduces the data rate on any one carrier, which promotes long bit periods. This frequency diversity yields great immunity to intersymbol interference, and multipath interference. Not only are adjacent bits interleaved over a wide frequency range, but convolutional coding corrects those errors that do occur. Individual broadcasters can select the bit-rate appropriate for the application (for example, 32 to 384 kbps) with varying levels of error correction.

Eureka 147's frequency diversity provides spectral efficiency that exceeds that of analog FM broadcasting. In addition, time interleaving combats fading experienced in mobile reception. The transmission power efficiency, as with many digital radio systems, is impressive; it can be 10 to 100 times more power efficient than FM broadcasting; a Eureka 147 station could cover a broadcast market with transmitter power of less than 1000 W. A principal feature of Eureka 147 is its ability to support both terrestrial and satellite delivery on the same frequency; the same receiver can be used to receive a program from either source. Block diagrams of a Eureka 147 transmitter and receiver are shown in Fig. 13-8.

Eureka 147 originally used MUSICAM bit rate reduction in its source coding to minimize the spectrum requirements. Subsequently, Eureka 147 developers adopted the ISO/MPEG-1 Layer II standard; at a rate of 128 kbps per channel, the compression does not impair the quality of the original audio signal. MUSICAM and ISO/MPEG are discussed in chapter 11.

One prototype Eureka 147 system, using L-band transmission, was evaluated in Canada. The COFDM used the following parameters: 7-MHz RF bandwidth, 448-quadrature phase shift keying, subcarriers with 15.625-kHz spacing, 80-μs symbol length with 16-μs guard interval, capacity to transmit in multiplex 33 monophonic channels (129 kbps) or 16 stereo pairs and 1 data channel. A transmitter with power of 150 W (1.5 kW ERP) total, or 9.4 W (94 W ERP) per stereo channel, produced a coverage range of 50 km, where ERP is effective radiated power. The propagation and reception were similar to that of FM and UHF broadcasting; a local FM station required 40 kW ERP for 70-km coverage. Multipath errors were generally absent.

In another Canadian test, fixed and mobile receivers performed signal strength measurements using a 50-W transmitter and 16-dB antenna to broadcast nine CD quality channels (with power of 200 W/channel) with reliable coverage to distances 45 km from the transmitter. In addition, Canadian tests verified Eureka's ability to provide a single frequency network in which multiple transmitters can operate on a single frequency, without interference in overlapping areas. The Canadian system also proposed a mixed mode of broadcasting in which a single receiver could receive either satellite or terrestrial digital audio broadcasts. In a test in London, a Eureka 147 transmitter with 100 W of power provided coverage over 95% of the London area, with antennas similar to those used in table radios.

Eureka 147 is inherently a wideband system, and requires a new spectrum allocation outside the existing commercial broadcast bands. The narrowest Eureka 147 configuration uses 1.5 MHz to transmit six stereo channels. In practice, a much wider band would be required for most applications. For example, up to 512 carriers might convey 16 stereo channels in a band that is 7 MHz wide. In other words, fully implemented Eureka 147 would occupy an entire radio band. Because spectral space

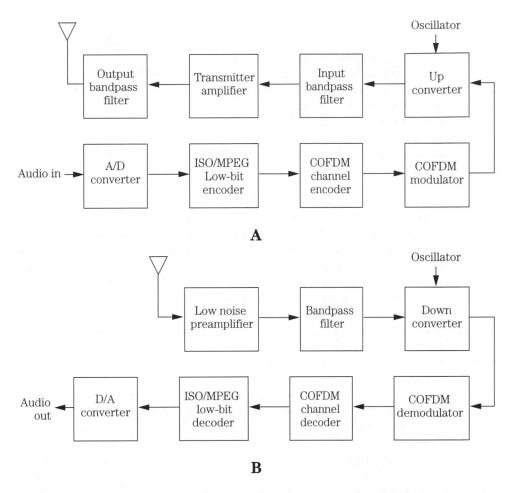

13-8 Eureka 147/DAB broadcasting system. A. Eureka transmitter. B. Eureka receiver.

is scarce, this poses a problem. Proponents have argued for allocation of the L-band (1500 MHz) for Eureka 147, but the U.S. government, for example, is unwilling to commit that space; in particular, the U.S. military uses that spectral space for aircraft telemetry. Other domestic 147 supporters have proposed operation in the S-band (2300 MHz); in general, Eureka 147 can operate in a number of bands, ranging from 30 MHz to 3 GHz; however, a 100-MHz to 1700-MHz range is preferred. Although some European countries have allocated the L-band for DAB, Germany and the United Kingdom have not. Germany has argued for DAB in the 200- to 230-MHz band, where it would replace upper VHF TV users. Under one plan, this space would be used temporarily until DAB market penetration justified replacing the FM band with DAB. Canada has extensively tested Eureka 147 in the L-band. In the U.S., although the FCC has authorized use of the S-band for digital satellite radio, lack of suitable spectral space remains an obstacle in the path of Eureka 147.

Other drawbacks exist. In particular, the need to combine stations leads to practical problems in some implementations. Eureka 147's designers, taking a European community bias, envisioned a satellite delivery system that would blanket Europe with a single footprint. Terrestrial transmitters operating on the same frequencies would be used mainly as gap fillers, operating on the same frequency. This monolithic approach is opposed in the U.S. where independent local programming is preferred. With satellite delivery of Eureka 147, the concept of local markets becomes more difficult to implement, while national stations become easier to implement. This would redefine the existing broadcast industry. To address this issue, researchers are exploring the use of Eureka in the FM and AM bands as an in-band system.

Eureka 147 could be used with terrestrial transmission in which local towers supplement satellite delivery, with local stations coexisting with national channels. In January 1991, the NAB endorsed such a system, and proposed that the L-band be allocated; existing AM and FM licensees would be given DAB space in the L-Band, before phasing out existing frequencies. The plan called for creation of "pods" in which each existing broadcaster would be given a digital channel; four stations would multiplex their signals over a 1.5-MHz-wide band. The power levels and location of pods would duplicate the coverage areas of existing stations. The NAB estimated that no more than 130 MHz of spectrum would be needed to accommodate all existing broadcasters in the new system. However, broadcasters did not accept the multiplexing arrangement and the potential for new stations it allowed, and many argued for an in-band DAB system that would allow existing stations to phase in DAB, yet still provide AM and FM transmission. In March 1991 the Department of Defense indicated that the L-band was not available. In the face of these actions, in January 1992, the NAB reversed its position and instead proposed development of an in-band digital radio system that would operate in the FM and AM bands, coexisting with analog FM and AM stations. The NAB generally opposes satellite delivery methods because they would negatively impact the infrastructure of terrestrial stations. Meanwhile, not bothered by America's political and commercial questions, other countries have argued that Eureka, practical problems aside, remains the best technical system available.

In-Band Digital Radio

Whereas most implementations of the Eureka 147 system occupy new digital audio broadcast bands outside existing FM (88 to 108 MHz) and AM (525 to 1705 kHz) bands, some U.S. manufacturers have developed in-band systems that transmit digital audio radio signals in existing FM and AM bands, along with analog radio signals. An in-band system offers commercial advantages, and would be simpler and cheaper to implement than a wideband system. In some implementations, the in-band digital system would provide twice the number of channels currently provided by analog broadcast means. However, such in-band systems would be incompatible with wideband Eureka systems, thus the proposal has delayed progress in other countries and deployment of a U.S. system. Any in-band system must equal the performance already demonstrated by the wideband Eureka system. For example, immunity to multipath interference must be demonstrated.

In-band systems use the existing AM and FM bands, and permit broadcasters to simultaneously transmit analog and digital programs on the same carriers. Digital signals are inherently highly immune to interference thus a digital receiver is able to reject the analog signals. However, it is more difficult for an analog receiver to reject the digital signal's interference. Coexistence can be achieved if the digital signal is broadcast at much lower power; because of the broadcast efficiency of DAR, a low-power signal can maintain existing coverage areas for digital receivers, and allow analog receivers to reject the interfering signal.

With an in-band on-channel (IBOC) system, DAR signals are superimposed on current FM and AM transmission bands (in some systems, DAR signals are placed on either side of the analog signal). In the U.S., FM radio stations are assigned a band-width of 240 kHz, and AM stations use 20.4-kHz bandwidths. In-band systems fit within the same bandwidth constraints, and furthermore, efficiently use the FCC regulated RF mask in which the channel's spectrum widens as power decreases. Specifically, if a DAR signal is 25 dB below the FM signal, it could occupy a 480-kHz bandwidth, as shown in Fig. 13-9A. In the case of AM, if the DAR signal is 25 dB below the AM signal, the band can be 40 kHz wide, as shown in Fig. 13-9B. Because the digital signal's power can be lower, it can thus efficiently use the entire frequency mask area. Clearly, because of the wider FM bandwidth, an FM in-band system is much easier to implement; rates of 256 kbps can be achieved. The narrow AM channels can limit DAR data rates to perhaps 128 or 96 kbps; in addition, existing AM radios are not as amenable to DAR signals as FM receivers. On the other hand, AM broadcast is not hampered by multipath problems, but multipath immunity is more difficult to achieve in a narrowband in-band FM system, compared to a wideband DAR system. In-band FM systems might require spatial diversity antennas on cars to combat multipath interference. As noted, any DAR system must rely on perceptual coding to reduce the channel data rate to 128 kbps or so, to allow the high-fidelity signal (along with nonaudio data) to be transmitted in the narrow bands available.

The IBOC method is highly attractive because it fits within much of the existing regulatory statutes and commercial interests. No modifications of existing AM and

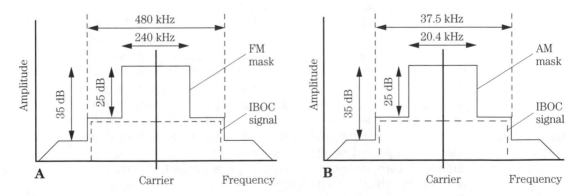

13-9 The Federal Communications Commission strictly defines the RF spectrum masks allowed to broadcasters. Any IBOC system must stay within the spectral mask. A. The FM spectrum mask. B. The AM spectrum mask.

FM receivers are required, and DAR receivers receive both analog and digital signals. Moreover, because digital signals are simply simulcast over existing equipment, start-up broadcasting costs are extremely low. An in-band system provides improved frequency response, and lower noise and distortion within existing coverage areas. Receivers can be designed so that if the digital signal fails, the radio would automatically switch to the analog signal.

Alternatively, in-band interstitial (IBI) systems transmit low power DAR signals on guardband frequencies adjacent to existing carriers; this helps to reduce the problems of differentiation between the types of signals. In a single-channel IBI system, the DAR signal is placed in one adjacent channel (upper or lower). Alternatively, both adjacent channels can be used; this would reduce the number of available stations, but frequency hopping, switching from carrier to carrier, can be used to reduce multiplex interference. In a single-channel multiplexed IBI system, various stations in a market multiplex their DAR signals, and they broadcast in adjacent channels across the band, providing greater frequency diversity, and protection against multipath interference.

The differentiation of the analog and digital signals presents technological challenges, particularly to an IBOC system. Specifically, the DAR signal must not interfere with the analog signal in existing receivers, and DAR receivers must use encryption methods to extract the DAR signal while ignoring the much stronger analog signal. FM receivers are good at rejecting amplitude noise; for example, their limiters would reject a DAR signal using ASK modulation. Existing FM receivers would see the weaker (30 dB or so) digital signal as noise, and reject it. With PSK modulation, the DAR signal might have to be 45 to 50 dB below the FM signal level; it is more difficult to extract the digital information from the analog signal. For example, an adaptive transversal filter could provide interference cancellation to eliminate the analog FM (or AM) signal so that on-channel digital information can be processed. Thanks to the industrial-military complex, signal extraction technology has been well developed; for example, the problem of retrieving signals in the presence of jamming signals has been carefully studied. In the case of IBOC, the problem is further simplified because the nature of the jamming signal (the analog signal) is known at the broadcast site, and can be determined at the receiver.

The idea of developing an IBOC DAR system was first proposed by Kintel Technologies. Its system relies on the FM capture effect to multiplex several signals on one channel; the modulation of the weaker signal is attenuated, and the stronger signal emerges. In this system, a lower-level digital carrier is mixed with the analog carrier. When in DAR mode, digital radios receive the combined signal then use cancellation in a phase-tracking circuit to attenuate the FM signal; the stronger DAR signal is captured by the receiver, and the remainder of the FM signal is eliminated. The DAR signal is 10 dB or lower relative to the FM signal, and uses FSK modulation. Additional signals can be multiplexed, at different power levels.

USA Digital Radio is an early developer of IBOC systems for both FM and AM DAB transmission. Their first IBOC system (Project Acorn) was publicly demonstrated in April 1991. A subsequent FM-IBOC system can be described as a narrowband, split-channel, spread-spectrum system. It uses MPEG Layer II coding for stereo audio transmission, and conveys an auxiliary data channel as well. A block di-

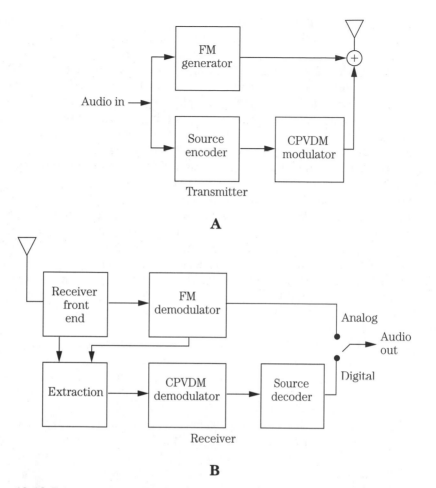

13-10 Prototype Acorn IBOC broadcasting system. A. Acorn transmitter. B. Acorn receiver.

agram of the system is shown in Fig. 13-10. Audio coding is continuously variable from 128 to 256 kbps and auxiliary data coding is variable up to 64 kbps; the modulation data rate is 384 kbps, with the difference given to error-correction coding. These variable source-coding rates allow flexibility in error-correction coding, providing a graceful degradation (gradual loss of dynamic range and frequency response as opposed to sudden muting) as bit errors increase under adverse conditions. Error-correction coding is hierarchical; important frame header information is heavily error-corrected, followed by exponent values, mantissa MSBs, and LSBs. In addition, low audio frequencies are more heavily protected than high frequencies.

The USA Digital Radio FM system uses 48 separate subchannels, placed both above and below the broadcast center frequency to provide frequency diversity. A void is maintained in the center of the spectrum of each subchannel waveform so that the analog FM signal is undisturbed. SCA signals are also unaffected. The subchannels are wideband, noiselike, and mutually orthogonal. Although the occupied bandwidth approaches 480 kHz, it remains within the FM emissions mask because the level is about 38 dB below the FM carrier signal. Each carrier provides 8 kbps with a bit width of about 100 μs. Data is coded with biphase keying. The system uses coded polyvector digital modulation (CPVDM), a method similar to the COFDM used in Eureka 147. When observed individually, each subchannel carrier has a spectrum that spans a 480-kHz bandwidth (with a 240-kHz void about the analog FM carrier). The center frequencies of the 48 subchannels continually shift; the reference signal driving the carriers is the analog FM deviation; the digital carriers move at the instantaneous rate of the analog FM signal, but do not interfere with it. The spread-spectrum movement of the DAR carriers within the band, and time interleaving, all reduce multipath interference from moving or stoplight fading.

In addition to separate subchannels, a wideband reference sounding waveform is injected into the modulation waveform; it assists subchannel acquisition and multipath equalization at the receiver. This standard bit pattern in the signal (occurring perhaps 40 times per second) is known to the receiver. The receiver can compare the received signal to the expected signal, calculate the response of the transmission path, and thus perform adaptive equalization to cancel the channel's effect and optimize reception. USA Digital Radio claims that a 100-W FM-IBOC DAB station can provide coverage equal to that of a 50-kW analog FM station. The system provides audio bandwidth of 20 kHz and a dynamic range of 96 dB.

The USA Digital Radio AM-IBOC system uses MPEG Layer II encoding at 96 kbps for joint stereo audio, and conveys a 2.4-kbps auxiliary data channel as well. When combined with error-correction data, the overall bit rate is 128 kbps, with an average efficiency of 3.2 bits per second per hertz. The resulting audio signal is reproduced with 15-kHz audio bandwidth and 96-dB dynamic range. The entire transmitted signal lies within the AM emissions low-power mask of 37.5 kHz, at a –25-dB level, and overlies the analog AM signal without interference. As in the FM system, adaptive equalization and phase correction, based on reference waveform information, are used to improve reliability. Using an IBOC DAR receiver, listeners can tune in AM, FM, or in-band digital channels.

At a meeting of the CCIR, virtually every country supported the adoption of Eureka 147 as a worldwide standard, except the United States. That opposition, supported by successful demonstrations of in-band systems, stalled any decision on the part of the CCIR. Critics argue that in-band DAR would be a minor improvement over AM and FM because of interference and crosstalk problems, especially in mobile environments. Instead, they argue that L-Band DAR should entirely replace AM and FM, because it would be more effective. They argue that if marketplace and political realities are used as the primary constraint, technological effectiveness will be compromised. However, the NAB has formally endorsed an in-band, on-channel system for the United States.

In 1994 and 1995 the Electronic Industries Association (EIA) and the National Radio Systems Committee (NRSC) tested digital radio systems from these developers: AT&T Bell Laboratories (IBAC in FM band), AT&T/Amati Communications (IBOC in FM band), Thomson Consumer Electronics (Eureka 147 COFDM at 1.5 GHz), USA Digital Radio (IBOC in FM and AM band), and Voice of America/Jet Propulsion Laboratory (DBS at 2.3 GHz). Ultimately, the FCC must determine which DAR technology to standardize in the United States.

14
CHAPTER

Digital Audio Workstations

Whereas in the past recording studios used a collection of diverse equipment—tape recorders, mixing desks, peripheral effects, and synthesis gear—today's workstations integrate these functions into a more efficient package. As with any technology, workstations have advantages and disadvantages, and are best suited to certain applications. To best utilize workstations, it is important to understand the environments for which they are designed. The technology of workstations is tied to that of digital signal processing and digital audio storage. The use of digital signal processing on a large scale for audio applications was pioneered by digital mixing consoles. The origins of workstations can thus be traced to this particular implementation. Workstations also draw from technology originally developed for applications such as console automation, synchronizers, MIDI software controllers, and microprocessor-based synthesis systems. In the future, workstation technology will increasingly integrate multimedia authoring and processing applications. In addition, soundcards for consumer and business applications have transformed many computer applications.

Digital Mixing Consoles

Increasingly sophisticated production values necessitate more flexible production equipment. However, the development of sophisticated analog mixing consoles leads to ergonomic obstacles. A large mixing desk has hundreds of controls spread over a large, acoustically unsuitable surface. In addition, the need to interface digital signal processing equipment and digital storage media with analog mixing circuitry negates much of the advantage of digital technology. The combination of higher-fidelity standards, greater user versatility, easier operation, and enhanced interfacing has led designers to the digital mixing console as a cost-effective solution. This technology is intended to both replace analog consoles and extend their performance and flexibility. Although some digital audio consoles approach the problems of audio production from a traditional, analog user standpoint, their development also serves as a proving ground for technology used in digital audio workstations.

Considerations for Digital Consoles

The design of a digital mixing console is quite complex. The device is, in effect, a vast digital signal processor, requiring perhaps 10^9 instructions per second. Although many of the obstacles present in analog technology are absent in a digital implementation, seemingly trivial exercises in signal processing might require sophisticated digital circuits. In addition, the task of real time computation of digital signal processing presents problems unique to digital architecture. In short, the digital manifestation of audio components requires a complete rethinking of analog architectures, and originality in the use of existing digital techniques.

A typical digital console system is shown in Fig. 14-1. Signals are converted to a digital format at the microphone panels so that lines between the studio and equipment room are free of analog degradation. By placing processing equipment in a room separated from the console's control surface, the bulk and ambient noise of the processing equipment can be closeted. Fiber-optic links can be used to interconnect the equipment.

A digital console avoids numerous problems encountered by its analog counterpart, but its simple task of providing the three basic functions of attenuating, mixing, and signal selection and routing entails greater design complexity. The problem is augmented by the requirement that all operations must be interfaced to the user's analog world. A software-based virtual mixer is much easier to design than one with

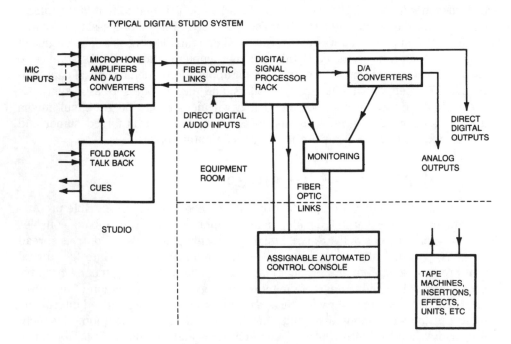

14-1 Interconnection of a digital mixing console in an audio studio. Neve, Ltd.

potentiometers and other physical comforts. On the other hand, tasks such as time delay for phase coherence of microphone inputs are easily provided. Of course, a digital console's software-defined processing promotes considerable flexibility in every facet of its operation.

The processing tasks of a digital console follow those of any DSP system, as described in chapter 15. The first fundamental task of a mixing console is gain control. In analog, this is realized with only a potentiometer; however, a digital preamplifier requires a potentiometer, an A/D converter to convert the analog position information of the variable resistor into digital form, and a multiplier to adjust the value of the digital audio data, as shown in Fig. 14-2A. The mixing console's second task, mixing, can be accomplished in the analog domain with several resistors and an operational amplifier. In a digital realization, this task requires a multiplexer and accumulator, as shown in Fig. 14-2B. The third task, signal selection and routing, is accomplished in analog with

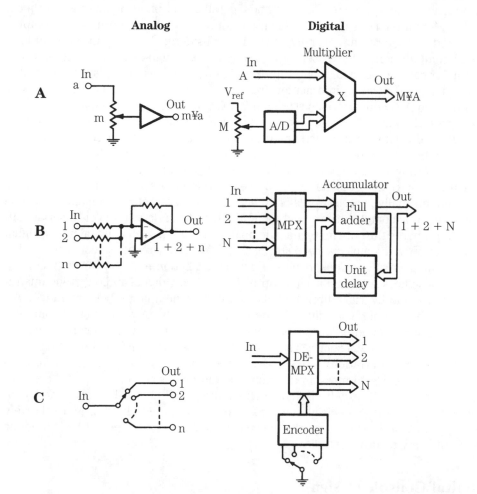

14-2 The three primary functions in signal processing can be realized in both analog and digital forms. A. Attenuating. B. Mixing. C. Selecting. Sakamoto, et al.

a multipole switch, but with digital technology requires a demultiplexer and encoding circuit to read the desired selection, as shown in Fig. 14-2C. Of course, all processing steps must be accomplished on each audio sample in each channel in real time, that is, within the span of one sample period (20.8 µs at a 48-kHz sampling frequency).

A requirement of any console is provision for extensive equalization faculties, including lowpass and highpass filters, presence, and shelving filters of various types. These can be designed using a variety of techniques, such as a cascade of biquadratic sections, a type of digital filter architecture. However, the fast processing speeds and necessity for long word length place great demands on the system. On the other hand, filter coefficients are readily stored in ROM, and no more than a few thousand characteristics are typically required for most applications.

The design of multipliers is critical in a digital audio processing system. Many types of hardware multipliers have been developed for many applications: serial-parallel multipliers using pipeline methods, parallel multipliers using array methods, and ROM multipliers using logarithm and dividing methods. Hardware cost, computing speed and computing accuracy must all be considered. By using an adder for low-speed computation such as user input, the amount of high-speed computing at the multiplier can be reduced. Input data from two channels is multiplexed by parallel processing, and position information from the balance control is converted at low speed by an A/D converter and stored in RAM. The digital position data is synchronized with the audio data and together they are supplied to an accumulator to successively add data words together. Alternatively, as discussed in chapter 15, DSP chips can be used to realize this and other audio circuits.

An overflow circuit might be included to scale the audio signal to prevent distortion at the multiplier. A digital signal processor that inputs and outputs 16-bit audio data can internally process words of 56 bits or more. The data is then applied to the multiplier to accomplish the actual manipulation of the data. Parallel to serial conversion prepares the data for digital and analog output. In such a digital mixer, signal deterioration in dynamic range, distortion, and frequency response could result due to internal calculation. Thus, realities such as truncation must be carefully considered by designers, as described in chapter 15. As in any digital audio system, quantization noise and overflow must be balanced to provide a large dynamic range. For example, the use of digital dither is prerequisite for low distortion signal computation. Otherwise, round-off distortion can become audible with complex routines.

The performance of such a system relative to cost is ultimately the deciding factor for market penetration. With the decreased cost of digital technology it has become cost effective to mass produce such audio processing units, using hardware selected from off-the-shelf electronics, including DSP chips. The combination of low-cost electronics, specially developed audio integrated circuits, and relatively large production runs has brought the cost of digital audio mixers within economic reach of many recording studios.

Digital Console Design

In many professional implementations, the digital console surface is separated from rack-mounted processing electronics, and interconnected by optical cable. The use of optical cable eliminates problems such as high-frequency loss, crosstalk, RFI (radio-frequency interference), and hum. For example, a fiber cable can use a MADI (AES10) protocol to carry 56 channels of digital audio over a 1.5-km distance. A console could provide 48 microphone inputs, 32 group outputs, 72 line level inputs, and 8 auxiliary sends. Two-channel I/O might adhere to the AES3 digital interface.

The channel processors are tailored for audio processing. One processor can be dedicated to the processing requirements of each audio input. Because of flexible signal routing within the processor as well as the overall system, unused channel processing capability can be applied elsewhere, for example in equalization of group outputs. The channel processor can use 24 bits, which is equivalent to a 144 dB S/N; thus, equalization can be performed without fear of prefader overload. The mixing processor might use 32 bits; this 192 dB of S/N is virtually overload proof and solves the analog problem of restricted headroom at a summation point. Time-division multiplexing allows efficient use of the bus structure. In the 20.8 μs between audio samples representing one channel, there is time for many other samples to travel the same bus for processing, for example, through equalizers or compressors. Multiplexing also eliminates the need for massively parallel patch bays; when source and destination are specified, the connection is handled internally.

An example of a channel processor is shown in Fig. 14-3. The arithmetic logic unit uses bit-slice processing with a typical instruction time of 100 ns. Processing speed is expedited by the use of pipeline techniques, which allow a new instruction to be presented while a previous one is being carried out. Tri-state buffers can be used to switch the bus to the correct device at the appropriate time. For example, a digital equalizer program can use a multiplier and coefficients stored in a register. Time-delay and addition operations required are performed in the arithmetic logic unit and RAM, and the intermediate result is sent to the multiplier. Correct routing of data is critical. Time manipulations of the signal are relatively simple, albeit dependent upon storage capacity. A console can provide up to 500 ms of delay per channel for insertion in feed-forward or delay paths to control arrival of signal times; in this way, phase-incoherent microphones can be brought into phase coherence.

Because the console is simply a remote control of the processing circuits located in the rack, no audio signal passes through the console surface. It is thus possible to offer assignable functions. Although the surface can emulate a conventional analog console with parallel controls, a fewer set of assignable controls can be used to manipulate all of the signal channels, using the basic control set as a selectable window to view and control all the mix elements. For example, after basic tracks have been recorded and equalized, those inputs can be assigned to virtual strips that are not assigned to physical controls, then individually reassigned back to physical controls as needed. In other words, the relationship between the number of physical channel strips and the number of console inputs and outputs is completely flexible; rather, the number of functions is defined by physical connections, and processing power in the rack. The console can provide a central control section that provides access to all of the assignable functions currently requested for a particular signal path.

Functions can be assigned to a channel, inserted in the signal path, and controlled from that channel's strip or elsewhere. Physical controls on a channel strip can provide any assigned function, with displays that reflect the value of the selected

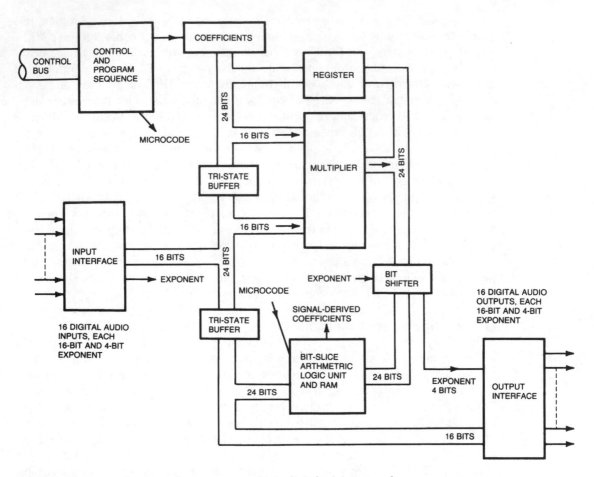

14-3 Architecture of a channel processor used in a digital mixing console. Neve, Ltd.

function. A set of controls might provide equalization, or auxiliary sends; in another example, one channel strip might be assigned to a mono, or stereo channel. As a session progresses from tracking to mix-down, the console can gradually be reconfigured, for example, adding more sends, then later creating subgroups. There is no need to limit controls to the equivalent fixed analog circuit parameters. Thus, rotary knobs, for example, might have no end stops and can be programmed for various functions, or resolution. For example, equalization might be accomplished in fractions of decibels, with selected values displayed in alphanumeric LEDs. Alternatively, a traditional analog console can be fitted with DSP processors, with the console itself merely providing a control surface.

Console set-up can be accomplished via an alphanumeric keyboard, and particular configurations can be saved on floppy disk, or preprogrammed for rapid change-over in a real-time application. Of course, flexibility would be more of a curse than a blessing if the operator were required to build a software console from scratch each time; therefore, using the concept of a "soft" signal path, multiple console preset configurations are available: track laying, mix-down, a combination of track laying and mix-down (for bounce-down, etc.), return to previous setting, and a fail-safe minimum mode in the event of system problems. A console configuration can be read from disk and the console completely reconfigured.

A video display typically shows graphic representations of console signal blocks as well as their order in the signal path; this is useful when default settings of delay, filter, equalization, dynamics and fader are varied. In addition, each path can be named, and its fader assignment shown, as well as its mute group, solo status, phase reverse, phantom power on/off, time delay, and other parameters. The video display is useful to the maintenance engineer; the console runs background diagnostics, and a problem can be pinpointed by stepping down to the appropriate level of screen information. The digital console thus provides the flexibility of digital processing with ergonomics surpassing that of analog consoles. The result is a console that offers superior production capability, and digital sound quality.

Digital Audio Workstations

A digital audio workstation is an integrated collection of hardware devices controlled by software programs to create an audio tasking system. It is based on central computer processing of digital audio signals; software control and display of signal processing, editing, and routing; random-access recording on hard drive or optical disk; and programmable output. In addition, to facilitate its use, the workstation should be highly interactive, and promote an intuitive environment for learning its operation. It should provide greater flexibility and efficiency, as well as fidelity and creativity, compared to the traditional assortment of studio gear. The early dictate that digital components be made to emulate analog ones severely restricted utility. Workstations provide a fresh approach to production needs.

Hard disk-based workstations consolidate storage, editing, production, and interfacing features. A single workstation can take the place of several pieces of traditional studio hardware, offering cost savings. More important, using random access and user friendliness, production time is decreased, and creative possibilities are enhanced. The large capacity recordability and random access make it a nearly ideal storage and production tool, albeit at a substantially higher cost than traditional cut and splice methods.

Workstation Features

A digital audio workstation must provide random access, multitrack recording and playback; nondestructive editing; digital signal processing for mixing, equalization, compression and reverberation; subframe synchronization to timecode and other time-base references; data back-up; networking; media removability; external machine control; sound-cue assembly; edit decision list I/O; analog and digital data I/O; and a dedicated work surface. To provide this integration of functions with necessary routing, a specialized, hybrid architecture is required. In most cases, this is accomplished with a personal computer, and dedicated audio processing electronics that are plugged into the personal computer's bus, or interfaced to it. In addition, a workstation must provide internal storage, and external I/O of analog and digital signals. In some cases, audio data can be loaded and unloaded from hard disk as a background operation.

Workstations can provide multitrack operation, using hard disk storage. A time-division multiplex bus is used to overcome limitations of a hard-wired bus structure. In this way, the number of tracks does not equal the number of audio outputs; a software system is thus much more flexible than a hard-wired system. In theory, a system could have any number of virtual tracks, flexibly directed to inputs and outputs. In practice, as data is distributed over a disk surface, access time limits the number of channels that can be output from a drive. Additional disk drives can increase the number of virtual tracks available; however, physical input/output connections ultimately impose a constraint. For example, a system might feature 256 virtual tracks (automated, for digital mixing) with 24 I/O channels (real tracks).

Workstations use a graphical interface, with most human action taking place with a mouse and keyboard; some systems provide a dedicated hardware controller that can remotely control the system. Although software packages differ, most systems provide standard "tape recorder" transport controls along with means to name autolocation points, and punch-in and punch-out indicators. Time scale indicators permit material to be measured in minutes, seconds, bars and beats, SMPTE timecode, or feet and frames. Grabber tools allow regions and tracks to be moved; moves can be precisely aligned and synchronized to events. Zoomer tools allow audio waveforms to be viewed at any resolution, down to the individual sample, for exact editing. Other features include fading, crossfading, gain change, normalization, tempo change, pitch change, time stretch and shrink, and morphing.

Workstations provide virtual mixing capabilities. A mixing console appears on the display, with both audio and MIDI tracks. Audio tracks can be manipulated with faders, pan pots, and equalization modules, and MIDI tracks addressed with volume and pan messages. Other console controls include mute, record, solo, output channel assignment, and automation; VU meters indicate signal present, level before clipping, and clipping status. Nondestructive bouncing allows tracks to be combined during production, prior to stereo mix-down.

In many cases, workstation functions are provided by plug-in cards that contain DSP chips to perform dedicated audio processing. In some cases, multimedia computers contain DSP chips on their mother boards; they can record and play 16-bit stereo audio directly. DSP chips are essential to workstation operation. This high-speed programmable device performs editing, mixing, filtering, reverberation, and other functions depending on the programs loaded into its memories. The system stores many such subroutines, providing many operations performed in an audio studio. Digital filters provide a number of filter types, using filter coefficients and audio data from the digital audio bus. The filter can provide its own smoothing function between previous and current filter settings. Some computers provide asynchronous disk I/O, which allows cooperative multitasking; audio throughput processing does not affect screen re-draws and other tasks. Multimedia computers such as these let users run Sound Manager and QuickTime software to create video programs with CD-quality audio without additional hardware. However, more sophisticated editing and processing does require additional hardware and software.

Although the majority of hard disk workstations use off-the-shelf Macintosh or IBM computers and provide recording, processing, and editing capabilities, some hard disk recorders are stand-alone products designed with a user interface that emulates traditional multitrack tape recorders. For example, a rack-mount recorder unit can contain multiple hard-disk drives, providing a half-hour of recording capability for each of 48 channels. A remote-control unit provides keyboard, track ball, and other controllers. SCSI interfaces can be used for additional disk drives. The hard-disk system provides random access, audio scratchpad, editing, punch-in, crossfading, and ability to set cue points and automatically play loops; however, as with any hard-disk system, finished material must be off-loaded to tape or other media. In many cases, 8-mm Exabyte tape is used to back-up data; these drives can run faster than real time to store and retrieve sound and other data files from a hard disk. Alternatively, DDS-DAT drives can be used. In some cases, the off-line storage operates in the background, continuously monitoring and archiving updates. With erasable optical drives, entire projects can be moved on and off the workstation by simply switching disks.

Most workstation computers use SCSI (Small Computer System Interface) connections. SCSI (pronounced "scuzzy") is a high-speed data transfer protocol that allows multiple devices to access information over a common 8-bit parallel bus. Transmitting (smart) devices initiate SCSI commands; for example, to send or request information from a remote device. Likewise, receiving (dumb) devices accept SCSI commands; for example, a hard disk can only receive commands. Some devices (sometimes called logical devices) are classified as transmitter/receivers; computers are grouped in this category.

The SCSI protocol allows up to eight devices to be daisy-chained together; each device is given a unique identification number (from 0 to 7); numbers can follow any order in the chain. A SCSI cable can extend to 6 meters. A device must have two SCSI ports to allow chaining, otherwise the device must fall at the end of the chain. Generally, the first and last physical devices (determined physically, not by identification number) in a chain must be terminated; intermediate devices should not be terminated. Termination can be internal or external; devices that are externally terminated allow greater liberty of placement in the chain. The basic SCSI data transmission rate is 12.8 Mbps, that is, 1.6 Mbyte/second; all data transfer is asynchronous. SCSI-2 and -3 permit higher data rates, with versions providing up to 80 Mbyte/second. Alternatively, the Enhanced-IDE/ATAPI interface can be used to connect computers and peripherals at speeds of 13.3 Mbyte/second over short (18 inch) cables. Fast ADA-2 hard-drive interfaces can operate at 16.6 Mbyte/second. However, unlike SCSI, these are simple interfaces that do not support intelligent multitasking. In many cases, transfer speed is limited by the computer bus itself; for example, an ISA bus is capable of only 3 Mbyte/second. To overcome many interconnection installation problems, the Plug and Play standard was devised; the operating system and system BIOS automatically configures jumper, IRQ, DMA address, SCSI IDs and other parameters for the plug-in device.

In any workstation, RAM provides working memory, but primary audio storage is handled remotely with hard disks and optical disks. The drives can be interfaced to the workstation via a SCSI port. Multiple SCSI controllers could be used to connect an entire bank of drives. An 800-Mbyte hard-disk drive holds about 139 minutes of audio data sampled at 48 kHz. An optical disk drive can provide 2 Gbytes or more of storage. Storage times are extended by about 9% when sampling at 44.1 kHz. Preferably, system software, edit processing data, stored crossfades, and other overhead data are stored on tracks in a separate disk drive. Operating parameters can be stored on a floppy disk. Backup for audio data can be provided with removable streaming tape cartridges, or optical disk formats. In addition, it is often useful to interconnect workstations with a local network, as described in chapter 10. An example of workstation subsystems is shown in Fig. 14-4.

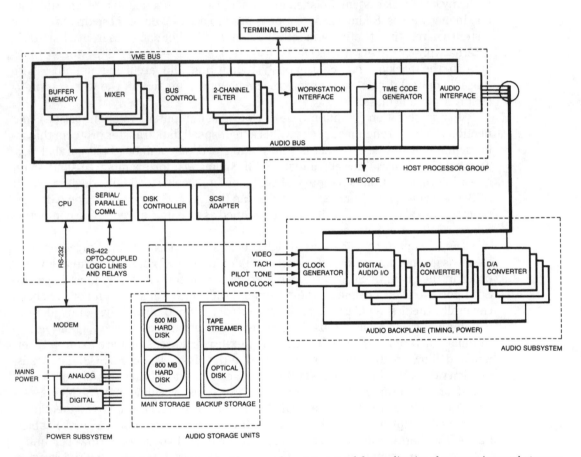

14-4 Architecture of the four primary hardware subsystems used for audio signal processing and storage in a workstation. Lexicon

Some workstations use a time-division multiplexing (TDM) digital audio bus to connect and provide routing between devices. It provides a software-controlled routing matrix with many sources and destinations including software modules and analog and digital external devices. The bus allows routing of 256 channels of 24-bit data at variable sample rates. Following initial installation and connection of devices, the TDM bus operates transparently to the user. In a workstation with plug-in cards, the bus is implemented with a piggyback bus card on each plug-in card, and the bus cards are connected via a ribbon cable. Within the bus itself, data words (up to 24 bits) are passed in parallel along the ribbon, and samples are conveyed at speeds to accommodate 256 channels within each sampling period. A receiver can extract samples from a specific channel slot, ignoring the remaining data stream.

Of course, even the most complete workstation still lacks total facility. There is always need to interface the workstation to peripheral gear, other workstations, and to the output storage medium. A high-quality I/O method is therefore critical to the workstation's overall performance. AES3, S/PDIF and other transmission protocols can link the elements in an all-digital studio. This directly benefits the workstation concept, as the nucleus of the all-digital studio.

Hard-Disk Storage

A length of tape provides a good medium to store data, particularly if the data occurs as a linear sequence, and will be retrieved in a linear sequence. On the other hand, if one wishes to manipulate the sequence of the recording, tape is far from ideal. The limitations of tape storage have been addressed by the development of magnetic hard-disk storage systems. Hard disks offer both efficient storage in themselves, as well as the important feature of random access. Using a large buffer memory, data can be located in any number of hard disks and assembled into final form. The success of the technique has encouraged a major move toward hard disk-based recorders.

Magnetic hard-disk drives using longitudinal recording are a staple of the computer industry and increasingly ubiquitous in the audio industry. Without the computer industry, a technology as sophisticated as the hard disk might never have been developed for the relatively thinly financed audio industry. However, given the availability and low cost of these drives, audio companies have not hesitated to take advantage of them. These drives (sometimes generically referred to as Winchester drives) store 40 Mbytes to 10 Gbytes (and more) of data in a sealed, nonremovable environment, at extremely low cost. Hard disks offer relatively fast access times and random access, the paramount requirements for audio editing.

A bit of hard disk mathematics: One kilobyte equals 1024 bytes. One megabyte equals 1024K. One 16-bit audio sample equals 2 bytes. Given 16-bit samples at a sampling frequency of 44.1 kHz, 5.1 Mbytes of memory will store 1 minute of audio. (Mbyte = sampling frequency × bits/sample × time × 60/1024/1024 thus 44100 × 16 × 60/8/1024/1024 = 5.1 Mbytes.) Similarly, it takes about 10 Mbyte to store 1 minute of stereo audio. For the record, a 1-hour, 24-track recording occupies over 7 Gbytes. In practice, a drive should have at least twice the capacity of the program itself; in this way data can be processed and copied without affecting the original recording. A 15-minute full motion, quarter screen video using data reduction, and accompanying audio tracks, might require a work space of 1 Gbyte. Clearly, unlike multitrack tape in which capacity is wasted on silences between musical parts, a hard disk only records the parts themselves, effectively increasing capacity.

In most systems, the hard disk medium is nonremovable; this greatly lowers manufacturing costs, simplifies the medium's design, and allows increased capacity. The storage disk is actually a series of disks, usually made of rigid aluminum alloy, stacked on a common spindle, as shown in Fig. 14-5. The disks are coated, top and bottom, with a magnetic material such as ferric oxide, with an aluminum oxide undercoat. Alternatively, metallic disks can be electroplated with a magnetic recording layer. These magnetic thin-film disks allow closer spacing of data tracks, providing greater data density and faster track access. Thin-film disks are more durable than conventional oxide disks because the data surface is harder; this helps them to resist head crashes.

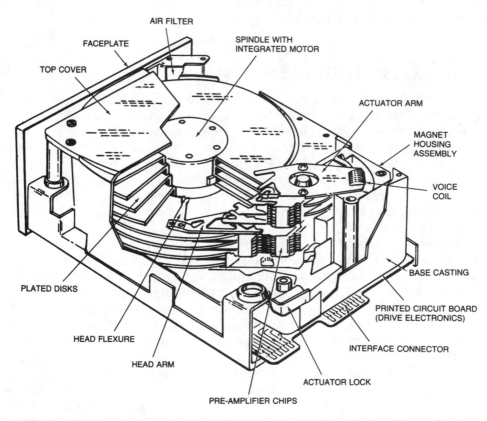

14-5 Construction of a computer hard disk drive showing disk cylinder, disks, and actuator arm.

Hard disks rotate whenever the unit is powered. This is because the mass of the system might require 10 to 30 seconds to reach proper rotational speed of 3600 to 7200 rpm. A series of read/write heads, one for each magnetic surface, are mounted on an arm called a head actuator. The actuator moves the heads across the disk surfaces in unison to seek data. In most designs only one head is used at a time (some drives used for digital video are an exception) thus read/write circuitry can be shared among all the heads. Unlike floppy disk drives, in which the head contacts the medium, hard disk heads float over the magnetic surfaces on a thin cushion of air, typically 20 μm or less. The head must be aerodynamically designed to provide proper flying height yet negotiate disk surface warping that could cause azimuth errors, and fly above disk contaminants. However, the flying height limits data density due to spacing loss. In the event of a head crash, the head touches the surface, causing it to burn (literally, crash and burn). This usually catastrophically damages both head and disks, necessitating, at best, a data-recovery procedure and repair at a service center.

To maintain correct head tolerances, drives must calibrate their mechanical systems according to changes in temperature. With automatic thermal recalibration, the drive simply interrupts data flow to perform this function; this is not a hardship with most data applications, but can cause an interruption in an audio or video signal. Newer drives use smart controllers that do not permit thermal recalibration when in use; these drives (sometimes called AV drives) are recommended for audio and video applications.

One disk surface in the pack acts as a servo surface, dedicated to nonuser data. It is read by the head actuator to identify the assembly's location relative to the radial disk surface. The use of a servo surface maintains accurate tracking despite thermal expansion and contraction of platters, a deviation on the order of the track pitch itself for temperature extremes. In some cases, a servo system counts embedded codes and generates a location signal, and outputs an error signal as well, to center the head on the desired track. Optical, variable reluctance, or eddy-current sensors can be used for track sensing.

All disk drives originally used heads with a wire-wrapped ferrite core; newer ferrite heads use metal-in-gap and double metal-in-gap technology. The former uses metal sputtered in the trailing edge of the recording gap to provide a well-defined record pulse and higher density; the latter adds additional magnetic material to further improve head response. Newer heads use thin-film technology to achieve very small gap areas, which allows track density of 2500 tracks/inch or more, as well as higher write frequencies. Thin-film heads can yield 500 Mbytes over two 3.5-inch platters. Some drives use magneto-resistive (MR) heads that use a nano-sized magnetic material in the read gap with a resistance that varies with magnetic flux. Typically, the same head is used for both reading and writing; precompensation equalization is used during writing. Erasing is performed by overwriting. Several types of head actuator designs are used; for example, a moving coil assembly can be used. The moving coil acts against a spring to position the head actuator on the disk surface. Alternatively, an electric motor and carriage arrangement, or mechanical lead screw could be used in the actuator.

Data on the disk surface is configured in concentric data tracks. Each track comprises one disk circumference for a given head position. The total tracks provided by all the heads at a given position is known as a cylinder—a strictly imaginary construction. Most drives segment data tracks into arcs known as sectors, with perhaps 17 sectors per track. A particular physical address within a sector, known as a block, storing perhaps 512 bytes, is identified by a cylinder (positioner address), head (surface address), and sector (rotational angle address). Although early hard disks used FM coding, this was wholly replaced by MFM coding, as well as other forms of coding such as 2/3 and 2/7 run length limited codes, for greater storage density.

Some drives are equipped with a park and lock feature to protect disks and their data from mechanical shock. This withdraws the head actuator from the disk data area when the unit is not powered. In some cases, a special part of the disk is specially designed to serve as a retraction area where the heads can land safely. Many hard-disk drives use heatsinks to dissipate heat and prevent heat build-up from the internal motors. In some cases, the enclosure is charged with helium to facilitate heat dissipation, and reduce disk drag.

Hard-disk drives were developed for computer applications where any error is considered fatal. Drives are assembled in a clean room. The atmosphere inside the drive housing is evacuated, and the unit hermetically sealed (with a filtered vent to equalize pressure). This protects the media from contamination. Media errors are greatly reduced by the sealed disk environment; however, an error correction encoding scheme is still needed in most applications. Manufactured disk defects, called bad blocks, are logged at the factory, and their locations are mapped in firmware so the drive controller will never write data to those defective addresses. Obviously, error-concealment techniques cannot be used.

Hard-disk diameters of 3½, and 5¼ inches are commonly used. Data can be output either in serial or parallel; the latter provides faster data transfer rates. For faster access times, disk-based systems can be designed to write data in a logically organized fashion. A method known as spiraling can be used to minimize interruptions in data transfer by reducing sector seek times at a track boundary. Overall, hard disks should provide a transfer rate of 1 to 4 Mbyte/second (1 Mbyte/second is necessary to write an ISO 9660 CD-ROM disc) and access time of 20 ms or less. For video data at 30 fps, depending on data reduction used, and screen size, an access time of 10 ms or less, and data transfer rate of 3.5 Mbyte/second is recommended.

Although removable hard disk systems are widely used, their capacity usually ranges from 40 to 270 Mbytes, insufficient recording capacity for most recording projects. One popular format holds 44 Mbytes with backward compatible 88-Mbyte disks. Removable disks holding 270 Mbytes are also available. When removability is required, optical disk storage is usually preferred. New hard-disk drive technologies permit ultrasmall PCMCIA drives; they use a head-to-media contact recording architecture, thin-film heads, and vertical recording for high data density. Average seek time is 3 ms.

In practice, the transfer rate of a hard disk is faster than that required for a digital audio channel. During playback the drive delivers bursts of data to the output buffer that in turn steadily delivers output data. The drive is free to access data randomly distributed on different platters. Similarly, given sufficient drive transfer rate, it is possible to record and play back multiple channels of audio. Most disk editing is done through an edit decision list in which in/out and other edit points are saved as data addresses; music plays from one address and as the edit point approaches, the system accesses the next music address from another disk location, joining them in real time through a crossfade. This allows nondestructive editing; the original data files are not altered. Original data can be backed up to another medium, or a finished recording can be output using the edit list.

Hard disks offer reliable storage of digital audio data, and the opportunity for comprehensive editing of the data. But most hard disks suffer from nonremovability, a serious drawback for many audio applications. This obstacle can be overcome by a variety of recordable optical disk technologies.

Multimedia

Formerly, the only sounds from a computer were the click of keys, and an occasional beep. That has changed, in large measure because of the introduction in 1987 of Apple's HyperCard, a tool for authoring interactive presentations. Today, many personal computers are equipped with soundcards and CD-ROM drives for entertainment, business communication, and education. A personal computer can be used to integrate audio, video, animation, and graphics and author sophisticated multimedia presentations. To permit use of such authoring and presentation software tools, computer hardware processing and storage capabilities have been improved, as have computer operating systems. For example, the MPC (Multimedia Personal Computer) platform specification was introduced by Microsoft Corporation, as part of Multimedia Extensions, included in Windows. The MPC standard calls for soundcards that can record and play 8- to 16-bit linear audio, as well as a software-controlled mixer to combine diverse sound sources and channels. In many cases, these cards include digital signal processing, polyphonic FM synthesis, speech synthesizer, RAM buffers, and I/O. In many cases, multiple levels of audio quality are available. Most multimedia software is produced for Macintosh or DOS/Windows computers; in some cases, titles can be presented on either platform.

There are a wide variety of soundcards available for plug-in to computer buses. With appropriate software, these cards often contain A/D and D/A converters to permit recording and playback of stereo 8- or 16-bit audio at sampling rates up to 44.1 kHz, as well as playback via wavetable synthesis, sampled sound, or FM synthesis; digital I/O, MIDI and CD-ROM interfaces; and software-controlled audio mixer, onboard amplifiers, and other features. Increasingly, computers contain many of these functions as built-in features. With wavetable synthesis, a particular waveform is stored in ROM, and looped through to create a continuous sound. Wavetable synthesizers can provide 32 voices of playback. A sampled sound synthesizer plays stored sound files—for example, .snd or AIFF. An FM synthesis chip can provide 20 instrument voices based on two operators, or 11 voices based on four operators. Some cards contain a DSP chip that allows hardware data reduction during recording and playback, and others provide resident nonreal-time software data reduction algorithms. In addition, some cards provide voice recognition capability. With a Windows operating system, for example, a card could be used to create, edit and play back .WAV files, and play back CD audio; MIDI files could be played using the FM or wavetable synthesizers.

Many users are anxious to add sound capabilities to their computers; however, proper software drivers must be selected or installed for proper operation. In some cases, soundcards suffer compatibility problems; parameters such as card I/O address, IRQ line, and DMA channel must be examined. Generally, after the card is installed, a diagnosis program sets nonconflicting system parameters; the card is then installed for the host operating system.

File Interchange Formats

In some applications, audio data is most easily exchanged by swapping physical formats. However, in some cases it is more efficient to transfer data directly between systems, particularly if the hardware formats are incompatible. File formats are used to provide compatibility between platforms so that digital audio data can be packaged, moved to other systems, and be compatibly processed or replayed. Some file formats also contain control data; for example, a file can contain an edit decision list with timecode and crossfade information, as well as equalization control.

Digital audio file formats allow sound files to be stored and transmitted; some popular formats include AIFF, SDII, QuickTime, WAVE, JPEG, MPEG, and OMF. The AIFF (Audio Interchange File Format) is native to platforms using Motorola processors, that is, Macintosh computers. AIFF is based on the EA IFF 85 standard. AIFF includes the AIFC format and is used for both compressed and uncompressed data. The format contains information on the number of interleaved channels, sample size, and sample rate, as well as the raw audio data. The AIFF format is used to exchange Macintosh sound files and is recognized by numerous software editing systems. Because sound files are stored together with other parameters, it is difficult to add data, for example, as in a multitrack overdub, without writing a new file. The SDII (Sound Designer II) format is also a Macintosh format; it stores audio data separately from file parameters. Both AIFF and SDII are limited to sound files; because they do not contain editing information, they are generally not used as multimedia file formats.

QuickTime is an extension to the Macintosh operating system; it is a file format with compression algorithms for processing multimedia files. It can be used to play videos on Macintosh and Windows computers. More generally, time-based files, including audio, animation and MIDI can be stored in documents similarly to text and graphics, synchronized and controlled, and replayed. Because of the time-base inherent in a video program, the video itself can be used to control preset actions. QuickTime movies can have multiple audio tracks; for example, different language soundtracks can accompany a video. Videos can be played on a Macintosh (without additional hardware) at 15 or 30 fps. However, frame rate, along with picture size and resolution, is often limited by hard disk data transfer rates. Sound is played back continuously; however, slower processors drop video frames to maintain audio synchronization. Hardware and software tools allow the user to record video clips to hard disk in real time, trim extraneous material, compress video, edit video, add audio tracks, then play the result as a QuickTime movie. In some cases, the system can be used as an off-line video editor, and used to create an edit decision list with timecode, or the finished product can be output directly to disk or videotape. Audio files with 16-bit, 44.1-kHz quality can be inserted in QuickTime movies; QuickTime also accepts MIDI data for playback. As noted, QuickTime is also available for Windows so that presentations developed on the Macintosh can be played on a PC.

HyperCard is an Apple software program that provides fundamental multimedia authoring capabilities. More specifically, it is a software tool used to create virtual stacks of cards linking the user to an interactive database. The top card in the stack is displayed on the screen; cards contain objects such as buttons, text and illustrations; the objects represent a series of instructions that describe an event; event scripts are written in HyperTalk, an English-like computer language. For example, to play a series of notes from one of four sound generators, we could use the Play command:

```
on mouseUp
play "harpsichord" d e f g a
end mouseUp
```

HyperTalk can be used to control audio events; three of the audio formats available in HyperCard are: .snd resources, QuickTime movies, and CD-Audio and CD-ROM. The .snd format is included in all HyperCard programs; audio material is loaded into the computer, and the Macintosh's sound control panel is used to copy, cut and paste, and name and save sound files as part of a stack. The HyperTalk "play/play stop" commands can be used to play the file from any script. A variety of X-Commands (XCMDs) have been devised to expand the capabilities of HyperCard; these code modules can be added as resources to a stack. For example, using XCMDs, external sound files (other than .snd) such as AIFF can be played; in addition, QuickTime movies can be played in HyperCard, using a call from a script. XCMDs can also be used to create scripts and stacks that control music CDs, as well as mixed-mode CDs incorporating both ROM and music tracks. Without question, HyperCard, and QuickTime, were pioneering tools that helped show the way to today's multimedia technology.

The RIFF WAVE (Resource Interchange File Format Waveform) audio file format is used on platforms with Intel processors, that is, IBM-PCs. The WAVE file interchange format is described in the Microsoft/IBM Multimedia Programming Interface and Data Specifications document. WAVE is used for uncompressed 8-, 12-, and 16-bit audio files. RIFF files organize blocks of data into sections called chunks; many audio formats can be stored in the file. For example, a format specific field can hold parameters used to specify a data-compressed file. RIFF data types are supported by Windows software. The VOC file format is used with Soundblaster cards on DOS computers; VOC defines eight block types that can vary in length; sampling frequency and word length are specified. The MFX data-exchange language converts one proprietary data format to another; information such as fader-level changes, channel groups, and mutes can be exchanged.

JPEG (Joint Photographic Experts Group) lossy video compression format is used primarily to reduce the size of still image files. Compression ratios of 20:1 to 30:1 can be achieved with little loss of quality, and much higher ratios are possible. Motion JPEG (MJPEG) can be used to store a series of data-reduced frames comprising a motion video; this is often used in video editors where individual frame quality is needed. Many proprietary JPEG formats are in use. The MPEG (Motion Picture Experts Group) lossy video compression methods are used primarily for motion video often with accompanying audio. Some frames are stored with great resolution, then intervening frames are stored as differences between frames; video compression ratios of 200:1 are possible. MPEG is discussed in more detail in chapter 11.

The OMF (Open Media Framework) interchange format allows exchange of content and description data. It encompasses audio, animation, graphics, text, video, as well as edit decision lists, crossfade profiles, and DSP data. APIs (application programming interfaces) translate file structures from proprietary formats to an OMF-compatible format. The audio specification supports AIFC and WAVE data. In some cases, bridges exist between formats. For example, given proper software, OMF video files can be played on a QuickTime system. OMF is described in more detail in chapter 10.

Most audio workstations are based on the Apple Macintosh or IBM-PC platforms. Very generally, the former are preferred for professional authoring, but the latter hold a wide margin in consumer preference thus are used for most presentations. The IBM-PC computer uses Intel processors; the Pentium replaced the 486 processor and offers faster processing time. The PowerPC processor, developed by Motorola, has the ability to run either Apple or IBM software applications, and is a high-performance RISC processor in its own right. When buying a computer, it is important to know what local buses it offers, so that peripheral cards can be plugged into the computer. Most IBM-PC computers contain the ISA (Industry Standard Architecture) local bus; it is the most widely used bus but its 11-Mbyte/second transfer rate is limiting. The ESIA (Extended ISA) local bus offers a 32-Mbyte/second rate and other improvements. The PCI (Peripherals Component Interconnect) local bus provides a maximum 132-Mbyte/second transfer rate, 32-bit pathways, good noise immunity, and efficiently integrates the computer's processor and memory with peripherals. The VESA (Video Electronics Standards Association) local bus is available on some computers, but has compatibility drawbacks. The PS/2 bus has not won widespread acceptance.

Workstation Applications

A workstation should be a multifunction device, limited by its hardware and software implementation, yet upgradable via modular expansion to perform other tasks. Ideally, all of these functions should fall under its command: signal processing, synthesis, editing, mixing and mastering, and storage. More specifically, a diverse range of production and post-production applications are addressed: music scoring, recording, video sweetening, sound design, effects edit-to-picture, Foley, ADR (automatic dialogue replacement) and mixing. To achieve this, a workstation can combine elements of a multitrack recorder, sequencer, drum machine, synthesizer, sampler, digital effects processor, and mixing board, with MIDI, SMPTE, and clock interfaces to audio and video equipment. In practice, most digital audio workstations specialize in more specific areas of application.

Soundtrack production for film and video benefits from the inherent nature of synchronization and random access in a workstation. Instantaneous lock-up and ability to lock to vari-speed timecode facilitates production, as does ability to slide individual tracks or cues back and forth, and ability to insert or delete musical passages while maintaining lock. Similarly, a workstation can fit sound effects to picture in slow motion while preserving synchronization.

In general, to achieve proper artistic balance, audio post-production work is divided into dialogue editing, music, effects, Foley, atmosphere, and mixing. In many cases, the audio elements for a feature film are largely re-created. A workstation's ability to deal with disparate elements independently, locate, overlay, and manipulate sound quickly, synthesize and process sound, adjust timing and duration of sounds, and nondestructively audition and edit sound make it ideal for this kind of application. In addition, there is no loss of audio quality in transferring from one digital medium to another.

In Foley, footsteps and other natural sound effects are created to fit a picture's requirements. For example, a stage with sand, gravel, and concrete, and water can be used to record footstep sounds in synchronization with the picture. With a workstation, the sounds can be recorded to disk or memory, where they can be easily edited and fitted. Alternatively, a library of sounds can be accessed in real time to fit the picture, thus eliminating the need for a Foley stage entirely. Hundreds of footsteps or other sounds can be sequenced, providing a wide variety of effects. Similarly, film and video requires ambient sound, or atmosphere, such as traffic sounds or cocktail party chatter. With a workstation, library sounds can be sequenced, then overlaid with other sounds and looped, to create a complex atmosphere, to be triggered by an edit list, or crossfaded with other atmospheres.

Hard and optical disk recording capabilities allow the workstation to act as a multitrack recorder. The benefits of random access are obvious; instantaneous fast forward, rewind, locate, and punch-in and -out expedite session work. Talent can no longer rest while the engineer rewinds tape; a session can move from one take to the next as fast as the engineer can hit the button. Likewise, software editing allows the user to jump from one cue to the next for fast, nondestructive edits.

Optical disk sound effects libraries provide on-line storage of indexed and cross-referenced sounds. Users can assemble a timecode hit list, then audition sounds and effects while locked to picture. Disk recording expedites dialogue replacement. Master takes can be assembled from multiple passes by setting cue points, then fitted back to picture at locations logged from the original synchronization master. Room ambience can be taken from location tapes, then looped and overlaid on re-recorded dialogue. Track space is automatically allocated by the system.

Composers and arrangers are attracted to workstations for writing and pre-production; sampled sounds can be mixed and enhanced to suit even the most complex orchestration. Notation, step editing, cut-and-paste, splice, bounce, slide, loop, copy, panning, chorus, tempo and key change, fade-ins and -outs all provide flexibility for different arrangements and production ideas.

A workstation can be used as a master MIDI controller and sequencer. The user can remap MIDI outputs, modify or remove messages such as aftertouch, transmit patch changes and volume commands as well as song position pointers. It can be advantageous to transfer MIDI sequences to the workstation because of its superior timing resolution. For example, a delay problem could be solved by sliding tracks in fractions of milliseconds. Inadequate acoustical sounds can be replaced with custom samples.

Workstations are designed to integrate with an SMPTE timecode system. SMPTE in- and out-points can be placed in a sequence to create a hit list. Offset information can be assigned flexibly for one or many events. Blank frame spaces can be inserted or deleted to shift events. Track times can be slid independently from times of other tracks, and sounds can be interchanged without altering the hit list in any other way.

Commercial production can be made more efficient. For example, an announcer can be recorded to memory, assigning each line to its own track. In this way, tags and inserts can be accommodated by shifting individual lines backward or forward; transfers and back-timing are eliminated. Likewise "doughnuts" can be produced by switching sounds, muting and soloing tracks, changing keys without changing tempos, cutting and pasting, and manipulating tracks with fade-ins and -outs. For broadcast, segments can be assigned to different tracks and triggered via timecode from the computer. In music production, for example, a vocal fix is easily accomplished by sampling the vocal to memory, bending the pitch, then flying it back to the master—an easy job when the workstation records timecode while sampling.

A catalog of workstation production examples would be extensive, but the nature of the workstation is evident. A workstation is, in essence, a memory recorder. It records not only sounds, but performance parameters as well. In this way, the system can manipulate the data in ways not available in traditional tape technology. Although a tape recorder can be considered as a one-dimensional device, a workstation is a three-dimensional one. Recorded audio information becomes a cue, an organized playback creates an event, and a timetable that schedules playback of cues is an event list. Thus, when recording, random access and editing (as well as synthesis) are combined under a unified controller; the benefit is more than tripled.

Hard-Disk Editing

One of the most basic and important functions of a workstation is its use as an audio editor. With random access storage, instantaneous auditioning, level adjustment, marking, and crossfading, nondestructive edit operations are efficiently performed. Many editing errors can be corrected with an undo command.

Using an edit cursor, clipboard, cut and paste and other tools, sample-accurate cutting, copying, pasting and splicing is easily accomplished. Edit points are located in ways analogous to analog tape recorders; sound is "scrubbed" back and forth until the edit point is found. In analog tape systems, tape must be physically moved back and forth across the heads, but in memory systems data is simply read from memory forward and back. In some cases, an edit point is assigned by entering a timecode number. Crossfade times can be automatically or manually selected.

Edit splices often contain four parameters: duration, mark point, crossfade contour, and level. Duration sets the time of the fade; it corresponds to the angle of an analog tape cut. The mark point identifies the edit position, and can be set to various points within the fade. Crossfade contour sets the gain-versus-time relationship across the edit. Although a linear contour sets the midpoint gain of each segment at –6 dB, other midpoint gains might be more suitable. Level sets the gain of any segments edited together to help match them. In most systems, these and other parameters can use default settings.

Most editing tasks can be broken down into cut, copy, replace, align, and loop operations. Cut and copy functions are used for most editing tasks. A cut edit moves marked audio to a selected location, and removes it from the previous location. However, cut edits can be broken down into four types. A basic cut combines two different segments. Two editing points are identified, and the segments joined. A cut/insert operation moves a marked segment to a marked destination point. Three edit points are thus required. A delete cut edit removes a segment marked by two edit points, shortening overall duration. A fourth cut operation, a wipe, is used to edit silence before or after a segment.

A copy edit places an identical duplicate of a marked audio section in another section. It thus leaves the original segment unchanged; the duration of the destination is changed, but not that of the source. A basic copy combines two segments. A copy/insert operation copies a marked segment to a destination marked in another segment. Three edit points are required.

A replace command exchanges a marked source section with a marked destination section, using four edit points. Three types of replace operations are performed. An exact replace copies the source segment and inserts it in place of the marked destination segment. Both segment durations remain the same. Because the duration of the destination segment is not changed, any three of the four edit points defines the operation. The fourth point could be automatically calculated. A relative replace edit operation permits the destination segment to be replaced with a source segment of a different duration; the location of one edit point is simply altered. A replace with silence operation writes silence over a segment. Both duration and timecode alignment are unchanged.

An align edit command slips sections relative to timecode, slaving them to a reference, or specifying an offset. Several types of align edits are used. A synchronization align edit is used to slave a segment to a reference timecode address. One edit point defines the synchronization reference alignment point in the timecode, and the other marks the segment timecode address to be aligned. A trim alignment is used to slip a segment relative to timecode; care must be taken not to overlap consecutive segments. An offset alignment changes the alignment between an external timecode and an internal timecode when slaving the workstation.

A loop command creates the equivalent of a tape loop in which a segment is seamlessly repeated. In effect, the segment is sequentially copied. The loop section is marked with duration and destination; the destination can be an unused track, or an existing segment.

When any edit is executed, the relevant parameters are stored in an edit list and recalled whenever that edit is performed. The audio source material is never altered. Edits can be easily revised; moreover, memory is conserved. For example, when a sound is copied, there is no need to rewrite the data. An extensive editing session would result in a short database of edit decisions and their parameters, as well as system configuration, assembled into an edit list. Note that in the above descriptions of editing operations, the various moves and copies are virtual, not physical.

In some cases, data-reduced files (such as MPEG-1 Layer I or II) can be editing directly without conversion to PCM; gain changes and crossfades are performed by individually changing the scale factor for each subband.

Audio for Video Workstations

In some implementations, digital audio workstations display digitized video "movies" for video editing, and synchronizing audio to picture. Using video capture tools, the movie can be displayed in a small insert window on the same screen as the audio tools; however, a full screen display on a second monitor (with dedicated video display card) is preferable. Users can prepare audio tracks for QuickTime moves, with random access to both audio and digital audio. Using authoring tools, audio and video materials can be combined into a final presentation, for example, on CD-ROM. Although the definitions have blurred, it is correct to classify video edit systems as linear, nonlinear, off-line, and on-line. Nonlinear systems are disk-based, and linear systems are videotape-based. Off-line systems are used to edit audio and video programs, then the generated edit decision list (EDL) can be transferred to a higher quality on-line video system for final assembly. In many cases, a cheaper off-line system is used for editing, and its EDL its transferred to a more sophisticated on-line system for creation of final materials. In other cases, and increasingly, on-line, nonlinear workstations provide all the tools, and production quality, for complete editing and post production.

Audio for video workstations offers a selection of frame rates and sampling frequencies, as well as pre-roll, post-roll and other video prerequisites. Some workstations also provide direct control over external videotape recorders. Video signals are recorded using data reduction algorithms to reduce throughput and storage demands; depending on the compression ratio, requirements can vary from 8 Mbytes/minute to over 50 Mbytes/minute. In many cases, video data on a hard disk should be defragmented (using an appropriate software utility) for more optimal reading and writing.

Depending on the application, either audio or video can be designated as the master. When picture is slaved to audio, for example, the movie will respond to audio transport commands such as play, rewind and fast forward. A picture can be scrubbed with frame accuracy, and audio dropped into place. Alternatively a user can park the movie at one location while listening to audio at another location. In any case, there is no waiting while audio or videotapes shuttle while assembling the program. Using machine control, the user can audition the audio program while watching the master videotape, then lay back the final synchronized audio program to a digital audio or video recorder.

During a video session, the user can capture video clips from an outside analog source. Similarly, audio clips can be captured from analog sources. Depending on the on-board audio, or soundcard used, audio can be captured in mono or stereo, at a variety of sampling rates, and 8- or 16-bit resolution. Similarly, source elements that are already digitized can be imported directly into the application; for example, sound files in the AIFF or WAVE format can be imported, or tracks can be imported from CD-Audio or CD-ROM. In addition, most systems allow audio and video files to be compressed, saving storage space.

Once clips are placed in the project window, authoring software can be used to audition and edit clips, and combine them into a movie with linked tracks. For example, the waveforms comprising audio tracks can be displayed, and specific nuances or errors processed with software tools. Audio and video can be linked and edited together, or unlinked and edited separately. In- and out-points and markers can be set, identifying timed transition events such as a fade. Editing is nondestructive; the recorded file is not manipulated, only the directions for replaying it; edit points can be revised ad infinitum. Edited video and audio clips can be placed relative to other clips using software tools, and audio levels can be varied. The finished project can be compiled into a QuickTime movie, for example, or with appropriate hardware can be recorded to external videotape or CD recorder.

Disk-based workstations offer a highly efficient method to integrate and expedite audio and multimedia functions, and have quickly and radically changed the techniques of music and video production. Recording, processing, editing, mixing, and other tasks can be efficiently performed on both audio and video material in one working environment. The increase in productivity, as well as creative possibilities, are enormous. In the same way that a word processor obsoletes a typewriter, an audio workstation obsoletes a tape recorder and peripherals for many applications.

15
CHAPTER

Digital Signal Processing

In many ways, digital signal processing (DSP) returns us to the elemental beginning of the discussion of digital audio. Although conversion, storage and other concerns are critical to a digitization system, it is the software-driven signal processing of digital audio data that is germane to the venture. Without the ability to manipulate the numbers that comprise digital audio data, its digitization and storage would not be useful for many applications. Moreover, a discussion of digital signal processing returns us to the roots of digital audio in that the technology is based on the same elemental mathematics that first occupied us. On the other hand, digital signal processing is a science far removed from simple logic circuits, with special algorithms required to achieve its aim of efficient signal manipulation.

Fundamentals of Digital Signal Processing

Digital signal processing is a technology used to analyze, manipulate, or generate signals in the digital domain. It uses the same principles that make digital recording possible, sampling and quantization; however, instead of providing a storage medium, it is a processing method. DSP is very similar to the technology used in computers and microprocessor systems; however, whereas a regular computer processes data, a DSP system processes signals. In particular, a signal is a time-based sequence in which the ordering of values is critical. A digital audio signal only makes sense, and can be processed properly, if the sequence is properly preserved. DSP is thus a special application of general data processing. Simply stated, DSP is a mathematical formula or algorithm that generates, changes or analyzes a bit stream signal.

A signal can be any natural or artificial phenomenon that varies as a function of some independent variable. For example, when the variable is time, then changes in barometric pressure, temperature, oil pressure, current, or voltage are all signals that can be recorded, transmitted, or manipulated either directly or indirectly. Their representation can be either analog or digital in nature, and both offer advantages and disadvantages.

Digital processing of acquired waveforms offers several advantages over processing of continuous-time signals. Fundamentally, the use of unambiguous discrete samples promotes: use of components with lower tolerances; predetermined accuracy; identically reproducible circuits; a theoretically unlimited number of successive operations on a sample; and reduced sensitivity to external effects such as noise, temperature and aging. The programmable nature of discrete-time signals permits changes in function without changes in hardware. Digital integrated circuits are small, highly reliable, low in cost, and capable of complex processing. Some operations implemented with digital processing are difficult or impossible with analog means. Examples include filters with linear phase, long-term uncorrupted memory, adaptive systems, image processing, error correction, and signal transformations. The latter includes time domain to frequency domain transformation with the discrete Fourier transform (DFT) and special mathematical processing such as the fast Fourier transform (FFT).

On the other hand, DSP has disadvantages. For example, the technology always requires power; there is no passive form of DSP circuitry. DSP cannot presently be used for very high frequency signals. Digital signal representation of a signal requires a larger bandwidth than the corresponding analog signal. DSP technology is expensive to develop. Circuits capable of performing fast computation are required. Finally, when used for analog applications, A/D and D/A conversion are required. In addition, the processing of very weak signals such as antenna signals or very strong signals such as those driving a loudspeaker, presents difficulties; digital signal processing thus requires appropriate amplification treatment of the signal.

DSP Applications

In the 1960s, signal processing relied on analog methods; electronic and mechanical devices processed signals in the continuous-time domain. Digital computers generally lacked the computational capabilities needed for DSP. In 1965, the invention of the fast Fourier transform to implement the discrete Fourier transform, and the advent of more powerful computers, inspired the development of theoretical discrete-time mathematics, and modern DSP.

Some of the earliest uses of digital signal processing included soil analysis in oil and gas exploration, and radio and radar astronomy using mainframe computers. With the development of specialized hardware, extensive applications in telecommunications were implemented, including modems, data transfer between computers, and vocoders and transmultiplexers in telephony. Medical science has used digital signal processing in processing of X ray and NMR (nuclear magnetic resonance) images. Image processing also is used for photographs received from orbiting satellites and deep space vehicles. Television studios use digital techniques to manipulate picture signals. Analytical instruments use digital signal transforms such as FFT for spectral and other analysis. The chemical industry uses digital signal processing for industrial process control. Digital signal processing has revolutionized professional audio in effects processing, interfacing, user control, and computer control. The consumer sees digital signal processing in the guise of multimedia computers, compact disc players, digital television receivers, as well as digital radio receivers and telephones.

DSP presents rich possibilities for audio applications. Error correction, multiplexing, sample rate conversion, speech and music synthesis, data compression and reduction, volume/fader/balance, filtering, adaptive equalization, dynamic compression and expansion, reverberation, ambience processing, time alignment, acoustic noise cancellation, mixing and editing, and acoustic analysis can all be performed with digital signal processing.

Discrete Systems

Digital audio signal processing is concerned with the manipulation of audio samples. Because those samples are digitally represented as numbers, digital audio signal processing is thus a science of calculation. Hence, any fundamental understanding of audio DSP must begin with its mathematical essence.

When the independent variable, such as time, is continuously variable, the signal is defined at every real value of time (t); the signal is thus a continuous time signal. For example, consider temperature changes through a 24-hour day. When the signal is only defined at discrete values of time (nT), the signal is a discrete-time signal. As observed in chapter 2, using the sampling theorem, any bandlimited continuous time function can be represented without loss as a discrete time signal. Although general discrete time signals and digital signals both consist of samples, a general discrete time signal can take any real value but a digital signal can only take a finite number of values. In digital audio, this requires approximation, or quantization.

Linearity and Time-Invariance

A discrete system is any system that accepts one or more discrete input signals $x(n)$ and produces one or more discrete output signals $y(n)$, in accordance with a set of operating rules. The input and output discrete time signals are represented by a sequence of numbers. If an analog signal $x(t)$ is sampled every T seconds, the discrete time signal is $x(nT)$, where n is an integer. Time can be normalized so that the signal is written as $x(n)$.

Two important criteria for discrete systems are linearity, and time-invariance. A linear system exhibits the property of superposition; the response of a linear system to a sum of signals is the sum of the responses to each individual input. That is, the input $x_1(n) + x_2(n)$ yields the output $y_1(n) + y_2(n)$. A linear system exhibits the property of homogeneity; the amplitude of the output of a linear system is proportional to that of the input. That is, an input $ax(n)$ yields the output $ay(n)$. Combining these properties, a linear discrete system with the input signal $ax_1(n) + bx_2(n)$ produces an output signal $ay_1(n) + by_2(n)$ where a and b are constants. The input signals are treated independently, output amplitude is proportional to that of the input, and no new signal components are introduced. As described in the following paragraphs, all z- transforms and Fourier transforms are linear.

A discrete time system is time-invariant if the input signal $x(n - k)$ produces an output signal $y(n - k)$ where k is an integer. In other words, a linear time-invariant discrete (LTD) system behaves the same way at all times; for example, an input delayed by k samples generates an output delayed by k samples.

A discrete system is causal if at any instant the output signal corresponding to any input signal is independent of the values of the input signal after that instant. In other words, there are no output values before there has been an input signal. The output does not depend on future inputs. As some theorists put it, a causal system doesn't laugh until after it has been tickled.

Impulse Response and Convolution

The impulse response is an important concept in many areas, including digital signal processing. The impulse response $h(t)$ gives a full description of a linear time-invariant discrete system in the time domain. Figure 15-1A shows that an LTD system, like any discrete system, converts an input signal into an output signal. However, an LTD has a special property such that when an impulse (a delta function) is applied to an LTD system, the output is the system's impulse response, as shown in Fig. 15-1B. The impulse response describes the system in the time domain, and can be used to reveal the frequency response of the system in the frequency domain. Practically speaking, most digital filters are LTD systems, and yield this property. A system is stable if any input signal of finite amplitude produces an output signal of finite amplitude. In other words, the sum of the absolute value of every input and the impulse response must yield a finite number. Useful discrete systems are stable.

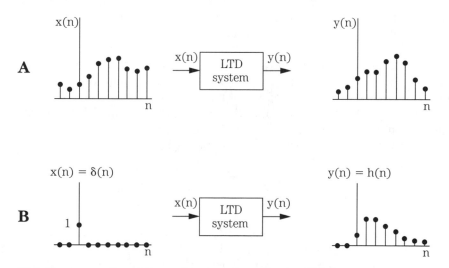

15-1 Two properties of linear time-invariant discrete (LTD) systems. A. LTD systems produce an output signal based on the input. B. An LTD system can be characterized by its impulse response, the output from a single pulse input. van den Enden and Verhoeckx

Furthermore, the impulse response can be sampled, and used to filter a signal. Audio samples themselves are impulses, represented as numbers. The signal could be filtered, for example, by using the samples as scaling values; all of the values of a filter's impulse response are multiplied by each signal value. This yields a series of filter impulse responses scaled to each signal sample. To obtain the result, each scaled filter impulse response is substituted for its multiplying signal sample. The filter response can extend over many samples; thus, several scaled values might overlap. When these are added together, the series of sums forms the new filtered signal values.

This is the process of convolution. The output of a linear system is the convolution of the input and the system's impulse response. Convolution is a time-domain process that is equivalent to the multiplication of the frequency responses of two networks. Convolution in one domain (such as the time domain) is equivalent to multiplication in the conjugate domain (such as frequency). Furthermore, the duality exists such that multiplication in the time domain is equivalent to convolution in the frequency domain.

Fundamentally, in convolution, samples (representing the signal at different sample times) are multiplied by weighting factors; these products are continually summed together to produce an output. An FIR oversampling filter (as described in chapter 4) provides a good example. A series of samples are multiplied by the coefficients that represent the impulse response of the filter, and these products are summed. The input time function has been convolved with the filter's impulse in the time domain. For example, the frequency response of an ideal lowpass filter can be achieved by using coefficients representing a time-domain $\sin(x)/x$ impulse response. The convolution of the input signal with coefficients results in a filtered output signal.

Recapitulating, the response of a linear and time-invariant system (such as a digital filter) over all time to an impulse is the system's impulse response; its response to an amplitude scaled input sample is a scaled impulse response; its response to a delayed impulse is a delayed impulse response. The input samples are comprised of a sequence of impulses of varying amplitude, each with a unique delay. Each input sample results in a scaled, time-delayed impulse response; by convolution, the system's output at any sample time is the sum of the partial impulse responses produced by the scaled and shifted inputs for that instant in time.

Because convolution is not an intuitive phenomenon, a graphical illustration of its nature might be useful. Consider the waveform in Fig. 15-2A. It can be divided into discrete pieces such that $x(t) = x_1(t) + x_2(t) + x_3(t) + \ldots$

In other words:

$$x(t) = \sum_{k=-\infty}^{\infty} x_k(t)$$

where $k = 1,2,3, \ldots$

Consider a network that produces an output $h(t)$ when a single piece of the waveform is input, as shown in Fig. 15-2B. The output $h(t)$ defines the network; from this single response we can find the network's response to any input. The network's complete response to the waveform can be found by adding its response to all of the input pieces. The response $h(t)$ to $x_1(t)$ is scaled by the amplitude of $x_1(t)$ and is output time-invariantly with $x_1(t)$. Similarly, the inputs that follow produce outputs that are scaled and delayed by the delay of the input, as shown in Fig. 15-2C. The sum of the individual responses is the full response to the input waveform:

$$y(n) = \sum_{k=1}^{\infty} h(k)\, x(n-k).$$

Equivalently,

$$y(n) = \sum_{k=1}^{\infty} x(k)\, h(n-k).$$

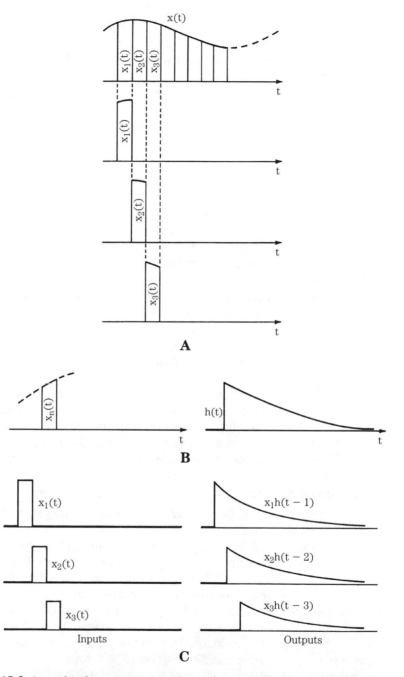

15-2 A graphical representation of convolution. A. The samples comprising a discrete signal may be considered singly. B. When applied to a discrete processing system such as a digital filter, each sample produces an output response. C. The overall response is the summation of the individual responses. Blesser

This is convolution, mathematically expressed as:

$$y(n) = h(n)*x(n) \text{ where } * \text{ denotes convolution.}$$

To view convolution in action, consider a series of snapshots of the terms present at five consecutive sample times:

$t = 0T$	$t = 1T$	$t = 2T$	$t = 3T$	$t = 4T$
$x_0 h_0$	$x_0 h_1$	$x_0 h_2$	$x_0 h_3$	$x_0 h_4$
	$x_1 h_0$	$x_1 h_1$	$x_1 h_2$	$x_1 h_3$
		$x_2 h_0$	$x_2 h_1$	$x_2 h_2$
			$x_3 h_0$	$x_3 h_1$
				$x_4 h_0$

The response is the sum of the terms in each column:

$$y_0 = x_0 h_0$$
$$y_1 = x_0 h_1 + x_1 h_0$$
$$y_2 = x_0 h_2 + x_1 h_1 + x_2 h_0$$
$$y_3 = x_0 h_3 + x_1 h_2 + x_2 h_1 + x_3 h_0$$
$$y_4 = x_0 h_4 + x_1 h_3 + x_2 h_2 + x_3 h_1 + x_4 h_0.$$

The convolved response is found by reversing the impulse response, and aligning h_0 with the current x sample to generate the ordered weighted product. The rest of the sequence is obtained by moving the reversed impulse response until it has passed through the duration of the samples of interest, be it finite or infinite in length.

More generally, when two waveforms are multiplied together, their spectra are convolved, and if two spectra are multiplied, their determining waveforms are multiplied. The response to any input waveform can be determined from the impulse response of the network, and its response to any part of the input waveform. As noted, the convolution of two signals in the time domain corresponds to multiplication of their Fourier transforms in the frequency domain (as well as the dual correspondence). The bottom line is that any signal can be considered to be a sum of impulses.

Complex Numbers

Analog and digital networks share a common mathematical basis. Fundamentally, whether the discussion is one of resistors, capacitors, and inductors, or scaling, delay, and addition (all linear, time-invariant elements), processors can be understood through complex numbers. A complex number z is any number that can be written in the form $z = x + jy$ where x and y are real numbers, and where x is the real part, and jy is the imaginary part of the complex number. An imaginary number is any real number multiplied by j, where j is the square root of -1. There is no number that when multiplied by itself gives a negative number, but mathematicians cleverly invented the concept of an imaginary number. (Mathematicians refer to it as i, but engineers use j, because i denotes current.) The form $x + jy$ is the rectangular form of a complex number, and represents the two-dimensional aspects of numbers. For example, the real part can denote distance, and the imaginary part can denote direction. A vector can be constructed, showing the indicated location.

A waveform can be described by a complex number. This is often expressed in polar form, with two parameters: r and θ. The form $re^{j\theta}$ also can be used. If a dot is placed on a circle and rotated, perhaps representing a waveform changing over time, the dot's location can be expressed by a complex number. A location of 45° would be expressed as $0.707 + 0.707j$. A location of 90° would be $0 + 1j$, 135° would be $-0.707 + 0.707j$, and 180° would be $-1 + 0j$. The size of the circle could be used to indicate the magnitude of the number.

The j operator can be used to convert between imaginary and real numbers. A real number multiplied by an imaginary number becomes complex, and an imaginary number multiplied by an imaginary number becomes real. Multiplication by a complex number is analogous to phase shifting; for example, multiplication by j represents a 90° phase shift, and multiplication by $0.707 + 0.707j$ represents a 45° phase shift. In the digital domain, phase shift is performed by time delay. A digital network comprised of delays can be analyzed by changing each delay to a phase shift. For example, a delay of 10° corresponds to the complex number $0.984 - 0.174j$. If the input signal is multiplied by this complex number, the output result would be a signal of the same magnitude, but delayed by 10°.

Mathematical Transforms

Signal processing, analog or digital, can be considered in either of two domains. Together, they offer two perspectives on a unified theory. For analog signals, the domains are time and frequency. For sampled signals, they are discrete time and discrete frequency. A transform is a mathematical tool used to move between the time and frequency domains. Continuous transforms are used with signals continuous in time and frequency; series transforms are applied to continuous time, discrete frequency signals; and discrete transforms are applied to discrete time and frequency signals.

The analog relationships between a continuous signal, its Fourier transform, and Laplace transform are shown in Fig. 15-3A. The discrete-time relationships between a discrete signal, its discrete Fourier transform, and z-transform are shown in Fig. 15-3B.

The Laplace transform is used to analyze continuous time and frequency signals; it maps a time domain function $x(t)$ into a frequency domain, complex frequency function $X(s)$; the Laplace transform takes the form:

$$X(s) = \int_{-\infty}^{\infty} x(t)e^{-st}dt$$

The inverse Laplace transform performs the reverse mapping. Laplace transforms are useful for analog design.

The Fourier transform is a special kind of Laplace transform; it maps a time domain function $x(t)$ into a frequency domain function $X(j\omega)$, where $X(j\omega)$ describes the spectrum (frequency response) of the signal $x(t)$. The Fourier transform takes the form:

$$X(j\omega) = \int_{-\infty}^{\infty} x(t)e^{-j\omega t}dt.$$

This equation (and the inverse Fourier transform), are identical to the Laplace transforms when $s = j\omega$; the Laplace transform equals the Fourier transform when the real part of s is zero. The Fourier series is a special case of the Fourier transform

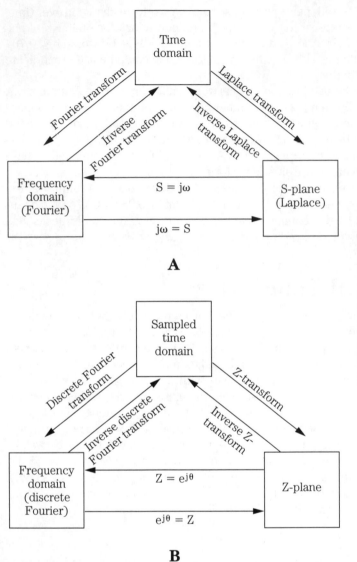

15-3
Transforms are used to mathematically convert a signal from one domain to another. A. Analog signals can be expressed in the time, frequency and *s*-plane domains. B. Discrete signals can be expressed in the sampled-time, frequency, and *z*-plane domains.

and results when a signal contains only discrete frequencies, and the signal is periodic in the time domain.

Figure 15-4 shows how transforms are used. Specifically, two methods can be used to compute an output signal: convolution in the time domain, and multiplication in the frequency domain. Although convolution is conceptually concise, in practice, the second method using transforms and multiplication in the frequency domain is usually preferable. Transforms also are invaluable in analyzing a signal, to determine its spectral characteristics. In either case, the effect of filtering a discrete signal can be predictably known.

The Fourier transform for discrete signals generates a continuous spectrum but is difficult to compute. Thus, a sampled spectrum for discrete time signals of finite

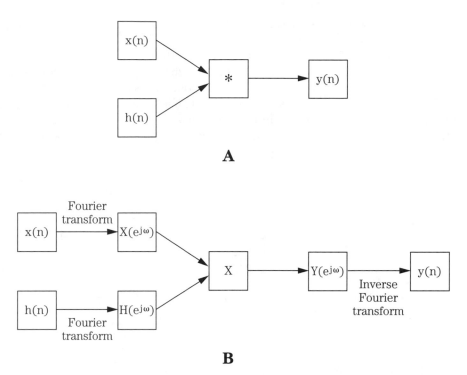

15-4 Given an input signal $x(n)$ and impulse response $h(n)$ the output signal $y(n)$ can be calculated through direct convolution, or Fourier transformation, multiplication, and inverse Fourier transformation. In practice, the latter method is often an easier calculation. A. Direct convolution. B. Fourier transformation, multiplication, and inverse Fourier transformation.

duration is implemented as the discrete Fourier transform (DFT). Just as the Fourier transform generates the spectrum of a continuous signal, the DFT generates the spectrum of a discrete signal, expressed as a set of harmonically related sinusoids with unique amplitude and phase. The DFT takes samples of a waveform and operates on them as if they were an infinitely long waveform comprised of sinusoids, harmonically related to a fundamental frequency corresponding to the original sample period. An inverse DFT can recover the original sampled signal.

The DFT is the Fourier transform of a sampled signal; when a finite number of samples (N) are considered, the N-point DFT transform is expressed as:

$$X(m) = \sum_{n=0}^{N-1} x(n)e^{-j(2\pi/N)mn}$$

The $X(m)$ term is often called bin m, and describes the amplitude of the frequencies in signal $x(n)$, computed at N equally spaced frequencies. The $m = 0$, or bin 0 term describes the dc content of the signal, and all other frequencies are all harmonically related to the fundamental frequency corresponding to $m = 1$, or bin 1. Bin numbers thus specify the harmonics that comprise the signal, and the amplitude in each bin describes the power spectrum (square of the amplitude). The DFT thus describes all the frequencies contained in signal $x(n)$; there are identical positive and negative frequencies; usually only the positive half is shown, and multiplied by 2 to obtain the actual amplitudes.

An example of DFT operations is shown in Fig. 15-5. The input signal to be analyzed is a simple periodic function $x(n) = \cos(2\pi n/6)$. The function is periodic over six samples because $x(n) = x(n + 6)$. Three N-point DFTs are used, with $N = 6$, 12 and 16. In the first two cases, N is equal to 6 or is an integer multiple of 6; a larger N yields greater spectral resolution. In the third case, $N = 16$, the discrete spectrum positions cannot exactly represent the input signal; spectral leakage occurs in all bins. In all cases, the spectrum is symmetrical.

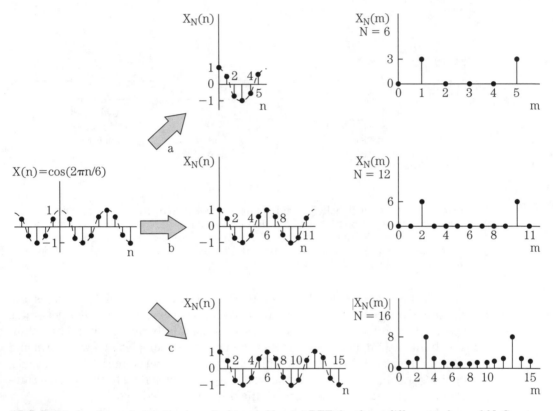

15-5 Example of a periodic signal applied to an N-point DFT, for three different values of N. Greater spectral resolution is obtained as N is increased. When N is not equal to an integral number of waveform periods, spectral leakage occurs. van den Enden and Verhoeckx

The DFT is computation-intensive, requiring N^2 complex multiplications and $N(N-1)$ complex additions. The DFT is often generated with the fast Fourier transform (FFT), a collection of fast and efficient algorithms for spectral computation that takes advantage of computational symmetries and redundancies in the DFT; it requires $N\log_2 N$ computations, 100 times fewer than DFT. The FFT can only be used when N is an integral power of 2; zero samples can be padded to satisfy this requirement. The FFT is not another type of transformation, but rather an efficient method of calculating the DFT. In general, a number of short length DFTs are calculated, then the results are combined. The FFT can be applied to various calculation methods and strategies, including analysis of signals and filter design.

The FFT will transform a time series, such as the impulse response of a network, into the real and imaginary parts of the impulse response in the frequency domain. In this way, the magnitude and phase of the network's transfer function can be obtained. An inverse FFT can produce a time domain signal. FFT filtering is accomplished through multiplication of spectra. The impulse response of the filter is transformed to the frequency domain. Real and imaginary arrays, obtained by FFT transformation of overlapping segments of the signal, are multiplied by filter arrays, and an inverse FFT produces a filtered signal. Because the FFT can be efficiently computed, it can be used as an alternative to time domain convolution if the overall number of multiplications is fewer.

The z-transform operates on discrete signals in the same way that the Laplace transform operates on continuous signals. In the same way that the Laplace transform is a generalization of the Fourier transform, the z-transform is a generalization of the DFT. Whereas the Fourier transform operates on a particular complex value, $e^{-j\omega}$, the z-transform operates with any complex value. When $z = e^{j\omega}$, the z-transform is identical to the Fourier transform. The DFT is thus a special case of the z-transform. The z-transform of a sequence $x(n)$ is defined as:

$$X(z) = \sum_{n=-\infty}^{\infty} x(n)z^{-n}$$

where z is a complex variable and z^{-1} represents a unit delay element. The z-transform has an inverse transform, often obtained through partial fraction expansion.

Whereas the DFT is used for literal operations, the z-transform is a mathematical tool used in digital signal processing theory. Convolution in the time domain is equivalent to multiplication in the z-domain. For example, we could take the z-transform of the convolution equation, such that the z-transform of an input multiplied by the z-transform of a filter's impulse response is equal to the z-transform of the filter's output. In other words, the ratio of the filter output transform to the filter input transform [that is, the transfer function, $H(z)$] is the z-transform of the impulse response. Furthermore, this ratio, the transfer function $H(z)$, is a fixed function determined by the filter. In the z-domain, given an impulse input, the transfer function equals the output.

Unit Circle and Region of Convergence

The Fourier transform of a discrete signal corresponds to the z-transform on the unit circle in the z-plane. The equation $z = e^{j\omega}$ defines the unit circle in the complex plane. The evaluation of the z-transform along the unit circle yields the function's frequency response.

The variable z is complex, and $X(z)$ is the function of the complex variable. The set of z in the complex plane for which the magnitude of $X(z)$ is finite is said to be in the region of convergence. The set of z in the complex plane for which the magnitude of $X(z)$ is infinite is said to diverge, and is outside the region of convergence. The function $X(z)$ is defined over the entire z-plane but is only valid in the region of convergence. The complex variable s is used to describe complex frequency; this is a function of the Laplace transform. S variables lie on the complex s-plane. The s-plane can be mapped to the z-plane; vertical lines on the s-plane map as circles in the z-plane.

Because there is a finite number of samples, practical systems must be designed within the region of convergence. The unit circle is the smallest region in the z-plane that falls within the region of convergence for all finite stable sequences. Poles must be placed inside the unit circle on the z-plane for proper stability. Improper placement of the poles constitutes an instability.

Mapping from the s-plane to the z-plane is an important process. Theoretically, this function allows the designer to choose an analog transfer function and find the z-transform of that function. Unfortunately, the s-plane generally does not map into the unit circle of the z-plane; stable analog filters, for example, do not always map into stable digital filters. This is avoided by multiplying by a transform constant, used to match analog and digital frequency response. There also is a nonlinear relationship between analog and digital break frequencies, which must be accounted for. The nonlinear effects are known as warping effects and the use of the constant is known as pre-warping the transfer function.

Often, a digital implementation can be derived from an existing analog representation. For example, a stable analog filter can be described by the system function $H(s)$. Its frequency response is found by evaluating $H(s)$ at points on the imaginary axis of the s-plane. In the function $H(s)$, s can be replaced by a rational function of z, which will map the imaginary axis of the s-plane onto the unit circle of the z-plane. The resulting system function $H(z)$ is evaluated along the unit circle and will take on the same values of $H(s)$ evaluated along its imaginary axis.

Poles and Zeros

Summarizing, the transfer function $H(z)$ of a linear, time-invariant discrete-time filter is defined to be the z-transform of the impulse response $h(n)$. The spectrum of a function is equal to the z-transform evaluated on the unit circle. The transfer function of a digital filter can be written in terms of its z-transform; this permits analysis in terms of the filter's poles and zeros. The roots of the numerator's polynomial of the transfer function are the zeros of the filter, and the denominator's roots are its poles. Mathematically, zeros make $H(z) = 0$, and poles make $H(z)$ nonanalytic. When the magnitude of $H(z)$ is plotted as a function of z, poles appear at a distance above the z-plane and zeros touch the z-plane. One might imagine the flat z-plane and above it a flexible contour, the magnitude transfer function, passing through the poles and zeros, with peaks on top of poles, and valleys centered on zeros. Tracing the rising and falling of the contour around the unit circle yields the frequency response. For example, the gain of a filter at any frequency can be measured by the magnitude of the contour. The phase shift at any frequency is the angle of the complex number that represents the system's response at that frequency.

If we plot $|z| = 1$ on the complex plane, we get the unit circle; $|z| > 1$ specifies all points on the complex plane that lie outside the unit circle; and $|z| < 1$ specifies all points inside it. The z-transform of a sequence can be represented by plotting the locations of the poles and zeros on the complex plane.

Figure 15-6A shows an example of a z-plane plot. Among other approaches, the response can be analyzed by examining the relationships between the pole and zero vectors. In the z-plane, angular frequency is represented as an angle, with a rotation of 360° corresponding to the sampling frequency. The Nyquist frequency is thus located at π in the figure. The example shows a single pole (X) and zero (O). The amplitude of the frequency response can be determined by dividing the magnitude of the zero vector by that of the pole vector. The frequency response from 0 to the Nyquist frequency is seen to be that of a lowpass filter, as shown in Fig. 15-6B. Similarly, the phase response can be determined by subtracting the argument of the pole

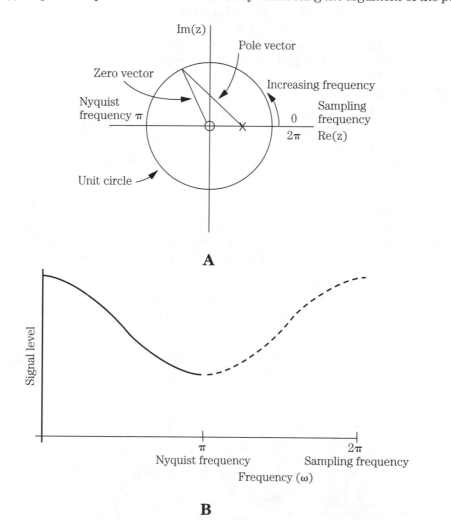

A

B

15-6 The frequency response of a filter can be obtained by dividing the magnitude of the zero vector by that of the pole vector. A. An example of a z-plane plot of a lowpass filter, showing the pole and zero locations. B. Examination of the plot reveals the filter's frequency response.

vector from that of the zero vector. As the positions of the pole and zero are varied, the response of the filter changes. For example, if the pole is moved along the negative real axis, the filter's response changes to that of a highpass filter.

Some general observations: Zeros are created by summing input samples, and poles are created by feedback. A filter's order equals the number of poles or zeros it exhibits, whichever is greater. A filter is stable only if all its poles are inside the unit circle of the z-plane. Zeros can lie anywhere. When all zeros lie inside the unit circle, the system is called a minimum-phase network. If all poles are inside the unit circle and all zeros are outside, and if poles and zeros are always reflections of one another in the unit circle, the system is a constant-amplitude, or all-pass network. If a system has zeros only, except for the origin, and they are reflected in pairs in the unit circle, the system is phase linear. No real function can have more zeros than poles. When the coefficients are real, poles and zeros occur in complex conjugate pairs; their plot is symmetrical across the real z-axis. The closer its location to the unit circle, the greater the effect of each pole and zero on frequency response.

DSP Elements

Successful DSP applications require sophisticated hardware and software. However, all DSP processing can be considered in three simple processing operations: summing, multiplication, and time delay, as shown in Fig. 15-7. With summing, multiple digital values are added to produce a single result. With multiplication, a gain change is accomplished by multiplying the sample value by a coefficient. With time delay $(n - 1)$, a digital value is stored for one sample period. The delay element (realized with shift registers or memory locations) is alternatively notated as z^{-1} because a delay of one sampling period in the time domain corresponds to multiplication by z^{-1} in the z-domain; thus $z^{-1}x(n) = x(n - 1)$. Delays can be cascaded, for example, a z^{-2} term describes a two-sample $(n - 2)$ delay. Although it is usually most convenient to

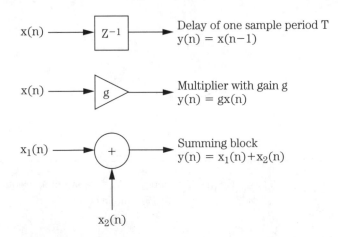

15-7 The three basic elements in any DSP system are delay, multiplication, and summation. They are combined to accomplish useful processing.

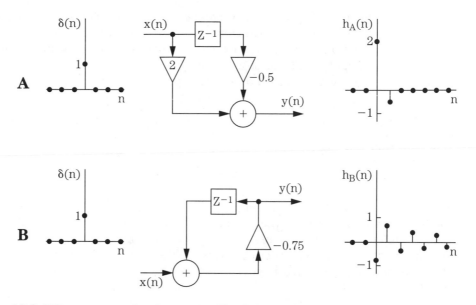

15-8 LTD systems can be characterized by their impulse responses. A. A simple non-recursive system and its impulse response. B. A simple recursive system and its impulse response. van den Enden and Verhoeckx

operate with sample numbers, the time of a delay can be obtained by taking nT, where T is the sampling interval. Figure 15-8 shows two examples of simple networks and their impulse responses; as described (see Fig. 15-1B). LTD systems such as these are completely described by the impulse response.

In practice, these elemental operations are performed many times for each sample, in specific configurations depending on the desired result. In this way, algorithms can be devised to perform operations useful to audio processing, such as reverberation, equalization, data compression, limiting, and noise removal. Of course, for real-time operation, all processing for each sample must be completed within one sampling period of 20 μs or so.

Digital Filters

Filtering (or equalization) is important in many audio applications. Analog filters using both passive and active designs shape the signal's frequency response and phase, as described by linear time-invariant differential equations. They describe the system's performance in the time domain. With digital filters, each sample is processed through a transfer function to affect the change in frequency response or phase. Operation is generally described in linear shift-invariant difference equations; they define how the discrete time signal behaves from moment to moment, in the time domain. At an infinitely high sampling rate, these equations would be identical to those used to describe analog filters. Digital filters can be designed from analog filters; such impulse-invariant design is useful for lowpass filters with a cutoff frequency far below the sampling rate. Other filter designs make use of transformations to convert characteristics of an analog filter to a digital filter. These transformations map the frequency range of the analog domain into the digital range, from 0 Hz to the Nyquist frequency.

A digital filter can be represented by a general difference equation:

$$y(n) + b_1 y(n-1) + b_2 y(n-2) + \dots b_N y(n-N) =$$

$$a_0 x(n) + a_1 x(n-1) + a_2 x(n-2) + \dots a_M x(n-M)$$

More efficiently, the equation can be written:

$$y(n) = \sum_{i=0}^{M} a_i x(n-i) - \sum_{i=1}^{N} b_i y(n-i)$$

where x is the input signal, y is the output signal, the constants a_i and b_i are the filter coefficients, and n represents the current sample time, the variable in the filter's equation. A difference equation is used to represent $y(n)$ as a function of the current input, previous inputs, and previous outputs. The filter's order is specified by the maximum time duration (in samples) used to generate the output. For example, the equation:

$$y(n) = x(n) - y(n-2) + 2x(n-2) + x(n-3)$$

is a third-order filter.

To implement a digital filter, the z-transform is applied to the difference equation so that it becomes:

$$Y(z) = \sum_{i=0}^{M} a_i z^{-i} X(z) - \sum_{i=1}^{N} b_i z^{-i} Y(z)$$

where z^{-i} is a unit of delay i in the time domain. Rewriting the equation, the transfer function $H(z)$ can be determined:

$$H(z) = \frac{Y(z)}{X(z)} = \frac{\sum\limits_{i=0}^{M} a_i z^{-i}}{\left(1 + \sum\limits_{i=1}^{N} b_i z^{-i}\right)}$$

As noted, the transfer function can be used to identify the filter's poles and zeros. Specifically, the roots (values that make the expression zero) of the numerator identify zeros, and roots of the denominator identify poles. Zeros constitute feedforward paths and poles constitute feedback paths. By tracing the contour along the unit circle, the frequency response of the filter can be determined.

A filter is canonical if it contains the minimum number of delay elements needed to achieve its output. If the values of the coefficients are changed, the filter's response is altered. A filter is stable if its impulse response approaches zero as n goes to infinity. Convolution provides the means for implementing a filter directly from the impulse response; convolving the input signal with the filter impulse response gives the filtered output. In other words, convolution acts as the difference equation, and the impulse response acts in place of the difference equation coefficients in representing the filter. The choice of using a difference equation or convolution in designing a filter depends on the filter's architecture, as well as the application.

FIR Filters

As noted, the general difference equation can be written:

$$y(n) + b_1 y(n-1) + b_2 y(n-2) + \dots + b_N y(n-N) =$$
$$a_0 x(n) + a_1 x(n-1) + a_2 x(n-2) + \dots + a_M x(n-M).$$

Consider the general difference equation without b_i terms:

$$y(n) = \sum_{i=0}^{M} a_i x(n-i)$$

and its transfer function in the z domain:

$$H(z) = \sum_{i=0}^{M} a_i z^{-i}.$$

There are no poles in this equation, hence no feedback elements. The result is a nonrecursive filter. Such a filter would take the form:

$$y(n) = ax(n) + bx(n-1) + cx(n-2) + dx(n-3)\dots$$

Any filter operating on a finite number of samples is known as a finite impulse response (FIR) filter.

As the name FIR implies, the impulse response has finite duration. Furthermore, an FIR filter can have only zeros outside the origin, it can have a linear phase, it responds to an impulse once, and it is always stable. Because it does not use feedback, it is called a nonrecursive filter. A nonrecursive structure is always an FIR; however, an FIR does not always use a nonrecursive structure.

Consider this introduction to the workings of FIR filters: we know that large differences between samples are indicative of high frequencies and small differences are indicative of low frequencies. A filter changes the differences between consecutive samples. The digital filter described by $y(n) = 0.5[x(n) + x(n-1)]$ makes the current output equal to half the current input plus half the previous input. Suppose this sequence is input: 1, 8, 6, 4, 1, 5, 3, 7; the difference between consecutive samples ranges from 2 to 7. The first two numbers enter the filter and are added and multiplied: $(1 + 8)(0.5) = 4.5$. The next computation is $(8 + 6)(0.5) = 7.0$. After the entire sequence has passed through the filter the sequence is: 4.5, 7, 5, 2.5, 3, 4, and 5. The new inter-sample difference ranges from 0.5 to 2.5; this filter averages the current sample with the previous sample. This averaging smoothes the output signal, thus attenuating high frequencies. In other words, the circuit is a lowpass filter.

More rigorously, the filter's difference equation is:

$$y(n) = 0.5[x(n) + x(n-1)].$$

Transformation to the z-domain yields:

$$Y(z) = 0.5[X(z) + z^{-1} X(z)].$$

The transfer function can be written:

$$H(z) = \frac{Y(z)}{X(z)} = \frac{(1 + z^{-1})}{2} = \frac{(z + 1)}{2z}.$$

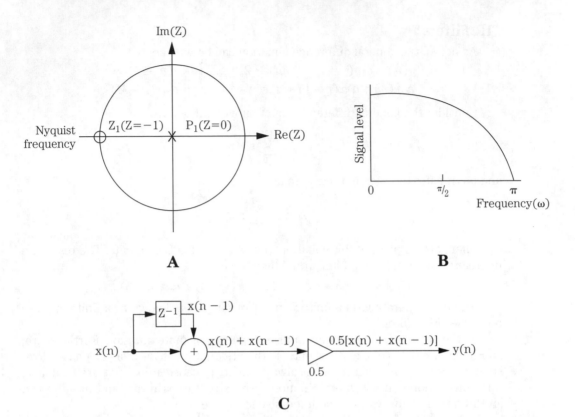

15-9 An example showing the response and structure of a digital lowpass filter. A. The pole and zero locations of the filter in the z-plane. B. The frequency response of the filter. C. Structure of the lowpass filter.

This indicates a zero at $z = -1$ and a pole at $z = 0$, as shown in Fig. 15-9A, an example suggested by Jayant Datta. Tracing the unit circle, the filter's frequency response is shown in Fig. 15-9B; it is indeed a lowpass filter. Finally, the difference equation can be realized with the algorithm shown in Fig. 15-9C.

Another example of a filter is one in which the output is formed by subtracting the past input from the present, and dividing by 2. In this way, small differences between samples (low-frequency components) are attenuated and large differences (high-frequency components) are accentuated. The equation for this filter is only slightly different from the previous example:

$$y(n) = 0.5[x(n) - x(n - 1)].$$

Transformation to the z-plane yields:

$$Y(z) = 0.5[X(z) - z^{-1}X(z)].$$

The transfer function can be written:

$$H(z) = \frac{Y(z)}{X(z)} = \frac{(1 - z^{-1})}{2} = \frac{(z - 1)}{2z}$$

This indicates a zero at $z = 1$ and a pole at $z = 0$, as shown in Fig. 15-10A. Tracing the unit circle, the filter's frequency response is shown in Fig. 15-10B; it is a highpass filter. The difference equation can be realized with the algorithm shown in Fig. 15-10C. This highpass filter's realization differs from that of the previous lowpass filter's realization only in the −1 multiplier. In both of these examples, the filter must store only one previous sample value; however, a filter could be designed to store a large (but finite) number of samples for use in calculating the response.

An FIR can be constructed as a multi-tapped digital filter, functioning as a building block for more sophisticated designs. The direct-form structure for realizing a digital FIR filter is shown in Fig. 15-11. This structure is an implementation of the convolution sum. To achieve a given frequency response, the impulse response coefficients of an FIR must be calculated. Simply truncating the extreme ends of the impulse response to obtain coefficients would result in an aperture effect and Gibbs phenomenon; the response will peak just below the cutoff frequency and ripples will appear in the passband and stopband. All digital filters have a finite bandwidth; in other words, in practice the impulse response must be truncated. Although the Fourier transform of an infinite (ideal) impulse response creates a rectangular pulse, a finite (real-world) impulse response creates a function exhibiting Gibbs phenomenon. This is not ringing as in analog systems, but the mark of a finite bandwidth system.

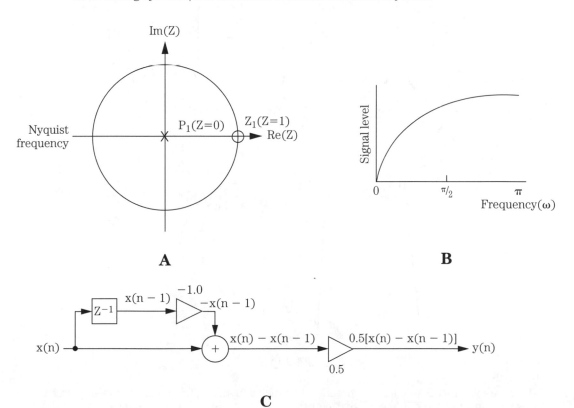

15-10 An example showing the response and structure of a digital highpass filter. A. The pole and zero locations of the filter in the z-plane. B. The frequency response of the filter. C. Structure of the highpass filter.

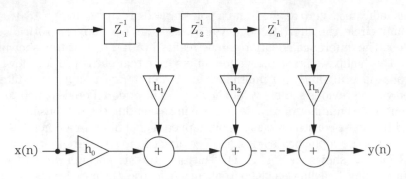

15-11 The direct-form structure for realizing an FIR filter. This multitapped structure implements the convolution sum.

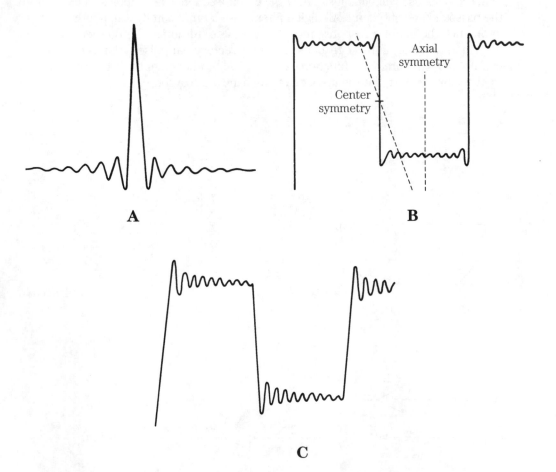

A

B

Axial symmetry

Center symmetry

C

15-12 Phase linearity is an important criterion for a digital filter. A. The impulse response of an audio lowpass linear phase FIR filter. B. Symmetrical square-wave response of an audio lowpass linear phase filter, showing both axial and center symmetry. C. Asymmetrical response of a non-phase-linear filter. Lagadec

Choice of coefficients determines the phase linearity of the resulting filter. For many audio applications, providing linear phase is important; this results in symmetry in the impulse response, as shown in Fig. 15-12A. The filter's constant delay versus frequency linearizes the phase response and results in a symmetrical output response. The steady-state response of a phase linear system to a square-wave input is shown in Fig. 15-12B; it displays center and axial symmetry. As noted, the Gibbs phenomenon dictates that a very fast transition must result in overshoot from the target values, and this is evident. When a system's phase response is nonlinear, the step response does not display symmetry, as in Fig. 15-12C.

The length of the impulse to be considered depends on frequency response and filter ripple. It is important to provide a smooth transition between samples that are relevant and those that are not. For example, the filter coefficients can be multiplied by a window function, a finite weighting sequence used to modify the infinite series of Fourier coefficients that define a given frequency response. Many DSP applications involve operation on a finite set of samples, truncated from a larger data record; this can cause side effects. For example, as noted, the difference between the ideal and actual filter lengths yields Gibbs phenomenon overshoot at transitions in the transfer function in the frequency domain. This can be reduced by multiplying the coefficients by a window function, but this also can change the transition bands of the transfer function. For example, a rectangular window function can be used to effectively gate the signal. The window length can only take on integer values, and the window length must be an integer multiple of the input period. The input signal must repeat itself over this integer number of samples. The method works well because the spacing of the nulls in the window transform are exactly the same as the spacing of the harmonics of the input signal. However, if the integer relationship is broken, and there is not an exact number of periods in the window, spectrum nulls do not correspond to harmonic frequencies and there is spectral leakage. Other window functions can be used to overcome spectral leakage; they are smoothly tapered to gradually reduce the amplitude of the input signal at the endpoints of the data record. They attenuate spectral leakage according to the energy of spectral energy outside their main lobe.

Alternatively, the desired response can be sampled, and the discrete Fourier transform coefficients computed. These are then related to the desired impulse response coefficients. The frequency response can be approximated, and the impulse response calculated from the inverse discrete Fourier transform. Still another approach is to derive a set of conditions for which the solution is optimal, using an algorithm providing an approximation, with minimal error, to the desired frequency response.

IIR Filters

The general difference equation contains $y(n)$ components that contribute to the output value; these are feedback elements that are delayed by a unit of time i, and describe a recursive filter. The feedback elements are described in the denominator of the transfer function; because the roots cause $H(z)$ to be undefined, certain feedback could cause the filter to be unstable. The poles contribute an exponential sequence to each pole's impulse response; when the output is fed back to the input, the output in theory will never reach zero; this allows the impulse to be infinite in duration. This type of filter is known as an infinite impulse response (IIR) filter.

Feedback provides a powerful method of recalling past samples. For example, an exponential time average filter adds the current input sample to the last output (as opposed to the previous sample) and divides the result by 2. The equation describing its operation is: $y(n) = x(n) + 0.5y(n - 1)$. This results in an exponentially decaying response in which each next output sample is ½ the previous sample value. The filter is called an infinite impulse response filter because of its infinite memory. In theory, the impulse response of an IIR filter lasts for an infinite time; its response never decays to zero. This type of filter is equivalent to an infinitely long FIR filter where:

$$y(n) = x(n) + 0.5x(n - 1) + 0.25x(n - 2) + 0.125x(n - 3) + ... + (0.5)^M x(n - M).$$

In other words, the filter adds one-half the current sample, one-fourth the previous sample, etc. The impulse response of a practical FIR filter decays exponentially, but it has a finite length thus cannot decay to zero.

In general, an IIR filter can be described as:

$$y(n) = ax(n) + by(n - 1).$$

When the value of b is increased relative to a, the lowpass filtering is augmented; that is, the cut-off frequency is lowered. The value of b must always be less than unity or the filter will become unstable; the signal level will increase and overflow will result.

An IIR filter can have both poles and zeros, can introduce phase shift, and can be unstable if one or more poles lie on or outside the unit circle. IIR filters cannot achieve linear phase except in the case when all poles in the transfer function lie on the unit circle. This is realized when the filter consists of a number of cascaded first-order sections. Because the output of an IIR is fed back as an input (with a scaling element), it is called a recursive filter. An IIR filter always has a recursive structure, but filters with a recursive structure are not always IIR filters. Any feedback loop must contain a delay element; otherwise, the value of a sample would have to be known before it is calculated—an impossibility.

Consider the IIR filter described by the equation:

$$y(n) = x(n) - x(n - 2) - 0.25y(n - 2)$$

It can be rewritten as:

$$y(n) + 0.25y(n - 2) = x(n) - x(n - 2)$$

Transformation to the z-plane yields:

$$Y(z) + 0.25z^{-2}Y(z) = X(z) - z^{-2}X(z).$$

The transfer function is:

$$H(z) = \frac{Y(z)}{X(z)} = \frac{(1 - z^2)}{(1 + 0.25z^{-2})} = \frac{(z^2 - 1)}{(z^2 + 0.25)}$$

$$= \frac{(z + 1)(z - 1)}{(z + 0.5j)(z - 0.5j)}.$$

There are zeros at $z = \pm 1$ and conjugate poles on the imaginary axis at $z = \pm 0.5j$, as shown on Fig. 15-13A. The bandpass response is shown in Fig. 15-13B. A realization of the filter is shown in Fig. 15-13C. Delay elements have been combined to sim-

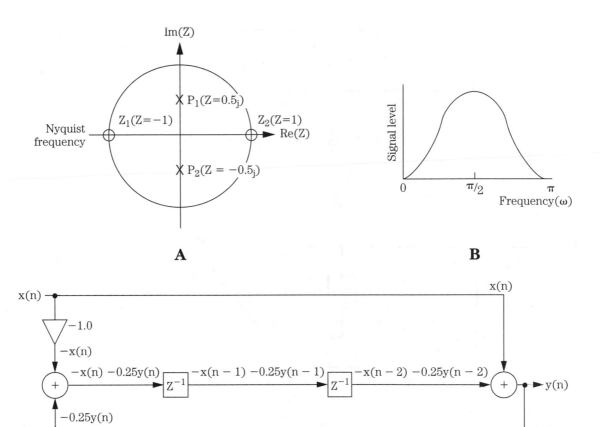

A

B

C

15-13 An example showing the response and structure of a digital bandpass filter. A. The pole and zero locations of the filter in the z-plane. B. The frequency response of the filter. C. Structure of the bandpass filter.

plify the design. Similarly, the difference equation $y(n) = x(n) + x(n-2) + 0.25y(n-2)$ also is an IIR filter. The development of its pole-zero plot, frequency response, and realization are left to the ambition of the reader.

In general, it is easier to design FIR filters with linear phase and stable operation than IIR filters with the same characteristics. However, IIR filters can achieve a steeper roll off than a FIR filter for a given number of coefficients. FIR filters require more stages, and hence greater computation, to achieve the same result. As with any digital processing circuit, noise must be considered; a filter's type, topology, arithmetic, and coefficient values all determine whether meaningful error will be introduced. For example, the exponential time average filter described above will generate considerable error if the value of b is set close to unity, for a low cut-off frequency.

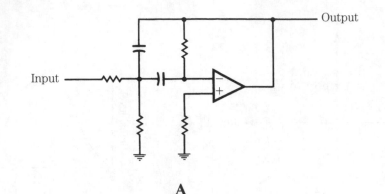

A

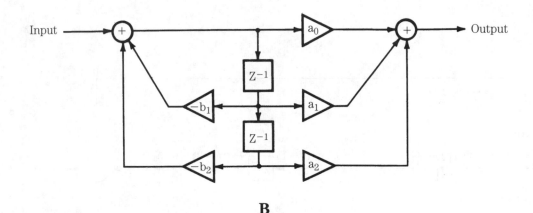

B

15-14 A comparison of second-order analog and digital filters. A. A second-order analog filter. B. IIR biquadratic second-order filter section. Tydelski

Filter Applications

An example of second-order analog filter is shown in Fig. 15-14A, and an IIR filter is shown in Fig. 15-14B; this is a bi-quadratic filter section. Coefficients determine the filter's response; in this example, with appropriate selection of the five multiplication coefficients, highpass, lowpass, bandpass, and shelving filters can be obtained. A digital audio processor might have several of these sections at its disposal. By providing a number of presets, users can easily select frequency response, bandwidth, and phase response of a filter. In this respect, a digital filter is more flexible than an analog filter that has relatively limited operating parameters. However, a digital filter requires considerable computation, particularly in the case of swept equalization. As the center frequency is moved, new coefficients must be calculated—not a trivial task. To avoid quantization effects (sometimes called zipper noise) filter coefficients and amplitude scaling coefficients must be updated at a theoretical rate equal to the sampling rate; in practice, an update rate equal to one-half or one-fourth the sampling rate is sufficient. To accomplish even this, coefficients are often obtained through linear interpolation; the range must be limited to ensure that filter poles do not momentarily pass outside the unit circle, causing transient instability.

Adaptive filters automatically adjust their parameters according to optimization criteria. They do not have fixed coefficients; instead, values are calculated during operation. Adaptive filters thus consist of a filter section and a control unit used to calculate coefficients. Often, the algorithm used to compute coefficients attempts to minimize the difference between the output signal and a reference signal. In general, any filter type can be used, but in practice, adaptive filters often use a transversal structure as well as lattice and ladder structures. Adaptive filters are used for applications such as echo and noise cancelers, adaptive line equalizers, and prediction.

A transversal filter is a FIR filter in which the output value depends on both the input value, and a number of previous input values held in memory. Inputs are multiplied by coefficients and summed by an adder at the output. Only the input values are stored in delay elements; there are no feedback networks used, hence it is an example of a nonrecursive filter. As described in chapter 4, this architecture is used extensively to implement lowpass filtering with oversampling.

In practice, digital oversampling filters often use a cascade of FIR filters, designed so the sampling rate of each filter is a power of two higher than the previous filter. The number of delay blocks (tap length) in the FIR filter determines the passband flatness, transition band slope and stopband rejection; there are $M + 1$ taps in a filter with M delay blocks. Most digital filters are dedicated chips; however, general purpose DSP chips can be used to run custom filter programs.

The block diagram of a dedicated digital filter (oversampling) chip is shown in Fig. 15-15. It demonstrates the practical implementation of DSP techniques. A central processor performs computation while peripheral circuits accomplish input/output and other functions. The filter's characteristic is determined by the coefficients stored in ROM; the multiplier/accumulator performs the essential arithmetic operations; the shifter manages data during multiplication; the RAM stores intermediate computation results; a microprogram stored in ROM controls the filter's operation. The coefficient word length determines filter accuracy, and stopband attenuation. A filter can have, for example, 293 taps and a 22-bit coefficient; this would yield a passband flat to within ±0.00001 dB, with stopband suppression greater than 120 dB. Word length of the audio data increases during multiplication (length is the sum of the input words); truncation would result in quantization error thus the data must be rounded or dithered. Noise shaping can be applied at the accumulator, using an IIR filter to redistribute the noise power, primarily placing it outside the audio band. Noise shaping is discussed in chapter 16.

Sources of Errors

The DSP computation required to process an audio signal can result in noise and distortion unless precautions are taken. In general, errors in digital processors can be classified as coefficient errors, limit cycle errors, overflow, truncation and round-off errors. Coefficient errors occur when a coefficient is not specified with sufficient accuracy; a resolution of 24 bits or more is required for computations on 16-bit audio samples. Limit cycle error might occur when a signal is removed from a filter, leaving a decaying sum. This decay might become zero or might oscillate at a constant amplitude, known as limit cycle oscillation. This effect can be eliminated, for example, by offsetting the filter's output so that truncation always produces a zero output.

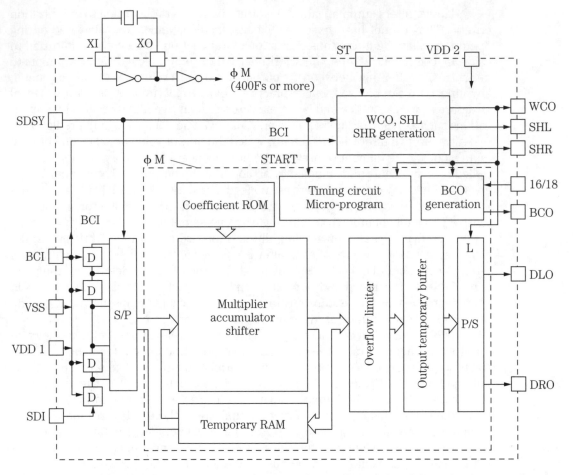

15-15 A functional block diagram showing the elements in a dedicated digital filter chip.

Overflow occurs when a register length is exceeded, resulting in a computational error. In the case of wraparound, when a 1 is added to the maximum value positive two's complement number, the result is the maximum value negative number. In short, the information has overflowed into a nonexistent bit. The drastic change in the amplitude of the output waveform would yield a loud pop if applied to a loudspeaker. To prevent this, saturating arithmetic can be used so that when the addition of two positive numbers would result in a negative number, the maximum positive sum is substituted instead. This results in clipping—a more satisfactory, or at least more benign, alternative. Alternatively, designers must provide sufficient digital headroom.

Truncation and round-off errors occur whenever the word length of a computed result is limited. Errors accumulate both inside the processor during calculation, and when word length is reduced for output through a D/A converter. However, A/D conversion always results in quantization error, and computation error can appear in different guises. For example, when two n-bit numbers are multiplied, the number of output bits will be $2n - 1$. Thus, multiplication almost doubles the number of bits required to represent the output. Although many hardware multipliers can perform double precision computation, a finite word length must be maintained following multiplication, thus limiting precision. Discarded data results in an error analogous to that of A/D quantization. To be properly modelled, multiplication must be followed by quantization; multiplication does not introduce error, but inability to keep the extra bits does.

Rather than truncate a word, for example, following multiplication, the value can be rounded off; that is, the word is taken to the nearest available value. This results in a peak error of 1/2 LSB, and an RMS value of $1/(12)^{1/2}$, or 0.288 LSB. This round-off error will accumulate over successive calculations. In general, the number of calculations must be large for significant error. However, in addition, dither information can be lost during computation. For example, when a properly dithered 16-bit word is input to a 32-bit processor, even though computation is of high precision, the output signal can be truncated to 16 bits for conversion through the output D/A converter. For example, a 16-bit signal that is delayed and scaled by a 12-dB attenuation would result in a 12-bit undithered signal. To overcome this, digital dithering to the resolution of the next processing (or recording) step should be used in a computation. For example, a 20-bit resolution signal must be dithered to 16 bits for output to a CD recorder. IIR and noise shaping filters with digital feedback can exhibit limit cycle oscillations with low level signals if gain reduction or certain equalization (resulting in gain changes) processing is performed; digital dither can be used to randomize these cycles.

John Vanderkooy and Stanley Lipshitz have shown that truncated or rounded digital words can be redithered with rectangular pdf or triangular pdf fractional numbers, as shown in Fig. 15-16. A rectangular pdf dither word D_1 is added to a digital audio word with integer part P_i and fractional part P_f. The carry bit dithers the rounding process in the same way that 1 LSB analog rectangular pdf dither affects an A/D converter. When a statistically independent rectangular pdf dither D_2 is added, triangular pdf dither results. This triangular pdf dither noise power is $Q^2/6$ and rounding noise power is $Q^2/12$ so total noise power is $Q^2/4$. The final sum has integer part S_i and fractional part S_f, which become S upon rounding.

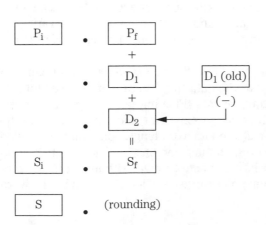

15-16
An example of digital redithering used during a truncation or rounding computation. Vanderkooy and Lipshitz

In cases of gain fading, triangular pdf appears to be a better choice than rectangular pdf because it eliminates noise modulation as well as distortion, at the expense of a slightly higher noise floor. To minimize audibility of this noise penalty, highpass triangular pdf dither can be most appropriate in rounding. The triangular pdf statistics are not changed; however, dither samples are correlated. Average dither noise power is $Q^2/6$, with no noise at 0 Hz and double the average value at the Nyquist frequency; hence the term: highpass dither. This shaping becomes more pronounced with noise increasingly shifted outside the audio band, as the oversampling ratio is increased, for example, by two or four times. The audible effect of a noise penalty is lessened when oversampling is used because in-band noise is relatively decreased proportional to the oversampling rate. Further reduction of the $Q^2/12$ requantization noise power can be achieved through noise shaping circuits, as described in chapter 16.

As noted, the problem of error sources is applicable to both audio samples as well as the computations used to determine other system operators, such as filter coefficients. For example, improperly computed filter coefficients could shift the locations of poles and zeros, thus altering the characteristics of the response. In some cases, an insufficiently defined coefficient can cause a stable IIR filter to become unstable. On the other hand, quantization of filter coefficients will not affect the linear operation of a circuit, or introduce artifacts that are affected by the input signal or that vary with time. The effect of coefficient errors in a filter is generally determined by the number of coefficients determining the location of each pole and zero. The fewer the coefficients, the lower the sensitivity. However, when poles and zeros are placed in locations where they are few, the effect of errors is greater.

DSP Integrated Circuits

A DSP chip is a specialized hardware module that performs digital signal processing under the control of software algorithms. DSP chips are stand-alone processors, often independent of host CPUs (central processing units), and are specially designed for operations used in certain spectral and numerical applications. For example, large numbers of multiplications are possible, as well as special addressing modes such as bit-reverse and circular addressing. When memory and input/output circuits are added, the result is an integrated digital signal processor. Such a general-purpose DSP chip is software programmable, and thus can be used for a variety of signal-processing applications. Alternatively, a custom signal processor can be designed to accomplish a specific task.

DSP chips are designed according to two arithmetic types, fixed integer and floating point, which define the format of the data they operate on. A fixed integer chip uses two's complement, binary integer data. Floating point chips use integer and floating point numbers (represented as an exponent and mantissa). The dynamic range of a fixed integer chip is based on its word length; data must be scaled to prevent overflow; this can increase programming complexity. The scientific notation used in a floating point chip allows larger dynamic range, without overflow problems. However, the resolution of floating point representation is limited by the word length of the exponent.

Digital audio applications require long word lengths and high operating speeds. To prevent distortion from round-off error, the internal word length must be 8 to 16 bits longer than the external word. In other words, for high quality applications, internal processing of 24 to 32 bits or more is required. A 24-bit DSP chip might require a 56-bit accumulator to prevent overflow when computing long convolution sums.

DSP chips often use a pipelining architecture so that several instructions can be paralleled. For example, a fetch (fetch instruction from memory and update program counter), decode (decode instruction and generate operand address), read (read operand from memory), and execute (perform necessary operations) can be effectively executed in one clock cycle with pipelining. A pipeline manager, aided by proficient user programming, helps ensure speedy processing.

DSP chips, like all computers, are comprised of input and output devices, an arithmetic unit, a control unit, and memory, interconnected by buses. All computers originally used a single sequential bus (von Neumann architecture), shared by data, memory addresses, and instructions. However, in a DSP chip a particularly large number of operations must be performed quickly for real-time operation. Thus, parallel bus structures are used (such as the Harvard architecture) that store data and instructions in separate memories and transfers them via separate buses. For example, a chip can have separate buses for program, data, and DMA, providing parallel program fetches, data reads, as well as DMA operations with slower peripherals.

When performing benchmark exercises, DSP chips outperform their general purpose microprocessor counterparts by a wide margin. For example, a 40-MHz 68040 processor can perform 4 MFLOPS (million floating-point operations per second), but a 40-MHz DSP chip such as the TMS320C30 will perform 40 MFLOPS.

A block diagram of a general purpose DSP chip is shown in Fig. 15-17; many DSP chips follow a similar architecture. The chip has seven components: multiply-accumulate unit, data address generator, data RAM, coefficient RAM, coefficient address generator, program control unit, and program ROM. Three buses interconnect these components: the data bus, the coefficient bus, and the control bus. In this example, the multiplier is asymmetrical; it multiplies 24-bit sample words by 12-bit coefficient words. The result of multiplication is carried out to 36 bits. For dynamic compression, the 12-bit words containing control information are derived from the signal itself; two words could be taken together to provide double precision when necessary. A 40-bit adder is used in this example; this adds the results of multiplications to other results stored in the 40-bit accumulator. Following addition in the ALU, words must be quantized to 24 bits before being placed on the data bus. Different methods of quantization can be applied.

Coefficients are taken from the coefficient RAM, loaded with values appropriate to the task at hand, and applied to the coefficient bus. Twenty-four-bit data samples are moved from the data bus to two data registers. Parallel and serial inputs and outputs, and data memory can be connected to the data bus. This short memory (64 words by 24 bits, in this case) performs the elementary delay operation. To speed multiple multiplications, pipelining is provided. Necessary subsequent data is fed to intermediate registers simultaneously with operations on current data.

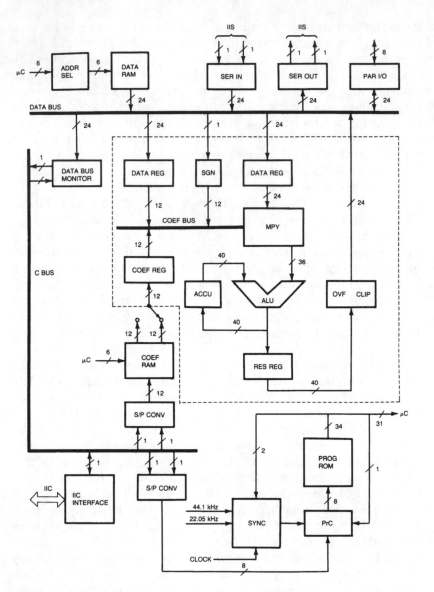

15-17 Digital signal processor chip. The section surrounded by a dashed line is the arithmetic unit where computation occurs. Independent buses are used for data, coefficients, and control. Philips

Accu	Accumulator register for intermediate results	IIC	Connection with the (external) IIC bus that carries
Addr Sel	Address Control for data memory	Interface	the signals to and from other ICs in accordance
ALU	Arithmetic logic unit		with a standard protocol
C Bus	Control bus	IIS	Standardized digital signal ('Inter-IC Signal')
Clock	Clock signal	Mpy	Multiplier (24 × 12 bits)
Coef Bus	Coefficient bus	Ovf Clip	Quantization and overflow circuit
Coef RAM	Random access memory for coefficients	Par I/O	Parallel input and output unit
Coef Reg	Coefficient register	PrC	Program counter
Data Bus	Data bus	Prog ROM	Read-only memory containing the program
Data Bus	Unit that monitors the traffic on the data bus	Res Reg	Results register
Monitor	for control purposes	Ser In, Out	Serial input and output units
Data RAM	Random-access memory for data	Sgn	Register for the sign bit
Data Reg	Data register	S/P Conv	Serial/parallel converter
IC	Integrated circuit	Sync	Synchronization circuit
IIC	Standardized control signal ('Inter-IC Control')	μC	Microcode

A Multimedia DSP Processor

The demands of multimedia are computation-intensive, requiring processing and movement of large quantities of data. Digital signal processors are able to efficiently perform all the audio, visual and communication computation chores. They have a high degree of parallelism to perform effectively simultaneous tasks (such as processing audio and video files), and balance performance with I/O to avoid bottlenecks. In short, such processors are well designed for multimedia signal processing tasks.

One such multimedia processing chip is the Motorola DSP96002 processor, named the Media Engine. It supports fast, high-resolution graphics, full-motion video, computer animation, and multichannel digital audio processing. The device is a 32-bit floating point DSP chip that exceeds the performance of the DSP5600x chip family with increased speed, dual input and output structure, and full compliance with the IEEE (Institute of Electrical and Electronic Engineers) standards for floating point mathematics, the same standard used in mainframe and supercomputer systems.

The DSP96002 has a clock rate of 33 MHz with a speed of 16 MIPS (million instructions per second). For example, the DSP96002 can execute a 1024-point FFT in less than 0.8 ms. The instruction throughput peaks at 165 MOPS (million operations per second), and 50 MFLOPS (million floating point operations per second) because several operating instructions can be performed in parallel with one instruction. For example, the CPU can perform the following operations: Floating-point multiplication; floating-point addition; floating-point subtraction; DMA transfer; load two registers for subsequent calculations; calculate address for two new pieces of data; and calculate source and destination addresses for the next transfer—all in less than 60 billionths of a second.

There are five separate data buses, three address buses, and a program instruction bus, all 32 bits wide. The buses provide a total internal bandwidth of more than 2 Gbps. There are ten 96-bit registers in the ALU that can be used as thirty 32-bit registers. The ALU supports integer arithmetic including a 32×32 multiplication with a full, nontruncated, 64-bit product. The DSP96002 has six on-chip memories, and can directly address up to 12 Gbytes of memory. Moreover, multiple DSP96002's can be linked to form processing arrays.

Of the chip's 223 pins, fully 162 are devoted to input/output communications. There are two identical input and output ports, each providing a 32-bit data path, 32-bit address path, and 19 control and handshaking lines. These ports are bidirectional, and can operate independently while computation continues. For example, one port can transfer video data while the other transfers audio data, both in the background of other real-time processing. Overall, throughput is 33 million words per second; this is equivalent to moving a 66,000-page document on and off the chip in one second. Especially important in audio processing is the DSP96002's fast-interrupt function that permits the chip to immediately take up a new task without storing information on the current task. The CPU can process over 2.78 million interrupts per second.

The programming model of the DSP96002 is virtually identical to the DSP5600x, and DSP5600x software can be ported to the DSP96002. Moreover, DSP96002 software can be retouched to run on the DSP5600x. The DSP96002 contains an on-chip emulator. Third party compilers enable programming in high level languages such as C and there is a third party real time operating system.

DSP Programming

A general-purpose software approach is often more expensive than dedicated hardware, but it is desirable because of the great flexibility that programmability provides for both DSP designers and users. The execution of software instructions is accomplished by the DSP chip; the DSP chip is like an engine, and the software instructions are the fuel. In this case, the DSP chip runs a complete software program on every audio sample as it passes through the chip. Although the architecture of a DSP chip determines its theoretical processing capabilities, actual performance also is largely affected by the structure and diversity of its instruction set.

Each DSP chip uses its own assembly language, and programming at that level is highly efficient. High-level languages (such as C) are easy to use, document, debug, and independent of hardware; however, they are less efficient and thus slower to execute, and do not take advantage of specialized chip hardware. Assembly languages are more efficient, execute faster, require less memory, and take advantage of special hardware functions; however, they are more difficult to program, read, debug, are hardware dependent, and labor intensive.

An assembly language program for a specific chip is written using the commands in the chip's instruction set; these instructions take advantage of the chip's specialized signal processing functions. Generally, there are four types of instructions: arithmetic, program control, memory access and transfer, and input/output. Instructions are programmed with mnemonics that identify the instruction, and reference a data field to be operated upon. Because many DSP chips operate within a host environment, user front-end programs are written in higher-level languages, reserving assembly language programming for the critical audio processing tasks.

An operation that is central to DSP programming is the multiply-accumulate command, often called MAC. Many algorithms call for two numbers to be multiplied, and the result summed with a previous operation. DSP chips feature a multiply-accumulate command that moves two numbers into position, multiplies them together, and accumulates the result, with rounding, all in one operation. To perform this efficiently, the arithmetic unit contains a multiplier/accumulator combination (see Fig. 15-17). This can calculate one subproduct and simultaneously add a previous subproduct to a sum, in one machine cycle, the shortest time period in a DSP chip. To accommodate this, DSP chips rely on a hardware multiplier to execute the multiply-accumulate operation. Operations such as sum of products and iterative operations can be performed efficiently.

As an example of assembly language programming, consider the FIR transversal filter shown in Fig. 15-18A. It can be described with this difference equation:

$$y(n) = x(n-4)h(4) + x(n-3)h(3) + x(n-2)h(2) + x(n-1)h(1) + x(n)h(0).$$

The five input audio sample values, five coefficients describing the impulse response at five sample times, and the output audio sample value will be stored in memory locations; data value $x(n)$ will be stored in memory location XN; $x(n-1)$ in XNM1; $y(n)$ in YN; $h(0)$ in H0, etc. The running total will be stored in the accumulator, as shown in Fig. 15-18B. In this case, intermediate calculations are held in the

$$y(n) = x(n-4)h(4) + x(n-3)h(3) + x(n-2)h(2) + x(n-1)h(1) + x(n)h(0)$$

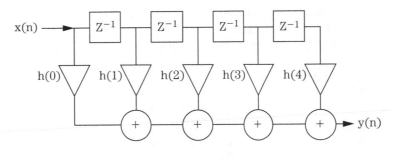

A

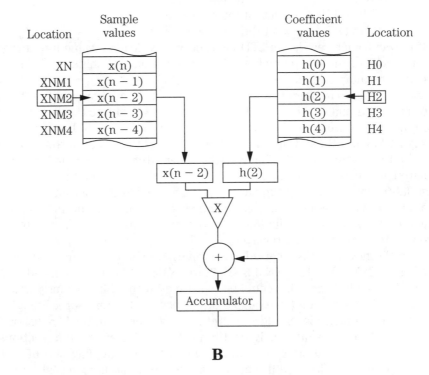

B

15-18 A five-coefficient FIR filter can be realized with assembly language code authored for a commercial DSP chip. A. Structure of the FIR filter. B. Audio sample and filter coefficient values stored in memory are multiplied and accumulated to form the output samples.

T register. The code to execute this filter on a Texas Instruments TMS320 chip, suggested by Matt Booty, is shown below:

```
1. NXTPT  IN XN,PA2      * get the new input value XN from port
2.        ZAC            * zero the accumulator
```

3.	LT XNM4	* x(n – 4)h(4)
4.	MPY H4	* multiply
5.	LTD XNM3	* x(n – 4)h(4) + x(n – 3)h(3)
6.	MPY H3	* multiply
7.	LTD XNM2	* similar to previous steps
8.	MPY H2	
9.	LTD XNM1	
10.	MPY H1	
11.	LTD XN	
12.	MPY H0	
13.	APAC	* add the result of the last multiply
		* to the accumulator
14.	SACH YN,1	* store the result in YN
15.	OUT YN,PA2	* output the response to port
16.	B NXTPT	* get the next point

Of particular interest is the LTD instruction that loads a value into a register, adds the result of the last multiply to the accumulator, and shifts the value to the next higher memory address.

Line 1 moves an input data word from an I/O port to memory location XN. Line 2 zeros the accumulator. Line 3 loads the past value XNM4 into the T register. Line 4 multiplies the contents of the T register with the coefficient in H4. Lines 5 and 6 multiply XNM3 and H3 and the LTD instruction adds the result of the Line 4 multiplication to the accumulator. Similarly, the other filter taps are multiplied and accumulated in Lines 7 through 12. Line 13 adds the final multiplication to the accumulator, so that the accumulator contains the filtered output value corresponding to the input value from Line 1. Line 14 transfers this output to YN. Line 15 transfers location YN to the I/O port. Line 16 returns the program to Line 1 where the next input value is received.

When the new input is received, past values are shifted one memory location; XN moves to XNM1, XNM1 to XNM2, XNM2 to XNM3, XNM3 to XNM4, and XNM4 is dropped. Although these shifts could be performed with additional instructions, as noted, the LTD instruction (an example of the power of parallel processing) shifts each value to the next higher address after it is transferred to the T register. After Line 11, the data values are ready for the next pass. Other program sections not shown would set up I/O ports, synchronize I/O with the sampling rate of external hardware, and store filter coefficients. This filter example uses straight-line code with separate steps for each filter tap. It is very fast for short filters, but longer filters would be more efficiently performed with looped algorithms. The decision of which is more efficient for a given filter is not always obvious.

The Motorola DSP5600x family of processors also can be used to perform DSP operations such as filtering. Efficiency stems from the DSP chip's ability to perform multiply-accumulate operations while simultaneously loading registers for the next multiply-accumulate operation. Further, hardware do loops and repeat instructions allow repetition of the multiply-accumulate operation.

To illustrate programming approaches, the difference equation for the five-coefficient FIR filter in the previous example (see Fig. 15-18) will be coded twice, in examples devised by Thomas Zudock. First, as in the previous example, the filter is implemented with the restriction that each operation must be executed independently in a straight-line fashion. Second, the filter is implemented using parallel move and looping capabilities to maximize efficiency as well as minimize code size.

First, some background on the DSP5600x family syntax and architecture: The DSP5600x has three parallel memories, x, y, and p. Typically, the x and y memories are used to hold data, and the p memory holds the program that performs the processing. The symbols r0 and r5 are address registers. They can be used as pointers to read or write values into any of the three memories. For example, the instruction "move x:(r0)+,x0" reads the value stored at the memory location pointed to by r0 in x memory into the x0 data register, then increments the r0 address register pointer to the data to be accessed. The x0, and y0 symbols are data registers, typically used to hold next data that is ready for a mathematical operation. The accumulator is denoted by a; it is the destination for mathematical operations. The instruction "mac x0,y0,a" is an example of the multiply-accumulate operation; the data registers x0 and y0 are multiplied and then summed with the value held in accumulator a.

In a straight-line coded algorithm implementing the FIR example, each step is executed independently. At the start, x0 is already loaded with a new sample, r0 points to the location in x memory to save that sample, and r5 points to the location in memory where h(0) is located. The FIR straight-line code is:

```
1.  move  x0,x:(r0) +      ;save x(n) in memory, increment r0
2.  move  y:(r5) + ,y0     ;get h(0) from memory, increment r5
3.  mpy   x0,y0,a          ;a = x0y0 = x(n)h(0)
4.  move  x:(r0) + ,x0     ;get x(n – 1) from x memory, increment r0
5.  move  y:(r5) + ,y0     ;get h(1) from y memory, increment r5
6.  mac   x0,y0,a          ;a = a + x0y0 = x(n)h(0) + x(n – 1)h(1)
7.  move  x:(r0) + ,x0     ;get x(n – 2) from x memory, increment r0
8.  move  y:(r5) + ,y0     ;get h(2) from y memory, increment r5
9.  mac   x0,y0,a          ;a = a + x0y0 = x(n)h(0) + x(n – 1)h(1) + …
                           ;… + x(n – 2)h(2)
10. move  x:(r0) + ,x0     ;get x(n – 3) from x memory, increment r0
11. move  y:(r5) + ,y0     ;get h(1) from y memory, increment r5
12. mac   x0,y0,a          ;a = a + x0y0 = x(n)h(0) + x(n – 1)h(1) + …
                           ;… + x(n – 2)h(2) + x(n – 3)h(3)
13. move  x:(r0) + ,x0     ;get x(n – 3) from x memory, increment r0
14. move  y:(r5) + ,y0     ;get h(1) from y memory, increment r5
15. macr  x0,y0,a          ;a = a + x0y0 = x(n)h(0) + x(n – 1)h(1) + …
                           ;… + x(n – 2)h(2) + x(n – 3)h(3) + …
                           ;… + x(n – 4)h(4), round to 24 bits.
16. lua(r0)–,r0            ;decrement r0
```

In line 1, the just-acquired sample x(n), located in x0, is moved into the x memory location pointed to by r0, and r0 is advanced to point to the next memory location, the previous sample. In line 2, the filter coefficient in y memory pointed to by r5, h(0), is read into data register y0, and r5 is incremented to point to the next filter coefficient, h(1). In line 3, x(n) and h(0) are multiplied and the result is stored in accumulator a. The initial conditions of the algorithm, and the status of algorithm after line 3 can be described:

Initial Status:

$x0 = x(n)$ the sample just acquired

	x memory		y memory
r0->	x(n – 5)	r5->	h(0)
	x(n – 1)		h(1)
	x(n – 2)		h(2)
	x(n – 3)		h(3)
	x(n – 4)		h(4)

After Line 3:

$a = x0y0 = x(n)h(0)$

	x memory		y memory
	x(n)		h(0)
r0->	x(n – 1)	r5->	h(1)
	x(n – 2)		h(2)
	x(n – 3)		h(3)
	x(n – 4)		h(4)

The remainder of the program continues similarly, with the next data value loaded into x0 and the next filter coefficient loaded into y0 to be multiplied and added to accumulator a. After line 16, the difference equation has been fully evaluated and the filtered output sample is in accumulator a. This status can be described:

After Line 15:

$$a = x0y0 = x(n)h(0) + x(n – 1)h(1) + x(n – 2)h(2) + x(n – 3)h(3)$$
$$+ x(n – 4)h(4)$$

	x memory		y memory
	x(n)>	r5->	h(0)
	x(n – 1)		h(1)
	x(n – 2)		h(2)
	x(n – 3)		h(3)
r0->	x(n – 4)		h(4)

After the next sample is acquired, the same process will be executed to generate the next filtered output sample. Address registers r0 and r5 have wrapped around to point to the needed data and filter coefficients. The registers are set up for modulo addressing with a modulus of five (because there are five filter taps). Instead of continuing to higher memory, they wrap around in a circular fashion when incremented or decremented to repeat the process again.

Although this code has evaluated the difference equation, the DSP architecture has not been optimally used; this filter can be written much more efficiently. Values stored in x and y memory can be accessed simultaneously with execution of one instruction. While values are being multiplied and accumulated, the next data value and filter coefficient can be simultaneously loaded in anticipation of the next calculation. Additionally, a hardware loop counter allows repetition of this operation, easing implementation of long difference equations. The operations needed to realize the same filter can be implemented with fewer instructions and in less time, as shown below. The FIR filter coded using parallel moves and looping is:

```
1. clr  a  x0,x:(r0)+  y:(r5)+,y0      ;initialize accumulator a to zero
                                       ;save x(n) in x memory, increment r0
                                       ;get h(0) from y memory, increment r5
2. rep  #4                             ;repeat the next instruction four times
3. mac  x0,y0,a  x:(r0)+,x0  y:(r5)+,y0  ;a = a + x(n – D)h(D) : D = 0,1,2,3
                                       ;get x(n – D + 1) from x memory, increment r0
                                       ;get h(D + 1) from memory, increment r5
4. macr  x0,y0,a  (r0)–                ;a = a + x(n – 4)h(4), round to 24 bits
                                       ;decrement r0
```

The parallel move and looping implementation is clearly more compact. The number of comments needed to describe each line of code is indicative of the power in each line. However, the code can be confusing because of its consolidation. As programmers become more experienced, use of parallel moves becomes familiar. Many programmers view the DSP5600x code as having three execution flows: the instruction execution, x memory accesses, and y memory accesses.

In most cases, the success of a DSP application depends on the talents of the human programmer. Software development costs are usually much greater than the hardware itself. In many cases, manufacturers supply libraries of functions such as FFTs, filters, and windows that are common to many DSP applications. To assist the development process, software development tools are often available. A text editor is used to write and modify assembly language source code. An assembler program translates assembly language source code into object code. A compiler translates programs written in high-level languages into object code. A linker combines assembled and compiled object programs with library routines and creates executable object code. The assembler and compiler use the special processing features of the DSP chip wherever possible. A simulator is used to emulate code on a host computer before running it on DSP hardware. A debugger is used to perform low-level debugging of DSP programs. In addition, DSP operating systems are available, providing programming environments similar to those used by general-purpose processors.

High-Level DSP Programming

New software environments permit straightforward design of DSP algorithms including custom algorithms and software for a variety of audio applications. One such software package, DSP Designer using the Z language, simplifies the design, analysis, simulation, and implementation of digital filters. In addition, the user can create, manipulate, and display complex test signal waveforms, and use Motorola development software to generate optimized code applications for the Motorola DSP5600x chip. With the appropriate DSP card, processed audio files can be played in real time.

Using the Z language, both single- and multi-band FIR and IIR filters, as well as arbitrary group delay IIR filters can be designed, modelling either the filter or the signal itself. Filter order is limited only by available memory. Floating-point filter/systems can be simulated, and optimized for speed. Sinusoids, random noise, and other signals can be created as input test generators. Several output waveforms can be displayed simultaneously in a variety of formats including graphics mode. A variety of signal file formats, such as ASCII text and compressed binary, can be used for signal editing, data storage, import/export, and so on. To simplify import/export, format information is stored in the file's resource fork, apart from signal data. Applications can be developed, and implemented as DSP5600x macros, and executed in real time with audio files.

The language frees the user from the chores of assembly language programming, instead operating at a much higher level. A number of software tools encompass a large number of tasks. For example, the RecordSignal tool records input signals, and the PlaySignal tool plays signals in real time through a DSP card generated using the Process56k or Build56k tools for use with Motorola DSP5600x and DSP96002 assemblers. The CreateFilterDSP tool quantizes and formats filter coefficients, with any specified digital filtering or custom DSP5600x programs. The TransformSignal tool computes the discrete Fourier transform of a specified input signal using the FFT, with 80-bit accuracy; in addition, windowing and scaling options are provided. The CreateSignal tool creates real or complex signal files, using algebraic expressions; a library of arithmetic operators and functions is available. FilterSignal filters a signal stream, PlotSignal displays one or more waveforms, and DesignFilter, DesignFIR, DesignIIR, DesignWindowFIR, and PlotFilter are all used for filter design and analysis.

For example, using the following three commands, a 5-kHz sinewave would be generated, sampling at 8 kHz; the resulting signal and aliasing components would be displayed in a spectral plot:

```
CreateSignal 'sine[5000]' -o sine5K.Signal -fs 8e3 -t0 0 -tu 0.1
TransformSignal sine5k.Signal -o 5kxfrm.Signal
PlotSignal -tl 0 -th 10e3 -show magnitude 5kxfrm.Signal
```

The Z language used to model DSP systems is similar to the C programming language, but is optimized for problems in the z domain. A Z program consists of an algebraic expression that specifies signal processing or calculations. For example, the following Z program will digitally dither a signal by adding spectrally shaped Gaussian noise to the audio waveform:

```
p = gaussian * 0.1;          # generate noise and adjust level
q = filter[h.filter](p);     # apply shaping filter to noise
x = input[x.Signal];         # read sample from input file
y = q + x;                   # add noise to input sample
output[y.Signal](y)          # write sum to output file
```

Similarly, delay, reverberation, equalization, and other devices can be modelled, tested, constructed in software, and then executed by the Motorola DSP5600x.

Specialized DSP Applications

In addition to digital filtering, some of the most powerful and creative applications of digital signal processing come in the form of specialized processing of audio signals. Building on the basic operations of multiplication and delay, sophisticated operations such as chorusing and phasing can be developed. Reverberation perhaps epitomizes the degree of time manipulation possible in the digital domain; it is possible to synthesize reverberation to both simulate natural acoustic environments, and create acoustic environments that could not physically exist. The power of digital signal processing also is clearly audible in the algorithms used for the enhancement of noisy signals.

Digital Delay

A delay block is a simple storage unit, such as a memory location. A sample is placed in memory, stored, then recalled some time later, and output. A delay unit can be described by the equation: $y(n) = x(n - m)$ where m is the delay in samples. Generally, when the delay is small, the frequency response of the signal is altered; when the delay is longer, an echo results. Just as in filtering, a simple delay can be used to create sophisticated effects. For example, Fig. 15-19A shows an echo circuit using a delay block. Delay mT is of duration m samples, and samples are multiplied by a gain coefficient (a scaling factor) less than unity. If the delay time is set between 10 and 50 ms, an echo results; with shorter fixed delays, a comb filter response results, as shown in Fig. 15-19B. Peaks and dips are equally spaced through the frequency response, from 0 Hz to the Nyquist frequency. The number of peaks depends on the delay time; the longer the delay, the more peaks.

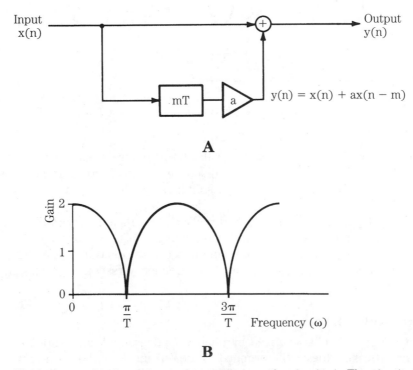

A

B

15-19 A delay block can be used to create an echo circuit. A. The circuit contains an mT delay, and gain stage. B. With shorter delay times, a comb filter response will result. Bloom, Berkhout, and Eggermont

If the delay time of the circuit in Fig. 15-19A is slowly varied between 0 and 10 ms, the time-varying comb filter creates a flanging effect. If the time delay is varied between 10 and 25 ms, a doubling effect is achieved, giving the impression of an accompanying voice. A chorus effect is provided when the signal is directed through several such blocks, with different delay variations.

A comb filter can be either recursive or nonrecursive. It cascades a series of delay elements, creating a new response. Mathematically, we see that a nonrecursive comb filter, such as the one described above, can be designed by adding the input sample to the same sample delayed: $y(n) = x(n) + ax(n - m)$ where m is the delay time in samples. A recursive comb filter creates a delay with feedback. The delayed signal is attenuated and fed back into the delay: $y(n) = ax(n) + by(n - m)$. This yields a response as shown in Fig. 15-20. The number of peaks depends on the duration of the delay; the longer the delay, the greater the number of peaks.

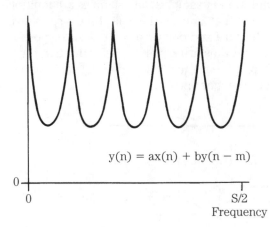

$$y(n) = ax(n) + by(n - m)$$

0

0   S/2

Frequency

15-20
A recursive comb filter creates a delay with feedback, yielding a toothed frequency response.

An all-pass filter is one that has a flat frequency response from 0 Hz to the Nyquist frequency; however, its phase response causes different frequencies to be delayed by different amounts. An all-pass filter can be described as: $y(n) = -ax(n) + x(n - 1) + by(n - 1)$.

If the delay in the above circuits is replaced by a digital all-pass filter or a cascade of all-pass filters, a phasing effect is achieved: $y(n) = -ax(n) + x(n - m) + by(n - m)$. The effect becomes more pronounced as the delay increases. The system exhibits nonuniformly spaced notches in its frequency response, varying independently in time.

Digital Reverberation

Reflections are characterized by relative loudness and delay. For example, in room acoustics, loudness is determined by the reflectivity of the boundary surfaces, and delay is determined by the size of the room. Digital reverberation is ideally suited to manipulate both of these parameters of an audio signal, to create acoustical environments. Because reverberation is comprised of a large number of sound paths, a digital reverberation circuit must similarly process many data streams.

Both reverberation and delay lines are fundamentally short-memory devices. A pure delay accepts an input signal and reproduces it later, possibly a number of times at various intervals. With reverberation, the signal is mixed repetitively with itself during storage at continually shorter intervals and decreasing amplitudes. In a delay line, the processor counts through RAM addresses sequentially, returning to the first address after the last has been reached. A write instruction is issued at each address, and the sampled input signal is routed to RAM. In this way, audio information is continually stored in RAM for a period of time until displaced by new information. During the time between write operations, multiple read instructions can be issued sequentially with different addresses. By adjusting the numerical differences, the delay times for the different signals can be determined.

In digital reverberation, the stored information must be read out a number of times, and multiplied by factors less then unity. The result is added together to produce the effect of superposition of reflections with decreasing intensity. The reverberation process can be represented as a feedback system with delay unit, multiplier, and summer. The processing program in a reverberation unit corresponds to a series and parallel combination of many such feedback systems (for example, 20 or more). Recursive configurations are often used. The single-zero unit reverberator in Fig. 15-21A generates an exponentially decreasing impulse response when the gain block is less than unity. It functions as a comb filter with peaks spaced by the reciprocal of the delay time. The echoes are spaced by the delay time, and the reverberation time can be given as: $RT = 3T/\log_{10}(a)$ where T is the time delay and a is the coefficient. Sections can be cascaded to yield more densely-spaced echoes; however, resonances and attenuations can result. Overall, it is not satisfactory as a reverberation device.

Alternatively, a reverberation section can be designed from an all-pass filter. The filter in Fig. 15-21B yields an all-pass response by adding part of the unreverberated signal to the output. Total gain through the section is unity. In this section, frequencies that are not near a resonance and thus not strongly reverberated are not attenuated. Thus, they can be reverberated by a following section. Other types of configurations are possible; for example, Fig. 15-21C shows an all-pole section of a reverberation circuit, which can be described as:

$$y(n) = -ax(n) + x(n - m) + ay(n - m).$$

The spacing between the equally spaced peaks in the frequency response is determined by the delay time, and their amplitude is set by the scaling coefficients.

One reverberation algorithm devised by Manfred Schroeder uses four reverberant comb filters in parallel followed by two reverberant all-pass filters in series, as shown in Fig. 15-22. The four comb filters, with time delays ranging from 30 to 45 ms, provide sustained reverberation, and the all-pass networks with shorter delay times contribute reverberation density. The combination of section types provides a relatively smooth frequency response, and permits adjustable reverberation times. Commercial implementations are often based on similar methods, with the exact algorithm held in secrecy.

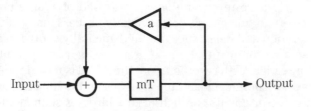

A A simple reverberation circuit derived from a comb filter.

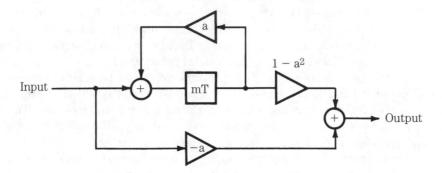

B A reverberation circuit derived from an all-pass filter.

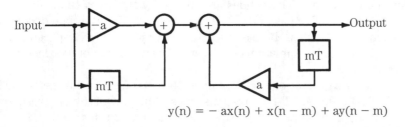

$$y(n) = -\,ax(n) + x(n - m) + ay(n - m)$$

C Reverberation circuit constructed from an all-pole section.

15-21 Reverberation algorithms can be constructed from recursive configurations. _{Blesser, et al.}

Loudspeaker Correction

Loudspeakers are far from perfect; their nonuniform frequency response, limited dynamic range, frequency-dependent directivity, and phase nonlinearity all degrade the audio signal. In addition, the listening room reinforces and cancels selected frequencies in different room locations, and contributes surface reflections, superimposing its own sonic signature on that of the recorded signal. Using DSP, correction signals can be applied to the audio signal; because they are the opposite to the errors in the acoustically reproduced signal, they theoretically cancel them.

Loudspeakers can be measured as they leave the assembly line, and errors such as nonuniform frequency response and phase nonlinearity can be corrected by DSP

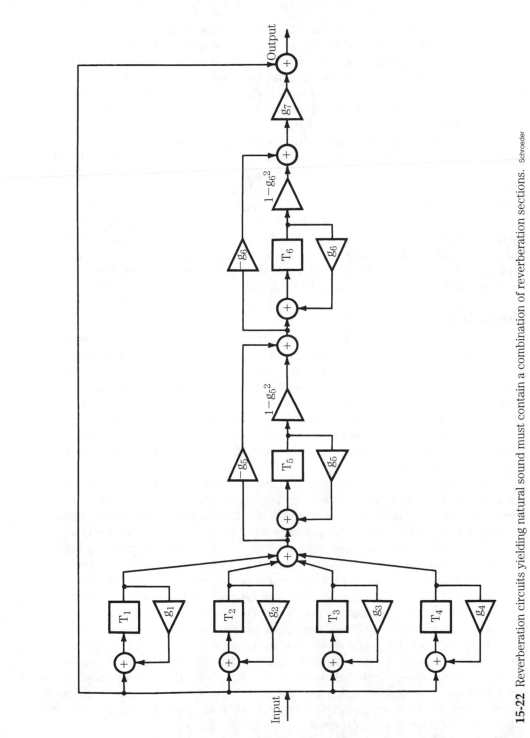

15-22 Reverberation circuits yielding natural sound must contain a combination of reverberation sections. Schroeder

processing. Because small variations exist from one loudspeaker to the next, the DSP program's coefficients can be optimized for each loudspeaker. Moreover, certain loudspeaker/room problems can be addressed. For example, floor-standing loudspeakers will have pre-determined relationships between the drivers, the cabinet, and the floor reflecting surface. The path length differences between direct and reflected sounds create a comb-filtered frequency response that can be corrected using DSP processing.

A dynamic approach also can be used in an adaptive loudspeaker/room correction system, in which the loudspeakers generate audio signals to correct the unwanted signals reflected from the room. Using DSP chips and embedded software programs, low-frequency phase delay, amplitude and phase errors throughout the audio band, and floor reflections can all be compensated for. Room acoustics correction starts with room analysis, performed on-site. Using a test signal, the loudspeaker/room characteristics are collected by an instrumentation microphone, and processed by a program that generates room-specific coefficients. The result is a smart loudspeaker that compensates for its own deficiencies, as well as anomalies introduced according to its placement in a particular room.

Noise Removal

Digital signal processing can be used to improve the quality of previously recorded material or restore a signal to a previous state, for example, by removing an echo. With DSP it is possible to characterize a noise signal and minimize its effect without affecting a music signal. For example, DSP can be used to reduce or remove noises such as clicks, pops, hum, tape hiss, and surface noise from an old recording. In addition, using methods borrowed from the field of artificial intelligence, signal lost due to tape drop-outs can be synthesized with great accuracy. Typically, noise removal is divided into two tasks, detection and elimination of impulsive noise such as clicks, and background noise reduction.

Interactive graphic displays can be used to locate impulsive disturbances; a declicking program analyzes frequency and amplitude information around the click, and synthesizes a signal over the area of the click. In contrast to tape editing, the exact duration of the performance is preserved. For example, Fig. 15-23 shows a music segment with a click, and the success of various de-clicking methods; a simple sample-and-hold function produces a plateau that is preferable to a loud click; with linear interpolation the click is replaced by a straight line connecting valid samples; using a signal model to measure local (six samples) signal characteristics, interpolation is improved; by increasing the number of samples to 120, de-clicking is further improved. Automatic de-clicking algorithms similarly perform interpolation over defects, but first must differentiate between unwanted clicks, and transient music information. Isolated clicks will exhibit short rise and decay times between amplitude extremes, but a series of interrelated clicks can be more difficult to identify. When more than one copy of a recording is available (or when the same signal is recorded on two sides of a groove), uncorrelated errors are more easily identified; however, different recordings must be precisely time-aligned.

A background noise-removal process can begin by dividing the audio spectrum into frequency bands, then performing analysis to determine content. The spectral

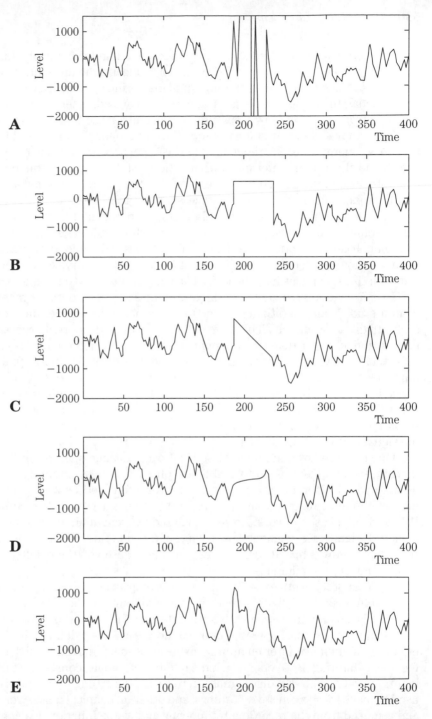

15-23 Examples showing how interpolation can be used to overcome an impulsive click. Higher-order interpolation can synthesize an essentially inaudible bridge. A. Original sample with click. B. Sample and hold with highpass click detection. C. Straight-line interpolation. D. Low-order interpolation. E. High-order interpolation.

composition of surface noise and hiss is determined and this fingerprint is used to develop an inverse function to remove the noise. Ideally, the fingerprint data is taken from a silent portion of the recording, perhaps during a pause. Because there is no music signal, the noise can be more accurately analyzed. Alternatively, samples can be taken from an area of low amplitude music, and a noise template applied.

For removal of steady state artifacts, the audio signal is considered in small sections; the energy in each frequency band is compared to that in the noise fingerprint's and the system determines what action to take in each frequency band. For example, at a particular point in the program, the music can dominate in a lower spectrum and the system can pass the signal in that band unprocessed, but hiss dominating at a higher frequency might trigger processing in that band. In many cases, some original noise is retained, because the result is generally more natural sounding. In some algorithms, a clean audio signal is estimated, then analyzed to create a masking curve; only noise that is not masked by the curve is subjected to noise removal; this minimizes introduction of artifacts or damage to the audio signal.

Hiss from a noisy analog recording, wind noise from an outdoor recording, hum from a studio's air conditioner, even the noise obscuring speech in a downed aircraft's flight recorder can all be reduced in a recording. In short, a processed recording can sound better than the original master recording. On the other hand, as with most technology, noise removal processing requires expertise in its application, and improper use degrades a recording. One question is the degree to which processing is applied. A 10 to 15% reduction in noise level can make the difference between an acceptable recording, and an unpleasantly noisy one. Additional noise removal can be problematic, even if it is only psychoacoustic tricks that make us think it is the audio signal that is being affected.

One noise-removal method devised by Roger Lagadec operates in the frequency domain, using a bank of up to 512 linear phase bandpass filters. It can be implemented with a nonrecursive polyphase network, followed by a FFT and a bank of half-band filters. Following analysis, reconstruction is accomplished with an inverse FFT and polyphase network. Noise is analyzed by examining its characteristics during short, signal-free segments, over long averaged periods of the audio signal, over the signal bandwidth, and across stereo channels. Based on the results, the gain of a band is adjusted to minimize noise.

Thomas Stockham's experiments on recordings made by Enrico Caruso in 1906 resulted in releases of digitally restored material in which those acoustic recordings were analyzed and processed with a blind deconvolution method, so-called because the nature of the signals operated upon cannot be precisely defined. In this case, the effect of an unknown filter on an unknown signal was removed by observing the effect of the filtering. By averaging a large number of signals, constant signals could be identified relative to dynamic signals. In this way, the strong resonances of the horn used to make these acoustic recordings, and other mechanical noise, were estimated and removed from the recording by applying an inverse function, leaving a restored audio signal.

In essence, the acoustic recording process was viewed as a filter; thus the music and the impulse response of the recording system were convolved. From this analysis of the playback, the original performance's spectrum was multiplied by that of the recording apparatus, and then inverse Fourier transformed to yield the signal actually present on the historic recordings. Correspondingly, the undesirable effects of the recording process were removed from the true spectrum of the performance. The computation of a correction filter using FFT methods was not a trivial task. A long-term average spectrum was needed for both the recording to be restored, and for a model, higher-fidelity recording. A one-minute selection of music required about 2500 FFTs for complete analysis. The difference between the averaged spectra of the old and new recordings was computed, and became the spectrum of the restoration filter. Restoration required multiplying segments of the recording's spectrum by the restoration spectrum and performing inverse FFTs, or by direct convolution using a filter impulse response obtained through inverse FFT.

Blind deconvolution uses techniques devised by Alan Oppenheim, known as generalized linearity or homomorphic signal processing. This class of signal processing is nonlinear, but is based upon a generalization of linear techniques. Convolved or multiplied signals are nonlinearly processed to yield additive representations, which in turn are processed with linear filters and returned via an inverse nonlinear operation to their original domain. These and other more advanced digital-signal processing topics are discussed in detail in other texts.

16
CHAPTER

Low-Bit Conversion and Noise Shaping

Although multibit linear PCM converters can be manipulated to decrease errors and improve low-level linearity, limitations in classical PCM converter architectures have stimulated development of low-bit converters. These systems are characterized by very high oversampling rates, noise shaping, and word lengths of one or a few number of bits. They demonstrate that conversion can be performed either with a high-resolution quantizer at a low sampling rate (as in multibit converters), or with a low-resolution quantizer at a high sampling rate (as in low-bit converters). Low-bit A/D and D/A converters both use conversion methods such as sigma-delta modulation with noise shaping, and process high sampling-rate signals with oversampling and decimation filters. These systems share the goal of translating nonideal converter errors into uncorrelated, benign noise. In addition, nonoversampling noise shaping is critical when reducing word length during a data transfer; for example, when transferring a 20-bit master recording to the 16-bit CD format.

Low-Bit Conversion

Conversion of multibit PCM audio data words, whether 16 or 18 bits, is a classic approach. A multibit system represents the analog waveform as an amplitude signal, storing information that measures the amplitude sample by sample. However, the method is flawed when quantization introduces differential nonlinearity errors in the amplitude representation. Moreover, because a multiplicity of bits are used to form the representation, and because each bit has an error unequal to the others, the overall error varies with each sample, and is thus difficult to correct. In practice, calibration procedures during manufacture, and sophisticated circuit design are required to achieve high performance and maintain it over the life of the converter. Understandably, manufacturers have sought to develop alternative conversion methods, including low-bit converters.

It is not easy to see how one bit (or a few) can replace 16 or more bits. Consider this analogy: multibit converters are like a row of light bulbs, each connected to a switch. Sixteen bulbs, for example, each with a different brightness, can be lighted in various combinations to achieve 2^{16}, or 65,536 different brightness levels. However, relative differences in individual bulb intensities will introduce error into the system. A certain switch combination will not always produce the desired room brightness. Similarly, multibit converters introduce error as they attempt to reproduce the audio signal.

Low-bit technology uses a wholly different approach. Instead of many bulbs and switches, only one bulb and one switch are used. Room brightness is varied by simply switching the bulb on and off. Dynamically, if the bulb is switched on and off equally, the room is at half brightness. If the bulb's on-time is increased, room brightness will increase. Similarly, low-bit converters use one bit to represent an audio amplitude, with very fast switching and very accurate timing. Low-bit technology is an inherently more precise method of representing an audio waveform.

Conventional PCM conversion divides the signal in multiple amplitude steps; however, low-bit conversion divides the signal in time, keeping amplitude changes constant. Nonintuitively, a high- or low-level pulse signal can represent an audio signal. For example, pulse-density modulation (PDM) can be used; Fig. 16-1 shows how a single constant-width pulse, with either a high or low level, can reconstruct a waveform; this is often called 1-bit conversion. Alternatively, a pulse-width modulation (PWM) (variations are pulse-edge and pulse-length modulation) signal can be used to reconstruct the output signal; these are called low-bit converters because the signal is typically quantized to four or fewer bits.

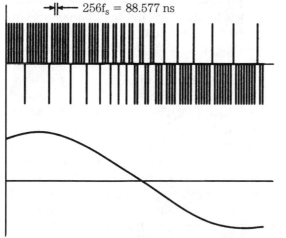
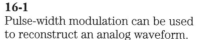

16-1
Pulse-width modulation can be used to reconstruct an analog waveform.

Low-bit conversion methods have become increasingly useful in digital audio products. For example, sigma-delta techniques are extremely competitive in A/D applications, because they obviate the need for brick-wall anti-aliasing filters. Although low-bit methods use familiar techniques such as oversampling, highly sophisticated processing is required to implement noise shaping, and decrease the high in-band noise levels otherwise present in low-bit conversion. A variety of low-bit A/D and D/A architectures have been devised, with different algorithms and orders of noise shaping.

Sigma-Delta Modulation

In pulse-code modulation, a signal is sampled and quantized into discrete steps; the maximum signal amplitude determines the maximum quantizer range. A PCM quantizer is represented in Fig. 16-2A. Quantization error is uniformly present across the Nyquist frequency band from 0 to $f_s/2$ Hz and cannot be removed from the signal; f_s is the sampling frequency. If quantization is performed at a higher sampling frequency $R \times f_s$ Hz where R is the oversampling rate, the error is spread across the band to $R \times f_s/2$, Hz hence the noise in the audio band is reduced by 3 dB for every factor of two oversampling.

As Max Hauser has pointed out, with a maximum amplitude sinusoidal input signal, oversampling will increase the signal-to-error ratio as follows:

$$S/E \text{ (dB)} = 6.02(N + 0.5L) + 1.76$$

where

N = the number of quantization bits
L = the number of octaves of oversampling.

For example, an oversampling A/D converter performs as well as a longer word length A/D converter, yielding a benefit of 0.5 bit/oversampling octave. However, the benefit is limited; for example, a 10-bit improvement would require an L of 20 octaves, an oversampling factor of one million. It is the aim of noise shaping to introduce a highpass function in the noise spectrum and thus improve oversampling performance.

Delta modulation and sigma-delta modulation (also called delta-sigma) were developed in the 1940s and 1960s, respectively, and used for voice telephony applications. Limitations prohibited their use in high quality music applications until the emergence of high-speed digital signal processing techniques in the 1980s. Differential pulse-code modulation (DPCM) is a technique in which the derivative of the signal is quantized. When signal changes between sample periods are small, the quantizer's word length can be reduced. With very high oversampling rates, the changes between sample periods are made very small, thus the quantizer can be reduced to low-bit. A 1-bit DPCM coder is known as a delta modulator (DM). In other words, DM codes the differences in the signal amplitude instead of the signal amplitude itself.

A delta-modulation encoder is shown in Fig. 16-2B; it is known as a single integration modulator. The analog input signal is compared to the integrated output pulses and the delta (difference) signal is applied to the quantizer. The quantizer generates a positive pulse when the difference signal is negative, and a negative pulse when the difference signal is positive. This difference error signal moves the integrator step by step closer to the present value input, tracking the derivative of the analog input signal. The integrator's output is a past approximation to the input, thus the coder operates similarly to other integrating feedback loops such as phase-locked loops.

A delta-modulation decoder is shown in Fig. 16-2C. This circuit consists of an integrator and a lowpass filter. When the 1-bit pulses are integrated using a time constant that is long compared to the sample period, a step waveform is produced. An

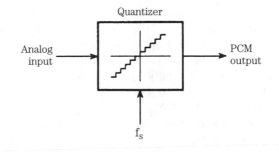

A Pulse-code modulation (PCM) converter.

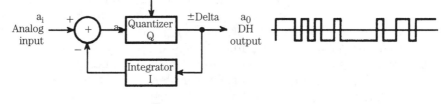

B Delta modulation (DM) encoder.

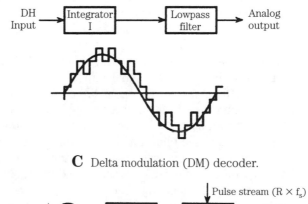

C Delta modulation (DM) decoder.

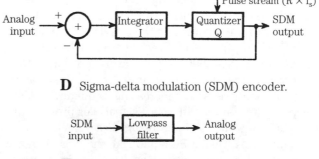

D Sigma-delta modulation (SDM) encoder.

SDM input → Lowpass filter → Analog output

E Sigma-delta modulation (SDM) decoder.

16-2 A comparison of modulation methods used in A/D and D/A conversion.

output analog waveform is produced by lowpass filtering this step waveform. Requantization error at the output of the integrator is white. As in PCM, oversampling decreases the error level by 3 dB for every factor of two oversampling. The dynamic range can be improved, that is, the requantization error made smaller, by making the delta (difference or step size) value smaller. The limit to which the delta can be reduced is given by the maximum derivative of the signal. The coded signal amplitude decreases at 6 dB/octave thus S/N decreases as signal frequency increases.

The maximum derivative occurs at maximum signal frequency and maximum signal amplitude. Exceeding this limit causes slope overload distortion. For music signals, the delta value must be high, resulting in high quantization error level. When the signal has reduced high-frequency content, as in speech, delta can be reduced. In any case, the success of DM hinges on assumptions about the nature of the encoded signal. This dependence of the dynamic range on the signal spectrum, and good performance only when the signal has lowpass characteristics, as well as correlated patterns at low signal levels, limits single integration DM applications.

To convert a maximum amplitude 16-bit word, a 1-bit modulator would have to perform 2^{16} toggles per conversion period; with a sampling frequency of 44.1 kHz, this would demand a toggle rate of approximately 2.9 GHz, an impossibility with today's technology. As the rate is slowed to accommodate hardware limitations, noise levels increase to an intolerable level. Looked at in another way, bit reduction at a high sampling frequency is required to output a low-bit signal from a high-bit source; this greatly degrades the signal's dynamic range.

Sigma-delta modulation (SDM) was developed to overcome the limitations of delta modulation. Sigma-delta systems quantize the delta (difference) between the current signal and the sigma (sum) of the previous difference. An integrator is placed at the input to the quantizer; signal amplitude is constant with increasing frequency. Like PCM, SDM quantizes the signal directly, and not its derivative as in DM. Thus the maximum quantizer range is determined by the maximum signal amplitude and is not dependent on signal spectrum. As with other low-bit coders, to achieve high resolution, high oversampling rates are required; for example, with an audio band of 24 kHz and 64 times oversampling, the internal sampling frequency rises to 3.072 MHz, thus quantization noise is spread from dc to 1.536 MHz. However, sigma-delta modulation adds noise-shaping benefits.

A first-order (single integration) sigma-delta modulation encoder is shown in Fig. 16-2D. The input to the quantizer is the integral of the difference between the input and the quantized output. The difference between the analog input signal and the digital approximation approaches zero; the average value of the clocked output tracks the analog input. There is little dc error in the output signal; the frequency spectrum of the quantizing error rises with increasing frequency (6 dB/octave). The integrator forms a lowpass filter on the difference signal thus providing low frequency feedback around the quantizer. This feedback results in a reduction of quantization noise at low (in-band) frequencies. Unlike PCM and DM, the noise is not white, but shaped by a first-order highpass characteristic as analyzed below. In practice, the in-band noise floor level is not satisfactory with first-order SDM. In addition, quantization noise is highly correlated in a first-order SDM. Further noise shaping must be achieved with higher-order (multiple integration) sigma-delta modulation coders.

A SDM decoder is shown in Fig. 16-2E; only a lowpass filter is required to decode the signal, to remove high-frequency (out-of-band) components. In other words, it averages the 1-bit signal to produce an analog waveform. Analog SDMs are used for A/D conversion, and digital SDMs are used for D/A conversion.

The signal and noise transfer functions for a first-order sigma-delta modulator are analyzed in Fig. 16-3. $X(z)$ is the z-transform of the input sequence and $Y(z)$ represents the output sequence. The quantization error is represented as white noise $N(z)$. For a zero noise source, the transfer function shows a lowpass characteristic. For a zero signal, the transfer function shows a highpass characteristic. In other words, as the loop integrates the difference between the input signal and the sampled signal, it lowpass filters the signal and highpass filters the noise. If the system is designed so the signal's frequency content is less than the filter's cutoff frequency, the signal will not be affected. Given a first-order noise-shaping loop, with a maximum amplitude sinusoidal input, the maximum signal-to-error ratio will be:

$$S/E \text{ (dB)} = 6.02(N + 1.5L) - 3.41$$

where

N = the number of quantization bits
L = the number of octaves of oversampling.

For example, an A/D converter with sigma-delta first-order noise shaping provides a benefit of 1.5 bits/octave compared to an oversampling converter without a noise-shaping loop.

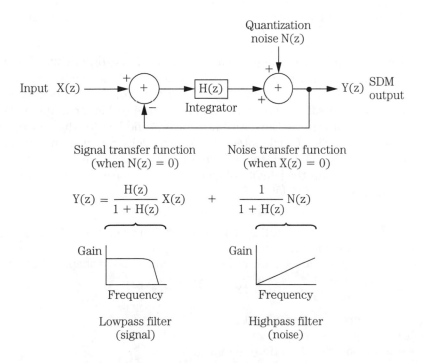

16-3 A z-transform analysis of a sigma-delta modulator. Hauser

The performance of a sigma-delta converter relies on both oversampling, and its noise-shaping characteristic. The quantization noise floor with 1-bit conversion falls from 0 to $f_s/2$ Hz and is quite high, as shown in Fig. 16-4. Quantization noise is reduced with an R oversampling ratio because noise is spread over a 0 to $f_a/2$ Hz spectrum where $f_a = R \times f_s$ Hz. With sigma-delta noise shaping, in-band noise (0 to $f_s/2$) is further decreased and out-of-band noise is increased.

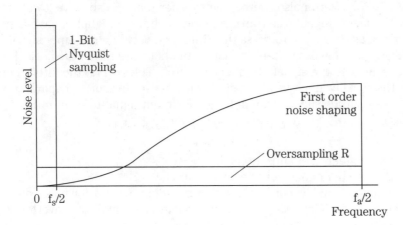

16-4 With 1-bit conversion, quantization noise is quite high. In-band noise is reduced with oversampling. With noise shaping, quantization noise is shifted away from the audio band, further reducing in-band noise.

Figure 16-5 summarizes the mathematical basis of first-order sigma-delta noise shaping. Quantization noise is assumed to be random, and the quantizer is modelled as an additive noise source. Note that the $(1 - z^{-1})$ factor doubles quantized noise power; however, the same factor also shifts the noise to higher frequencies. This sigma-delta modulator forms the basis for many A/D and D/A low-bit converters.

As noted, first-order (single integration) sigma-delta modulation is usually not satisfactory for high-fidelity systems. Higher order loops further decrease in-band quantization noise, with the penalty of increased total noise power. For example, a second-order loop would yield:

$$S/E \text{ (dB)} = 6.02(N + 2.5L) - 11.14.$$

This provides a benefit of 2.5 bits/octave, with a fixed-noise penalty approximately equal to two equivalent bits.

The input/output characteristic of a basic sigma-delta noise shaper of nth order is:

$$Y(z) = X(z) + (1 - z^{-1})^n N(z)$$

where
   $Y(z)$ = the noise-shaped output
   $X(z)$ = the input signal,
     n = the order of the differentiation,
   $N(z)$ = the quantization noise (assumed to be white)

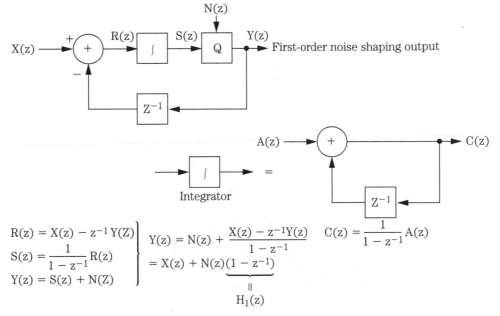

$$R(z) = X(z) - z^{-1}Y(Z)$$
$$S(z) = \frac{1}{1 - z^{-1}}R(z)$$
$$Y(z) = S(z) + N(Z)$$

$$Y(z) = N(z) + \frac{X(z) - z^{-1}Y(z)}{1 - z^{-1}}$$
$$= X(z) + N(z)\underbrace{(1 - z^{-1})}_{\parallel}$$
$$H_1(z)$$

$$C(z) = \frac{1}{1 - z^{-1}}A(z)$$

Where $N(z)$ = requantization noise,
T_a = period of noise shaper sampling frequency.

$$z = e^{j\omega T_a} = \cos \omega T_a - j\sin \omega T_a$$

$$H_1(z) = 1 - z^{-1} = 1 - \cos \omega T_a + j\sin \omega T_a$$

$$|H_1(z)| = \sqrt{2(1 - \cos \omega T_a)} = 2|\sin (\frac{\omega T_a}{2})| = 2|\sin(\frac{\pi f}{f_a})|$$

16-5 Analysis of a first-order sigma-delta noise shaper.

This characteristic can be theoretically comprised of n cascaded digital differentiators. As n increases, the slope in frequency of the shaping function increases, thus it is more effective in suppressing low frequency noise. However, the out-of-band noise could overly burden subsequent analog filters. A successful noise-shaping circuit thus seeks to balance a high oversampling rate with noise-shaping order to reduce in-band noise and shift it away from the audible range. Higher order noise-shaping loops can remove even more in-band noise overall, but relatively more noise is present near the Nyquist frequency. Hence these algorithms are more effective at high over-sampling rates so there is more spectral space between the highest audio frequency and the Nyquist frequency; this allows very simple analog lowpass filters to be used.

Using first-order and higher-order noise-shaping algorithms, a series of noise-shaping curves can be generated, as shown in Fig. 16-6. As higher orders of noise shaping are used, the in-band noise level is decreased. The frequency response curves described by sigma-delta noise-shaping equal unity value at $f_a/6$ Hz where f_a is the noise-shaping oversampling frequency. Noise is reduced only for $f < f_a/6$ Hz, and increased for $f_a/6 < f < f_a/2$ Hz. The noise level reaches a maximum at $f_a/2$ Hz.

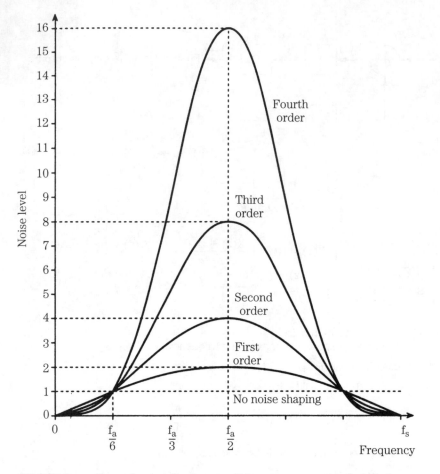

16-6 Higher orders of noise shaping result in more pronounced shifts in re-quantization noise.

As the oversampling rate is increased, the portion of the curve in the audio band is relatively reduced; although the shape of the noise curve remains the same, high oversampling rates relatively decrease in-band noise.

In a traditional noise-shaper design, the poles of the loop filter are at 0 Hz, as in an ideal integrator; this results in zeros in the audio band. In some noise-shaper designs, a technique called zero shifting is used to modify the rising noise spectrum by shifting one or more zeros to the edge of the audio band (for example, 18 kHz). For example, when two zeros are shifted in a third-order noise filter, noise in the range from 13 kHz to 20 kHz can be reduced, but increased below 13 kHz. Overall, the noise measurement is enhanced. However, suppression of idle patterns and thresholding effects can be diminished, thus the zero-shifting technique must be used with care.

Idling Patterns

The low-level linearity of low-order (particularly first-order) sigma-delta noise-shaping circuits can be degraded by idling patterns. Given a zero input signal, a noise shaper can output a regular 1010 pattern. A very low-level input might result in a similar pattern, disturbed by double 1s and 0s. If the period of the repetition of such patterns is long enough, they might fall in the audio baseband, being audible as a deterministic or oscillatory tone, rather than as noise. Because they occur when the channel is idling, these nonlinear patterns are called idling patterns, and result in idle channel noise. The double codes will be generated, or not, depending on the duration of the input signal; the phenomenon is especially characteristic of low-amplitude, high-frequency sinewaves. Because the phenomenon has a frequency dependent threshold level, below which the signal is not coded, the effect is sometimes called thresholding.

First-order sigma-delta noise shapers particularly exhibit these effects because of their stable 1010 patterns. Higher-order noise shapers are much less prone to the problem because their output patterns are less stable. However, in many multistage designs, the effect can occur in each of the cascaded low-order stages. Thus, it is important to add a dither signal in the first stage to disturb any fixed patterns and remove the correlation. Dither is applied most effectively in low-bit converters, and less effectively in 1-bit converters.

One-Bit D/A Conversion with Second-Order Noise Shaping

One implementation of a true 1-bit D/A conversion method is comprised of three elements: oversampling, second-order sigma-delta noise shaping, and pulse-density modulation output. The sampling frequency is increased from 44.1 kHz to 11.2896 MHz, an increase of 256 times. At the same time, the 16-bit signal is converted to a 1-bit signal that reconstructs the audio waveform. The requantization error of the output signal is corrected by feedback; instead of outputting a signal with conventional quantization error, the error undergoes sigma-delta processing to attenuate its in-band level.

The output bit, operating at a frequency of 11.2896 MHz, is converted to an analog signal using a simple switched capacitor network. Specifically, a capacitor is charged and discharged according to the 1 or 0 value of the data; the result is an analog waveform that reflects the encoded waveform through time averaging of the output bit. The network's operation is accurate, and hence the error of the signal is low. There are only positive and negative full-scale reference points; errors in the reference values will generate a gain offset error, but not a linearity error. The offset error can easily be removed. In practice, nonlinearities could result from idle patterns in the noise-shaping circuitry.

Figure 16-7 represents the operation of the 1-bit PDM converter; it performs noise shaping through feedback loops and generates a 1-bit signal for conversion into analog. The noise shaper consists of two integration (filter) loops to reduce in-band requantization noise. The output (H) of the quantizer is +1 if its input is positive (MSB = 0), and –1 if its input is negative (MSB = 1); the 1-bit code output from the quantizer is simply a sign bit. Following a limiting operation designed to prevent overflow, the remainder of each sample is fed back as a quantization error. The error

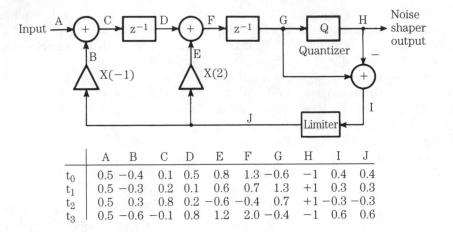

	A	B	C	D	E	F	G	H	I	J
t_0	0.5	−0.4	0.1	0.5	0.8	1.3	−0.6	−1	0.4	0.4
t_1	0.5	−0.3	0.2	0.1	0.6	0.7	1.3	+1	0.3	0.3
t_2	0.5	0.3	0.8	0.2	−0.6	−0.4	0.7	+1	−0.3	−0.3
t_3	0.5	−0.6	−0.1	0.8	1.2	2.0	−0.4	−1	0.6	0.6

16-7 Operation of a second-order noise-shaping circuit. Philips

signal (I) is fed back into the double integration loops. Values inside the loop exceed the unit value; in other words, wider data buses are required. In this case, a 21-bit data bus is used within the loop; signals are processed in two's complement form. Also, if large values are input to the circuit, the limiter would be needed to prevent overloading of the loops. Ideally, with no input signal, the coder should output only a tone at $R \times f_s/2$ Hz where R is the oversampling rate. However, idling patterns can also occur at additional frequencies. To overcome this, dither can be added to the input data so the circuit always operates with a changing signal even when the audio signal is zero or dc.

Figure 16-8 shows the complete system, including the 1-bit PDM noise-shaper modelled above. The first of the three oversampling stages performs four-times oversampling to attenuate image spectra; in addition, first-order noise shaping is performed in the filter. The second stage performs 32-times oversampling. A dither signal (–0 dB at 352 kHz) is added to prevent idling patterns from causing nonlinearity. Two-times oversampling is performed in the third stage. This 17-bit signal (dither adds one bit to the original 16-bit signal) undergoes second-order noise shaping as described above, and a single bit is output from the quantizer. Finally, D/A conversion is accomplished at a 1-bit D/A converter via pulse-density modulation that outputs two valued (±) data at 256-times oversampling, or 11.2896 MHz. A third-order analog lowpass filter removes out-of-band high-frequency components.

The output signal conveys the audio waveform through the density of pulses above and below zero (see Fig. 16-1); this pulse-density modulation signal is converted into an analog signal using a switched dual-capacitor network. Two control signals representing the data stream's logic 0 and logic 1 values control the switching of the capacitors, subject to a clock pulse. During the negative half of the clock, the first capacitor discharges while the second capacitor charges. During the positive half, if the data is a logic 1, the first capacitor is charged by taking a fixed amount of charge from the summing node of an operational amplifier. If the data is logic 0, a fixed charge is transferred into the summing node from the second capacitor. In this

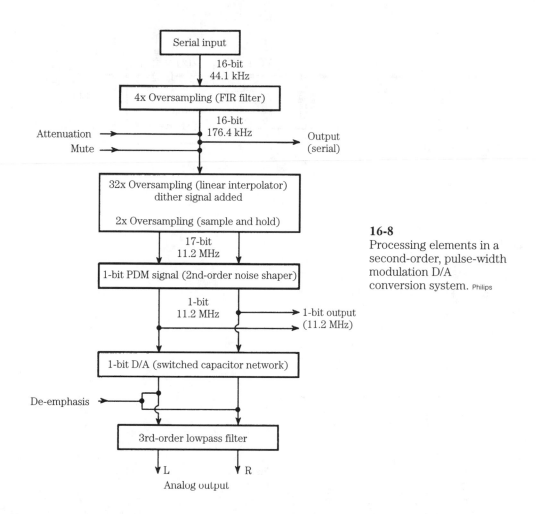

16-8
Processing elements in a second-order, pulse-width modulation D/A conversion system. Philips

way, there are only + and – full scale reference points, and intermediate points are determined by time averaging. There is no MSB change around zero, for example, because zero is represented by an equal number of positive and negative full scale pulses. Zero-cross distortion is thus eliminated. This Bitstream method was developed by Phillips N.V.

In this 1-bit converter, the quantization noise introduced by the word-length reduction is spectrally shaped by a lowpass feedback loop around the quantizer (see Fig. 16-7). Second-order noise shaping is performed:

$$Y(z) = X(z) + (1 - z^{-1})^2 N(z)$$

where $Y(z)$ is the noise-shaped output,

$\quad X(z)$ is the input signal,

$\quad N(z)$ is the quantization noise.

The requantization noise of the output signal is corrected by feedback; noise shaping attenuates its in-band level. As a result, the spectrum of the noise in the out-

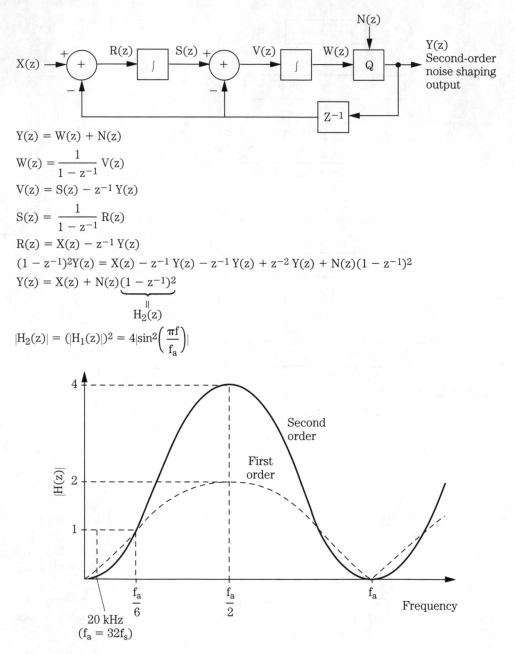

$$Y(z) = W(z) + N(z)$$

$$W(z) = \frac{1}{1 - z^{-1}} V(z)$$

$$V(z) = S(z) - z^{-1} Y(z)$$

$$S(z) = \frac{1}{1 - z^{-1}} R(z)$$

$$R(z) = X(z) - z^{-1} Y(z)$$

$$(1 - z^{-1})^2 Y(z) = X(z) - z^{-1} Y(z) - z^{-1} Y(z) + z^{-2} Y(z) + N(z)(1 - z^{-1})^2$$

$$Y(z) = X(z) + N(z)\underbrace{(1 - z^{-1})^2}_{\substack{\| \\ H_2(z)}}$$

$$|H_2(z)| = (|H_1(z)|)^2 = 4\left|\sin^2\left(\frac{\pi f}{f_a}\right)\right|$$

16-9 Analysis of a second-order noise shaper.

put signal is shifted away from the audio band. Figure 16-9 summarizes the mathematical basis of second-order noise shaping.

Low-Bit D/A Conversion with Third-Order Noise Shaping

One-bit coders with orders higher than two use nonlinear feedback loops that are only conditionally stable and require special design techniques such as limiting to prevent overload, or circuit resetting to prevent oscillation. This can happen when an overload occurs and effectively reduces the magnitude of loop gain, lowering the crossover frequency, where phase shift is too large for stability. As Max Hauser has pointed out, when a loop filter $H(z)$ has three or more integrations, its phase shift can be 180° at the frequency where the loop gain magnitude reaches unity at the crossover frequency. Higher-order noise shapers overcome this with a more complex loop architecture, often using multistage noise shaping; the loop filter $H(z)$ provides a high-order lowpass response at low baseband frequencies, but gain drops to a first- or second-order lowpass response nearer the crossover frequency. This approach provides good in-band noise shaping, with sufficient conditional stability.

The MASH system is a multistage third-order noise-shaping method. One implementation of this design accepts 16-bit words at a nominal sampling frequency, and a digital filter performs 8-times oversampling and outputs 24-bit words. Noise-shaping circuits output 11-valued data, at a 32-times oversampling rate. D/A conversion is accomplished via PWM (pulse-width modulation), outputting the low-bit data at a 768-times oversampling rate.

As noted, generally, if noise-shaping circuits exceed second-order they can be prone to oscillation; to avoid such errors, this third-order implementation uses a multistage configuration. A simplified schematic for the complete noise shaper is shown in Fig. 16-10; it contains a first-order noise shaper in parallel with a second-order noise shaper. The input signal is applied to quantizer Q1 after the error signal through the delay block is subtracted from the input. The signal output from the first loop is also applied to the second loop. The output of quantizer Q2 is differentiated and added to the output of the first loop to form the final output signal. Thus, the requantization error of the first loop is requantized by the second, and canceled by adding the requantized noise to the first loop's signal. The outputs of each stage can be characterized as follows:

$$Y_1(z) = X(z) + (1 - z^{-1})\, N_1(z)$$
$$Y_2(z) = -N_1(z) + (1 - z^{-1})^2\, N_2(z)$$

where $X(z)$ is the input signal, the quantization errors of the local quantizers Q_1 and Q_2 are $N_1(z)$ and $N_2(z)$ respectively, and $Y_1(z)$ and $Y_2(z)$ are the outputs of stages 1 and 2 respectively.

When both sides of the second equation are multiplied by $(1 - z^{-1})$ and this is added to the first equation, observe that the quantization error of the first stage can

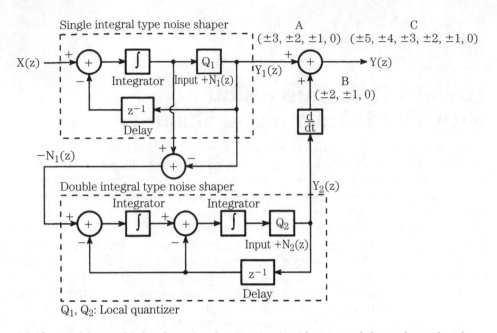

16-10 A multistage third-order noise shaping circuit with output of eleven data values before PWM reconstruction. <small>Matsushita Electric</small>

be canceled. By passing the output of the second stage through a differentiator and adding it to the output of the first stage, the overall circuit output is:

$$Y(z) = X(z) + (1 - z^{-1})^3 N_2(z)$$

In other words, the quantization error $N_2(z)$ is output with a third-order differential characteristic (18 dB/octave), achieving reduced in-band noise compared to first- and second-order characteristics.

Input data is linearly requantized into a multibit output digital signal with seven values (± 3, ± 2, ± 1, and 0) at the main loop, and at the sub-loop the requantization error is requantized into five values (± 2, ± 1, and 0). When these output values are added together, the digital signal output from the circuit represents eleven values (± 5, ± 4, ± 3, ± 2, ± 1, 0). These different data values are shown graphically in Fig. 16-11. Using a vertical scale to represent amplitude of the values, it can be seen that the main loop outputs seven values of rough accuracy, and the subloop outputs five values with high frequency content, used to eliminate the requantization error of the main loop. When summed, eleven values are output from the shaper to reconstruct the audio signal.

The final element in the system is D/A conversion. The 11-valued signal is converted into pulses, each with a width corresponding to one value, as shown in Fig. 16-12A. This can be accomplished by applying the 4-bit output of the shaper to a ROM to map 11 amplitude steps into 22 time steps with constant amplitude. For example, the figure shows the PWM waveforms resulting from the 0, +3, and –3 output values. In actuality, waveforms representing ± 5, ± 4, ± 3, ± 2, ± 1, and 0 are all output.

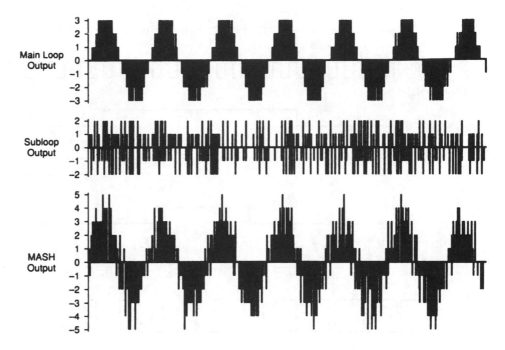

16-11 A graphical representation of the data values in a multistage noise shaper.
Matsushita Electric

The widest pulses translate into a large positive output, and the narrowest pulses translate into a large negative output, as shown in Fig. 16-12B. The width of the pulses carries the vital information; the amplitude of this signal can only be high or low; at this point the signal has the form of PWM binary data. Because timing accuracy can be achieved through crystal oscillators, the widths are very accurate, and hence signal error is low. The relatively coarse quantization permits accurate pulse timing by synchronizing pulse edges to the oversampling clock. Positive- and negative-going pulses are output, to cancel common noise. This 33.8688-MHz ($768 \times f_s$) low-bit data forms a PWM representation of the waveform; Figure 16-13 shows the spectrum of a 20-kHz input signal. Proof of performance can be evaluated by measuring the in-band noise of the system; it is below −100 dB. MASH was co-developed by Matsushita Electric Industrial and Nippon Telegraph and Telephone Corporation. Figure 16-14 summarizes the mathematical basis of third-order noise shaping.

Low-Bit D/A Conversion with Quasi Fourth-Order Noise Shaping

Victor Advanced Noise Shaping (VANS) is an example of a low-bit D/A converter architecture using eight-times oversampling, a quasi fourth-order noise shaper, and pulse-edge modulation conversion. The noise shaper uses four loop filters in a configuration that yields in-band performance equivalent to fourth-order noise shaping.

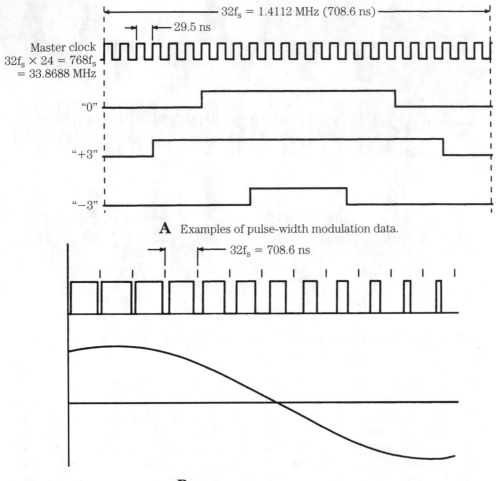

A Examples of pulse-width modulation data.

B Reconstruction of analog waveform.

16-12 Pulse-width modulation data is output from a MASH converter.

The VANS circuit is designed to operate like a fourth-order noise shaper at audible frequencies, gradually shifting toward second-order noise shaping at higher frequencies. This provides stability, yet improves performance in the audio band.

Thirty-two times oversampling is performed, and the output clock frequency is 16.9344 MHz ($384 \times f_s$). With pulse edge modulation, input data is converted into a binary pulse train with 15 discrete values (± 7, ± 6, ± 5, ± 4, ± 3, ± 2, ± 1, 0). A differential configuration is used in which the rise of the leading edge of a pulse, and the fall of the trailing edge of a pulse are output by two independent pulse edge modulation converters, as shown in Fig. 16-15A. This determines the width of the pulse. Two converters output pulse trains A and C based on the input signal, and an analog subtractor generates a composite (A-C) signal determined by the leading and trailing

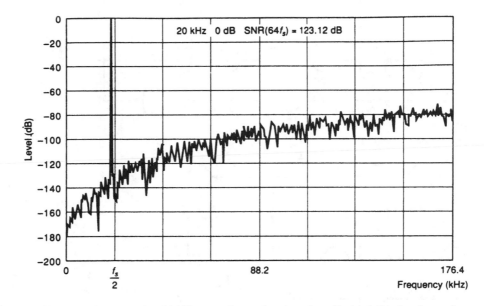

16-13 Reproduction of a 20-kHz waveform showing the effect of third-order noise shaping. _{Matsushita Electric}

edges of the pulse trains. This signal can take either a positive or negative value, as shown in Fig. 16-15B. For example, data representing a –1 value would generate a short negative-going pulse, but data representing a +5 value would generate a longer positive-going pulse. When time averaged, these values create the analog waveform, as in pulse-width modulation. VANS pulse edge-conversion method was devised by Victor Company of Japan. Figure 16-16 summarizes the mathematical basis of this quasi fourth-order noise shaping.

Low-Bit A/D Conversion

Digital audio recorders have traditionally relied on successive approximation A/D conversion. These A/D converters compare the unknown input with accurately known fractions of a reference voltage. Starting with the largest fraction and rejecting any fraction that causes the sum to be larger than the unknown input, k iterations are required for a k-bit word conversion. The input oversampling rates (and conversely, the order of the input filters) are limited by the relatively low speed at which these A/D converters can operate. Hence, brick-wall filters are used. Conventional A/D converters, either directly or through associated circuitry such as brick-wall filters, can contribute substantial distortion to the signal.

One way to improve the linearity of conversion is to increase word length; thus, longer word length multibit A/D converters have been introduced. These converters improve performance, but resolution is generally constrained to 18 bits. Thus a variety of oversampling chips, using low-bit architectures, have been introduced to remedy the ills of conventional input filtering and A/D conversion. First- and second-order

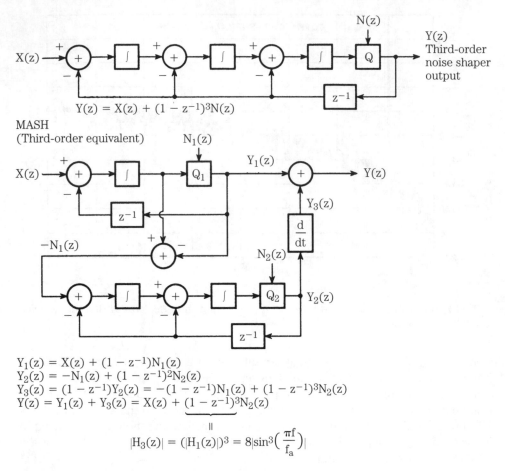

$$Y(z) = X(z) + (1 - z^{-1})^3 N(z)$$

MASH
(Third-order equivalent)

$$Y_1(z) = X(z) + (1 - z^{-1})N_1(z)$$
$$Y_2(z) = -N_1(z) + (1 - z^{-1})^2 N_2(z)$$
$$Y_3(z) = (1 - z^{-1})Y_2(z) = -(1 - z^{-1})N_1(z) + (1 - z^{-1})^3 N_2(z)$$
$$Y(z) = Y_1(z) + Y_3(z) = X(z) + \underbrace{(1 - z^{-1})^3 N_2(z)}$$
$$\|$$
$$|H_3(z)| = (|H_1(z)|)^3 = 8|\sin^3\left(\frac{\pi f}{f_a}\right)|$$

16-14 Analysis of a third-order noise shaper.

A/D converters provide limited quality, and idling patterns can produce audible tones in the noise floor. Attention has turned to higher-order A/D converters that give good performance and are free of idling patterns. Care must be taken to prevent oscillation from modulation overload.

In theory, oversampling A/D conversion is simple: the input signal is first passed through a simple RC analog anti-aliasing filter, and then sampled at a very high rate to extend the Nyquist frequency. After quantization, the signal passes through a digital filter to prevent aliasing and reduce the sampling frequency to a standard frequency (that is, 44.1 or 48 kHz) for storage or processing using normal methods.

In practice, other factors play a role. Only coarse quantization is possible at the highly oversampled rate; this results in a high noise floor. Although noise is spread over a large oversampled spectrum, it is unsatisfactorily high. Noise shaping must be used to reduce in-band noise. In addition, a conventional digital filter with satisfactory passband response and stopband attenuation cannot operate at this highly oversampled rate. Rather, a digital decimation filter, operating as a lowpass filter, is used;

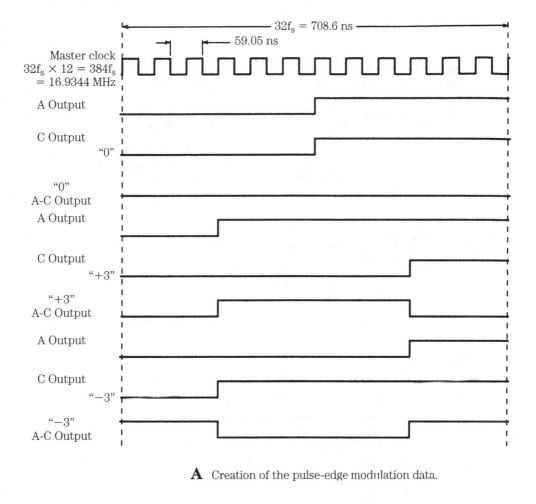

A Creation of the pulse-edge modulation data.

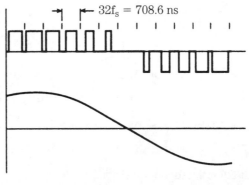

B Reconstruction of the analog waveform.

16-15 The VANS architecture uses a differential configuration to determine rising and falling edges of the output pulse. A. Creation of the pulse-edge modulation data. B. Reconstruction of the analog waveform. Victor Company of Japan

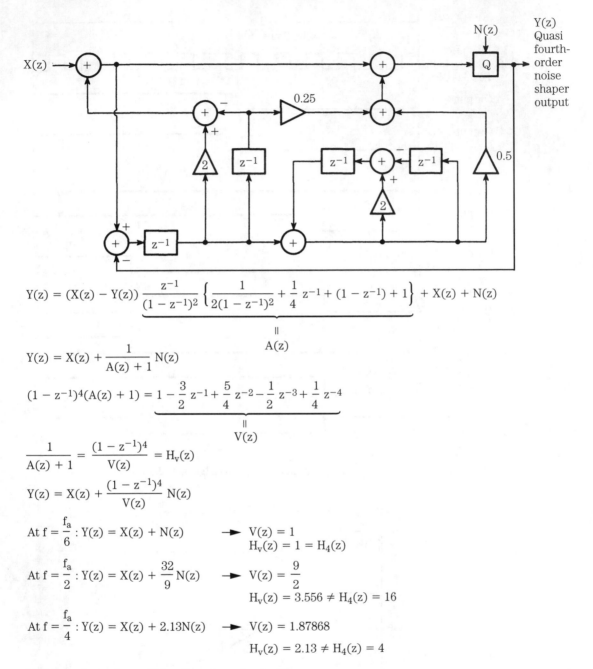

$$Y(z) = (X(z) - Y(z)) \underbrace{\frac{z^{-1}}{(1 - z^{-1})^2} \left\{ \frac{1}{2(1 - z^{-1})^2} + \frac{1}{4} z^{-1} + (1 - z^{-1}) + 1 \right\}}_{\substack{\| \\ A(z)}} + X(z) + N(z)$$

$$Y(z) = X(z) + \frac{1}{A(z) + 1} N(z)$$

$$(1 - z^{-1})^4 (A(z) + 1) = \underbrace{1 - \frac{3}{2} z^{-1} + \frac{5}{4} z^{-2} - \frac{1}{2} z^{-3} + \frac{1}{4} z^{-4}}_{\substack{\| \\ V(z)}}$$

$$\frac{1}{A(z) + 1} = \frac{(1 - z^{-1})^4}{V(z)} = H_v(z)$$

$$Y(z) = X(z) + \frac{(1 - z^{-1})^4}{V(z)} N(z)$$

At $f = \dfrac{f_a}{6}$: $Y(z) = X(z) + N(z)$ $\longrightarrow$ $V(z) = 1$
$\phantom{At f = \dfrac{f_a}{6} : Y(z) = X(z) + N(z) \longrightarrow}$ $H_v(z) = 1 = H_4(z)$

At $f = \dfrac{f_a}{2}$: $Y(z) = X(z) + \dfrac{32}{9} N(z)$ $\longrightarrow$ $V(z) = \dfrac{9}{2}$
$\phantom{At f = \dfrac{f_a}{2} : Y(z) = X(z) + \dfrac{32}{9} N(z) \longrightarrow}$ $H_v(z) = 3.556 \neq H_4(z) = 16$

At $f = \dfrac{f_a}{4}$: $Y(z) = X(z) + 2.13 N(z)$ $\longrightarrow$ $V(z) = 1.87868$
$\phantom{At f = \dfrac{f_a}{4} : Y(z) = X(z) + 2.13 N(z) \longrightarrow}$ $H_v(z) = 2.13 \neq H_4(z) = 4$

16-16 Analysis of a quasi fourth-order noise shaper.

its computation requirements are far easier. When a low-bit quantizer is used, in conjunction with noise shaping, the decimation filter must remove out-of-band quantization noise; this effectively increases the resolution of the digital output. An analog lowpass filter is required at the input to remove the frequency components that cannot be removed by the digital filter; however, because the preliminary sampling rate is high, the analog lowpass filter is low order. The filter must remove any frequency components outside the audio band to prevent aliasing between the audio signals and the resulting lower sampling rate. This would occur when the output of the digital filter is resampled (undersampled) at the lower downstream sampling rate.

Oversampling A/D converters are unusual in that the basic A/D elements of anti-alias filtering, sampling, and quantization are merged throughout the subsections of the converter. For example, anti-alias filtering occurs in both the input analog filter, and in the digital decimation filter. Although conventional A/D converters only perform quantization, oversampling A/D converters are complete signal acquisition interfaces.

A diagram illustrating oversampling A/D conversion is shown in Fig. 16-17. The input signal is first passed through a simple analog anti-aliasing filter, and the input signal is sampled at a very fast rate (for example, $f_a = 64 \times f_s$) to extend the Nyquist frequency. The signal is applied to a coarse quantizer such as a sigma-delta converter, which adds (shaped) noise to the signal. The digital data is lowpass filtered with a cutoff at the Nyquist frequency; this removes out-of-band noise components to prevent anti-aliasing. Finally, the signal is resampled at a lower rate (for example, 44.1 or 48 kHz) for storage or processing using normal methods. A decimation lowpass filter bandlimits the wideband signal (to 20 kHz in Fig. 16-17) so that aliasing will not occur when the signal is subsampled at the lower output frequency. A sample-and-hold circuit is not needed because an input sample can be taken during every internal clock cycle, but in successive approxi-

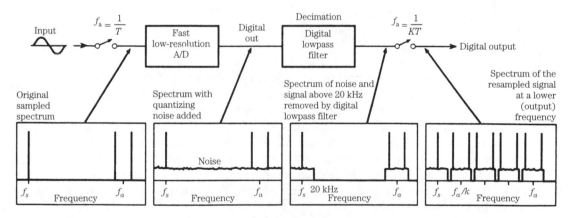

16-17 Diagram showing the theory of oversampling A/D conversion. Adams

mation converters the sampled analog value must be held for the number of clock cycles equal to the number of bits being converted.

Sigma-Delta A/D Modulator

A sigma-delta modulator can be used to create the low-bit coding from the low-pass filtered input analog signal. A first-order sigma-delta A/D modulator is shown in Fig. 16-18. The modulator accepts a sampled analog signal, performs quantizing and outputs, for example, a 1-bit signal. A low-resolution (1-bit quantizer) D/A converter operating at a high sampling rate is placed in a feedback loop. The input to the loop filter is the difference between the input signal and the quantized output converted back to an analog signal; this difference is theoretically equal to the quantization error. Because a coarse (1-bit A/D) quantizer is used, quantization error at sampling time is large. The coarse output signal is averaged by the decimation filter, interpolating over several samples (64 or so) to achieve a precise result. High resolution (manifested as dynamic range) is achieved through noise shaping. The noise shaping in a sigma-delta circuit is the inverse of the transfer function of the $(1 - z^{-1})^{-1}$ filter. A filter with higher gain at low frequencies is thus desired to attenuate audio band noise. This transfer function is essentially a highpass filter; noise is thus shifted to a higher frequency. Because the input sampling rate is high, a simple one-pole RC anti-alias filter suffices.

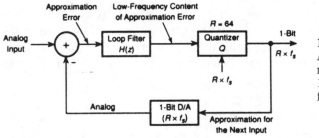

16-18
A first-order sigma-delta modulation circuit showing a 1-bit D/A converter in the feedback loop.

Instead of a 1-bit code, converters might produce a low-bit word of three or four bits using, for example, a sigma-delta modulator modified to contain a multibit quantizer. The dynamic range increases in proportion to the resolution of the quantizer; however, this must be balanced against operating speed. Because the output is proportional to the signal's amplitude rather than slope, it is like a PCM converter. Unlike a conventional PCM converter, the noise floor rises with increasing frequency. Alternatively, a differential pulse code modulator differs from a delta modulator only in that the error signal is quantized to more than one bit. For example, a flash converter could be used inside the loop.

Numerous sigma-delta methods have been applied to A/D conversion, all using a high input sample rate, and noise shaping: Single and dual integrator loops, cascaded first-order sigma-delta loops, and multi-bit quantizers with loop filters. The first two methods use true 1-bit coders with inherent linearity. The third method uses several bits, and noise is reduced in proportion to the number of quantizer levels used. However the converter's linearity depends on the linearity of the quantizer. In any case, noise performance hinges on the oversampling rate and order of noise shaping used. Some converter architectures use several first- or second-order sigma-delta coders in combination to achieve higher order, stable noise shaping.

Given a second-order sigma-delta modulator, Charles Thompson has demonstrated that M-bit resolution requires an oversampling rate:

$$R = \left[\left(\frac{\pi^2}{5^{1/2}}\right) \times 10^{6M/20}\right]^{2/5}$$

where R is the oversampling rate defined by:

$$R = \frac{f_a}{f_s}$$

where f_s is the output sampling frequency

f_a is the oversampling frequency.

Thus, 16-bit resolution would require an oversampling rate of 150. A 100-kHz output sampling frequency would necessitate a filter sampling frequency of 15 MHz; this is difficult to achieve. If the order of noise shaping is raised to third-order, the required oversampling rate is described by:

$$R = \left[\left(\frac{\pi^3}{7^{1/2}}\right) \times 10^{6M/20}\right]^{2/7}$$

Thus, the required oversampling ratio is 48; this is well within practical design limits.

Depending on its order and design, a sigma-delta feedback loop generally consists of the following operations: subtraction of output from input to find the approximation error, filtering to extract the low-frequency content of the approximation error, low-bit D/A conversion of the output code into a signal to subtract it from input analog signal, and quantization to output a low-bit approximation for the next input sample. In practice, a third-order loop can be used to shape the noise toward higher frequencies, where it is removed by the subsequent decimation (undersampling) filter. As with any noise-shaping loop, the signal must be properly dithered to overcome idling tones and other artifacts. In some cases, a dither signal can be applied so that its fundamental and harmonics can be removed by the decimation filter.

Decimation filter

As Robert Adams has pointed out, oversampling converters provide high resolution not by decreasing the error between the analog input and the digital output, but by making the error occur more often. In this way the error spectrum moves beyond the audio passband and although total noise power is high, in-band noise power is low. The high bit rate is reduced to more manageable rates through decimation in which a discrete time signal is sampled at a rate lower than the original rate. Decimation provides both an averaging (lowpass) filter, and rate reduction; it can be described through a simple example. Sixteen 1-bit values could be reduced through a 16:1 decimation to a single multibit value; for example, values 1,0,1,0,0,1,0,1,1,0,1,1,1,1,0,0 would be decimated to 9/16, or 0.5625. Because there is only one (multibit) output value for every 16 input values, the decimator has decreased the sampling rate by 16:1. As Sangil Park has shown, it is also important to note that decimation has increased resolution; in this example, the input signal is only one bit, but the decimation (averaging) process yields 4-bit resolution ($2^4 = 16$) while reducing the sampling rate. Thus oversampling followed by decimation demonstrates how speed can be exchanged for resolution. The meaning of the word decimation, incidently, originally referred to losing one-tenth of an army in battle.

The decimation process lowpass filters the signal and noise in the low-bit code, bandlimiting the 1-bit code prior to sample rate reduction to remove alias components. Decimation also replaces the low-bit coding with 16-bit coding, for example, at a lower sampling rate. However, the computation rate of the filter is not trivial; output samples cannot be discarded (providing decimation) until the filtering computation is complete.

Ideally, the decimation filter would provide a sharp lowpass cutoff at half the output sampling frequency, thus upholding the Nyquist sampling theorem. However, as Robert Adams has shown, this is not practical; for example, a FIR filter would require many coefficients because of the high ratio of input sampling rate to output sampling rate. A practical approach uses two or more stages of decimation, operating at intermediate sampling frequencies. For example, the first decimation stage might be a low-order, high-speed filter, and the second stage a high-order, low-speed filter. If the first stage resamples at an intermediate frequency f_i, it would appear that all frequencies above $f_i/2$ must be rejected to prevent subsequent aliasing. However, only certain portions of the spectrum will alias in the audio band, thus the decimation filter need only attenuate those frequency bands. In particular, these alias bands can be identified:

$$f_{alias} = I \times f_i \pm BW \text{ Hz}$$

where I = any integer,

f_i = the decimation filter's intermediate resampling frequency,

BW = the audio bandwidth (for example, 20 kHz).

For example, if $f_i = 96$ kHz, the bands of interest will lie at $96, 2 \times 96, 3 \times 96$ kHz, etc., each occupying a width of 40 kHz. The decimation filter can be designed so that its frequencies of maximum attenuation will coincide with these potentially aliasing frequency bands. A filter with pockets of attenuation, rather than attenuation across the entire stopband, is much easier to implement. As the sampling rate is decreased from one stage to the next, the pockets become proportionally wider and filter complexity increases, but intense computation is performed at the slower rate. In this way, each filter must only reject the signals that would be aliased by the immediate next decimation. Subsequent filters will reject signals that would alias with later decimation. As Sangil Park points out, a comb filter is an expedient choice because its design does not require a multiplier (all coefficients are unity). However, comb filters cannot wholly remove out-of-band quantization noise so they are followed by additional filter stages of other design. These additional stages can also be needed to compensate for high-frequency drooping caused by the comb filter. A final filter, operating at the slowest sampling rate, could provide a true lowpass characteristic, and correct any frequency-response deviations. A comb filter of length R is an FIR filter with coefficients equal to unity; its transfer function is:

$$H(z) = \sum_{n=0}^{R-1} z^{-n}$$

In other words, this expression shows a moving average. For example, if $R = 4$:

$$y(n) = x(n) + x(n-1) + x(n-2) + x(n-3)$$

In recursive form, the transfer function can be written as:

$$H(z) = \frac{(1 - z^{-R})}{(1 - z^{-1})}$$

This can be expressed in terms of integration followed by differentiation:

$$Y(z) = (1 - z^{-1})^{-1}(1 - z^{-R})X(z)$$

This single-stage comb filter decimator can be easily realized, as shown in Fig. 16-19A. Not only is no storage required for the filter coefficients, but the burden of intermediate computations is decreased owing to the low sampling rate at the differentiator. In addition, the same topology can be used for higher orders of rate change. As noted, in practice a single comb filter stage does not provide sufficient stopband attenuation to prevent aliasing thus cascaded stages are often used, as shown in Fig. 16-19B. In this example, four sections are cascaded, requiring eight data registers and $4(R+1)$ additions per input sample. As noted, the comb filter is designed for maximum attenuation at higher frequency components that would alias after rate decimation. Figure 16-19C shows the spectrum with first-, second-, third-, and fourth-order cascaded comb filter sections.

In some decimator designs, the cascaded comb filter is followed by a FIR filter; the intermediate-rate output from the comb filter is further decimated and the FIR section provides sharp filtering when the sampling frequency is reduced to nominal values (for example, 44.1 kHz). The decimation factor is typically lower in the FIR section as compared to that in the comb filter section; however, the FIR must provide extreme stopband attenuation. In addition, the FIR section can provide compensation for audio band droop caused by the comb filter. FIR computation also provides linear phase response.

Consider an example in which low-bit coding takes place at 64×44.1 kHz = 2.8224 MHz. The decimation filter can have two stages. With a $64 \times f_s$ Hz input bit stream, the first stage can generate a multibit output sample at a sampling frequency of $2 \times f_s$ Hz. The second stage of the decimation filter can use a multibit multiplier with convolution performed at the output sampling frequency of f_s Hz. In all, the decimation filter provides a stopband from 20 kHz to the half-sampling frequency of 1.4112 MHz. The analog filter at the system's input is modest, perhaps first- or second-order, ensuring phase linearity in the audio band.

The use of low-bit coding as the intermediate phase of A/D conversion simplifies the filter design. For example, a new output sample is not required for every input bit. Because the decimation factor is 64 (in this example), an output is required only for every 64 input bits. In practice, the decimation filtering might be carried out in two stages. A FIR filter would commonly be used for down-sampling, because its nonrecursive operation would simplify computation to one sample every $1/f_s$ second. Following decimation, the result can be rounded to 16 bits, and output at a 44.1-kHz sampling frequency. Figure 16-20 summarizes the operation of a low-bit A/D converter in the frequency domain.

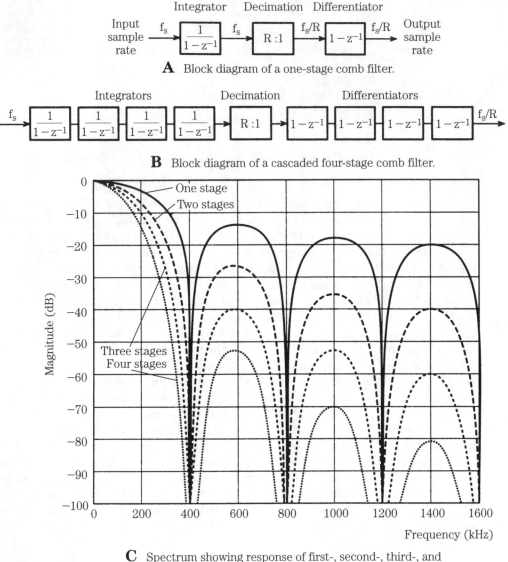

A Block diagram of a one-stage comb filter.

B Block diagram of a cascaded four-stage comb filter.

C Spectrum showing response of first-, second-, third-, and fourth-order cascaded comb filter sections.

16-19 Use of comb filters for decimation. Park

Digital audio equipment containing A/D (and D/A) converters must have a stable sampling clock that in turn is phase locked to a distributed master clock. The individual clocks must have very low jitter levels to prevent generated sidebands from rising to audibility. For example, a 16-bit A/D converter would require jitter of less than 250 ps. Jitter is proportionally greater per period for a sigma-delta A/D converter than a multibit converter. Amplitude errors attributable to jitter increase as the input signal frequency increases; however, because the slew rate of the input signal is equal in

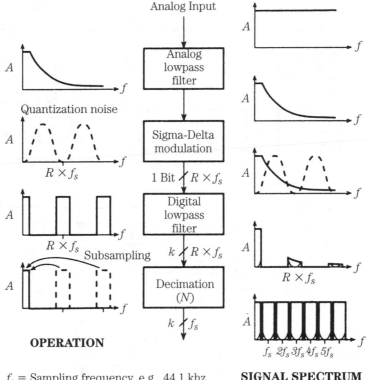

f_s = Sampling frequency, e.g., 44.1 khz
k = Number of bits/sample, e.g., 16
R = Oversampling Rate

16-20 Summary of spectral characteristics of a 1-bit A/D converter.
Philips

either type of converter, the amplitude error resulting from sinusoidal jitter is also equal in both cases. In the case of noise-induced jitter, added noise is distributed over the sigma-delta converter's increased Nyquist frequency range and lowpass filtered by the decimation circuit. Hence overall in-band jitter-induced noise is less than in a conventional converter. Thus analysis would show that oversampling sigma-delta A/D converters are no more sensitive to sinusoidal jitter than a conventional converter, and are less susceptible to random noise clock jitter. However, actual performance depends on a converter's design. Time-base correction is discussed in chapter 4.

A Low-Bit A/D Converter Chip

The block diagram of a sigma-delta A/D converter chip is shown in Fig. 16-21. It is a linear 16-bit converter, using 64-times oversampling, providing output sampling frequencies up to 100 kHz, operating up to 6.4 MHz. The use of sigma-delta processing obviates the need for a brick-wall anti-aliasing filter and sample-and-hold circuit. As with other sigma-delta A/D converters, the input signal is oversampled to extend

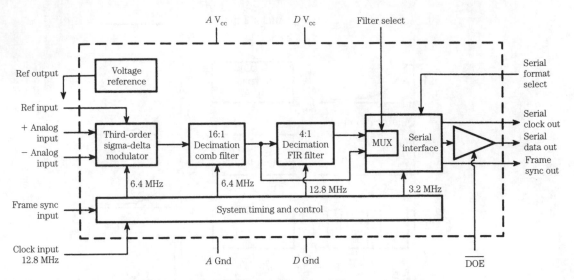

16-21 Internal block diagram of a DSP56ADC16 sigma-delta A/D converter. Kloker, et al.

the noise spectrum well beyond the audio band. Noise shaping reduces noise in the audio band, and lowpass filtering removes out-of-band quantization noise. Finally, the signal is decimated to reduce the sample rate commensurate with the audio band and increase resolution.

The converter is designed around four major blocks: third-order sigma-delta modulator and noise shaper, 16:1 decimation comb filter, 4:1 decimation FIR filter, and serial interface. The third-order noise shaper places an 18 dB/octave characteristic on the quantization noise. The analog front end to the converter consists of three differential, switched-capacitor, linear integrators. Filtering and decimation are performed in two steps to reduce the complexity of the digital filter. For example, to achieve the desired stopband attenuation and filter steepness, a single stage FIR with over 2800 taps would be required. Use of a multirate decimation filter system also allows a dual mode application. The output of the modulator is filtered by a fourth-order comb filter and decimated; the sampling rate is decreased by a factor of 16:1. A comb filter is used because it contains only adders and delay, without need for multiplication. The first stage comb filter accomplishes initial filtering as well as decimation of the input sampling rate by a factor of 16:1. Its z-domain transfer function can be expressed as:

$$H(z) = \frac{(1 - z^{-16})^4}{(1 - z^{-1})^4}$$

The equivalent frequency domain transfer function is:

$$H(f) = \left[\frac{1 \sin (16\pi f/f_s)}{16 \sin (\pi f/f_s)} \right]^4$$

where f_s Hz is the filter sampling frequency.

An FIR filter is used to decimate the signal by a 4:1 factor with a lowpass response. Overall, a 64:1 decimation ratio is achieved; in other words, 63 of every 64 output samples are discarded. A stopband attenuation of –96 dB is achieved. To compensate for the response (passband droop) of the fourth-order comb filter, the FIR uses an inverse equalization response to achieve an overall flat response. FIR images occur at multiples of the comb filter output sampling rate; these are also zeros in the fourth-order comb response. The FIR stopband attenuates the comb response, leaving a negligible alias component at the overlap of the two responses. In all, this digital filter section is the equivalent of a 30th-order analog Bessel filter. The output sampling frequency is 100 kHz, with 16-bit resolution and S/N ratio of 90 dB.

Because the cutoff frequencies of the comb and FIR filters are scaled by the input sampling rate, the converter can be used with any arbitrary sampling rate without changing component values. For further flexibility, this A/D converter chip is designed so the 16:1 comb filter can be connected directly to a serial output. This permits operation at faster speed (output sampling frequency of 400 kHz) at the expense of lower resolution (12 bit, and S/N of 72 dB). This is useful for ultrasonic applications and where lower resolution is tolerable. A general application for this chip using its full resolution is shown in Fig. 16-22; the A/D converter is connected to a DSP processor. The DSP56ADC16 A/D converter was developed by Motorola.

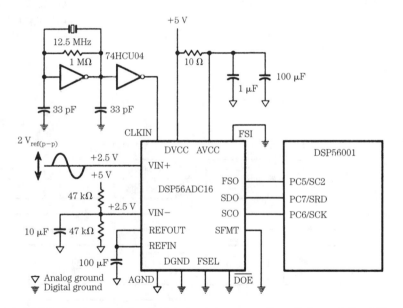

16-22 Application circuit showing interconnection of sigma-delta A/D converter (single-ended mode) and DSP processor. Motorola

A Low-Bit A/D-D/A Converter Chip

Because of the high degree of integration permitted by sigma-delta conversion methods, it is possible to place a linear, 16-bit sigma-delta analog-to-digital and digital-to-analog converter on a single chip. One such chip permits input-output sampling frequencies up to 50 kHz with 16-bit resolution, and frequencies of 100 kHz with 12-bit resolution. Third-order noise shaping is used on the A/D side, and fourth-order noise shaping is used on the D/A side. The A/D section uses 64-times over-sampling, and 64-times decimation. A digital compensation circuit is used to equalize the response to within ±0.025-dB ripple in the passband, with phase linearity. The D/A section uses two digital anti-imaging interpolation filters, along with a FIR compensation filter for flat passband response. The D/A section provides a 1-bit output signal. An analog sixth-order Bessel lowpass filter is provided on-chip, as is a temperature-compensated voltage reference for stable coding and clocking. This reference can operate in a master/slave configuration to ensure gain matching/tracking between multiple devices. Likewise sampling coherency can be preserved between multiple converter chips to ensure interchannel phase accuracy. Digital data can be shifted into and out of the converters with either MSB or LSB first. A SSI bus can be implemented in several different modes.

The DSP56ADA16 provides a dynamic range of 96 dB and signal-to-noise ratio of 90 dB. A block diagram of the DSP56ADA16 is shown in Fig. 16-23. As with all sigma-delta converters, this converter pair is based on digital filtering techniques, thus approximately 90% of the chip is given to digital circuitry; this promotes compatibility, reliability, increased functionality, and reduced chip cost. Two of these chips forms a complete conversion circuit for a stereo signal, and together with a DSP5600x chip form a complete digital signal processing system. The DSP56ADA16 was developed by Motorola.

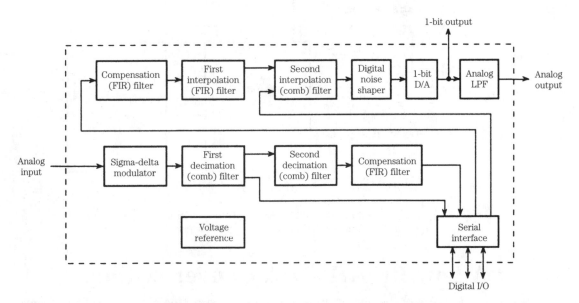

16-23 Block diagram of a DSP56ADA16 sigma-delta analog-to-digital and digital-to-analog converter chip.
Motorola

Noise Shaping of Nonoversampling Quantization Error

As noted, noise shaping is prerequisite in any low-bit system, to preserve dynamic range when a signal is represented with a reduced number of bits. For example, the noise-shaping characteristic of sigma-delta converters allows 1-bit quantization. However, noise shaping can be applied in a variety of ways. For example, a noise-shaping feedback loop can be placed around a quantizer, as shown in Fig. 16-24. This noise-shaping loop uses the known characteristics of the error generated by the word length reduction (requantization) to alter the spectrum of the requantization noise error. Recursion places the error information back into the signal, much like negative feedback is used to reduce distortion in analog amplifiers. The quantizer's output error is fed back through a filter and subtracted from the quantizer's input. Because only the difference between the input and output of the quantizer is fed back, the input signal is not affected. The configuration alters the frequency response of the error signal, but not that of the audio signal, it has the effect of passing the noise through the filter, not the signal.

However, with proper dither, the error is white, and the $H(z)$ filter in the feedback loop spectrally shapes the output error by $1 - H(z)$; that is, the output error e becomes: $[1 - H(z)]e$. The noise is shaped by the inverse of the loop transfer function; when a low-pass filter is placed in the loop, the noise spectrum rises with frequency. A filter with high gain at low frequencies yields improved baseband attenuation of noise; higher-order functions provide a higher-order difference operation on quantizer error, with greater attenuation of baseband noise. The frequency response of the requantization noise can be creatively manipulated by the filter in the feedback loop. For example, the filter's parameters could be dynamically adapted so that the error noise is always optimally masked by the audio signal. The feedback loop must incorporate at least a one-sample z^{-1} delay; the error cannot be processed until after it has been created by quantization. Theory also dictates that $1 - H(z)$ must be minimum phase (all poles and zeros within the z-plane unit circle) to preserve the capacity of the channel.

Referring again to Fig. 16-24, John Vanderkooy and Stanley Lipshitz have pointed out that $H(z)$ represents a loop error that is subtracted from the input at each next sample. This corrects for any such errors on average and gives a highpass shape to both quantization and dither signals present inside the loop. A digital dither signal applied as shown (inside the shaping loop) is identical to a highpass filtered dither signal applied at a point outside the loop prior to the quantizer. Figure 16-25A shows the spectrum of the quantized output of an undithered noise shaper when a 937.5-Hz signal of 1 LSB peak amplitude (approximately –90.3 dB) is passed though an undithered requantizer. The spectrum shows many correlated errors with this low-level input signal. When triangular pdf digital dither is applied, a highly uncorrelated spectrum results, as shown in Fig. 16-25B. The quantizer and the dither signal noise are both shaped by the loop. A rectangular pdf dither signal could be applied, but could result in noise modulation and limit cycle oscillation. Alternatively, a highpass triangular pdf dither could be applied; requantization noise is shaped as before,

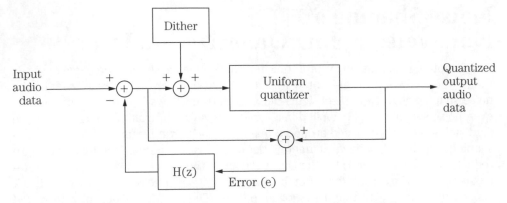

16-24 A requantization topology showing dithering and noise shaping. This processing reduces quantization distortion artifacts and can be used to reduce the noise floor in perceptually critical frequency regions.

but the higher frequency dither signal is shaped to even higher frequencies. However, correlation can result in higher overall noise. In this example, triangular pdf dither with a white spectrum appears to yield the best results.

Psychoacoustically Optimized Noise Shaping

It is the goal of noise-shaping systems to dither the audio signal, then shape quantization noise to yield a less audible noise floor. These systems consider the fact that total noise power does not fully describe audibility of noise; perceived loudness also depends on spectral characteristics. Oversampling noise shapers reduce audioband quantization noise and increase noise beyond the audio band, where it is inaudible. Nonoversampling noise shapers only redistribute noise energy within the audio band itself. For example, the difference in quantization noise between a 20-bit input signal and 16-bit output signal can be reshaped to minimize its audibility. In particular, psychoacoustically optimized noise-shaping systems use a feedback filter designed to shape the noise according to an equal loudness contour or other perceptual weighting function. In addition, such systems can use masking properties to conceal requantization noise.

Sixteen-bit master recordings are not adequate for subsequent replication on 16-bit CDs. For example, when using a digital console or hard-disk workstation to add equalization, change levels, or perform other digital signal processing, error accumulates in the 16th bit due to computation. It is desirable to use a longer word length, such as 20 bits, that allows processing prior to 16-bit storage. Furthermore, with proper transfer, much information contained in the four LSBs can be conveyed in the upper 16 bits. However, the problem of transferring 20 bits to 16 bits is not trivial. Simple truncation of the four least-significant bits greatly increases distortion. If the 16th bit is rounded, the improvement is only modest. It is thus important to redither the signal during the requantization that occurs in the transfer; this provides the same benefits as dithering during the original recording. If the most significant bit has not been exercised in the recording, it is possible to bit-shift the entire

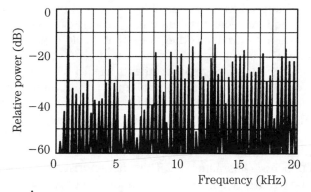

A Spectrum of signal with undithered noise shaper.

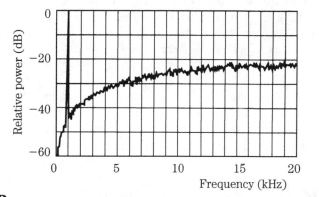

B Spectrum of signal with triangular pdf-dithered noise shaper.

16-25 Dither profoundly affects the spectrum of the signal output from a noise-shaping circuit. Vanderkooy and Lipshitz

program upward, thus preserving more of the dynamic range. This is accomplished with a simple gain change in the digital domain. It can be argued that in some cases, for example, when transferring from an analog master tape, a 20-bit interface and noise shaping are not needed because the tape's noise floor makes it self-dithering. However, even then it is important to preserve the analog noise floor, which contains useful audio information.

Nonoversampling noise-shaping systems are often used when converting a professional master recording to a consumer format such as CD. With linear conversion, and dither, a 16-bit recording can provide a distortion floor below −110 dB. Noise shaping cannot decrease total unweighted noise, but given a 20-bit master tape, subjective performance can be improved by decreasing noise in the critical 1- to 5-kHz region, at the expense of increasing noise in the noncritical 15-kHz region, and increasing total unweighted noise power as well. Because noise shaping removes requantization noise in the most critical region, this noise cannot mask audible details, thus improving subjective resolution. However, the benefit is realized only when output D/A converters exhibit sufficient low-level linearity, and high S/N ratio is available. Indeed, any subsequent requantization must preserve the most critical noise floor improvements, and not introduce other noise that would negate the advantage of a shaped noise floor. For example, 19-bit resolution in D/A converters can be required to fully preserve noise-shaping improvements in a 16-bit recording.

When reducing word length, the audio signal must be redithered for a level appropriate for the receiving medium, for example, 16 bits for CD storage; white triangular pdf dither can be used. A nonoversampling noise-shaping loop redistributes the spectrum of the requantization noise. As noted earlier in this chapter, sigma-delta noise shapers used in highly oversampled converters yield a contour with a gradually increasing spectral characteristic. This characteristic will not specifically reduce noise in the 1- to 5-kHz region. To take advantage of psychoacoustics, higher-order shapers are used in nonoversampling shapers to form more complicated weighting functions. In this way, the perceptually weighted output noise power is minimized. A digital filter $H(z)$ in a feedback loop (see Fig. 16-24) accomplishes this, in which the filter coefficients determine a response so that the output noise is weighted by $1 - H(z)$, the inverse of the desired psychoacoustic weighting function. The resulting weighted spectrum ideally produces a noise floor that is equally audible at all frequencies.

As Robert Wannamaker suggests, a suitable filter design begins with selection of a weighting function. This design curve is inverted, and normalized to yield a zero average spectral power density that represents the squared magnitude of the frequency response of the minimum-phase noise shaper. The desired response is specified, and an inverse Fourier transform is applied to produce an impulse response. The response is windowed to produce a number of filter coefficients corresponding to $1 - H(z)$; $H(z)$ is derived from this, yielding a FIR filter.

Theory shows that as very high-order filters $H(z)$ are used to approximate the optimal filter weighting function, the unweighted noise power increases, tending toward infinity with an infinite filter order. For example, although an optimal approximation might yield a 27-dB decrease in audible weighted noise (using an F-weighting curve that reflects the ear's high frequency roll off), other weighting functions must be devised, with more modest performance. For example, using a nine-coefficient FIR shaping filter, perceived noise can be decreased by 17 dB compared to unshaped requantization noise; total unweighted noise power is increased a reasonable 18 dB compared to an unshaped spectrum. In other words, the output is subjectively as quiet as an unshaped truncated signal with an additional three bits; in this way, 19-bit audio data can be successfully transferred to a 16-bit CD.

The balance of decrease in audible noise versus increase in total noise (at higher inaudible frequencies) is delicate. For example, a very high total noise power might register on digital audio meters or damage tweeters, and some listeners suggest that aggressively boosted high-frequency noise produces artifacts, or perhaps masks otherwise audible information. In practice, depending on the design, the weighting function often approximates a proprietary contour. For example, Fig. 16-26 shows a proprietary noise-shaping contour, plotted with linear frequency for clarity. In some cases, this curve is fixed; in other cases, the curve is adaptively varied according to signal conditions. Similarly, in some designs, an adaptive dither signal is correlated

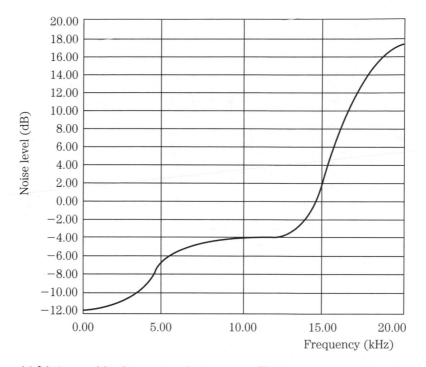

16-26 An equal-loudness noise-shaping curve. This frequency response plot uses a linear scale to better illustrate the high-frequency contour. Akune, et al.

to the audio signal so the audio signal masks the added dither noise. For example, the audio signal can be spectrally analyzed so that dither frequencies slightly higher in frequency can be generated.

Figure 16-27 shows a 1-kHz sinewave with –90-dB amplitude; measurements are made with a 16-kHz lowpass filter, to approximate the ear's averaging response. A 20-bit recording is quite accurate; when truncated to 16-bits, quantization is clearly evident; when dithered (±1 LSB triangular pdf) to 16-bits, quantization noise is alleviated, but noise is increased; when noise shaping is applied, the noise in this lowpass filtered measurement is reduced. This 16-bit representation is quite similar to the original 20-bit representation. Figure 16-28 shows the spectrum of the same –90-dB sinewave, with the four representations. The 20-bit recording has low error and noise; truncation creates severe quantization error; dithering removes the error but increases noise; noise shaping reduces low- and mid-frequency noise, with an increase at higher frequencies.

In one implementation of a psychoacoustic noise shaper, adaptive error-feedback filters are used to optimize the requantization noise spectrum according to equal loudness contours as well as masking analysis of the input signal. An algorithm analyzes the signal's masking properties to calculate simultaneous masking curves. These are adaptively combined with equal loudness curves to calculate the noise-shaping filter's coefficients, to yield the desired contour. This balance is dynamically and continuously varied according to the power of the input signal; for example,

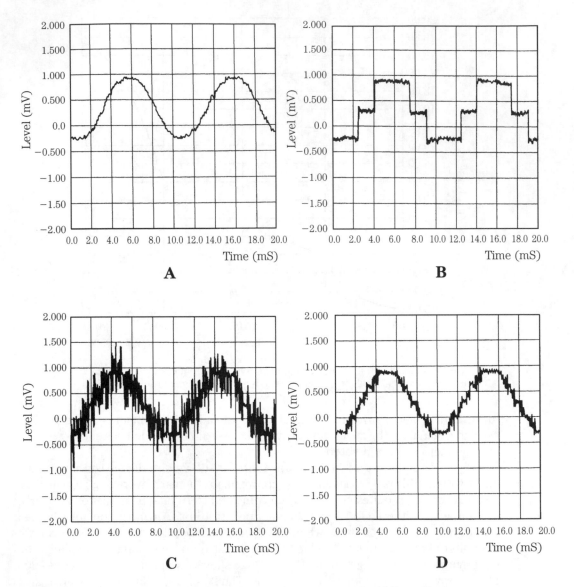

16-27 An example of noise shaping showing a 1-kHz sinewave with –90-B amplitude; measurements are made with a 16-kHz lowpass filter. A. Original 20-bit recording. B. Truncated 16-bit signal. C. Dithered 16-bit signal. D. Noise shaping preserves information in the lower 4 bits. Sony Corporation

when power is low, masking is minimal, so the equal loudness contour is used. Conversely, when power is high, masking is prevalent so the masking contour is more prominently used. The input signal is converted into critical bands, convolved with critical band masking curves, and converted to linear frequency to form the masking contour and hence the noise-shaping contour. In other words, masking analysis follows the same processing steps as used in perceptual coding.

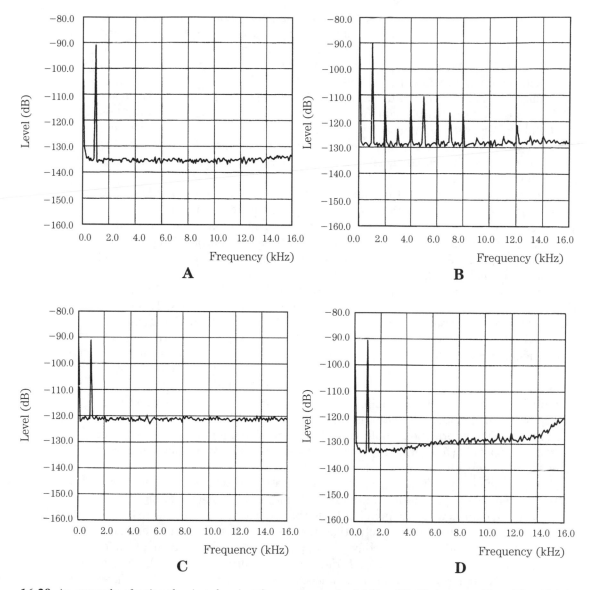

16-28 An example of noise shaping showing the spectrum of a 1 kHz, –90-dB sinewave (from Fig. 16-27). A. Original 20-bit recording. B. Truncated 16-bit signal. C. Dithered 16-bit signal. D. Noise shaping reduces low and mid frequency noise, with an increase at higher frequencies. Sony Corporation

Buried Data Technique

With proper dithering and noise shaping, dynamic range can be improved. However, processing can also be applied to use this dynamic range for purposes other than conventional audio headroom. Michael Gerzon and Peter Craven have demonstrated how variable-rate data can be "buried" in a data stream. The data is coded with psychoacoustic considerations so the data is inaudible under the masking curve of the audio program; the added data signal is randomized to appear like shaped noise. For example, the method could be used to place new information on conventional audio CDs, without significantly degrading the quality of the audio program. In particular, the coding technique replaces several of the least-significant bits of the 16-bit format with independent data. Clearly, if unrelated data simply displaced audio data, and the disc was played in a conventional CD player, the result would be unlistenable. For example, nonstandard data in the four least-significant bits would add about 27 dB of noise to the music, as well as distortion caused by truncating the 16-bit audio signal. The buried data method makes buried data discs compatible with conventional CD players.

The buried data is first coded to be pseudo-random, to make it noise-like. This signal is used as subtractive dither to remove the artifacts caused by quantization; specifically, the data dither is subtracted prior to quantization, then added after quantization, replacing the several least-significant bits of the output signal. In addition, noise shaping is applied in a loop around the quantizer to lower the perceived noise, as shown in Fig. 16-29. As a result, the noise created by four bits of buried data per channel (conveying 352.8 kbps with stereo channels) is reduced to yield an overall S/N ratio of about 91 dB, a level that is similar to conventional CDs. Two bits of buried data provides a buried channel rate of 176.4 kbps, while maintaining a S/N ratio of 103 dB. The method could variably "steal" bits from the original program only when their absence will be psychoacoustically masked by the music signal. The noise-shaping characteristic is varied according to the analyzed masking properties of the signal. The overall buried data rate could exceed 500 kbps, with 800 kbps possible during loud passages, depending on the music program. Combining methods, for example, buried data might consist of two 2-bit fixed channels, and a variable rate channel; side information would indicate the variable data rate. A buried data CD could be played in a regular CD player; the fidelity of music with limited dynamic range might not be affected at all.

More significantly, a CD player with appropriate decoding (or a player outputting buried data to an external decoder) could play the original music signal, and process buried data as well. The possibilities for buried data are numerous; many audio improvements can be more useful than the lost dynamic range. For example, buried 4-bit data could be used to convey multiple (5.1 channel) audio channels for surround sound playback; the main left/rights channels are conventionally coded, the buried data carries four additional channels. A 5.1 disc would compatibly deliver stereo reproduction with a conventional CD player, and surround sound with a 5.1 CD player. Alternatively, one or two bits of buried data could carry dynamic range compression or expansion information. Depending on the playback circumstances, the dynamic range of the music could be adjusted for the most desirable characteristics. Because the range algorithms are calculated prior to playback, they are much more effective than conventional real-time dynamic processing. Buried data could convey additional high-frequency information above the Nyquist frequency, and provide a gentle bandlimiting roll-off rate. Any of these applications could be combined, within the limits of the buried data's rate. For example, two ambience channels and dynamic range control data could be delivered simultaneously.

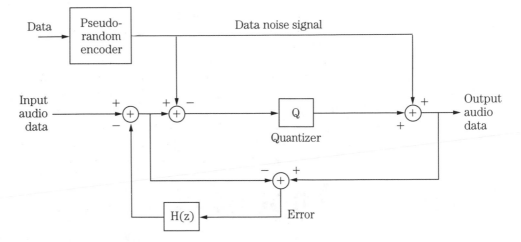

16-29 A buried channel encoder converts added data to a pseudo-random noise signal, which is used as a dither signal. This is subtracted from the audio signal prior to quantization and added to the signal after quantization. Noise shaping is performed around the quantizer.
Gerzon and Craven

Conclusion

In addition to obsoleting brick-wall analog filters, low-bit A/D converters surpass conventional multibit A/D converters by achieving increased resolution. Specifically, in-band noise can be made quite small. This benefit is provided by SDM; the same circuit that codes the signal into a low-bit stream also shifts the out-of-band noise components. Similarly, highly oversampling D/A converters using noise shaping and low-bit conversion largely surpass the performance of multibit D/A converters. In phase linearity, amplitude linearity, noise, long-term stability, and other parameters, A/D and D/A converters using low-bit architectures offer significant advantages. Noise shaping is also critical when reducing word length during data transfer; with nonoversampling noise shaping and dither, 19 bits of perceived resolution can be coded in a 16-bit storage medium. These applications all underscore the power of digital signal processing.

Appendix

The Sampling Theorem

Discrete time sampling is founded on the concept of a rectangular impulse of infinitesimal width. In practice, the width of a rectangular pulse is considered to be of finite width τ. Although data signals are often characterized by their time-domain properties, the transmission channel is usually best described by its frequency-domain properties. Specifically, it is important to know the bandwidth required for transmission of a sampled signal. The Fourier transform describes a time-domain function in the frequency domain. Given a single rectangular pulse of duration τ, the transformation of the pulse yields a $\sin(x)/x$ function.

This $\sin(x)/x$ function is composed of a fundamental cosine wave and its harmonics, its maximum value occurs at $x = 0$, and it approaches zero as x approaches $\pm \infty$. The width of the center lobe is exactly at $2/\tau$, and the frequency response passes through zero at multiples of $1/\tau$. Importantly, it demonstrates the fundamental nature of sampling as a modulation process; the frequency pattern of the function shows that the rectangular time pulse modulates the amplitude of a carrier frequency. The center frequency can be shifted without altering the shape of the envelope. Clearly, this spectrum extends to infinity thus ideal transmission of the pulse would require a system with infinite bandwidth. However, only the central lobe is required thus a finite bandwidth will suffice.

Given an understanding of the properties of a single pulse, it is useful to examine a series of such pulses with a periodic repetition of T. This leads to the creation of a practical sampling signal as a periodic series of pulses of fixed amplitude and finite width. The frequency spectrum of this function is defined at discrete values of n; that is, as equally spaced spectral lines with amplitudes corresponding to the discrete frequency components. Spectral lines are spaced according to the period T. They fall within a |sin(x)/x| envelope that is determined by the pulse duration τ, duty ratio τ/T, and pulse amplitude with zero-crossings at frequencies that are multiples of 1/τ.

The spectral response of a series of sampling pulses thus creates spectral lines with amplitudes that follow the same contour as that of a single pulse. The spectrum bandwidth is not affected by the pulse repetition frequency; rather, the bandwidth is determined by the pulse width τ. The shorter the duration of the pulse, the greater the frequency spread of the bandwidth. It is the case that transmission of narrow pulses requires a channel with higher bandwidth. From a frequency-domain standpoint, wider pulses might appear advantageous; however, as viewed in the time domain, narrow pulses permit a greater repetition rate and, for example, permit time multiplexing of channels. In any case it is not a higher repetition rate that necessitates higher bandwidth, but the narrow width of the pulses. Similarly, aperture error can be minimized by decreasing the duration of the pulse width. In the case of ideal sampling with a pulse of infinitesimal width and infinite bandwidth, its spectral lines are placed at multiples of the sampling rate, as in natural sampling; however, the amplitudes of the lines remain constant across the spectrum.

Given a sampling signal, it is possible to define the sampled signal as the multiplication of the sampling signal, and the message signal. Moreover, we can obtain an expression for the frequency spectrum of the sampled signal. The multiplication of these two time-domain functions can be represented as the convolution of their spectra. The spectrum of the sampled signal contains both positive and negative sidebands centered at the impulses defined by the sampling function, and placed at multiples of the sampling frequency. The spectra are strictly bandlimited. In addition, their amplitude again follows the sin(x)/x contour predicted by the Fourier transform of the sampling signal. The spectrum of the original message signal is repeated at multiples of the sampling frequency within the envelope of the sampled signal. When proper signal bandlimiting is provided, the spectrum repeats itself without overlap; if the signal's bandwidth is less than the Nyquist half-sampling frequency, the image sidebands are separated by a guard band. Note that complete information of the message signal is held in each sideband. The complete signal can be retrieved by removing higher frequency sideband spectra, leaving only the first sideband. As noted, complete information is contained in each sideband, thus, for example, a negative sideband could theoretically be used. The sin(x)/x function occurs repeatedly in sampling theory and in fact is often called the sampling function.

Given that any practical channel is bandlimited, it is important to know the maximum transmission rate afforded by a channel. Nyquist demonstrated that a message of S Hz can be completely characterized by samples taken at a frequency of $2S$ Hz. Moreover, the sin(x)/x function can be used as an interpolation function to reconstruct the original signal from the sample values. Each sample is multiplied by its interpolation function, and added to the functions of all other samples to obtain the signal waveform. Importantly, the sin(x)/x function represents the response of an ideal lowpass filter of bandwidth S Hz. In other words, the original signal can be reconstructed exactly by passing the representing samples through a lowpass filter with a bandwidth of S Hz. Thus, as Nyquist stated, a bandlimited signal can be completely reconstructed from samples. This is the key component that permits the transformation of analog signals and digital sequences. The following paragraphs summarize the sampling theorem.

The sampling process defines the values $f(nT)$ of $f(t)$ at regular time intervals. This is equivalent to a multiplication of $f(t)$ and $\delta_S(t)$, as shown in Fig. A-1. Therefore:

$$f_S(t) = \sum_{n=-\infty}^{\infty} Tf(nT)\delta(t - nT)$$

where $\delta(t)$ is a delta function. The Fourier transform $F_S(\omega)$ of $f_S(t)$ is:

$$F_S(\omega) = \int_{-\infty}^{\infty} \sum_{n=-\infty}^{\infty} Tf(nT)\delta(t - nT)e^{-j\omega t}dt$$

$$= \sum_{n=-\infty}^{\infty} F(\omega + n\omega_S)$$

where $\omega_S = 2\pi/T$. When we multiply two functions in time, we are convolving their transforms in the frequency domain. For this reason, we see the spectrum $F(\omega)$ repeated at multiples of the sampling rate.

We can recover $f(t)$ from $F_S(\omega)$ by first multiplying it with a gating function $G(\omega)$, as shown in Fig. A-2. We have:

$$F(\omega) = F_S(\omega)G(\omega)$$

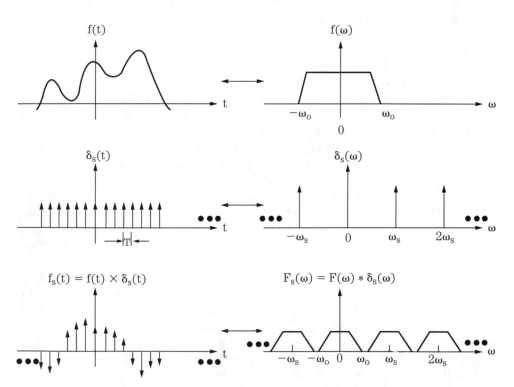

A-1 The sampling process.

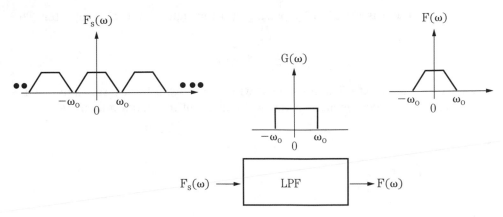

A-2 Recovery of $f(t)$ through filtering.

That is, we are filtering $F_S(\omega)$. Using the fact that the inverse transform of $G(\omega)$ is:

$$\frac{\sin \omega_o t}{\pi t}$$

and if $F_S(\omega) \leftrightarrow f_S(t)$ then and $G(\omega) \leftrightarrow g(t)$, then

$$F_S(\omega)G(\omega) \leftrightarrow f_S(t)*g(t)$$

where $*$ denotes convolution, and we obtain:

$$f(t) = \sum_{n=-\infty}^{\infty} Tf(nT)\delta(t - nT) * \frac{\sin\omega_o t}{T_0\omega_o t/2}$$

$$= \sum_{n=-\infty}^{\infty} Tf(nT) \frac{\sin \omega_o(t - nT)}{T_0\omega_o(t - nT)/2}$$

or

$$f(t) = \sum_{n=-\infty}^{\infty} f(nT) \frac{\sin \omega_o(t - nT)}{\omega_o(t - nT)}$$

where

$$\frac{T}{T_o/2} = 1$$

This result, known as the sampling theorem, relates the samples $f(nT)$ taken at regular intervals to the function $f(t)$. The same result also can be interpreted in the following way: $f(t)$ is represented by the Fourier series, which has the sampling function:

$$\frac{\sin (x)}{x}$$

as its basis, and each coordinate is weighted by $f(nT)$. Note that we can only reconstruct the original waveform $f(t)$ from the sampled values if it is bandlimited. In practice, this condition is satisfied by passing $f(t)$ through an anti-aliasing filter. The quantity

$$\frac{1}{T} = 2\left(\frac{1}{T_o}\right)$$

is called the Nyquist rate. This also can be written as $f_s = 2f_0$. Hence, the sampling frequency should be twice as high as the maximum input frequency anticipated.

Bibliography

1 Sound and Numbers

Backus, J., *The Acoustical Foundations of Music*, W.W. Norton, 1969.

Bartee, T.C., ed., *Data Communications, Networks, and Systems*, Howard W. Sams, 1985.

Bartee, T.C., *Digital Computer Fundamentals*, McGraw-Hill, 1981.

Blesser, B.A., "Elementary and Basic Aspects of Digital Audio," *AES Digital Audio Collected Papers*, Rye, 1983.

Booth, T.L., *Digital Networks and Computer Systems*, John Wiley and Sons, 1971.

Eargle, J., *Handbook of Recording Engineering*, 2nd ed., Van Nostrand Reinhold, 1992.

Gilchrist, N.H.C., "Digital Audio Impairments and Measurements," *AES Digital Audio Collected Papers*, Rye, 1983.

Kinsler, L.E., A.R. Frey, A.B. Coppens, and J.V. Sanders, *Fundamentals of Acoustics*, 3rd ed., John Wiley and Sons, 1982.

Morris, R.L., and J.R. Miller, *Designing with TTL Integrated Circuits*, McGraw-Hill, 1971.

Osborne, A., *An Introduction to Microcomputers - Volume One*, Adam Osborne and Associates, 1977.

Roth, Jr., C.H., *Fundamentals of Logic Design*, West, 1979.

Short, K.L., *Microprocessors and Programmed Logic*, Prentice-Hall, 1981.

Streitmatter, G.A., and V. Fiore, *Microprocessors, Theory and Applications*, Reston, 1982.

Strong, W.J., and G.R. Plitnik, *Music, Speech, High Fidelity*, Soundprint, 1983.

Woram, J.W., *Sound Recording Handbook*, Howard W. Sams, 1989.

2 Fundamentals of Digital Audio

Adams, R.W., "Nonuniform Sampling of Audio Signals," *JAES*, vol. 40. no. 11, November, 1992.

Blesser, B.A., "Digitization of Audio: A Comprehensive Examination of Theory, Implementation, and Current Practice," *JAES*, vol. 26, no. 10, October, 1978.

Cauchy, A.L., "Memoire sur Diverses Formules d'Analyse," *Comptes Rendus Acad. Sci. Paris*, vol. 12, 1841.

Clarke, A.B., and R.L. Disney, *Probability and Random Processes for Engineers and Scientists*, John Wiley and Sons, 1970.

Jerri, A.J., "The Shannon Sampling Theorem - Its Various Extensions and Applications: A Tutorial Review," *Proc. IEEE*, vol. 65, no. 11, November, 1977.

Karl, J.H., *An Introduction to Digital Signal Processing*, Academic Press, 1989.

Kotelnikov, V.A., "On the Transmission Capacity of "Ether" and Wire in Electrocommunications," *Izd. Red. Upr. Svyazi RKKA*, Moscow, 1933.

Lipshitz, S.P., R.A. Wannamaker, and J. Vanderkooy, "Quantization and Dither: A Theoretical Survey," *JAES*, vol. 40, no. 5, May, 1992.

Maher, R.C., "On the Nature of Granulation Noise in Uniform Quantization Systems," *JAES*, vol. 40, no. 1/2, January/February, 1992.

Nyquist, H., "Certain Factors Affecting Telegraph Speed," *Bell Sys. Tech. Journal*, vol. 3, no. 2, April, 1924.

Nyquist, H., "Certain Topics in Telegraph Transmission Theory," *Trans. AIEE*, vol. 47, no. 2, April, 1928.

Ogura, K., "On a Certain Transcendental Integral Function in the Theory of Interpolation," *Tohoku Mathematics Journal*, vol. 17, 1920.

Schuchman, L. "Dither Signals and Their Effect on Quantization Noise," *IEEE Trans. Communication Tech.*, vol. COM-12, December, 1964.

Shannon, C.E., "A Mathematical Theory of Communication," *Bell Sys. Tech. Journal*, vol. 27, October, 1948.

Stockham, Jr., T.G., "The Promise of Digital Audio," *AES Digital Audio Collected Papers*, Rye, 1983.

Talambiras, R., "Some Considerations in the Design of Wide-Dynamic-Range Audio Digitizing Systems," *AES* preprint 1226, Los Angeles, May, 1977.

Tanabe, H., and T. Wakuri, "On the Quality of Some Digital Audio Equipment Measured by the High Accuracy Dynamic Distortion Measuring System," *AES* preprint 1909, Anaheim, October, 1982.

Vanderkooy, J., and S.P. Lipshitz, "Dither in Digital Audio," *JAES*, vol. 35, no. 12, December, 1987.

Vanderkooy, J., and S.P. Lipshitz, "Resolution Below the Least Significant Bit in Digital Audio Systems with Dither," *JAES*, vol. 32, no. 3, March, 1984, Erratum, *JAES*, vol. 32, no. 11, November, 1984.

Watkinson, J., *The D-2 Digital Video Recorder*, Focal Press, 1990.

Whittaker, E.T., "On the Functions which are represented by the Expansions of the Interpolation-Theory," *Proc. R. Soc. Edinburgh*, vol. 35, 1915.

Zayed, A.I., *Advances in Shannon's Sampling Theorem*, CRC Press, 1993.

3   Digital Audio Recording

Behr, M.I., and N. S. Blessum, "Technique for Reducing Effects of Pulse Crowding in Magnetic Recording," *IEEE Trans. Magnetics*, vol. MAG-8, no. 3, September, 1972.

Black, H.S., *Modulation Theory*, Van Nostrand Reinhold, 1953.

Blesser, B.A., "Advanced Analog-to-Digital Conversion and Filtering: Data Conversion," *AES Digital Audio Collected Papers*, Rye, 1983.

Blesser, B.A., "Digitization of Audio: A Comprehensive Examination of Theory, Implementation, and Current Practice," *JAES*, vol. 26, no. 10, October, 1978.

Blesser, B.A., and F.F. Lee, "An Audio Delay System Using Digital Technology," *JAES*, vol. 19, no. 5., May, 1971.

Blesser, B.A., and B.N Locanthi, "The Application of Narrow-Band Dither Operating at the Nyquist Frequency in Digital Systems to Provide Improved Signal-to-Noise Ratio over Conventional Dithering," *JAES*, vol. 35, no. 6. June, 1987.

Carr, J.J., *Digital Interfacing with an Analog World*, TAB Books, 1978.

Davidson, M., et al., "High Density Magnetic Recording Using Digital Block Codes of Low Disparity," *IEEE Trans. Magnetics*, vol. MAG-12, no. 5, September, 1976.

Doi, T.T., "Channel Codings for Digital Audio Recordings," *JAES*, vol. 31, no. 4, April, 1983.

Doi, T.T., "Recent Progress in Digital Audio Technology," *AES Digital Audio Collected Papers*, Rye, 1983.

Endoh, N., M. Katoh, and K. Ogi, "Channel Coding for a Stationary Head PCM Tape Recorder," *AES* preprint 2009, New York, October, 1983.

Finger, R.A., "On the Use of Computer Generated Dithered Test Signals," *JAES*, vol. 35, no. 6, June, 1987.

Gersho, A., "Quantization," *IEEE Commun. Soc. Mag.*, vol. 15, September, 1977.

Gilchrist, N.H.C., "The Subjective Effect and Measurement of ADC-DAC Transfer Characteristic Discontinuity," *JAES*, vol. 36, no. 9, September, 1988.

Hamill, D.C., "Transient Response of Audio Filters," *Wireless World*, August, 1981.

Haykin, S., *Communication Systems*, John Wiley and Sons, 1983.

Heemskerk, J.P.J., and K.A. Schouhamer Immink, "Compact Disc System Aspects and Modulation," *Philips Tech. Rev.*, vol. 40, no. 6, 1982.

Hiroshi, I. et al., "Pulse-Code Modulation Recording System," *JAES*, vol. 21, no. 7, September, 1973.

Hnatek, E.R., *A User's Handbook of D/A and A/D Converters*, John Wiley and Sons, 1976.

Hoeschele, D, *Analog-to-Digital, Digital-to-Analog Conversion Techniques*, John Wiley and Sons, 1968.

Horiguchi. T, and K. Morita, "An Optimization of Modulation Codes in Digital Recording," *IEEE Trans. Magnetics*, vol. MAG-12, no. 6, November, 1976.

Immink, K.A., et al., "Method of Coding Binary Data," U.S. Patent 4,501,000, February 19, 1985.

Iwamura, H., et al., "Pulse-Code-Modulation Recording System," *JAES*, vol. 21, no. 9, September, 1973.

Jacoby, G.V., "A New Look-Ahead Code for Increased Data Density," *IEEE Trans. Magnetics*, vol. MAG-13, no. 5, September, 1977.

Jayant, N., and L. Rabiner, "The Application of Dither to the Quantization of Speech Signals," *Bell Sys. Tech. Journal*, vol. 51, 1972.

Kam, J.J. van der, "A Digital 'Decimating' Filter for Analog-To-Digital Conversion of Hi-Fi Audio Signals," *Philips Tech. Rev.*, vol. 42, no. 6/7, 1986.

Korn, I., *Digital Communications*, Van Nostrand Reinhold, 1985.

Krause, M., and H. Petersen, "How Can the Headroom of Digital Recordings Be Used Optimally?" *AES* preprint 2799, Hamburg, March, 1989.

Lagadec, R., and T.G. Stockham, Jr., "Dispersive Models for A-to-D and D-to-A Conversion Systems," *AES* preprint 2097, Paris, March, 1984.

Lindholm, D.A., "Power Spectra of Channel Codes for Digital Magnetic Recording," *IEEE Trans. Magnetics*, vol. MAG-14, no. 5, September, 1978.

Lindsey, W.C., and M.K. Simon, *Telecommunications Systems Engineering*, Prentice-Hall, 1973.

MacArthur, J. "20/20 Vision," *Studio Sound*, January, 1993.

Marchant, A.B., *Optical Recording: A Technical Overview*, Addison-Wesley, 1990.

Mathews, M., *The Technology of Computer Music*, MIT press, 1969.

Matick, R.E., *Computer Storage Systems and Technology*, John Wiley and Sons, 1977.

Meyer, J., "Time Correction of Anti-Aliasing Filters Used in Digital Audio Systems," *JAES*, vol. 32, no. 3, March, 1984.

Miller, J.W., "DC Free Encoding for Data Transmission System," U.S. Patent 4,027,335, May 31, 1977.

Morris, D.J., *Pulse Code Formats for Fiber Optical Data Communication*, Marcel Dekker, 1983.

Muraoka, T., Y. Yamada, and M. Yamazaki, "Sampling Frequency Considerations in Digital Audio Standards," *JAES*, vol. 26, no. 4, April, 1978., Erratum, *JAES*, vol. 26, no. 7/8, July/August, 1978.

Myers, J.P., and A. Feinburg, "High-Quality Professional Recording Using New Digital Techniques," *JAES*, vol. 20, no. 10, October, 1972.

Nakajima, H., T.T. Doi, J. Fukuda, and A. Iga, *Digital Audio Technology*, TAB Books, 1983.

Ogawa, H., and K.A. Schouhamer Immink, "EFM - The Modulation Method for the Compact Disc Digital Audio System," *AES Digital Audio Collected Papers*, Rye, 1983.

Owen, F.F.E., *PCM and Digital Transmission Systems*, McGraw-Hill, 1982.

Patel, A.M., "Zero-Modulation Encoding in Magnetic Recording," *IBM Journal of Research and Development*, July, 1975.

Peled, A., and B. Liu, *Digital Signal Processing; Theory, Design, and Implementation*, John Wiley and Sons, 1976.

Picot, J.P., *Introduction a l'Audio Numerique*, Editions Frequencies, 1984.

Preis, D., and P.J. Bloom, "Perception of Phase Distortion in Anti-Alias Filters," *AES* preprint 2008, New York, October, 1983.

Rabiner, L.R., and B. Gold, *Theory and Applications of Digital Signal Processing*, Prentice-Hall, 1975.

Salman, W.P., and M.S. Solotareff, *Le Filtrage Numerique*, Eyrolles, 1978.

Sato, N. "PCM Recorder - A New Type of Audio Magnetic Tape Recorder," *JAES*, vol. 21, no. 9, September, 1973.

Shannon, C.E., "Communication in the Presence of Noise," *Proc. Institute of Radio Engineers*, vol. 37, 1949.

Takahashi, Y., et al., "Study and Evaluation of New Method of ADPCM Encoding," *AES* preprint 2813, Hamburg, March, 1989.

Takashi, T., et al., "A Coding Method in Digital Magnetic Recording," *IEEE Trans. Magnetics*, vol. MAG-8, no. 3, September, 1972.

Widrow, B., "A Study of Rough Amplitude Quantization by Means of Nyquist Sampling Theory," *IRE Trans. Circuit Theory*, vol. CT-3, December, 1956.

Wong, P.W., "Quantization Noise, Fixed-Point Multiplicative Roundoff Noise, and Dithering," *IEEE Trans. ASSP*, vol. 38, no. 2, February, 1990.

4 Digital Audio Reproduction

Adams, R.W., "Clock Jitter, D/A Converters, and Sample-Rate Conversion," *The Audio Critic*, no. 21, Spring, 1994.

Adams, R.W., "Design and Implementation of an Audio 18-Bit Analog-to-Digital Converter Using Oversampling Techniques," *JAES*, vol. 34, no. 3, March, 1986.

Baldwin, G.L., and S.K. Tewksbury, "Linear Delta Modulator Integrated Circuit with 17-Mbit/s Sampling Rate," *IEEE Trans. Communications*, vol. COM-22, no. 7, July, 1974.

Blesser, B.A., "Digitization of Audio: A Comprehensive Examination of Theory, Implementation, and Current Practice," *JAES*, vol. 26, no. 10, October, 1978.

Blesser, B.A., "The Floating Point System," *dB Magazine*, May, 1981.

Blesser, B.A., "Upconverting D/A," *dB magazine*, November, 1983.

Bristow-Johnson, R., "Effect of DAC Deglitching on Frequency Response," *JAES*, vol. 36, no. 11, November, 1988.

Charbonnier, A., and J. Petit, "Sub-Band ADPCM Coding for High Quality Audio Signals," *IEEE ICASSP*, 1988.

Couch, L., *Digital and Analog Communication Systems*, Macmillan, 1983.

Dijkmans, E.C., and P.J.A. Naus, "The Next Step Towards Ideal A/D and D/A Converters," *Proc. AES 7th International Conference*, Toronto, May, 1989.

Fielder, L.D., "Evaluation of the Audible Noise and Distortion Produced by Digital Audio Converters," *JAES*, vol. 35, no. 7/8, July/August, 1987.

Finger, R.A., "Review of Frequencies and Levels for Digital Audio Performance Measurements," *JAES*, vol. 34, no. 1/2, January/February, 1986.

Gundry, K.J., D.P. Robinson, and C.C. Todd, "Recent Developments in Digital Audio Techniques," *AES* preprint 1956, Eindhoven, March, 1983.

Halbert, J.M., and M.A. Shill, "An 18-Bit Digital-to-Analog Converter for High Performance Digital Audio Applications," *JAES*, vol. 36, no. 6, June, 1988.

Harris, S., "The Effects of Sampling Clock Jitter on Nyquist Sampling Analog-to-Digital Converters", and on Oversampling Delta-Sigma ADCs," *JAES*, vol. 38, no. 7/8, July/August, 1990.

Kakiuchi, S., et al., "Application of Oversampling A/D and D/A Conversion Techniques to R-DAT," *AES* preprint 2520, New York, October, 1987.

Lipshitz, S.P., and J. Vanderkooy, "Are Digital-to-Analog Converters Getting Worse?," *AES* preprint 2586, Paris, March, 1988.

Nagata, A., et al., "Over-Sampling Filter for Digital Audio Use," *AES* preprint 2289, New York, October, 1985.

Naylor, J.R., "A Dual Monolithic 18-Bit Analog-to-Digital Converter for Digital Audio Applications," *Proc. AES 7th International Conference*, Toronto, May, 1989.

Nishiguchi, N., K. Akagiri, and T. Suzuki, "A New Audio Bit Rate Reduction System For the CD-I Format," *AES* preprint 2375, Los Angeles, November, 1986.

Oppenheim, A.V., ed., *Applications of Digital Signal Processing*, Prentice-Hall, 1978.

Pohlmann, K.C., *The Compact Disc Handbook*, 2nd ed., A-R Editions, 1992.

Pohlmann, K.C., "Multibit Conversion," *Advanced Digital Audio*, Pohlmann, ed., Howard W. Sams, 1991.

Pohlmann, K.C., "Pulse Modulation and Sampling Systems," *Advanced Digital Audio*, Pohlmann, ed., Howard W. Sams, 1991.

Proakis, J., *Digital Communications*, McGraw-Hill, 1983.

Roden, M.S., *Analog and Digital Communication Systems*, Prentice-Hall, 1985.

Schindler, H.R., "Delta Modulation," *IEEE Spectrum*, October, 1970.

Schott, W., "Philips Oversampling System for Compact Disc Decoding," *Audio Magazine*, vol. 68, no. 4, April, 1984.

Shelton, W. T. "Progress Towards a System of Synchronization in Digital Audio," *AES* preprint 2484, London, March, 1987.

Steele, R., *Delta Modulation Systems*, Halsted Press, 1975.

Stockham, Jr., T.G., "A/D and D/A Converters: Their Effect on Digital Audio Fidelity," *Digital Signal Processing*, Rabiner and Rader, eds., IEEE Press, 1972.

Sun, M.T., and L. Wu, "Efficient Design of the Oversampling Filter for Digital Audio Applications," *AES* preprint 2378, Los Angeles, November, 1986.

Takasaki, Y., *Digital Transmission Design and Jitter Analysis*, Artech House, 1991.

Trischitta, P.R., and E.L. Varma, *Jitter in Digital Transmission Systems*, Artech House, 1989.

Van de Plassche, R.J., and E.C. Dijkmans, "A Monolithic 16 Bit D/A Conversion System for Digital Audio," *AES Digital Audio Collected Papers*, Rye, 1983.

Yamada, M., and K. Odaka, "A New Audio Digital Filter with Compensation of Phase for A/D and D/A Conversion," *AES* preprint 2528, New York, October, 1987.

5   Error Correction

Berlekamp, E.R., *Algebraic Coding Theory*, McGraw-Hill, 1968.

Berlekamp, E.R., "Error Correcting Code for Digital Audio," *AES Digital Audio Collected Papers*, Rye, 1983.

Buddine, L., and E. Young, *The Brady Guide to CD-ROM*, Prentice-Hall, 1987.

Cabot, R.C., "Measuring AES-EBU Digital Audio Interfaces," *JAES*, vol. 38, no. 6, June, 1990.

Clark, Jr., G.C., and J.B. Cain, *Error-Correction Coding for Digital Communications*, Plenum Press, 1981.

Doi, T.T., "Error Correction for Digital Audio Recordings," *AES Digital Audio Collected Papers*, Rye, 1983.

Feher, K., *Telecommunications Measurements, Analysis and Instrumentation*, Prentice-Hall, 1987.

Gallager, R.G., *Information Theory and Reliable Communication*, John Wiley and Sons, 1968.

Hagelbarger, D.W., "Recurrent Codes: Easily Mechanized, Burst-Correcting, Binary Codes," *Bell Sys. Tech. Journal*, vol. 38, no. 4, July, 1959.

Hamming, R.W., *Coding and Information Theory*, Prentice-Hall, 1980.

Hamming, R.W., "Error Detecting and Error Correcting Codes," *Bell Sys. Tech. Journal*, vol. 29, no. 1, January, 1950.

Hoeve, H., J. Timmermans, and L.B. Vries, "Error Correction and Concealment in the Compact Disc System," *Philips Tech. Rev.*, vol. 40, No. 6, 1982.

Imai, H. ed, *Essentials of Error-Control Coding Techniques*, Academic Press, 1990.

Lin, S., *An Introduction to Error-Correcting Codes*, Prentice-Hall, 1970.

Maher, R.C., "A Method for Extrapolation of Missing Digital Audio Data," *JAES*, vol. 42, no. 5, May, 1994.

McEliece, R.J., *The Theory of Information and Coding*, Addison-Wesley, 1977.

Odaka, K., et al., "Error Correctable Data Transmission Method," U.S. Patent 4,413,340, November 1, 1983.

Peterson, W.W., "Error-Correcting Codes," *Scientific American*, vol. 206, no. 2, February, 1962.

Reed, I.S., and G. Solomon, "Polynomial Codes over Certain Finite Fields," *J. SIAM*, vol. 8. 1960.

Shenton, D., E. DeBenedictis, and B.N. Locanthi, "Improved Reed-Solomon Decoding Using Multiple Pass Decoding," *AES* preprint 2035, New York, October, 1983.

Silver, S.L., "Correcting Tape Errors in Digital Magnetic Recording," *dB Magazine*, November 1980.

Viterbi, A.J., "Coding and Interleaving for Correcting Burst and Random Errors in Recording Media," *AES Digital Audio Collected Papers*, Rye, 1983.

Viterbi, A.J., *Coherent Communication*, McGraw-Hill, 1966.

Vries, L.B., and K. Odaka, "CIRC - The Error Correcting Code for the Compact Disc Digital Audio System," *AES Digital Audio Collected Papers*, Rye, 1983.

Watkinson, J., "Inside CD, Part 4," *Hi-Fi News & Record Review*, February, 1987.

6 Magnetic Tape Storage

Alesis Corporation, "ADAT Eight Track Professional Digital Audio Recorder Reference Manual," Alesis Corporation, 1994.

Barr, K., et al., "Format for Recording Digital Audio onto Magnetic Tape with Enhanced Editing and Error Correction Capability," U.S. Patent 5,321,561, June 14, 1994.

Eguchi, T., and J.H. Wilkinson, "The 4:2:2 Component Digital VTR," *International Broadcast Engineer,* September, 1986.

Gregory, S., *Introduction to the 4:2:2 Digital Tape Recorder*, Pentech Press, 1989.

Gross, L.S., *The New Television Technologies*, William C. Brown, 1983.

Imakoshi, S., et al., "Thin Film Heads for Multi-Track Tape Recorders," *AES* preprint 2287, New York, October, 1985.

Itoh, S., et al., "PCM Multitrack Format on 8 mm Video," *IEEE Trans. Consumer Electronics*, CE-31, no. 3, August, 1985.

Johnson, Jr., C.E., "The Promise of Perpendicular Magnetic Recording," *Byte Magazine*, March, 1983.

Jorgensen, F., *The Complete Handbook of Magnetic Recording*, 3rd ed., TAB Books, 1988.

Kogure, T., Dol, T.T., and Lagadec, R., *The DASH Format: An Overview*, AES preprint 2038, New York, October, 1983.

Lagadec, R., H.P. Girsberger, and C. Brandes, "Design of a Professional 2-Channel Stationary-Head Digital Audio Recorder," *AES* preprint 2095, Paris, March, 1984.

Lagadec, R., and M. Schneider, "A Professional, 2-Channel 15-ips DASH Recorder," *AES* preprint 2259, Anaheim, May, 1985.

Lemke, J.V., "The State of the Art in High-Density Magnetic Recording," *AES Digital Audio Collected Papers*, Rye, 1983.

Lowman, C., *Magnetic Recording*, McGraw-Hill, 1972.

Petersen, G., *Modular Digital Multitracks*, Mix Publications, 1994.

Pohlmann, K.C., and J. Monforte, "Field Test: Sony PCM-3324S Digital 24-Track Recorder," *Mix Magazine*, vol. 16, no. 8, 1992.

Simmons, W., "Analog Mastering Tape Versus Digital Mastering Tape," *dB Magazine*, January, 1983.

Suesada, K., et al., "D-5: ½-inch Full Bit Rate Component VTR Format," *SMPTE Journal*, August, 1994.

Takayama, J., and S.P. Burgess, "Enhancement to One-Inch VTRs," *IEE Conference Publication*, 1986.

Tamaka, K., "Tape Formats and Multi-Track Formats," *AES Digital Audio Collected Papers*, Rye, 1983.

TEAC Corporation, "DA-88 Digital Audio Tape Deck Technical Information (Circuit Descriptions)," *Tascam*, TEAC Professional Division, 1994.

Watkinson, J., "Digital Audio Recorders," *JAES*, vol. 36, no. 6, June, 1988.

Whitaker, J., "Hard Disk Recording Technology," *Recording Engineer/Producer*, March, 1988.

White, G., *Video Recording*, Butterworth and Co., 1972.

Wilton, P., "The Sony ¾-Inch Digital Audio System," *International Broadcast Engineer*, November, 1987.

7 Digital Audio Tape (DAT)

Adachi, T., et al., "A Fast Random Accessing Scheme for R-DAT," *IEEE Trans. Consumer Electronics*, vol. CE-33, no. 3, August, 1987.

Arai, T., et al., "Digital Signal Processing Technology for R-DAT," *IEEE Trans. Consumer Electronics*, vol. CE-32, no. 3, August, 1986.

Fukami, T., et al., "New LSIs for a Rotary-Head Digital Audio Tape Recorder (R-DAT) and Their Digital Signal Processing," *AES* preprint 2379, Los Angeles, November, 1986.

Hitomi, A., and T. Takai, "Servo Technology of R-DAT," *IEEE Trans. Consumer Electronics*, vol. CE-32, no. 3, August, 1986.

Itoh, F., et al., "Magnetic Tape and Cartridge of R-DAT," *IEEE Trans. Consumer Electronics*, vol. CE-32, no. 3, August, 1986.

Lagadec, R. "R-DAT and Professional Audio," *AES* preprint 2558, New York, October, 1987.

Nakajima, H., and M. Kosaka, "The DAT Conference, Its Activities and Results," *IEEE Trans. Consumer Electronics*, vol. CE-32, no. 3, August, 1986.

Nakajima, H., and K. Odaka, "A Rotary Head High Density Digital Audio Tape Recorder," *IEEE Trans. Consumer Electronics*, vol. CE-29, no. 3, August, 1983.

Ohtake, N., et al., "Magnetic Recording Characteristics of R-DAT," *IEEE Trans. Consumers Electronics*, vol. CE-32, no. 4, November, 1986.

van Gestel, W.J., H.G. de Haan, and T.G.J.A. Martens, "Digital Magnetic-Tape Recording and Reproduction," *Audio Engineering Handbook*, Benson, ed., McGraw-Hill, 1988.

Watkinson, J., *RDAT*, Focal Press, 1991.

8   Optical Storage and Transmission

Ajemian, R.G., "Fiber-Optic Connector Considerations for Professional Audio," *JAES*, vol. 40, no. 6, June, 1992.

Ajemian, R.G., and A.B. Grundy, "Fiber-Optics - The New Medium for Audio: A Tutorial," *JAES*, vol. 38, no. 3, March, 1990.

Allard, F.C., *Fiber Optics Handbook for Engineers and Scientists*, McGraw-Hill, 1990.

Amphenol Fiber Optic Designer's Handbook, Amphenol Products, F122-00188, 1987.

Baack, C., *Optical Wideband Transmission Systems*, CRC Press, 1986.

Baker, D.G., *Fiber Optic Design and Applications*, Reston Publishing Co., 1985.

Baker, D.G., *Monomode Fiber Optic Design with Local-Area Network Applications*, Van Nostrand Reinhold, 1987.

Blake, L., "Digital Sound in the Cinema," *Mix Magazine*, vol. 17, no. 11, November, 1993.

Bouwhuis, G., et al., *Principles of Optical Disc Systems*, Adam Hilger, 1985.

Bradley, A., *Optical Storage for Computers: Technology and Application*, Ellis Horwood, 1989.

Cheo, P.K., *Fiber Optics, Devices and Systems*, Prentice-Hall, 1985.

Cherin, A.H., *An Introduction to Optical Fibers*, McGraw-Hill, 1983.

Daley, J.C., *Fiber Optics*, CRC Press, 1984.

Dick, B., "Building Fiber-Optic Transmission Systems - Parts 1,2,3" *Broadcast Engineering*, November, 1991, December, January, 1992.

Doi, T.T., T. Itoh, and H. Ogawa, "A Long Play Digital Audio Disc System," *AES* preprint 1442, Brussels, March, 1979.

Freese, R.P., "Optical Disks Become Erasable," *IEEE Spectrum*, February, 1988.

Geckeler, S., *Optical Transmission Systems*, Artech House, 1987.

Halley, P., *Fibre Optic Systems*, John Wiley and Sons, 1987.

Hartmann, M., B. Jacobs, and J. Braat, "Erasable Magneto-Optical Recording," *Philips Tech. Rev.*, vol. 42, no. 2, August, 1985.

Howes, M.J., and D.V. Morgan, *Optical Fibre Communications*, John Wiley and Sons, 1980.

Izawa, T., and S. Sudo, *Optical Fibers: Materials and Fabrication*, KTK Scientific Publishers, 1987.

Jeunhomme, L.B., *Single-Mode Fiber Optics, Principles and Applications*, Marcel Dekker, 1983.

Jones, Jr., W.B., *Introduction to Optical Fiber Communication Systems*, Holt, Reinhart and Winston, 1988.

Kao, C.K., *Optical Fiber Systems*, McGraw-Hill, 1982.

Karley, B.A., "Fiber Optics," *Advanced Digital Audio*, Pohlmann, ed., Howard W. Sams, 1991.

Keiser, G., *Optical Fiber Communications*, McGraw-Hill, 1983.

Koechner, W., *Solid-State Laser Engineering*, Springer Series in Optical Sciences, Springer-Verlag, 1988.

Kurahashi, A., et al., "Development of an Erasable Magneto-Optical Digital Audio Recorder," *AES* preprint 2296, New York, October, 1985.

Lin, C., *Optoelectronic Technology and Lightwave Communications Systems*, Van Nostrand Reinhold, 1989.

Mahlke, G., and P. Gossing, *Fiber Optic Cables: Fundamentals, Cable Technology, Installation Practice*, John Wiley and Sons, 1987.

Marshall, G. F., *Laser Beam Scanning, Opto-Mechanical Devices, Systems, and Data Storage Optics*, Marcel Dekker, 1985.

Meyer-Arendt, J.R., *Introduction to Classical and Modern Optics*, Prentice-Hall, 1972.

Midwinter, J.E., *Optical Fibers for Transmission*, John Wiley and Sons, 1979.

Miller, C.M., *Optical Fiber Splices and Connectors, Theory and Method*, Marcel Dekker, 1986.

Morgan, J., *Introduction to University Physics*, vol. 2, Allyn and Bacon, 1964.

Murata, H., *Handbook of Optical Fibers and Cables*, Marcel Dekker, 1988.

Murata, S., et al., "Multimedia Type Digital Audio Disc System," *IEEE Trans. Consumer Electronics*, vol. 35, no. 3, August, 1989.

Nöldeke, C. "Compact Disc Diffraction," *The Physics Teacher*, October, 1990.

Palais, J.C., *Fiber Optic Communications*, Prentice-Hall, 1984.

Paulson, C.R., "Fiber Optic Transmission Systems," *National Association of Broadcasters Engineering Handbook*, 8th ed., NAB, 1992.

Personick, S.D., *Fiber Optics Technology and Applications*, Plenum Press, 1985.

Personick, S.D., *Optical Fiber Transmission Systems*, Plenum Press, 1981.

Pohl, R.W., *Einfuhrung in die Optik*, Springer Verlag, Berlin, 1943.

Pohlmann, K.C., *The Compact Disc Handbook*, 2nd ed., A-R Editions, 1992.

Pohlmann, K.C. "Optical Storage Technologies," *Mix Magazine*, vol. 16, no. 7, July, 1992.

Sakura, S., et al., "Fiber Optics Links for Digital Audio Interface," *IEEE Trans. Consumer Electronics*, vol. CE-34, no. 3, August, 1988.

Schouhamer Immink, K., and J. Braat, "Experiments Toward an Erasable Compact Disc Digital Audio System." *JAES*, vol. 32, no. 7/8, July/August, 1984.

Seippel, R.G., *Fiber Optics*, Reston Publishing Co., 1984.

Senior, J.M., *Optical Fiber Communications, Principles and Practice*, Prentice-Hall, 1985.

Shevlin, T., "Fiber Optic Networks: Applications for Professional Audio," *Professional Sound*, October, 1994.

Talbot, D., "Fiber-Optic Transmission and Professional Audio," *JAES*, vol. 42, no. 5, May, 1994.

Thomas, G.E., "Future Trends in Optical Recording," *Philips Tech. Rev.*, vol. 44, no. 2, 1988.

Uhlig, R.E., "Feasibility of Digital Sound on Motion Picture Film," *Proc. AES 7th International Conference*, Toronto, May, 1989.

Varela, A., "Film Sound Goes Digital," *Post*, September, 1990.

Verdeyen, J.T., *Laser Electronics*, Prentice-Hall, 1981.

Webb, R.H., *Elementary Wave Optics*, Academic Press, 1969.

Yariv, A., *Optical Electronics*, 3rd ed., CBS College Publishing, 1985.

9 The Compact Disc

Baert, L., L. Theunissen, and G. Vergult, *Digital Audio and Compact Disc Technology*, 2nd ed., Butterworth-Heinemann Ltd, 1992.

Bouwhuis, G., et al., *Principles of Optical Disc Systems*, Adam Hilger Ltd., 1985.

Carasso, M.G., et al., "Disc-Shaped Optically Readable Record Carrier Used as a Data Storage Medium," U.S. Patent 4,238,843, December 9, 1980.

Carasso, M.G., J.B.H. Peck, and J.P. Sinjou, "The Compact Disc Digital Audio System," *Philips Tech. Rev.*, vol. 40, no. 6, 1982.

Goedhart, D., R.J. van de Plassche, and E.F. Stikvoort, "Digital-to-Analog Conversion in Playing a Compact Disc," *Philips Tech. Rev.*, vol. 40, no. 6, 1982.

Heemskerk, J.P.J., and K.A. Schouhamer Immink, "Compact Disc System Aspects and Modulation," *Philips Tech. Rev.*, vol. 40, no. 6, 1982.

IEC 908: *Compact Disc Digital Audio System*, 1987.

Isailovic, J., *Videodisc and Optical Memory Systems*, Prentice-Hall, 1985.

ISO 9660: 1988 (E), *Information Processing - Volume and File Structure of CD-ROM for Information Interchange*, 1988.

ISO/IEC 10149: 1989 (E), *Information Technology - Data Interchange on Read-Only 120 mm Optical Data Disks (CD-ROM)*, 1989.

Lambert, S., and S. Ropiequet, *CD-ROM, The New Papyrus*, Microsoft Press, 1986.

Matull, J., "IC's for Compact Disc Decoders," *Electrical Components and Applications*, May, 1982.

Microsoft *MS-DOS CD-ROM Extensions documentation*, version 2.20; Microsoft Corporation, 1990.

Miyaoka, S., "Manufacturing Technology of the Compact Disc," *AES Digital Audio Collected Papers*, Rye, 1983.

Nakajima, H., and H. Ogawa, *Compact Disc Technology*, Ohmsha Ltd., 1992.

Ogawa, H., K. Odaka, and M. Yamamoto, "Digital Disk Recording and Reproduction," *Audio Engineering Handbook*, Benson, ed., McGraw-Hill, 1988.

Ogawa, H., and K.A. Schouhamer Immink, "EFM - The Modulation Method for the Compact Disc Digital Audio System," *AES Digital Audio Collected Papers*, Rye, 1983.

Oppenheim, C., *CD-ROM Fundamentals to Applications*, Butterworths, 1988.

Pahwa, A., *The CD-Recordable Bible*, Eight Bit Books, 1994.

Philips International, Inc., *Compact Disc-Interactive: A Designer's Overview*, McGraw-Hill, 1988.

Pohlmann, K.C., "The Compact Disc Formats: Technology and Applications," *JAES*, vol. 36, no. 4, April, 1988.

Pohlmann, K.C., *The Compact Disc Handbook*, 2nd ed., A-R Editions, 1992.

Roth, J.P., *Essential Guide to CD-ROM*, Meckler Publishing, 1986.

Sekiguchi, K., Y. Maruyama, and M. Tsubaki, "An Extension of the CD Mastering System Format For CD-ROM Mastering," *AES* preprint 2557, New York, October, 1987.

Sherman, C. ed. *The CD-ROM Handbook*, 2nd ed., McGraw-Hill, 1988.

van der Meer, J., "The Full Motion System for CD-I," *IEEE Trans. Consumer Electronics*, vol. 38, no. 4, November, 1992.

Verkaik, W., "Compact Disc (CD) Manufacturing - An Industrial Process," *AES Digital Audio Collected Papers*, Rye, 1983.

10 Interconnection

Adams, R., and T. Kwan, "Theory and VLSI Architectures for Asynchronous Sample-Rate Converters," *JAES*, vol. 41, no. 7/8, July/August, 1993.

"AES Recommended Practice for Digital Audio Engineering - Serial Transmission Format for Two-Channel Linearly Represented Digital Audio Data," *JAES*, vol. 40, no. 3, March, 1992.

AES3-1985, "AES Recommended Practice for Digital Audio Engineering - Serial Transmission Format for Linearly Represented Digital Audio Data," *JAES*, vol. 33, no. 12, December, 1985.

"AES3 Interface Guidelines Document AES-2ID: Progress Report by the SC-2-2 Working Group on Digital Input-Output of the SC-2 Subcommittee on Digital Audio," *JAES*, vol. 42, no. 3, March, 1994.

"AES3 Interface Guidelines Document AES-2ID: Second Progress Report by the SC-2-2 Working Group on Digital Input-Output of the SC-2 Subcommittee on Digital Audio," *JAES*, vol. 42, no. 5, May, 1994.

AES5-1984, "AES Recommended Practice for Professional Digital Audio Applications Employing Pulse-Code Modulation - Preferred Sampling Frequencies," *JAES*, vol. 32, no. 10, October, 1984.

AES10-1991, "AES Recommended Practice for Digital Audio Engineering - Serial Multichannel Audio Digital Interface (MADI)," *JAES*, vol. 39, no. 5, May, 1991.

AES11-1991, "AES Recommended Practice for Digital Audio Engineering - Synchronization of Digital Audio Equipment in Studio Operations," *JAES*, vol. 39, no. 3, March, 1991.

AES17-1991, "AES Standard Method for Digital Audio Engineering - Measurement of Digital Audio Equipment," *JAES*, vol. 39, no. 12, December, 1991.

AES18-1992, "AES Recommended Practice for Digital Audio Engineering - Format for the User Data Channel of the AES Digital Audio Interface," *JAES*, vol. 40, no. 3, March, 1992.

Barr, K., et al., "Method and Apparatus for Providing a Digital Audio Interface Protocol," U.S. Patent 5,297,181, March 22, 1994.

Cabot, R.C., "Measuring AES-EBU Digital Audio Interfaces," *JAES*, vol. 38, no. 6, June, 1990.

Cabot, R.C., "Testing Digital Audio Devices in the Digital Domain," *AES* preprint 2800, Hamburg, March, 1989.

Chan, C., "Monitoring Digital Audio/Video Signals," *Broadcast Engineering*, November, 1994.

Dunn, C., and M.O.J. Hawksford, "Is the AES/EBU/SPDIF Digital Audio Interface Flawed?" *AES* preprint 3360, San Francisco, October, 1992.

EBU (European Broadcasting Union), *Specification of the Digital Audio Interface*, EBU Doc. Tech., 3250.

Finger, R.A., "The Revised Two-Channel Digital Audio Interface," *JAES*, vol. 40, no. 3, March, 1992.

Haynes, D., "Tying It All Together: Synchronization Issues for All-Digital Studios," *Mix Magazine*, vol. 16, no. 7, July, 1992.

Kirby, D.G., "Twisted-Pair Cables for AES/EBU Digital Audio Signals," *JAES*, vol. 43, no. 3, March, 1995.

Koch, A., R. Lagadec, and D. Pelloni, "Method and Apparatus for Converting an Input Scanning Sequence into an Output Scanning Sequence," U.S. Patent 4,825,398, April, 1989.

Krol, E., *The Whole Internet User's Guide & Catalog*, O'Reilly & Associates, Inc., 1992.

Lagadec, R. "Digital Sampling Frequency Conversion," *AES Digital Audio Collected Papers*, Rye, 1983.

Lagadec, R., "Scanning Frequency Synchronization Method and Apparatus," U.S. Patent 4,780,892, October, 1988.

Lagadec, R., and H. Kunz, "Process and Apparatus for Translating the Sampling Rate of a Sampling Sequence," U.S. Patent 4,748,578, May, 1988.

Lagadec, R., and G.J. McNally, "Labels and their Formatting in Digital Audio Recording and Transmission," *AES* preprint 2003, New York, October, 1983.

Lambert, M., "Digital Audio Interfaces," *JAES*, vol. 38, no. 9, September, 1990.

Miller, M.A., *Internetworking: A Guide to Network Communications*, M&T Books, 1991.

"OMF Interchange Specification, Version 1.0," *Avid Technology*, May, 1993.

Rabiner, L.R., "Digital Techniques for Changing the Sampling Rate of a Signal," *AES Digital Audio Collected Papers*, Rye, 1983.

Robjohns, H., "Digital Interconnections - Parts 1–2," *Audio Media*, August, September, 1994.

Rumsey, F., "Audio Programme Interchange: Networks, File Formats, and Real-Time Transfer," *AES* preprint 3737, New York, October, 1993.

Rumsey, F., *Digital Audio Operations*, Focal Press, 1991.

Sanchez, C.W., "An Understanding and Implementation of the SCMS Serial Copy Management System for Digital Audio Transmission," *JAES*, vol. 42, no. 3, March, 1994.

Shelton, W. T. "Synchronization of Digital Audio," *Proc. AES 7th International Conference*, Toronto, May, 1989.

Smith, R. J., and M. Gibbs, *Navigating the Internet*, Howard W. Sams, 1994.

"Technical Reference Document for Digital Audio Recorders," *Copyright Law Reports*, No. 16,080, Commerce Clearing House, Inc. 1992.

11 Perceptual Coding

Ahmed, N., T. Natarajan, and K.R. Rao, "Discrete Cosine Transform," *IEEE Trans. Comput.* vol. C-23, no. 1, January, 1974.

Allen, J., "Cochlear Modelling," *IEEE ASSP Mag.*, vol. 2, no. 1, January, 1985.

Audio Precision, "Testing Reduced Bit-Rate Codecs Using the System One DSP Program CODEC.DSP," *Tech Notes* TN-14, Beaverton, 1994.

Baron, S., and W.R. Wilson, "MPEG Overview," *SMPTE Journal*, June, 1994.

Beerends, J.G., and J.A. Stemerdink, "A Perceptual Audio Quality Measure Based on a Psychoacoustic Sound Representation," *JAES*, vol. 40, no. 12, December, 1992.

Brandenburg, K., "Evaluation of Quality for Audio Encoding at Low Bit Rates," *AES* preprint 2433, London, March, 1987.

Brandenburg, K., "High Quality Sound Coding at 2.5 Bits/sample," *AES* preprint 2582, Paris, March, 1988.

Brandenburg, K., "Perceptual Models for the Prediction of Sound Quality of Low Bit-Rate Codecs," *Proc. AES 12th International Conference*, Copenhagen, June, 1993.

Brandenburg, K., et al., "ASPEC: Adaptive Spectral Entropy Coding of High Quality Music Signals," *AES* preprint 3011, Paris, February, 1991.

Brandenburg, K., and D. Seitzer, "Low Bit Rate Coding of High-Quality Digital Audio: Algorithms and Evaluation of Quality," *Proc. AES 7th International Conference*, Toronto, May, 1989.

Brandenburg, K., and T. Sporer, "NMR and Masking Flag: Evaluation of Quality Using Perceptual Criteria," *Proc. AES 11th International Conference*, Portland, May, 1992.

Brandenburg, K., and G. Stoll, "ISO-MPEG-1 Audio: A Generic Standard for Coding of High-Quality Digital Audio," *JAES*, vol. 42, no. 10, October, 1994.

Cabot, R.C., "Performance Assessment of Reduced Bit Rate Codecs," *AES UK Conference*, London, May, 1994.

Cambridge, P., and M. Todd, "Audio Data Compression Techniques," *AES* preprint 3584, Berlin, March, 1993.

Campbell M., and C. Greated, *The Musician's Guide to Acoustics*, Schirmer Books, 1987.

Capellini, V., *Data Compression and Error Control Techniques with Applications*, Academic Press, 1985.

Cellier, C., P. Chenes, and M. Rossi, "Lossless Audio Data Compression for Real Time Applications," *AES* preprint 3780, New York, October, 1993.

Cho, N.I, and S.U. Lee, "DCT Algorithms for VLSI Parallel Implementations," *IEEE Trans. ASSP*, vol. 38, no. 1, January, 1990.

Colomes. C., et al., "A Perceptual Model Applied to Audio Bit-Rate Reduction," *AES* preprint 3742, New York, October, 1993.

Cox, R.V., "The Design of Uniformly and Nonuniformly Spaced Pseudoquadrature Mirror Filters," *IEEE Trans. ASSP*, vol. ASSP-34, no. 5, October, 1986.

Crochiere, R.E., "On The Design of Sub-Band Coders for Low-Bit-Rate Speech Communication," *Bell Sys. Tech. Journal*, vol. 56, no. 5, May June, 1977.

Crochiere, R.E., "Sub-Band Coding," *Bell Sys. Tech. Journal*, vol. 60, no. 7, September, 1981.

Datta, J., "Study of Window Performance with Respect to the Auditory Masking Curve for Low Bit-Rate Coding Applications," *AES* preprint 3370, San Francisco, October, 1992.

Davidson, G., L.D. Fielder, and M. Antill, "High-Quality Audio Transform Coding at 128 kbits/s," *Proc. IEEE International Conference ASSP*, Albuquerque, 1990.

Davidson, G, L.D. Fielder, and M. Antill, "Low Complexity Transform Coder for Satellite Link Applications," *AES* preprint 2966, Los Angeles, September, 1990.

Davis, M. "The AC-3 Multichannel Coder," *AES* preprint 3774, New York, October, 1993.

Davisson, L.D., and R.M. Gray, ed., *Data Compression*, Dowden, Hutchinson & Ross, 1976.

Deutsch, D., "Auditory Illusions, Handedness, and the Spatial Environment," *JAES*, vol. 31, no. 9, September, 1983.

Eberlein, E., et al., "Layer III: A Flexible Coding Standard," *AES* preprint 3493, Berlin, March, 1993.

Egan, J.P., and H. W. Hake, "On the Masking Pattern of a Simple Auditory Stimulus," *JASA*, vol. 22, no. 5, September, 1950.

Elder, A.G., and S.G. Turner, "A Real-Time PC-Based Implementation of AC-2 Digital Audio Compression," *AES* preprint 3773, New York, October, 1983.

Feiten, B., "Spectral Properties of Audio Signals and Masking with Aspect to Bit Rate Reduction," *AES* preprint 2795, Hamburg, March, 1989.

Fielder, L.D., "Evaluation of the Audible Distortion and Noise Produced by Digital Audio Converters," *JAES*, vol. 35, no. 7/8, July/August, 1987.

Fielder, L.D., "Human Auditory Capabilities and their Consequences in Digital-Audio Converter Design," *Proc. AES 7th International Conference*, Toronto, May, 1989.

Fielder, L.D., and G.A. Davidson, "AC-2: A Family of Low Complexity Transform Based Music Coders," *Proc. AES 10th International Conference*, London, September, 1991.

Finger, R.A., "DCC Format" *Matsushita Technical Lecture*, Osaka, October 15, 1991.

Finger, R.A., "Video CD: A Coding Challenge," *Audio Magazine*, vol. 78, no. 12, December, 1994.

Forshay, S.E., "Audio Data Compression," *Broadcast Engineering*, September, 1994.

Galand, C.R., and H.J. Nussbaumer, "New Quadrature Mirror Filter Structures," *IEEE Trans. ASSP*, vol. ASSP-32, no. 3, June, 1984.

Gerzon, M., "The Gentle Art of Digital Squashing," *Studio Sound*, May, 1990.

Gerzon, M., "Problems of Error Masking in Audio Data Compression Systems," *AES* Preprint 3013, Paris, February, 1991.

Grewin, C., "Methods for Quality Assessment of Low Bit-Rate Audio Codecs," *Proc. AES 12th International Conference*, Copenhagen, June, 1993.

Grusec, T., L. Thibault, and R.J. Beaton, "Sensitive Methodologies for the Subjective Evaluation of High Quality Audio Coding Systems," *Proc. AES UK DSP Conference*, London, September, 1992.

Held, G., *Data Compression: Techniques and Applications, Hardware and Software Considerations*, 3rd. ed., John Wiley and Sons, 1991.

Herre, J., et al., "Analysis Tool for Real Time Measurements Using Perceptual Criteria," *Proc. AES 11th International Conference*, Portland, May, 1992.

Humes, L.E., "Psychoacoustic Foundations of Clinical Audiology," *Handbook of Clinical Audiology*, 3rd ed., Katz, ed., Williams and Wilkins, 1985.

ISO/IEC 11172-3. "International Standard: Coding of Moving Pictures and Associated Audio for Digital Storage Media at up to about 1.5 Mbit/s."

Jayant, N.S., and P. Noll, *Digital Coding of Waveforms: Principles and Applications to Speech and Video*, Prentice-Hall, 1984.

Jerger, J., ed., *Modern Developments in Audiology*, 2nd ed., Academic Press, 1973.

Johnston, J.D., "Transform Coding of Audio Signals Using Perceptual Noise Criteria," *IEEE J. Sel. Areas in Comm.*, Vol. 6, no. 2, February, 1988.

Kate, W.R., et al., "5-Channel MUSICAM Codec," *AES* preprint 3671, Berlin, March, 1993.

Katz, J., "Clinical Audiology," *Handbook of Clinical Audiology*, 3rd ed., Katz, ed., Williams and Wilkins, 1985.

Kerkhof, L. van de, "Compatible 5.1 Channel Extension to the MPEG Layer II Audio Coding Standard," *Proc. Tirrenia International Workshop on Digital Communications*, Pisa, September, 1993.

Keyhl, M., J. Herre, and C. Schmidmer, "NMR Measurements of Consumer Recording Devices Which Use Low Bit-Rate Audio Coding," *AES* preprint 3616, Berlin, March, 1993.

Krasner, M.A., "Digital Encoding of Speech and Audio Signals Based on the Perceptual Requirements of the Auditory System," *MIT Lincoln Laboratory, Technical Report* 535, June, 1979.

LeGall, D., "MPEG - A Video Compression Standard for Multimedia Applications," *Comm. ACM*, vol. 34, no. 4, April, 1991.

Lokhoff, G.C.P., "DCC - Digital Compact Cassette," *IEEE Trans. Consumer Electronics*, vol. 37, no. 3, August, 1991.

Lokhoff, G.C.P., "Precision Adaptive Subband Coding (PASC) for the Digital Compact Cassette (DCC)," *IEEE Trans. Consumer Electronics*, vol. 38, no. 4, November, 1992.

Lookabaugh, T., and M. Perkins, "Application of the Princen-Bradley Filter Bank to Speech and Image Compression," *IEEE Trans. ASSP*, vol. 38, no. 11, November, 1990.

Lyman, S., "An Introduction to Audio Subjective Testing," *CBC Engineering Review*, vol. 33, 1993–94.

Malvar, H.S., "Lapped Transforms for Efficient Transform/Subband Coding," *IEEE Trans. ASSP*, vol. 38, no. 6, June, 1990.

Moore, B.C.J., "Characterization of Simultaneous, Forward and Backward Masking," *Proc. AES 12th International Conference*, Copenhagen, June, 1993.

NAB Guide to Advanced Television Systems, 2nd ed., National Association of Broadcasters, 1991.

Nguyen, T.Q., and P.P. Vaidyanathan, "Two-Channel Perfect-Reconstruction FIR QMF Structures which Yield Linear-Phase Analysis and Synthesis Filters," *IEEE Trans. ASSP.* vol. 37, no. 5, May, 1989.

Paillard, B., et al., "PERCEVAL: Perceptual Evaluation of the Quality of Audio Signals," *JAES*, vol. 40, no. 1/2, January/February, 1992.

Pohlmann, K.C., "The PASC Algorithm, Part 1," *Mix Magazine*, vol. 16, no. 3, March, 1992.

Princen, J., and A. Bradley, "Analysis/Synthesis Filter Band Design Based on Time-Domain Aliasing Cancellation," *IEEE Trans. ASSP*, vol. ASSP-34, no. 5, October, 1986.

Princen, J., A. Johnson, and A. Bradley, "Subband/Transform Coding Using Filter Band Designs Based on Time Domain Aliasing Cancellation," *Proc. IEEE International Conference ASSP*, Dallas, 1987.

Radocy, R.E., and J.D. Boyle, *Psychological Foundations of Musical Behavior*, 2nd ed., Charles C. Thomas, 1988.

Rault, J.B., et al., "MUSICAM (ISO/MPEG Audio) Very Low Bit-Rate Coding at Reduced Sampling Frequency," *AES* preprint 3741, New York, October, 1993.

Schroeder, E.F., and W. Voessing, "High Quality Digital Audio Encoding with 3.0 Bits/sample using Adaptive Transform Coding," *AES* preprint 2321, Montreaux, March, 1986.

Seitzer, D., K. Brandenburg, and R. Kapust, "Real-Time Implementation of Low Complexity Adaptive Transform Coder," *AES* preprint 2581, Paris, March, 1988.

Shannon, C.E., "A Mathematical Theory of Communication," *Bell Sys. Tech. Journal*, vol. 27, no. 3, July, 1948.

Smythe, M., and S. Smythe, "Apt-X100: A Low-Delay, Low Bit-Rate, Sub-Band ADPCM Audio Coder for Broadcasting," *Proc. AES 10th International Conference*, London, September, 1991.

Sporer, T., and K. Brandenburg, "Constraints of Filter Banks Used for Perceptual Measurement," *JAES*, vol. 43, no. 3, March, 1995.

Sporer, T., U. Gbur, J. Herre, and R. Kapust, "Evaluating a Measurement System," *JAES*, vol. 43, no. 5, May, 1995.

Stautner, J.P., "Scalable Audio Compression for Mixed Computing Environments," *AES* preprint 3357, San Francisco, October, 1992.

Stoll, G., "A Perceptual Coding Technique Offering the Best Compromise between Quality, Bit-Rate, and Complexity for DSB," *AES* preprint 3458, Berlin, March, 1993.

Stoll, G., et al., "Generic Architecture of the ISO/MPEG Audio Layer I and II: Compatible Developments to Improve the Quality and Addition of New Features," *AES* preprint 3697, New York, October, 1993.

Stoll, G., M. Link, and G. Thiele, "Masking-Pattern Adapted Subband Coding: Use of the Dynamic Bit-Rate Margin," *AES* preprint 2585, Paris, March, 1988.

Storer, J.A., and M. Cohn, ed., *Proc. of the Data Compression Conference*, Snowbird, UT, IEEE Computer Society Press, March, 1992.

Sun, H., "Hierarchical Decoder for MPEG Compressed Video Data," *IEEE Trans. Consumer Electronics*, vol. 39, no. 3, August, 1993.

Thiele, G., M. Link, and G. Stoll, "Low Bit Rate Coding of High Quality Audio Signals," *AES* preprint 2432, London, March, 1987.

Thiele, G., M. Link, and G. Stoll, "Low Bit-Rate Coding of High Quality Audio Signals: An Introduction to the MASCAM System," *EBU Review, Technical, UHF Satellite Sound Broadcasting*, no. 230, August, 1988.

Tobias, J.S., *Foundations of Modern Auditory Theory*, Vol. 1, Academic Press, New York, 1970.

Todd, C.C., et al., "AC-3: Flexible Perceptual Coding for Audio Transmission and Storage," *AES* preprint 3796, Amsterdam, February, 1994.

Trahiotis, C., "Progress and Pitfalls Associated with Scientific Measures of Auditory Acuity," *AES Digital Audio Collected Papers*, Rye, 1983.

United States Advanced Television Systems Committee, "Digital Audio Compression (AC-3)," *ATSC Draft Standard*, Doc. T3/S7-016, July 25, 1994.

Vaidyanathan, P.P., "Multirate Digital Filters, Filter Banks, Polyphase Networks, and Applications: A Tutorial," *Proc. IEEE*, vol. 78, no. 1, January, 1990.

Vaidyanathan, P.P., *Multirate Systems and Filter Banks*, Prentice-Hall, 1993.

Wever, E.G., and M. Lawrence, *Physiological Acoustics*, Princeton University Press, 1954.

Wirtz, G.C., "Digital Compact Cassette: Audio Coding Technique," *AES* preprint 3216, New York, October, 1991.

Wirtz, G.C., "Digital Compact Cassette: Background and System Description," *AES* preprint 3215, New York, October, 1991.

Witten, J.H., R.M. Neal, and J.G. Cleary, "Arithmetic Coding for Data Compression," *Communication of the ACM*, June, 1987.

Yen Pan, D. "Digital Audio Compression," *Digital Technical Journal*, vol. 5, no. 2, Spring, 1993.

Ziv, J., and A. Lempel, "A Universal Algorithm for Sequential Data Compression," *IEEE Trans. Information Theory*, vol. IT-23, no. 3, May, 1977.

Ziv, J., and A. Lempel, "Compression of Individual Sequences via Variable-Rate Coding," *IEEE Trans. Information Theory*, vol. IT-24, no. 5, September, 1978.

Zwicker, E. "Subdivision of the Audible Frequency Range into Critical Bands," *JASA*, vol. 33, no. 2, February, 1961.

Zwicker, E., and H. Fastl, *Psychoacoustics*, Springer-Verlag, Berlin, 1990.

Zwicker, E., and U.T. Zwicker, "Audio Engineering and Psychoacoustics: Matching Signals to the Final Receiver, The Human Auditory System," *JAES*, vol. 39, no. 3, March, 1991.

12 The MiniDisc

AT&T Bell Labs, *"ASPEC,"* Doc. No. 89/205, ISO-IEC/JTC1/SC2/WG8 MPEG-AUDIO, October 18, 1989.

Brannon, C., and J. Macdonald, "Mastering for MiniDisc Software," Digital Audio Disc Corporation, unpublished, 1992.

Esteban, D., and C. Galand, "Application of Quadrature Mirror Filters to Split Band Voice Coding Schemes," *Proc. IEEE International Conference ASSP*, Hartford, CT, 1977.

Ishida, Y., et al., "On The Development of MiniDisc Players," *IEEE Trans. Consumer Electronics*, vol. 39, no. 3, August, 1993.

Kawakami, D., "The Sony MiniDisc (MD)," *Broadcast Engineering*, February, 1993.

Maeda, Y., "MiniDisc System," *J. Acoustical Society of Japan*, vol. 49, no. 4, April, 1993.

Pohlmann, K. C., "MiniDisc Technology, Parts 1–5," *Mix Magazine*, vol. 16, no. 11, November, 1992 - vol. 17, no. 3, March, 1993.

Ranada, D., "Inside MiniDisc," *Stereo Review*, vol. 58, no. 3, March, 1993.

Sony Corporation, "A Guide to the MiniDisc Mastering System Format Converter Address Generator," Sony Audio Product Division, Broadcast Products Group, 1993.

Sony Corporation, "MiniDisc Specifications," Digital Audio Disc Corporation, 1993.

Sony Corporation, "Optical Pickup for MiniDisc System," Sony Corporation, 1992.

Sony Corporation, "Overview to the Technology behind MiniDisc," Audio Development Group, 1992.

Sony Corporation, "Recordable MiniDisc Technical Information," MiniDisc Division, Recording Media Group, 1992.

Sugiyama, A., et al., "Adaptive Transform Coding with an Adaptive Block Size (ATCABS)," *Proc. IEEE International Conference ASSP*, Albuquerque, NM, 1990.

Tsutsui, K., et al., "ATRAC: Adaptive Transform Acoustic Coding for MiniDisc," *AES* preprint 3456, San Francisco, October, 1992.

Vaidyanathan, P.P., "Quadrature Mirror Filter Banks, M-Band Extensions and Perfect-Reconstruction Techniques," *IEEE ASSP Mag.*, vol. 4, no. 3, July, 1987.

Veldhuis, R., M. Breeuwer, and R. van der Waal, "Subband Coding of Digital Audio Signals without Loss of Quality," *Proc. IEEE International Conference ASSP*, Glasgow, 1989.

13 Digital Audio Broadcasting

Blonstein, L., *Communication Satellites*, Halsted Press, 1988.

Chen, Z., J. Wang, and K. Feher, "Effect of HPA Non-linearities on Crosstalk and Performance of Digital Radio Systems," *IEEE Trans. Broadcasting*, vol. 34, no. 3, September, 1988.

Conway, F., and W. Kwong, "CBS Engineering Experimentation with DAB," *CBC Engineering Review*, vol. 31, 1991.

Conway, F., and J.C. Lee, "Digital Radio Broadcasting Service Considerations in Canada and the Requirement for an International System and Frequency Band Standard," *CBC Engineering Review*, vol. 33, 1993–94.

Conway, F., and B. Sawyer, "Canadian Broadcasting Corporation Experiments with L-Band for Terrestrial Digital Radio Broadcasting," *CBC Engineering Review*, vol. 32, 1992–93.

Cook, Jr., J.H., G. Springer, and J.B. Vespoli, "Satellite Earth Stations," *National Association of Broadcasters Engineering Handbook*, 8th ed., NAB, 1992.

Dick, B., "Satellite Transmission: C-Band vs. Ku-Band," *Sound & Video Contractor*, June 20, 1988.

Douglas, R.L., *Satellite Communications Technology*, Prentice-Hall, 1988.

Elbert, B.R., *Introduction to Satellite Communication*, Artech House, 1987.

Elliott, C., "High-Quality Multimedia Conferencing through a Long-Haul Packet Network," *ACM Multimedia*, 1993.

Feher, K., *Advanced Digital Communications Systems and Signal Processing Techniques*, Prentice-Hall, 1987.

Feher, K., *Digital Communication Satellite/Earth Station Engineering*, Prentice-Hall, 1983.

Forrest, J.R., "Commercial Broadcasting for Europe," *IEEE Trans. Broadcasting*, vol. 34, no. 4, December, 1988.

Fujimoto, M., et al., "Small and Light Weight DBS and FSS Converters," *IEEE Trans. Consumer Electronics*, vol. 36, no. 3, August, 1990.

Heymann, R., et al., "A Multipurpose Four IC Satellite Concept," *IEEE Trans. Consumer Electronics*, vol. 36, no. 3, August, 1990.

Karley, B.A., "Digital Audio Satellite Broadcasting," *Advanced Digital Audio*, Pohlmann, ed., Howard W. Sams, 1991.

Killen, H.B., *Digital Communications with Fiber Optics and Satellite Applications*, Prentice-Hall, 1988.

Klank, O., and D. Rottman, "DSR-Receiver for Digital Sound Broadcasting via the European Satellites TV-SAT/DF," *IEEE Trans. Consumer Electronics*, vol. 35, no. 3, August, 1989.

Konishi, Y., and Y. Fukuoka, "Satellite Receiver Technologies," *IEEE Trans. Broadcasting*, vol. 34, no. 4, December, 1988.

Konishi, Y., "Special Issue on Satellite Broadcasting," *IEEE Trans. Broadcasting*, vol. 34, no. 4, December, 1988.

Langhans, R., and M. Shumila, "Digital Audio Transmission System Using Satellite Distribution," *AES* preprint 2018, New York, October, 1983.

Le Floch, B., R. Halbert-Lassalle, and D. Castelain, "Digital Sound Broadcasting to Mobile Receivers," *IEEE Trans. Consumer Electronics*, vol. 35, no. 3, August, 1989.

Matsushita, M., and S. Yokoyama, "Experience on Operating a DBS System (DB-2) in Japan," *IEEE Trans. Broadcasting*, vol. 34, no. 4, December, 1988.

McNally, G.W., "Digital Audio in Broadcasting," *IEEE ASSP Mag.*, vol. 2, no. 4, October, 1985.

Miller, J.E., "Application of Coding and Diversity to UHF Satellite Sound Broadcasting Systems," *IEEE Trans. Broadcasting*, vol. 34, no. 4, December, 1988.

Muller-Romer, F., "Directions in Digital Audio Broadcasting," *JAES*, vol. 41, no. 3, March, 1993.

National Association of Broadcasters, "Digital Audio Broadcasting: Status Report and Outlook," *NAB*, Washington DC, 1990.

National Association of Broadcasters, "Understanding DAB: A Guide for Broadcast Managers and Engineers," *NAB*, Washington, DC, 1992.

Pizzi, S., "Digital Audio Applications in Radio Broadcasting," *Proc. AES 7th International Conference*, Toronto, May, 1989.

Pizzi, S., *Digital Radio Basics*, Telephony Intertec, 1992.

Pohlmann, K.C., "The DAB Debate," *Mix Magazine*, vol. 15, no. 9, September, 1991.

Pohlmann, K.C., "Eureka 147," *Mix Magazine*, vol. 17, no. 5, May, 1993.

Pohlmann, K.C., "In-Band Digital Radio," *Mix Magazine*, vol. 17, no. 6, June, 1993.

Sukow, R., et al., "Radio's Digital Evolution," *Broadcasting*, October 17, 1988.

14 Digital Audio Workstations

Bagnaschi, C.L., "A Magnetic Storage Disk-Based Digital Audio Recording, Editing, and Processing System," *AES* preprint 2505, New York, October, 1987.

Baudot, M.D., "Hardware Design of a Digital Mixer for Musical Applications," *AES* preprint 2506, New York, October, 1987.

Chan, C., "Hard Drives," *Broadcast Engineering*, September, 1994.

De Lancie, P., "Audio in Mac Authoring," *Mix Magazine*, vol. 18, no. 7, July, 1994.

Elen, R.G., "The Integration of Large-Scale Studio Systems," *Recording Engineer/Producer*, February, 1988.

Ingebretsen, R.B., and T.G. Stockham, Jr., "Random Access Editing of Digital Audio," *JAES*, vol. 32, no. 3, March, 1984.

Jones, M.H., et al., "The Digital Sound Mixing Desk - Opportunities and Challenges," *IBC*, Brighton, September, 1982.

Jostin, P., "The Future of the Recording Studio," *Studio Sound*, August, 1988.

Kitagawa, K., et al., "A Proto Model of a Digital Audio Control Center," *AES* preprint 2204, New York, October, 1983.

Lambert, M., "Defining a Digital Audio Workstation," *Mix Magazine*, vol. 18, no. 7, July, 1994.

Lidbetter, P.S., "Digital Tape Transfer Console," *AES* preprint 2276, New York, October, 1985.

McNally, G.W., "Fast Edit Point Location and Cueing in Disc-Based Digital Audio System," *AES* preprint 2232, Anaheim, May, 1985.

McNally, G.W., P.S. Gaskell, and A.J. Stirling, "Digital Audio Editing," *AES* preprint 2214, Hamburg, March, 1985.

Moorer, J.A., "The Lucasfilm Audio Signal Processor," *Computer Music Journal*, Fall, 1982.

Moorer, J.A., and J. Borish, "An Optical Disk Recording, Archiving, and Editing Device for Digital Audio Signal Processing," *AES* preprint 2376, Los Angeles, November, 1986.

Moorer, J.A., et al., "The Digital Audio Processing Station: A New Concept in Audio Postproduction," *JAES*, vol. 34, no. 6, June, 1986.

Sakamoto, N., S. Yamaguchi, and A. Kurahashi, "A Professional Digital Audio Mixer," *JAES*, vol. 30, no. 1/2, January/February, 1982.

Schwartz, R., "File Interchange Formats," *Mix Magazine*, vol. 18, no. 7, July, 1994.

Snell, J.M., "Professional Real-Time Signal Processor for Synthesis, Sampling, Mixing, and Recording," *AES* preprint 2508, New York, October, 1987.

Spencer-Allen, K., "DSP at CTS," *Studio Sound*, March, 1985.

Wilcox, M., "Riding the Bus," *Mix Magazine*, vol. 17, no. 10, October, 1993.

15 Digital Signal Processing

Adams, R.W., "A New Windowing Technique for Digital Harmonic-Distortion Measurement," *JAES*, vol. 36, no. 5, May, 1988.

Berkhout, P.J., and L.D.J. Eggermont, "Digital Audio Systems," *IEEE ASSP Mag.*, vol. 2, no. 4, October, 1985.

Berkovitz, R., "Digital Equalization of Audio Systems," *AES Digital Audio Collected Papers*, Rye, 1983.

Betts, D., and G. Reid, "DSP and Audio Restoration," *Studio Sound*, March, 1993.

Blesser, B.A., K. Baeder, and R. Zaorski, "A Real-Time Digital Computer for Simulating Audio Systems," *JAES*, vol. 23. no. 9, November, 1975.

Bloom, P.J., "High-Quality Digital Audio in the Entertainment Industry: An Overview of Achievements and Challenges," *IEEE ASSP Mag.*, vol. 2, no. 4, October, 1985.

Booty, M. "Digital Signal Processing: Programming and Interfacing," *Advanced Digital Audio*, Pohlmann, ed., Howard W. Sams, 1991.

Cabot, R., "Practical Performance of Digital Systems," *Recording Engineer/Producer*, March, 1988.

Datta, J., "Digital Signal Processing: Theory," *Advanced Digital Audio*, Pohlmann, ed. Howard W. Sams, 1991.

Dattorro, J., "The Implementation of Recursive Digital Filters for High Fidelity Audio," *JAES*, vol. 36, no. 11, November, 1988.

Dattorro, J., "Using Digital Signal Processor Chips in a Stereo Audio Time Compressor/Expander," *AES* preprint 2500, New York, October, 1987.

Elliot, S.J., and P.A. Nelson, "Multiple-Point Equalization in a Room Using Adaptive Digital Filters," *JAES*, vol. 37, no. 11, November, 1989.

El-Sharkawy, M., *Real Time Digital Signal Processing Applications with Motorola's DSP56000 Family*, Prentice-Hall, 1990.

Griesinger, D., "Practical Processors and Programs for Digital Reverberation," *Proc. AES 7th International Conference*, Toronto, May, 1989.

Griesinger, D., "Theory and Design of a Digital Audio Signal Processor for Home Use," *JAES*, vol. 37, no. 1/2, January/February, 1989.

Hamada, O., N. Kitazato, and T. Nakagami, "Digital Signal Processing LSIs Suitable for Digital Audio Equipment," *AES* preprint 2269, New York, October, 1985.

Hamming, R.W., *Digital Filters*, Prentice-Hall, 1977.

Hutchings, H.J., "Digital Filters Explained," *Electronics & Wireless World*, December, 1985.

IEEE, "Programs for Digital Signal Processing," *IEEE Trans. ASSP DSP Committee*, IEEE Press, 1979.

Jackson, L.B., *Digital Filters and Signal Processing*, Kluwer Academic Publishers, 1986.

Jensen, J.A., "A New Principle for an All-Digital Preamplifier and Equalizer," *JAES*, vol. 35, no. 12, December, 1987.

Kalliris, G., et al., "Z Language, A New DSP Dedicated Programming Environment," *AES* preprint 3514, Berlin, March, 1993.

Lagadec, R., "Measuring the Phase Linearity of Digital Audio Systems," *AES* preprint 2040, New York, October, 1983.

Leventhal, L.A., *6809 Assembly Language Programming*, Osborne, McGraw-Hill, 1981.

Lindemann, E., "DSP Architectures for the Digital Audio Workstation," *AES* preprint 2498, New York, October, 1987.

Lindquist, C.S., *Adaptive and Digital Signal Processing*, Vol. 2, Steward and Sons, 1989.

Menesi, B., and F. Takacs, "Processing of Audio Signals with Extended Precision by TMS 32010," *AES* preprint 2475, London, March, 1987.

Moorer, J.A., "The Audio Signal Processor: The Next Step in Digital Audio," *AES Digital Audio Collected Papers*, Rye, 1983.

Morris, R., *Digital Signal Processing Software*, Carleton University, 1983.

Motorola, "DSP56001 and DSP56000 Data Sheets and Applications Notes," Motorola Microprocessor Products Group.

Mourjopoulos, J., et al., "Noisy Audio Signal Enhancement Using Subjective Spectra," *AES* preprint 3240, Vienna, March, 1992.

Oppenheim, A.V., ed., *Applications of Digital Signal Processing*, Prentice-Hall, 1978.

Oppenheim, A.V., and R.W. Schafer, *Digital Signal Processing*, Prentice-Hall, 1975.

Parks, T.W., and C.S. Burrus, *Digital Filter Design*, John Wiley and Sons, 1987.

Peek, J.B.H., "Digital Signal Processing - Growth of a Technology," *Philips Tech. Rev.*, vol. 42, no. 4, 1985.

Peled, A., and B. Liu, *Digital Signal Processing: Theory, Design and Applications*, Robert E. Krieger Publishing, 1985.

Persoon, E.H.J., and C.J.B. Vandenbulcke, "Digital Audio: Examples of the Application of the ASP Integrated Signal Processor," *Philips Tech. Rev.*, vol. 42, no. 6/7, 1986.

Pohlmann, K.C., "Digital Mixing Consoles," *Mix Magazine*, vol. 9, no. 9, September, 1985.

Pohlmann, K.C., "Multiple-Accumulate Commands," *Mix Magazine*, vol. 16, no. 10, October, 1992.

Pohlmann, K.C., and T. Tanner, "Zola," *Mix Magazine*, vol. 16, no. 8, August, 1992.

Rabiner, L.R., and B. Gold, *Theory and Application of Digital Signal Processing*, Prentice-Hall, 1975.

Rich, D.A., "The Present State of CD Player Technology," *The Audio Critic*, vol. 15, Spring/Winter, 1990–1.

Robinson, E.A., and M.T. Silvia, *Digital Signal Processing and Time Series Analysis*, Holden Day, 1978.

Schroeder, M.R., "Natural Sounding Artificial Reverberation," *JAES*, vol. 10, no. 7, July, 1962.

Schroeder, M.R., "Improved Quasi-Stereophony and 'Colorless' Artificial Reverberation," *JASA*, vol. 33, August, 1961.

Schroeder, M.R., and B.S. Atal, "Computer Simulation of Sound Transmissions in Rooms," *IEEE International Convention Record*, Pt. 7, 1963.

Schuck, P.L., "Digital FIR Filters for Loudspeaker Crossover Networks II: Implementation Example," *Proc. AES 7th International Conference*, Toronto, May, 1989.

Shapton, D., and M. Mattingley-Scott, "True Digital Audio Mixers," *Recording Engineer/Producer*, February, 1989.

Snell, J.M., "Professional Real-Time Signal Processor for Synthesis, Sampling, Mixing, and Recording," *AES* preprint 2508, New York, October, 1987.

Stockham, Jr., T.G., T.M. Cannon, and R.B. Ingebretsen, "Blind Deconvolution through Digital Signal Processing," *Proc. IEEE*, vol. 63, no. 4, April, 1975.

Strawn, J., ed., *Digital Audio Signal Processing*, A-R Editions, 1985.

Texas Instruments, "Digital Signal Processing Applications with the TMS320 Family: Theory, Algorithms, and Implementations," Texas Instruments, Inc., 1990.

Texas Instruments, "Second Generation TMS320 User's Guide," Texas Instruments, Inc., 1989.

Tydelski, P., "Equalizer Trends: Digital Filtering," *Recording Engineer/Producer*, February, 1988.

van den Enden, A.W.M., and N.A.M. Verhoeckx, "Digital Signal Processing: Theoretical Background," *Philips Tech. Rev.*, vol. 42, no. 4, December, 1985.

van Meerbergen, J.L., "Developments in the Integrated Digital Signal Processors, and the PCB 5010," *Philips Tech. Rev.*, vol. 44, no. 1, 1988.

Varga, I., "Adaptive Filtering for Noise Reduction in Audio Signals," *AES* preprint 3247, Vienna, March, 1992.

Vaseghi, S.V., and R. Frayling-Cork, "Restoration of Old Gramophone Recordings," *JAES*, vol. 40, no. 10, October, 1992.

Wilson, R., G. Adams, and J. Scott, "Application of Digital Filters to Loudspeaker Crossover Networks," *JAES*, vol. 37, no. 6, June, 1989.

Zucker, I., "Reproducing Architectural Acoustical Effects Using Digital Soundfield Processing," *Proc. AES 7th International Conference*, Toronto, May, 1989.

16 Low-Bit Conversion and Noise Shaping

Adams, R.W., "An IC Chip Set for 20-Bit A/D Conversion," *JAES*, vol. 38, no. 6, June, 1990.

Adams, R.W., "Companded Predictive Delta Modulation: A Low-Cost Conversion Technique for Digital Recording," *JAES*, vol. 32, no. 9, September, 1984.

Adams, R.W., "Design and Implementation of an Audio 18-Bit Analog-to-Digital Converter Using Oversampling Techniques," *JAES*, vol. 34, no. 3, March, 1986.

Adams, R.W., et al., "Theory and Practical Implementation of a Fifth-Order Sigma-Delta A/D Converter," *JAES*, vol. 39, no. 7/8, July/August, 1991.

Akune, M., R. Heddle, and K. Akagiri, "Super Bit Mapping: Psychologically Optimized Digital Recording," *AES* preprint 3371, San Francisco, October, 1992.

Ardalan, S.H., "Analysis of Delta-Sigma Modulators with Bandlimited Gaussian Inputs," *Proc. of IEEE Conference*, ASSP, vol. III, 1988.

Ardalan, S.H., and J.J. Paulos, "An Analysis of Nonlinear Behavior in Delta-Sigma Modulators," *IEEE Trans. Circuits and Systems*, vol. CAS-34, no. 6, June, 1987.

Boser, B.E., and B.A. Wooley, "The Design of Sigma-Delta Modulation Analog-to-Digital Converters," *IEEE Journal of Solid State Circuits*, vol. 23, no. 6, December, 1988.

Carley, L.R., "An Oversampling Analog-to-Digital Converter Topology for High-Resolution Signal Acquisition Systems," *IEEE Trans. Circuits and Systems*, vol. CAS-34, no. 1, January, 1987.

Craven, P., "Toward the 24-Bit DAC: Novel Noise-Shaping Topologies Incorporating Correction for the Nonlinearity in a PWM Output Stage," *JAES*, vol. 41, no. 5, May, 1993.

Crochiere, R.E., and L.R. Rabiner, "Interpolation and Decimation of Digital Signals - A Tutorial Review," *Proc. IEEE*, vol. 69, no. 3, March, 1981.

Darling, T.F., and M.O.J. Hawksford, "Oversampled Analog-To-Digital Conversion for Digital Audio Systems," *JAES*, vol. 38, no. 12, December, 1990.

Gerzon, M.A., and P.G. Craven, "A High-Rate Buried-Data Channel for Audio CD," *JAES*, vol. 43, no. 1/2, January/February, 1995.

Gerzon, M.A., et al., "Psychoacoustic Noise Shaped Improvements in CD and Other Linear Digital Media," *AES* preprint 3501, Berlin, March, 1993.

Goldberg, J.M., and M.B. Sandler, "Noise Shaping and Pulse-Width Modulation for an All-Digital Audio Power Amplifier," *JAES*, vol. 39, no. 6, June, 1991.

Harris, S., "The Effects of Sampling Clock Jitter on Nyquist Sampling Analog-to-Digital Converters, and on Oversampling Delta-Sigma ADCs," *JAES*, vol. 38, no. 7/8, July/August, 1990.

Harris, S., "How to Achieve Optimum Performance from Delta-Sigma A/D and D/A Converters," *JAES*, vol. 41, no. 10, October, 1993.

Hauser, M.W., "Principles of Oversampling A/D Conversion," *JAES*, vol. 39, no. 1/2, January/February, 1991.

Hauser, M.W., and R.W. Brodersen, "Monolithic Decimation Filtering for Custom Delta-Sigma A/D Converters," *Proc. IEEE Conference*, ASSP, vol. III, 1988.

Hawksford, M.O.J., "Chaos, Oversampling, and Noise Shaping in Digital-to-Analog Conversion," *JAES*, vol. 37, no. 12, December, 1989.

Hawksford, M.O.J., "Dynamic Model-Based Linearization of Quantized Pulse-Width Modulation for Applications in Digital-to-Analog Conversion and Digital Power Amplifier Systems." *JAES*, vol. 40, no. 4, April, 1992.

Hawksford, M.O.J., and W. Wingerter, "Oversampling Filter Design in Noise-Shaping Digital-to-Analog Conversion," *JAES*, vol. 38, no. 11, November, 1990.

Kam, J.J. van der, "A Digital 'Decimating' Filter for Analog-to-Digital Conversion of Hi-Fi Signals," *Philips Tech. Rev.*, vol. 42, no. 6/7, April, 1986.

Kloker, K.L., B.L. Lindsley, and C.D. Thompson, "VLSI Architectures for Digital Audio Signal Processing," *Proc. AES 7th International Conference*, Toronto, May, 1989.

Komamura, M., "Wide-Band and Wide-Dynamic-Range Recording and Reproduction of Digital Audio," *JAES*, vol. 34, no. 1/2, January/February, 1995.

Kuroda, N., JVC Corporation, personal correspondence, November, 1989.

Lipshitz, S.P., J. Vanderkooy, and R.A. Wannamaker, "Minimally Audible Noise Shaping," *JAES*, vol. 39, no. 11, November, 1991.

Lipshitz, S.P., R.A. Wannamaker, and J. Vanderkooy, "Dithered Noise Shapers and Recursive Digital Filters," *AES* preprint 3515, Berlin, March, 1993.

Matsuya, Y., et al., "A 16-Bit Oversampling A/D Conversion Technology Using Triple-Integration Noise Shaping," *IEEE Journal Solid-State Circuits*, vol. SC-22, no. 6, December, 1987.

Motorola, "DSP56ADC16 16-Bit Sigma-Delta Analog-to-Digital Converter," *Motorola Semiconductor Technical Data*, Ref. DSP56ADC16/D, 1989.

Naus, P.J.A., et al., "Low Signal-Level Distortion in Sigma-Delta Modulators," *AES* preprint 2584, Paris, March, 1988.

Ning, H., A. Buzo, and F. Kuhlmann, "Multi-Loop Sigma-Delta Quantization: Spectral Analysis," *Proc. IEEE Conference, ASSP*, vol. III, 1988.

Oomen, A.W.J., et al., "A Variable-Bit-Rate Buried-Data Channel for Compact Disc," *JAES*, vol. 34, no. 1/2, January/February, 1995.

Park, S., "Multistage Halfband Filter Design for Improving Effective Resolution from Sigma-Delta Analog-to-Digital Converters," *AES* preprint 3008, New York, September, 1990.

Park, S., "Principles of Sigma-Delta Modulation for Analog-to-Digital Converters," *Motorola Applications Note APR8/D*, 1990.

Richards, M., "Improvements in Oversampling Analogue to Digital Converters," *AES* preprint 2588, Paris, March, 1988.

Seitzer, D., et al., "Low Bit Rate Codecs for Audio Signals Implementation in Real Time," *AES* preprint 2707, New York, November, 1988.

Spinnler, W., et al., "VLSI Implementation Aspects of Low Bit Rate Codecs for High Quality Audio Channels," *AES* preprint 2750, Hamburg, March, 1989.

Stikvoort, E.F., "Higher Order One Bit Coder for Audio Applications," *AES* preprint 2583, Paris, March, 1988.

Stikvoort, E.F., "Some Remarks on the Stability and Performance of the Noise Shaper or Sigma-Delta Modulator," *IEEE Trans. Communications*, vol. 36, no. 10, October, 1988.

Stuart, J.R., and R.J. Wilson, "Dynamic Range Enhancement Using Noise-Shaped Dither Applied to Signals with and without Pre-Emphasis," *AES* preprint 3871, Amsterdam, February, 1994.

Thompson, C.D, "A VLSI Sigma-Delta A/D Converter for Audio and Signal Processing Applications," *Proc. IEEE Conference, ASSP*, May, 1989.

Uchimura, K., et al., "Oversampling A-to-D and D-to-A Converters with Multistage Noise Shaping Modulators," *IEEE Trans. ASSP*, vol. 36, no. 12, December, 1988.

Vanderkooy, J., and S.P. Lipshitz, "Digital Dither: Signal Processing with Resolution Far Below the Least Significant Bit," *Proc. AES 7th International Conference*, Toronto, May, 1989.

Wannamaker, R.A. "Psychoacoustically Optimal Noise Shaping," *JAES*, vol. 40, no. 7/8, July/August, 1992.

Welland, D.R, et al., "A Stereo 16-Bit Delta-Sigma A/D Converter for Digital Audio," *JAES*, vol. 37, no. 6, June, 1989.

Wong, P.W., and R.M. Gray, "FIR Filters with Sigma-Delta Modulation Encoding," *IEEE Trans. ASSP*, vol. 38, no. 6, June, 1990.

Index

Illustrations are in **boldface.**

About the Author

Ken C. Pohlmann is a professor and director of the music engineering programs at the University of Miami in Coral Gables, Florida. He is also president of Hammer Laboratories, a company devoted to the research, development, and testing of new audio technology. Internationally known as an author, consultant, expert witness, and lecturer in the field of digital audio, he received the Audio Engineering Society's Fellowship Award for his work. He has written over 1,200 articles on audio topics, and is author of *The Compact Disc Handbook*, Second Edition, editor and coauthor of *Advanced Digital Audio*, and coauthor of *Writing for New Media: The Essential Guide to Writing for Interactive Media, CD-ROMs, and the Web*.